VOLUME 5

NORTH AMERICAN
P-51 MUSTANG

By Frederick A. Johnsen

specialtypress
PUBLISHERS AND WHOLESALERS

Published by
Specialty Press Publishers and Wholesalers
11481 Kost Dam Road
North Branch, MN 55056
United States of America
(612) 583-3239

Distributed in the UK and Europe by
Airlife Publishing Ltd.
101 Longden Road
Shrewsbury
SY3 9EB
England

ISBN 0-933424-68-X

Designed by Greg Compton

Printed in the United States of America

TABLE OF CONTENTS

THE NORTH AMERICAN P-51 MUSTANG

FOREWORD

It has been my pleasure to fly the North American P-51 Mustang in air shows for more than three decades.

During that time, I have come to know the Mustang inside and out. And that inside look is what makes this WarbirdTech volume about the P-51 Mustang uniquely interesting and useful. Excerpted drawings from original technical manuals, interpretive photo captions, and text backed up by official documentation give the reader more than just another picture book about the magnificent Mustang.

I've known author Fred Johnsen since he was a college student, photographing and writing about air shows in the Pacific Northwest in the 1960s and 1970s. Therefore it is with pleasure that I introduce his book, about the Mustang aircraft that I have grown to know so well over much of that same span of years.

My association with North American Aviation afforded a wonderful opportunity when company president Lee Atwood bought a slick refurbished surplus P-51 from Cavalier Aircraft in Florida for me to fly at air shows in the early 1960s. Of all the different North American aircraft I have flown in demonstrations, it gives me great satisfaction to be so closely associated with the sleek, powerful, and capable P-51.

Even as I have coaxed demanding maneuvers from my Mustang at air shows for years, those performances stand as a testimonial to the innovators at North American Aviation who designed and built the Mustang in the urgency of wartime, as well as the thousands of pilots who honed their skills in the P-51 under fire, backed up by maintenance people who kept the Mustangs flying. So please sit back and enjoy this book as a tribute to the Mustang airplane, and the people who gave it life and capitalized on its superior abilities.

ROBERT A. "BOB" HOOVER
1996

Ever-dapper, Bob Hoover watched the Abbotsford International Air Show from the wing of his trademark P-51 in the mid-1970s. (Frederick A. Johnsen)

PREFACE

CREATIVE PEOPLE MADE IT POSSIBLE

Mustang! The name conjures images of wild, muscular horses living a spirited existence in the expansive American West. No doubt that was exactly what was intended when North American Aviation's sleekly-sculpted P-51 fighter was given the same name. By any standard, the P-51 Mustang rates as one of the major success stories of World War Two. With an inspired airframe from the start, the aircraft only got better as the Rolls Royce Merlin engine was mated to it, delivering performance at altitude that made the P-51 a scourge to enemies around the world.

But this performance had a price tag. The underslung coolant scoop that also acted as a propulsive force to aid the Mustang's speed was a terrifying ram brake in ditchings, prompting advice from the British to avoid ditching a Mustang unless no alternative remained. The addition of more fuel in the fuselage, which did so much to make the Mustang an extraordinary long-range escort fighter, also produced

some undesirable aft center-of-gravity characteristics until that fuel was burned off in flight.

But the first thing you are likely to hear from any Mustang veteran is praise for the machine. Its vices could be overcome or accommodated as part of the overall package.

Many authors have written volumes about the P-51. This offering, in the WarbirdTech Series, offers a look at what made the Mustang great, and what humbled it occasionally.

Many people assisted with this project. Thanks to the U.S. Air Force Academy Special Collections (Duane Reed), Paul Fackler, Tom Foote, Lowell Ford, Bob Guilford, Steve Hinton, Howie Keefe, Don Keller (Air Depot), Fred LePage, Dave Menard, Jim Morrow, L.M.

Myers, Carl Scholl (Aero Trader), Carl Schuler, Bob, Dave and Jeff Sturges (Columbia Airmotive), Herb Tollefson, Ray Wagner (San Diego Aerospace Museum), Walter Wright, R.A. "Bob" Hoover, and all who helped.

Several good references about aspects of the P-51 story are available. An incredible genealogy of Mustangs, as well as other warbirds, appears in *Warbirds Worldwide Directory*, by John Chapman and Geoff Goodall, edited by Paul A. Coggan. Like felines, some of the surviving Mustangs have at least nine lives.

Some abbreviations appearing in the caption credits include: USAF (U.S. Air Force), AAF (Army Air Forces), NAA (North American Aviation), and SDAM (San Diego Aerospace Museum).

FREDERICK A. JOHNSEN
1996

Graceful simplicity and economy of purpose is evident in this side view of the NA-73X prototype for the P-51 series. Salient Mustang features are already evident, from the angular tail to the ventral radiator coolant scoop, although the scoop underwent several iterations in subsequent models. (NAA/SDAM)

TEAM1WORK

WHEN ENGINEERING CREATED ART

If there exists one icon above all others symbolizing American fighters of World War Two, it is North American Aviation's calculatingly-sculpted P-51 Mustang. In 1940, the British Purchasing Commission approached North American Aviation (NAA) about setting up another production line for Curtiss P-40 variants which the British used in combat. NAA president J.H. "Dutch" Kindelberger preferred to have his company supply the British with an entirely new design instead of a franchised Curtiss product; one reason given was a difference in production methods that NAA officials said would make the P-40 more difficult to build in North American's facility.

An added attraction to Kindelberger's suggestion was the ability to weave wartime lessons into the new design instead of merely expanding on a prewar fighter. The task of selling the British Purchasing Commission on this unbuilt NAA dream plane was handed to North American Aviation vice president J. Lee Atwood, a perceptive engineer in his own right, who met with members of the commission in New York. Backing Atwood up was the sound reputation of NAA with the British, who were already impressed with quantity deliveries of Harvard trainers from North American's Inglewood, California, plant. The British were interested in seeing NAA design and build the prototype of the new fighter.

Part of the lore of the Mustang says North American Aviation was obligated to produce the new prototype in only 120 days; historian Ray Wagner says no documentary evidence has come to his attention to support this.[1] Whether apocryphal or not, the story of the short deadline captures the spirit of the times which saw NAA hustle to produce their promising fighter quickly. The ultimate success of the Mustang was a synergy of many ideas and design practices. Salient features that progressively made the Mustang a winner included its use of a laminar flow wing airfoil; the use of stand-off inlets to gather air outside the plane's boundary layer; the boost in forward thrust provided by the ventral radiator system; employment of mathematics to compute optimum streamlining; and the ultimate advantage provided later by mating the Mustang airframe in 1942 with the remarkable Rolls Royce Merlin V-12 engine with two-stage supercharging blower.

In late April 1940, NAA preliminary designers executed a profile drawing of their new warplane,

NA-73X used a curved Plexiglas windscreen that caused distortion; subsequent Mustangs had a flat center pane. Pre-war American fighters tended to sport curved front windscreens, sometimes backed by add-on flat armor glass inside the cockpit. Only the P-39 retained this style throughout its production life, as the P-38, P-40, P-47, P-51, P-61, and P-63 all used variations on a flat armor glass front windscreen at some point during production. (SDAM)

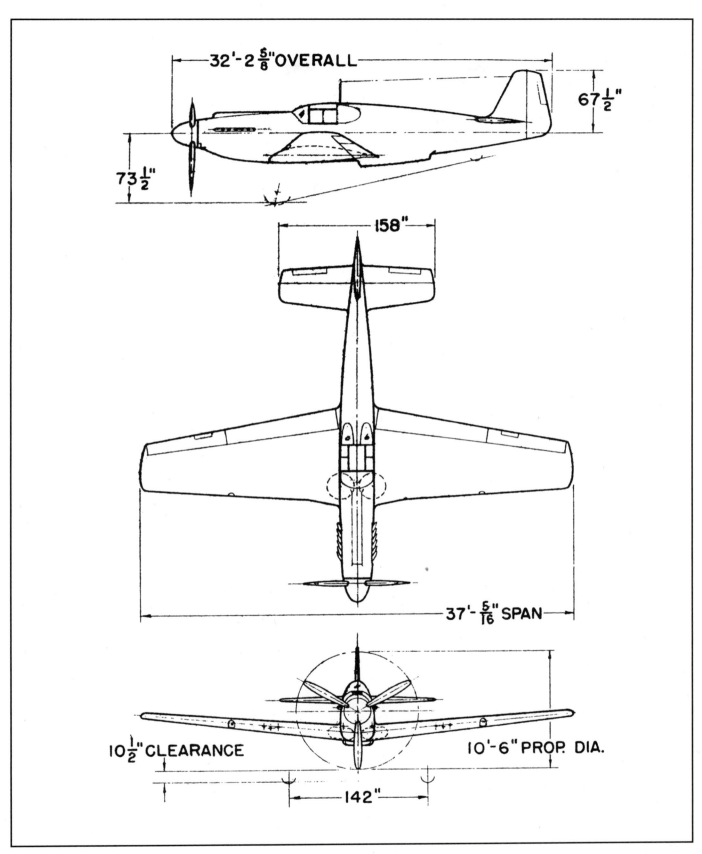

Early NA-73 three-view shows early scoops, curved windscreen, as wind tunnel tested in September 1940. (GALCIT Report 286-A)

Polished wooden NA-73 model at the GALCIT wind tunnel of the California Institute of Technology in Pasadena shows early ventral radiator inlet configuration, and short nose carburetor inlet. GALCIT was a key research facility used by major American aircraft manufacturers before and during World War Two. Early NA-73 tests at GALCIT were complemented by other tests at the slightly-larger University of Washington Aeronautical Laboratory (UWAL), in Seattle, Washington. (GALCIT photo courtesy Jerry Landry)

incorporating a list of British requirements. The British responded positively to this preliminary work, signaling the beginning of serious engineering and design of what was to become the P-51 Mustang. NAA wisely streamlined the design process, procuring parts without resorting to traditional requisitioning bureaucracy. A contemporary news release said: "In this flexible set-up, paper work and red tape were forgotten. Inter-office memos took the place of official orders and even of drawings." Workers were dispatched to stand by for special parts being fabricated off-site, thereby minimizing the time before those parts could be added to the prototype aircraft.[2]

The Mustang's designers clearly understood what must be done to make a successful fighter in the over-400 MPH range. The use of an inline engine kept frontal area to a minimum; ironically, this began as the same basic Allison V-1710 powerplant of the P-40 that Kindelberger had rejected. Fully enclosed retractable landing gear was deemed a must for streamlining, and the bugaboo of compressibility shock waves at high speed and high altitude was addressed as well. In several instances, NAA engineers were willing to embrace new technologies and ideas to foster their fast fighter in the limited days given them. A signature of the Mustang was its pioneering use of a laminar flow airfoil based on

Not quite the end of the line for the first Mustang, this crash landing made by NAA pilot Paul Balfour on November 20, 1940, followed stoppage of the Allison engine at low altitude. Balfour was not seriously hurt; the NA-73X was rebuilt, although its usefulness, as a handmade prototype, was limited and finally came to an end the following July when the aircraft was retired. Lengthening of the carburetor scoop atop the nose, accompanied by raising the lip of the carburetor inlet off the nose contour into undisturbed air, resolved the problem that stalled the engine that day. (SDAM)

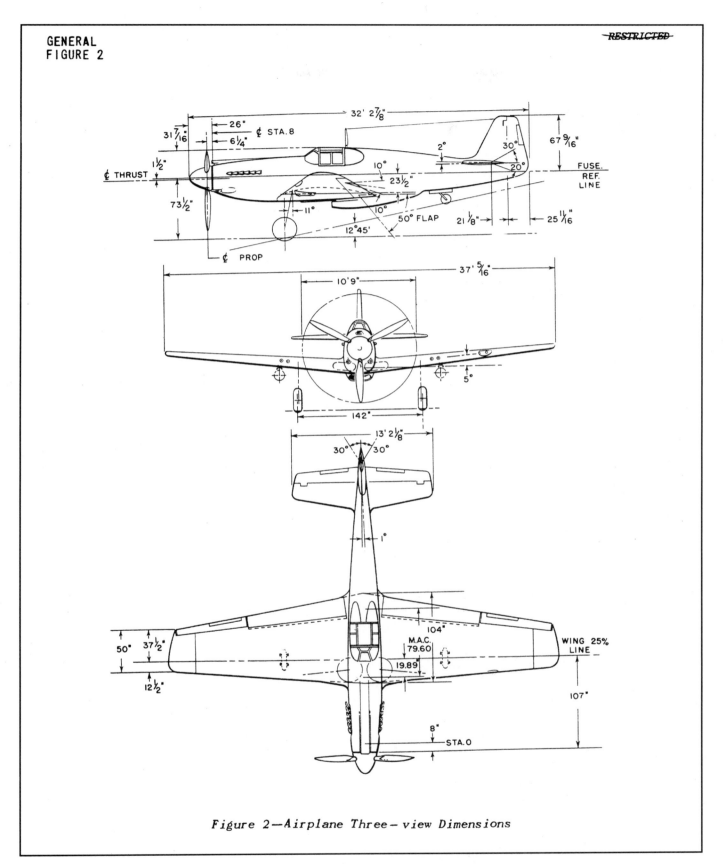

Figure 2—Airplane Three-view Dimensions

A-36A drawings show many of the same dimensions as NA-73 prototype; ventral and nose air scoops were elongated by this time.

Close-up of the crumpled left wing of the NA-73X following its engine-out landing in a plowed field suggests the three wing gun ports may have been painted on for appearances on this testbed airframe. Early radiator inlet and exhaust gate are discernible. (SDAM)

research by the National Advisory Committee for Aeronautics. Untried in production, the laminar wing promised dramatic reductions in drag. NAA chief design engineer Edgar Schmued and the company's aerodynamics section chief Edward Horkey put their faith in laminar flow, and went to bat willing to risk the entire compressed development project on NAA's ability to perfect a laminar flow wing design in time. Kindelberger agreed, but insisted Schmued must be poised to draft a conventional wing in a 30-day period in case laminar flow did not pan out.

Ultimately, NAA's laminar flow design for the Mustang departed from the original NACA research. First tested in the California Institute of Technology wind tunnel in Pasadena, an early NAA laminar flow wing showed bad stall traits, illustrated by tufts attached to the wing that lifted to show areas of turbulent, non-laminar airflow. A revised wing still showed problems in the Cal Tech wind tunnel, and engineers began to wonder if the confines of the tunnel itself was the problem, reverberating disturbed airflow back over the wingtips. As a control test, Ed Horkey shipped the wooden wing model by airliner

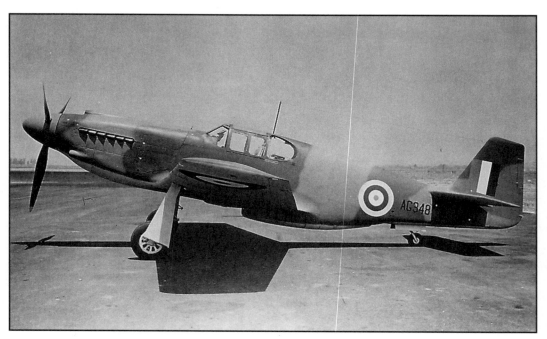

Bearing Royal Air Force number AG348, this early Mustang I was built with the old short carburetor scoop, soon changed after RAF pilots experienced problems similar to those which caused the NA-73X engine failure. This was the fourth production Mustang. (NAA/SDAM collection)

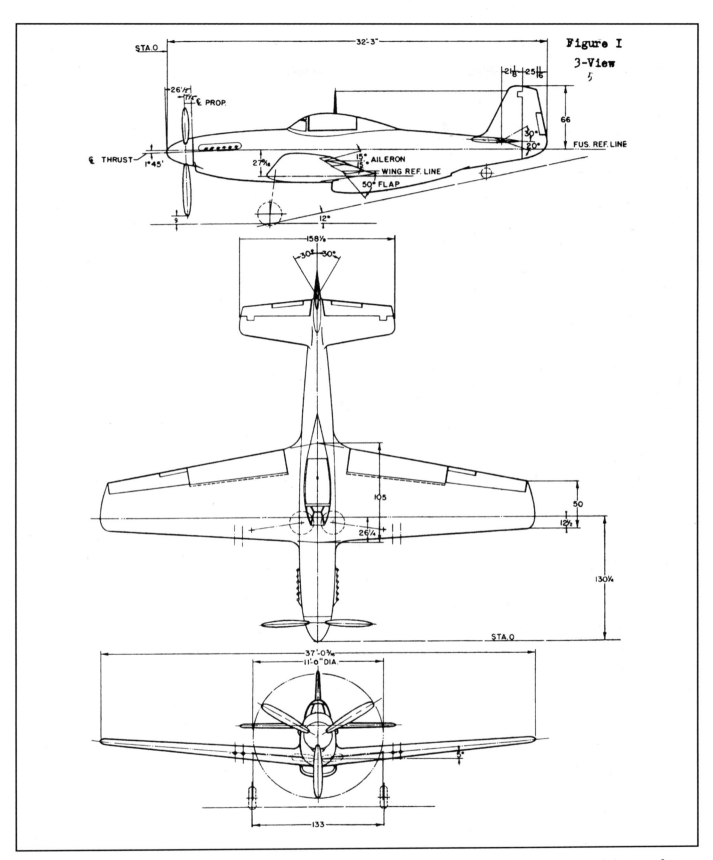

Figure I
3-View

Lightweight XP-51 variants, in early design stages, were envisioned with a semi-bubble canopy reminiscent of some FW-190 canopies. Small mainwheels and lack of extended inboard wing leading edge are evident.

Three factory views of an XP-51 show the revised and lengthened carburetor inlet atop the nose, the placement of .50-caliber machine guns in cheek positions beside the Allison engine, and wing gun ports for two inboard .50-caliber and four .30-caliber machine guns. Curtiss Electric propeller was installed. (NAA/SDAM)

to the larger University of Washington wind tunnel, where validation was obtained for the NAA laminar flow design. The airflow remained "attached," or laminar, over about 40 percent of the wing chord of the Mustang, which was much higher than on conventional airfoils of the era. This reduced the compressibility effects.

The benefits of laminar flow could be degraded by surface irregularities. Early in the Mustang's service life, British crews flying Mustang I fighters on ground attack sorties over continental Europe used measures to keep their airplanes' wings smooth. A USAAF study of British Mustang operations noted in August 1943 that pilots and ground crews were "encouraged to keep the wings polished and free from scratches. In fact, no one is allowed to climb up on the wings without a pad in place. The pilots enter from the front stepping on the wing at only two designated spots."[3] Not all Mustang users were so fastidious.

First version of the Mustang's windscreen was a molded Plexiglas design that smoothed out some drag-producing surfaces, but unforeseen to the designers, the curved windscreen distorted the view of the ground and complicated landings in the Mustang. A more conventional flat windscreen with gently curved side panels was used instead. Inside the cockpit, designers faced the challenge of installing all the equipment a fighter pilot would require, in the narrow cross section afforded by the streamlined inline engine up front. A wartime paper about the Mustang explained: "As finally completed, the Mustang cockpit allowed just enough room for a pilot to sit com-

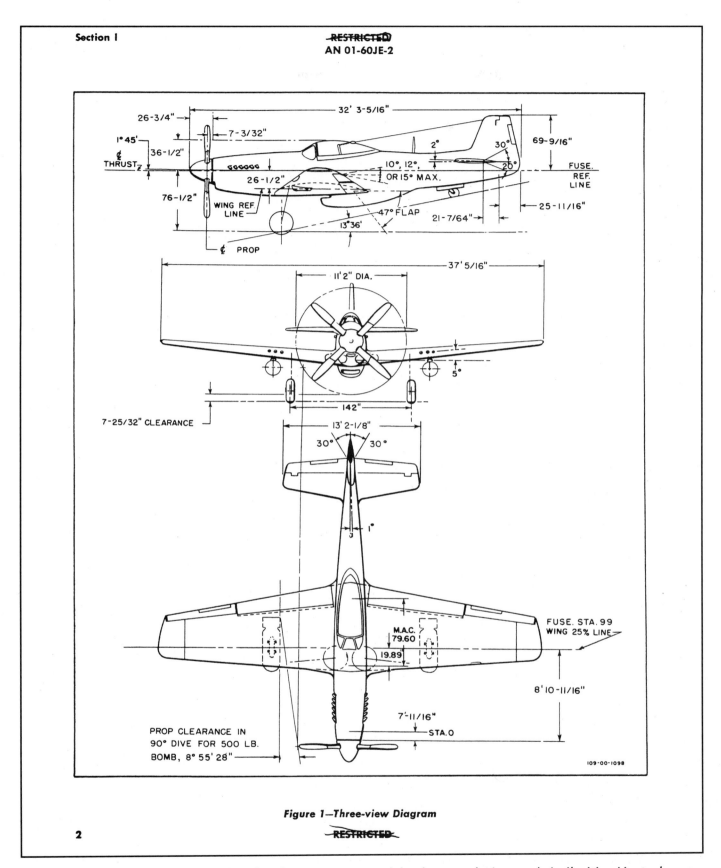

Figure 1—Three-view Diagram

P-51D drawings, when compared with other Mustang models, show evolution and similarities. Ventral scoop metamorphosis is evident throughout the design life of the Mustang.

NORTH AMERICAN
P-51 MUSTANG

Two examples from Mustang I production were kept by the USAAF, and called XP-51. One outlived the rigors of wartime testing and flew under the sponsorship of the Experimental Aircraft Association (EAA) during the late 1970s; as of this writing, this XP-51, the oldest Mustang extant, is displayed at the EAA's museum in Oshkosh, Wisconsin. (Frederick A. Johnsen)

fortably, yet all controls, instruments, and equipment were within easy reach."[4]

The form-fitting streamlining that was the aesthetic hallmark of the P-51 was figured, literally, with mathematical precision by NAA engineers Roy Liming and Carter Hartley. This was said to be the first application of mathematical second degree curve technology, which provided calculations to determine the best streamlining between two points on the airframe. As a wartime paper noted: "The fact that the Mustang was the first plane in the world to benefit from this new streamlining technique explains to some degree the aerodynamic efficiency of its fuselage design and empennage and wing fairings." Not all aspects of the Mustang were calculated correctly in advance of the first flight. Early on, the location of the carburetor air inlet for Allison-engine Mustangs, atop the nose, suffered from varying volumes of air being ingested, instead of the required uniform flow at all speed ranges. Study showed the problem to be a combination of boundary layer interference and pulsing from the passage of the propeller blades ahead of the inlet. By raising the inlet slightly, the boundary layer problem was solved; by extending the inlet forward, the pulsing phenomenon was mitigated, and the Allison performed well under all speed ranges after that. The high speed of the Mustang caused another unexpected phenomenon when an airfoil-shaped radio mast was applied originally. Similar to the mast used successfully on the slower North American O-47, the Mustang's airfoil mast was snapping off in high-speed flight. NAA engineers concluded the mast's airfoil, like a small wing placed vertically, was generating sideways lift. This displaced the mast to the side until its own strength sprang it back, when reverse lift carried it beyond neutral, setting up a rapidly diverging oscillation that snapped the mast off. Next installation was a round mast, which did not break off, but which robbed the Mustang of six to nine miles an hour. A modi-

The second straight P-51 (41-37321) on the North American Aviation flightline in 1942 shows early-style radiator exit gate open beneath fuselage insignia. Triangle within circle on tail is NAA emblem. Production P-51 (with no suffix letter) deleted nose guns, typically carrying four long-barreled 20MM cannons in the wings, although not installed in this aircraft when the photo was taken. (NAA)

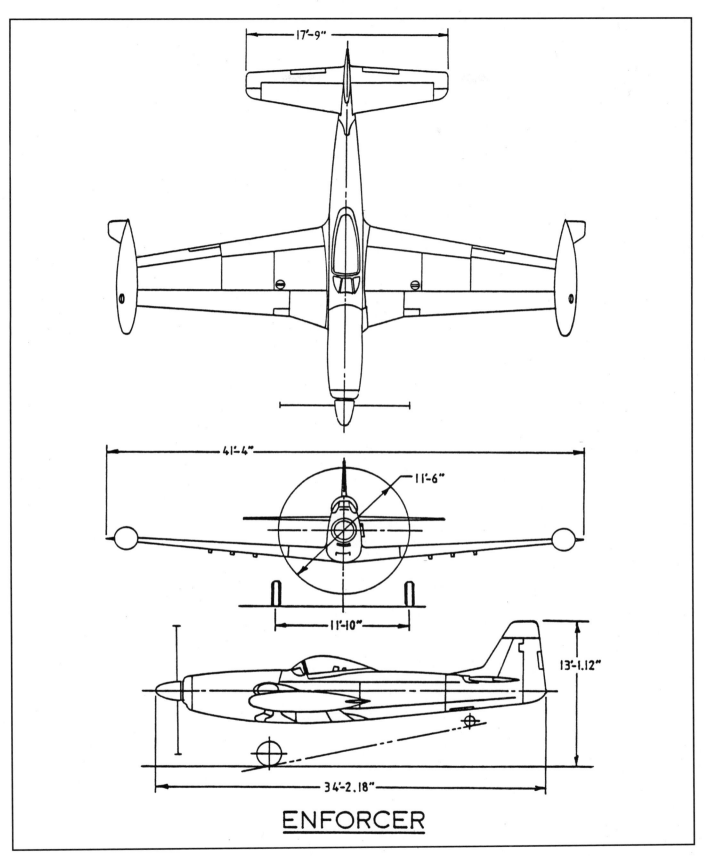

17'-9"

41'-4"

11'-6"

11'-10"

13'-1.12"

34'-2.18"

ENFORCER

The turboprop Enforcer was an effort to gain the last measure of combat utility from the P-51 airframe. Enlarged horizontal tail surfaces are evident. Enforcer was about two feet longer overall than the P-51D.

P-51 carried complement of 20mm cannons in wings when this photo was taken in 1942. Five hundred rounds of 20mm ammunition could be carried by the P-51. (SDAM)

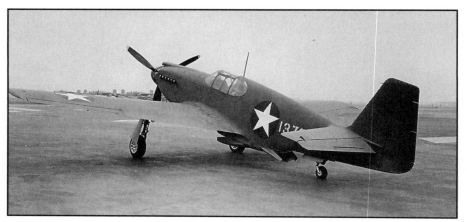

Rear three-quarter view of a P-51 silhouettes stand-off carburetor inlet, and shows ventral radiator inlet and outlet lowered. (NAA/SDAM)

Armorers load heavy 20mm ammunition in the wings of a P-51, 1942. (NAA). Unusual for American combat aircraft is relatively hard demarcation line between olive drab upper surfaces and gray undersurfaces, usually blended with feathering overspray. (NAA).

fied, rounded, yet streamlined, mast similar to that of the Spitfire was next tested, but it departed the Mustang above 300 miles an hour. A wartime Mustang paper explained: "Finally one of the engineers had a steel tube flattened and tried it on the Mustang as an aerial mast, its narrow axis parallel to the fuselage. Miraculously, it worked, and resulted in a negligible loss of only ½ m.p.h. in speed. The most optimistic estimate of lost speed for the first streamline section tried had been four m.p.h." The result was a steel mast almost round at the base, and tapered to a flat section, made from heat-treated steel tubing.[5]

To cradle the Allison engine, Art Chester devised a built-up aluminum engine mount instead of the traditional steel tubing structure. The Allison (and later, the Merlin) powerplant of the Mustang was closely cowled, taking full advantage of this engine style's small frontal area. NAA planners desired to keep the frontal area small, and placed oil and engine coolant radiators in a belly scoop beneath the wing center section, where the resulting drag would be less than in a chin installation as was used on the P-40. As first flown, the Mustang's radiator inlet proved insufficient to keep the engine running cool. Wind tunnel tests isolated the problem as disturbed airflow along the undersurface of the wing. By redesigning the inlet to stand off from the fuselage about an inch from the bottom of the wing, undisturbed air was ingested, resulting in greater cooling efficiency.

According to Edward Horkey, the aft ventral placement of the coolant scoop was influenced by

NORTH AMERICAN AVIATION PART NUMBERS

1...	73-44002-10	SPINNER
2...	73-31011-100	NOSE RING COWLING
3...	83-31073-100	ENGINE TOP COWLING
4...	73-31071	ENGINE INTERMEDIATE COWLING
5...	73-31068	LOWER CENTER COWLING
6...	73-310155-50	BOTTOM FRONT COWLING
7...	73-31098	BOTTOM REAR COWLING
8...	73-31099	LOWER INTERMEDIATE REAR COWLING
9...	73-310100	UPPER INTERMEDIATE REAR COWLING
10...	73-31072	ENGINE TOP AFT COWLING
11...	73-31102-30	FIREWALL
12...	83-31826	WINDSHIELD ASSEMBLY
13...	97-31107	FUSELAGE SIDE PANEL
14...	73-31848-10	COCKPIT PORT SIDE EXIT HATCH
15...	73-31835	COCKPIT STARBOARD EXIT HATCH
16...	73-31829	COCKPIT UPPER EXIT HATCH
17...	97-31122	FUSELAGE TOP DECK
18...	73-31830	COCKPIT REAR PANEL
19...	97-310119	RADIATOR FRONT SCOOP FAIRING
20...	97-31022	FORWARD RADIATOR AIR DUCT
21...	73-46050	RADIATOR
22...	97-31025	REAR SCOOP
23...	73-31083	UPPER DOME AFT AIR DUCT
24...	97-31024	RADIATOR DRAIN ACCESS DOOR
25...	97-31021	RADIATOR LOWER ACCESS DOOR
26...	83-10007	WING TO FUSELAGE FILLET
27...	97-34101	TAIL WHEEL STRUT
28...	73-31066	TAIL WHEEL DOOR
29...	97-31108	FUSELAGE REAR SECTION
30...	73-21001	HORIZONTAL STABILIZER
31...	73-22001	ELEVATOR
32...	73-23001	VERTICAL STABILIZER
33...	73-24001	RUDDER
34...	83-24004	RUDDER TRIM TAB
35...	83-22004	ELEVATOR TRIM TAB
36...	97-14300	WING RIB STATION 0
37...	73-10023	WING CENTER BULKHEAD
38...	97-14051	AMMUNITION BAY DOOR
39...	73-18001	WING FLAP
40...	97-14052	GUN BAY DOOR AFT

41...	97-14050	GUN BAY DOOR FORWARD
42...	83-16005	AILERON TRIM TAB
43...	73-16000	AILERON
44...	97-14000	OUTER WING PANEL
45...	97-19002	LOWER DIVE BRAKES
46...	83-14011	LEFT WING TIP
47...	73-14011	RIGHT WING TIP
48...	73-33102	LANDING GEAR SHOCK STRUT
49...	73-33302	LANDING GEAR FAIRING
50...	73-14032	LANDING GEAR WING COVER
51...	73-14032-12	WING LANDING GEAR ACCESS DOOR
52...	73-33301	WING LANDING GEAR FAIRING DOOR
53...	73-14060	FUEL TANK DOOR
54...	97-63002	BOMB RACK
55...	97-14122	LANDING LIGHT COVER
56...	97-19001	UPPER DIVE BRAKE ASSEMBLY
57...	97-31029	RECOGNITION DEVICE COVER
58...	97-31031	UPPER FUSELAGE ACCESS DOOR

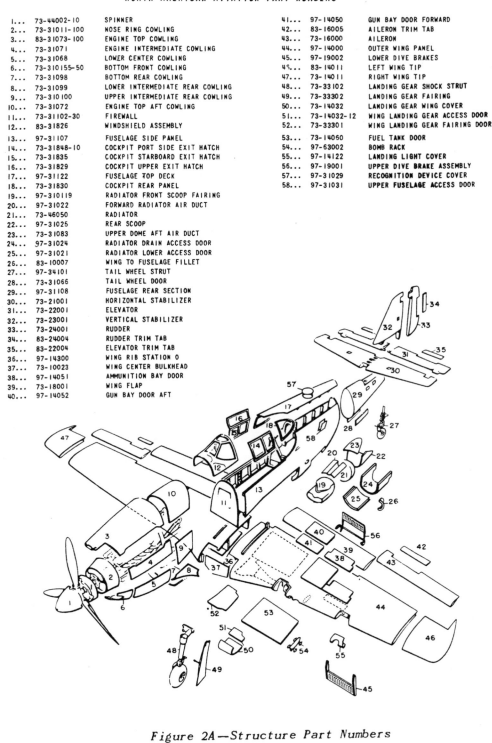

Figure 2A—Structure Part Numbers

A-36 exploded view depicts major assemblies. Dive brakes (part numbers 45 and 56) were unique to the A-36 variant.

The first A-36A (42-83663) was photographed in 1942. A-36 used four .50-caliber guns in the wings and two in the lower nose, plus bomb shackles, making it a potent ground attack weapon. (NAA)

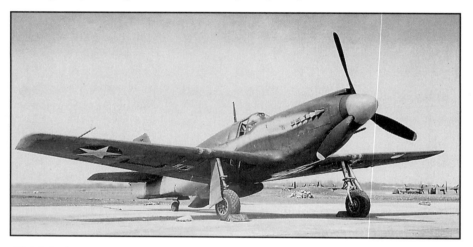

Thick light-colored smudging of exhaust shows airflow pattern on an A-36, rising slightly as it leaves the exhaust stacks, due to airflow over the wing, and then tucking under the horizontal stabilizer. (SDAM)

the large size of the radiator, making a chin location untenable.[6]

Years later, Lee Atwood, whose persuasions to the British Purchasing Commission gave the Mustang its chance, described British research into a phenomenon of radiator cooling that could be manipulated to provide forward thrust to an aircraft. Called the Meredith Effect, the boost in propulsion could be realized by varying the size of the exit opening for air after it passed through the radiator. This heated air, constricted as it exited the radiator, developed enough pressure and thrust, Atwood later estimated, to approximate an additional 200 horsepower for the Mustang.[7]

Whether or not the Meredith Effect influenced initial Mustang design rationale, the result of the Mustang's coolant scoop exit thrust was beneficial to the aircraft's performance.

DITCHING NOT DESIRED

There was a downside to NAA's efficient ventral radiator scoop on the Mustang. British experience showed some Mustangs disappeared on overwater flights. Based on eyewitness reports and model tests, the British concluded, "the ditching performance of the Mustang is so bad that pilots should bale out on every occasion if sufficient height exists to do this," according to a report filed by the Royal Aircraft Establishment at

Formation of three A-36s over Southern California shows typical early use of fuselage location for serial numbers on A-36s and P-51s. Some B-models still were made with fuselage numbers, but during B-model production, tail numbers were applied. (NAA)

P-51 Series

P-51B/C exploded view shows wing gun ports for only two .50-caliber weapons in each wing. Hinged top canopy facilitated access from left side of razorback Mustangs.

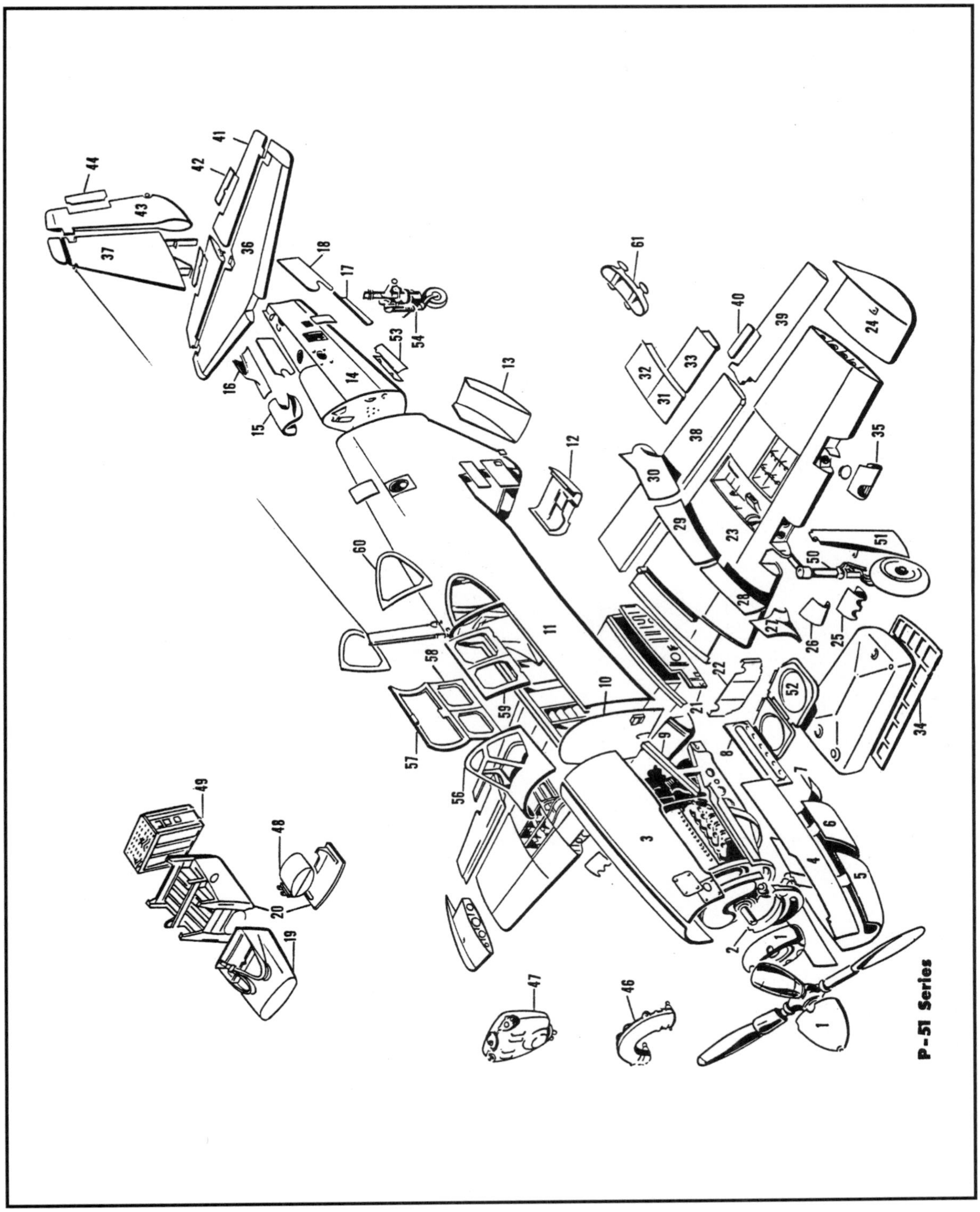

NORTH AMERICAN
P-51 MUSTANG

19

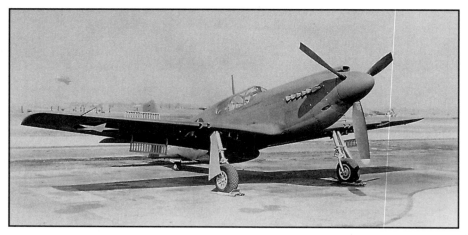

A-36 with dive brakes extended above and below wings also has empty nose gun ports. (SDAM)

The third P-51A (43-6005) shows clean nose lines with no armament there; four .50-caliber machine guns were carried in the wings; bomb shackles were under the wings. British used P-51A as Mustang II. (NAA/SDAM)

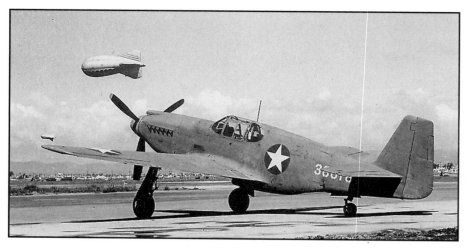

A familiar fixture in California skies near war production plants, barrage balloons float silently in the background as a North American Aviation photographer captures a P-51A on film. A-model Mustang was powered by a V-1710-81 engine—last P-51 production variant to ride behind an Allison.

Farnborough, England in December 1943. The belly radiator acted like a scoop, ramming water in and causing a ditching Mustang to tuck under and dive beneath the water rapidly, with deceleration as high as 8g. The British study was not simple bashing of an American airplane; previous British experience had also shown the Spitfire and Hurricane, heroes of the Battle of Britain, to be bad in water landings as well.

The USAAF Pilot Training Manual for the P-51 Mustang, dated August 15, 1945, bluntly instructed: "Never attempt to ditch the P-51 except as a last resort. Fighter planes are not designed to float on water, and the P-51 has an even greater tendency to dive because of the airscoop underneath. It will go down in 1½ to 2 seconds." The manual continued: "It is possible to ditch the P-51 successfully and it has been done on several occasions. However, it is a hazardous business."[8]

The manual offers a glimpse into the advice given new Mustang pilots: "If trouble arises during an over-water flight, and if you're sure that you can't reach land, don't hesitate to bail out. You won't be able to save the airplane by a water landing, nor will you provide yourself with any useful equipment, as would be the case with a larger airplane. So you had best abandon ship in the air.

If you're at an extremely low altitude, pull the airplane up at a steep angle, throw off the safety belt and shoulder straps and go out over the right side. Even if you're flying only 50 feet above the water, or less, you have sufficient speed at the minimum cruising rate to pull up to 500 feet, and from that altitude you can make a safe jump.

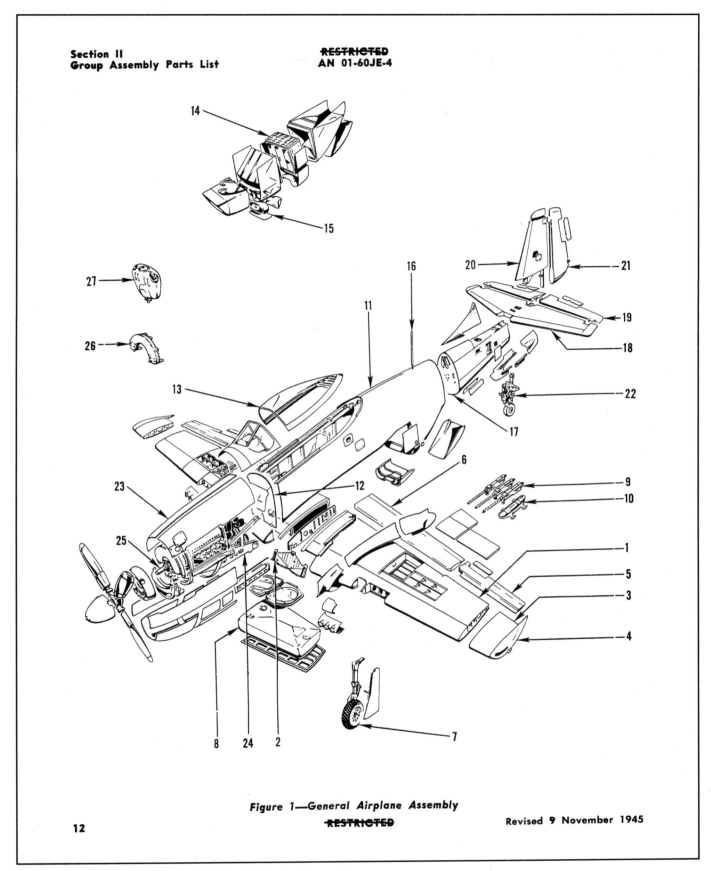

Figure 1—General Airplane Assembly

Revised 9 November 1945

12

P-51D exploded view shows six .50-caliber machine guns (part 9) and underwing shackle (part 10).

NORTH AMERICAN
P-51 MUSTANG

21

Mustang design studies included this mock-up of a center-engine variant mounting a Rolls Royce Griffon powerplant. (SDAM)

The important thing to remember is to make as steep a pull-up as possible and get out at as high an altitude as you can.

If there is a fire, or if for any other reason it is advisable to go out on the left side rather than the right side, don't hesitate to do so. The right side is recommended only because the slipstream helps you in clearing the airplane.

If it isn't possible to get up high enough to make a successful parachute drop, remember that the P-51 **can** be ditched successfully…

…If the wind is less than 35 MPH, touch down parallel with the lines of wave crests and troughs. Ditch into the wind only if its velocity is over 35 MPH, or if the sea is flat…

…Keep the wheels up, and use flaps in proportion to available power in order to obtain minimum forward speed with minimum rate of descent. Approach in 3-point attitude, and observe the following procedure:

1. Lower the seat, duck your head, and jettison the canopy.

2. Jettison tanks or bombs, if you're carrying any.

3. Unfasten the parachute harness.

4. Make sure that your shoulder harness and safety belt are locked and tight.

5. Maintain an airspeed of 120 MPH.

6. Cut the switches just before impact.

7. Touch down in normal landing attitude. Deceleration following contact will be very violent.

Once the airplane stops you won't have more than 2 seconds…" At this point, the pilot was instructed to jump out and extricate the life raft from the parachute harness, and to keep wearing the Mae West life preserver as well.[9]

Called Mustang X, several early airframes received Rolls Royce Merlin engines in England, proving the merit of this installation. Deep chin inlet characterized the Mustang X. (Peter M. Bowers collection via SDAM)

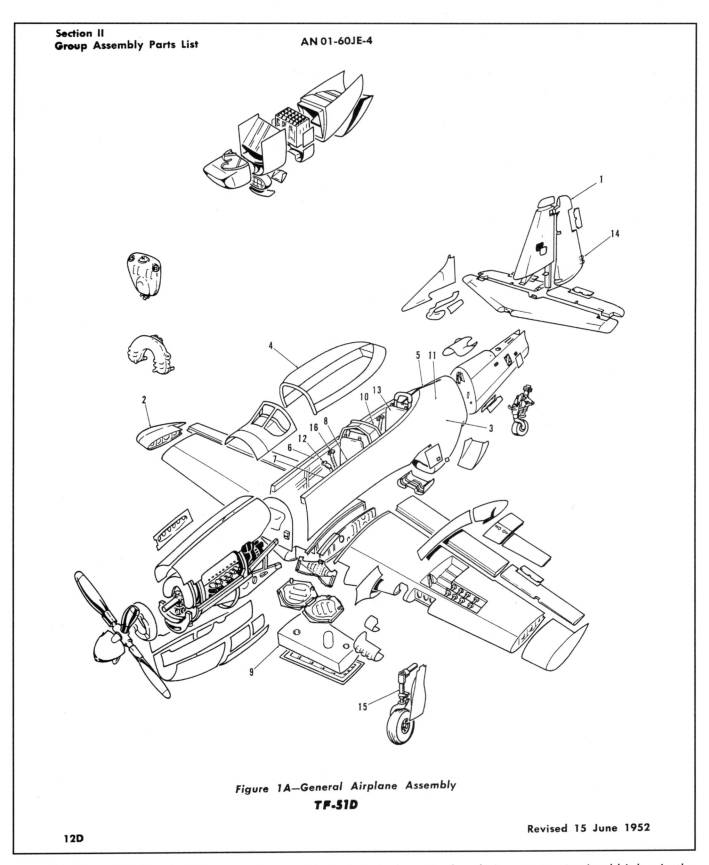

Figure 1A—General Airplane Assembly
TF-51D

Revised 15 June 1952

12D

TF-51D had modified cockpit for second seat with dual controls; revised cockpit canopy remained higher in the back for headroom, and had thicker canopy rail at rear end than single-seat Mustangs.

Wind tunnel test for Merlin-powered XP-51B used deep chin-mounted carburetor scoop that extended below nose contours. (GALCIT/Cal Tech)

On October 26, 1940, the first NA-73 was borne aloft on its new laminar-flow wings. This aircraft made a few flights before it was felled by a carburetion anomaly, coming to earth in a field and flipping on its back. Though some accounts say the first Mustang was scrapped after its somersault, evidence exists to show it was re-introduced on the assembly line and extensively refurbished.[11] The ultimate scrapping of the prototype Mustang after it was repaired and flown, accumulating a total of 45 flights, may have been prompted by the hand-built nature of this first of the breed, and the limits that placed on its serviceability and interoperability with other Mustangs.

If the instructions on ditching the Mustang have a sobering tone, they nonetheless exemplify a universal trait of good fliers, who never give up in an emergency.

READY, SET, GO

American governmental approval to sell the Mustang as an export to Britain was granted in early May 1940, with the proviso that two samples, built in addition to the initial production batch, be sold to the Air Corps for evaluation.[10] As North American Aviation's NA-73, the first airframe was ready on time, but stood idle awaiting arrival of the intended engine.

The first production Mustang I flew April 23, 1941, according to test pilot logs.[12] The fourth plane from this batch (and the second to fly, on May 20) became the USAAF's first XP-51, flown to Wright Field in the latter part of August. Armament included two .50-caliber machine guns firing from the underside of the nose, two more .50-calibers in the wings, and four outboard wing-mounted .30-caliber weapons. Quickly evident was the Mustang I's superlative low-level performance. The British increased their order, no doubt mindful of the pressing need for close air support in campaigns like the one being waged against General Erwin Rommel's tanks in north Africa at the time. Following the XP-51s in series nomenclature in 1941 were 150 straight P-51s ordered in July[13], similar but packing four long-barreled 20MM wing cannons. Ninety-three went to the RAF as Mustang IAs; 55 acquired a

As built, the XP-51B had the deep chin scoop and a ventral inlet that had an opening perpendicular to the undersurface of the wing. Subsequent problems, ranging from overheating to rumbling in the radiator inlet, led to a revision that clearly put the inlet down out of the boundary layer, and angled the lip. (NAA)

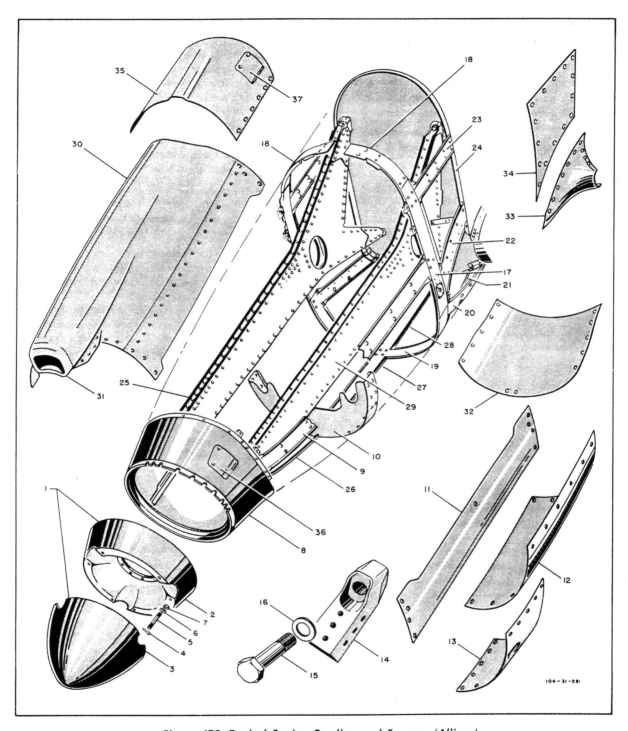

Figure 478—Typical Engine Cowling and Formers (Allison)

422

Sleek streamlining for Allison-engined Mustangs was only broken by elevated carburetor scoop atop nose.

P-51Bs at rest under camouflage netting at Inglewood show a feature of the landing gear— two Mustangs closest to camera have inner landing gear doors open, as they would be during retraction/extension cycle. Distant P-51B has inner doors closed; in flight, the doors opened to allow the wheels to pass, and then closed again for streamlining.

pair of K-24 cameras to become F-6A photo reconnaissance aircraft. Technically, the first operational use by the USAAF of Mustangs was with the 154th Observation Squadron, flying F-6As on April 9, 1943.[14]

DON'T CALL IT A MESSERSCHMITT

The Mustang's squared wingtips, early razorback configuration, and closely-packed inline engine configuration bore a passing resemblance to the Messerschmitt Me-109. According to a dispatch filed by a correspondent in 1942, when the first Mustang crossed the English channel and streaked over Europe, Axis guns and planes did not fire at it. The Mustang supposedly flew over German positions uncontested. Subsequently, other new Mustangs in trials over Great Britain were fired at by British anti-aircraft batteries, much to the surprise and chagrin of the pilots. The problem in both cases was laid to a resemblance between the Mustang and Germany's Messerschmitt Me-109, especially when seen in silhouette or illuminated in such a way that made markings difficult to register.[15]

From this casual similarity in appearance between the two antagonists, according to a wartime dispatch, rumors started in England and flowed back to the United States that the Mustang was designed by a

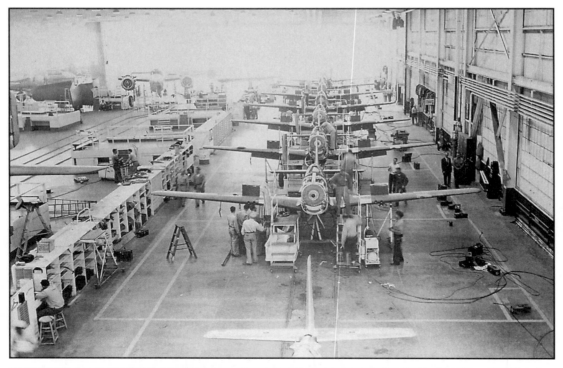

Four-gun P-51Bs receive attention on the Inglewood assembly line next to a production run of B-25s. Gun bay doors are open on the tops of the Mustangs' wings. (NAA)

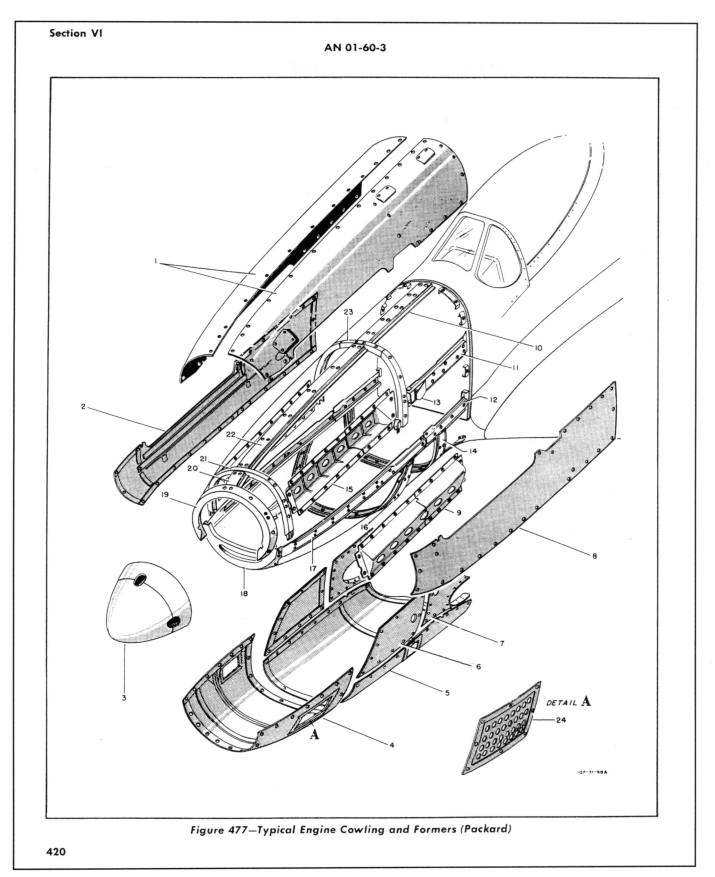

Figure 477—Typical Engine Cowling and Formers (Packard)

Merlin Mustang cowling on P-51D included side dust screens for carburetor (detail A).

NORTH AMERICAN
P-51 MUSTANG

A P-51B tested bulging camera stores. (SDAM)

USAAF portrait of a P-51B-5 at Wright Field shows placement of large landing light in left wing leading edge; pitot mast rides below right wing in undisturbed air. (USAF photo)

P-51B fuselages in castered dollies share shop space with AT-6 Texan trainers at Inglewood. (NAA/SDAM)

pair of German refugees who formerly were designers for Willy Messerschmitt. North American Aviation Company officials took steps to deny this legend of imitation in the creation of the Mustang. The dispatch took pains to explain "ex-Germans" on NAA's design team, saying that North American Aviation said there were never any ex-Messerschmitt designers working on the Mustang design. Some ex-Germans working for North American all hailed from the pre-Messerschmitt era of aviation, the release noted. The dispatch said some engineers who came to the United States with Anthony Fokker after World War One remained in the Fokker organization as it was merged into General Aviation Company and later into NAA. Ed Schmued, chief of North American's designers, was described as an ex-Austrian who served as an officer in the Austrian Air Force in World War One. An American citizen, Schmued, along with project engineer Ken Bowen, who became assistant factory manager of North American's Dallas, Texas plant, were pivotal in the design of the Mustang. Bowen's background was listed as a former British citizen who had served in the RAF.[16]

If news stories succeeded in squelching rumors of copycat designing in the Mustang, the P-51 still was mistaken for an Me-109 long after. European Mustangs often adopted distinctive bands painted around the tail surfaces and wings as quick-reference features to distinguish them from Messerschmitts.

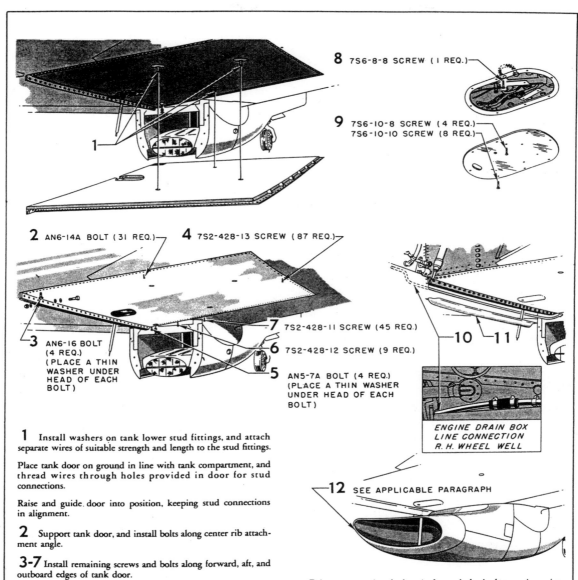

8 7S6-8-8 SCREW (I REQ.)

9 7S6-10-8 SCREW (4 REQ.)
7S6-10-10 SCREW (8 REQ.)

2 AN6-14A BOLT (31 REQ.)

4 7S2-428-13 SCREW (87 REQ.)

3 AN6-16 BOLT (4 REQ.) (PLACE A THIN WASHER UNDER HEAD OF EACH BOLT)

7 7S2-428-11 SCREW (45 REQ.)

6 7S2-428-12 SCREW (9 REQ.)

5 AN5-7A BOLT (4 REQ.) (PLACE A THIN WASHER UNDER HEAD OF EACH BOLT)

10 **11**

ENGINE DRAIN BOX LINE CONNECTION R. H. WHEEL WELL

12 SEE APPLICABLE PARAGRAPH

1 Install washers on tank lower stud fittings, and attach separate wires of suitable strength and length to the stud fittings.

Place tank door on ground in line with tank compartment, and thread wires through holes provided in door for stud connections.

Raise and guide door into position, keeping stud connections in alignment.

2 Support tank door, and install bolts along center rib attachment angle.

3-7 Install remaining screws and bolts along forward, aft, and outboard edges of tank door.

8 Connect bonding braid from booster pump to tank door.

9 Install booster pump access door.

10 Install engine drain box drain line.

11 Install fairing over lower wing center bolting angle.

12 Install radiator air inlet scoop.

REMOVAL: Essentially the reverse of installation procedure, with the following exceptions:

Prior to removing fuel tank doors, jack airplane, using wing jacking points at lower surface of each wing section immediately outboard of bomb racks, and jacking point on wing center rib.

Weight of airplane must be supported at center jacking point, with outer jacking points being used for balance only.

CAUTION

The foregoing jacking procedure should be closely followed, as the fuel tank doors form a structural part of the wing. Distortion and misalignment may result from improper support. To prevent sinking when jacking on soft surface, place suitable platform beneath jacking stand.

109-10-246

Figure 86—Installing Fuel Tank Doors

RESTRICTED

Drawings depict P-51D wing joint, and fairing applied to joint angle (item 11); access door for wing fuel tank (item 2) was bolted in place first.

NORTH AMERICAN

P-51 MUSTANG

A-36 Dive-Bombed Its Way Into History

The early success with ground attack missions in the Mustang I boded well for the development of speed-brake equipped A-36 dive bomber variants—the most deliberate and extensive makeover of an American fighter into a dive bomber during World War Two. (Prewar Air Corps planning deliberately omitted bombing equipment from fighters, to keep ground commanders from attempting to siphon off fighter assets for close-support duties. The A-36 represented a change in primary mission, and mission designation as an attack aircraft instead of a pursuit. Ultimately, all major USAAF fighters of the war were made bomb-capable, and special-purpose AAF dive bombers largely gave way to multi-role fighters.) The A-36 was built with dive brakes that extended above and below the wing surfaces, unique in Mustang production. Able to carry a 500-pound bomb beneath each wing, the A-36 had four wing-mounted and two nose-mounted .50-caliber machine guns with which to intimidate and demolish ground targets, or for its own aerial defense. A-36s started construction in the spring of 1942, being completed and beginning delivery in October of that year. The installed Allison V-1710-87 engine of the A-36 gave it a top speed, without external stores, of 366 miles an hour; when carrying a pair of 500-pound bombs at 5,000 feet, the A-36 could reach 310 miles an hour—substantially faster than purpose-built dive bomber airframes riding behind radial engines. The 27th Fighter Bomber Group inaugurated combat missions with the A-36 on June 6, 1943, reaching out to strike Italian targets from Tunisia. With a service ceiling of 27,000 feet, the A-36 remained a credible dive bomber, but still lacked the range and performance to suggest itself as an escort fighter.

North American Aviation applied the model number NA-105 to several lightweight Mustang variants including the XP-51F (43-43332 shown), swinging a three-blade prop and topping out at 466 miles an hour at 29,000 feet. Use of smaller, lighter, mainwheels allowed leading edge of wing to be made without the characteristic fillet near the fuselage as used on previous Mustangs. NAA photo numbers for these XP-51F photos uses 105 nomenclature; NAA photos of lightweight XP-51G, also Model 105, use nomenclature of 105A, suggesting this was a company distinction between model designations for the F and G.

The leapfrogging development of combat aircraft in World War Two saw the P-51A delivered to the USAAF in the spring and summer of 1943, relying

on four wing-mounted .50-caliber guns. Riding behind an Allison V-1710-81 engine, the P-51A-model retained underwing shackles of the A-36, but had an improved top speed of 390 miles an hour at 20,000 feet, and a service ceiling of 31,350 feet. The shackles could carry drop tanks; clearly the P-51 was evolving toward its destiny as the best escort fighter of World War Two. USAAF P-51As flew combat in Asia, beginning in the fall of 1943.

MERLIN'S MAGIC FOR THE B-MODEL

NAA engineers investigated the possibility of mating their state-of-the-art Mustang airframe with Britain's superlative Rolls Royce Merlin engine, a powerplant with a two-stage mechanical supercharger that was unequaled at the time. Ultimately, the first blending of Mustang and Merlin took place in England, where Rolls Royce received several Mustang Is to convert. The first of these flew in 1942. NAA undertook a Merlin modification program, initially under the designation XP-78, later changed to XP-51B. The B-model also incorporated revised ailerons.

The stand-off belly scoop that allowed undisturbed air to be ingested for cooling was introduced on the B-model. This salient design feature is attributed to NAA aerodynamics engineer Irv Ashkenas during test sessions at the Cal Tech wind tunnel.

First XP-51G (43-43335) shows short vertical tail similar to that of earlier Mustangs; elongated cockpit canopy, and five-blade Rotol wooden propeller. P-51G boasted more than 470 miles an hour at 20,750 feet.

An Inglewood P-51D (44-13366) was built without the dorsal fin of later D-models; some Mustangs, including some razorbacks, were retrofitted with dorsal fins. Aft fuselage fuel tank cap is visible near rear of canopy frame. (USAF photo from Malcolm Gougon collection)

P-51D shows Swiss-cheese vent in lower part of nose that was alternate air inlet with filtration for dusty operations; front chin inlet could be baffled off to cause air intake for carburetor to pass through these side-mounted filter openings. In later years, many owners of civilian Mustangs have removed this feature as no longer needed.

Second XP-51G (43-43336) was earmarked for England, and fitted with four-blade prop when photo was taken February 26, 1945. Vertical fin appears to have increased height on this example. (NAA/SDAM)

The B-model introduced a hallmark of Merlin Mustangs by placing the carburetor inlet in the "chin" location instead of on top of the nose as had been the practice with Allison Mustangs. The results were exciting—the P-51B could attain 440 miles an hour at 30,000 feet, and had a service ceiling of 42,000 feet. Still not possessing the range needed for escort duties deep into German territory, the B-model was fitted with additional fuel storage behind the cockpit, serviced by a receptacle high on the left side of the fuselage. This raised total internal fuel capacity from 184 to 269 gallons; underwing drop tanks could add another 220 gallons to the total. In March 1944, P-51Bs escorted bombers all the way to Berlin and back—strategic bombardment now had the protective canopy it needed to carry the war to the heart of Germany.

Upon arrival in the United Kingdom, a P-51B for the RAF (Mustang III) was inspected on October 19, 1943, by a host of Royal Air Force, British industry, and USAAF representatives at Hamble. A British RAF examination report on the Mustang III noted its two wing racks were cleared for up to a 1,000-pound bomb on each rack, adding: "The installation makes provision for twin lug stores or drop tanks; and selective fusing, nose and tail, for American bombs."[17]

The RAF report mentioned the impending American application in

Capitalizing on the lightweight strides made with NAA Model NA-105 Mustang models, the P-51H (foreground) was the last version of the single-engine Mustang to enter quantity production. Noticeably taller tail with vertical fin cap, redesigned ventral scoop, and generally different fuselage and wing contours distinguish the H-model from the late P-51D-NA flying formation in the photo. (USAF photo)

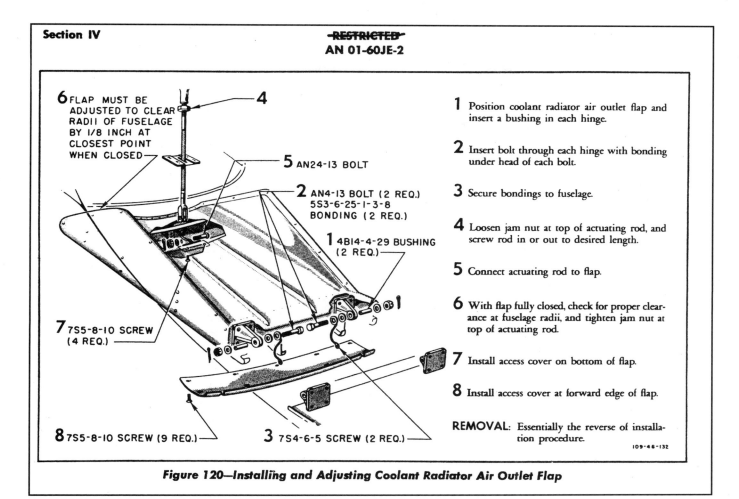

6 FLAP MUST BE ADJUSTED TO CLEAR RADII OF FUSELAGE BY 1/8 INCH AT CLOSEST POINT WHEN CLOSED

4

5 AN24-13 BOLT

2 AN4-13 BOLT (2 REQ.)
5S3-6-25-1-3-8 BONDING (2 REQ.)

1 4B14-4-29 BUSHING (2 REQ.)

7 7S5-8-10 SCREW (4 REQ.)

8 7S5-8-10 SCREW (9 REQ.)

3 7S4-6-5 SCREW (2 REQ.)

1 Position coolant radiator air outlet flap and insert a bushing in each hinge.

2 Insert bolt through each hinge with bonding under head of each bolt.

3 Secure bondings to fuselage.

4 Loosen jam nut at top of actuating rod, and screw rod in or out to desired length.

5 Connect actuating rod to flap.

6 With flap fully closed, check for proper clearance at fuselage radii, and tighten jam nut at top of actuating rod.

7 Install access cover on bottom of flap.

8 Install access cover at forward edge of flap.

REMOVAL: Essentially the reverse of installation procedure.

109-46-132

Figure 120—Installing and Adjusting Coolant Radiator Air Outlet Flap

P-51D ventral coolant radiator outlet flap installation; by adjusting the size of the outlet, variations in forward thrust could be achieved as a byproduct to good engine cooling.

1944 of a sliding "balloon" canopy to future Mustangs. Meanwhile, "the 'Malcolm' Balloon Sliding Hood developed for Mustang aircraft is to be applied retrospectively to all Mustang III aircraft," the report noted, with priority going to

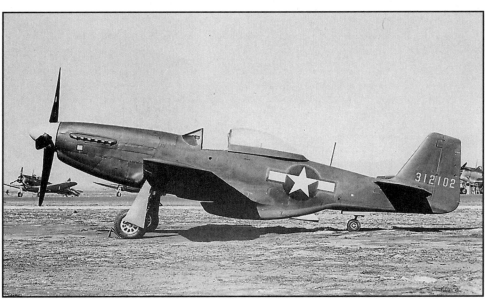

Its serial number (43-12102) verifies this is a P-51B; the bubble canopy and revised windscreen shows it to be one of two B-models that became prototypes for the P-51D. Far greater visibility and headroom resulted; an unwanted side effect was reduced stability due to the lost aft fuselage side area. Most P-51Ds incorporated a dorsal fin to correct for this. Another clue that this is a modified B-model is the absence of a fuel cap in the rear fuselage near the top left part of the national insignia; later B-models introduced a fuel tank in that location to boost range. (NAA)

Fastest of all the Mustangs, the Allison-engined XP-51J could attain 491 miles an hour at 27,400 feet. Sleek nose contour without chin carburetor inlet was possible when carburetor air source was relocated in ventral radiator scoop. Use of photo identification numbers 105B on NAA pictures of the XP-51J may signify how this version of the same Model 105 was distinguished from other NA-105 variants including the P-51F and G models. (SDAM)

those Mustang IIIs used for fighter duties. Additionally, the RAF report commented: "It is understood that this modification will also be applied to USAAF Mustang III aircraft in (the) UK." The British-designed Malcolm hood was a bulging blown canopy that afforded pilots better visibility than the more narrow confines of the razorback Mustang as delivered from the factory. But the ultimate answer for Mustang pilot visibility was the full-blown bubble canopy and cut-down rear fuselage introduced in production on the P-51D. Photos of USAAF razorback P-51s in Europe show frequent evidence of the use of Malcolm hoods.[18]

The redesigned radiators on the P-51B used metals different from earlier Mustangs. The British inspection report for the B-model acknowledged information from the United States that said a special mixture of glycol coolant was needed because of rapid corrosion and deterioration of the main intercooler radiator. Until the special glycol mix was available, the Merlin engine was limited to 50 inches of boost. The British report also made note of air cleaners that were to be installed beginning with the 126th B-model, adding: "Early aircraft are accepted without this modification." This may refer to dust filters, for desert operations, that were installed in the lower sides of the engine cowling, behind panels with rows of holes. These were alternate air inlets that could be used to filter engine carburetor air in dusty climates; photos of early P-51Bs show smooth-skinned nose cowling without this addition.[19]

DEFINING THE MUSTANG WITH THE P-51D

P-51Bs from NAA's Inglewood, California, factory and 1,750 similar P-51Cs from the NAA Dallas assembly line were the last of the razorback Mustangs. Improved visibility to the rear was a key to fighter pilots' survival, and a bubble canopy on a cut-down fuselage was the answer for the Mustang. Building on late B- and C-model upgrades, including the use of six wing-mounted .50-caliber machine guns, the P-51D employed the V-1650-7 version of the Merlin, turning a four-blade Hamilton-Standard propeller. Virtually identical P-51Ks built at Dallas had Aeroproducts propellers. Output of D-models was high; Inglewood tallied 6,502 P-51D-NA versions, while Dallas built 1,454 P-51D-NTs, as well as the 1,337 similar K-models.

As first introduced, the P-51D's cut-down rear fuselage afforded less area than that of razorback

The first NAA model NA-126 P-51H (44-64160) was photographed with a tail of intermediate height, similar to that of the XP-51J, with no vertical fin cap above the metal-skinned rudder. (SDAM)

Mustangs, and hence provided less directional stability. Addition of a dorsal fin effectively fixed the problem, and added its own aesthetic to the lines of the P-51D.

As F-6D and F-6K, photo reconnaissance versions of the P-51D and P-51K, respectively, packed a K-22, K-17, and K-24 camera for their missions.

LIGHTWEIGHTS PROMISED SPEED

As P-51Bs and Cs were battling above Germany, and the P-51D was unfolding as the next production variant, NAA engineers undertook efforts to lighten the Mustang. Even the thoroughbred could be overtaken by future designs if North American Aviation grew careless. As early as January 1943, before production P-51Bs were delivered, NAA proposed a new lightweight NA-105 model; that July, the USAAF gave a contract ordering five prototypes. NAA carved away at the Mustang airframe, taking away the wing root leading edge fillet characteristic of earlier P-51s, using smaller landing wheels and narrower landing gear doors. Two of the machine guns and their attending mounts and ammunition were stripped from the lightweights. The results were far more than a makeover; the first example, the XP-51F, riding behind a three-blade Aeroproducts propeller, was a new airplane. Topping out at 466 miles an hour, three F-models were built, one being sent to Great Britain. The pair of XP-51Gs used five-bladed Rotol propellers to coax 472 miles an hour top speed at 20,750 feet. In June 1944, two more lightweight prototypes were added to the wish list—the XP-51Js.

Banking P-51H shows simplified wing leading edge, plus underwing hardpoints for a total of six zero-length rocket launchers and two drop tanks or bombs. (NAA)

SPEEDING TO OBLIVION: P-51J

Among the lightweight Mustang airframes produced in an effort to improve even further on the design's greatness was the short-lived P-51J. The two J-models reunited the P-51 with an Allison engine, this time the impressive V-1710-119 with two-stage blower. At last, the promise of the Allison V-12 aircraft engine was realized, as the V-1710-119, coupled with a lightened airframe, gave the P-51J the

The second P-51H had an enlarged vertical fin that extended over the rudder, characterizing production H-models. (NAA/SDAM)

P-51D was fitted with two ramjet engines beneath the wings.

enter mass production. Top speed was 487 miles an hour, provided by a V-1650-9 Merlin engine. The war ended when 555 P-51Hs were finished at Inglewood, and the balance of a 2,000-plane contract was canceled. Only one similar P-51M was completed at Dallas before that plant's 1,600-aircraft order was shut down. Also canceled was the P-51L powered by a Merlin V-1650-11.

almost unbelievable speed of 491 miles an hour at 27,400 feet. It was the fastest of any Mustang variant. When it first flew on April 23, 1945, the P-51J handily outsped the Bell P-59 Airacomet jet. The vaunted Lockheed P-80A Shooting Star, already flying, could boast 558 miles an hour at sea level, but this dwindled to only 508 miles an hour at 30,000 feet.[20] The reciprocating-engine P-51J was a contender in the early jet world.

In the absence of hard data and correspondence, speculation about the fate of the incredible J-model Mustang is tantalizing. At least one researcher suggests the P-51J was a victim of its own success. It represented the zenith in reciprocating fighter engine and airframe design at a time when turbojets, in their infancy, represented the future. To have a prop-driven fighter share the skies with P-80s, and be nearly their equal in speed and more than a match in endurance, could be a liability for the builders of the jet Air Force. So the theory goes, rather than spend time and money on a capable prop fighter that repre-

sented the end of one era, the Air Force shunted the P-51J aside to foster development of jets—the beginning of the future.[21]

At any rate, North American's Dallas, Texas, factory was discussed as a site to build 1,000 P-80As—not P-51Js—under contract before the end of the war scaled that back to Lockheed's home plant in Burbank only.[22]

The P-51J featured a nearly chinless nose contour, with the engine air inlet collocated in the ventral scoop for the coolant system. Narrow main gear doors and no leading edge root flair suggested some common ground with other lightweight Mustang variants, while the teardrop bubble canopy looked enormously long on the J-model airframe.

Last of the Single Engine Production Mustangs

Using attributes of the lightweight prototypes, the P-51H, which first flew on the third day of February 1945, was the last P-51 to

The P-51H could still post a speed of 450 miles an hour while toting a pair of 500-pound bombs, and the armament was returned to six .50-caliber machine guns. The 555 completed H-models never saw combat, although they equipped postwar units in the active-duty U.S. Air Force as well as stateside Air National Guard organizations during the Korean war. The P-51H presided over the technology transformation from propeller-driven fighters to turbojets; another North American product, the jet-propelled F-86, carried on the tradition of fighter excellence in the U.S. Air Force that typified the NAA Mustang.

North American Aviation's development of the Mustang line continued, on paper at least, with a tricycle gear proposal using a forward swept wing and a Westinghouse turbojet engine in the aft fuselage, augmenting an Allison V-1710 in the nose. It was to have used tricycle gear and a P-51H cockpit layout, but such a hybrid fighter did not materialize.

Given the nomenclature NA

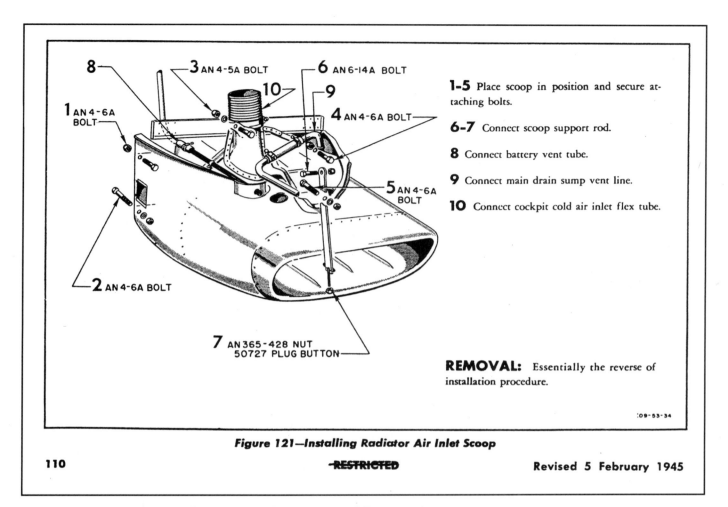

1-5 Place scoop in position and secure attaching bolts.

6-7 Connect scoop support rod.

8 Connect battery vent tube.

9 Connect main drain sump vent line.

10 Connect cockpit cold air inlet flex tube.

REMOVAL: Essentially the reverse of installation procedure.

:09-53-34

Figure 121—Installing Radiator Air Inlet Scoop

110   Revised 5 February 1945

P-51D angled radiator air inlet scoop used a support rod (items 6, 7).

Model Number RD-1410, the swept-forward wing Mustang was intended to capitalize on the ability of a piston-engine fighter to be smaller than the size required of a fuel-guzzling jet of that vintage. Envisioned as a penetration fighter, the aircraft's jet engine would be used for short durations as required in combat.

NAA aerodynamicist Edward Horkey said wing sweep decreased drag as Mach number increased, while still allowing enough wing thickness to house armament and landing gear inside the wing. Swept wings, whether forward or aft, presented some problems in low-speed stability and control. The forward sweep initially appeared to be easier to deal with in treating these problems. But the radical Mustang model's forward swept wing was dogged by twisting problems under load.23 Clearly, bright North American Aviation engineers learned from the experience with the swept-forward Mustang venture, and applied a refined knowledge of aft-swept wings to that company's milestone F-86 and F-100 jet fighters.

[1] From margin notes made to a draft of this manuscript by San Diego Aerospace Museum archivist Ray Wagner, July 1996. [2] "North American P-51 Mustang," news release, unsigned and undated (contemporary with World War Two), held at the Air Force Historical Research Center, Maxwell AFB, Alabama. [3] "British Army Cooperation Tactical Employment of the Mustang I (P-51)," by Brig Gen Charles F. Born, Asst. Chief of Staff, A-3, Headquarters, Northwest African Strategic Air Forces, 26 Aug 1943. [4] "North American P-51 Mustang," news release, unsigned and undated (contemporary with World War Two), held at the Air Force Historical Research Center, Maxwell AFB, Alabama. [5] *Ibid.* [6] "The P-51—The Real Story," by Edward Horkey, *American Aviation Historical Society Journal*, Vol. 41, No. 3, Fall 1996. [7] "The 'Spitfire' and the 'Mustang': The Meredith Mystery," by J. Leland Atwood, *USAF Museum Foundation Friends Magazine.* [8] *Pilot Training Manual for the P-51 Mustang*, HQ, AAF, Washington, DC, Aug 15, 1945. [9] *Ibid.* [10] From conversation between the author and San Diego Aerospace Museum archivist Ray Wagner, July 18, 1996. [11] From conversation between the author and P-51 researcher Lowell Ford, June 1996. [12] From margin notes and correspondence with Ray Wagner, July 1996. [13] *Ibid.* [14] Ray Wagner, *American Combat Planes*, Doubleday, Garden City, New York, 1968. [15] Obert Ruark, NEA Service Washington Correspondent dispatch (untitled), Sept. 9, 1942. [16] *Ibid.* [17] Royal Air Force Report on Examination of Aircraft, Mustang III (P.51-B), Oct 19, 1943. [18] *Ibid.* [19] *Ibid.* [20] Ray Wagner, *American Combat Planes*, Doubleday, Garden City, New York, 1968. [21] Discussion about P-51J between the author and P-51 researcher Lowell Ford, June 1996. [22] Ray Wagner, *American Combat Planes*, Doubleday, Garden City, New York, 1968. [23] "The P-51—The Real Story," by Edward Horkey, *American Aviation Historical Society Journal*, Vol. 41, No. 3, Fall 1996.

MUSTANGS 2 IN SERVICE

The magnificent Mustang entered combat in 1942, and North American Aviation (NAA) engineers continued to refine the design for the remainder of the war, keeping the P-51 a cutting-edge piston-engine fighter all the way. Only jets posed a serious threat to Mustang dominance, and even the vaunted Messerschmitt Me-262s of the Luftwaffe fell victim to skillful P-51 pilots who exploited the early jets' notoriously slow acceleration characteristics. Mustangs were in use virtually daily; samples of the Mustangs' participation in the Second World War include the following:

On August 19, 1942, Royal Canadian Air Force (RCAF) Mustangs supported the abortive Dieppe invasion of continental Europe.

By June 6, 1943, USAAF A-36s of the Northwest African Air Forces (NAAF) were part of the Allied offensive effort directed against the island of Pantelleria. Next month, on the Eighth of July, A-36s ranged over a variety of Sicilian targets, including a marshaling yard, sulfur plant, railroads, highways, trucks, and a train.[1]

Allison-powered A-36s were suitable ground attack aircraft that saw considerable service in the Mediterranean Theater of Operations, but the full promise of the Mustang only began to be realized with the introduction in combat of the razorback P-51B.

Ninth Air Force's IX Fighter Command received assignment of its first tactical fighter organization, the P-51-equipped 354th Fighter Group, on November 8, 1943.

On December 13, for the first time Eighth Air Force P-51s reached their maximum escort range while providing protection for about 649 B-24s and B-17s attacking targets in Germany, including Bremen, Hamburg, and Kiel. On December 17, 1943, the 40th anniversary of the Wright brothers' history-making flight, 12th Air Force P-51s joined P-40s in strafing a ship near Trpanj, while 12th AF A-36s and P-40s bombed a variety of Italian targets that day.[2]

The first day of 1944 saw 10th Air Force, in the China-Burma-India Theater, dispatch 15 P-51s and 11 A-36s to attack the Japanese-held airfield at Myitkyina. On January 11, 1944, seven P-51s from 14th Air Force joined five P-40s to intercept a second wave of Japanese medium bombers and fighters attacking the airfield at Suichwan; the mixed gaggle of American fighters claimed three medium bombers downed.

A-36As rode, 20 at a time, on the decks of T2 tankers bound for Europe from New Jersey. These new attack aircraft flew to Newark where they were barged to a loading pier. Censor blotted out stenciling on aircraft to minimize information given out with the photography during the war. (SDAM)

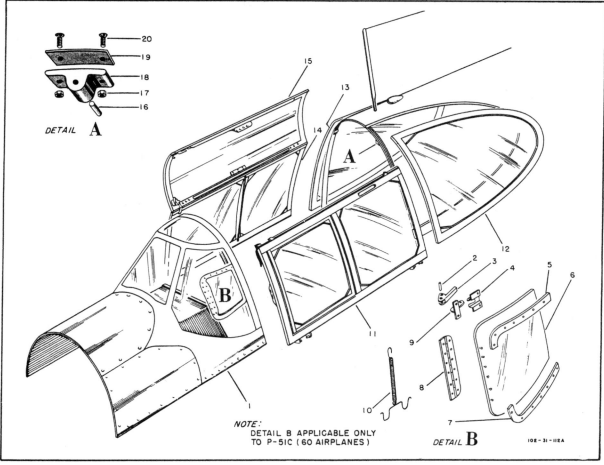

DETAIL **A**

DETAIL **B**

NOTE:
DETAIL B APPLICABLE ONLY
TO P-51C (60 AIRPLANES)

102-31-112A

REF. NO.	PART NO.	TITLE	REF. NO.	PART NO.	TITLE
1	83-31826-300	Windshield Assem.—Cockpit Encl.		99-318102	Hook—Side Glass Open Position
	83-31828	Glass—Windshield Front Armor Plate		73-52448	Spring—Side Glass Open Position Hook
	83-318180	Glass—Windshield Upper		7S4-8-8	Screw
	83-31827-1	Glass—Windshield Side RH		AC365-832	Nut
	99-31827-2	Glass—Windshield Side LH	11	73-31848-20	Panel Assem.—Cockpit Encl. LH
	99-31827	Glass Assem.—Windshield Side LH	12	102-31830	Panel Assem.—Cockpit Enclosure Rear LH
2	99-318141	Pin—Side Glass Handle	13	102-31830-1	Panel Assem.—Cockpit Enclosure Rear RH
3	99-318140	Handle—Left Side Glass Door Latch	14	73-318144-2	Panel Assem.—Exit Hatch Top & Right Side
4	99-318139	Bracket—Side Glass Door Latch		73-31835-10	Panel Assem.—Exit Hatch RH
5	99-318135-3	Retainer—Side Glass Inner	15	73-31829	Panel Assem.—Exit Hatch Upper
6	99-31827-3	Transparent Sheet—Left Side Glass Door	16	73-31271-2	Pin—Side Panel Attaching
7	99-318135-2	Retainer—Side Glass Inner		73-31271-4	Pin—Side Panel Attaching
8	99-318137	Hinge—Side Glass Door	17	83-318182	Nut—Retainer Attachment Front
	7S5-6-8	Screw		AC365-832	Nut—Retainer Attachment Rear
	7S5-6-9	Screw	18	73-31271	Fitting—Exit Hatch Attaching RH
	AN936-A6	Washer		73-31271-3	Fitting—Exit Hatch Attaching LH
	AN365-632	Nut	19	83-318179	Shim—Exit Hatch Attaching Retainer
9	99-318138	Fitting—Side Glass Door Latch	20	7S5-8-8	Screw—Front
10	99-318105	Hook Assem.—Side Glass Open Position		5C4-832-10	Screw—Rear
				AN936-A416	Washer—Front

Figure 425—Typical Cockpit Enclosure—P-51C and Earlier Series Airplanes.

377

Details of razorback Mustang canopy show top hinging canopy and fold-down left side window panel.

Photo recon F-6B (43-6174) of the 67th Tactical Reconnaissance Group began life as part of the P-51A contract. It was photographed at LeMolay, France in August 1944. Small camera mission symbols form two rows beneath the exhaust stacks. (Fred LePage)

P-51A in the China-Burma-India (CBI) Theater used triple bazooka tubes to increase ground attack potency.

On January 17, 1944, 10th Air Force had A-36s and P-51s in the air, supporting ground troops near Taro and in the area of Shaduzup-Ngamaw Ga. A-36s of 12th Air Force continued to hit transportation targets and enemy guns north of Rome, and also in support of the U.S. Fifth Army's efforts in the area of the expanding Garigliano bridgehead on January 19. During this period, both 10th and 12th Air Forces kept A-36s well-employed against ground targets in their areas of responsibility.

January 24, 1944, marked the date on which the British and Americans in England formally agreed to emphasize placement of P-51s in Eighth Air Force for long-range escort of heavy bombers; this would ultimately lead to the Eighth Air Force equipping most of its fighter units with Mustangs and sending its P-38s and P-47s to Ninth Air Force.[3]

On the first day of February 1944, 10th Air Force put up a force of 32 P-51s and A-36s, joined by a single B-25, to rake over the main Japanese-held airfield at Myitkyina, following which some of the attacking force strafed a transport depot at Radhapur and a storage area.

February 11, 1944, saw the first of many P-51s join Eighth Air Force's VIII Fighter Command. On February 14, P-51s and A-36s from 10th Air Force executed about 70 sorties against diverse ground targets in Burma in a pattern repeated in this stage of the war. On March 2, A-36s and P-40s from 12th Air Force targeted troops and guns throughout the contested Anzio area in Italy. That same day saw five P-51s from 10th Air Force bomb artillery positions in the vicinity of Maingkwan.

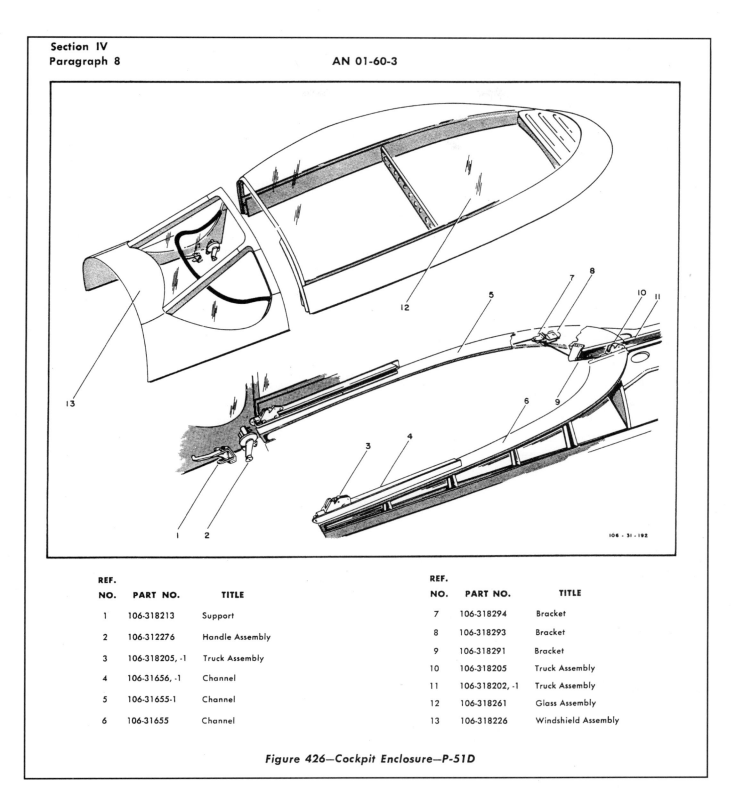

REF. NO.	PART NO.	TITLE	REF. NO.	PART NO.	TITLE
1	106-318213	Support	7	106-318294	Bracket
2	106-312276	Handle Assembly	8	106-318293	Bracket
3	106-318205, -1	Truck Assembly	9	106-318291	Bracket
4	106-31656, -1	Channel	10	106-318205	Truck Assembly
5	106-31655-1	Channel	11	106-318202, -1	Truck Assembly
6	106-31655	Channel	12	106-318261	Glass Assembly
			13	106-318226	Windshield Assembly

Figure 426—Cockpit Enclosure—P-51D

P-51D canopy and windscreen were completely redesigned from earlier variants, providing greater visibility and headroom.

On the sixth day of March, cannon-equipped A-36s from 12th Air Force performed armed reconnaissance over roads and rail lines northeast of Rome, dropping bombs on train cars at Capranica and targeting vehicles as well. On March 8, 23 P-51s from 10th Air Force went after Japanese-held airfields at Shwebo, Anisakan, and Onbauk, demolishing more than 30 enemy aircraft. Though superlative

Bazookas remained an option for P-51Ds, as seen in company photo of 44-14886.

in aerial combat, Mustangs continued to contribute to the Allied war effort with ground attacks as well. On March 15, 1944, Ninth Air Force was released from its first priority obligation to assist the Eighth Air Force, although Ninth AF P-51s would continue to escort Eighth Air Force heavy bombers as required. March 21 saw 41 P-51s from Eighth Air Force sweep southern France in a mission that netted 21 Axis planes destroyed. That same day,

12th Air Force A-36s performed resupply sorties as they dropped food in the vicinity of Cassino. In ensuing days, the A-36s would revert to attacking enemy troop concentrations, guns, and other communications targets in the Cassino area. On March 26, a combined force of about 140 Ninth Air Force P-51s and P-47s dive-bombed the marshaling yards at Creil and military targets in France.

On April 5, 1944, the fighter power of Eighth Air Force was unleashed on airfields and other ground targets in western Europe and Germany as a combined total of more than 450 P-51s, P-38s and P-47s hunted there. During much of April, 10th Air Force P-51s and A-36s were part of the mix of aircraft supporting ground troops in the area of Mawlu, and attacking ground targets in the Mogaung Valley. On April 21, a flight of four 10th Air Force P-51s took out a bridge at Shweli. The campaign against the Luftwaffe continued on April 23 when a mixed bag of 346 Eighth Air Force P-51s, P-47s, and P-38s mounted sorties against airfields and other targets in northern France, Belgium, and northwest Germany. That same day, Ninth Air Force logged about 1,000 P-47 and P-51 dive-bombing sorties against many targets in France and the Low Countries. April 28 saw 10 P-51s from 14th Air Force escort 26 B-24 Liberators in attacks on Yellow River bridges and a nearby Japanese storage area.

Fifteenth Air Force put up 62 P-51s to escort more than 420 B-24s and B-17s on their way to bomb marshaling yards in Bucharest on May 7, 1944; 53 Mustangs provided return escort. May 11 saw two dozen P-51s from 10th Air Force rampage over airfields at Meiktila, Anisakan, and Heho, downing 13 Japanese airplanes in the vicinity. Next day, 21 Mustangs from 10th AF revisited the fields at Meiktila and Heho, claiming eight more Japanese interceptors shot down. On May 19, a force of 11 P-51s from 14th Air

Sharkmouthed P-51B (43-12404) undergoes an engine run at Kunming, China, 1944, with a utility Stearman trainer in the background. (John Houser via San Diego Aerospace Museum collection)

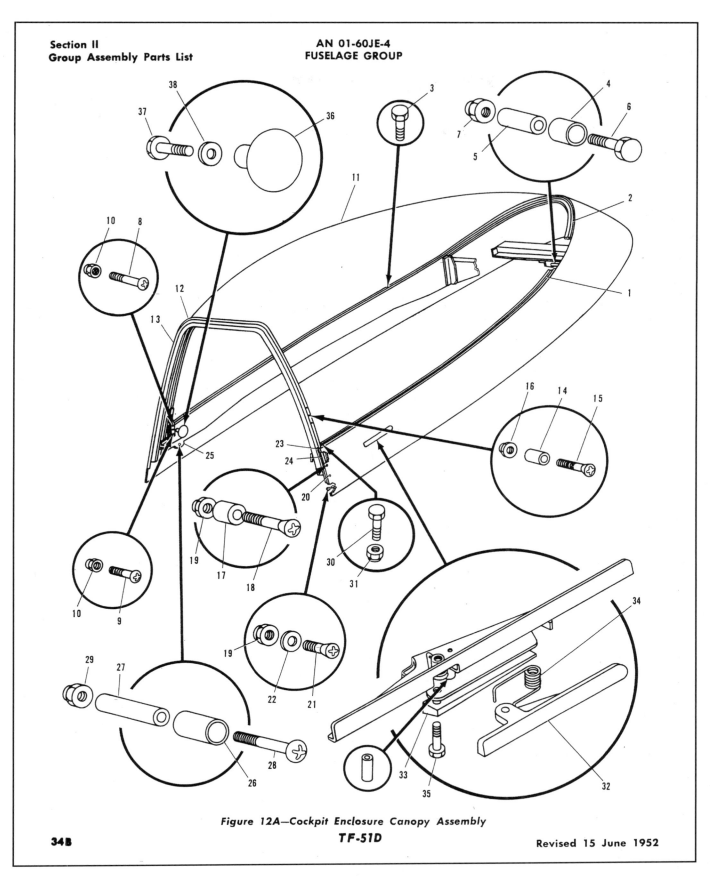

Figure 12A—Cockpit Enclosure Canopy Assembly

TF-51D

Revised 15 June 1952

TF-51D canopy used modified bottom frame.

NORTH AMERICAN
P-51 MUSTANG

Nationalist Chinese razorback Mustang leads a camouflaged bubble-top P-51 down the assembly line. Shroud placed around exhaust stacks on Merlin engine hangs from underwing shackle, awaiting installation as workers tinker in engine bay. (SDAM)

Force bombed a village near Anking, resulting in fires and secondary explosions. Four A-36s from 10th Air Force joined P-40s in a ground attack on Japanese gun positions, supply caches, and troops in the Myitkyina area on May 23. On May 30, eight P-51s from 14th Air Force attacked various railroad targets as the Mustangs ranged over Peking, Chengting, Pingting, Linfen, and Puchou. Other 14th AF P-51s joined P-38s in attacking and damaging installations at one end of the Nanchang bridge that day.

On June 2, 1944, the first shuttle bombing mission, relying on Soviet cooperation for landing fields after hitting targets deep in Axis territory, was launched by 15th Air Force. Seventy P-51s escorted 130 B-17s on this effort, as the heavy bombers hit the marshaling yards at

Representing the swelling tide of American airpower over Europe, P-51Bs of the 357th Fighter Group cruise with drop tanks attached. Airplane nearest camera has B6 lettering for 363rd Fighter Squadron; Mustang coded C5 flew with 364th FS. A mixture of Malcolm and factory canopies is evident. White band on tail and nose is quick recognition device to distinguish Mustang from Messerschmitt Me-109. (Fred LePage collection)

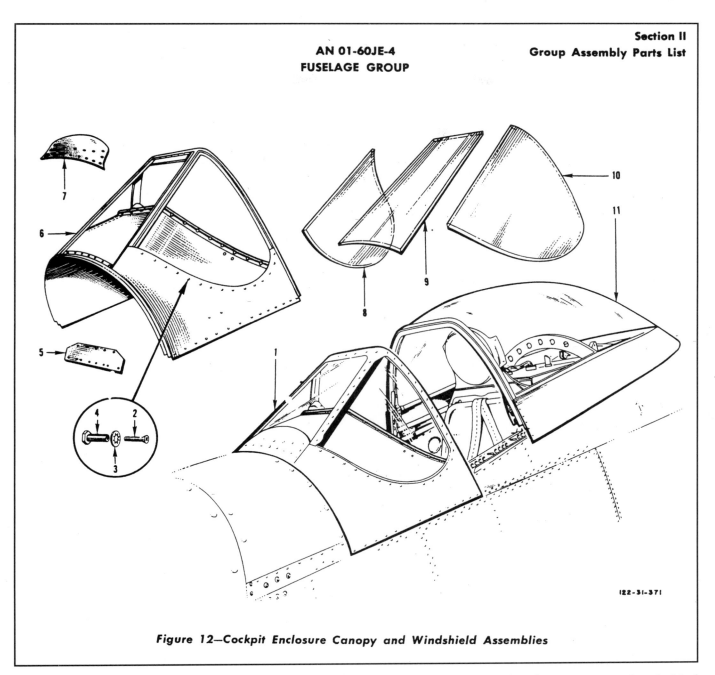

122-31-371

Figure 12—Cockpit Enclosure Canopy and Windshield Assemblies

Line art from the P-51D illustrated parts manual shows glass panes of windscreen, headrest on armor plate behind pilot, and curved canopy stiffener.

Debreczen. The Mustangs landed at Piryatin, the B-17s at other Soviet airfields, at the end of that mission. On June 6, 42 of the P-51s that flew to the Soviet Union on June 2 joined B-17s in another shuttle raid to the enemy airfield at Galati before returning to Soviet shuttle bases. Two P-51s were lost that day in the shuttle foray. June 6 also marked the Allied invasion at Normandy; Mustangs, as well as other tactical aircraft, would sport variations on black-and-white invasion stripes for months, to alert friendly ground forces that these were Allied aircraft. On June 11, 60 escort P-51s from 15th Air Force accompanied 126 B-17s as the American warplanes departed Russian shuttle bases to return to Italy; 121 of the B-17s bombed an airfield at Focsani on the way home, thus ending the first shuttle mission of Operation Frantic.

On June 21, Eighth Air Force launched its first shuttle bombing mission under Operation Frantic, with a choreographed hand-off of

Rollover accident involving a checkertail 325th Fighter Group Mustang shows checkers extended to undersides of horizontal tail surfaces. (USAF photo)

B-17s from escorting P-47s to P-51s over Stendal, who escorted the bombers over the target—a synthetic oil plant at Ruhland. The P-51s were relieved 50 miles southeast of Poznan by 65 more Mustangs that accompanied the Flying Fortresses into the Soviet Union. About 50 miles southeast of Brest Litovsk, German fighters attacked the formation; six Luftwaffe planes fell, for the loss of one P-51. The

remaining 64 Mustangs landed at Piryatin. That night, German bombers destroyed 47 B-17s and damaged others at Poltava; the Mustangs and surviving B-17s were moved farther east into the Soviet Union on June 22 for protection, thereby avoiding a German strike at Piryatin and Mirgorod the night of the 22nd. On the 25th of June, the Mustangs and B-17s returned to Poltava and Mirgorod to be

armed and fueled for a mission that was canceled by weather; the aircraft returned to their dispersal bases for safety. Next day, 55 of the Mustangs in the Soviet Union escorted B-17s that bombed targets at Drohobycz before flying on to Foggia, Italy. Fifteenth Air Force P-51s met the formation after the bomb drop, and escorted them back to Italy. Weather kept the Eighth Air Force's shuttle warriors in Italy for a few days, where, on July 2, 41 of the Eighth's Mustangs joined 15th AF fellows in escorting bombers to Budapest, meeting aerial opposition. The Eighth's shuttle Mustangs again flew escort out of Italy on July 3; on the fifth of the month, 42 of these Mustangs returned to the United Kingdom; 10 more followed the next day, and one arrived several days after.

Meanwhile, on June 23, Eighth Air Force sent 161 Mustangs from four fighter groups to escort heavy bombers attacking a dozen Crossbow German missile launching sites in western Europe. After this, the Mustangs descended to ravage rail and road targets in the vicinity of Paris, claiming 14 vehicles, three locomotives, and about 100 railcars destroyed. The only Mustang lost on the mission was struck by debris from an exploding ammunition train. On July 9, P-51s from 15th Air Force swept over Ploesti during heavy-bomber attacks on oil refineries there. In the

In full wrap-around Normandy invasion stripes, P-51Bs or Cs form a pastoral mid-1944 portrait. Stripes on upper surfaces gradually came off as the year matured. (Barrett Tillman collection)

WARBIRD**TECH**
SERIES

China-Burma-India Theater in the summer of 1944, P-51s and A-36s continued a pattern of ground attacks that utilized the Mustangs even on those occasions when there were no aerial opponents for them to challenge. July 25 saw 34 Mustangs from 15th Air Force and 33 P-38s, flying from Russian shuttle bases, attack a German airfield at Mielec, and then return to Russia. The massive build-up of P-51 escort fighters in Eighth Air Force was manifested July 31, 1944, when five P-51 fighter groups escorted 651 B-17s to German targets, while eight Mustang groups covered the bombers' return leg home.

In response to the first direct Soviet request for air strikes by the USAAF, on August 1, 1944, 15th Air Force sent about 70 P-51s and P-38s to attack the airfield and town of Focsani, with the fighters landing at shuttle basses in the Soviet Union afterward. On August 6, Eighth Air Force Mustang groups again relay-escorted B-17s on a shuttle bombing mission. Anticipating the invasion of southern France by Allied troops in August, more than 100 P-51 sorties were logged by 15th Air Force on August 12, as the Mustangs strafed German radar sites and other coastal observation facilities in that part of France, in an effort to blind German forces to the impending invasion. Return attacks on coastal observation and radar sites were made on subsequent days. On August 27, Eighth Air Force put up an impressive 11 P-51 groups for bomber escort and ground strafing duties; 10 Mustangs were lost in that effort. Next day, Eighth Air Force lost 16 P-51s during ground attack operations.

On September 13, 1944, Eighth Air Force P-51s claimed 33 enemy aircraft downed and 20 more destroyed on the ground, for a loss of nine Mustangs. The ability to employ the P-51 as an escort fighter or as a fighter-bomber allowed commanders flexibility in maximizing the utility of their Mustangs for much of the remainder of the war. On December 8, 1944, a force of 14 P-51s from 14th Air Force hit targets at Nanking, including the airfield; the Mustang fliers claimed destruction of two locomotives, a freighter, and 24 aircraft.

As 1945 unfolded, Eighth AF bombers and fighters, including P-51s, sometimes made use of airfields on continental Europe as the war pressed ever closer to Germany. On the second day of February, 15th Air Force dispatched 33 P-51s to strafe an airfield at Kurilovec, while 14 more Mustangs provided top cover. Eleven more 15th AF P-51s flew escort for a Royal Air Force supply-dropping mission to Yugoslavia that day. On February 7, 11 P-51s from 14th Air Force took out a bridge at Hengshan. On March 1, Mustangs from Eighth AF performed a double-barreled mission, escorting heavy bombers to marshaling yard targets in south-

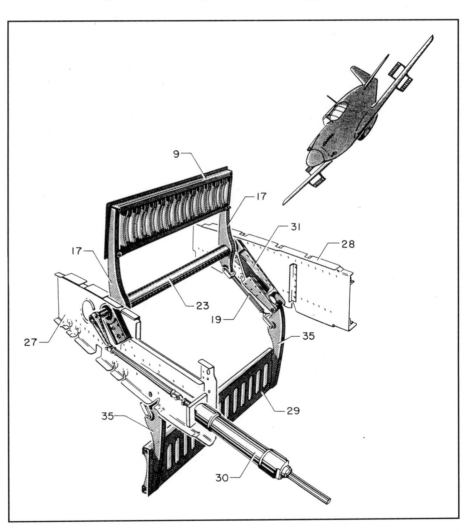

A-36 dive brake mechanism forced slotted panels to extend above and below each wing. Some dive brakes may have been disabled by combat units; regular P-51s also served as dive bombers without air brakes.

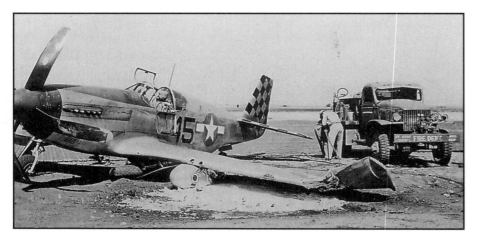

Fire-suppressing foam stopped the threat of fire from a drop tank that appears to have been punctured by its pylon when the left main gear collapsed on this 325th Fighter Group P-51 in Italy. (USAAF photo)

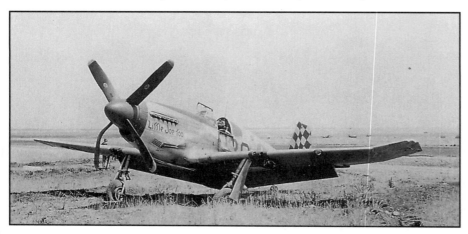

Mustang wingtips were not meant to withstand impact with the ground, and easily bent up as on this 325th Fighter Group razorback Mustang, Little Joe Too, *in Italy. (USAF)*

west Germany, after which a large part of the P-51 force was released to strafe airfields and transportation facilities. Following the historic flag-raising by days, 28 P-51s from Seventh Air Force landed on Iwo Jima March 6, 1945. (By March 11, these Mustangs were bombing Susaki and strafing Kitamura and Okimura.) On the 11th of March, 14 P-51 groups from Eighth Air Force provided close escort for a total of 1,212 heavy bombers going after several targets in Germany including Kiel, Bremen, and Hamburg. March saw several 15th Air Force P-51 missions launched to strafe train traffic in Austria and Germany.

On April 1, 1945, a force of 52 P-51s from 15th Air Force strafed trains in Prague, Plzen, and vicinity. On April 2, 14th Air Force sent 32 P-51s to attack airfields in the Shanghai area. The first time P-51s from VII Fighter Command escorted B-29s to Japan came on April 7, 1945, when 91 Mustangs made the mission, claiming 21 enemy aircraft downed. On April 23, P-51s from 15th Air Force escorted recon flights and B-25 missions against targets in northern Italy. On May 7, 1945, the German High Command surrendered unconditionally, effective May 9.

May 17 saw FEAF P-51s and B-25s cause damage to a variety of targets during sweeps over Formosa. May 29, 1945, marked the first time

Funny Face, *probably from the 21st Fighter Group in the Pacific, sports a Kilroy cartoon on the front of the drop tank under its left wing. A common method of mounting the P-51 was to step on the main tire and up to the wing; hence, nearby drop tanks were marked NO STEP. (Paul N. Fackler collection)*

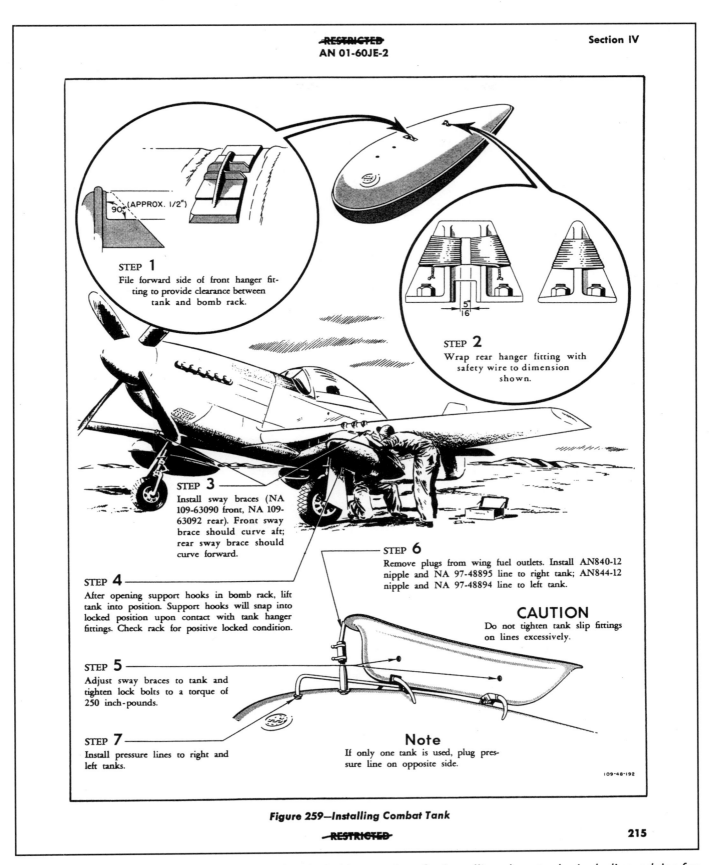

STEP **1**
File forward side of front hanger fitting to provide clearance between tank and bomb rack.

STEP **2**
Wrap rear hanger fitting with safety wire to dimension shown.

STEP **3**
Install sway braces (NA 109-63090 front, NA 109-63092 rear). Front sway brace should curve aft; rear sway brace should curve forward.

STEP **4**
After opening support hooks in bomb rack, lift tank into position. Support hooks will snap into locked position upon contact with tank hanger fittings. Check rack for positive locked condition.

STEP **5**
Adjust sway braces to tank and tighten lock bolts to a torque of 250 inch-pounds.

STEP **6**
Remove plugs from wing fuel outlets. Install AN840-12 nipple and NA 97-48895 line to right tank; AN844-12 nipple and NA 97-48894 line to left tank.

CAUTION
Do not tighten tank slip fittings on lines excessively.

STEP **7**
Install pressure lines to right and left tanks.

Note
If only one tank is used, plug pressure line on opposite side.

109-48-192

Figure 259—Installing Combat Tank

A P-51D erection and maintenance manual included instructions for installing drop tanks, including advice for plugging pressure lines on the opposite wing if only one tank was installed.

NORTH AMERICAN
P-51 MUSTANG

VII Fighter Command P-51s escorted 20th Air Force B-29s on a fire-bombing mission, with 101 Mustangs shepherding 454 Superfortresses over Yokohama. When a Japanese fighter force estimated at 150 aircraft attack the formation, seven B-29s and three P-51s were lost. The Mustangs claimed 26 Japanese fighters shot down in the action, while the B-29s claimed six more downed fighters. On June 1, a force of 148 P-51s encountered severe turbulence en route to rendezvous with B-29s bound for Osaka. Many Mustangs collided; 27 were lost. Twenty-seven others in the P-51 formation were able to press on to rendezvous with the Superfortresses and escorted them over the target.

Fifth Air Force fighters made their first mission over Japan on July 3, 1945, as P-51s destroyed Japanese floatplanes in the Fukuoka harbor area. Next day, FEAF P-51s flew a major sweep of Kyushu. On July 16, FEAF Mustangs and B-25s supported ground troops in the vicinity of Baguio east of Manila in the Philippines.

As late as August 11, 1945, nine P-51s from 14th Air Force logged ground attacks against Japanese troops, trains, and river vessels near Tehsien, Chenhsien, and Hengyang.

On August 15, 1945, all offensive operations against Japan ceased; the official surrender document was signed September 2 in Tokyo Bay, aboard the battleship USS *Missouri*. The end of World War Two marked the last major use of Mustangs as dogfighters, although the loitering time of the prop-driven P-51s would make Mustangs handy ground attack aircraft for several years to come.

HITCH-HIKING RESCUE IN GERMANY

On March 18, 1945, as Mustangs of the crack Fourth Fighter Group zipped over an airfield in German territory, flak punctured the P-51 of

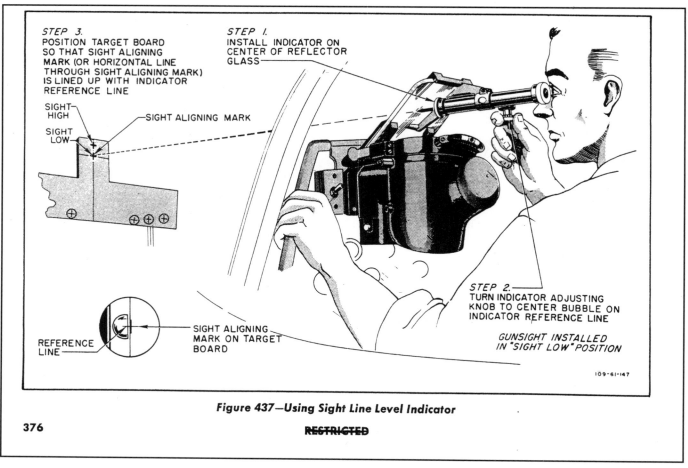

STEP 3.
POSITION TARGET BOARD SO THAT SIGHT ALIGNING MARK (OR HORIZONTAL LINE THROUGH SIGHT ALIGNING MARK) IS LINED UP WITH INDICATOR REFERENCE LINE

SIGHT HIGH
SIGHT LOW
SIGHT ALIGNING MARK

STEP I.
INSTALL INDICATOR ON CENTER OF REFLECTOR GLASS

STEP 2.
TURN INDICATOR ADJUSTING KNOB TO CENTER BUBBLE ON INDICATOR REFERENCE LINE

GUNSIGHT INSTALLED IN "SIGHT LOW" POSITION

REFERENCE LINE
SIGHT ALIGNING MARK ON TARGET BOARD

109-61-147

Figure 437—Using Sight Line Level Indicator

376

P-51s could be boresighted for gunfire convergence customized for particular purposes, doctrine, or preferences. Adjustments could account for "the flight attitude of the airplane (angle of attack of the fuselage reference line) for the desired attacking speed, weight, and G acceleration," according to a Mustang erection and maintenance manual. (Carl Scholl/Aero Trader)

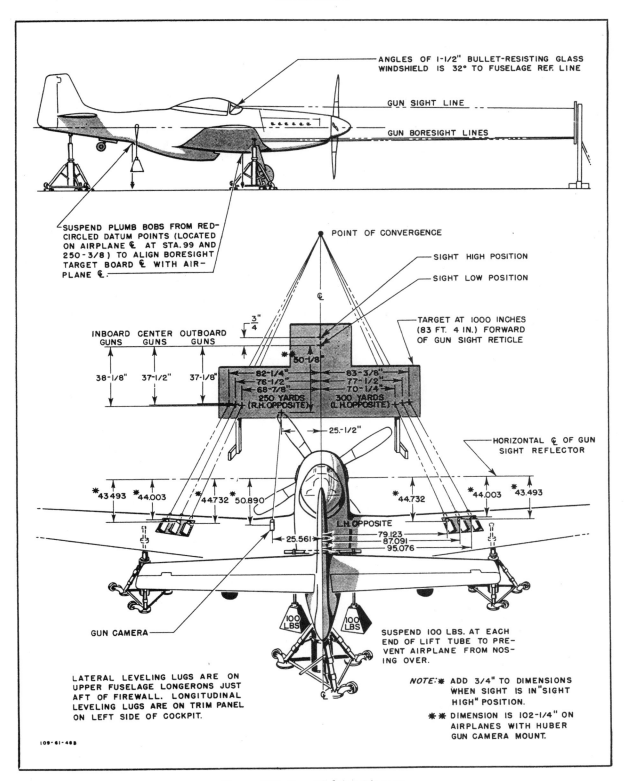

Figure 435—Bore Sighting Diagram

Re-enacting their harrowing piggyback rescue flight out of Germany, Lt. George D. Green sat in the lap of Maj. Pierce W. McKennon, whom Green rescued by landing near the major after a bailout not far from Berlin. Green and McKennon shared one oxygen mask on the flight home when weather forced them to fly as high as 18,000 feet. (USAAF photo)

Maj. Pierce W. McKennon, commander of the 335th Fighter Squadron. With damage to his plane's oil system, Major McKennon contemplated his second bailout over enemy territory since the summer of 1944.

With a matter-of-fact "See you later, fellas," the major jettisoned his plane's canopy and pushed the control stick forward, expecting the negative G-loading to float him free of the Mustang. When his G-suit

Apparent split canopy suggests this may be a field-modified two-seat P-51D, used by the 31st Fighter Group in Italy late in 1945. (Allen Troupe collection)

snagged in the plane, major McKennon was nearly doubled back by the slipstream as he was momentarily held fast before clearing the disabled Mustang and riding down under a parachute canopy. About an hour after noon, he was on the ground in a field about 40 miles north of Berlin, with two men and a leashed police dog approaching him.[4]

Lt. George D. Green watched the drama from his P-51. As other Mustangs dropped down to strafe the approaching Germans, Lieutenant Green prepared to land his fighter in the field to rescue the squadron CO. The unit history noted: "Green made an extraordinarily short landing. McKennon ran to his ship. McKennon detached the drop tanks while Green got rid of his parachute." A moment's confusion reigned as the two pilots figured out the best way to ride piggyback out of Germany. "McKennon being the biggest, he sat down in the cockpit and Green sat in his lap," the official history reported. Green piloted the Mustang and effected a takeoff, but left his landing gear extended as others in the group radioed "Get your wheels up."[5]

The 550-mile ride home gave the cramped fliers time to contemplate their lack of any parachutes, and only one oxygen mask, which Lieutenant Green used as he flew. When weather forced the fliers up to 18,000 feet, Green shared the oxygen mask with McKennon. Peeling off sharply over the Fourth Group's home base, Lieutenant Green radioed the tower to clear the runway. Queried if he were declaring an emergency, Lieutenant Green is said to have responded, "I guess so. We've got two in this crate."[6]

AN 01-60JE-4
ARMAMENT GROUP

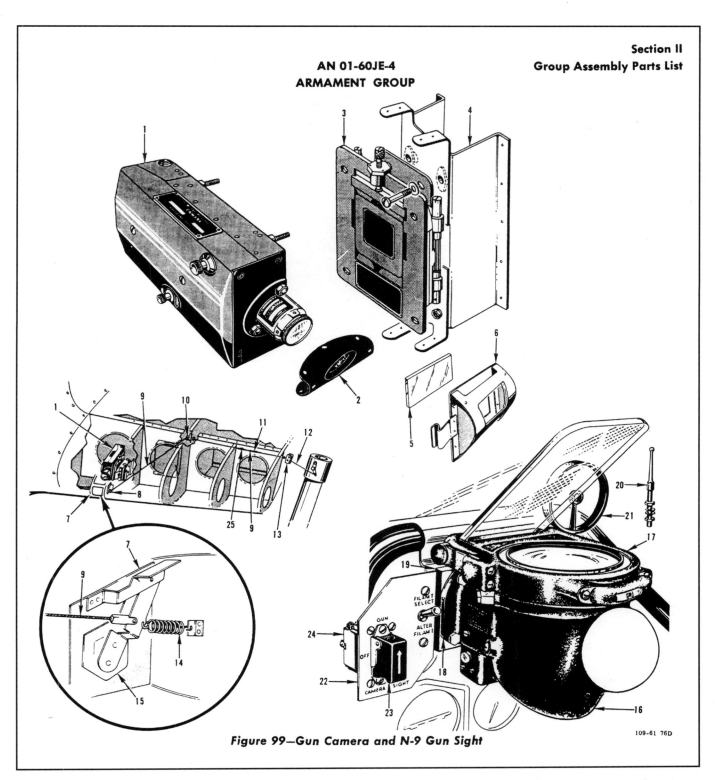

Figure 99—Gun Camera and N-9 Gun Sight

109-61 76D

F-51D parts manual depicts N-9 gunsight with back-up metal ring and bead sight available (parts 20 and 21). Gun camera mounted in leading edge of left wing near root.

BRITISH USED MUSTANG I TO DISRUPT TRANSPORTATION

British Army Cooperation Units (ultimately absorbed into Royal Air Force Fighter Command in the last half of 1943) used Allison-powered Mustang I and IA aircraft to strafe German trains, barges, and transportation in western Europe, using the Mustang's already-legendary range to reach into Germany on

First Lt. Felix J. Kirkpatrick of the 302nd Fighter Squadron in Italy was photographed at the completion of his tour of duty. Protective armor plate behind seat is visible. Inside of canopy framing on razorback Mustangs typically was painted dark green to minimize distracting reflections. (USAAF)

occasion. Originally, these British Mustangs performed low-altitude photo reconnaissance missions, with one vertical camera, and one oblique camera pointing aft out the left side of the Mustang from a hole in the left side window behind the pilot. Carrying a combination of .50-caliber and .30-caliber machine guns, these Mustangs were potent attackers of transportation targets, and the reconnaissance mission increasingly took on an offensive capability until it was developed into a strategic effort aimed at enemy transportation targets. With a fuel capacity of 180 gallons, the Mustang I was already considered a long-range aircraft by standards of the day pre-dating the arrival of the P-51B. The Allison engine was found to oper-

Portrait of 302nd Fighter Squadron pilot 1Lt. George J. Haley in his P-51D in Italy shows how much the bubble canopy bulged beyond the canopy frame. Edge contour of protective armor plate behind seat changed from configuration used on razorback Mustangs. (USAF)

ate efficiently at lower RPMs than Merlins, further adding to the range of these aircraft. A USAAF study of British Mustang I ground attack operations noted: "This aircraft is powered by the Allison 1710-39 engine having a rated power of 1150 H.P. at 3000 R.P.M. and 44 inches Hg. at 12,000 ft. The engine was originally equipped with an automatic boost control limiting the manifold pressure at the lower altitudes to 44 inches. The British remove this so as to get the vastly increased performance at lower altitudes thru the judicious use of over-boost. As has been mentioned before, they have had exceptionally good service out of these engines and due to its smoothness at low RPM's, they are able to operate it so as to obtain a remarkably low fuel consumption giving them an operational range greater than any single engine fighter they possess (the fact that the Merlin engine will not run well below 1600 prevents them from obtaining an equivalent low fuel consumption and therefore limits its usefulness for similar operations.)" The British experience with ground-attack Allison-engined Mustangs prompted this testimonial to the V-1710 in a 1943 USAAF study: "The British have operated at full throttle at sea level (72 inches Hg.) for as much as 20 min. at a time without hurting the engines. According to them, the Allison is averaging 1500 hours between bearing failures as compared to 500 to 600 hrs for the Merlin. The Allison, they have found, will drag them home even with the bearings ruined."[7]

Tagged "Rhubarbs," the ground-attack missions of the British Mustang I and IA aircraft were carefully choreographed to cross the continental coastline where flak was

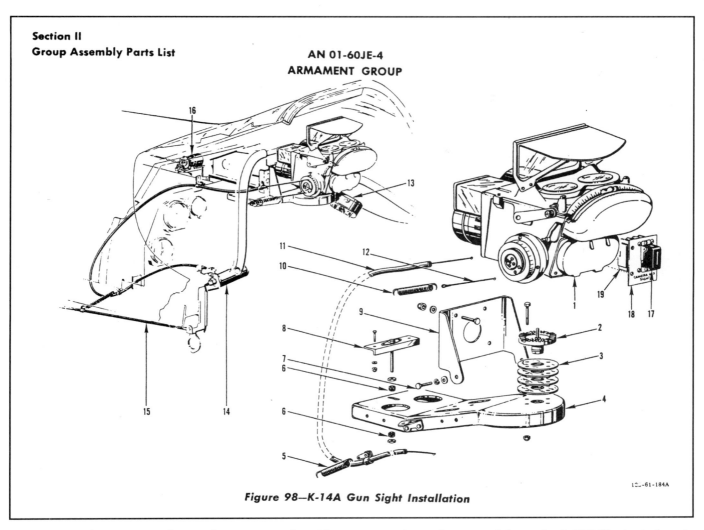

AN 01-60JE-4
ARMAMENT GROUP

Figure 98—K-14A Gun Sight Installation

K-14A gunsight was one of several options used on Mustangs, as shown in artwork from the P-51D illustrated parts book. (Carl Scholl/Aero Trader)

expected to be light, diving and strafing in an effort to suppress even those defenses. Then, the flight of Mustangs, often composed of groups of two-ship elements, raced at tree-top level, using terrain-masking as much as possible. Pre-arranged zig-zags were flown precisely, to throw off any planned Luftwaffe interceptions by denying German observers a predictable flight path for the hedge-hopping Mustangs. As described in a USAAF evaluation: "The flight from the home base to within 40 miles of the point of crossing the enemy coast is made at 200 IAS [indicated airspeed]... at between 25 to 50

Goodwiggle was a 100th Fighter Squadron P-51 flown by 2 Lt. Christopher W. Newman. (USAF)

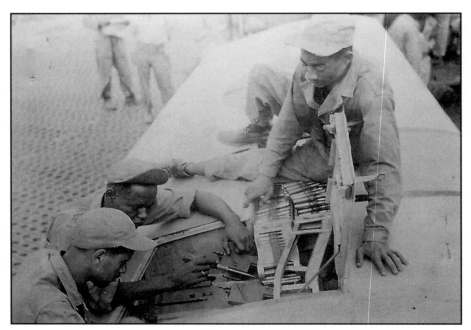

Armorers from the 99th Fighter Squadron worked on the canted guns in a razorback Mustang in Italy. Mechanic in the center has his left hand on a gun heater, a valuable accessory at altitude. Angled mounting of guns in P-51Bs and Cs led to jamming problems, and D-models had guns positioned upright. (USAF)

feet altitude. Upon reaching the above-mentioned point, the power is increased to maximum cruising (250-275 MPH…) and left there during the entire time over enemy territory and until 40 miles away from enemy coast on the return trip." At minimum altitudes, it took trained eyes to pick out targets flashing by. The USAAF study noted: "Experience and alertness are required to pick out these targets in time to make an attack. It has been found necessary for inexperienced pilots to fly at not over 250 MPH until they acquire the necessary skill and experience. It has also been found that depressing the flaps 5 degrees will have little effect on the speed, but it will change the (attitude) of the aircraft so that targets can be more easily seen over the nose."[8]

Low cloud cover was a bonus, allowing the Mustangs to slip out of view. The USAAF report said: "For operations deep into Germany 10/10 clouds at not over 1500 ft. is required while 6/10 to 7/10 clouds at 1500 ft. is allowable for operations into Holland, Belgium and France." Attacks on steam locomo-

tives were effective with .50-caliber fire. The USAAF report, perhaps optimistically, noted: "It is felt that with the present load on the enemy shops and the possible shortage of the high quality steel necessary for the boiler tubes, that a locomotive which has been holed by .50 cal. machine gun fire will be out of service from 3 weeks to 6 months depending on the location with reference to repair facilities. In some cases the locomotive explodes; if it does not explode, often the escaping steam blows the fire out of the fire box into the cab. The repetition of these attacks has definitely made the profession of locomotive engineer unpopular in that part of Europe within range of the Mustangs." Although the Rhubarbs often were too low, fast, and unpredictable to allow the Luftwaffe to mount meaningful interception, the possibility always existed, and Mustang fliers on Rhubarbs were taught to use their planes' superior speed at low altitude to run away from German

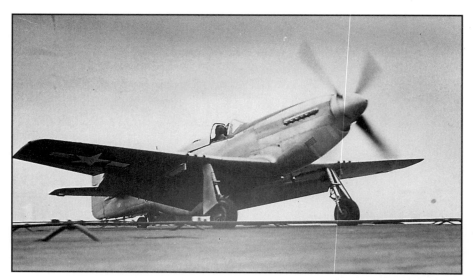

On Nov. 15, 1944, U.S. Navy pilot Lt. R.M. Elder operated a P-51D aboard the USS Shangri-La (CV-38). U.S. Navy had a historical resistance to liquid-cooled engines, due at least in part to the added logistics burdens they would place on the limited space and resources of an aircraft carrier. (U.S. Navy via Peter M. Bowers collection)

ARMAMENT GROUP

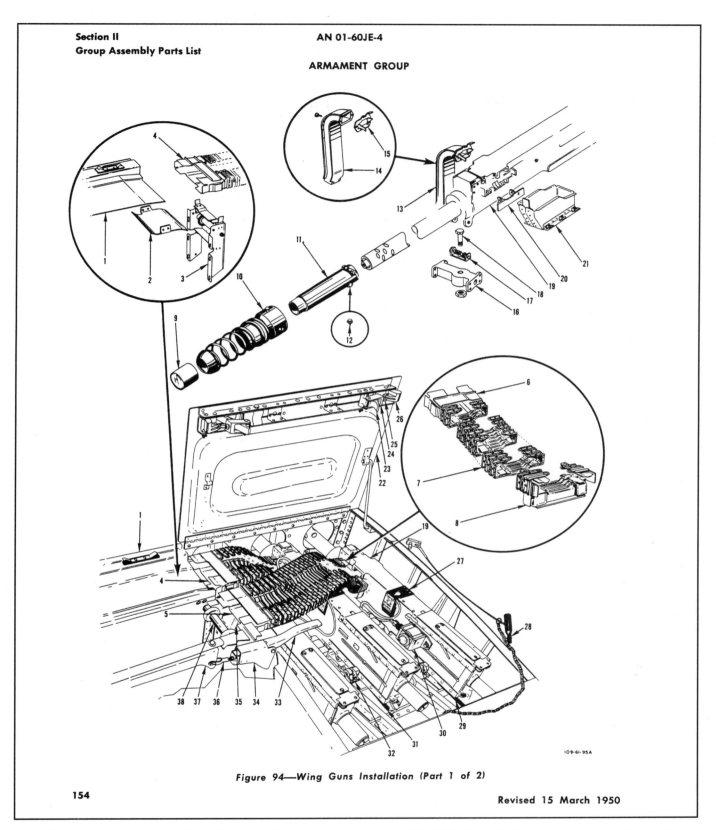

Figure 94—Wing Guns Installation (Part 1 of 2)

Revised 15 March 1950

109-61-95A

Upright mounting of .50-caliber M-2 machine guns in the wings of P-51Ds helped eliminate some earlier feed and jamming problems when guns had been canted. Staggering of far right gun receiver allows flexible feed chute access. Part 27 is a style of gun heater used on many aircraft applications. Parts 13-15 are link ejection chute components. Civilian Mustang owners sometimes make use of the wing gun bays as compact baggage holds.

NORTH AMERICAN
P-51 MUSTANG

Marines on Iwo Jima inspected a P-51D that moved up to Motoyama Airfield No. 1 to bring the war closer to the Japanese. (USMC/SDAM)

fighters whenever possible, since the mission was ground attack. As the USAAF study reported: "They are instructed in the use of the flaps in combat to reduce their turning radius (which with flaps is shorter than the ME-109 or FW-190). At least one FW-190 has been made to spin in through the use of a small amount of flap by the Mustang when engaged in a turning contest at low altitude; the 190 tried to tighten his turn to keep the Mustang in his sights after the pilot had dropped his flaps slightly but spun out of the turn."[9]

The British pilots donned goggles whenever over enemy territory to protect from splintering windscreens and canopies; they wore flight suits over street clothes and carried escape and evasion supplies including civilian passport photos designed to make the fliers look like residents of the countries over which they were operating. They were taught how to avoid being conspicuous. The AAF report said: "It has been found that the poor people of a country are always more ready than any other class to help in escaping." The pilots were encouraged to carry a personal weapon other than a gun. Sometimes, they would carry two compasses—one that was fairly obvious in case of capture, and another more concealed for escape use. As the Mustang I pilot departed the operations room for a sortie, "the last thing he fastens on himself is a sheath knife placed outside everything and in easy reach so that if a chance hit should cause his 'Mae West' to inflate while in the air, he can puncture it."[10] A cramped Mustang cockpit at low altitude over German-held territory was no place to wrestle a bulging deployed life preserver.

A-36 OPERATIONS DESCRIBED

A wartime description of A-36 dive bomber operations in the Mediterranean said the A-36 in a dive had a shrill scream even more haunting than that of the storied Stuka. With speed and maneuverability beyond the limits of the fixed-gear Stuka, the A-36 was a tactical and psychological force to be reckoned with. Stories surfaced about Italian troops being pummeled into hysteria by repeated A-36 assaults. In typical dive bomber fashion, many A-36 pilots rolled

Angels' Playmate still carried the black horizontal stabilizer identification markings intended to differentiate it from an Me-109 when photographed in a grassy field. (N.L. Avery via SDAM)

inverted and pulled the stick back, half-rolling into a steep dive over their intended target. After releasing its two 500-pound bombs, the A-36 handily doubled as a strafer, with six .50-caliber machine guns. And over Salerno, A-36s pinch-hit for purpose-built fighters by flying cover for troops, and downing several German fighters in air-to-air combat. The A-36 briefly was accorded the popular nickname "Invader" (though this is usually associated with the long-lived twin-engine Douglas A-26).[11]

MUSTANG VERSUS ZEKE

In April 1945, Allied Technical Air Intelligence Center (TAIC) Report Number 38 cited comparisons of performance between the P-51D-5 and a captured Mitsubishi 52, code-named Zeke. The comparison was made by the AAF Proving Ground Command. The captured Zeke was in nearly new condition, allowing for significant flight comparisons to be made with the P-51D and other AAF fighters, although the report noted, "certain airframes (sic) discrepancies prevented obtaining maximum speed and climb performance."

The P-51D, as well as the P-38J-25, and P-47D-30 were found to be "greatly superior" to the Zeke 52 in maximum level flight speed at tested altitudes of 10,000 and 25,000 feet. So much faster were the AAF fighters that speed comparisons at other altitudes were deemed needless. The P-51D was clocked at about 80 miles an hour TAS (True Airspeed) faster than the Zeke 52 at 10,000 feet, and about 95 miles an hour faster than the Mitsubishi at 25,000 feet. The AAF report said: "Due to advantages in speed, acceleration and high speed climb, all

Boxer Joe Louis, then a staff sergeant, sat in a P-51C-10-NT of the 332nd Fighter Group, and showed how cramped the original razorback Mustang canopy could be. Capt. Joseph D. Elsberry gave the prizefighter a tour of the Mustang. (USAF)

three AAF fighters were able to maintain the offensive in individual combat with the Zeke 52, and to break off combat at will." But there was still life in the old Mitsubishi design, and the comparison found: "The Zeke 52 is greatly superior to all three AAF fighters in radius of turn and general maneuverability at low speeds."[12]

The report urged pilots of AAF fighters including the P-51D to "take advantage of high speed performance superiority when engaging the Zeke 52 in combat; speed

Fifth Air Force P-51D carries one Japanese flag victory symbol. Black identification band on aft fuselage was painted when radiator exit gate was open, as evidenced by paint on the gate and overspray beyond the part that was masked. (SDAM)

Following an inflight fire, P-51D 44-15237 was foamed on Sept. 27, 1944, at Sarasota, Florida. (SDAM)

should be kept well above 200 IAS (Indicated Airspeed; AAF airspeed indicators were in miles per hour) during all combat; 'hit and run' tactics should be used whenever possible, and following the Zeke through any continued turning maneuvers must be strictly avoided." With full military loads carried in the Mustang and the Zeke for combat tests at 10,000 and 25,000 feet, the Japanese fighter was better at all turning circle comparisons including diving and climbing spirals, as well as in general low-speed maneuverability. Dogfight challenges between the P-51D and the Zeke 52 included engagements with the two fighters approaching each other, as well as with the two planes taking turns being about 2,000 feet above and behind the other aircraft. "In every case, the Zeke was forced on the defensive after combat started," the report said. Shallow dives and high speed climbs enabled the faster Mustang to disengage combat and re-enter it at will, giving the Zeke only a quick shot when the nimble Mitsubishi turned into the attack pass

by the P-51D. "Only when the AAF fighters slowed down or turned after a pass could the Zeke get in a shot (other than head-on defensive shooting). The Zeke could easily get in firing position and stay on the tail of AAF fighters through all low speed maneuvers." When engaged in chandelle turns, the P-51 and other AAF fighter pilots in the tests "were unable to keep their sights on the Zeke."[13]

In level turns at 10,000 and 25,000 feet, the Zeke was able to get an advantage over the P-51D in less than one full 360-degree turn. When the P-51D and the Zeke 52 engaged in level flight acceleration tests from a line abreast position at 10,000 feet and a starting speed of 200 IAS, the P-51 at the end of one minute at full power enjoyed a lead estimated at 400 yards; after two minutes, this lead had grown to 1,500 yards. At 25,000 feet, with an initial speed of 190 IAS, the P-51D's estimated lead was 300 yards after one minute and about 1,000 yards after two minutes of full power. In dive comparison tests begun at 200

IAS, the P-51D quickly accelerated beyond the Zeke 52, which reached its selected redline airspeed of 325 IAS in 27 seconds at 10,000 feet, at which time the Mustang had a lead of about 200 yards. At both test altitudes of 10,000 and 25,000 feet, the Zeke 52 enjoyed slightly better aileron rolling ability than the P-51D at speeds below 220 IAS. Above that speed, the Mustang was superior because of increasing control forces felt by the Zeke pilot. The Mustang won zoom contests from level flight as well as from a dive at both test altitudes. Amplifying why the P-51D should not engage a Zeke 52 in climbing or diving spirals, the report said: "Climbing and diving spirals were executed at 10,000 and 25,000 feet, with either airplane alternately leading in a line astern formation. Results were the same at both altitudes. The Zeke could stay in range within the P-51D's turn during either a climbing or diving spiral. With the Zeke in the lead position at the start of a spiral, the P-51D could hold the initial advantage for only a short time."[14]

MUSTANG CONTRIBUTED TO SUPERSONIC UNDERSTANDING

Maj. Frederic A. Borsodi was a P-40 combat veteran subsequently assigned to fighter test duties at Wright Field where he observed the phenomenon of a sonic shock wave propagating on the upper surface of a Mustang in a test dive in July 1944. Purpose of the dive was to further understand compressibility, the acceleration of airflow over the top of a wing to sonic speeds even though the aircraft's speed is still subsonic. Compressibility led to turbulent airflow that characteristically buffeted tail surfaces, and induced a tuck-under

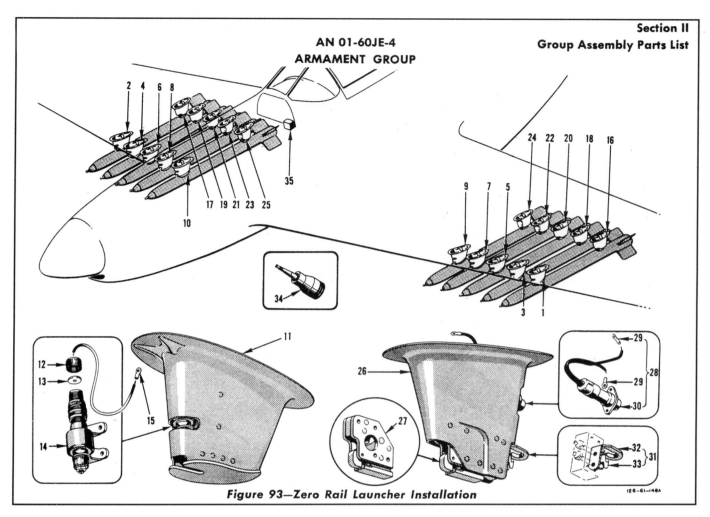

Figure 93—Zero Rail Launcher Installation

126-61-148A

P-51D was fitted with 10 zero-length launchers for five-inch high velocity aircraft rockets (HVARs), as shown in the Dash-4 illustrated parts book. Unlike earlier rail launchers, zero-length launchers freed the rocket after traveling forward about one inch to clear the lugs.

pitching moment, making recovery from dives difficult and sometimes life-threatening. Major Borsodi is credited as the first pilot to see a sonic shock wave shimmer atop his P-51's wing during a compressibility dive. He subsequently had the Mustang fitted with a motion-picture camera trained over the wing, and repeated the event on film. The wave moved aft as speed increased, and crept forward until dissipating as the Mustang slowed down.[15]

The Mustang's laminar flow wing inherently inhibited the effects of compressibility better than other airfoil designs of the era by keeping airflow attached for a greater portion of the chord (front-to-back measurement) of the wing. Yet the P-51 was still susceptible to compressibility tuck-under and shudder, and the P-51 pilot's manual included detailed instruction on dive and speed management. The manual somewhat ominously advised: "It is possible to come out of compressibility safely if you don't go into it too far." As a safety reminder, the P-51 had a variable redline speed based on altitude. Because the speed of sound varies with altitude, the onset of compressibility occurred at different speeds as well. The Mustang pilot's manual explained: "At sea level, sound travels 760 MPH. At 30,000 feet, sound travels 680 MPH. The higher you are, therefore, the sooner you approach the speed of sound. And, the higher you are, the lower your safe IAS [Indicated Airspeed]."[16]

The maximum redline speed for the P-51 was posted at 505 miles an hour indicated airspeed, according to a 1945 pilot's manual. This diminished to a top IAS of only 260 miles an hour at 40,000 feet, as the accompanying table shows:

P-51 MAXIMUM ALLOWABLE DIVING AIRSPEED

Altitude	Maximum Safe Airspeed	
	IAS	TAS
5,000 ft.	505 MPH	560 MPH
10,000 ft.	480 MPH	550 MPH
15,000 ft.	440 MPH	540 MPH
20,000 ft.	400 MPH	530 MPH
30,000 ft.	330 MPH	510 MPH
35,000 ft.	290 MPH	500 MPH
40,000 ft.	260 MPH	495 MPH

Above 5,000 feet, it was possible to attain compressibility in a P-51 before reaching the redline speed of 505 MPH marked on the airspeed indicator; hence the need for a "variable redline speed" governed by altitude. The disparity between Indicated Airspeed and True Airspeed (TAS) is evident; at an IAS of 260 miles an hour, the P-51 is actually traveling 495 miles an hour TAS.[17]

Ironically, a compressibility dive contained a crucial element for recovery, because as the P-51 entered warmer, denser air at lower altitudes, the speed of sound increased, and compressibility dissipated. However, an unchecked dive could result in compressibility shock wave vibrations severe enough to dismember an aircraft, and if recovery were attempted too late, the plane would impact the ground. The Mustang pilot's manual described the onset of compressibility: "In your P-51, the first effect of compressibility that you feel is a 'nibbling' at the stick—the stick will occasionally jump slightly in your hand. If you don't check the airspeed, this will develop into a definite 'walking' stick—the stick will 'walk' back and forth and you won't be able to control it. At this stage the airplane is beginning to porpoise—that is, to pitch up and down in a violent rhythm like a porpoise. As the airplane accelerates further, the porpoising will become increasingly violent… Once the airplane begins porpoising, you won't be able to anticipate its porpoising movements by any counter-movements of the stick. Anything you do in this regard merely makes the situation worse. Or you may develop an aggravated case of reversibility—the control forces reverse, as they do when your fuselage tank is full and you have to push forward on the stick in a dive to keep the airplane from pulling out too abruptly."[18]

Aircraft contemporary with the P-51 entered compressibility at different speeds, based on design elements. Some aircraft experienced sonic airflow, and hence compressibility, as they reached 65 percent of the speed of sound. The percentage at which an aircraft encountered compressibility is its critical Mach number. The Mustang pilot's manual noted: "The P-51 has one of the highest critical Mach numbers of any airplane now in combat. It can be dived to beyond 75 percent of the speed of sound before going into compressibility." While in the grip of compressibility, the Mustang manual instructed, "you have virtually no control over your airplane. While in compressibility you can aggravate your situation; you can make it a lot worse. But outside of cutting off the power (if it isn't already off) and holding the stick as steady as possible, there's nothing you can do to help the situation… All you can do is ride it through until you decelerate enough and lose altitude to the point where your speed is below the red line speed as given in the table. This usually means an uncontrolled dive of between 8,000 and 12,000 feet, depending upon circumstances… Only after you have lost enough speed and altitude, do you come out of compressibility and regain control of your airplane. At that point—with the airplane

Earmarked at the time for preservation, this P-51D carried a sign used on several Air Force aircraft in the immediate postwar period, urging recruitment. (USAF/SDAM)

WARBIRDTECH
SERIES

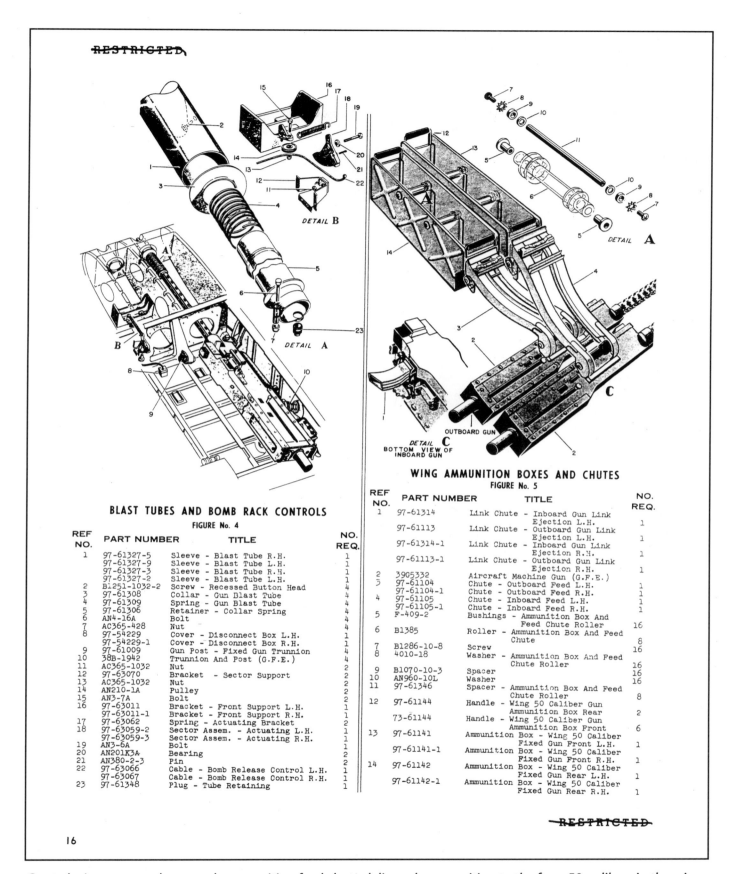

BLAST TUBES AND BOMB RACK CONTROLS
FIGURE No. 4

REF NO.	PART NUMBER	TITLE	NO. REQ.
1	97-61327-5	Sleeve - Blast Tube R.H.	1
	97-61327-9	Sleeve - Blast Tube L.H.	1
	97-61327-3	Sleeve - Blast Tube R.H.	1
	97-61327-2	Sleeve - Blast Tube L.H.	1
2	B1251-1032-2	Screw - Recessed Button Head	4
3	97-61308	Collar - Gun Blast Tube	4
4	97-61309	Spring - Gun Blast Tube	4
5	97-61306	Retainer - Collar Spring	4
6	AN4-16A	Bolt	4
7	AC365-428	Nut	4
8	97-54229	Cover - Disconnect Box L.H.	1
	97-54229-1	Cover - Disconnect Box R.H.	1
9	97-61009	Gun Post - Fixed Gun Trunnion	4
10	38B-1942	Trunnion And Post (G.F.E.)	4
11	AC365-1032	Nut	2
12	97-63070	Bracket - Sector Support	2
13	AC365-1032	Nut	2
14	AN210-1A	Pulley	2
15	AN3-7A	Bolt	2
16	97-63011	Bracket - Front Support L.H.	1
	97-63011-1	Bracket - Front Support R.H.	1
17	97-63062	Spring - Actuating Bracket	2
18	97-63059-2	Sector Assem. - Actuating L.H.	1
	97-63059-3	Sector Assem. - Actuating R.H.	1
19	AN3-6A	Bolt	1
20	AN201K3A	Bearing	2
21	AN380-2-3	Pin	2
22	97-63066	Cable - Bomb Release Control L.H.	1
	97-63067	Cable - Bomb Release Control R.H.	1
23	97-61348	Plug - Tube Retaining	1

WING AMMUNITION BOXES AND CHUTES
FIGURE No. 5

REF NO.	PART NUMBER	TITLE	NO. REQ.
1	97-61314	Link Chute - Inboard Gun Link Ejection L.H.	1
	97-61113	Link Chute - Outboard Gun Link Ejection L.H.	1
	97-61314-1	Link Chute - Inboard Gun Link Ejection R.H.	1
	97-61113-1	Link Chute - Outboard Gun Link Ejection R.H.	1
2	39G5332	Aircraft Machine Gun (G.F.E.)	
3	97-61104	Chute - Outboard Feed L.H.	1
	97-61104-1	Chute - Outboard Feed R.H.	1
4	97-61105	Chute - Inboard Feed L.H.	1
	97-61105-1	Chute - Inboard Feed R.H.	1
5	F-409-2	Bushings - Ammunition Box And Feed Chute Roller	16
6	B1385	Roller - Ammunition Box And Feed Chute	8
7	B1286-10-8	Screw	16
8	4010-18	Washer - Ammunition Box And Feed Chute Roller	16
9	B1070-10-3	Spacer	16
10	AN960-10L	Washer	16
11	97-61346	Spacer - Ammunition Box And Feed Chute Roller	8
12	97-61144	Handle - Wing 50 Caliber Gun Ammunition Box Rear	2
	73-61144	Handle - Wing 50 Caliber Gun Ammunition Box Front	6
13	97-61141	Ammunition Box - Wing 50 Caliber Fixed Gun Front L.H.	1
	97-61141-1	Ammunition Box - Wing 50 Caliber Fixed Gun Front R.H.	1
14	97-61142	Ammunition Box - Wing 50 Caliber Fixed Gun Rear L.H.	1
	97-61142-1	Ammunition Box - Wing 50 Caliber Fixed Gun Rear R.H.	1

Canted wing guns and a curved ammunition feed chute delivered ammunition to the four .50-calibers in the wings of many razorback P-51s, as seen in this P-51A artwork.

again completely under your control—you can begin to come out of your dive." The P-51 manual depicted a steep dive in which a pilot did not cut power soon enough after entering compressibility above 20,000 feet; his recovery, after descending 13,000 feet to come out of compressibility, required 9,000 feet for a safe pullout; he only had 8,500 feet to go, and impacted the ground, illustrating the death grip compressibility could impose on a P-51 if its symptoms were not recognized and counteracted promptly. Steep dives were worse for prolonging recovery.[19]

A succinct compressibility recovery procedure for P-51 pilots was posted in the flight manual, prefaced with advice: "If you ever get into compressibility in a high-speed dive, don't get excited. Keep calm, and follow this recommended recovery procedure:

1. Cut the power immediately. To get out of compressibility you've got to lose airspeed, so cut your throttle back.

2. Release a slight amount of the forward pressure you're holding on the stick.

3. Don't allow the airplane to yaw. Never deliberately yaw it to slow the airplane down.

4. Hold the stick as steady as you possibly can. Don't attempt to anticipate the porpoising movement by counter-movements of the stick.

5. As the airplane slowly but steadily decelerates with power off, and you get into the lower altitudes where the speed of sound is greater, the porpoising stops and you regain complete control of the airplane.

6. Pull out of the dive in a normal recovery. Don't pull out abruptly. Take it as easy as altitude permits.

Notice in the above procedure that you don't need to use the elevator trim tab. It isn't needed."[20]

To counter some of the effects of compressibility, late P-51Ds and P-51Ks were delivered with metal-clad elevators and a decreased angle of incidence to the horizontal stabilizer. Plans called for modifying existing airplanes to these standards, although it is not recorded how many modifications were actually carried out. Pilots were urged to be sure they knew if they were flying a modified airplane because of changes in flight characteristics in the realm of compressibility. In modified P-51s, porpoising was eliminated up to at least Mach .80, at the expense of worsened elevator characteristics requiring greater stick forces to maintain pitch in a dive at high Mach numbers or to initiate pullout. The modified airplanes still were placarded with a limiting Mach number of .75. The manual advised pilots of modified Mustangs: "You won't feel serious compressibility effects if you keep your diving speed below .75 Mach number, and recovery can be made without difficulty. Exceeding that Mach number will bring on vibration of the stick, vibration of the airplane, and a wallowing motion caused by low directional stability. This means that you must start a smooth recovery. Do not wait or try to ride the dive to a lower altitude because that technique is not necessary with this airplane; smooth recovery is possible at any altitude sufficiently high."[21]

P-51C equivalent, this RAF Mustang Mk III used Normandy invasion stripes as did its USAAF counterparts in mid-1944. Malcolm hood bulges above original canopy size. (SDAM)

[1] Kit C. Carter and Robert Mueller, compilers, *Combat Chronology, 1941-1945—U.S. Army Air Forces in World War II*, Center for Air Force History, Washington, DC, 1991. [2] *Ibid.* [3] *Ibid.* [4] History report, Fourth Fighter Group, March 1945, submitted to Commanding General, Eighth Air Force, 1 April 1945. [5] *Ibid.* [6] *Ibid.* [7] "British Army Cooperation Tactical Employment of the Mustang I (P-51)," by Brig Gen Charles F. Born, Asst. Chief of Staff, A-3, Headquarters, Northwest African Strategic Air Forces, 26 Aug 1943. [8] *Ibid.* [9] *Ibid.* [10] *Ibid.* [11] "Those Screaming A-36's," *Skyline* magazine, May-June 1944, Pp. 8-9. [12] "Comparative Performance Between Zeke 52 and the P-38, P-51, P-47," *Technical Air Intelligence Report #38* By Army Air Forces Proving Ground Command, Eglin Field, Florida, April 1945. [13] *Ibid.* [14] *Ibid.* [15] Richard A. Morley, "Fred Borsodi: Profile of a Test Pilot, Engineer, Pilot, Patriot," *Journal, American Aviation Historical Society*, Summer 1996, (Pp. 121-124). [16] *Pilot Training Manual for the P-51 Mustang*, HQ, AAF, Washington, DC, Aug 15, 1945. [17] *Ibid.* [18] *Ibid.* [19] *Ibid.* [20] *Ibid.* [21] *Ibid.*

HORSE OF A DIFFERENT COLOR

THE MUSTANG IN COLOR

Early British orders for Mustangs ensured the type would fly typically variegated camouflage schemes employed by the Royal Air Force. The more somber olive drab and gray coated USAAF Mustangs until natural metal finish became standard during razorback Merlin Mustang production. Some units, especially over Europe in 1944, reapplied partial camouflage to the upper surfaces of their P-51s.

After the war, civilian P-51 operators exceeded the colorful markings of wartime Mustang units with highly imaginative paint schemes

Fire-breathing TF-51D comes to life during the Merced, California, fly-in, June 1978. Flames dissipated and engine settled into a throaty idle moments after the photo was taken. Extra travel of the dual-control Mustang's canopy is evident. (Frederick A. Johnsen)

P-51B over England shows paint discoloration on inboard wing panels, indicating obliteration of upper-surface invasion stripes. White identification stripes prevailed, in an effort to distinguish Mustangs from Messerschmitts.

applied to racing aircraft, while business-plane Mustangs refurbished by Cavalier Aircraft carried a distinguished two-tone scheme that became a Cavalier recognition feature.

The newest combat camouflage scheme to adorn a Mustang variant was the Air Force-style European One green and gray scheme applied to two Piper Enforcer turboprop prototypes that still flew in the first half of the 1980s.

Perhaps the best evidence of the Mustang's inherent aesthetics is the fact it is difficult to paint one badly; the sleek design seems to forgive whatever paint is applied to it.

With cowling sections removed, the Merlin on a 364th Fighter Group P-51D receives attention in a post-D-Day Kodachrome. (Mark Brown/USAFA)

Red-accented TF-51D (44-84666) used small postwar 'U.S. Air Force' lettering on tail. (R. Arnold via Dave Menard)

Pressed paper drop tanks and a code letter 'A' that obliterates most of the serial number accent the Mustang nearest camera as elements of the 364th Fighter Group prepare for takeoff, probably in August or later in 1944. (Mark Brown /USAFA)

For years in the 1970s, Howie Keefe campaigned his brightly-painted P-51D Miss America at air shows as well as air races. Sponsors and subtle markings variations evolved over the years since this photo was taken near Abbotsford, British Columbia, in August 1971. (Frederick A. Johnsen)

Ben Hall raced P-51D N5482V before it was acquired by Mike Loening. Hall and his Mustang were popular at air shows in the Northwest United States, including this Pacific Northwest Aviation Historical Foundation (PNAHF) open house at Seattle's Boeing Field on November 12, 1966. (Frederick A. Johnsen)

Record-setting P-82 Betty Jo was retired to the U.S. Air Force Museum. Parked outside at the old museum location, the Twin Mustang looked like this in 1960. For many years since, this aircraft has been displayed indoors. (Sommerich collection via Jim Morrow)

A Dallas-built P-51D (44-84948) shared ramp space with a Bell P-59 Airacomet jet, as the zenith in piston-engine fighters met the jet age in its infancy. (W.J. Balogh via Dave Menard)

F-82 survived the scrapper to go on permanent display instead at Lackland Air Force Base, San Antonio, Texas, where it was photographed in July 1994. (Frederick A. Johnsen)

P-51D at McChord Field, Washington, gleamed at the rainy exit from one of the base's huge hangars in February 1946. (Photo by Carl Schuler)

HOT AND COLD WARS

LONGEVITY PROVES MUSTANG'S STATUS AS A CLASSIC

The U.S. Air Force at the end of World War Two held a surplus of many types of warplanes; a surplus that allowed for picking and choosing what aircraft types to retain and what types to put out to pasture. The P-51 stayed on, as an Air National Guard fighter-bomber, as well as in some active-duty units. But the total number of Mustangs needed for postwar U.S. Air Force requirements was less than the surviving wartime output, making some P-51s available for foreign countries and civilian buyers.

P-51s served the Air National Guard (ANG) for 11 years beginning in 1946. They were the most plentiful fighters in the early ANG postwar period, equipping about 75 Guard squadrons at one time or another before the last ANG F-51 stood down in 1957.[1]

When North Korea invaded the south on June 25, 1950, the Air Force rallied almost immediately. F-51s were sent in quantity to Korea, ultimately flown by U.S. Air Force, Republic of Korea (ROK) Air Force, and other United Nations' countries' pilots in air-to-ground and some air-to-air combat. Early in the war, range for ground attack aircraft was an issue as many Far East Air Forces' (FEAF) airplanes operated out of Japan initially. The prop-driven F-51 Mustang offered range, loitering ability, and hard points for bombs and rockets—all desirable in Korean combat. Early combat in Korea found the F-80 jets from Japan at that time unable to carry napalm bombs that were useful against enemy T-34 tanks; until the jets were modified to carry these bombs, Mustangs were the logical answer. Thirty-six F-51s in storage in Japan were readied for combat over Korea, partly re-equipping two

squadrons in July 1950, and moving up to Taegu and Pohang in South Korea. From here the Mustangs could cover any target in South Korea. More F-51s were requested to be sent from the United States, and the aircraft carrier USS *Boxer* ferried 145 Mustangs to the fray in July 1950.[2] The urgent need for Mustangs by active duty Air Force units saw 296 F-51s pulled from Air National Guard units that summer, for use by the active forces in Korea.[3]

As combat over Korea evolved, in the period between August 3 and September 23, 1950, a Fifth Air Force tally showed the loss of 45 F-51s and one F-82 on all types of sorties. Other Fifth AF losses in that period were only eight F-80s and three Douglas B-26s. F-51s were soon found less than ideal for night interdiction sorties because muzzle flashes from the wing-mounted

Partial cloud cover over the San Francisco Bay area accents a California Air National Guard F-51H with twin antenna mast installation aft of cockpit, and radio direction-finding (DF) loop antenna housed inside the Plexiglas canopy behind the hard-helmeted pilot. (William T. Larkins via Peter M. Bowers collection)

California ANG F-51H sports a black panel around and aft of the exhaust stubs to minimize appearance of exhaust stains. Small mainwheels and slim main gear doors characteristic of the lightweight Mustang variants are evident in this view. (Tom Foote collection)

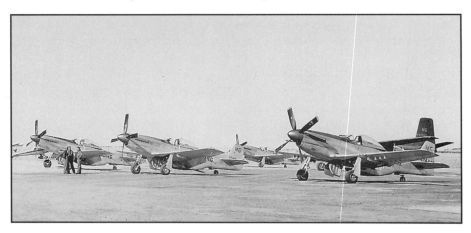

P-51Ds of the Arizona Air National Guard had propeller spinners painted copper; Arizona is the Copper State. (Ken Shake)

.50-caliber machine guns hindered the pilots' night vision. By day, Mustangs browsed the roads of Korea, looking for targets.[4]

When the USAF prepared an operations analysis of F-51 Korean War battle damage covering the early period between September 8, 1950, and June 9, 1951, some illuminating vignettes were preserved: The peril of ditching a Mustang hit home again on October 8, 1950, when the pilot of an F-51 tried to ditch in the ocean following engine failure. The report tersely noted: "Pilot stated engine failure; attempted to ditch but was not seen after aircraft hit water." On November 3, 1950, F-51 number 427 collided with debris from an enemy Yak fighter that was downed by another Mustang. Number 427 sustained damage to the coolant scoop requiring eight man-hours to fix. On the morning of November 27, 1950, F-51 number 45-11560 was engaged in strafing a road in the vicinity of Kwangsongdong. The Mustang struck a ridge east of the road, glancing off and rolling twice before hitting the ground, still rolling and tearing itself apart in flames, a victim of the peculiar perils of low-level aerial warfare.[5]

One of the early users of F-51Ds over Korea was the 12th Fighter Bomber Squadron of the 18th Fighter Bomber Group. The squadrons of the group were formerly equipped with F-80Cs at

Squadron emblem replaced U.S. national insignia on fuselage of this Arizona National Guard P-51D in the early postwar era; later, Guard Mustangs carried more standard star-and-bar markings on fuselages as well as wings. (Bodie via SDAM)

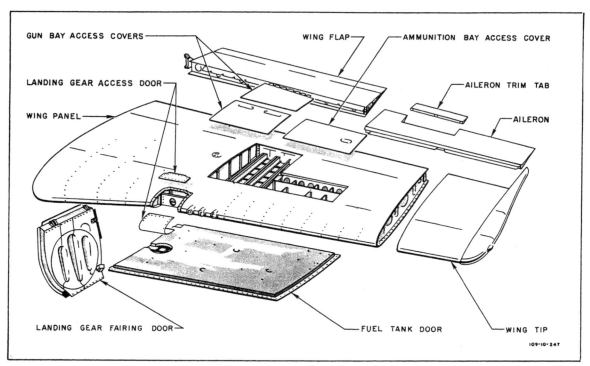

GUN BAY ACCESS COVERS

WING FLAP

AMMUNITION BAY ACCESS COVER

LANDING GEAR ACCESS DOOR

AILERON TRIM TAB

WING PANEL

AILERON

LANDING GEAR FAIRING DOOR

FUEL TANK DOOR

WING TIP

109-10-247

Figure 84—Wing Panel Assembly

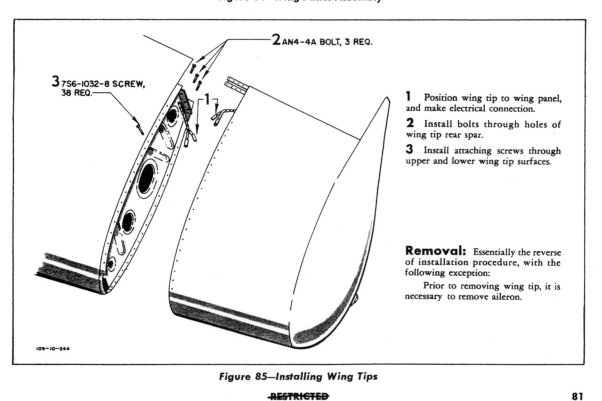

2 AN4-4A BOLT, 3 REQ.

3 7S6-1032-8 SCREW, 38 REQ.

1

1 Position wing tip to wing panel, and make electrical connection.

2 Install bolts through holes of wing tip rear spar.

3 Install attaching screws through upper and lower wing tip surfaces.

Removal: Essentially the reverse of installation procedure, with the following exception:

Prior to removing wing tip, it is necessary to remove aileron.

109-10-244

Figure 85—Installing Wing Tips

Line art from P-51D erection and maintenance manual shows removable wingtip which lent itself to clipping for racing purposes.

NORTH AMERICAN
P-51 MUSTANG

For export to Uruguay, this refurbished P-51D (possibly 44-63559) was parked at California's Pacific Airmotive in a postwar era when Mustangs were viable weapons for smaller air forces. (Bodie)

Clark Air Base in the Philippines. Leaving the jet aircraft behind, the unit moved to Ashiya Air base, Japan, where it received its F-51Ds before moving to airfields K-9 and, evidently, K-10, in Korea around September 9, 1950. The 12th squadron had previous experience with F-51s before converting to F-80s in the Philippines. "About 85 percent of the pilots flying the F-51D aircraft had World War II experience," a squadron operational analysis noted. The Mustangs of the 12th Fighter Bomber Squadron carried the standard six .50-caliber machine guns and 1,800 rounds of ammunition in the wings. Varying ordnance loads could include six underwing rockets and two napalm tanks or six rockets and two bombs. Alternately, the F-51Ds could be configured for long range missions by carrying only four rockets and two 110-gallon drop tanks. Short missions could rely on internally tanking only 265 gallons of gas; the addition of the drop tanks boosted the fuel total to 485 gallons.[6]

The 12th FBS tallied and described its operations for the month of February 1951: "During the month of February most of the 12th Fighter Bomber Squadron missions were armed reconnaissance, specifically in an interdiction role. Mission objective was to seek out and destroy enemy vehicles, supply concentrations, and enemy troops. In addition the squadron was committed for alerts, primarily in a close support role." A flight profile for the F-51Ds of the unit often began with engine-start five to 10 minutes before takeoff. The report noted: "Single ship takeoff is necessary due to the condition of runway at this base." At K-10, the F-51s used a sod runway 4,200 feet long and 175 feet wide, according to the operations analysis. Once airborne, two, four, or more Mustangs made the mission. After forming up over

Royal Canadian Air Force P-51D (RCAF 9273) carried the red maple leaf insignia with white inside blue circle when photographed. Number 9273 may have been allocated more than once to RCAF Mustangs. (SDAM)

RCAF Mustang (9256) carries identifiers AW-X on left side of fuselage. Circular gas cap for aft fuselage tank is evident at rear of canopy frame. (Bodie/SDAM)

Using RCAF marking with no white surrounding the red maple leaf is Mustang IV number 9552, carrying underwing drop tank/bomb pylons, but no rocket launchers. (Bodie/SDAM)

the airfield, a typical mission of four F-51Ds would assume a diamond formation, slipping into a fingertip formation nearing the target. (Fingertip or "finger four" formation describes a vee formation with planes staggered much as the tips of the four fingers on the hand when held out straight ahead.) When the 12th squadron compiled its analysis in February 1951, the combat situation meant typical distance to reach close-support and armed reconnaissance targets was 180 miles from base; longer reconnaissance missions could be 200 to 400 miles.[7]

During the month of February 1951, the 12th FBS did not engage in any air-to-air action. For ground attacks, the squadron analysis noted: "Suitability of the F-51D aircraft for type of operation carried out is very good, but its coolant system is vulnerable to ground fire." During the month, the 12th Fighter Bomber Squadron posted an average of 26 aircraft assigned, logging an aggregate of 1,616 flying hours for the month, which averaged out

to 62 hours per F-51. This activity consumed 104,164 gallons of gas on combat missions. Effective sorties for the month were 460. Seventy-six percent of the squadron's aircraft were in commission. Of three F-51s lost by the squadron that February, one was in combat and two were listed as operational losses. Five Merlin engines were changed during the month. The .50-caliber machine guns of the

12th Fighter Bomber Squadron expended 401,970 rounds in February, while 2,242 rockets were fired and 668 napalm tanks were released. Lower in usage were bombs, with only a dozen 500-pound general purpose bombs and four 260-pound fragmentation bombs dropped that month.[8] The 12th Fighter Bomber Squadron's operations analysis for February 1951 concluded: "The F-51D is a

Passing a sea of drop tanks, F-51Ds taxi for a Korean War mission. Mustang nearest camera (44-84910) was reported to have crashed and burned on takeoff March 6, 1952. (Tom Foote collection)

South African Air Force Mustangs flew combat in Korea as part of the United Nations effort to repel communist North Koreans. (SDAM)

very suitable aircraft for close support tactical work. Its range and ability to stay in the target area for sustained periods enable pilots to pick out definite targets."[9] The piston-engine war horse of World War Two still had some strengths the early-jet Air Force needed, and appreciated, in Korea.

The Air Force assigned an operations analyst to review F-51 operations in Korea covering the period between October 1951 and March 1952. The mission for F-51s was described by Fifth Air Force as "day tactical air close support and day interdiction bombing." The operations analyst added: "In addition to their regular mission F-51s are often used for cover in air rescue operations. Their main targets are personnel, gun positions, and rails. Armament used consists of .50-caliber ammunition and HE bombs. They normally do not have counter-air enemy opposition; however, they receive heavy damage from ground fire due to low-level operations."[10]

The report noted the 18th Fighter Bomber Wing's responsibility for the F-51 mission in Korea, staging from an advance base at Hoengsong, and using a rear base at Chinhae for maintenance. A chart in the report tallied F-51 losses in Korea from a variety of causes, between June 1, 1951, and April 27, 1952, showing 84 outright losses of Mustangs, and a total of lost or damaged F-51s at 352 incidents. (The 18th FBW continued using F-51s until beginning the conversion to

Snow had to be cleared from this Republic of Korea Air Force (ROKAF) F-51D, armed with 5-inch HVAR rockets and general-purpose bombs. Three circles under the wing, outboard of the Korean insignia, are recognition lights in different colors. Wing insignia shows variation on bars, with no blue edge on either end. (SDAM)

In the transition period for postwar Air Force markings and designations, this Inglewood P-51D carried 1947-introduced stars with red bars, but the buzz number on the fuselage still used the letters 'PF' indicating a Pursuit, instead of the later 'FF' for fighter. The second letter 'F' was used to designate single-engine Mustangs, and the last three numbers of the serial were applied after the letters. Buzz numbers, in theory at least, allowed for positive identification of aircraft by people unfamiliar with types; if they could remember PF or later FF, it was certain they were identifying a Mustang. Other aircraft types had different identifying letters in the buzz number scheme introduced in 1945. F-82s were tagged FQ. (SDAM)

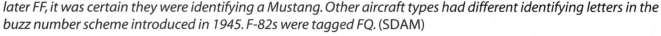

F-86s in January 1953, after the publication date of this report and charts.) For the period covered in the report, 18th Wing F-51s took hits from air-to-air engagements three times between June 1 and June 21, 1951 and once in September 1951. But the vast majority of damage sustained by the F-51s was from ground-to-air fire, representing 329 of the 352 listed incidents. Other causes were listed as self-inflicted, 11 times, and no known cause, eight times.[11]

Extracts from a compilation of 18th Fighter Bomber Wing F-51 losses in Korea between January 1951 and April 30, 1952, help paint a picture of the rigors of that war. Other losses during this period included reassignments, transfers for "rebirth" as noted in the original report, and single-letter loss codes that did not always elaborate on circumstances:[12]

Date Lost	Serial No.
Remarks	

| 16 Jan 51 | 44-13253 |
| Crash-landed in friendly territory | |

| 1 Mar 51 | 45-11362 |
| Crashed behind enemy lines | |

| 5 Apr 51 | 44-73592 |
| Lost to combat | |

| 5 Apr 51 | 44-74460 |
| Pilot bailed out at 37 deg. 43' Lat; 126 deg. 46' Long. | |

| 9 Apr 51 | 44-74381 |
| Lost to combat behind enemy lines | |

| 11 Apr 51 | 44-74943 |
| Crashed on takeoff at K-13; reclamation by KAMU to be accomplished | |

| 14 Apr 51 | 44-74401 |
| Lost behind enemy lines | |

| 19 Apr 51 | 44-74154 |
| Lost to combat | |

| 25 Apr 51 | 45-11420 |
| Lost in enemy territory | |

| 26 Apr 51 | 44-74484 |
| Crashed into enemy territory | |

| 30 Apr 51 | 44-15236 |
| Crashed into enemy lines; lost | |

| 30 Apr 51 | 44-74905A |
| Crashed just south of Han River; KAMU requested to reclaim | |

| 7 May 51 | 44-73050 |
| Landed at K-16 on fire | |

| 11 May 51 | 44-74727 |
| Crashed into friendly territory; KAMU asked to reclaim | |

| 13 May 51 | 44-72740 |
| Crash-landed in friendly territory | |

| 17 May 51 | 44-73995 |
| Crashed in enemy territory when coolant was lost | |

| 17 May 51 | 44-74622 |
| Crashed into water off end of K-10 runway | |

| 18 May 51 | 45-11379 |
| Mushed into ground on takeoff | |

| 19 May 51 | 44-84913 |
| Crashed and burned behind enemy lines | |

| 23 May 51 | 44-74539 |
| Lost behind enemy lines | |

| 25 May 51 | 44-73116 |
| Lost to combat - behind enemy lines | |

| 29 May 51 | 44-74416 |
| Lost behind enemy lines | |

| 2 Jun 51 | 44-74177 |
| Lost to enemy action | |

| 1 Jul 51 | 44-74611 |
| Crashed and burned at K-46 | |

Bearing race number 45, P-51D (44-72400) featured a clean chin profile in the manner of the XP-51J; but power was provided by a Merlin variant instead of the J's Allison. Carburetor intake was below engine to the rear of standard location. More radical still was the removal of the ventral radiator intake, replaced by leading edge inlets in the wings, where sliced P-39 radiators were fitted in the gun bays. Photo circa 1947-49. (Peter M. Bowers collection via SDAM)

3 Jul 51 44-74392	9 Nov 51 44-74369	20 Mar 52 44-74032
Crashed on landing; code A	Crashed on takeoff at K-46	Lost to battle damage and bad weather

3 Jul 51   44-74392
Crashed on landing; code A

5 Jul 51   44-73868
Crashed into friendly territory

5 Jul 51   45-11365
Ran off end of runway at K-46

5 Jul 51   45-11407
Crashed behind enemy lines

7 Jul 51   44-74488
Crashed into enemy territory

9 Jul 51   44-74137
Crashed on takeoff

11 Jul 51   44-74495
Left landing gear could not extend; pilot bailed out

18 Jul 51   44-74408
Crashed on landing; code N

30 Jul 51   44-84908
Lost to combat

2 Aug 51   44-74442
Lost behind enemy lines

5 Aug 51   44-84939
Lost to code N; aircraft crashed upon collision

7 Sep 51   44-73242
Ran off end of runway at K-10

9 Nov 51   44-74369
Crashed on takeoff at K-46

3 Dec 51   44-74343
Crashed in friendly territory; inaccessible to crash equipment

20 Dec 51   44-84868
Takeoff mishap at K-46

8 Feb 52   45-11602
Crashed on takeoff at K-46

19 Feb 52   44-74412
Engine failure short of field

1 Mar 52   44-72055
Extensive battle damage - lost to KAMU

4 Mar 52   44-74384
Lost to enemy action

6 Mar 52   44-84910
Crashed on takeoff; burned

8 Mar 52   44-73994
Crashed behind enemy lines

9 Mar 52   44-72726
Crashed behind enemy lines

15 Mar 52   44-72091
Lost to combat - behind enemy lines

18 Mar 52   45-11350
Crashed into water off end of K-10 runway on takeoff

20 Mar 52   44-74032
Lost to battle damage and bad weather

21 Mar 52   44-73898
Crashed and burned - total loss

1 Apr 52   44-84945
Lost to enemy action

2 Apr 52   44-73983
Lost to combat behind enemy lines

5 Apr 52   44-72914
Crashed into sea - lost through enemy action

5 Apr 52   44-74643
Lost to enemy action

10 Apr 52   44-73648
Lost behind enemy lines

10 Apr 52   44-84792
Lost behind enemy lines

12 Apr 52   44-74730
Crashed into friendly territory; KAMU advised

13 Apr 52   45-11363
Lost behind enemy lines

13 Apr 52   45-11736
Enemy action; behind enemy lines

20 Apr 52   44-74378
Lost to combat behind enemy lines

30 Apr 52   44-74029
Crashed into enemy territory

30 Apr 52   44-74509
Lost behind enemy lines

Large capacity drop tanks added range to a postwar P-51D. Canopy frame, prop spinner, rudder tip, wingtip, and horizontal tail tip are painted, probably red. (SDAM)

Who wouldn't want their own P-51 Mustang? The vaunted fighter that did so much to win World War Two was a genuine icon of American victory. Its performance knocked on the doors of early jet statistics, and its no-fat airframe was sculpted in a way that evoked images of the lean wild horse for which it was named. The immediate postwar air races were populated with Mustangs ranging from Bendix entrant NX1204V, a straight P-51 (41-37426), to Bendix racer number 15, A-36A (42-83665), civil registration N39502, that was later restored to military configuration for the U.S. Air Force Museum. Other razorback P-51Bs and Cs entered the civil market in limited numbers, but the benchmark P-51D and nearly identical P-51K made up the bulk of civilian-owned Mustangs.

North American Aviation test pilot Robert A. "Bob" Hoover became an air show legend for his precise P-51D aerobatics, and trademark hesitation rolls and one-wheel landings. After adding a North American Rockwell Shrike Commander business

Stripped from the firewall forward, stored F-51Ds yielded parts. (SDAM)

Snug-fitting Merlin engine and engine-mount details are revealed on uncowled F-51D-30-NA (44-74656A) assigned to Nellis Air Force Base, Nevada, when the photo was taken, probably in the early 1950s. Landing light is visible in the wheel well.

In October 1955, an F-51D with vertical fin extension used by NACA at the Dryden Flight Research Center on Rogers Dry Lake in California posed with a NACA Superfortress mother ship.

Last USAF Mustang?

Early in May 1955, the Palmdale, California newspaper reported on what was believed to be the last active F-51D in the Air Force inventory departing service that year. Identified as number 107, piloted by Capt. Robert F. Titus, the Mustang was ferried from the Naval Auxiliary Air Station at El Centro, [California] to a storage and reclamation compound of the Sacramento Air Materiel Area. According to the article, this F-51D was retired with 1,371 hours logged in jobs including training test pilots at Wright Field, Ohio. Its last two years of service included carrying telemetry and parachute test devices on behalf of the 6511th Parachute Test Group at El Centro.[14]

plane to his routine in about 1970, Hoover often booked the military Mustang and the civilian Aero Commander at the same air show, moving from the realm of high-powered warbirds to sleek business aircraft in a smooth show of airmanship. Though sometimes flying borrowed Mustangs at air shows if his regular mounts were unavailable, Bob Hoover has been associated, since 1972, with P-51D (44-74739) registration number N51RH, registered successively since that time to North American Rockwell, Rockwell International, and later to Evergreen International, under whose sponsorship Hoover has flown demonstrations.[13]

Last American Military Mustang Served Army

Honors of being the last North American Mustang in U.S. military service go to F-51D 44-72990, flown up to February 7, 1978, by the U.S. Army as a chase plane for the Cheyenne and other helicopter programs including the YUH-60 Blackhawk. This Mustang was acquired

NACA-148 was emblazoned on the underside of the left wing of a tall-tail F-51D used by the National Advisory Committee for Aeronautics at Dryden Flight Research Center, in the Mojave Desert of California in the mid-1950s.

from the civilian market in 1967 by the Army, and initially assigned to Fort Rucker, Alabama. Later, it was transferred to the Army's aviation test facility at Edwards Air Force Base, California. Number 44-72990 was accepted by the USAAF on February 23, 1945. Postwar service included a stint with the 82nd Fighter Wing at Grenier Field in 1949-50. On January 23, 1951, this aircraft was assigned to the Royal Canadian Air Force's Canadian Air Defense Command, and given the Canadian serial number 9283. By December 1956, this Mustang was out of Canadian service and in storage. Between 1959 and 1967, several civilian owners kept the plane, including Stan Kurzet in California, who owned it before the Army bought it. An Army spokesman associated with the program said a Mustang was selected for pacing helicopters because it was deemed the best aircraft capable of pacing and chasing the Cheyenne through its various speeds and altitudes. On February 7, 1978, this Mustang began a cross-country flight from Edwards Air Force Base to Fort Rucker, and a berth in the Army Aviation Museum there.[15]

Chuck Hall's P-51D (44-84961) looked like this in 1965 in its hangar at Paine Field, Everett, Washington, before metamorphosis as an air racer. (Frederick A. Johnsen)

CAVALIER MUSTANGS FOR WAR AND PEACE

In Florida, Cavalier Aircraft Corporation decided the sleek F-51 offered promise as a business and sport plane years before there was a recognized warbird movement in civilian circles. Cavalier Mustangs

Race team member Bob Patterson held the original wingtip in place to show what had been clipped from Chuck Hall's racing P-51 (N7715C) at Paine Field, Washington, in an effort to increase its competitiveness, circa 1969. (Frederick A. Johnsen)

By about 1969, Chuck Hall's P-51 had racing number 5 on the tail, a silver, green, and yellow paint scheme, and clipped wingtips. (Frederick A. Johnsen)

Continued modifications to racer number 5 included building up a turtledeck to fair into a cut-down canopy, fashioned by turning the original sliding canopy around backward to become the windscreen. (Frederick A. Johnsen)

were typically distinguished by the use of a taller vertical fin, reminiscent of that used on the P-51H, and made by extending the lines of the regular D-model fin above the rudder. Some Cavalier conversions used centerline-mounted tip tanks for greater range; most featured a jumpseat behind the pilot's seat. Sleek commercial paint schemes on Cavalier conversions typically used a demarcation line sweeping up from the chin and along the fuselage, with a band on the vertical tail surfaces, executed in the best of business aircraft style. As restored warbird

Passing through subsequent owners, racer number 5 ultimately emerged as the Red Baron "RB-51," with a Griffon engine turning contra-rotating propellers, and a vertical fin of broader chord. In 1979 this aircraft set a piston engine speed record of more than 499 miles an hour. Sustaining major damage in a mishap at the Reno National Championship Air Races in September 1979, portions of this long-lived Mustang went into a P-51 resurrection. (Wings Publishing Co.)

Mustangs came into vogue, some Cavalier Mustangs reverted to a more military appearance once more.

In 1967, the U.S. Air Force bought several militarized F-51Ds from Cavalier, who by this time had bought the rights to the Mustang from North American Aviation. The remanufactured military Cavalier Mustangs had the trademark tall tail, plus provision for six .50-caliber guns in the wings and hardpoints for six high-velocity aircraft rockets (HVARs) and two 1,000-pound bombs. Destined for distribution to central American countries under the Military Assistance Program, at least some of the 1967 Mustangs were painted glossy gray overall and given

U.S. Army F-51 chase plane carried tail number 0-72990 (originally 44-72990) circa 1967 when used to observe helicopters under test in Alabama and California. High canopy for greater headroom in rear seat is reminiscent of TF-51, but canopy rail is standard F-51 style. Paint blocked intense overhead sun from entering canopy. After retirement, this aircraft was put in the U.S. Army Aviation Museum at Fort Rucker, Alabama.

Mike Loening's red, white, and black P-51D N5482V in the sage brush at Reno after an emergency landing during the National Championship Air Races in 1971. Using an Aeroproducts hollow propeller, the blades crumpled and kinked as they bent on impact. This aircraft previously had been operated by Ben Hall out of Everett, Washington, in a yellow and black paint scheme. (Frederick A. Johnsen)

U.S. Air Force markings. New 1967 serial numbers were assigned to the aircraft.[16]

Several of the military Cavalier F-51Ds came back to the United States and Canada as civilian aircraft after ending their service in Latin America. Known Cavalier military Mustangs include:

67-14865, Bolivian Air Force, possibly stored for Bolivian museum.

67-14866, Bolivian Air Force, to Alberta, Canada as civil warbird.

67-22579, Bolivian Air Force, to Canada and then U.S. civil owner by 1987.

67-22580, Bolivian Air Force, to Alberta, Canada by 1977.

67-22581, Bolivian Air Force, to Alberta, Canada, by 1977; still flown in Canadian registration C-GMUS, nickname "What's Up Doc?," as of 1995.

68-15795, to the U.S. Air Force Museum program by 1984.

At least one other Cavalier Mk. 2 F-51D military conversion, formerly number 405 with the air force of El Salvador, was brought to the United States as a civil aircraft in 1974.

A Cavalier P-51D identified both as 44-74827 and 72-1541 is reported to be an aircraft delivered to Indonesia, later winding up in the Royal New Zealand Air Force Museum.[17]

Painted to represent a Texas Air National Guard F-51D, Ed Messick of the Confederate Air Force flew N51MR during the 1976 Confederate Air Force air show at Harlingen, Texas. In 1989, this aircraft sustained damage in a mishap at Santa Monica, California. (Frederick A. Johnsen)

ENFORCER—MUSTANG'S LAST HURRAH

Cavalier made a bold attempt to keep the Mustang magic alive for the military by mounting a Dart turboprop

The skies are filled with warbirds at the Experimental Aircraft Association (EAA) fly-in convention at Oshkosh, Wisconsin, each summer. In 1979, a P-51 and an AT-6 Texan made mock strafing runs as two more Mustangs raised their tailwheels from the Oshkosh runway during the air show. Mustangs remain favorites at air shows around the world. (Frederick A. Johnsen)

WARBIRDTECH
S E R I E S

engine in an F-51D airframe, and altering the wing for more modern hardpoints for a variety of stores including pod-mounted guns instead of the .50-calibers in the wings. Hopes for a U.S. Air Force purchase of the turboprop version dimmed, and Piper Aircraft bought rights to this version, naming it the PA-48 Enforcer. Two Enforcers were campaigned again by Piper in an effort to win a contract from the United States, as a possible MAP aircraft for other countries.

In 1979, Congress approved funding for evaluation of the Enforcer.[18] Ultimately, the Air Force declined the Enforcer, which at least one pilot said had a blind spot under its long nose during some types of bomb deliveries. The two Enforcer examples, made with substantial portions of existing D-model Mustang airframes as well as some new construction, were preserved by the U.S. Air Force Museum system, tributes to the Mustang and the postwar engineers and builders who saw an opportunity for one more encore using this design coupled with modern technology.

The end of U.S. military Mustangs, whether measured by the Army's chase planes, Cavalier's MAP versions, or the civil-registered Piper Enforcers, only added more lore and luster to the Mustang story, a propeller-driven fighter that continued to serve, in the United States and abroad, well into the jet age.

Bearing Canadian civil registration C-GMUS, Cavalier F-51D Mustang number 67-22581, carries a Cavalier data plate showing its new serial number and a manufacture date of Feb. 12, 1968. With vertical fin extension, this Mustang flew with the Bolivian Air Force before being imported by civilian owners into Canada. (Frederick A. Johnsen)

[1] Rene Francillon, *The Air Guard*, AeroGraph 2, Motorbooks International, Osceola, Wisconsin, ca. 1983. [2] Eduard Mark, *Aerial Interdiction in Three Wars*, Center for Air Force History, Washington, DC, 1994. [3] Charles Joseph Gross, *Prelude to the Total Force: The Air National Guard, 1943 - 1969*, Office of Air Force History, Washington, DC, 1985. [4] Eduard Mark, *Aerial Interdiction in Three Wars*, Center for Air Force History, Washington, DC, 1994. [5] Air Force Operations Analysis, "Korean Battle Damage, F-51, 8 September 1950—9 June 1951," IR-7-52, AF 421031, 18 Feb 52. [6] Operations Analysis Section, Headquarters, 12th Fighter Bomber Squadron, 18th Fighter Bomber Group, "Operational Analysis of F-51D Aircraft in Combat," 3 March 1951. [7] *Ibid.* [8] *Ibid.* [9] *Ibid.* [10] Operations Analysis Report No. 10, "Aircraft Service Performance Evaluation Maintenance Workloads Generated in Korean Combat, Volume 5, F-51 Operations and Maintenance Workloads," by Irvin J. Kessler, Operations Analyst, Hq, USAF, Operations Analysis Division, Directorate of Operations, Deputy Chief of Staff, Operations, Headquarters, USAF, Washington, DC, 8 July 1952. [11] *Ibid.* [12] *Ibid.* [13] John Chapman and Geoff Goodall, *Warbirds Worldwide Directory*, Warbirds Worldwide Limited, Mansfield, England, 1989. [14] "Last F-51D Leaves Base," Palmdale Enterprise, May 5, 1955. [15] U.S. Air Force Flight Test Center news release (untitled), about retirement of the Army's last Mustang. [16] Peter M. Bowers and Gordon Swanborough, *United States Military Aircraft Since 1908*, Putnam, London, 1971. [17] John Chapman and Geoff Goodall, *Warbirds Worldwide Directory*, Warbirds Worldwide Limited, Mansfield, England, 1989. [18] *Echelon*, Jul-Aug 1979.

2 TIMES 51 4 EQUALS 82

In the era of the Second World War, twin engine fighter evolution in America took the form of twin-boom designs like the P-38 and P-61, conventional layout like the too-late-for-combat F7F Tigercat, and—most radical of all—two complete fuselages joined at the wing and tail, as was done with the XP-82 Twin Mustang. The Twin Mustang, although obviously related to the P-51, is not merely two conventional Mustang fuselages wedded by the factory. Longer than a P-51, the P-82 rested on two inwardly-retracting mainwheels and two retracting tail wheels—one in the rear of each fuselage—giving the Twin Mustang a four-point tail-low stance on the ground. Simultaneously developed for Merlin or Allison engines, the P-82 promised long range, heavy firepower, and two pilots to take turns on long escort missions. With the weight of two complete fuselages sharing less than two complete sets of wings, the Twin Mustang could be a handful on landing, with a formidable sink rate.

In January 1944, North American Aviation approached the Air Materiel Command with a proposal: NAA perceived the need for long-range escort fighters to accompany super bombers whose ranges were promising to stretch beyond that of current fighters. Negotiations that month led to a contract to procure two XP-82s powered by V-1650 Merlin engines and two XP-82As riding behind Allison V-1710-119 powerplants. Cost of the four airplanes, plus a static article and related items, was in excess of $4 million.[1]

The two XP-82s led the way to a short production run of Merlin-powered P-82B versions. The Allison-engined XP-82As ultimately were canceled as prototypes because the intended production Allison-version, the P-82E (sometimes referenced as the P-82Z) was nearing completion before the V-1710-119 engines were available for the prototype XP-82As.[2]

The P-82C was a Merlin-engined B-model (44-65169) converted to a night fighter by addition of SCR720 radar in the central pod; the P-82D was another converted B-model (44-65170) that was a night fighter equipped with APS-4 radar. The righthand cockpit became home to the radar operator. Twenty Merlin-powered P-82Bs were built before construction switched to 100 Allison-engined P-82E escort fighters, 100 P-82F night fighters with APS-4 radar, and 50 P-82Gs with SCR720 radar. The powerplants used were Allison V-1710-143 and -145 variants in production aircraft. In June 1948, the designations of these Twin Mus-

One of only 20 P-82Bs built, number 44-65163 shows exhaust stack shrouds similar to Merlin-powered P-51s. Buzz number used second letter Q to designate Twin Mustangs. (Via Tom Foote)

tangs were changed to the respective models of F-82 instead of P-82.[3]

North American had a mock-up ready for AAF inspection from 19-23 June 1944. Eleven months later, the engineering acceptance inspection on the first XP-82, number 44-83886, took place at the NAA plant. Engine accessibility for replacement was demonstrated, as noted in an Air Force summary: "During the course of the inspection the contractor was required to demonstrate removal and reinstallation of one powerplant. The crew used for this demonstration was unfamiliar with this installation and completely removed and reinstalled the powerplant in 28½ minutes. When the engine had been removed, the oil tank and heat exchanger were removed and reinstalled in 15 minutes. Accordingly, the total operation of removing everything forward of the firewall and reinstalling same required 43½ minutes with a crew of six engine mechanics."[4] The lessons of the war had obviously been applied to the XP-82's design, making maintenance chores less onerous than on some older designs.

Vital statistics for the XP-82 included an overall length of 39 feet, a wingspan of 50 feet, 11 inches, and a total wing area of 408 square feet. Unlike the P-51, where the wings were joined under the centerline of the fuselage, the XP-82 featured outer wing panels that mated to a center wing stub outboard of each fuselage. The wing center section was configured to carry internally six .50-caliber machine guns. Interconnected controls allowed the XP-82 to be flown from either cockpit; an early design premise said the pilots could take turns on long escort missions.[5]

Opposite-rotating paddle-bladed Aeroproducts propellers are evident on this six-gun toting P-82E at McChord Air Force Base in 1948. A hundred E-model Twin Mustangs were delivered as escort fighters for Strategic Air Command bombers. (Photo by Herb Tollefson)

F-82E shows unusual curved main landing gear doors, necessitated when mainwheels were placed under the fuselages, so doors had to conform to fuselage contours. Two underwing pylons for drop tanks were fitted under each wing of some F-82s. Allison-engined E-model used different exhaust stack configuration than Merlin. (Tom Foote collection)

XP-82 number 44-83886, the Twin Mustang used for the acceptance inspection, first took flight on June 12, 1945, with an NAA pilot at the controls.[6] An Air Force pilot flew it on July 6, 1945. These early sorties revealed the XP-82 to have satisfactory flight characteristics; following further tests by NAA, the Army Air Forces accepted this aircraft on August 30, 1945—after the cessation of hostilities in the Pacific, but a few days before signing of the official surrender treaty. At this point, the XP-82 was bailed back to the contractor, NAA, who conducted airworthiness and stability flight tests. For the next year and a half,

F-82G (46-377), North American model NAA-150, carries elaborate art on left drop tank, suggesting the tank was not to be dropped casually. Red arctic tail and wing panels were intended to make aircraft operating over snow stand out in the event of a forced landing. (Tom Foote collection)

Nightfighting F-82F (46-408) of the 52nd Fighter Group shows star-spangled vertical tail paint scheme. Radome pod extended beyond noses of F-82F's twin fuselages. (Tom Foote collection)

Glossy black F-82F (46-415) rode behind Allison V-1710-143/145 engines. Flame-hiding exhaust stacks are discernible.

NAA had this XP-82 on bailment before the aircraft was turned over to the National Advisory Committee for Aeronautics (NACA), who used this Twin Mustang at its Cleveland, Ohio, laboratory to conduct airborne tests of a ramjet, with the jet powerplant suspended beneath the wing center section. The next XP-82, number 44-83887, first flew August 30, 1945, at a takeoff weight of 18,410 pounds. The lefthand Merlin engine was rough running on this and subsequent tests, prompting NAA to make engineering changes to correct a power surge problem. Beginning March 18, 1946, Air Materiel Command Flight Test Division pilots went to the NAA plant to conduct performance tests on the XP-82.[7]

As early as December 1945, the AAF asked North American Aviation to install M-3 guns in the wings of both XP-82s, as well as in the eight-gun armament nacelle mounted beneath the center wing section. By this time, the .50-caliber machine gun used in so many American warplanes had evolved to the M-3 version, with performance improvements and some external differences from the older standard M-2. Bailment of the number two XP-82 was extended to allow NAA the opportunity to install M-3 guns. Following this, the aircraft was flown to Eglin Field, Florida, for tactical evaluation.[8] (Production F-82s did not use the centerline gun pod; radar was fitted on all-weather variants in place of the gun pod. Evidence also suggests older-style M-2 guns were retained by at least some production F-82s.)

The Allison-powered F-82Es formed the U.S. Air Force's only escort wing. Fourteen F-82Hs were winterized from earlier F- and G-models to serve in Alaska. (Unlike missions in temperate climates where aircraft might be exposed to cold temperatures at high altitude for a period of hours, and then return to moderate temperatures again, the environment of Alaska and other arctic regions demanded special configuring for aircraft that became "cold-soaked" by continuous exposure to freezing temperatures.)

The F-82s were acknowledged stop-gap cold-warriors. A February 1948 Air Force technical report noted: "Following the end of World War Two, a production program was set up with certain fighters designated to be procured as interim fighters. The XP-82A (Allison-powered) fell in this category and were to be procured in limited quantities and designated P-82Z airplanes."[9] The Allison F-82s ultimately filled the all-weather/night fighter role, relieving the older Northrop Black Widow until jets like the F-94 were ready for service.

F-82B (44-65172) was testbed for reconnaissance photo pod evaluated at Eglin Field in 1948. (USAF/SDAM)

The few Merlin-engined Twin Mustangs did not enter line service as operational fighters. One of these F-82Bs, christened "Betty Jo," showed off its long legs in a nonstop flight of more than 5,000 miles from Hawaii to New York, averaging more than 340 miles an hour en route. The advent of the Korean War saw Allison-engined Twin Mustangs step in to do what they were purchased for—fill in until the advent of jets with their all-weather capabilities. With a long loitering time, F-82Gs were useful early in the war. The first air-to-air victories by U.S. warplanes over North Korean aircraft occurred on June 27, 1950, when two F-82Gs of the 68th Fighter (All Weather) Squadron downed a Yak apiece.

Construction of the photo pod for the F-82B shows forward-angling camera in place in framework. Removal of large four-blade propellers probably facilitated work on the project. Vestiges of B-model gun ports in center wing can be seen behind the pod framework. (SDAM)

FAMOUS FLIERS TESTED F-82 IRREVERSIBLE CONTROLS

At Edwards Air Force Base between September 11 and November 7, 1950, a roster of test pilots evaluated F-82E (46-260) after it had been fitted with an irreversible control system with variable artificial feel. The Twin Mustang was a test airframe only; some of the pilots commented it was the wrong airframe for such a test, and that a jet fighter should be substituted for higher speeds. Irreversible controls prevented air loads from returning control surfaces to neutral against the stick and rudder forces applied by the pilot. Artificial feel was used to give the pilot some sense of control input feedback—feedback that would have been supplied by air loads on strictly mechanically-linked control surfaces. The testbed F-82E was altered with the substitution of an irreversible hydraulic power-operated control system, along with elevator, aileron, and rudder variable artificial feel,

Evidently gaining unofficial status as an "RF-82B," the testbed Twin Mustang photo reconnaissance aircraft appears to have additional oblique camera ports in the fuselage, impinging on the national insignia. B-model had shorter vertical fins than E-model. (Hendrix/SDAM)

F-82B shows single elevator trim tab in center trailing edge of the control surface. Rudders are metal-clad. Twin tailwheels gave F-82 a four-point stance. (SDAM)

replacing the aircraft's normal surface control boost system.[10]

Most notable about this test was the pantheon of test pilots who flew the F-82E in the short period of the evaluation. The list includes: Brig. Gen. Albert Boyd, Lt. Col. Fred J. Ascani, Maj. Frank K. Everest, Jr., Maj. Jack L. Ridley, Capt. Charles E. Yeager, Jr., Capt. James W. Andrew, Capt. William A. Bailey, Capt. Russell M. Roth, Capt. Arthur Murray, Capt. W.W. Seller, Jr., 1st Lt. Fitzhugh Fulton, and 1st Lt. James S. Nash.[11]

The F-82 Twin Mustang was the last piston-engine fighter built by North American Aviation, and the last piston-engine fighter bought by the U.S. Air Force. The Allison variants showcased a high-altitude powerplant that exceeded the V-1710s of wartime P-38s, P-39s, and P-40s, although there evidently remained some disagreement over the choice of Allisons versus Merlins on the operational Twin Mustangs.

F-82B with narrow experimental photo reconnaissance pod shows dihedral in outer wing panels; placement of landing gear under each fuselage.

[1] "Final Report on the Procurement, Inspection, Testing, and Acceptance of North American Model XP-82 and XP-82A Airplanes," U.S. Air Force Technical Report No. 5673, by Werner R. Rankin, Project Engineer, 19 Feb 1948. [2] Ibid. [3] Peter M. Bowers and Gordon Swanborough, United States Military Aircraft Since 1908, Putnam, London, 1971. [4] "Final Report on the Procurement, Inspection, Testing, and Acceptance of North American Model XP-82 and XP-82A Airplanes," U.S. Air Force Technical Report No. 5673, by Werner R. Rankin, Project Engineer, 19 Feb 1948. [5] Ibid. [6] From correspondence and margin notes made to a draft of this manuscript by Ray Wagner, July 1996. [7] "Final Report on the Procurement, Inspection, Testing, and Acceptance of North American Model XP-82 and XP-82A Airplanes," U.S. Air Force Technical Report No. 5673, by Werner R. Rankin, Project Engineer, 19 Feb 1948. [8] Ibid. [9] Ibid. [10] "F-82E Variable Boost Flight Test," U.S. Air Force Air Materiel Command Memorandum Report EMR 50-39, 18 Dec 1950. [11] Ibid.

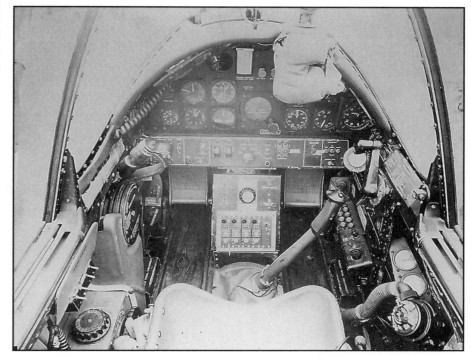

Righthand cockpit of F-82B photo pod testbed (44-65172), where photo operations were made. Large knob to left of seat is rudder trim wheel. (SDAM)

THE COLOR OF VICTORY

MUSTANG PAINT AND MARKINGS

The P-51 entered the war in camouflage, and emerged in gleaming bare aluminum, testimony to the overwhelming aerial victory scored by the Allies that made concealment unnecessary. The prototype NA-73 was gleaming bare aluminum, with a U.S. civil registration number applied as NAA tested their new product in 1940. As early as the end of January 1944, natural aluminum P-51s were leaving the factory, typically with olive drab anti-glare panels extending from the windscreen framing up to the nose. In service, some fighter groups chose to over-ride the anti-glare panel by painting squadron colors in its place, as with the red and blue diamonds of many 356th Fighter Group Mustangs, or variations of black and yellow checks on Mustangs of the 353rd Fighter Group, or black and white checks on some 78th Fighter Group P-51s. Other Eighth and Ninth AF P-51s sometimes sported solid color anti-glare panels, as in the decorative blue markings of the 352nd and 370th Fighter Groups.

Early razorback P-51Bs in England suffered an identity crisis, as eager Allied pilots and gunners mistook them for Me-109s. As applied to olive drab and gray B-model Mustangs, recognition markings to distinguish them from Messerschmitts included white prop spinner and the first foot of nose cowling; a 12-inch white band around the vertical tail; and five-inch white bands around the horizontal tail surfaces and wings. With the advent of natural aluminum Mustangs, the markings were applied in black. Some individuality pertained in the appli-

Typhoon McGoon of the 357th Fighter Group in England in 1944 used white recognition markings to distinguish it from a Messerschmitt Me-109. Residue from fuel spill can be seen below aft fuselage gas cap, behind cockpit. (Fred LePage collection)

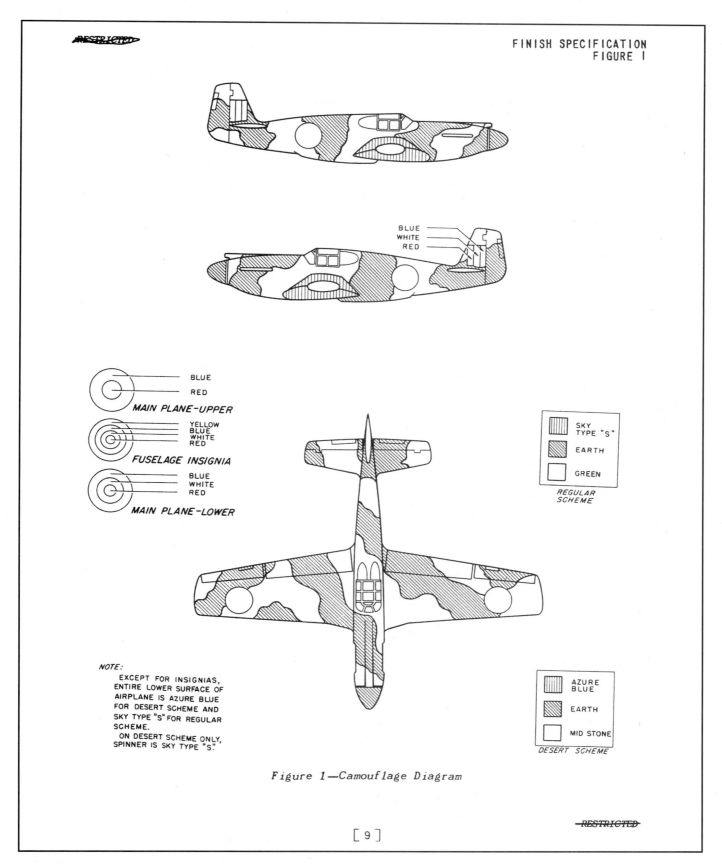

BLUE
WHITE
RED

BLUE
RED
MAIN PLANE-UPPER

YELLOW
BLUE
WHITE
RED
FUSELAGE INSIGNIA

BLUE
WHITE
RED
MAIN PLANE-LOWER

SKY
TYPE "S"

EARTH

GREEN

*REGULAR
SCHEME*

NOTE:
EXCEPT FOR INSIGNIAS,
ENTIRE LOWER SURFACE OF
AIRPLANE IS AZURE BLUE
FOR DESERT SCHEME AND
SKY TYPE "S" FOR REGULAR
SCHEME.
ON DESERT SCHEME ONLY,
SPINNER IS SKY TYPE "S".

AZURE
BLUE

EARTH

MID STONE

DESERT SCHEME

Figure 1—Camouflage Diagram

RESTRICTED

*Contained in an A-36 manual, this three-view drawing explains early RAF Mustang camouflage and insignia
scheme. Variations were provided for regular or desert service.*

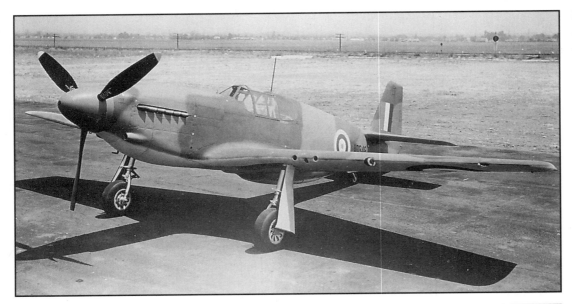

cation and subsequent removal of these markings, which became less frequently used as the war progressed.[1]

While ensuring their fighter-pilot individuality with colorful markings, Mustang units in Eighth Air Force heeded instructions for application of invasion stripes just prior to the Normandy landings of June 6, 1944. As early as April 1944, the plan for invasion stripes called for five bands of black and white encircling aft fuselages and top and bottom wing surfaces of any aircraft likely to be flying low enough to be seen from the ground. Actual painting was not to be done until just prior to the invasion. In July, units began the second phase of Normandy

RAF Mustang I (serial AG-348) was photographed from all sides at NAA factory to depict British camouflage. Landing light in wing leading edge later was relocated to wheel well. (NAA/SDAM)

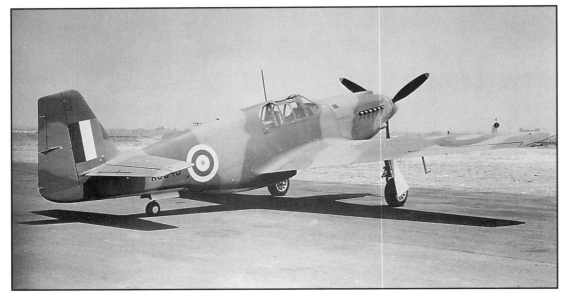

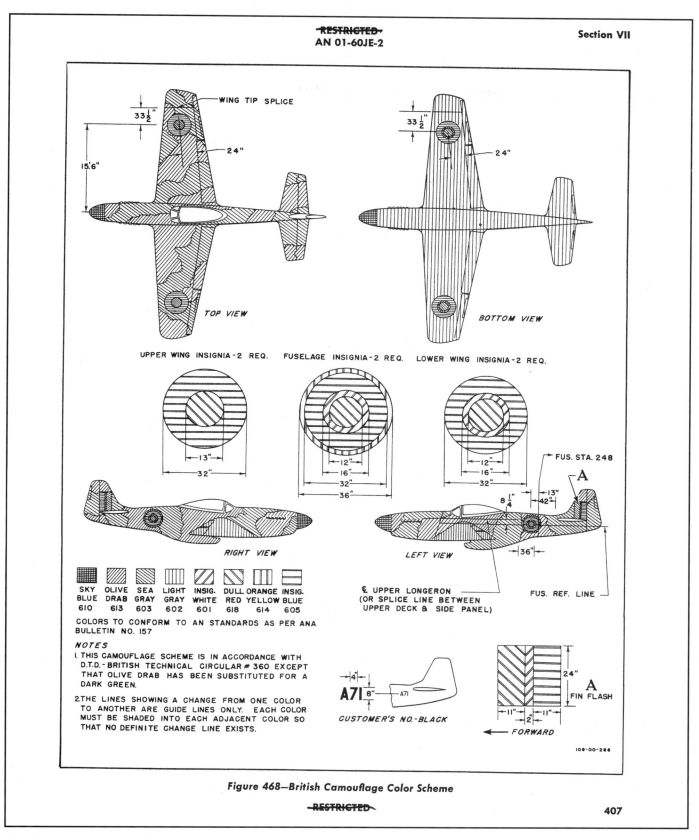

Figure 468—British Camouflage Color Scheme

P-51D/Mustang IV Royal Air Force paint and markings followed same basic outlines as earlier Mustangs, although using sea gray and olive drab for the upper surfaces, with the olive drab substituting for the usual British dark green in those areas. (Carl Scholl/Aero Trader)

NORTH AMERICAN
P-51 MUSTANG

93

invasion stripes, by removing or covering the stripes on the upper surfaces of the wings and fuselage, to diminish the visibility of the aircraft from above, while retaining undersurface stripes for the benefit of friendly troops on the ground who might otherwise mistake the Allied aircraft for German airplanes. Late in August 1944, the underwing stripes were to be taken off, and by December 6, 1944, Supreme Headquarters Allied Expeditionary Force (SHAEF) called for the removal of all invasion stripes.[2]

Creativity flourished in the application, and in the removal, of Normandy invasion stripes. Some units took the markings as temporary necessities, and applied them quickly and without particular regard for neatness. Other P-51s carried neatly-defined invasion stripes equal in quality to their other markings. When removal was ordered, some stripes were stripped from P-51s, while others were overpainted with aluminum silver paint. In some instances, olive or dark blue panels covered the upper-surface stripes; this gave a characteristic look to post-Normandy Mustangs of the 361st Fighter Group.

With the occupation of Germany, some P-51s (and other aircraft) stationed there were given red-yel-

P-51B (43-6638) flew with 355th Fighter Squadron of 9th Air Force's 354th Fighter Group. Cockpit close-ups reveal fuzzy edges of casually-sprayed code letter 'G'; bomb and fighter mission symbols portray a busy combat career. Pilots show typical variations on flight clothing. During the war, it was common to wear a wool flightsuit over regular uniform. (SDAM)

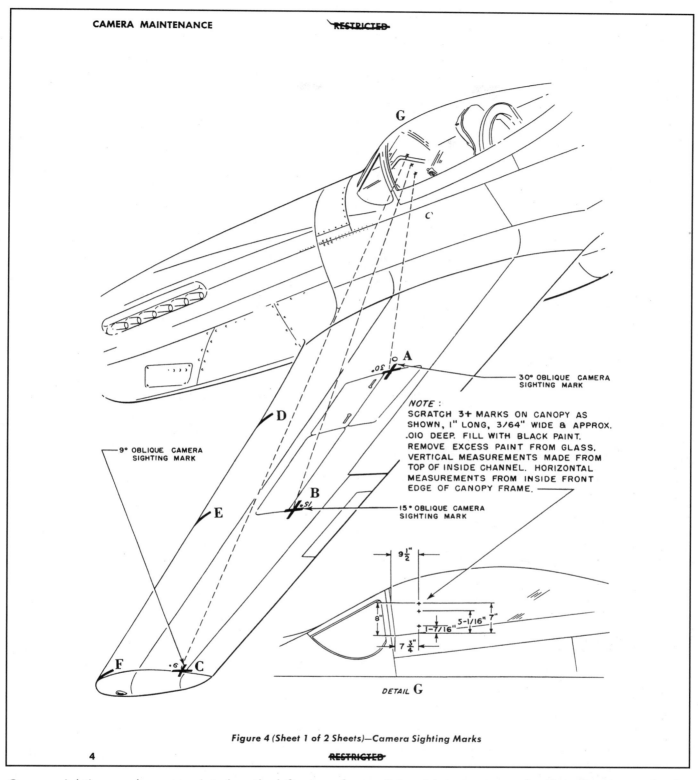

NOTE:
SCRATCH 3+ MARKS ON CANOPY AS
SHOWN, 1" LONG, 3/64" WIDE & APPROX.
.010 DEEP. FILL WITH BLACK PAINT.
REMOVE EXCESS PAINT FROM GLASS.
VERTICAL MEASUREMENTS MADE FROM
TOP OF INSIDE CHANNEL. HORIZONTAL
MEASUREMENTS FROM INSIDE FRONT
EDGE OF CANOPY FRAME.

30° OBLIQUE CAMERA
SIGHTING MARK

9° OBLIQUE CAMERA
SIGHTING MARK

15° OBLIQUE CAMERA
SIGHTING MARK

DETAIL G

Figure 4 (Sheet 1 of 2 Sheets)—Camera Sighting Marks

Camera sighting marks were painted on the left wing of some F-6s, with crosses scratched into the canopy for the pilot to align his recon Mustang in the proper angle of bank to point the cameras at their intended subject. A manual excerpt showed exactly where and how large such markings should be. The crosses on the wing were spaced to aim cameras with oblique angles ranging from 30 degrees for the inboard mark to 15 degrees for the middle mark and 9 degrees for the outboard cross. If a K-22 camera was installed, it could only be mounted for a 16-degree angle, requiring some interpolation by the pilot.

low-red fuselage bands to identify them as part of the occupying force in 1945.

To facilitate accurate oblique angle reconnaissance photography, some F-6 variants had aiming markings painted on the upper surface of the left wing, with aligning crosses scratched into the Plexiglas canopy on the left side. By aligning two appropriate marks between the canopy and the wing, the pilot could be sure of aiming his fixed cameras in the right direction.

In the Pacific, some Fifth Air Force P-51s carried classic red-white-and-blue rudder striping in 1945, as Fifth AF used this decoration on several types of aircraft. Air

354th Fighter Group P-51B (43-6638) with grimace carried vestiges of invasion stripes when photographed. Filled gun ports suggest this may have been a hack non-combat aircraft when the photos were taken. (SDAM)

F-6D, produced by using a P-51D-NA (44-15453), carried cameras behind cockpit, photographing through circular windows in sides and bottom of fuselage. Direction-finding antenna atop aft fuselage frequently accompanied reconnaissance aircraft, where precise navigation was often vital to mission success. (Peter M. Bowers)

Piper PA-48 Enforcers were evaluated at Edwards Air Force Base; no production ensued. The House Armed Services Committee approved a $6 million appropriation for development and demonstration of the Enforcer in 1979. Long nose of the Enforcer was not favored by at least one pilot who said it made bomb runs difficult to sight. Nonetheless, this turboprop renaissance for the venerable Mustang proved that the design still had plenty of kick, and that Yankee ingenuity was alive and well.

Sweet Mary (44-72138) may have flown with the 31st Fighter Group occupying Germany when she folded her left main gear on Dec. 21, 1946. Remnants of three swastika kill symbols appear on the left side of the canopy frame. Bands around aft fuselage are probably red-yellow-red occupation markings.

Commando Mustangs in the China-Burma-India Theater made use of a series of narrow diagonal bands on the aft fuselage for identification.

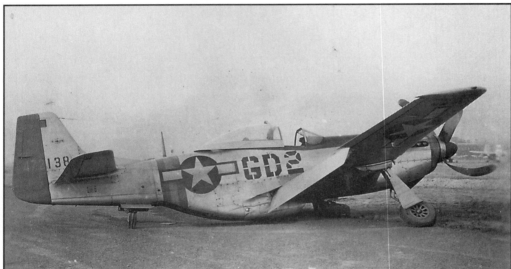

By the time of the Korean war, P-51Ds assigned to the Republic of Korea Air Force (ROKAF) imposed the Korean national insignia within the borders of U.S. national insignia, replacing the star, but retaining the red and white flanking bars of the era.

¹ Roger A. Freeman, *The Mighty Eighth—A History of the U.S. 8th Army Air Force*, Doubleday, Garden City, New York, 1970. ² Dana Bell, *Air Force Colors, Volume 2, ETO & MTO*, 1942-45, Squadron/Signal, Carrollton, Texas, 1980.

North American Aviation designers pondered forward-swept wing technology and the combined use of reciprocating and turbojet engines in a radical airplane with unmistakable Mustang origins, circa 1945-46. Though not built, the concept had evolved on paper far enough to indicate the use of six wing-mounted machine guns, with the natural stagger induced by the 30-degree forward sweep of the wing allowing easy ammunition feed access to all three weapons in each wing. In a move reminiscent of Northrop technology, thought was given to putting spoilers on the wings along with conventional ailerons to boost roll rate. The design was proposed using the cockpit of the P-51H. The back of the pilot's seat was to be nested against the canted front wall of a fuel tank holding a little over 150 gallons. In the nose, designers envisioned an Allison V-1710-G6R engine, turning a four-blade propeller and sharing space with a nosewheel. A ram air inlet on the left side of the nose would feed the piston engine. Cut into either side of the lower nose surface were inlets for the Allison's oil cooler and engine coolant radiators, with exits in two notched steps in the belly beneath the wing. A second ram air inlet on the side of the fuselage beneath the cockpit was to sustain a Westinghouse 19XB-28 jet engine, with its exhaust beneath the tail. Just as the Ryan Fireball was a Navy stop-gap postwar aircraft combining the acceleration benefits of a propeller with the high-end speed gains provided by a turbojet, so might this Mustang derivative have found a temporary niche until full-blown jet fighters fulfilled the role. Wingspan was envisioned as about 35-and-a-half feet; length was supposed to be 37 feet, 7 inches.

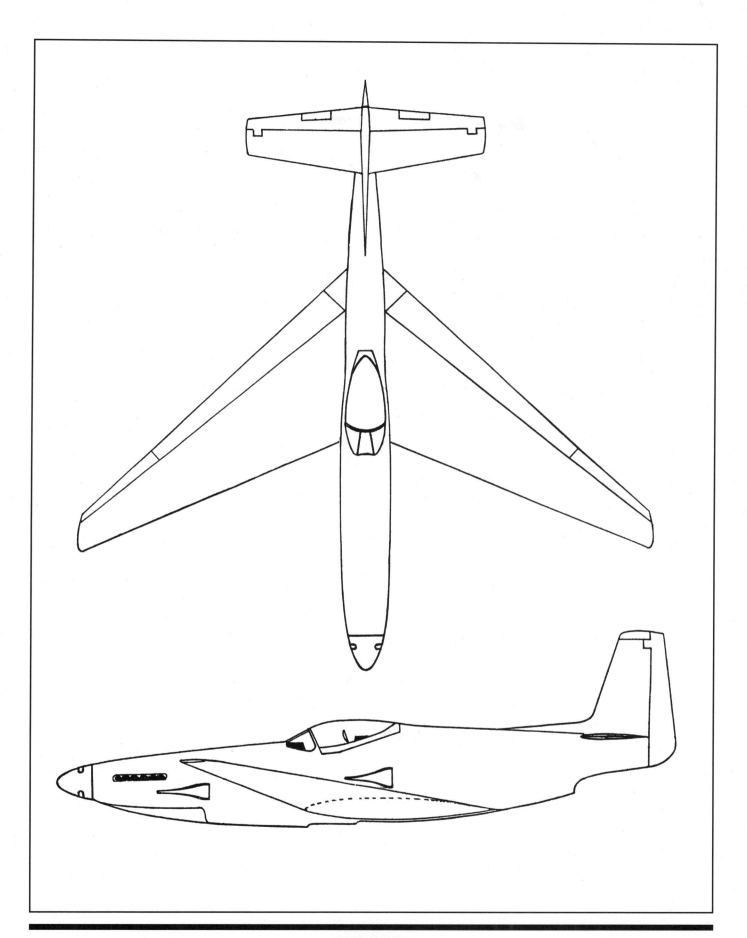

Significant Dates

October 26, 1940
First flight of NA-73X (Mustang prototype).

April 23, 1941
First flight of first production model Mustang I.

May 20, 1941
First flight of XP-51.

July 27, 1942
First operational Mustang sortie flown by RAF Army Co-operation Command.

August 19, 1942
RAF Mustangs supported Dieppe raid on European continent by assault troops.

November 30, 1942
First flight of XP-51B.

November 17, 1943
First flight of XP-51D, modified from a P-51B.

December 1, 1943
First Merlin-powered P-51s delivered to Eighth AF in United Kingdom.

December 13, 1943
First Eighth AF Merlin Mustang escort mission, to Kiel and return.

March 1944
Merlin-engined P-51s first accompanied B-17s and B-24s all the way to Berlin and back, altering the air defense equation over Europe.

October 12, 1944
Capt. Charles E. "Chuck" Yeager downed five German fighters, including two Me-109s that collided trying to avoid Yeager's attack.

November 27, 1944
Capt. Chuck Yeager downed four German fighters, becoming a double ace with 11 victories at that time, finishing the war with 13 credits, including a jet Me-262.

February 3, 1945
First flight of P-51H.

April 7, 1945
P-51Ds made first land-based fighter attack on Tokyo.

April 23, 1945
First flight of Allison-powered XP-51J.

June 12, 1945
First flight of XP-82 Twin Mustang.

June 1947
Deliveries of surplus Mustangs to Royal Canadian Air Force (RCAF) began.

June 27, 1950
First North Korean aircraft downed by U.S. warplane fell to an F-82G Twin Mustang.

February 7, 1978
Last Mustang in U.S. military service, a U.S. Army chase aircraft, departed Edwards Air Force Base, California, for retirement in the U.S. Army Aviation Museum at Fort Rucker, Alabama.

MATHEMATICS PLUS

HBJ **Harcourt Brace Jovanovich, Inc.**
Orlando Austin San Diego Chicago Dallas New York

Printed in the United States of America
ISBN 0-15-300143-7
4 5 6 7 8 9 10   048   95   94   93   92

ACKNOWLEDGMENTS

Some computer lessons in this book are based on AppleWorks® by Claris Corporation.
© 1989 by Claris Corporation. All rights reserved. Claris is a registered trademark of Claris Corporation.
AppleWorks is a registered trademark of Apple Computer, Inc. licensed to Claris Corporation.
Apple is a registered trademark of Apple Computer, Inc.

Logo lessons in this book present the Terrapin Logo version. Terrapin
is a registered trademark of Terrapin Software, Inc.

AUTHORS

Grace M. Burton
Professor, Department of Curricular Studies
University of North Carolina at Wilmington
Wilmington, North Carolina

Jerome D. Kaplan
Professor of Education
Seton Hall University
South Orange, New Jersey

Martha H. Hopkins
Associate Professor
University of Central Florida
Orlando, Florida

Leonard Kennedy
Professor Emeritus
California State University at Sacramento
Sacramento, California

Howard C. Johnson
Chair, Mathematics Education
Professor of Mathematics and Mathematics Education
Syracuse University
Syracuse, New York

Karen A. Schultz
Professor, Mathematics Education
Georgia State University
Atlanta, Georgia

SENIOR EDITORIAL ADVISOR

Francis (Skip) Fennell
Professor of Education
Western Maryland College
Westminister, Maryland

ADVISORS

Janet S. Abbott
Curriculum Coordinator
Chula Vista Elementary School District
Chula Vista, California

Genevieve M. Knight
Professor of Mathematics
Coppin State College
Baltimore, Maryland

Dorothy S. Strong
Director K–12 Mathematics
Chicago Public Schools
Chicago, Illinois

Don S. Balka
Professor
Saint Mary's College
Notre Dame, Indiana

Charles Lamb
Associate Professor
University of Texas at Austin
Austin, Texas

Steven Tipps
West Foundation Professor
Midwestern State University
Wichita Falls, Texas

Gilbert Cuevas
Professor of Education
University of Miami
Miami, Florida

Marsha W. Lilly
Mathematics Coordinator, K–12
Alief Independent School District
Alief, Texas

David Wells
Retired Assistant Superintendent
for Instruction
Pontiac, Michigan

Michael C. Hynes
Professor
University of Central Florida
Orlando, Florida

Sid Rachlin
Professor
University of Hawaii
Honolulu, Hawaii

▶▶▶▶▶▶▶▶▶

Contents

4 **Dividing Whole Numbers and Decimals**   94
THEME: *Life at School*

Multiplying and Dividing Fractions   234
THEME: *Celebrating Holidays*

Geometry   **340**
THEME: *Nature—the Environment*

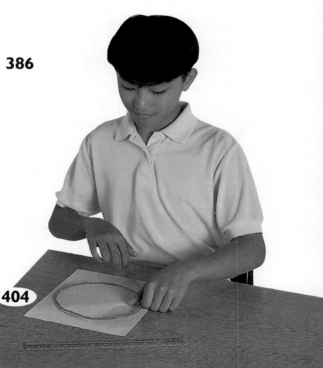

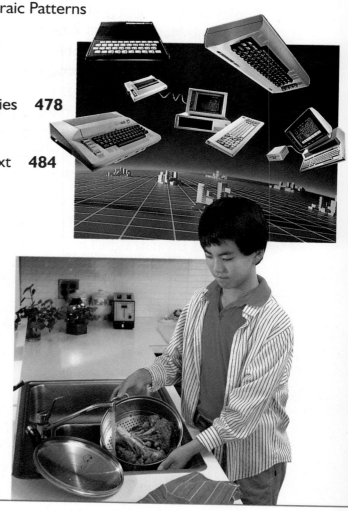

Welcome to MATHEMATICS PLUS

Mathematics is an important part of your daily life. You use it at school, at home, and everywhere you go. As you study math this year, think about how the ideas you are learning help you with other school subjects and with your everyday activities.

This year you are going to use ideas you have already learned in interesting, new ways. You will learn more about how to solve problems. You will also learn how to use the calculator and the computer as problem-solving tools. You will use whole numbers, fractions, and decimals to solve problems. You will explore ideas about the perimeter and area of plane figures and about the volume of solid figures. You will learn more about collecting, organizing, and analyzing data. You will explore ideas that will help you understand algebra. You will learn more about how to estimate and how to use an estimate to check that an answer is reasonable.

Math is fun! You will work in groups to share what you are learning. You will have fun solving the puzzles and problems in the **Math Fun Magazine** at the back of this book.

This year
you can make mathematics
a learning adventure!

The Authors

How Do You Use Math Every Day?

People use math to help them do many things. Here are some things you do in which you use math.

shop	weigh
count	measure
share	save
build	cook
travel	tell time
compare	keep score
estimate	predict

Talk about how the people in the photographs are using math. Share with your classmates some of the ways you use math at school, at home, and everywhere you go.

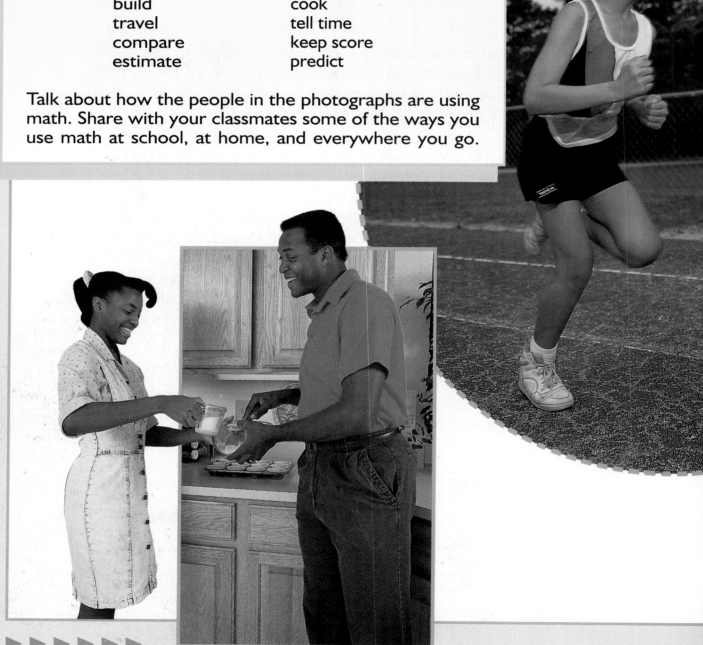

Solving Problems

You use math every day to solve problems. In this book you will learn how to solve problems by asking yourself questions. These questions will help you

- UNDERSTAND the problem.
- PLAN a solution.
- SOLVE the problem.
- LOOK BACK and check your solution.

Kevin has a problem to solve. Read his problem slowly and carefully.

Kevin won first prize in a photography contest. The prize is a $100.00 gift certificate from Shutterbug Camera Shop. He plans to buy a tripod that costs $57.98 and a camera bag that costs $27.29. How much of the prize money will he have left to spend on film?

How can Kevin find out? Think along with Kevin as he solves the problem.

▶ ▶ ▶ ▶ ▶ ▶ ▶ ▶

Understand the Problem

First, Kevin must UNDERSTAND the problem.

He restates the problem to himself. He wants to be sure he knows what the problem is about. Then he asks himself these questions.

What must I find?
I must find how much I will have left to spend on film after I buy the tripod and camera bag I want.

What facts do I have?
The gift certificate is worth $100.00. The tripod costs $57.98. The camera bag costs $27.29.

How would you restate Kevin's problem in your own words?

Plan a Solution

Then, Kevin must PLAN how to solve his problem.

He thinks about the ways he solves problems. He chooses one of these strategies.

- Draw a picture
- Make a model
- Work backward
- Guess and check
- Write a number sentence
- Make a table or graph

Then he makes a plan by asking himself these questions.

How can I solve the problem?
Since I must find how much money I will have left after purchasing two items, I can write a number sentence to solve the problem.

What number sentence should I write?

price of tripod + price of camera bag = total spent

I can then subtract the total from the $100.00 to find how much I will have left for film.

What other plan could Kevin have made?

Next, Kevin must SOLVE the problem.

He must decide how to solve the problem. He must decide whether to use mental math, a calculator, or paper and pencil to find the answer.

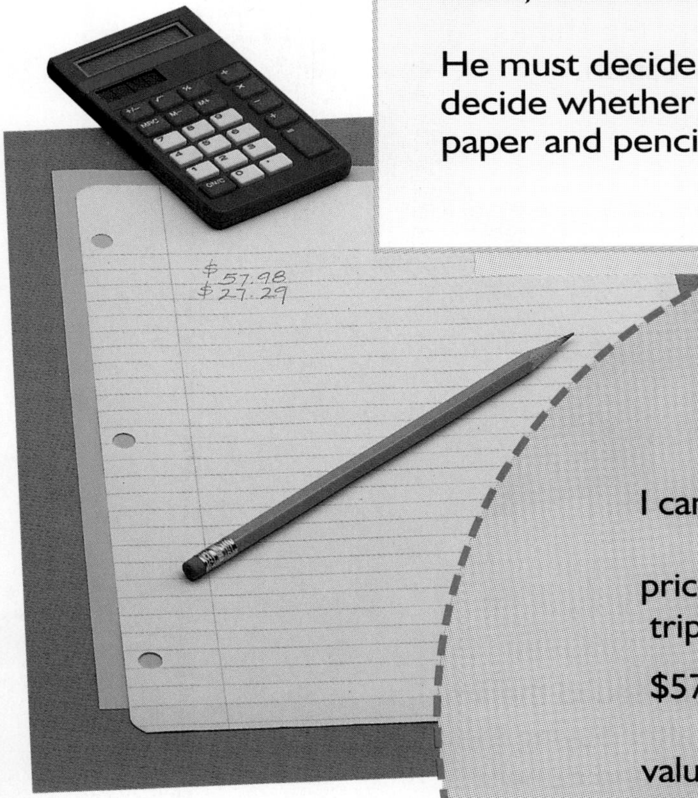

$57.98
$27.29

I can use a calculator to find the answer.

price of tripod	+	price of camera bag	=	total spent
$57.98	(+)	$27.29	(=)	(85.27)

value of gift certificate		total spent		amount left for film
$100.00	(−)	$85.27	(=)	(14.73)

Why do you think Kevin chose a calculator to solve the problem? What method would you choose?

▶ ▶ ▶ ▶ ▶ ▶ ▶ ▶ ▶

Look Back

Last, Kevin can LOOK BACK and check whether his answer is correct.

He thinks about a way to check his answer. He thinks about whether his solution answers the question.

He asks himself these questions.

How can I check my answer?
I can add the prices of the tripod and the camera bag and the amount I have left for film. If the total is $100, then my answer is correct.

Does my solution answer the question?
Since I found the amount left after buying the tripod and camera bag with the $100 gift certificate, my solution answers the question.

How else could Kevin check his answer?

Kevin solved his problem. He used math to help him find how much money he will have left from his $100 gift certificate.

In Mathematics Plus you will learn to be a problem solver!

▶▶▶▶▶▶▶▶

How Will You Learn Math?

In Mathematics Plus you will learn math in different ways. All of the ways to learn involve *thinking*.

WORKING TOGETHER

- Listen carefully to other people's ideas.
- Encourage others to share their ideas.
- Discuss ideas in a friendly way.
- Plan how your group is going to share the work.

You will learn math by

- working with a group.
- modeling problems, using objects and diagrams.
- listening to your teacher and your classmates.
- talking about math ideas.
- writing about math ideas.
- recording the meanings of new words.
- choosing problem-solving strategies.
- making decisions about how to solve problems.
- using math in school, at home, and everywhere.

1

PLACE VALUE
WHOLE NUMBERS
AND
DECIMALS

Did you know ...

... that people who work in highly technical fields use both very large and very small numbers?

Talk About It

Analysts predict that NASA's budget in the year 2000 will exceed twenty-three billion dollars. While accountants work with this large amount, engineers may be working with intervals of time that are smaller than one ten-thousandth of a second. How can you write these numbers in standard form?

Numeration systems are ways of counting and naming numbers. Here are three different ways to represent the number in a dozen.

- Which way of representing the number in a dozen is most familiar to you?

Ancient Egyptians used everyday objects as symbols to name numbers.

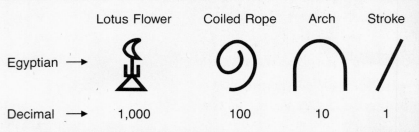

	Lotus Flower	Coiled Rope	Arch	Stroke
Egyptian →				
Decimal →	1,000	100	10	1

The Egyptian system was based on groups of 10. Numbers were formed by writing a series of symbols.

 → 1,428

- Tell the decimal value of each Egyptian number.

A.    B.

- How would you write the day of the month on which you were born, using the Egyptian system?

- How would you write the year you were born using the Egyptian system?

Comparing Numeration Systems

The people of ancient Rome used letters as symbols to name numbers.

Roman →	M	D	C	L	X	V	I
Decimal →	1,000	500	100	50	10	5	1

Roman numerals are read from left to right. You add or subtract the value of each symbol to find the value of the number. A symbol can be repeated only three times.

If the value of the symbols from left to right decreases or stays the same, you add.

CLVI → 156   MCXXIII → 1,123

If the value of the symbols from left to right increases, you subtract.

XC → 90   CMIV → 904

- Tell whether to add or to subtract to find the value of the number.

a. LXV   b. CD   c. MCMXC

- How would you write the year you were born using Roman numerals?

Talk About It

▶ How is the Roman system like the Egyptian system?

▶ How is the Roman system different from the Egyptian system?

3

Comparing Numeration Systems

The numeration system you use is called a **decimal system** because it is based on ten numerals: 0, 1, 2, 3, 4, 5, 6, 7, 8, and 9. You use place value and these numerals to name numbers.

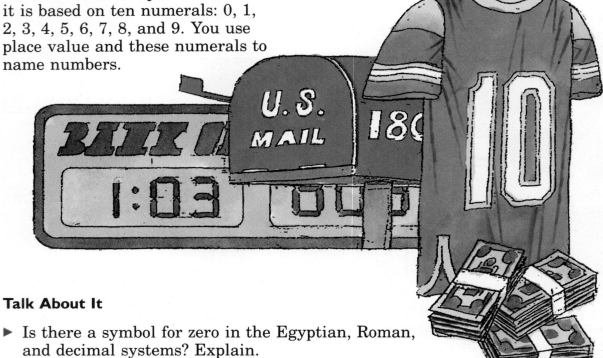

Talk About It

▶ Is there a symbol for zero in the Egyptian, Roman, and decimal systems? Explain.

▶ Which systems repeat symbols to show greater values?

▶ Which system uses place value?

▶ In which systems is the order of the symbols important?

▶ How many symbols are needed in each system to write the current year?

Check for Understanding

Write the Roman numeral and the Egyptian numeral.

1. 8   **2.** 24   **3.** 35   **4.** 101   **5.** 1,000

Write the decimal numeral.

6. XXXIV   **7.** ⌃⌃⌃∩∩⦚//// ⁄⁄⁄⁄⁄   **8.** MCMXXV   **9.** ⌃⌃∩∩//// ⁄⁄⁄⁄⁄

10. ⊃∩∩///   **11.** DCCXLV   **12.** ⌃⦾⦾/////   **13.** MXII

Practice

Copy and complete the table.

14. Decimal	38	☐	☐	1,432	☐	☐
15. Roman	☐	CXLVII	☐	☐	MCCMXLV	☐
16. Egyptian	☐	☐	୨୨∩∩	☐	☐	𓏤∩∩/// / 𓏤∩∩///

Mixed Applications

17. When will you be sixteen years old? Write the year in the decimal system, the Roman system, and the Egyptian system.

18. The decimal number 215 means $200 + 10 + 5$. Do the values of the 2 and the 1 change if you change the order of the digits? Explain your answer.

19. By pressing ⟨1⟩ ⟨+⟩ ⟨=⟩ and then ⟨=⟩ repeatedly on a calculator, Liz can count the beats to music while she listens. Use a calculator. How quickly can you count to 500?

20. **Number Sense** Create your own number system. Make a table to explain your symbols. Then use your number system to write your age and the year you were born.

COMPUTER CONNECTION

You can use any number as a base to make up a numeration system. Sometimes computer programmers use a base-8 system in which only the digits 0, 1, 2, 3, 4, 5, 6, and 7 are used to name numbers.

Base 10:	1	2	3	4	5	6	7	8	9	10 ... 16 24 32 ...
Base 8:	1	2	3	4	5	6	7	10	11	12 ... 20 30 40 ...

21. Use the table to explain each example.

A. $9_{10} \longrightarrow 11_8$

   base 10   base 8

B. $21_8 \longrightarrow 17_{10}$

22. Write the base-8 equivalent.
$13_{10} \longrightarrow$ ☐

23. Write the base-10 equivalent.
$32_8 \longrightarrow$ ☐

24. Write your age in base 8.

25. Write the number of days in September in base 8.

Name an advantage of the decimal system.

WRAP UP...

Joe estimates that it will take about 800 truckloads of sand to repair a ten-mile stretch of beach.

Eight hundred truckloads will contain about 122,039,680,000 grains of sand.

The chart can help you read and write large numbers. Notice that commas separate each three-digit period.

A tablespoon contains about 2,400 grains of sand.

A cubic foot contains about 353,100 grains of sand.

Place Value											
Billions			Millions			Thousands			Ones		
Hundreds	Tens	Ones	Hundreds	Tens	Ones	Hundreds	Tens	Ones	Hundreds	Tens	Ones
1	2	2	0	3	9	6	8	0	0	0	0

A dump truck contains about 152,549,600 grains of sand.

Read:

Short Word Form → 122 billion, 39 million, 680 thousand

Word Form → one hundred twenty-two billion, thirty-nine million, six hundred eighty thousand

Write:

Standard Form → 122,039,680,000

Expanded Form → 100,000,000,000 + 20,000,000,000 + 2,000,000,000 + 30,000,000 + 9,000,000 + 600,000 + 80,000

Talk About It

▶ What is the value of the underlined digit in the number 42,736?

▶ What are some careers in which people use large numbers?

Check for Understanding

Write the value of the underlined digit.

1. 45,301,276,489   2. 174,057   3. 18,426   4. 77,100,264,993   5. 694,132

6

Practice

Write the value of the underlined digit.

6. 43,8<u>7</u>5,000

7. 5<u>2</u>1,976,000

8. 881,7<u>6</u>4

9. 43,0<u>4</u>1,000,000

10. 5,432,0<u>1</u>4

11. 3<u>9</u>8,004,213

12. 2,6<u>6</u>4,902,000

13. <u>4</u>2,908,000,000

14. 9,087,6<u>5</u>4,321

Write the number in short word form.

15. 3,603,542

16. 36,542,000

17. 507,090,000

18. 103,058,200,753

19. 45,034,126

20. 3,043,987,000

21. 356,080

22. 6,780,200,000

Write the number in standard form.

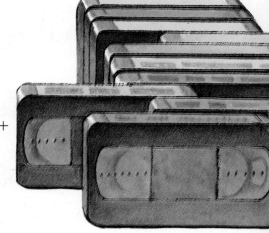

23. twenty-six billion, three hundred fourteen million, one hundred ten thousand, nine hundred ninety-six

24. eight million, twenty-four thousand, two hundred one

25. 500 billion, 24 thousand, 12

26. 1,000,000,000 + 2,000,000 + 800,000 + 70,000 + 4,000 + 300 + 50 + 8

27. 6,000,000 + 400,000 + 60,000 + 8,000

Mixed Applications

28. The circulation of a magazine is eight million, ninety-one thousand, seven hundred fifty-one. Write the number in standard form.

29. A movie studio reports that rentals of a video are 2,000,000 + 600,000 + 50,000 + 7,000 + 800. Write the number in word form.

30. **Number Sense** How is the value of each place in a decimal number related to the value of the place at its right?

31. **Logical Reasoning** Three box labels read as follows: **(a)** Pen is here, **(b)** Pen is not here, and **(c)** Pen is in Box **a.** Only one label is correct. In which box is the pen?

How do you know that the values of 160,000 and 100,600 are not the same?

UNDERSTANDING SMALL NUMBERS

Ancient Romans developed the first concrete used in construction. The concrete we use today is a similar mixture of water, cement, and hard materials, such as sand. Engineers measure the size of the grains of sand to help determine the strength of the concrete. A grain of sand may be as small as 0.0025 inch in diameter.

The place-value chart for whole numbers can be expanded to help you read and write decimal numbers.

Place Value				
Ones	Tenths	Hundredths	Thousandths	Ten-Thousandths
0	0	0	2	5

Read:

Word Form → twenty-five ten-thousandths
Short Word Form → 25 ten-thousandths

Sometimes people read a number by saying the digits. → zero point zero zero two five

Write:

Standard Form → 0.0025

Talk About It

▶ Why do people say the number by reading the digits?

▶ What are some careers in which people use small numbers?

Check for Understanding

Write the number in short word form.

1. 0.3421   2. 0.87   3. 0.8905

4. 0.739   5. 0.73   6. 1.034

Write the value of the underlined digit.

7. 4.5   8. 0.214   9. 0.03   10. 0.005   11. 0.0001

Practice

Write the number in standard form.

12. 45 hundredths

13. eight hundredths

14. two hundred one and two thousandths

15. seven ten-thousandths

Copy and complete the table.

	Standard Form	Short Word Form	Word Form
16.	0.4	■	■
17.	■	■	thirty-two and eight tenths
18.	■	35 thousandths	■
19.	43.0834	■	■
20.	■	80 and 9 hundredths	■
21.	■	■	one hundred twenty-one ten-thousandths

Mixed Applications

22. A grain of coarse sand may be as large as eighty-three thousandths inch. Write the number in standard form.

23. The world's smallest cut diamond is 0.0009 inch in diameter and weighs 0.0012 carat. Write both numbers in short word form.

VISUAL THINKING

About how much of each geometric figure is shaded? Write **a, b,** or **c.**

24.

a. 0.3   **b.** 0.6   **c.** 0.9

25.

a. 0.3   **b.** 0.6   **c.** 0.9

26.
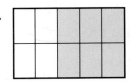
a. 0.3   **b.** 0.6   **c.** 0.9

How do you know that 2.3 and 2.003 are not the same?

Sue is a buyer for a men's clothing chain. Her inventory shows the numbers of shirts still in the store. The smaller the number in the Total column of the inventory, the more popular the shirt.

Inventory			
Item: <u>Men's Shirts</u>		Date: <u>Nov. 2, 1991</u>	
Identification	Color	Size	Total
# 0723001	red	sm.	12,010
# 0723002	red	med.	12,583
# 0723003	red	lg.	12,924
# 0723004	blue	sm.	11,403
# 0723005	blue	med.	10,010
# 0723006	blue	lg.	12,031
# 0723007	green	sm.	13,040
# 0723008	green	med.	13,001
# 0723009	green	lg.	13,945

- Which size red shirt is the most popular?

- Which color shirt is the least popular?

- Which shirt is the most popular of all?

You can use these symbols when you compare and order numbers.

$<$ means "is less than."
$>$ means "is greater than."

Example List the numbers of large shirts in the inventory in order from least to greatest.

$12,031 < 12,924 < 13,945$

Talk About It

▶ Would you solve the problem differently if you were asked to order the numbers of large shirts from greatest to least? Explain your answer.

▶ How do you use comparison to order numbers?

Check for Understanding

Compare the numbers. Write $<$, $>$, or $=$.

1. 8,234 ● 8,324   **2.** 42,697 ● 42,079   **3.** 23,431 ● 23,431   **4.** 9.550 ● 9.55

Write the numbers in order from least to greatest. Use $<$.

5. 42,697; 42,079; 42,597   **6.** 45.7; 45.57; 45.07   **7.** 2.05; 2.07; 2.01

Practice

Compare the numbers. Write <, >, or =.

8. 23.001 ⬤ 23.010   **9.** 5,788 ⬤ 5,787   **10.** 41.030 ⬤ 41.03   **11.** 13,945.2 ⬤ 13,954.6

12. 17.099 ⬤ 17.090   **13.** 4.707 ⬤ 4.770   **14.** 0.21 ⬤ 0.22   **15.** 5.401 ⬤ 5.4010

Write the numbers in order from greatest to least. Use >.

16. 23,511; 23,611; 23,116   **17.** 0.0009; 9; 0.009; 0.09   **18.** 423,173; 423,317; 423,137

19. 0.001; 0.101; 0.011   **20.** 6,552; 6,525; 6,255   **21.** 5.004; 5.040; 5.005

Mixed Applications

Use the inventory on page 10 for Exercises 22–23.

22. Write in order from greatest to least the numbers of medium-sized shirts. Use >.

23. Write in order from least to greatest the numbers of all the shirts in the inventory. Use <.

LOGICAL REASONING

Use the table for Exercise 24 a–c.

24. Sue is saving shares of Regal stock. She keeps a list of the average yearly values so that she knows whether the value of her stock is increasing or decreasing.

Average Yearly Values of Regal Stock

Year	Value
1986	$12.075
1987	$13.106
1988	$12.100
1989	$12.195
1990	$12.989

a. Which year would have been the best year to buy some stock? Why?

b. Which year would have been the best year to sell some stock? Why?

c. Explain how Sue's stock has changed in value from 1986 to 1990.

Name a career in which people must compare and order numbers.

WRAP UP...

PROBLEM Solving

Dr. Lee's list shows the average daily calorie consumption of nine clients. Suppose that the most active clients consume the greatest number of calories. How can you show the data in a way that Dr. Lee can easily see which clients are most active?

If you have access to a database program, you can use a computer to organize the data.

Client	Calories Consumed
Ellen	2,641
Frank	3,089
Juan	2,915
Karen	3,140
Lani	2,689
Louis	2,908
Maria	2,402
Ron	2,654
Wayne	3,273

► UNDERSTAND

What are you asked to do?

What information are you given?

► PLAN

How will you solve the problem?

You can make a table in which you list the clients in order by the number of calories they consumed.

► SOLVE

How can you make a table?

List the clients in order from greatest to least number of calories consumed. Label the columns and title the table.

Use the data in the table to see which clients are most active.

Daily Calorie Consumption	
Client	**Calories Consumed**
Wayne	3,273
Karen	3,140
Frank	3,089
Juan	2,915
Louis	2,908
Lani	2,689
Ron	2,654
Ellen	2,641
Maria	2,402

► LOOK BACK

How can you check your solution?

WHAT IF... ...you were asked who consumed the least number of calories? What would be your answer?

 Connection, pages 488–489

Apply

(1) Make a table to organize the meteorologist's report of average January temperatures and amounts of precipitation in four cities.

Report: In Chicago the average temperature is 21°F, and the average precipitation is 1.6 inches. In Los Angeles the temperature is 57°F, and the precipitation is 3.7 inches. In Atlanta the temperature is 42°F, and the precipitation is 4.9 inches. In Dallas the temperature is 44°F, and the precipitation is 1.7 inches.

Use your table for Exercises 2–5.

(2) Which of the four cities have average temperatures between 40°F and 50°F?

(3) Which two cities have about the same average amount of precipitation?

(4) List the average temperatures in order from coldest to warmest. Use <.

(5) Compare the average amount of precipitation in Chicago with that in Atlanta. Use < or >.

Mixed Applications

STRATEGIES
- Make and Use a Table
- Guess and Check
- Draw a Picture
- Act It Out

Choose a strategy and solve.

(6) Every day Carrie drives 7 miles to work and 5 miles to a health club. Then she takes the same route home. How many miles does she drive each day?

(7) W, X, and Y each stand for different whole numbers. If $W + X + Y < Z$, can Z equal 2? Can Z equal 7? Can Z equal 10? Justify your answers.

(8) Al is a commercial artist who uses colored pencils to sketch. How many pencils does Al have if all of them are blue except 2, all of them are yellow except 2, and all of them are red except 2?

(9) Leonard wants to buy a pen and a pencil that together cost $15. The pen costs $10 more than the pencil. How much does the pencil cost?

WRITER'S CORNER

(10) Use the information in the table you made in Exercise 1. Write word problems that can be solved by comparing both the temperatures and the amounts of precipitation.

Sara estimates her company's average annual sales by rounding to the nearest ten-thousand dollars to make a pictograph for a presentation.

Look at the 1975 sales. The estimated amount is $80,000. What could the actual sales for 1975 be?

Think: What is the least amount that rounds to $80,000?
What is the greatest amount that rounds to $80,000?

Average Annual Sales	
Year	**Amount**
1975	🏀🏀🏀🏀
1980	🏀🏀🏀🏀◖
1985	🏀🏀🏀🏀🏀🏀◖
1990	🏀🏀🏀🏀🏀🏀🏀🏀

🏀 = $20,000

Least amount: $75,000   Greatest amount: $84,999

So, the actual sales for 1975 could range from $75,000 to $84,999.

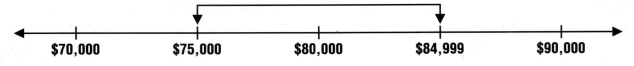

A. For 1990 the sales could range from $155,000 to $164,999.

B. For 1980 the sales could range from $85,000 to $94,999.

Talk About It

▶ Why do you think Sara used estimated amounts in the pictograph?

▶ Why do you think Sara decided to round to ten thousands rather than to hundreds?

▶ In what everyday situations are estimates commonly used?

Check for Understanding

The number has been rounded to the place indicated. Write the range of numbers that round to the given number.

1. 500
   hundreds

2. 750
   tens

3. 1,000,000
   millions

4. 3,600
   hundreds

5. 6,000,000,000
   billions

6. $0.60
   ten cents

7. 12,000
   thousands

8. 1,530,000
   thousands

Practice

Estimate by rounding to the place indicated.

9. 92
tens

10. $12.58
10 cents

11. 229
hundreds

12. $43.25
10 cents

13. $15.75
dollar

The number has been rounded to the place indicated.
Write the range of numbers that round to the given number.

14. 76,000
thousand

15. 80,000
ten thousand

16. 900,000
hundred thousand

17. 23,000,000
million

18. 500,000,000
hundred million

19. $3.50
ten cents

20. Use the digits 3, 4, 5, 6, 6, and 6.
Write two numbers that each round
to 500 when you round them to the
nearest hundred.

21. Use the digits 2, 3, 4, 5, 9, 9, 9, and
9. Write two numbers that each
round to 3,000 when you round
them to the nearest thousand.

Mixed Applications

Use the pictograph on page 14 for Exercise 22.

22. Compare the sales for 1975 with
those for 1990. Which statement is
true? **(a)** Sales are about the same.
(b) Sales have doubled.

23. Find Data Ask ten classmates what
size shoes they wear. Make a list of
the data you collect.

24. Organize Data List the shoe sizes
★ from Exercise 22 in order from
largest to smallest. Make a
pictograph to display your data.
Check students' pictographs.

MIXED REVIEW

Write the number in short word form.

1. 5,066

2. 0.02

3. 0.5432

4. 0.087

5. 600,002

6. 2.011

Write the numbers in order from greatest to least. Use >.

7. 43,231; 43,132; 43,223

8. 5.02; 5.0202; 5.022

9. 0.049; 0.005; 0.0489

What is meant by "a range"
of estimates?

Use scrap paper to plan your table.

1. Suppose you will give a report about the Egyptian, Roman, and decimal numeration systems. Make a table to show the symbols and their values.

2. Write the Roman numeral MCM in decimal form.

3. Write the decimal number 34 using Roman numerals.

4. A pattern of numbers begins with 0. If each number in the pattern is 5 more than the number before, what are the fourth and the fifth numbers in the pattern?

Write the value of the underlined digit.

5. 26,098,751,084

6. 26,098,751,084

7. 956.07134

Write the number in short word form.

8. 7,011,011

9. 6,005,000,031

10. 3.0028

Write the number in word form.

11. 15,010,003

12. 14,012,000,005

13. 9.0017

Write the number in standard form.

14. 102 million and twelve hundredths

15. 57 billion and ten thousandths

16. twenty and two ten-thousandths

Write the numbers from least to greatest. Use <.

17. 5.2, 5.13, 5.123

18. 6.07, 6.7, 6.007

19. 7.06, 7.1, 7.024

Estimate by rounding to the place indicated.

20. 29,683,425,000 millions

21. 29,683,425,000 billions

22. 523.098647 ten-thousandths

Write the range of numbers that round to the given number.

23. 25,000 thousands

24. 500 hundreds

25. 45,000,000 millions

26. 50 tens

27. 6,000,000 millions

28. 640,000 ten-thousands

Spotlight ON PROBLEM SOLVING

Understand
Plan
Solve
Look Back

Draw Conclusions from Data

Data is collected for many reasons. Analyze the data in the table and draw conclusions.

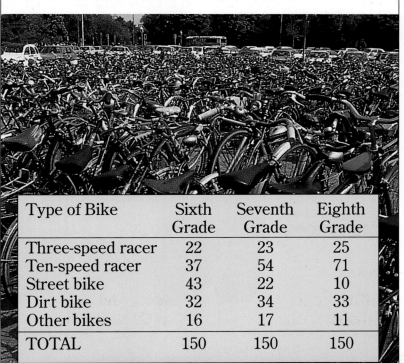

Type of Bike	Sixth Grade	Seventh Grade	Eighth Grade
Three-speed racer	22	23	25
Ten-speed racer	37	54	71
Street bike	43	22	10
Dirt bike	32	34	33
Other bikes	16	17	11
TOTAL	150	150	150

Talk About It

A. Which type of bike is most popular? Which is least popular?

B. What is the most popular bike among sixth graders?

C. Are younger students more likely or less likely to prefer ten-speed racers?

D. Which bike or bikes seem about equally popular at all the grades?

E. Why are street bikes less popular at the upper grades?

F. Draw your own conclusion based on the data in the table. Make sure you can defend your conclusion.

Apply

Can you draw these conclusions?

Discuss these statements with a classmate and answer *yes* or *no*.

1. Ninth graders who own bikes will most likely own ten-speed racers.
2. The three-speed racer is most popular among girls.
3. All students own bikes.
4. About 1 out of 5 students owns a dirt bike.

ORDER OF OPERATIONS

When Melvin leaves for work, he must choose to put his car in forward gear or reverse gear.

- In which gear should Melvin put his car first?

- Why is it important which gear Melvin chooses first?

In many areas of life, the order in which you perform tasks has a dramatic impact on the results. The same is true in math. To avoid confusion, mathematicians agree on this order of operations.

1. Perform all operations inside the parentheses first.

2. Multiply and divide from left to right.

3. Add and subtract from left to right.

Example

$$2 + (12 \div 3) \quad \longleftarrow \text{ Perform operation inside parentheses.}$$
$$\downarrow \qquad \downarrow$$
$$2 + \qquad 4$$
$$2 + \qquad 4 \quad = 6 \longleftarrow \text{ Then add.}$$

More Examples

A. $50 - 10 \times 3 \quad \longleftarrow$ Multiply.
$50 - 30 = 20 \longleftarrow$ Subtract.

B. $4 + 3 \times 5 - 6 \quad \longleftarrow$ Multiply.
$4 + 15 - 6 \qquad \longleftarrow$ Add.
$19 - 6 = 13 \qquad \longleftarrow$ Subtract.

- How can you rewrite Example **A** so that the correct answer is 120?

Check for Understanding

Tell which operation to perform first.

1. $(3 - 2) \times 5$ **2.** $25 \div 5 - 3$ **3.** $3 + 3 \times 5$ **4.** $7 \times 9 + 3$

Solve.

5. $30 - 15 \div 3$ **6.** $12 + (5 \times 6)$ **7.** $(7 \times 8) \div 2$ **8.** $(5 \times 4 + 13) \div 11$

Practice

Tell which operation to perform first.

9. $7 \times 9 + 8$ **10.** $4 \times (3 + 8)$ **11.** $25 - 3 \times 5$ **12.** $25 - 15 \div 5$

13. $6 + 9 - 5$ **14.** $12 \div 3 - 4$ **15.** $5 \times 4 \div 2$ **16.** $9 + 49 \div 7$

Solve.

17. $(4 + 3) \times 8$ **18.** $8 \times 9 + 7$ **19.** $36 - 7 \times 2$

20. $54 - 81 \div 9$ **21.** $12 + 11 \div 11$ **22.** $63 \div 7 - 2$

23. $144 \div (12 - 8)$ **24.** $(5 + 4) \times (10 - 3)$ **25.** $300 \div (23 - 8)$

26. Rewrite Exercise 10 so that the answer is 20.

27. Rewrite Exercise 12 so that the answer is 2.

28. Rewrite Exercise 23 so that the answer is 4.

29. Rewrite Exercise 24 so that the answer is 42.

Use the digit 7 four times and the order of operations to write problems that have the following answers.

30. 126 **31.** 4 **32.** 10 **33.** 490

Mixed Applications

34. Sam can score 15 points in 5 minutes. May can score twice as many in 5 minutes. How many total points can they score in 5 minutes?

35. May scores 15 fewer points than Ray, who scores 45 points. Fay scores half as many points as May. How many points does Fay score?

36. **Make Up a Problem** Write a word problem that can only be solved by using two operations.

37. **Number Sense • Mental Math** Mr. Jones teaches 5 classes of 25 students each. In his classes 100 students are sixth graders. How many students are not sixth graders?

Why do you think it is important to agree on an order of operations?

WRAP UP...

Numbers can be written in many forms. For example, you can rename 81 by using nines and threes as factors.

$$81 = 9 \times 9 \qquad 81 = 9 \times 3 \times 3 \qquad 81 = 3 \times 3 \times 3 \times 3$$

WORK TOGETHER

Building Understanding

Use base-ten blocks to explore writing numbers using powers and exponents.

One hundred

Ten

One thousand

Talk About It

▶ How can you rename 100 using tens as factors?

▶ How can you rename 1,000 using tens and hundreds as factors?

▶ How can you rename 1,000 using only tens as factors?

▶ How many times is 10 used as a factor of 1,000?

Another way to write 1,000, or $10 \times 10 \times 10$, is to use an exponent. An **exponent** shows how many times a number called the **base** is used as a factor.

Example

$$\underset{\text{base}}{\overset{\overset{\text{exponent}}{\downarrow}}{10}}{}^{3} = \underbrace{10 \times 10 \times 10}_{\text{factors}} = \underset{\substack{\text{number in}\\\text{standard form}}}{1{,}000}$$

Write: 10^3. **Read:** "ten to the third power," or "ten cubed."

Making the Connection

Compare a multiple of 10 written in exponent form with the same multiple of 10 written in standard form. You will find an interesting pattern.

Copy and complete the place-value chart.

Place Value

Power of Ten	Millions H	Millions T	Millions O	Thousands H	Thousands T	Thousands O	Ones H	Ones T	Ones O
1. 10^1								▦	▦
2. ▦							1	0	0
3. ▦						1	0	0	0
4. 10^4					▦	▦	▦	▦	▦
5. 10^5				▦	▦	▦	▦	▦	▦
6. ▦			1	0	0	0	0	0	0

Look at the pattern of zeros in the numbers written in standard form.

7. In the table, what power of 10 results in the least number of zeros when the number is written in standard form?

8. In the table, what power of 10 results in the greatest number of zeros when the number is written in standard form?

9. How does the exponent of a power of 10 compare with the number of zeros in the number written in standard form?

10. A googol is the term used for 10^{100}. How many zeros are in a googol?

Checking Understanding

Tell how many zeros will be in the number when written in standard form.

11. 10^7 **12.** 10^{11} **13.** ten cubed   **14.** ten to the tenth power

Write the number in standard form.

15. ten to the ninth power   **16.** 10^8 **17.** $10 \times 10 \times 10 \times 10 \times 10$

EXPLORING

Squares and Square Roots

Do you know that 100 is one of many numbers that are called perfect squares?

WORK TOGETHER

You know that 10 × 10, or 10^2, is equal to 100.

A number is a **perfect square** if it is the square of a whole number. The numbers 9, 25, and 100 are perfect squares.

Use unit cubes to model each square.

Draw a square using the number of square units given. Describe the lengths of two sides as factors.

Talk About It

▶ How many square units are in each square?

▶ How can you rename the number of square units in each square by using the lengths of two sides as factors?

▶ How many equal factors are in each square?

a. 4   b. 36   c. 49   d. 64

When you find the two equal factors of a number, you are finding the **square root**, $\sqrt{}$, of the number.

Example   What is $\sqrt{16}$?   Arrange 16 blocks to model the square. Find the two equal factors of 16.

$$4 \times 4 = 16$$
$$\text{So, } \sqrt{16} = 4.$$

▶ How does a square differ from a square root?

22

Making the Connection

You can use a calculator to find squares and square roots.

Use a calculator to find the square of a number.

Example

What is 15^2?   15 $\boxed{\times}$ $\boxed{=}$ $\boxed{225.}$

So, 15^2 is 225.

Use a calculator to find the square root of a number.

Example

What is $\sqrt{625}$?   625 $\boxed{\sqrt{}}$ $\boxed{25.}$

So, $\sqrt{625} = 25$.

1. Since 2 is the square root of 4 and 3 is the square root of 9, would you estimate $\sqrt{5}$ to be closer to 2 or to 3? Defend your answer.

2. Use a calculator. What is $\sqrt{5}$?

Checking Understanding

Use a calculator. Write the square in standard form or the square root of the number in standard form.

3. 50^2 **4.** 30^2 **5.** 5.5^2 **6.** 5.05^2

7. $\sqrt{121}$ **8.** $\sqrt{49}$ **9.** $\sqrt{0.49}$ **10.** $\sqrt{0.0049}$

11. 3.7^2 **12.** $\sqrt{146.41}$ **13.** 7.07^2 **14.** $\sqrt{5{,}580.09}$

MIXED REVIEW

Round to the place indicated.

1. $1.87
   ten cents

2. 6,561
   thousands

3. 25,789
   ten thousands

4. 622.411
   hundredths

Tell which operation to perform first. Then solve.

5. $144 \div 12 - 8$ **6.** $(25 + 15) \div 5$ **7.** $30 \times 4 - 12$ **8.** $7 + 45 \div 15 - 2$

9. $30 \times (12 - 6)$ **10.** $640 \div 10 + 2$ **11.** $1.5 \times (17 - 7)$ **12.** $(13 + 59) \div 8$

PROBLEM *Solving*

Luisa writes training manuals for new employees. The notepad shows the total number of pages she has written by the end of each week. If she continues this pattern, how many pages will she have written by the end of the seventh week?

week 1 = 10 pages
week 2 = 16 pages
week 3 = 23 pages
week 4 = 31 pages

▶ **UNDERSTAND**

What are you asked to find?

What information are you given?

▶ **PLAN**

How can you solve the problem?

Make a table to show the number of pages written by the end of each week.

Week	1	2	3	4	5	6	7
Pages Written	10	16	23	31	■	■	■

+ 6 + 7 + 8 + ? + ? + ?

Look for a pattern.

Week 1 = 10 pages
Week 2 = 10 pages + 6 pages
Week 3 = 16 pages + 7 pages
Week 4 = 23 pages + 8 pages

The pattern shows the number of pages increasing by 6, 7, 8. . . .

▶ **SOLVE**

How can you carry out your plan?

Extend the table to Week 7.

Week	1	2	3	4	5	6	7
Pages Written	10	16	23	31	40	50	61

So, Luisa will have written 61 pages by the end of the seventh week.

▶ **LOOK BACK**

How can you check your answer?

WHAT
IF . . .

. . . Luisa has written 15 pages by the end of the first week, 26 the second, 36 the third, and 45 the fourth week? If she continues this pattern, how many pages will she write by the end of Week 8?

Connection, pages 478–479

Apply

Find the pattern. Then solve.

1 Jason has used 15 blocks to build the first 5 steps of a staircase. How many blocks will he need to build a staircase with 10 steps?

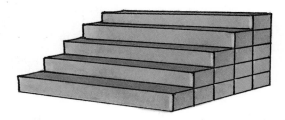

2 A landscaper plants 10 rosebushes the first year. He adds 2 every year after that. How many in all does he plant during 6 years?

3 How many puzzles will you solve on the tenth day if you solve 1 the first day and then solve 2 more puzzles each day than you did the day before?

| Mixed Applications | STRATEGIES | • Find a Pattern • Draw a Picture • Use a Table • Act It Out |

Choose a strategy and solve.

4 **Making Choices** Monte will work for his aunt this summer. She has given him the option of being paid (**a**) a total of $20 or (**b**) $1 the first day, $2 the second, $3 the third, and so on for 8 days. For which option will Monte be paid more?

5 Vic works in a pet store. His job is to feed the animals. He feeds the fish first and the reptiles last. He feeds the cats before the dogs and the dogs after the birds. Which animals does Vic feed just before he feeds the reptiles?

6 Ria has a fifty-cent coin. She asks a clerk to give her 6 coins as change. What combination of coins could the clerk give Ria?

7 Suppose Ria had asked the clerk to give her 8 coins as change for a fifty-cent coin. What coins could the clerk give Ria?

Use the table for Exercises 8–11.

8 If the quality of each car is the same, which is the best buy?

9 If the quality of each car is the same, which is the worst buy?

10 Is the price of the Vigro greater than or less than the price of the Tiger?

11 List in order from greatest to least the prices of the Hawk, Tiger, and Vigro.

Car	Price
Hawk	$12,430
Tiger	$14,489
Vigro	$13,999

CHAPTER REVIEW

Vocabulary Check

Choose a word or words from the box to complete each sentence.

Using new words in sentences helps you learn them.

base
exponent
perfect square
square root
standard

1. The number 2,136 is written in __?__ form. *(page 6)*

2. The __?__ shows how many times the __?__ is used as a factor. *(page 20)*

3. A number is a __?__ if it is the square of a whole number. *(page 22)*

4. When you find the two equal factors of a number, you are finding the __?__ of the number. *(page 22)*

Concept Check

5. In which numeration systems is the order of the symbols important—the decimal, the Roman, or the Egyptian system? *(pages 2, 3, 4)*

6. If you were rounding the amount of your $4.75 weekly allowance in order to estimate the total for the year, would you round to the nearest dollar or ten dollars? *(page 14)*

7. Which numeration system uses place value—the decimal, the Roman, or the Egyptian system? *(page 4)*

8. Explain the order of operations. *(page 18)*

9. What does 10^4 mean? *(page 20)*

10. How does a square differ from a square root? *(page 22)*

The number has been rounded to the place indicated.
Write the range of numbers that round to the given number. *(page 14)*

11. 35,000,000
    millions

12. $0.80
    ten cents

13. 100
    hundreds

Tell which operation to perform first. *(page 18)*

14. $5 \times (45 - 25)$

15. $12 + 6 \times 8$

16. $(26 + 12) \div 7$

Tell how many zeros will be in the number when written in standard form. *(page 20)*

17. ten cubed

18. ten squared

19. ten to the ninth power

Skill Check

Write the value of the underlined digit. *(pages 6, 8)*

20. 5,0<u>3</u>0,000,000

21. <u>5</u>,030,000,000

22. 12.008<u>6</u>

Write the number in short word form. *(pages 6, 8)*

23. 6,300,000

24. 6,300,000,000

25. 2.0014

Write the numbers from least to greatest. Use <. *(page 10)*

26. 1.10, 1.01, 1.001

27. 2.04, 2.4, 2.014

28. 3.5, 3.25, 3.185

Estimate by rounding to the place indicated. *(page 14)*

29. 9,705,128,004
billions

30. 9,705,128,004
millions

31. 59,238.60057
ten-thousandths

Use the order of operations. Solve. *(page 18)*

32. $5 \times 3 + 4 \div 2$

33. $35 - 3 \times 6 \div 2$

34. $4 + (6 - 10 \div 5) \times 4$

35. $12 \div 4 + (20 - 11)$

36. $4 \times 5 \div (6 - 2)$

37. $(7 + 6) + (9 \times 5)$

Write the number in standard form. *(pages 20, 22)*

38. 10^7

39. 10^3

40. $\sqrt{100}$

41. 4^2

Problem-Solving Check

Use the table for Exercises 42–43. *(pages 12, 24)*

42. Liz uses the table to make plant food at a nursery. If the pattern continues, how many teaspoons of concentrate will she use with 8 quarts of water?

43. How many teaspoons of concentrate will Liz use with $4\frac{1}{2}$ quarts of water?

44. Make a table that shows the formula so that 4 teaspoons are used with 1 quart of water.

Plant-Food Formula					
Teaspoons of Concentrate	2	4	6	8	10
Quarts of Water	1	2	3	4	5

CHAPTER TEST

Write the value of the underlined digit.

1. 529.01035

2. 67,018,932,005

3. 67,018,932.005

Write the number in short word form.

4. 4,907,000,000

5. 49,007,000

6. 12.0015

Write the numbers from greatest to least. Use >.

7. 0.71, 0.17, 0.07

8. 1.09, 1.9, 1.009

9. 4.210, 4.012, 4.030

Write the range of numbers that round to the given number.

10. 730
    tens

11. 500
    hundreds

12. 47,000
    thousands

13. 150,000
    ten-thousands

14. 19,000,000
    millions

15. 19,000,000,000
    billions

Tell which operation to perform first. Then solve.

16. $19 - 5 \times 4 \div 2$

17. $5 \times 2 + 9 \div 3$

18. $12 + (15 - 5 \div 5) \times 2$

Write the number in standard form.

19. 10^4

20. $\sqrt{4}$

21. 5^2

22. ten cubed

Use the table for Exercises 23–25. Solve.

23. The table shows the increase in the number of employees at Top Hardware over four years. If the pattern continues, how many employees will Top Hardware have in the year 1998?

24. How many more employees did Top Hardware have in 1991 than it had in 1988?

25. If the pattern continues, how many more employees will Top Hardware have in 2000 than it had in 1990?

Always read problems carefully.

Top Hardware's Growth				
Year 19 ___	88	89	90	91
Number of Employees	5	7	9	11

Teamwork P-R-O-J-E-C-T

Start a Business

Suppose you are going to open a business that sells school supplies. You will need to fill these positions:

Decide Determine which team member or members will fill each position. If there are other jobs that need to be done, decide which members of your team will fill those positions.

Do Each team member should make a list of five or six responsibilities that his or her position might require.

Share Compare the responsibilities of the positions. If more than one person feels responsible for a task, decide as a group which person should accept the responsibility.

Directors
(those who decide which supplies to sell)

Purchasers
(those who order the supplies)

Accountants
(those who keep track of expenses and profits)

Salespeople
(those who sell the supplies)

Work with your teammates to plan your business.

Talk About It

☐ **How would the person filling each position use numbers in the course of his or her work?**

☐ **Why is it important that all the group members work together in the business?**

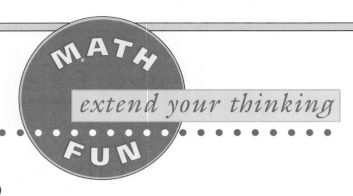

Decimal High

To play this game, you will need an opponent, a deck of 20 cards labeled with the numbers 0 through 9 twice, and a game board similar to the one shown. The object of the game is to make the greater decimal number. Shuffle the cards and place them facedown in a stack.

The players take turns drawing a card from the stack and placing it faceup in one of the spaces on the game board. A player who draws a zero has three choices: place the zero on the board, switch any two digits already on the board to create a larger number, or move any one card from its space to an empty space. If the zero is not placed on the board, it is set aside. Play continues until the players fill all the spaces on the game board. The player with the greater decimal number wins the round, and the player who wins two out of three rounds wins the game.

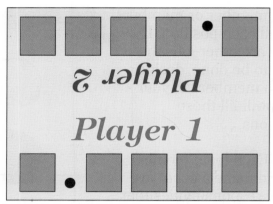

Challenge

Number Sense

Which numbers in the chart have equal value? Find one set of "twins" and one set of "triplets" by determining the value of the numbers.

2^2	2^4	6^2
2^3	1^4	4^2
4^3	1^2	8^2
1^3	10^2	3^4
5^2	3^1	5^3
3^3	3^2	2^6
	3^5	
	2^5	

Logical Reasoning

This five-digit number is 20,000 when rounded to the nearest ten thousand. The number contains consecutive digits whose sum is 10. The digit in the hundreds place is the least. The tens digit is less than the thousands digit and the ones digit. What is the number?

CUMULATIVE REVIEW

Write the letter of the correct answer.

1. Which is the value of the underlined digit? 20,000,000,000

   A. 20 thousand
   B. 20 million
   C. 20 billion
   D. 20 trillion

2. Which is the short word form for 0.0005?

   A. 5 tenths
   B. 5/1,000ths
   C. 5 ten-thousandths
   D. 5/100,000

3. Which is one million two in standard form?

   A. 1,000,000.2
   B. 1,000,002
   C. 1,200,000
   D. not here

4. Which is four and fourteen ten-thousandths in standard form?

   A. 4.00014
   B. 4.0014
   C. 414,000
   D. not here

5. Which is two hundred and two thousandths in standard form?

   A. 0.202
   B. 200.002
   C. 200.2
   D. 202,000

6. Which is listed in order from least to greatest?

   A. 0.8, 0.9, 0.08
   B. 0.8, 0.08, 0.9
   C. 0.08, 0.8, 0.9
   D. not here

7. Which is 4.089765 rounded to the ten-thousandths place?

   A. 4.08977
   B. 4.089
   C. 4.0898
   D. 4.09

8. $4 \times 5 + 6 \div 2$

   A. 13
   B. 22
   C. 23
   D. 36

9. $25 + (12 - 6 \div 3) \times 2$

   A. 29
   B. 54
   C. 70
   D. not here

10. Which is the value of 10^3?

    A. 30
    B. 100
    C. 1,000
    D. 3,000

11. When does bus fare cost most?

Bus Schedule	
Time	Cost
9 A.M.–6 P.M.	$12.50
6 P.M.–10 P.M.	$12.05
10 P.M.–12 P.M.	$12.55

    A. 6 P.M.–10 P.M.
    B. 9 A.M.–6 P.M.
    C. 10 P.M.–12 P.M.
    D. $12.55

12. Rob is trying to figure out a number series. The first three numbers are 3, 7, and 11. If the pattern continues, which will be the fourth and the fifth numbers in the series?

    A. 11 and 15
    B. 13 and 17
    C. 15 and 19
    D. 19 and 23

2

ADDING AND SUBTRACTING
WHOLE NUMBERS
AND
DECIMALS

Did you know ...

... that in college basketball a woman holds the overall record for most career points?

Talk About It

Pearl Moore, with 4,061 points, holds the women's record for most points scored during a college basketball career, while Travis Grant, with 4,045 points, holds the men's record. How can you find how many more points Pearl Moore scored than Travis Grant?

In the first four basketball games of the season, Wes scored 16, 9, 11, and 24 points. How many points did he score in all?

$16 + 9 + 11 + 24$

The properties of addition can help you find pairs of addends that are easy to add using mental math.

$16 + 9 + 11 + 24$
$16 + 24 + 9 + 11$ ← Commutative
$(16 + 24) + (9 + 11)$ ← Associative
$40 + 20 = 60$ ← Use mental math.

So, Wes scored 60 points in four games.

Properties of Addition

Commutative Property
Numbers can be added in any order.
$7 + 16 = 16 + 7$

Zero Property
The sum of any number and zero is that number.
$36 + 0 = 36$

Associative Property
Addends can be grouped differently. The sum is always the same.
$(23 + 20) + 36 = 23 + (20 + 36)$
$43 + 36 = 23 + 56$
$79 = 79$

Another Strategy

When you use **compensation**, you make adding and subtracting simple and quick by changing one addend to a multiple of ten and adjusting the other addend to keep the balance.

Addition Example
How many points did Wes score in the first two games?

$16 + 9$
$(16 - 1) + (9 + 1)$
$15 + 10 = 25$

So, Wes scored 25 points in the first two games.

Subtraction Example
How many more points did Wes score in the fourth game than in the first game?

$24 - 16$ ← $16 + 4 = 20$
$(24 + 4) - (16 + 4)$ ← Compensate.
$28 - 20 = 8$

So, Wes scored 8 more points in the fourth game.

Recall that addition and subtraction are **inverse**, or opposite, operations.

Talk About It

► How can you use compensation when you add?

► How can you use compensation when you subtract?

► Explain how you can use the Commutative and Associative Properties to find the sum $18 + 24 + 76 + 12$.

Check for Understanding

Use mental math and the properties of addition to find the missing addend. Name the property you use.

1. $6 + \blacksquare = 6$

2. $(17 + 3) + \blacksquare = 5 + (17 + 3)$

3. $3 + (4 + \blacksquare) = (3 + 4) + 6$

Use compensation to solve. Show your work.

4. $19 + 8$

5. $8 + 24$

6. $67 + 15$

7. $67 - 38$

8. $21 - 17 - 4$

9. $41 - 29$

10. $127 + 115$

11. $82 - 36$

Practice

Find the sum or difference. Use mental math when possible.

12. $46 - 46$

13. $17 + (3 + 20)$

14. $4 + 23 + 76$

15. $34 + (6 + 23)$

16. $(14 + 22) + 8$

17. $35 + 33 + 5$

18. $92 + 66 + 8$

19. $49 - 21 - 0$

20. $(6 + 22) + 8$

21. $75 + 46 + 25$

22. $42 - 36$

23. $92 - 14$

24. $43 + (17 + 8)$

25. $81 - 25$

26. $11 + 20 + 49$

27. $33 - 28$

Mixed Applications

Write a number sentence that shows the property used. Then solve.

28. Chee had 14 team pennants. Then he won 6 at a fair, and friends gave him 3 more. How many pennants does Chee have?

29. Bea sold 4 bowls of chili, 16 hamburgers, and 20 orders of french fries. How many items did she sell altogether?

30. **Logical Reasoning** Use the map.

   a. Name the cities missing on the road sign.

   b. Tell where the sign is located.

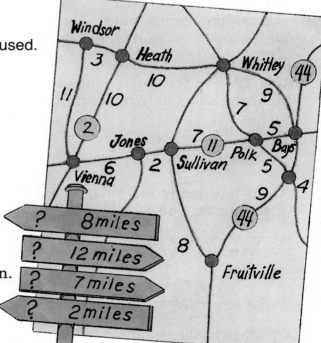

What is one advantage of knowing and using the properties of addition?

WRAP UP...

ESTIMATING
Sums and Differences

You estimate sums or differences when an exact answer is not needed or when you want to check the reasonableness of an answer.

Keena determines that Daley Thompson scored 17,293 total points. Is her answer reasonable?

Olympic Decathlon Champions		
Name	**Points**	**Date**
Bruce Jenner, U.S.	8,617	1976
Daley Thompson, U.K.	8,495	1980
Daley Thompson, U.K.	8,798	1984
Christian Schenk, E. Ger.	8,488	1988

You can use the front digits.

Add front digits. Then adjust.

$$\begin{array}{r} 8{,}495 \\ +\ 8{,}798 \\ \hline 16{,}000 \end{array}$$ ← estimate

$495 + 798 \approx 1{,}300$

≈ means "is approximately equal to."

$16{,}000 + 1{,}300 = 17{,}300$ ← adjusted estimate

You can use rounding.

Round.

$$\begin{array}{r} 8{,}495 \rightarrow 8{,}000 \\ +8{,}798 \rightarrow 9{,}000 \\ \hline 17{,}000 \end{array}$$

Since 17,293 is close to the estimate, Keena's answer is reasonable.

- How would the example using rounding change if you rounded to the nearest hundred?

You can determine whether an estimated sum is an overestimate or an underestimate.

If both rounded addends are greater than the exact addends, the estimate is an **overestimate.**

$$\begin{array}{r} 8{,}495 \rightarrow 8{,}500 \\ +8{,}798 \rightarrow 8{,}800 \\ \hline 17{,}300 \end{array}$$

If both rounded addends are less than the exact addends, the estimate is an **underestimate.**

$$\begin{array}{r} 8{,}445 \rightarrow 8{,}400 \\ +8{,}732 \rightarrow 8{,}700 \\ \hline 17{,}100 \end{array}$$

The place to which you round depends on the situation.

About how many more points did Bruce Jenner score than Christian Schenk?

Estimate the difference by rounding.

$$\begin{array}{r} 8{,}617 \rightarrow 8{,}600 \\ -8{,}488 \rightarrow 8{,}500 \\ \hline 100 \end{array}$$

So, Bruce Jenner scored about 100 more points.

- How can you use front-end digits to estimate the difference?

Check for Understanding

Use front-end estimation to estimate the sum or difference.

1. $\begin{array}{r} 1,072 \\ +2,550 \\ \hline \end{array}$
2. $\begin{array}{r} 3,244 \\ -2,124 \\ \hline \end{array}$
3. $\begin{array}{r} 8,025 \\ -2,284 \\ \hline \end{array}$
4. $\begin{array}{r} 4,668 \\ +6,432 \\ \hline \end{array}$
5. $\begin{array}{r} 7,312 \\ -4,583 \\ \hline \end{array}$

Round to the nearest thousand. Then estimate the sum or difference.

6. $\begin{array}{r} 1,854 \\ +5,187 \\ \hline \end{array}$
7. $\begin{array}{r} 6,443 \\ +7,248 \\ \hline \end{array}$
8. $\begin{array}{r} 6,153 \\ -5,075 \\ \hline \end{array}$
9. $\begin{array}{r} 5,231 \\ -2,139 \\ \hline \end{array}$
10. $\begin{array}{r} 5,167 \\ +6,860 \\ \hline \end{array}$

Practice

Tell whether the estimate is an overestimate or an underestimate.

11. $6,321 + 8,239 \approx 14,000$
12. $13,772 + 6,559 \approx 21,000$
13. $61,864 + 32,901 \approx 90,000$
14. $82,142 + 23,031 \approx 100,000$

Use front-end estimation to estimate the sum or difference.

15. $\begin{array}{r} 7,320 \\ +9,989 \\ \hline \end{array}$
16. $\begin{array}{r} 7,381 \\ -3,547 \\ \hline \end{array}$
17. $\begin{array}{r} 5,933 \\ -3,642 \\ \hline \end{array}$
18. $\begin{array}{r} 1,754 \\ +3,748 \\ \hline \end{array}$
19. $\begin{array}{r} 2,329 \\ +7,673 \\ \hline \end{array}$

Round to estimate the sum or difference.

20. $\begin{array}{r} 27,681 \\ -23,216 \\ \hline \end{array}$
21. $\begin{array}{r} 21,050 \\ -12,155 \\ \hline \end{array}$
22. $\begin{array}{r} 61,240 \\ +27,545 \\ \hline \end{array}$
23. $\begin{array}{r} 93,685 \\ +93,216 \\ \hline \end{array}$
24. $\begin{array}{r} 28,803 \\ -17,901 \\ \hline \end{array}$

Mixed Applications

25. Lu says that by driving 14,879 miles and 37,640 miles, she has driven a total of 40,640 miles. Is her calculation reasonable? Explain.

26. **Number Sense** Nancy ran 3 miles farther than Fran. Together they ran 17 miles. How far did Nancy run?

27. Three duffel bags weigh 49, 53, and 77 pounds. About how much is the total weight of the three bags?

28. **Write a Question** Use the facts in the table on page 36. Write a question that can be solved by estimating the sum.

If you reheat a plate of food in a microwave, should you overestimate or underestimate the cooking time?

W R A P
UP...

CONNECTING ADDITION AND SUBTRACTION

Since addition and subtraction are inverse, or opposite, operations, you can subtract to check addition and add to check subtraction.

Michael Jordan scored 3,041, 2,868, and 2,633 points in three years. How many total points did he score in the three years?

Add.
$$\begin{array}{r} 3,041 \\ 2,868 \\ +2,633 \\ \hline 8,542 \end{array}$$

Subtract to check.
$$\begin{array}{r} 8,542 \\ -2,633 \\ \hline 5,909 \\ -2,868 \\ \hline 3,041 \end{array}$$ ← sum
← addend

← addend

← addend

So, Michael Jordan scored a total of 8,542 points in three years.

In his best year, Wilt Chamberlain scored a total of 4,029 points. How many more points did Chamberlain score in his best year than Jordan did in the year he scored 3,041 points?

Subtract.
$$\begin{array}{r} 4,029 \\ -3,041 \\ \hline 988 \end{array}$$

Add to check.
$$\begin{array}{r} 988 \\ +3,041 \\ \hline 4,029 \end{array}$$

So, Chamberlain scored 988 more points than Jordan.

Talk About It

▶ Why are two subtraction operations necessary to check the total points Jordan scored?

▶ Name one other way you could check the answer in each example.

Check for Understanding

Find the sum or difference. Use the inverse operation to check your answer.

1. $\begin{array}{r} 657 \\ -549 \\ \hline \end{array}$

2. $\begin{array}{r} 923 \\ +578 \\ \hline \end{array}$

3. $\begin{array}{r} 3,342 \\ -1,849 \\ \hline \end{array}$

4. $\begin{array}{r} 54,321 \\ -37,768 \\ \hline \end{array}$

5. $\begin{array}{r} 156,123 \\ 82,878 \\ +717,797 \\ \hline \end{array}$

Practice

Find the sum or difference. Use the inverse operation to check.

6.	768 +867	7.	535 −396	8.	357 −258	9.	6,273 +3,958	10.	7,632 −5,498

11.	54,652 −27,468	12.	19,233 − 6,988	13.	25,532 +33,468	14.	113,411 −109,424	15.	636,721 −365,290

16.	257 38 +766	17.	3,431 1,567 + 989	18.	78,465 5,821 +12,473	19.	131,522 2,945 + 76,798	20.	1,454,982 153,375 +5,662,866

Find the missing digits.

21.
```
  4 8 , 1 ▩ 0
+ ▩ 4 , 2 5 4
─────────────
  6 ▩ , 3 7 ▩
```

22.
```
  ▩ , 9 ▩ 2
− 3 , 5 5 ▩
───────────
  3 , ▩ 2 1
```

Mixed Applications

23. The Eagles scored 85 points. The Bobcats scored 114 points. Jan says the Bobcats won by 28 points. Is she correct? Justify your answer.

24. Lamont and Robert scored a total of 621 points this season. Since Robert scored 276 points, he will win the high-scorer award. Is this true? Justify your answer.

MIXED REVIEW

Use mental math and the properties of addition to find the missing addend.

1. $7 + ▩ = 6 + 7$

2. $5 + 0 = ▩$

3. $9 + (1 + ▩) = (9 + 1) + 8$

Use front-end estimation to estimate the sum or difference.

4.	3,240 +3,685	5.	7,673 −5,113	6.	8,203 +2,451	7.	4,186 −1,157	8.	6,223 −3,779

Round to the nearest thousand. Then estimate the sum or difference.

9.	7,548 −3,250	10.	1,972 +9,127	11.	19,201 −12,713	12.	15,126 +14,921	13.	26,130 −21,860

Why is it a good idea to estimate an answer before you use a calculator to add or subtract?

WRAP
UP...

Amy plans to spend $25 for a jogging outfit, $15 for a compact disc, $10 for a birthday present for her brother, and $5 for lunch. How much money should Amy take to the mall?

You can use estimation, paper and pencil, mental math, or a calculator to solve problems. To decide which to use, think about the numbers involved, the questions asked, and the time and tools available to you.

▶ UNDERSTAND

What are you asked to find?

What information are you given?

▶ PLAN

What will you do to solve the problem? Since you need to find the total cost of the items, you will add.

▶ SOLVE

What method of computation can you use? Since the amounts are in multiples of 5 dollars, you can use mental math. Use the Associative Property of Addition to group numbers so that they are easy to add.

$$(\$25 + \$5) + (\$10 + \$15)$$
$$\quad\downarrow \qquad\qquad \downarrow$$
$$\$30 \quad + \quad \$25 = \$55$$

So, Amy should take $55 to the mall.

▶ LOOK BACK

How can you check your answer?

WHAT IF... ... Amy must make sure she has enough money to buy items that cost $8.89, $14.67, and $14.14? What method could she use?

Spotlight ON PROBLEM SOLVING

Look for Patterns and Relationships

Sometimes you need to find patterns or relationships to solve a problem. First, compare the parts you are given. Then, determine how the parts relate to one another.

Example Football-jersey numbers indicate the positions of the players. Quarterbacks generally wear numbers from 7 through 19. Running backs wear numbers from 20 through 49. Centers usually wear numbers in the 50's, guards in the 60's, tackles in the 70's, and ends in the 80's.

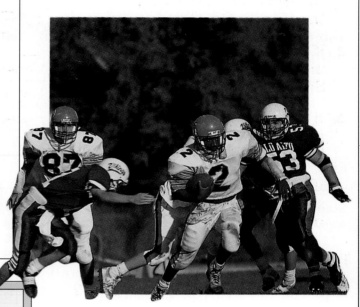

Talk About It

A. Hap wears 65, Ned 68, and Ted 64. What position do they play?

B. Seth said that his number is 13 less than Ned's. What position does Seth play?

C. The numbers of the team's three running backs total 86. Each number is even, and two of the numbers are in the 20's. What are the three numbers?

D. The tight end's number is 8 times as large as that of the quarterback. The quarterback's number is an odd number between 10 and 20. What are the numbers of the two players?

Apply

Solve. Use the system for numbering football jerseys.

1. Three quarterbacks wear odd numbers greater than 5 but less than 17. None of the numbers can be divided by 3. What are the three numbers?

2. Make a list of the offensive positions on a football team, and assign jersey numbers to each position.

3. Each of three running backs wears a jersey with the same two digits in the number. What are the three numbers?

4. Two tackles wear jersey numbers that total 152. Each jersey has an even number. What are the two numbers?

ADDING DECIMALS

The Dodd Middle School relay team won the 400-meter relay at a local meet. Ken ran his leg of the race in 15 seconds, Josh ran his in 14.75 seconds, Bill ran his in 13.125 seconds, and Bobby ran his in 12.8 seconds. What was the team's winning time?

You could round to the nearest whole number to estimate the sum.

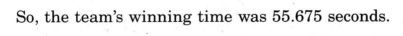

15 + 14.75 + 13.125 + 12.8

15 + 15 + 13 + 13 = 56 ← estimate

Find the sum.

Step 1 Align the decimal points.	**Step 2** Place the decimal point. Then add.
15　　or　15.000 Placing zeros to the 14.75　　　14.750 right of the decimal 13.125　　 13.125 point does not +12.8　　 +12.800 change the value 　　　　　　　　　　　of the decimal.	15 14.75 13.125 +12.8 ——— 55.675

So, the team's winning time was 55.675 seconds.

Talk About It

▶ How do you know it is acceptable to rewrite 15 as 15.000, 14.75 as 14.750, and 12.8 as 12.800?

▶ Why do you align the decimal points?

Check for Understanding

Find the sum.

1. $18 + $2.95 + $13.30

2. 14.4 + 231.67 + 24.699

3. 63.403 + 2.661

4. 763.114
17.58
+ 0.066

5. $304.42
+ 18.09

6. 420
76.3
+ 8.5

7. 260
103.403
+254.906

8. 25.01
115.9
+ 87.99

Practice

Place the decimal point in the sum.

9. $76.551 + 24.59 + 0.054 = 101195$

10. $123.98 + 0.873 + 10.0059 = 1348589$

11. $48.9 + 31.092 + 0.87 = 80862$

12. $0.1209 + 0.236 + 0.279 = 06359$

Find the sum.

13. $6.25 + 4.794$

14. $0.29 + 6.68$

15. $9.3 + 3.708$

16. $\$30.03 + \$40.54$

17. $67.1 + 2.693$

18. $4.6 + 75.188$

19.
$$\begin{array}{r} 76.6 \\ 55.66 \\ +32.666 \\ \hline \end{array}$$

20.
$$\begin{array}{r} 6.72 \\ 44.5 \\ + \ 0.77 \\ \hline \end{array}$$

21.
$$\begin{array}{r} 6{,}453.5 \\ 960.11 \\ + \ \ 431.7 \\ \hline \end{array}$$

22.
$$\begin{array}{r} \$423.12 \\ 33.42 \\ + \ \ 777.74 \\ \hline \end{array}$$

23.
$$\begin{array}{r} 54.01 \\ 9.3 \\ +68.776 \\ \hline \end{array}$$

24. $\$72.44 + \$33.93$

25. $4.12 + 832 + 209.7$

26. $\$0.12 + \$53.91 + \$43$

27. $40.2 + 753.01 + 2{,}562 + 0.96$

Mixed Applications

Solve. Use the table for Exercises 28–31.

Month	Jan.	Feb.	Mar.	Apr.	May	June	July	Aug.	Sept.	Oct.	Nov.	Dec.
Rainfall (inches)	2.2	3	3.55	4.2	3.45	2.7	0.84	0.4	10.1	2	1.9	2.3

28. How much rain fell during the first three months of the year?

29. How much rain fell during the last three months of the year?

30. How much rain fell during the three wettest months?

31. How much rain fell during the three driest months?

32. Logical Reasoning Look at the problems $3.2 + 9.7$ and $32 + 97$. How are they similar? Which problem has the greater sum?

33. Analyze Data Use the table. When do you think outdoor athletic contests were rained out? When could you have left your umbrella at home?

Name an everyday situation in which you add decimals.

SUBTRACTING DECIMALS

Arie Luyendyk drove a record 185.984 miles per hour (mph) to win the Indianapolis 500. The next fastest time was clocked four years earlier when Bobby Rahal drove 170.72 mph. How much faster is Luyendyk's time?

Estimate. You could use the front digits and then adjust if needed.

185.984 − 170.72   Since 0.984 ≈ 1, 0.72 ≈ 1, and 1 − 1 = 0,
   ↓   ↓   no adjustment is needed.
185 − 170 = 15

Find the difference.

Step 1 Align the decimal points.	**Step 2** Place the decimal point. Then subtract.
185.984 or 185.984 −170.72 −170.720	185.984 −170.72 ‾‾‾‾‾‾ 15.264

So, Luyendyk's time is 15.264 mph faster.

Examples

A. 24.02   B. 15.007   C. 36.1
   − 7.3   −12.22   − 9.73
  ‾‾‾‾‾   ‾‾‾‾‾‾   ‾‾‾‾‾
  16.72   2.787   26.37

- How can you check your subtraction?

Check for Understanding

Find the difference.

1. 4.2 − 0.12   2. 63.039 − 29.84   3. 739.4 − 56.2

4. 26.32 − 17.15   5. 481.201 − 256.893   6. 261.92 − 89.796

7. 42.03   8. 78.02   9. 34.7   10. 12.77   11. 77.95
  − 9.859   − 6.437   − 0.938   − 8.435   −41.5

Practice

Place the decimal point in the difference.

12. $98.5 - 6.09 = 9241$ **13.** $4.85 - 0.485 = 4365$ **14.** $680.2 - 92.4 = 5878$

Find the difference.

15. $5.23 - 0.986$ **16.** $83.12 - 8.6$ **17.** $101.23 - 8.7$

18. $9 - 6.23$ **19.** $0.54 - 0.054$ **20.** $23.5 - 9.6719$

21. $0.67 - 0.2103$ **22.** $41.08 - 8.7$ **23.** $31.02 - 7.8643$

24. $23 - 0.76$ **25.** $6.398 - 4.885$ **26.** $6.5 - 3.92$

27. $8.703 - 4.29$ **28.** $9.7 - 3.872$ **29.** $86.49 - 3.295$

30.
$$\begin{array}{r} 65.05 \\ -\ \ 5.2 \\ \hline \end{array}$$
31.
$$\begin{array}{r} 0.9 \\ -0.04 \\ \hline \end{array}$$
32.
$$\begin{array}{r} 74.7 \\ -\ 0.987 \\ \hline \end{array}$$
33.
$$\begin{array}{r} 86.49 \\ -\ 4.32 \\ \hline \end{array}$$
34.
$$\begin{array}{r} 9.183 \\ -7.041 \\ \hline \end{array}$$

Mixed Applications

35. Last year Maria did an average of 87.5 sit-ups. This year her average is 93.7 sit-ups. How much has her average improved?

36. Juan used 2.6 pounds of a 7-pound block of clay to sculpt a wrestler. He also gave away 1.5 pounds. How much clay was left?

37. Find Data Use an encyclopedia, an almanac, or another reference book to find and list five facts about your favorite sport.

38. Make Up a Problem Use the facts you found in Exercise 37 to write a problem that can be solved using addition or subtraction.

NUMBER SENSE

39. Copy the puzzle. Fill the yellow boxes with addition or subtraction signs so that the computations both across and down are equal to 18.4.

3.4		8.4		6.6
7.3		14.6		3.5
7.7		4.6		15.3

Name an everyday situation in which you subtract decimals.

WRAP UP...

USING CALCULATOR MEMORY

Use the memory keys on a calculator when you need to perform more than one operation to solve a problem.

Press MRC twice to clear the memory.   ← Always clear the memory first.

M+ adds a number to the memory.   MRC recalls the number.

Example   A checkbook balance shows how much money is in a checking account. Amounts of deposits are added to the balance. Amounts of checks are subtracted. Wade ٧es a calculator to check his checkbook balance.

Date	Check Number	Checks issued to or Deposit received from	Amount of Deposit	Amount of Check	Balance
4/19		beginning balance			$302.35
4/20		salary	487.24		
4/25	738	Northern Telephone Co.		37.45	
4/26	739	Abe's Oriental grocery		78.43	
4/27		salary	515.31		
4/27	740	Clyde's car loan Co.		256.25	
4/28	741	Luyfat Health Club		178.98	
4/30	742	Hi-Roll Savings Bank		400.00	353.79

sum of beginning balance and deposits − total checks = balance
(302.35 + 487.24 + 515.31) − (37.45 + 78.43 + 256.25 + 178.98 + 400.00)

First, Wade totals the checks. Then, he adds the total to the memory.

37.45 [+] 78.43 [+] 256.25 [+] 178.98 [+] 400 [=] [M+] ^M | 951.11 |

Next, he finds the sum of the beginning balance and the deposits.

302.35 [+] 487.24 [+] 515.31 [=] ^M | 1304.9 |

To subtract his checks, he presses [−] [MRC] [=] ^M | 353.79 | .

So, Wade's checkbook balance is $353.79.

• Was the final balance shown in the checkbook correct?

• How can Wade add another check to the memory?

Check for Understanding

Solve. Use a calculator with memory keys.

1. $(21.75 + 3.45 + 52.57 + 31.49 + 25.75) - (54.31 + 5.43 + 62.98)$

2. $(121,657 + 476,474 + 11,980) - (54,321 + 45,231 + 35,798)$

Practice

Find the balance. Use a calculator with memory keys.

3.

Checks	Deposits
$ 50.25	$851.67
136.29	
525.78	245.25
354.11	
Balance:	

4.

Checks	Deposits
$475.38	$1,200.00
84.76	
162.04	
260.52	68.52
Balance:	

5.

Checks	Deposits
$267.54	$750.80
192.48	
12.29	750.80
722.76	
Balance:	

Mixed Applications

6. In his collection of blocks, Dan has 375 red, 226 blue, 415 yellow, and 387 green blocks. He wants to build a castle that calls for 927 blocks, and a drawbridge with 368 blocks. How many blocks will be left?

7. Kate has $5.00, and Sue gives her $12.00 more for these groceries: cereal, $3.87; bread, $1.29; milk, $2.56; chicken, $5.39; broccoli, $1.78; and juice, $1.98. How much change will Kate receive?

LOGICAL REASONING

You can use a calculator and your knowledge of place value to perform operations with numbers in the hundred-millions place and greater.

Example $354,956,588 \rightarrow$ 354 million + 956,588
$+ \ 466,355,244 \rightarrow$ 466 million + 355,244

Use a calculator.

$354 + 466 = \boxed{820.}$ (million)

$956,588 + 355,244 = \boxed{1311832.}$

Use paper and pencil.

$820,000,000 + 1,311,832 = 821,311,832$

Use a calculator to solve.

8. $684,923,317 + 722,196,442$

9. $1,234,567,890 - 987,654,321$

Name a way you can use the memory keys on a calculator.

A football team scored 3 more points in the second half than they had scored in the first half of a game. How many points did the team score in the second half?

If the team had scored 7 points in the first half, you could write the numerical expression $7 + 3$ to solve the problem. Since you do not know the number of points scored in the first half, you can use a letter, or **variable**, to write an algebraic expression.

Use p for the number of points scored in the first half.

word expression ⟶ 3 more than the number of points scored in the first half

algebraic expression ⟶ $p + 3$

So, the team scored $p + 3$ points in the second half.

Talk About It

▶ How does the algebraic expression differ from the word expression?

▶ If the team had scored 3 fewer points in the second half, what algebraic expression would you have written?

The table shows examples of word expressions and algebraic expressions.

Word Expression	Algebraic Expression
Four more than a number x The sum of 8.6 and a number p	$x + 4$ $8.6 + p$
Nine less than a number y Seven fewer than a number d	$y - 9$ $d - 7$

Check for Understanding

Write an algebraic expression for the word expression.

1. seven more than a number y

2. four less than a number n

3. the sum of a number x and 15

4. nine fewer than a number s

Practice

Write an algebraic expression for the word expression.

5. 30 more than a number b

6. k fewer than 115.75

7. 26 less than a number p

8. w less than 97

9. 12 fewer than a number t

10. the sum of 55 and a number n

11. the sum of 3.2 and a number s

12. d more than 52

Write a word expression for the algebraic expression.

13. $23 + u$

14. $45 - q$

15. $t - 11.075$

16. $b + 452.5$

17. $43.7 + a$

18. $65 - y$

19. $z + 2.5$

20. $b - 67$

21. $w + 12$

22. $x - 5.5$

Mixed Applications

23. James scored 46 more free throws than Nathan. Let n represent the number of free throws Nathan scored. Write an algebraic expression that represents the number of free throws James scored.

24. Which decimal number is greatest, 1.02, 1.20, or 1.022? Which of these numbers is least?

25. June gave Sara $5. Let d represent the amount June had before she gave money to Sara. Write an algebraic expression that represents how much money June had left.

26. Number Sense • Estimation In his best game, a halfback rushed for 9 yards, 21 yards, 17 yards, and 58 yards. About how many total yards did he rush?

Write an algebraic expression that tells how much more time you spend in math class than you spend eating lunch. **WRAP UP...**

EVALUATING EXPRESSIONS

Each day Juana missed the same number of free throws no matter how many she attempted. She kept this record.

Attempted	10	15	18	24	28	f
Scored	4	9	12	18	22	?

- What pattern does the table show?

- If f represents the number of free throws attempted, what algebraic expression represents the number scored?

Suppose Juana attempts 16 free throws.
How many will she score?

Use 16 for f in the expression $f - 6$. $\rightarrow f - 6$
$16 - 6 = 10$

So, Juana will score 10 free throws.

When you replace the variable with a number and perform the operation in an algebraic expression, you are **evaluating**, or finding the value of, the expression.

Example   Evaluate $x + 6$, for $x = 7$.

Step 1 Replace the variable with the number 7. $x + 6 = 7 + 6$	**Step 2** Perform the operation. $7 + 6 = 13$

More Examples   Evaluate the expressions for $b = 4.5$ and $c = 12$.

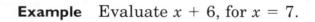

A. $32 - b$
$32 - 4.5 = 27.5$

B. $c + 13$
$12 + 13 = 25$

C. $(c + b) - 2.3$
$(12 + 4.5) - 2.3 = 14.2$

Check for Understanding

Evaluate the expression.

1. $n + 25$, for $n = 7$

2. $w - 13$, for $w = 72$

3. $33 - t$, for $t = 19$

4. $n + 25$, for $n = 2$

5. $w - 13$, for $w = 26$

6. $y - 9.8$, for $y = 21$

Practice

Evaluate the expression $p + 35.57$ for each value of p.

7. $p = 21.42$ **8.** $p = 19.09$ **9.** $p = 43.35$ **10.** $p = 87.09$ **11.** $p = 98.88$

Evaluate the expression $113.25 - p$ for each value of p.

12. $p = 13.89$ **13.** $p = 46.25$ **14.** $p = 51.5$ **15.** $p = 79.93$ **16.** $p = 98.88$

Evaluate the expression.

17. $a - 35$, for $a = 52$ **18.** $a + 7.9$, for $a = 5.2$ **19.** $72 - b$, for $b = 26$

20. $57 + b$, for $b = 64$ **21.** $45.2 - c$, for $c = 36.7$ **22.** $643 + c$, for $c = 597$

23. $65 - k$, for $k = 65$ **24.** $23.8 + k$, for $k = 0$ **25.** $d - 72$, for $d = 72$

26. $(5 + t) + 12$, for $t = 8$ **27.** $(t - 25) + 14$, for $t = 72$

28. $(2.6 + 5.9) + d$, for $d = 11.4$ **29.** $d - (7.8 + 6.5)$, for $d = 15.1$

30. $37 - (41 - f)$, for $f = 13.5$ **31.** $45 - (f + 12.2)$, for $f = 23.7$

32. $m + (2.45 + 5.73)$, for $m = 9.56$ **33.** $(m - 11.3) - 17.8$, for $m = 51.1$

Mixed Applications

Write and evaluate the algebraic expressions for Exercises 34–35.

34. A balcony ticket for a show costs $3.75 less than an orchestra ticket. How much does an orchestra ticket cost if a balcony ticket costs $14.25?

35. Isaac ran 37.6 meters farther than Drew in a contest to raise money for a charity. How far did Drew run if Isaac ran 463.5 meters?

36. Number Sense A number palindrome, such as 545, reads the same when you reverse the digits. You can often make a palindrome by adding a number and its reverse, such as $324 + 423 = 747$. Use 143 and 12,342 to make palindromes.

37. Logical Reasoning Tiffany, Deidre, Liza, Bette, and Lori are runners. Bette can outrun Liza and Tiffany, but Deidre can outrun Bette. Liza can outrun Lori, but Deidre can outrun Liza. Which one of the girls is the fastest runner?

If the value of the variable changes, will the value of the expression remain the same? Why?

WRAP UP...

EXPLORING

Addition and Subtraction Equations

WORK TOGETHER

Building Understanding

An **equation** is a number sentence. The equals sign shows that expressions on both sides represent the same number. Some equations contain algebraic expressions.

$$2 + 6 = 8 \qquad 8 = 17 - 9$$

$$n + 5 = 11 \qquad 8 = 12 - x$$

Think of an equation as a balanced scale. If you add the same number to both sides or subtract the same number from both sides, you can maintain the balance and solve the equation.

You can use a balance scale and counters to explore equations.

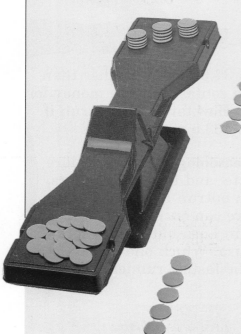

Talk About It

Look at the photo above.

► What is an expression that tells the number of counters on the left side of the scale? Use the variable c.

► How many counters are on the right side of the scale?

► Are the sides of the scale equal?

► What is an equation that tells the relationship between one side of the scale and the other?

Look at the photo to the left.

► How many counters were taken from each side?

► How many counters are now on the right side of the balanced scale?

► Since the scale has the same number of counters on each side, how many counters must be on the left side, or what is the value of c?

Making the Connection

By using a balance scale, you solved the equation $c + 5 = 20$ and found that $c = 15$.

1. What operation did you use to solve the equation and find the value of c?

2. What is the inverse of addition?

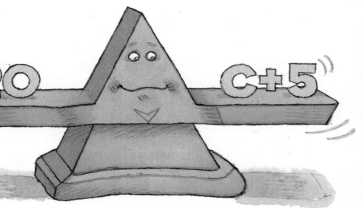

Suppose you were asked to solve the equation $c - 5 = 20$.

3. What is the inverse of subtraction?

4. What operation would you use to solve the equation?

5. How would you solve the equation and find the value of c?

Checking Understanding

Tell how to solve the equation.

6. $x + 7 = 21$

7. $y - 6 = 18$

8. $p + 26 = 47$

9. $1.5 + a = 7.75$

10. $t + 19 = 54$

11. $b - 5.25 = 14.75$

12. $c - 9.7 = 4.2$

13. $23.7 + d = 28$

14. $k + 31.8 = 51.8$

Use inverse operations. Solve the equations.

15. $x + 10 = 20$

16. $7 + b = 17$

17. $t - 5 = 20$

MIXED REVIEW

Find the sum or difference.

1. $\begin{array}{r} 8{,}394 \\ +\,2{,}493 \\ \hline \end{array}$

2. $\begin{array}{r} 98{,}763 \\ -\,97{,}873 \\ \hline \end{array}$

3. $\begin{array}{r} 75.364 \\ +\,75.463 \\ \hline \end{array}$

4. $\begin{array}{r} 325{,}433 \\ -\,245{,}349 \\ \hline \end{array}$

5. $\begin{array}{r} 75.335 \\ -\,33.965 \\ \hline \end{array}$

Write an algebraic expression for the word expression.

6. 11 more than a number b

7. 6 fewer than a number c

8. the sum of t and 3.7

9. y less than 6.2

Of the 25 hockey games the Redbirds played, they tied 3 games and won 2 more than they lost. How many games did the Redbirds win?

Guess and check is a good strategy to use when more than one condition must be met to find the solution.

► **UNDERSTAND**

What are you asked to find?

What information are you given?

► **PLAN**

What strategy will you choose?

Guess an answer that satisfies the first condition. Check to see if your answer satisfies the other conditions. If not, guess again.

► **SOLVE**

How will you carry out your plan?

Make a table to keep a record of your guesses and checks. Try to guess in an organized way so that each of your guesses comes closer and closer to the exact answer.

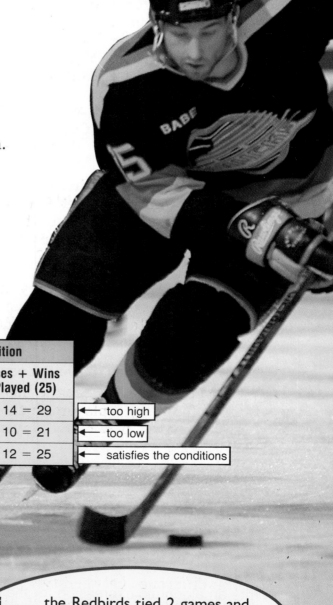

Given	Guess	Condition	Condition	
Games Tied	Games Lost	Games Lost + 2 = Games Won	Ties + Losses + Wins = Games Played (25)	
3	12	12 + 2 = 14	3 + 12 + 14 = 29	← too high
3	8	8 + 2 = 10	3 + 8 + 10 = 21	← too low
3	10	10 + 2 = 12	3 + 10 + 12 = 25	← satisfies the conditions

So, the Redbirds won 12 games.

► **LOOK BACK**

How does the table help you find the answer?

WHAT IF... ... the Redbirds tied 2 games and won 3 more than they lost? How many games did they lose?

58

Apply

Solve. Use the strategy *guess and check*.
Record your guesses and checks.

1. Of the 40 photographers and reporters attending a soccer game, there are 16 more photographers than reporters. How many reporters are there?

2. Mary and Bill collect baseball cards. Mary has 7 more cards than Bill. Together they have a total of 31 cards. How many baseball cards does Bill have?

Mixed Applications

STRATEGIES
- Guess and Check
- Find a Pattern
- Make and Use a Table
- Act It Out

Choose a strategy and solve.

3. Akim exercises 15 minutes in week one, 30 minutes in week two, and 45 minutes in week three. If this pattern continues, how long will Akim exercise in week six?

4. Of the 95 sixth graders and seventh graders going on a field trip, there are 27 more sixth graders than seventh graders. How many sixth graders are going on the trip?

5. A park has canoes that carry either 3 or 4 people. There are 5 canoes carrying a total of 17 people. How many four-person canoes are there?

6. Joyce runs 0.5 kilometer the first day. She adds 0.5 kilometer each day as she trains for a 10-kilometer race. On what day will Joyce run 10 kilometers?

7. Orange City Little League has 1 coach for every 9 players. If there are 8 coaches, how many players are there?

8. Chad has 11 coins in his pocket. He has only dimes and quarters. The sum of the coins is $2. How many quarters does Chad have?

9. A square garden decorates a stadium entrance. If 144 square yards of plastic covers the garden, what is the length of each side?

10. Janine walks 7 blocks south, 3 blocks east, 5 blocks north, and 8 blocks west. How many blocks has she walked when she crosses her own path?

11. The difference between two numbers is 37. Their sum is 215. What are the numbers?

12. The sum of Paco's and José's ages is 14. Paco is 2 years older than José. What are their ages?

More Practice, Lesson 2.12, page H41

CHAPTER REVIEW

Vocabulary Check

Choose a word from the box to complete each sentence.

algebraic
compensation
equation
evaluating
inverse
variable

1. When you use __?__, you change one addend to a multiple of ten and adjust the other addend by the same amount. *(page 34)*

2. Addition and subtraction are __?__ operations. *(page 34)*

3. A(n) __?__ expression contains a letter of the alphabet. The letter is called a __?__ and is used to represent a number. *(page 52)*

4. When you replace the variable with a number and perform the operation in an algebraic expression, you are __?__ the expression. *(page 54)*

5. In a(n) __?__, or number sentence, the equals sign shows that expressions on both sides represent the same number. *(page 56)*

Concept Check

6. How can you tell whether an estimated sum is an overestimate or an underestimate? *(page 36)*

7. Does the value change or remain the same if you add zeros to the right of a decimal? Explain. *(page 46)*

8. How can you check your answer to a subtraction problem? *(page 38)*

Write an algebraic expression for the word expression. *(page 52)*

9. four more than a number a

10. two fewer than a number c

11. a number n plus 15

12. 25 minus a number z

13. x less than 36

14. b more than 12

Tell what operation you would use to solve the equation. *(page 56)*

15. $h + 15 = 35$

16. $y - 25 = 15$

17. $b - 9 = 45$

18. $25 + b = 43$

Skill Check

Estimate the sum or difference. Then tell whether the sum is an overestimate or an underestimate. *(pages 36, 42)*

How I round determines my estimate.

19. $6.72 - 0.991$

20. $25.342 + 12.25$

21. $1.17 - 0.142$

22. $4.19 + 9.3$

23. $12.6 - 9.714$

24. $28.15 + 17.393$

Find the sum or difference. *(pages 34, 38, 46, 48)*

25. $18 + 12$

26. $12 + 16 + 14$

27. $35 - 17$

28. $56.34 - 38.76$

29. $745 - 259$

30. $811 - 622$

31. $8,140 + 9,205$

32. $8,771 - 2,846$

33. $3.9 + 6.78$

Write an algebraic expression for the word expression. *(page 52)*

34. 14 more than a number n

35. 1.6 less than a number c

Write a word expression for the algebraic expression. *(page 52)*

36. $10 - w$

37. $z + 1.7$

38. $d - 26$

Evaluate the expression. *(page 54)*

39. $n - 8$, for $n = 17$

40. $m + 12$, for $m = 9$

41. $2.1 - k$, for $k = 1.09$

42. $b + 9$, for $b = 7.5$

43. $y - 3.7$, for $y = 9.2$

44. $11.03 + n$, for $n = 9.19$

Problem-Solving Check *(pages 40, 58)*

45. The attendance at the state fair for four days was 168,254; 245,589; 214,520; and 179,065. What was the total attendance? What method of computation did you use?

46. Elsa gave the clerk $10.00 to pay for a package of apples that cost $2.95. How much change did Elsa receive? What method of computation did you use?

47. The sum of Sandy's and Trina's ages is 15. Trina is 3 years older than Sandy. What are Sandy's and Trina's ages?

48. The difference between two numbers is 38. The sum of the two numbers is 212. What are the numbers?

CHAPTER TEST

Estimate the sum or difference. Tell whether the sum is an underestimate or an overestimate.

Read the directions carefully.

1. $9,759 + 7,800$

2. $8.3 - 2.761$

3. $14.13 + 5.086$

4. $3.94 - 0.6$

5. $36.86 + 14.7$

6. $11.05 - 2.006$

Find the sum or difference.

7. $52 - 28$

8. $17 + 25 + 23$

9. $7.02 - 5.25$

10. $23.3 + 38.19$

11. $634 - 598$

12. $4,757 + 2,364$

Write an algebraic expression for the word expression.

13. 7 more than a number j

14. 1.2 less than a number e

15. a number k fewer than 12

16. a number t more than 35

Evaluate the expression.

17. $n - 5$, for $n = 11$

18. $m + 17$, for $m = 4$

19. $6 - k$, for $k = 1.27$

Solve.

20. The attendance at the last four football games was 18,277; 19,975; 22,107; and 16,964. What was the total attendance?

21. Shelly has 8 more football cards than Kirk. They have a total of 32 cards. How many football cards does Kirk have?

22. Amy works at a bakery. She just received a raise from $5.35 an hour to $6.00 an hour. How much was Amy's raise?

23. The difference between two numbers is 15. The sum of the two numbers is 155. What are the numbers?

24. What operation would you use to find the value of x in the equation $x - 4 = 10$?

25. What operation would you use to find the value of b in the equation $25 + b = 75$?

MENTAL-MATH STRATEGIES
for Multiplication

Lou used 13 packages of light bulbs to replace burned-out lights around a civic center. If each package contained 4 bulbs, how many bulbs did Lou use?

You can use mental math and the Distributive Property to make a simpler problem.

$$
\begin{aligned}
4 \times 13 &= 4 \times (10 + 3) \\
&= (4 \times 10) + (4 \times 3) \\
&= 40 + 12 \\
&= 52 \leftarrow \text{So, Lou used 52 bulbs.}
\end{aligned}
$$

You can also use mental math to solve multiplication problems by changing the order of factors or by grouping factors.

$$
\begin{aligned}
(2 \times 8) \times 5 &= (8 \times 2) \times 5 \leftarrow \text{Commutative} \\
&= 8 \times (2 \times 5) \leftarrow \text{Associative} \\
&= 8 \times 10 \\
&= 80
\end{aligned}
$$

Talk About It

▶ How can you use the Property of One and mental math to solve problems?

▶ How can you use the Zero Property and mental math to solve problems?

▶ Suppose Lou had used 28 packages of light bulbs. How could you find the total number of bulbs he used?

Check for Understanding

Use the properties of multiplication and mental math to find the product.

1. 3×42

2. $9 \times (8 - 8)$

3. $1 \times (6 \times 7)$

4. $(2 \times 9) \times 5$

Properties of Multiplication

Distributive Property

A factor can be thought of as the sum of addends. Each addend can be multiplied by the other factor without changing the product.

$$
\begin{aligned}
2 \times 37 &= 2 \times (30 + 7) \\
&= (2 \times 30) + (2 \times 7) \\
&= 60 + 14 \\
&= 74
\end{aligned}
$$

Commutative Property

Factors can be multiplied in any order without changing the product.

$$
\begin{aligned}
3 \times 4 &= 4 \times 3 \\
12 &= 12
\end{aligned}
$$

Associative Property

Factors can be grouped in any way without changing the product.

$$
\begin{aligned}
(6 \times 5) \times 3 &= 6 \times (5 \times 3) \\
30 \times 3 &= 6 \times 15 \\
90 &= 90
\end{aligned}
$$

Property of One

The product of any factor and 1 is the factor.

$$17 \times 1 = 17$$

Zero Property

The product of any factor and zero is zero.

$$99 \times 0 = 0$$

Practice

Write a number sentence that illustrates each property of multiplication.

5. Zero   **6.** Commutative   **7.** One   **8.** Associative   **9.** Distributive

Find the missing factor. Name the property used.

10. $26 \times 37 = \blacksquare \times 26$

11. $42 \times \blacksquare = 0$

12. $24 \times 31 = \blacksquare \times 24$

13. $16 \times 1 = \blacksquare$

14. $67 \times \blacksquare = 67$

15. $\blacksquare \times 6 = (4 \times 6) + (3 \times 6)$

16. $(3 \times 5) \times \blacksquare = 3 \times (5 \times 2)$

17. $1 \times 32 = \blacksquare$

18. $6 \times (4 \times 9) = (4 \times \blacksquare) \times 6$

19. $\blacksquare \times 13 = (6 \times 4) + (6 \times 9)$

20. $0 \times 25 = \blacksquare$

21. $48 \times 7 = (6 \times \blacksquare) \times 7$

Use mental math and the properties of multiplication to find the product.

22. $7 \times 2 \times 5$

23. $23 \times 3 \times 0$

24. 48×5

25. 35×4

26. $4 \times 25 \times 1$

27. 4×21

28. $3 \times 8 \times 5$

29. 13×9

30. $5 \times 4 \times 9$

31. 5×16

32. $22 \times 2 \times 0$

33. 28×8

34. 4×130

35. $3 \times 9 \times 10$

36. $11 \times 4 \times 2$

37. $12 \times 1 \times 12$

Mixed Applications

38. A flower shop has 5 vases on each of 3 shelves. Each vase holds 24 roses. What is the total number of roses on the shelves? Write a number sentence using one of the properties of multiplication. Then solve.

39. **Logical Reasoning** Dea will multiply several different numbers by 12. Next, she will divide each product by 2 twice and then by 3. What will the results be?

40. **Number Sense ● Estimation** Kyle made 3 trips to recycling centers. He took 383 cans, 521 cans, and 415 cans. About how many cans did Kyle take to the recycling centers?

How can you use the properties to multiply 9×510?

ESTIMATING PRODUCTS

The civic theater group is performing at a local theater. The theater has 48 rows of 28 seats each. About how many programs should be printed for the performance?

- Are you asked to find an exact answer or an estimate? How do you know?

One way to estimate a product is to round each factor.

Round and multiply.

$$\begin{array}{r} 48 \rightarrow 50 \\ \times 28 \rightarrow \times 30 \\ \hline 1{,}500 \end{array}$$

Sometimes you may need to know whether your estimate is an overestimate or an underestimate.

Both rounded factors are greater than the exact factors. So, 1,500 is an overestimate.

- Why might you want to overestimate the number of programs to print?

So, about 1,500 programs should be printed.

More Examples

Estimate.

$$\begin{array}{r} 104 \rightarrow 100 \\ \times 34 \rightarrow \times 30 \\ \hline 3{,}000 \end{array}$$

Both rounded factors are less than the exact factors. So, 3,000 is an underestimate.

$$\begin{array}{r} 1{,}975 \rightarrow 2{,}000 \\ \times 423 \rightarrow \times 400 \\ \hline 800{,}000 \end{array}$$

One rounded factor is greater than the exact factor, and one is less. You cannot tell whether 800,000 is an overestimate or an underestimate.

- Name a situation in which you might want to overestimate a product.

Check for Understanding

Estimate the product. Tell whether your estimate is an overestimate or an underestimate.

1. 345×6 **2.** 68×49 **3.** 495×275 **4.** $5{,}396 \times 422$ **5.** $9{,}164 \times 523$

Practice

Choose the best estimate. Write **a, b,** or **c.**

6. 375×185	**a.** 40,000	**b.** 100,000	**c.** 80,000
7. 536×54	**a.** 40,000	**b.** 20,000	**c.** 25,000
8. $2,654 \times 7$	**a.** 30,000	**b.** 14,000	**c.** 21,000
9. $5,560 \times 239$	**a.** 1,200,000	**b.** 1,000,000	**c.** 1,800,000
10. $1,850 \times 46$	**a.** 50,000	**b.** 100,000	**c.** 800,000

Estimate the product.

11.	**12.**	**13.**	**14.**	**15.**
$\begin{array}{r} 53 \\ \times\ 7 \\ \hline \end{array}$	$\begin{array}{r} 78 \\ \times\ 5 \\ \hline \end{array}$	$\begin{array}{r} \$21 \\ \times\ 9 \\ \hline \end{array}$	$\begin{array}{r} 189 \\ \times\ 6 \\ \hline \end{array}$	$\begin{array}{r} 232 \\ \times\ 4 \\ \hline \end{array}$

16.	**17.**	**18.**	**19.**	**20.**
$\begin{array}{r} 459 \\ \times\ 9 \\ \hline \end{array}$	$\begin{array}{r} 7,951 \\ \times\ 3 \\ \hline \end{array}$	$\begin{array}{r} 78 \\ \times 87 \\ \hline \end{array}$	$\begin{array}{r} 542 \\ \times\ 41 \\ \hline \end{array}$	$\begin{array}{r} 873 \\ \times 429 \\ \hline \end{array}$

Estimate to compare. Use < or >.

21. $32 \times 21 \ \bullet \ 600$ **22.** $47 \times 39 \ \bullet \ 2,000$ **23.** $9 \times 17 \ \bullet \ 200$

24. $123 \times 62 \ \bullet \ 6,000$ **25.** $50 \times 38 \ \bullet \ 2,000$ **26.** $246 \times 41 \ \bullet \ 8,000$

Mixed Applications

27. A group of 22 students has tickets to 7 performances by an ethnic dance company. About how many tickets do the students have in all?

28. A theater was filled to capacity for 627 shows. The theater holds 2,398 people. About how many people attended the shows?

29. A total of 7 buses will be driven to a football game. Each bus holds 42 students. About how many students can ride the buses to the game?

30. Each of 8 vendors has an umbrella. Each umbrella has 9 spokes. Attached to each spoke are 4 dolls. About how many dolls are there?

31. Making Choices Tonisha has a list of groceries to buy within her budget. Should she overestimate or underestimate the cost? Explain.

32. Write a Question A small-town college has an enrollment of 1,342 students. A city college has an enrollment of 12,078 students.

Why would you want to know whether an estimate is an underestimate or an overestimate?

MULTIPLYING
by Two- and Three-Digit Numbers

Baker Stadium, which holds 1,952 people, was filled to capacity for 23 games. What is the total number of people who attended the games?

Estimate. $1,952 \times 23 \longrightarrow 2,000 \times 20 = 40,000$

$1,952 \times 23 \approx 40,000$

Multiply.

Step 1	Step 2	Step 3
Multiply by the ones.	Multiply by the tens.	Add the partial products.
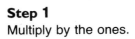	1 1	
1,952	1,952	1,952
× 23	× 23	× 23
5 856 ← 3 × 1,952	5 856	5 856
	39 040 ← 20 × 1,952	39 04
	You may omit the zero placeholder.	44,896

Since 44,896 is close to the estimate of 40,000, the answer is reasonable.

So, the total number of people who attended the games is 44,896.

Another Example $3,823 \times 408$

Estimate. $4,000 \times 400 = 1,600,000$

Multiply.
$$
\begin{array}{r}
3,823 \\
\times \quad 408 \\
\hline
30\ 584 \leftarrow 8 \times 3,823 \\
1\ 529\ 2 \leftarrow 400 \times 3,823 \\
\hline
1,559,784
\end{array}
$$

- Why are there two partial products for 408?

Check for Understanding

Find the product.

1. 42	2. 96	3. 1,637	4. 2,586	5. 23,556	6. 15,025
×17	×24	× 34	× 41	× 270	× 136

Practice

Estimate the product. If your estimate is greater than 200,000, use a calculator to find the exact answer.

7. 859
   × 34

8. 3,813
   × 508

9. 511
   × 16

10. 4,763
    × 20

11. 4,887
    × 75

12. 6,502 × 507   13. 683 × 75   14. 3,873 × 48   15. 178 × 498

Find the product.

16. 67
    × 23

17. 67
    × 85

18. 1,723
    × 44

19. 2,246
    × 906

20. 35,631
    × 74

21. 432
    × 336

22. 4,375
    × 697

23. 3,421
    × 56

24. 65,322
    × 635

25. 153,543
    × 732

Mixed Applications

26. Mary likes to exercise at a health club. She does 35 sit-ups in each workout. How many sit-ups will Mary do in 135 workouts? 4725

27. Inez manages 112 apartments. Each rents for $485 a month. If they were all leased in May, how much rent did Inez collect?

28. **Number Sense • Mental Math** There are 24 hours in a day. How many hours are in a 7-day week? 168

29. **Make Up a Problem** Write a problem about city life that must be solved by adding 4 three-digit numbers.

SCIENCE CONNECTION

At the science museum, Elise learned that light travels about 299,793 kilometers per second through space and about 225,408 kilometers per second through water.

30. About how far does light travel through space in 100 seconds? through water in 10 seconds?

31. About how much faster does light travel through space than it travels through water?

Are the number of partial products always the same as the number of digits being multiplied? Explain.

WRAP UP...

Don wants a bicycle to ride to and from school. The bicycle costs $290. Don has saved $225. He earns $40 a week working at a supermarket. He has three options.

Option 1: Don can save until he has $290 to buy the bicycle.

Option 2: Don can pay $90 down and $19 a month for a year.

Option 3: Don can pay nothing down and $28 a month for a year.

Which option should Don choose?

Sometimes solving a problem involves making a decision based on the situation.

▶ **UNDERSTAND**

What are you asked to find?

What information are you given?

▶ **PLAN**

How will you solve the problem?

You need to find the total amount Don would pay with each option and to compare the advantages and disadvantages.

▶ **SOLVE**

How will you carry out your plan?

Find the total amount Don would pay with each option. Consider the following:

A. With which option would Don spend the least?

B. With which options would Don get the bicycle right away?

C. Does Don make enough money to afford each option?

D. Would Don's monthly payment be smaller with Option 2 or with Option 3?

- If you were Don, which option would you choose? Why?

▶ **LOOK BACK**

Do your reasons make sense considering Don's situation? Explain.

WHAT IF... ... you wanted to buy a bicycle? What options would you consider?

Apply

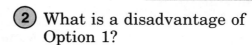

Yoko wants to buy a home video system that costs $250. She has $225 in a savings account. She earns $35 a week. Yoko considers these options.

Option 1: Continue to save until she can pay for the system in full

Option 2: Pay $65 down and $20 per month for 12 months

Option 3: Pay nothing down and $26 per month for 12 months

1 How much will the video system cost using Option 3?

2 What is a disadvantage of Option 1?

3 Which option will Yoko choose if she wants to keep all the money in her savings account?

4 Which option will Yoko choose if she wants to pay the lesser amount of money each month?

5 What is a reason for Yoko to choose Option 2?

6 What is a reason for Yoko to choose Option 1?

Mixed Applications

STRATEGIES • Guess and Check • Find a Pattern • Write a Number Sentence • Draw a Diagram

Choose a strategy and solve.

7 Joel withdrew $13 the first week, $16 the second, $20 the third, $25 the fourth, and $31 the fifth. If this pattern continues, how much will he withdraw the seventh week?

8 Sol and Sergio own a total of 59 books. Sergio owns 11 more books than Sol. How many books does Sergio own?

9 Jean has 3 times as many pens as Joan. If Joan has 5 blue pens and 2 red pens, how many pens does Jean have?

10 April is making a number puzzle. The first five numbers are 2, 6, 18, 54, and 162. If the pattern continues, what is the next number?

11 Rae has 72 inches of ribbon to wrap around a package that is 11 inches around. If she wraps the package 4 times, how much ribbon will she have left?

12 It takes Rich 5 minutes to take out the garbage, 2 times that long to vacuum, and 3 times as long to dust as to vacuum. How long does it take Rich to do all three chores?

WRITER'S CORNER

13 Use the options for Exercises 1–6. Write a paragraph telling which option you would choose. State your reasons.

ESTIMATING DECIMAL PRODUCTS

You can estimate decimal products in the same way you estimate whole-number products. Estimate decimal products when an exact answer is not needed or to determine the reasonableness of an answer.

Una earns $4.52 an hour at a local radio station. About how much does she earn for working 37.5 hours?

Estimate. $4.52 × 37.5

> Round $4.52 to the nearest dollar. Round 37.5 to the nearest ten.

$$\$5 \times 40 = \$200$$

So, Una earns about $200.00.

Una estimates she earns about $100 for working 19.5 hours. Using a calculator, she finds that her exact earnings are $881.40.

- Is Una's estimate reasonable?
- Is Una's calculation reasonable?
- What mistake did Una make?

You can also use estimation to place the decimal point in a product.

A hit song is 3.42 minutes long. If a radio station plays the song 8 times in one day, how many total minutes is the song on the air?

Estimate to place the decimal in the product.

$$
\begin{array}{cc}
3.42 & 3 \\
\times\ 8 & \times\ 8 \\
\hline
2736 & 24 \\
\end{array}
$$

Since the estimate is 24, place the decimal point after the 7.

So, the song is on the air for 27.36 minutes.

Check for Understanding

Choose the best estimate. Write **a, b,** or **c**.

1. 12.6 × 45   a. 690   b. 500   c. 400

2. $119.56 × 38   a. $4,000   b. $8,000   c. $3,000

3. 91.06 × 7.3   a. 9,000   b. 450   c. 630

Use estimation to place the decimal point in the product.

4. 6.19 × 75 = 46425   5. 435.7 × 8.9 = 387773   6. 14 × 2.713 = 37982

Practice

Estimate. Choose the correct product. Write **a, b,** or **c.**

7. 178 × 4.89
   a. 870.42
   b. 87.042
   c. 8.7042

8. 7.925 × 234
   a. 18,544.500
   b. 1,854.450
   c. 185.445

9. 83.7 × 19
   a. 159.03
   b. 15.903
   c. 1,590.3

10. 2.273 × 3.6
   a. 0.8182
   b. 8.1828
   c. 81.828

Estimate the product.

11. 5.23 × 9

12. 72.9 × 8.5

13. 1.3 × 6.4

14. 2.3 × 98.4

15. 38.7 × 1.7

16. 7.05 × 6.8

17. 51.2 × 0.9

18. 27.2 × 12.1

Mixed Applications

Solve. Use the table for Exercises 19–20.

19. Leroy bought 2.5 yards of cotton and 5.75 yards of corduroy. About how much did he spend?

20. If Karen bought 6 yards of acetate and Barbara bought 3.5 yards of cotton, who spent more money?

Fabrics on Sale	
Fabric	Price per Yard
Corduroy	$3.29
Cotton	$1.97
Polyester	$3.98
Acetate	$4.98

21. **Number Sense ● Mental Math** The pep club sells balloons for $2.00 each. If members have sold a total of 150 balloons, what is the total amount of their sales?

22. **Number Sense ● Estimation** Frank calculates that if nails cost $1.09 a pound, 4.25 pounds will cost $4.63. Is Frank's calculation reasonable? Explain.

PATTERNS AND RELATIONSHIPS

Look at the patterns of zeros.

4 × 6	= 24	3.51 × 10	= 35.1
40 × 6	= 240	3.51 × 100	= 351
40 × 60	= 2,400	3.51 × 1,000	= 3,510
400 × 60	= 24,000	3.51 × 10,000	= 35,100
400 × 600	= 240,000	3.51 × 100,000	= 351,000

23. How does the number of zeros in the whole-number factors compare with the number of zeros in the product?

24. State a rule for multiplying by multiples of 10.

25. State a rule for multiplying decimals by powers of 10.

How does estimating help you place the decimal point in the product?

WRAP UP...

1. John and Sue run a total of 21 miles every morning. Sue runs 3 more miles than John. How many miles does each run?

When you *guess and check,* record your guesses.

2. Sara is 6 years younger than Richard. Sara and Richard have a combined age of 18. Bob and Sara have a combined age of 14. How old are Sara, Bob, and Richard?

Use the situation in the box for Exercises 3–4.

3. Which option would cost Lee the least amount of money?

4. How much more money would Lee pay for the microwave if he chose Option C instead of Option B?

> Lee earns $5 a week. He has saved $155. He wants to buy a microwave that costs $180. He can (a) save until he has $180, (b) pay $75 down and $15 a month for 12 months, or (c) pay $25 a month for 12 months.

Find the sum or difference.

5. $9.201 + 76.8$

6. $42.93 - 0.861$

7. $24.9 + 89.075$

8. $91.37 - 6.798$

9. $\begin{array}{r} \$21.25 \\ 52.86 \\ +\ \ 0.04 \\ \hline \end{array}$

10. $\begin{array}{r} 9.768 \\ -5.332 \\ \hline \end{array}$

11. $\begin{array}{r} 2.32 \\ 69.1 \\ +\ 0.33 \\ \hline \end{array}$

12. $\begin{array}{r} 2,541.6 \\ 913.81 \\ +\ \ 692.34 \\ \hline \end{array}$

Write an algebraic expression for the word expression.

13. 2 more than a number b

14. 30 less than an amount p

15. k fewer than 210

Tell what operation to use to solve the equation.

16. $x + 2 = 25$

17. $y - 8 = 10$

18. $b - 4.5 = 12.8$

19. $68.4 + c = 93$

Estimate the product. Tell whether the estimate is an overestimate or an underestimate.

20. 63×112

21. $1,937 \times 791$

22. 42.1×2.4

23. 99.7×17.82

Find the product.

24. $\begin{array}{r} 61 \\ \times 18 \\ \hline \end{array}$

25. $\begin{array}{r} 1,563 \\ \times\ \ \ \ 67 \\ \hline \end{array}$

26. $\begin{array}{r} 852 \\ \times 353 \\ \hline \end{array}$

27. $\begin{array}{r} 46,924 \\ \times\ \ \ \ \ 812 \\ \hline \end{array}$

Spotlight ON

PROBLEM SOLVING

Understand
Plan
Solve
Look Back

Consider All Possibilities

Some problems may be solved by reading the information provided, considering the possible responses, and eliminating the responses that do not work.

Dot, Skip, Sam, and Joyce ran in the Jogtown 10-kilometer (km) race. Dot's best time for 10 km is 39 minutes (min). Skip predicted he would run the race in about 42 min. Sam expected to run the race in 45 to 48 min. Last year Joyce ran the race in 47 min 10 seconds (sec). This year Dot's time was 1 min more than her best 10-km time. Joyce ran the race in 1 min 45 sec less than she did last year. Sam's time for the race was greater than he had expected. Skip's prediction was accurate.

Talk About It

Work together to determine whether the results below are possible or impossible.

A. Dot ran the race in 40 min.

B. Joyce's time was 48 min 55 sec.

C. Sam's time was between 48 min 1 sec and 50 min.

D. Sam's time was less than Joyce's time.

E. Dot averaged better than $4\frac{1}{2}$ min per km.

F. Dot won the race.

Apply

Indicate which of the results are possible. Be prepared to defend your responses.

1. **Dot beat Sam by at least 5 min.**
2. **Skip ran the race in 43 min.**
3. **Joyce may have beaten Sam by as much as 3 min.**
4. **All runners finished the race in 50 min or less.**

79

Di is a meteorologist. She will buy sandwiches for $2.95, $3.00, $2.75, and $3.25 from a vending machine at the television station where she works. About how much money does she need?

Step 1	Step 2
Round to the nearest dollar.	The addends cluster around the same rounded dollar amount. Multiply it by the number of addends.
$2.95 → $3.00 $3.00 → $3.00 $2.75 → $3.00 $3.25 → $3.00	$4 \times \$3.00 = \$12.00$ $\$2.95 + \$3.00 + \$2.75 + \$3.25 \approx \$12.00$

So, Di needs about $12.00 to pay for the sandwiches.

- Why is multiplying more useful than adding to estimate the sum of a large number of addends that cluster around the same rounded number?

Another Example

Di made this table to show the average monthly rainfall in Albany, New York. About how much is the total rainfall in Albany in a year?

Jan.	Feb.	Mar.	Apr.	May	June	July	Aug.	Sept.	Oct.	Nov.	Dec.
2.4	2.3	3.0	2.9	3.3	3.3	3.0	3.3	3.2	2.9	3.0	3.0

2.4 + 2.3 + 3.0 + 2.9 + 3.3 + 3.3 + 3.0 + 3.3 + 3.2 + 2.9 + 3.0 + 3.0

$2 \times 2 = 4$ $10 \times 3 = 30$

$4 + 30 = 34$

So, the rainfall in Albany is about 34 inches a year.

Check for Understanding

Use mental math and multiplication to estimate the sum.

1.	0.66 0.79 +1.15	2.	5.21 4.95 +5.45	3.	29.51 27.48 +28.00	4.	9.54 9.78 +9.98	5.	2,450 1,544 2,333 +1,872

Practice

Use mental math and multiplication to estimate the sum.

6.	7.	8.	9.	10.
200	775	5,923	27,032	43,002
185	798	6,221	26,898	42,756
213	802	6,313	24,772	43,135
+221	+787	+6,400	+27,125	+42,999

11.	12.	13.	14.	15.
$2.35	9.07	0.9	87.333	62.005
2.15	9.2	1.02	87.002	61.9
1.98	8.7	0.8	86.701	62.1
1.75	8.821	0.76	87.114	62.355
+ 2.00	+8.88	+1.17	+87.101	+61.8882

16.	17.	18.	19.	20.
0.009	7.2	492	21,823	700,234
0.01	6.3	405	19,934	697,782
0.011	6.2	395	21,009	175
+0.008	+6.1	+501	+19,073	+709,145

Mixed Applications

21. Tyrone is a courier. The list below shows his earnings for six months. About how much did Tyrone earn in this time period?

Jan. $1,895.45	Apr. $1,901.67
Feb. $1,793.33	May $2,113.75
Mar. $2,045.45	June $1,754.91

22. Leslee gives dance lessons at a studio. Her daily schedule is listed below. About how many hours does Leslee teach in one week?

Mon. 3:30 to 7	Thurs. 4 to 8
Tues. 4 to 8:15	Fri. 2 to 6
Wed. 3:30 to 7:30	Sat. 1 to 5

MIXED REVIEW

Find the product. Round money amounts to the nearest cent.

1. 7×192

2. $9,125 \times 611$

3. $\$3.77 \times 8$

4. 76.3×3.67

5.	6.	7.	8.	9.
1,009	56,521	$462.55	22.5	3.72
× 599	× 0.9	× 12.15	× 0.033	×1.005

Evaluate the expression.

10. $95 + b$, for $b = 39$

11. $k - 13.3$, for $k = 24.1$

12. $2 + (x - 8)$, for $x = 32$

How is clustering similar to rounding?

WRAP UP...

MULTIPLYING DECIMALS

Mac adds 16.3 ounces of tint to a gallon of paint. How much tint will Mac need for 132.5 gallons of paint?

Step 1 Choose compatible numbers. Estimate the product.	**Step 2** Multiply.	**Step 3** Use the estimate to place the decimal point.
132.5×16.3 $\downarrow \qquad \downarrow$ $100 \quad \times 20 = 2,000$	$\begin{array}{r} 132.5 \\ \times \quad 16.3 \\ \hline 397\,5 \\ 7950 \\ 1325 \\ \hline 21597\,5 \end{array}$	$132.5 \times 16.3 \approx 2,000$ The estimate is in the thousands, so place the decimal after the 9. $132.5 \times 16.3 = 2,159.75$

So, Mac will need 2,159.75 ounces of tint.

More Examples

A. 81×7.23

Estimate. $80 \times 7 = 560$
Multiply.
Use paper and pencil.

$$\begin{array}{r} 7.23 \\ \times \quad 81 \\ \hline 7\,23 \\ 578\,4 \\ \hline 585\,63 \end{array} \longrightarrow 585.63$$

B. $7.9 \times \$2.35$

Estimate. $8 \times \$2 = \$16$
Multiply.
Use a calculator.

7.9 ☓ 2.35 ＝ [18.565]

$= \$18.57$
↑
Round money amounts to the nearest cent.

- Look at the decimal places in the factors and the product in Example **A** and in the example at the top of the page. State a rule for placing the decimal point in the product when multiplying decimals.

Check for Understanding

Tell how many decimal places will be in the product. Find the product.

1. $\begin{array}{r} 24.82 \\ \times \quad 5.6 \end{array}$	**2.** $\begin{array}{r} 288.7 \\ \times \quad 0.52 \end{array}$	**3.** $\begin{array}{r} 1.42 \\ \times 0.74 \end{array}$	**4.** $\begin{array}{r} 64.32 \\ \times \quad 20.5 \end{array}$	**5.** $\begin{array}{r} 18.88 \\ \times \quad 1.75 \end{array}$

Practice

Estimate to place the decimal point in the product.

6. $5.7 \times 2.4 = 1368$

7. $1.57 \times 5.5 = 8635$

8. $5.656 \times 8.8 = 497728$

9. $0.44 \times 2.6 = 1144$

10. $0.58 \times 0.89 = 05162$

11. $2.981 \times 0.2 = 05962$

12.
$$\begin{array}{r} 20.74 \\ \times\ \ \ 4.4 \\ \hline 91256 \end{array}$$

13.
$$\begin{array}{r} 78 \\ \times 4.6 \\ \hline 3588 \end{array}$$

14.
$$\begin{array}{r} 1.564 \\ \times\ \ \ 0.9 \\ \hline 14076 \end{array}$$

15.
$$\begin{array}{r} 9.67 \\ \times 54.2 \\ \hline 524114 \end{array}$$

16.
$$\begin{array}{r} 45.2 \\ \times\ 165 \\ \hline 74580 \end{array}$$

Find the product. Round money amounts to the nearest cent.

17.
$$\begin{array}{r} 5.8 \\ \times 2.5 \\ \hline \end{array}$$

18.
$$\begin{array}{r} 3.456 \\ \times\ \ \ 4.1 \\ \hline \end{array}$$

19.
$$\begin{array}{r} 345.6 \\ \times\ \ \ 4.1 \\ \hline \end{array}$$

20.
$$\begin{array}{r} \$14.85 \\ \times\ \ \ \ \ 8.5 \\ \hline \end{array}$$

21.
$$\begin{array}{r} 43.6 \\ \times 0.09 \\ \hline \end{array}$$

22.
$$\begin{array}{r} 58.87 \\ \times\ \ \ 38 \\ \hline \end{array}$$

23.
$$\begin{array}{r} \$13.87 \\ \times\ \ \ \ 0.7 \\ \hline \end{array}$$

24.
$$\begin{array}{r} \$763.08 \\ \times\ \ \ \ \ 6.06 \\ \hline \end{array}$$

25.
$$\begin{array}{r} \$543.99 \\ \times\ \ \ \ \ 0.5 \\ \hline \end{array}$$

26.
$$\begin{array}{r} 0.98 \\ \times 0.4 \\ \hline \end{array}$$

27. 14.8×64

28. $\$127.10 \times 4.9$

29. 842.7×1.82

30. 6.49×73

31. 52.33×6.7

32. 0.75×0.25

33. $8{,}392 \times 5.005$

34. 1.5×0.005

Mixed Applications

35. Joe buys ground beef for $1.78 a pound. To the nearest cent, how much will he pay for 3.8 pounds of ground beef?

36. Sam uses 1.5 pounds of cold cuts to make a 6-foot sub. If he makes 2.5, or $2\frac{1}{2}$, subs, how many pounds of cold cuts will he use?

37. Analyze Data The deli charges $1.32 for a sandwich and $0.85 for a salad. If Mel spent $5.66, how many sandwiches and salads did he buy?

38. Number Sense ● Estimation Rachael bought 3.2 pounds of pears at $1.89 a pound, 1.9 pounds of plums at $0.99 a pound, and 2.7 pounds of apples at $1.76 a pound. About how much did Rachael spend for fruit?

What two methods can you use to place the decimal point in the product?

ZEROS IN THE PRODUCT

Students touring a power plant learned that operating a television costs $0.037 an hour. How much does operating a television for 0.75, or $\frac{3}{4}$ hour cost?

- Will your answer be more than or less than $0.037? Explain.

Remember: The number of decimal places in the product equals the sum of the decimal places in the factors.

Step 1	Step 2
Multiply as with whole numbers.	Place the decimal point. Write a zero to hold the correct number of places. Place the dollar sign.

Step 1

$$\begin{array}{r} \$0.037 \\ \times\quad 0.75 \\ \hline 185 \\ 259 \\ \hline 2775 \end{array}$$

Step 2

$$\begin{array}{r} \$0.037 \leftarrow \text{3 decimal places} \\ \times\quad 0.75 \leftarrow \text{2 decimal places} \\ \hline 185 \\ 259 \\ \hline \$0.02775 \leftarrow \text{5 decimal places} \end{array}$$

So, the cost of operating a television for 0.75 hour is $0.02775. To the nearest cent, the cost is $0.03.

Another Example

$$\begin{array}{r} 0.0025 \leftarrow \text{4 decimal places} \\ \times\qquad 8 \leftarrow \text{0 decimal places} \\ \hline 0.0200 \leftarrow \text{4 decimal places} \end{array}$$

- Which zeros are holding places in the product?

Check for Understanding

Choose the correct product. Write **a**, **b**, or **c**.

1. 4.8×0.06 **a.** 0.0288   **b.** 0.288   **c.** 0.00288

2. 0.08×453 **a.** 0.03624   **b.** 0.3624   **c.** 36.24

Find the product.

3. $\begin{array}{r} \$2.40 \\ \times\quad 0.2 \\ \hline \end{array}$ 4. $\begin{array}{r} 0.03 \\ \times\quad 0.8 \\ \hline \end{array}$ 5. $\begin{array}{r} 0.0056 \\ \times\quad 4.2 \\ \hline \end{array}$ 6. $\begin{array}{r} 0.056 \\ \times\quad 100 \\ \hline \end{array}$ 7. $\begin{array}{r} \$5.04 \\ \times\quad 305 \\ \hline \end{array}$

Practice

Place the decimal point in the product.
Write zeros where necessary.

8. 0.03
    × 5.8
    ―――
    174

9. 0.002
    × 43.6
    ―――
    872

10. 0.037
    × 4.8
    ―――
    1776

11. 1.84
    × 0.5
    ―――
    92

12. 0.0007
    × 36
    ―――
    252

Find the product.

13. 0.038
    × 8
    ―――

14. 54.88
    × 30.7
    ―――

15. 0.08
    × 9
    ―――

16. 25.68
    × 0.04
    ―――

17. 0.98
    × 702
    ―――

18. 0.032
    × 0.4
    ―――

19. 0.0036
    × 587
    ―――

20. 7.5
    × 0.6
    ―――

21. 0.43
    × 2.08
    ―――

22. 0.003
    × 59.8
    ―――

23. 4.6×100

24. 0.031×10

25. $0.0097 \times 1,000$

26. 0.654×100

27. $16.9 \times 1,000$

28. 276.4×10

Mixed Applications

29. Perfume comes in sample packages of 0.025 ounce. What is the total amount of perfume in a box of 24 sample packages?

30. **Number Sense** Nutritionists say we need 0.0017 gram of riboflavin every day. How much do we need in a week?

MIXED REVIEW

Estimate the sum or difference.

1. $12.76 - 8.25$

2. $49.01 - 14.67$

3. $9.18 - 0.97$

4. $10.341 + 0.882$

Estimate. If your estimate is greater than 100,000, find the exact answer.

5. 17×14

6. 21×52

7. 3.7×209

8. $\$5.25 \times 476$

9. 236×722

When do you place zeros in the product?

PROBLEM *Solving*

Thirty students at Brook Middle School held a car wash to raise money for a trip to Los Angeles. They charged $1.95 for each car. They washed 93 cars on Saturday and 65 cars on Sunday. How much money did they earn for the trip?

When there is a main question and a hidden question, you may need two or more operations to solve the problem.

▶ **UNDERSTAND**

What are you asked to find?

What information are you given?

▶ **PLAN**

How will you solve the problem?
You need to multiply the total number of cars washed by $1.95.

To do this, you must first answer the hidden question: What was the total number of cars washed?

▶ **SOLVE**

How will you carry out your plan?
First, add to find the total number of cars washed.

93 ⊞ 65 ⊟ | 158. | M+

The students washed 158 cars.

Then, multiply to find the amount of money earned.

1.95 ⊠ MRC ⊟ | M 308.1 |

So, the students earned $308.10.

▶ **LOOK BACK**

How can you check your solution by solving the problem in a different way?

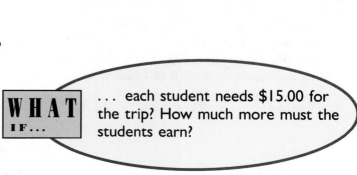

WHAT **IF...** ... each student needs $15.00 for the trip? How much more must the students earn?

Apply

Melissa plans to hang a shelf in her room. She finds a kit with all the parts for $15.25. The prices of the separate parts are $7.50 for the wood, $4.80 for the brackets, and $1.75 for the screws.

(1) Which is less expensive, the kit or the separate shelf parts?

(2) What is the difference in price between the kit and the separate shelf parts?

Mixed Applications ▶ **STRATEGIES** • Write a Number Sentence • Find a Pattern • Draw a Picture • Make a Table

Choose a strategy and solve.

(3) Francine is making a cabinet for a shop project. She buys 3 boards at $1.75 each and 4 hinges at $0.99 each. What is the total cost of the supplies?

(4) Leon runs 2 miles the first week, 3 miles the second, 5 miles the third, and 8 miles the fourth. If he continues this pattern, when will he run 23 miles?

(5) Teo scored 98 on a math test. On the next test, he scored 16 fewer points. On a third test, he scored 92. What is the difference between Teo's highest and lowest scores?

(6) Carol bought 2.3 pounds of bananas at $0.47 a pound and 3.4 pounds of grapes at $0.89 a pound. How much more money did Carol spend for grapes than she spent for bananas?

(7) Mr. Soni and his family consume 3 pounds of potatoes each day. If Mr. Soni buys a 50-pound sack of potatoes, how many days will it take the family to consume 24 pounds of the potatoes?

(8) A taxicab travels 5 miles west, 2 miles south, 1 mile west, 4 miles north, 8 miles east, 1 mile south, and then 10 miles west. How far has the taxicab traveled when it crosses its own path?

(9) Lin sold 43 pairs of shoes. Frances sold twice as many as Lin. How many pairs of shoes did they sell?

(10) Mrs. Schultz bought bread for $0.98, eggs for $1.17, ground turkey for $3.18, and carrots for $0.55. She gave the clerk $10.03. How much change should Mrs. Shultz receive?

Vocabulary Check

Choose a word from the box to complete each sentence.

| Associative |
| Distributive |
| overestimate |
| underestimate |
| zero |

1. If you rewrite the multiplication problem 24×7 as $(20 \times 7) + (4 \times 7)$, you are using the __?__ Property of Multiplication. *(page 68)*

2. An answer will be an __?__ if both rounded factors are less than the exact factors. *(page 70)*

3. The product of any number and zero is __?__ . *(page 68)*

4. The __?__ Property of Multiplication states that factors can be grouped in any way without changing the product. *(page 68)*

5. An answer will be an __?__ if both rounded factors are greater than the exact factors. *(page 70)*

Concept Check

6. Will you always be able to determine whether an estimate is an overestimate or an underestimate? Explain. *(page 70)*

7. How can you use estimation to place the decimal point in a product? *(page 76)*

8. Why is it sometimes necessary to add zeros to decimal products? *(page 84)*

9. How can you estimate the sum of several addends that cluster around the same number? *(page 80)*

10. State a rule for multiplying by multiples of 10. *(page 77)*

11. State a rule for multiplying decimals by powers of 10. *(page 77)*

> To answer Exercise 6, think about the rounded factor in relation to the exact factor.

Place the decimal point in the product. Write zeros where necessary. *(pages 82, 84)*

12. $2.11 \times \$62.53 = \$13194$

13. $16.079 \times 0.53 = 852187$

14. $0.23 \times 0.06 = 138$

15. $4.25 \times 0.003 = 1275$

Skill Check

Estimate the product. *(pages 70, 76)*

16. 62
$\times$ 18

17. 6,324
$\times$ 430

18. 60.09
$\times$ 1.18

19. 273.65
$\times$ 46.89

Use mental math and multiplication to estimate the sum. *(page 80)*

20. 795
812
834
783
+779

21. 26,091
26,234
25,957
+25,684

22. 0.008
0.013
0.01
+0.007

23. 42.32
41.98
41.18
+41.86

Find the product. *(pages 72, 82, 84)*

24. 26
$\times$ 54

25. 2,913
$\times$ 62

26. 864
$\times$ 795

27. 169,846
$\times$ 392

28. 6.7
$\times$ 2.8

29. $41.80
$\times$ 7.1

30. 914.03
$\times$ 5.06

31. 1.82
$\times$ 0.006

32. 824
$\times$ 309

33. 3,089
$\times$ 725

34. 4.06
$\times$ 7.33

35. 61.8
$\times$ 0.09

Problem-Solving Check

Use the information in the box for Exercises 36–37. *(pages 74, 86)*

> Ramon wants to buy a garage-door opener. He has these options.
> Option A: $149.99 for the opener
> $78.50 for installation
> Option B: $170.99 for the opener
> no installation service
> Option C: $199.99 for the opener
> $25.00 for installation

36. Which option is the least expensive if Ramon must have the garage-door opener installed?

37. Which option should Ramon choose if he wants to install the garage-door opener himself?

38. A taxi charged Rachel $7.75 to take her to school and $8.45 to take her to the arena. How much did she spend if she made round trips to both places?

39. Every week, Elsa drives 45 miles on Monday, 17 miles on Tuesday, 88 miles on Wednesday, and 12 miles on Friday. How many miles does she drive in 4 weeks?

Estimate the product.

1. $91
  × 6

2. 84
  ×29

3. 39,871
  × 4,215

Rounding is a good strategy to use here.

4. 73.8
  × 9.7

5. 2.4
  ×6.7

6. 6.89
  ×2.71

Find the product.

7. 5.5 × 100

8. 0.086 × 10

9. 214
  × 48

10. 6,275
  × 363

11. 59
  ×82

12. 345
  ×453

13. 0.6899
  × 0.11

14. $35.82
  × 73

15. 267.1
  × 2.08

16. $136.54
  × 80.5

Use mental math and multiplication to estimate the sum.

17. 294
318
288
326
+301

18. 7.9
8.1
7.895
8.075
+7.722

19. 6,098
5,880
6,209
6,379
+5,722

20. 3.701
4.01
3.9
3.88
+4.2

Solve. Use the information in the table for Exercises 21–23.

Flash Video Rental Policy	
$2.99	1 movie for 1 day
$0.99	each additional day
$3.79	5 additional days

21. Maria rented a video on Friday. She still has it on Tuesday. She wants to save money. Should she return the video now or wait until Thursday?

22. What would be Maria's total bill if she rented 3 videos and kept them for 6 days?

23. Star Video charges $7.00 per movie for 7 days. Which store charges less to rent for a week?

24. Cindy spends $2.59 a day to buy breakfast on Monday through Friday on her way to work. How much does she spend in 2 weeks?

25. A 4-line newspaper advertisement costs $0.80 a line during the week and $1.10 a line on the weekend. How much does it cost to advertise for a week?

Teamwork P·R·O·J·E·C·T

Write a Guidebook

When new people move to your community, how do they locate restaurants, theaters, museums, sporting events, and other community activities? Work with your teammates to plan a guidebook about places to go to and things to do in your community.

▲ *Decide*

As a team, brainstorm ideas for your guidebook. List categories of places and events you will include.

▲ *Do*

As a team, divide the list of categories among your team members. Have each team member research a category and select places and appropriate events.

Conduct interviews or use other sources of information to write a brief description of each place or event. Include

- important data, such as prices, dates and times of operation, and telephone numbers.

- Work together to design, write, and assemble your guidebook.

▲ *Share*

Exchange guidebooks. Tell what new things you have discovered about your community.

Talk About It

Could you combine pages from each team's guidebook to assemble one book for new students at your school?

Would your school newspaper or newsletter be interested in publishing some of your guidebook information?

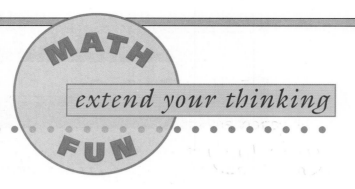

Mail-Order Shopping

J. J.'s SPORTS EQUIPMENT				
Catalog Number	Quantity	Name of Item	Price Each	Total Price
VH-44612	2	Sleeping Bag	86.25	
VK-52908	5	Cooking kit	17.60	
VK-71782	24	Can of cooking fuel	5.35	

Postage Chart				Total for Items
Orders up to $5.00 Orders from $5.01 to $15.00 Orders from $15.01 to $50.00	$0.95 $1.35 $2.95	Orders from $50.01 to $100.00 Orders over $100.00	$4.35 $5.50	Total Cost

To purchase by mail, you usually have to fill out a form. Study the order form Carl has started to fill out. Fill in the last column by multiplying the quantity by the price of each item. Add postage according to the postage chart.

Find a mail-order catalog and make up a mail-order form similar to the one above. List 3 items that you would like to buy. Specify 15 of one item, 23 of the second item, and 9 of the third item. Complete your order form. What is the total cost of your order?

Challenge

Logical Reasoning

Use the clues to find the number.

1. The product of the digits is 0.
2. It is $< (7 \times 9) + 2$.
3. It is $> 8 \times 5$.
4. It is a multiple of 5.
5. It is a multiple of 6.

What is the number?

Patterns

This is a multiples triangle. Complete the fifth row in the triangle.

```
        1
      2   4
    3   6   9
  4   8  12  16
```

What patterns can you find in the triangle? What would be the last number in row one hundred?

Write the letter of the correct answer.

1. What is twelve ten-thousandths written in standard form?

  A. 0.0012   **B.** 0.012
  C. 12.0000   **D.** not here

2. Which shows 86.4278 rounded to the nearest thousandth?

  A. 8.6427   **B.** 8.64278
  C. 86.42   **D.** 86.428

3. $2 + 7 \times 5$

  A. 35   **B.** 37
  C. 45   **D.** not here

4. What is the value of 10^6?

  A. 0.6   **B.** 60
  C. 100,000   **D.** 1,000,000

5. Which is the best estimate?
$12.94 + 7.18$

  A. 19   **B.** 20
  C. 21   **D.** 70

6. $6.924 - 4.58$

  A. 1.344   **B.** 2.34
  C. 2.344   **D.** 2.434

7. Choose an algebraic expression for 32 less than x.

  A. $32 - x$ **B.** 32
  C. $x - 32$ **D.** $32 + x$

8. Evaluate the expression
$24 - (8 + t)$, for $t = 11$.

  A. 4   **B.** 5
  C. 6   **D.** 27

9. Choose the best estimate.
$5,378 \times 621$

  A. 5,000   **B.** 30,000
  C. 300,000   **D.** 3,000,000

10. Place the decimal point in the product. 5.963×2.34

  A. 1.395342   **B.** 139.5342
  C. 1,395.342   **D.** not here

11. 2.7×0.0099

  A. 0.002672   **B.** 0.02672
  C. 0.02673   **D.** 0.2673

12. $120 \div 12 - 8$

  A. 2   **B.** 4
  C. 20   **D.** 30

13. Wanda works for $4.80 an hour for 3 hours each day of the week. About how many days must she work to earn $105.00?

  A. 4 days   **B.** 7 days
  C. 9 days   **D.** 10 days

14. Dave and Mark have a total of 35 bus tokens. If Dave has 7 more than Mark, how many bus tokens does Mark have?

  A. 14 bus tokens   **B.** 17 bus tokens
  C. 18 bus tokens   **D.** 21 bus tokens

DIVIDING
WHOLE NUMBERS
AND
DECIMALS

Did you know . . .

. . . that about 40,000,000 students attend elementary and secondary schools in the United States each year?

How can you determine the average number of students who attend elementary and secondary schools in each of the 50 states?

DIVISIBILITY

A number is **divisible** by another number if the quotient is a whole number and the remainder is zero.

Remember that a number is divisible by 3 if the sum of the digits of the number is divisible by 3. Use what you know about divisibility by 3 to explore divisibility by 9.

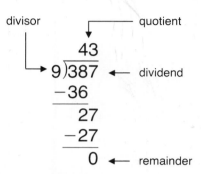

Talk About It

▶ What is the sum of the digits of the number 387? Is the sum divisible by 3? Is the sum divisible by 9?

▶ Use a calculator. Find 5 three-digit numbers that are divisible by 3. Find the sum of the digits of each number. Is each sum divisible by 9?

▶ If the sum of the digits of a number is divisible by 9, is the number divisible by 9?

▶ Are numbers that are divisible by 9 also divisible by 3? Are numbers that are divisible by 3 always divisible by 9? Why or why not?

Example A new school cafeteria will hold 396 students. Designers plan to use tables that seat 9 students each. Will there be exactly enough tables for 396 students?

Think: Is 396 divisible by 9?
Sum of the digits: $3 + 9 + 6 = 18$ ← 18 is divisible by 9.

So, there will be exactly enough tables for 396 students.

Learning divisibility rules can help you develop number sense.

Divisibility Rules	
A whole number is divisible by	
2	if it ends in 0, 2, 4, 6, or 8.
3	if the sum of its digits is divisible by 3.
5	if it ends in 0 or 5.
9	if the sum of its digits is divisible by 9.
10	if it ends in 0.

Check for Understanding

Determine whether the number is divisible by 2, 3, 5, 9, or 10.
Write all that apply.

1. 540   **2.** 621   **3.** 1,655   **4.** 457   **5.** 346

Practice

Complete the table. Write *yes* or *no*.

Number	2	3	5	9	10	Number	2	3	5	9	10
6. 3,750	?	?	?	?	?	**7.** 9,882	?	?	?	?	?
8. 4,516	?	?	?	?	?	**9.** 18,270	?	?	?	?	?
10. 2,604	?	?	?	?	?	**11.** 63,405	?	?	?	?	?

Mixed Applications

For Exercises 12–13, choose the correct answer. Write **a**, **b**, or **c**.

12. Tanya's class wants to sit together at an assembly. If each row has 9 seats and the class fills up 3 rows with 1 extra student, how many students are in the class?

   a. 39 students   **b.** 36 students   **c.** 28 students

13. In social studies class, students learn that the largest cattle ranches are in the Southwest. If the number of acres in the largest ranch is divisible by 2, which number could it be?

   a. 40,000 acres   **b.** 34,389 acres   **c.** 39,605 acres

14. Number Sense   Write *true* or *false* for each statement.

   a. Some numbers that are divisible by 5 are even numbers.

   b. Any number that is divisible by 3 is also divisible by 9.

   c. If a number is divisible by 10, it is divisible by 5.

   d. Some numbers that are divisible by 10 are odd numbers.

If a number is divisible by 9 and 10, is it also divisible by 2, 3, and 5? Why or why not?

WRAP UP...

ESTIMATING
Whole-Number Quotients

When you estimate a quotient, you can use rounding or compatible numbers. **Compatible numbers** divide without a remainder, are close to the actual numbers, and are easy to compute mentally.

Estimate. $6,134 \div 35$

Use compatible numbers.   Round.

$6,134 \div 35$ $6,134 \div 35$
$6,000 \div 30 = 200$ ← estimate $6,000 \div 40 = 150$ ← estimate

Talk About It

▶ Which estimate would be easier to compute by using mental math?

▶ When choosing numbers to estimate, why choose compatible numbers?

Remember to estimate when an exact answer is not needed or to determine the reasonableness of an answer.

Example   Ann knows that 34 sixth graders can attend the computer lab each hour. She determines that 1,654 students can attend the lab once in 69 hours. Is this reasonable?

Estimate by using compatible numbers.

$$34\overline{)1,654} \longrightarrow 40\overline{)1,600}^{\ \ 40} \leftarrow \text{estimate}$$

So, Ann's answer of 69 hours is not reasonable.

Talk About It

▶ Why would you not use rounding to estimate the quotient of 1,654 divided by 34?

Check for Understanding

Tell whether you would use compatible numbers or rounding to estimate. Justify your choice. Then estimate the quotient.

1. $7,344 \div 8$ 2. $9\overline{)2,945}$ 3. $12,353 \div 17$ 4. $22\overline{)23,650}$ 5. $53,350 \div 23$

Practice

Choose the best estimate. Write **a**, **b**, or **c**.

6. 5)345
   a. 55
   b. 70
   c. 30

7. 18)46,170
   a. 2,500
   b. 3,000
   c. 5,000

8. 5,474 ÷ 23
   a. 300
   b. 200
   c. 2,000

9. 7)749
   a. 10
   b. 170
   c. 100

10. 861 ÷ 41
   a. 20
   b. 30
   c. 40

Estimate the quotient.

11. 647 ÷ 7
12. 569 ÷ 3
13. 3,532 ÷ 8
14. 2,435 ÷ 7
15. 1,406 ÷ 6

16. 482 ÷ 7
17. 6,321 ÷ 9
18. 968 ÷ 47
19. 3,456 ÷ 432
20. 5,765 ÷ 26

21. 12)23,143
22. 30)2,552
23. 26)573
24. 57)4,339
25. 46)5,199

26. 8)4,396
27. 7)5,276
28. 72)647
29. 46)3,321
30. 12)3,786

31. 8)639
32. 5)885
33. 3)943
34. 8)752
35. 6)431

36. 9)889
37. 64)25,012
38. 37)3,663
39. 17)1,432
40. 58)32,557

Mixed Applications

41. A social studies book has 414 pages. If each chapter is about 35 pages, about how many chapters are in the social studies book?

42. A cafeteria prepares 145 celery sticks to serve 42 students. About how many celery sticks are served to each student?

43. **Number Sense ● Mental Math** Sally sold 9 boxes of pencils at the school bookstore. If each box contained 200 pencils, how many pencils did Sally sell?

44. **Making Choices** Frank can buy a package of 8 ball point pens for $14.96, or he can buy the same ball point pens for $1.75 each. If Frank needs 8 ball point pens, which choice is the better buy?

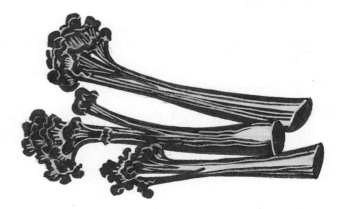

Is 273 ÷ 7 easier to estimate using rounding or compatible numbers?

There are 7 lockers per unit at Thomas Jefferson Middle School. How many units does it take to give each of 586 students a locker?

Estimate.

You can use your estimate to determine about how many digits will be in the exact quotient.

$$\overset{80}{7)586} \xrightarrow{\text{ }} \overset{80}{7)560} \quad \longleftarrow \text{ estimate}$$

Since the estimate is 80, or 8 tens, you know the first digit will probably be in the tens place, and there will probably be two digits in the quotient.

Divide.

Step 1	**Step 2**	**Step 3**
Since the first digit will be in the tens place, divide the 58 tens. Think: $7 \times 8 = 56$.	Bring down the ones. Divide the 26 ones. Think: $7 \times 3 = 21$. Record the remainder.	Use the inverse operation, multiplication, to check. Remember to add the remainder.

Step 1

$$\begin{array}{r} 8 \\ 7)\overline{586} \\ -56 \\ \hline 2 \end{array}$$ Multiply.

Subtract. Compare. $2 < 7$

Step 2

$$\begin{array}{r} 83 \text{ r5} \\ 7)\overline{586} \\ -56\downarrow \\ \hline 26 \\ -21 \\ \hline 5 \end{array}$$ ← More than 83 are needed.

Multiply.

Subtract. Compare. $5 < 7$

Step 3

$$\begin{array}{r} 83 \quad \longleftarrow \text{ quotient} \\ \times \quad 7 \quad \longleftarrow \text{ divisor} \\ \hline 581 \\ + \quad 5 \quad \longleftarrow \text{ remainder} \\ \hline 586 \quad \longleftarrow \text{ dividend} \end{array}$$

So, it takes 84 units to give each student a locker.

Talk About It

▶ How does estimating a quotient help you find the exact quotient?

▶ How does the fact that multiplication and division are inverse operations help you find quotients?

Check for Understanding

Estimate. Tell about how many digits will be in the exact quotient.

1. $8)\overline{427}$ 2. $2)\overline{874}$ 3. $4)\overline{3,324}$ 4. $7)\overline{232}$ 5. $9)\overline{843}$

Practice

Estimate the quotient.

6. $5\overline{)39}$ **7.** $4\overline{)125}$ **8.** $7\overline{)506}$ **9.** $8\overline{)816}$ **10.** $7{,}123 \div 4$

11. $311 \div 4$ **12.** $1{,}600 \div 5$ **13.** $16{,}543 \div 9$ **14.** $1{,}158 \div 6$ **15.** $587 \div 2$

16. $624 \div 16$ **17.** $51{,}222 \div 5$ **18.** $13{,}721 \div 7$ **19.** $5{,}500 \div 7$ **20.** $24{,}135 \div 6$

Find the quotient.

21. $4\overline{)552}$ **22.** $8\overline{)1{,}989}$ **23.** $8\overline{)568}$ **24.** $3\overline{)6{,}612}$ **25.** $9\overline{)6{,}234}$

26. $5{,}440 \div 8$ **27.** $699 \div 3$ **28.** $67{,}663 \div 6$ **29.** $1{,}845 \div 9$ **30.** $1{,}242 \div 3$

31. $8\overline{)3{,}376}$ **32.** $3\overline{)3{,}912}$ **33.** $6\overline{)49{,}307}$ **34.** $2\overline{)6{,}323}$ **35.** $6\overline{)548}$

Mixed Applications

36. A bus made 6 trips of 242 miles each. What is the total number of miles the bus traveled?

37. A teacher has 273 milligrams of a chemical to divide equally into 3 solutions. How much will the teacher add to each solution?

MATH CONNECTION

When you multiply and divide each part of the dividend mentally, you are using a method called short division.

Divide the first digit. Write the remainder next to the second digit. The remainder and the second digit become the next number to divide. Repeat until you have completed the division.

Example

$$\overset{1}{8\overline{)9\,^{1}9\ \ 5}} \rightarrow \overset{1\ 2}{8\overline{)9\,^{1}9\,^{3}5}} \rightarrow \overset{1\ 2\ 4\ r3}{8\overline{)9\,^{1}9\,^{3}5}}$$

Divide. Use short division.

38. $5\overline{)240}$ **39.** $7\overline{)1{,}680}$ **40.** $9\overline{)28{,}125}$ **41.** $4\overline{)4{,}933}$ **42.** $8\overline{)3{,}655}$

Why do you estimate a quotient?

Cheerleaders will stretch a band of ribbon along a 2,748-foot fence surrounding a football field. If the ribbon comes in 13-foot rolls, how many rolls of ribbon will the cheerleaders need?

Estimate to place the first digit in the quotient.
$2,748 \div 13 \rightarrow 2,600 \div 13 = 200$

Divide.

Step 1	**Step 2**	**Step 3**
Since the first digit will be in the hundreds place, divide the 27 hundreds. Think: 13 × 2 = 26.	Bring down the tens. Divide the 14 tens. Think: 13 × 1 = 13.	Bring down the ones. Divide the 18 ones. Record the remainder.
$$\begin{array}{r} 2 \\ 13\overline{)2,748} \\ -26 \\ \hline 1 \end{array}$$	$$\begin{array}{r} 21 \\ 13\overline{)2,748} \\ -26\downarrow \\ \hline 14 \\ -13 \\ \hline 1 \end{array}$$	$$\begin{array}{r} 211\ r5 \\ 13\overline{)2,748} \\ -26 \\ \hline 14 \\ -13\downarrow \\ \hline 18 \\ -13 \\ \hline 5 \end{array}$$

• Why do the cheerleaders need more than 211 rolls of ribbon?

Since they cannot buy part of a roll, the cheerleaders will need 212 rolls of ribbon.

Examples Sometimes you need to correct the quotient.

A.
$$\begin{array}{r} 9 \\ 23\overline{)200} \\ -207 \end{array}$$
Since 207 > 200, the digit in the quotient is too large.

B.
$$\begin{array}{r} 5 \\ 38\overline{)232} \\ -190 \\ \hline 42 \end{array}$$
Since 42 > 38, the digit in the quotient is too small.

Check for Understanding

Tell whether you need to correct the first digit in the quotient. Write *yes* or *no*.

1. $13\overline{)241}$ with quotient 2

2. $91\overline{)420}$ with quotient 4

3. $56\overline{)5,765}$ with quotient 1

4. $62\overline{)36,743}$ with quotient 6

5. $67\overline{)32,264}$ with quotient 4

Practice

Estimate the quotient.

6. $13\overline{)254}$
7. $52\overline{)123}$
8. $56\overline{)5,834}$
9. $13\overline{)4,145}$

10. $91\overline{)440}$
11. $36,043 \div 62$
12. $12\overline{)2,564}$
13. $91,654 \div 32$

Find the quotient.

14. $35\overline{)140}$
15. $13\overline{)117}$
16. $42\overline{)892}$
17. $29\overline{)261}$

18. $74\overline{)4,736}$
19. $38\overline{)8,174}$
20. $41\overline{)11,316}$
21. $6,552 \div 91$

22. $1,579 \div 81$
23. $42,032 \div 71$
24. $22,120 \div 35$
25. $2,744 \div 49$

26. $54\overline{)1,512}$
27. $66\overline{)15,972}$
28. $97\overline{)96,708}$
29. $28\overline{)67,815}$

Complete the table. You may want to use a calculator.

	Divisor	Dividend	Quotient		Divisor	Dividend	Quotient
30.	36	4,752	■	**31.**	46	460	■
32.	42	■	56	**33.**	97	87,979	■
34.	■	456	38	**35.**	■	3,858	6

Mixed Applications

36. A total of 288 students will play intramural basketball. Into how many teams of 12 can the students be grouped?

37. The principal at Division Middle School has ordered 1,170 desks to divide equally among 45 classrooms. How many desks will be in each classroom?

38. **Find Data** Use a recent almanac to find information about the number of students and the number of school districts in your state.

39. **Make Up a Problem** Use the data you found in Exercise 38 to write a word problem that can be solved using division.

How do you know that a digit in the quotient is too large? too small?

A teacher will distribute 288 new books among several classes of 24 students each. If every student in each class is given a new book, how many classes will have new books?

▶ UNDERSTAND

What are you asked to find?

What information are you given?

▶ PLAN

What strategy will you use?

Since you know that 288 books will be distributed among groups of 24, you can write a division number sentence.

▶ SOLVE

How can you carry out your plan?

Write a division number sentence.
$288 \div 24 = n$

Estimate.

$$288 \div 24$$
$$\downarrow \qquad \downarrow$$
$$300 \div 20 = 15$$

Use a calculator to solve.

$288 \boxed{\div} 24 \boxed{=} \boxed{12.}$

So, 12 classes will receive new books.

▶ LOOK BACK

How do you know your solution is reasonable?

WHAT IF... ... you were asked to find the total number of students in 3 of the classes? What number sentence would you write to solve the problem?

Apply

Write a number sentence. Then solve.

1 Elizabeth and Mary's school bus averages 328 miles on 41 gallons of gasoline. How many miles does the school bus average on 1 gallon of gasoline?

2 A band teacher is buying 341 sets of sheet music for members of the middle school band. If the sheet music costs $1.79 a set, what is the total cost?

Mixed Applications ➤ **STRATEGIES** • Find a Pattern • Use a Table • Guess and Check • Write a Number Sentence

Choose a strategy and solve.

3 Tran is sorting pencils. There are 7 more red pencils than blue pencils in a total of 39 pencils. How many are blue?

4 Julio makes $5.25 an hour working as an assistant to the school librarian. How much will Julio make if he works 36 hours?

5 Of the 2,048 students who competed in a spelling bee, 1,024 were eliminated the first day, 512 the second, and 256 the third. If this pattern continued, on what day did the last two students in the spelling bee compete?

6 Use the table below. If the pattern continues, how far will 6 runners run on the fifth day?

Each Runner's Training Schedule					
Day	1	2	3	4	5
Miles	2	6	10	14	▪

7 Janet ran 0.5 mile on Monday, 0.6 mile on Tuesday, and 0.7 mile on Wednesday. If she continues this pattern, how far will Janet run on Friday?

8 Alonzo scored 12 three-point shots and 14 two-point shots in three basketball games. How many total points did Alonzo score?

9 Marissa has 19 coins to spend at a soccer game. She has only dimes and quarters. The value of the coins is $4. How many dimes does Marissa have?

10 Jill has worked 4 more than 3 times as many problems as Dave. Wayne has worked 2 times as many as Dave. If Wayne has worked 28 problems, how many problems has Jill worked?

A total of 27 members of a band-booster club sold 8,235 bumper stickers. What is the average number sold by each member?

Estimate. $8{,}235 \div 27 \rightarrow 9{,}000 \div 30 = 300$

Divide.

Step 1	**Step 2**	**Step 3**
Since the first digit will be in the hundreds place, divide the 82 hundreds.	Bring down the tens. Divide the 13 tens. Think: 27 > 13. Write 0 in the quotient.	Bring down the ones. Divide the 135 ones. Use compatible numbers.

Step 1

$$
\begin{array}{r}
3 \\
27{\overline{)8{,}235}} \\
-81 \\
\hline
1
\end{array}
$$

Think:
$30 \times 3 = 90$
or
$25 \times 3 = 75$

Step 2

$$
\begin{array}{r}
30 \\
27{\overline{)8{,}235}} \\
-81\downarrow \\
\hline
13 \\
-0 \\
\hline
13
\end{array}
$$

Step 3

$$
\begin{array}{r}
305 \\
27{\overline{)8{,}235}} \\
-81 \\
\hline
13 \\
-0\downarrow \\
\hline
135 \\
-135 \\
\hline
0
\end{array}
$$

Think:
$30 \times 5 = 150$
or
$25 \times 5 = 125$

So, each member sold an average of 305 bumper stickers. Since 305 is close to 300, the answer is reasonable.

- When do you write zero in the quotient?

- How can you use your estimate to determine whether a zero has been omitted?

Check for Understanding

Choose the correct quotient. Write **a**, **b**, or **c**.

1. $8{\overline{)5{,}624}}$
  a. 703
  b. 730
  c. 73

2. $41{\overline{)8{,}614}}$
  a. 21 r4
  b. 201 r4
  c. 210 r4

3. $16{\overline{)992}}$
  a. 602
  b. 62
  c. 620

4. $24{\overline{)14{,}172}}$
  a. 50 r12
  b. 590 r12
  c. 509 r12

5. $63{\overline{)25{,}666}}$
  a. 740 r25
  b. 470 r25
  c. 407 r25

Find the quotient.

6. $72{\overline{)2{,}884}}$

7. $7{\overline{)8{,}421}}$

8. $8{\overline{)8{,}724}}$

9. $12{\overline{)2{,}439}}$

Practice

Find the quotient.

10. $7\overline{)2{,}821}$ **11.** $6\overline{)12{,}014}$ **12.** $9\overline{)7{,}020}$ **13.** $4\overline{)3{,}603}$

14. $43\overline{)8{,}772}$ **15.** $8\overline{)4{,}803}$ **16.** $32\overline{)22{,}432}$ **17.** $63\overline{)5{,}100}$

18. $6\overline{)7{,}204}$ **19.** $21\overline{)5{,}260}$ **20.** $5\overline{)4{,}304}$ **21.** $9\overline{)8{,}197}$

22. $47\overline{)14{,}326}$ **23.** $17\overline{)17{,}599}$ **24.** $70\overline{)4{,}925}$ **25.** $41\overline{)8{,}561}$

Use inverse operations to complete the table.

	Divisor	Dividend	Quotient
26.	24	14,544	■
27.	■	16,012	4,003
28.	9	■	60 r7
29.	45	4,815	■

Mixed Applications

30. Davis Middle School library has 62,525 cards in its card catalog. If there are 5 cards for each book, how many books are in the library?

31. **Number Sense • Estimation** A school library must put 35,099 books on 130 shelves. Which numbers would you use to estimate the quotient: $35{,}000 \div 130$, $36{,}000 \div 120$, or $35{,}000 \div 150$? Why?

MIXED REVIEW

Determine whether the number is divisible by 2, 3, 5, 9, or 10. Write all that apply.

1. 650 **2.** 315 **3.** 2,048 **4.** 6,561

Use multiplication to estimate the sum.

5. $3.1 + 2.8 + 3.3 + 2.75$ **6.** $99.11 + 100.32 + 97.954 + 102.004$

Find the quotient.

7. $7\overline{)392}$ **8.** $2{,}835 \div 9$ **9.** $57\overline{)684}$ **10.** $1{,}470 \div 98$

Why do you write a zero in the quotient?

1. Tasha sold 234 school newspapers for $0.05 each. If each newspaper cost $0.03 to print, what was the profit from Tasha's sales?

2. Barbara baked 10 dozen muffins for the 36 newspaper club members. If each member has 3 muffins, how many muffins will be left?

3. Students use a hand-run press to print the school newspaper. The press can print 24 pages every 30 minutes. If the press runs 210 minutes a day, how long will it take to print 504 pages?

When computing with money, I must place the decimal point correctly.

4. The school newspaper staff pays $0.03 for every page printed. If the staff decides to print 945 copies of a 4-page newspaper next month, how much will the printing cost?

Estimate the product or the quotient.

5. 9.8×41
6. 279.63×12.2
7. $5,432 \times 61.89$
8. $5,958.24 \times 3.9$

9. $642 \div 27$
10. $946 \div 34$
11. $5,391 \div 94$
12. $7,986 \div 11$

Place the decimal point in the product.

13. $6.8 \times 3.4 = 2312$
14. $5.3 \times 0.07 = 0371$
15. $800 \times 1.8 = 14400$

Find the product.

16. 9.7×5.2
17. $4,562 \times 7.5$
18. 0.066×100
19. $1,321.95 \times 0.38$

20. $3.029 \times 1,000$
21. 754.2×0.98
22. 33.2×21.5
23. 624×9.7

Determine whether the number is divisible by 2, 3, 5, 9, or 10. Write all that apply.

24. 270
25. 16,833
26. 62,390
27. 53,865

Find the quotient.

28. $984 \div 4$
29. $826 \div 6$
30. $3,691 \div 5$
31. $4,251 \div 6$

32. $68,242 \div 2$
33. $276 \div 45$
34. $1,207 \div 90$
35. $7,928 \div 12$

36. $18,496 \div 4$
37. $16,905 \div 42$
38. $62,863 \div 99$
39. $75,342 \div 60$

Spotlight ON PROBLEM SOLVING

Understand
Plan
Solve
Look Back

*E*valuate the Reasonableness of an Answer

An important part of solving any problem is checking whether or not your answer is reasonable. ▼

The drama class sold 65 tickets for a total of $48.75. Using a calculator, Peggy determined that 1 ticket cost $7.50. Is her answer reasonable?

To evaluate Peggy's answer, use estimation. If each ticket had cost $1.00, the total amount collected would have been $65.00. Since the drama class collected only $48.75, each ticket must have cost less than $1.00. So, $7.50 per ticket is not a reasonable answer.

Talk About It

What mistake do you think Peggy made when she used the calculator?

In what other way can you check whether the answer is reasonable?

Apply

Choose the most reasonable answer without solving. Write *a*, *b*, or *c*. Explain your choice.

1. There are 120 boys at camp. If 8 boys occupy each cabin, what is the total number of cabins occupied by the boys?

a. 95 cabins   b. 15 cabins   c. 150 cabins

2. If a contractor can build a garage in 27 days, how many garages can the contractor build in 297 days?

a. 11 garages b. 4 garages c. 19 garages

3. Five people will share equally in profits from the sale of a warehouse. If the selling price is $27,835, how much will each person receive?

a. $15,567   b. $1,067   c. $5,567

4. Susan buys 4 airline tickets to San Francisco, California. Each costs $289. What is the total cost of the tickets?

a. $945   b. $1,156   c. $1,428

DIVIDING DECIMALS
by Whole Numbers

Mario's father drives Mario and two friends to school track meets. If his car travels 103.6 miles on 4 gallons of gasoline, how many miles does it travel on 1 gallon of gasoline?

Estimate to place the first digit in the quotient.

$$103.6 \div 4 \quad \longrightarrow \quad 100 \div 4 = 25$$

Divide.

Step 1	**Step 2**
Place a decimal point above the decimal point in the dividend.	Divide as with whole numbers.

$4\overline{)103.6}$

So, the car travels 25.9 miles on 1 gallon of gasoline.

- You can also use short division.

Example $6.797 \div 7$

Round to estimate.   Use short division.

$\begin{array}{r} 1 \\ 7\overline{)7} \end{array}$ 6.797 rounded to the nearest whole number is 7.

$\begin{array}{r} 0.9\ 71 \\ 7\overline{)6.7^497} \end{array}$ Since the quotient is less than 1, place 0 in the ones place.

Check for Understanding

Choose the correct quotient without computing. Write **a, b,** or **c.**

1. $23\overline{)181.47}$

   a. 0.789
   b. 78.9
   c. 7.89

2. $59\overline{)164.02}$

   a. 27.8
   b. 2.78
   c. 0.278

3. $87\overline{)4.785}$

   a. 0.055
   b. 0.0055
   c. 0.55

4. $36\overline{)2.7972}$

   a. 0.0777
   b. 0.777
   c. 7.77

Practice

Place the decimal point in the quotient.

5. $270.585 \div 63 = 4295$ **6.** $11.919 \div 87 = 137$ **7.** $1591.2 \div 39 = 408$

Find the quotient.

8. $5)\overline{21.5}$ **9.** $2)\overline{\$30.72}$ **10.** $8)\overline{\$31.20}$ **11.** $11)\overline{3.96}$

12. $9)\overline{38.601}$ **13.** $12)\overline{7.2}$ **14.** $7)\overline{33.6}$ **15.** $11)\overline{394.46}$

16. $24)\overline{7.44}$ **17.** $82)\overline{59.86}$ **18.** $17)\overline{85.51}$ **19.** $31)\overline{111.6}$

20. $41)\overline{70.643}$ **21.** $37)\overline{99.9}$ **22.** $47)\overline{86.48}$ **23.** $53)\overline{79.5}$

24. $173.6 \div 8$ **25.** $7.1139 \div 69$ **26.** $70.95 \div 15$ **27.** $474.75 \div 75$

Mixed Applications

28. A total of 31 students signed up for a weekend computer course. They paid a total of $1,418.25. How much did each student pay?

29. A 6-story school building is 19.2 meters high. If each story of the school building is the same height, how high is each story?

30. **Logical Reasoning** Fluorine is one of the gaseous elements. Nine molecules of fluorine weigh 638.154 atomic mass units. How much do 2 molecules of fluorine weigh?

31. **Making Choices** A computer store sells two brands of diskettes of equal quality. Brand A costs $9.23 for 12. Brand B sells for $0.98 each. Which brand is the better buy?

When dividing a decimal by a whole number, why do you need a decimal point in the quotient?

WRAP UP...

In science class Jan learns that it takes 4 hours to move a space shuttle 3.4 miles from the assembly building to the launch pad. How far is the shuttle moved in 1 hour?

Estimate. Use compatible numbers.

$$4\overline{)3.4} \longrightarrow \overset{0.8}{4\overline{)3.2}}$$

Sometimes you must place zeros to the right of the decimal in a dividend to complete a division problem. Since 3.4 and 3.40 are equivalent, you can place a zero to the right of the decimal.

Divide.

Step 1	**Step 2**
Place the decimal point and divide.	Place a zero in the hundredths place. Continue to divide until the remainder is 0.

Step 1:

$$\begin{array}{r} 0.8 \\ 4\overline{)3.4} \\ -3\,2 \\ \hline 2 \end{array}$$

Step 2:

$$\begin{array}{r} 0.85 \\ 4\overline{)3.40} \\ -3\,2\downarrow \\ \hline 20 \\ -20 \\ \hline 0 \end{array}$$

So, the shuttle is moved 0.85 mile in 1 hour.

- Why do you place zeros to the right of the decimal in a dividend?

Zeros are sometimes needed to hold places in decimal quotients just as zeros are sometimes needed in whole-number quotients.

Example

$$\begin{array}{r} 0.026 \\ 5\overline{)0.130} \\ -10 \\ \hline 30 \\ -30 \\ \hline 0 \end{array}$$

Zeros show that there are no whole numbers and no tenths in the quotient.

Check for Understanding

Place the decimal point in the quotient. Add zeros to divide until the remainder is zero.

1. $4.50 \div 2 = 225$

2. $1.610 \div 5 = 322$

3. $0.1040 \div 65 = 16$

4. $0.924 \div 6 = 154$

5. $0.060 \div 4 = 15$

6. $2.135 \div 7 = 305$

Divide until the remainder is zero.

7. $5\overline{)1.61}$

8. $2\overline{)9.87}$

9. $8\overline{)7.9}$

10. $42\overline{)50.19}$

11. $16\overline{)119}$

Practice

Divide until the remainder is zero.

12. $8\overline{)0.7}$

13. $16\overline{)11}$

14. $18\overline{)40.5}$

15. $32\overline{)5.6}$

16. $4\overline{)21.5}$

17. $65\overline{)1.04}$

18. $4\overline{)3.4}$

19. $16\overline{)27}$

20. $98\overline{)121.03}$

21. $4\overline{)0.85}$

22. $342 \div 48$

23. $0.93 \div 6$

24. $0.47 \div 5$

25. $31.5 \div 84$

Mixed Applications

26. In home economics class, Ian made 8 hamburgers for lunch, using 2.8 pounds of ground beef. How much ground beef was in each hamburger?

27. When she set the table for lunch, Jean poured 0.5 liter of milk into each of 4 glasses. What is the total amount of milk she poured?

LOGICAL REASONING

Tell whether each item was bought at Joe's or at Bob's.

28. Sara bought 1 apple for $0.30.

29. Mont bought 1 orange for $0.37.

30. Ira bought 1 pear for $0.43.

31. Ward bought 2 apples for $0.80.

	Apples 3 for	Oranges 3 for	Pears 4 for
Joe's	$0.89	$1.29	$1.69
Bob's	$1.19	$1.09	$1.45

Why do you place zeros to the right of the decimal in some division problems?

WRAP UP...

Tonya can walk 0.05 of a mile around the school track in 1 minute (min). If she maintains this pace, how far can she walk in 10 min? in 100 min? in 1,000 min?

Notice the pattern that occurs when you multiply decimals by powers of 10.

10^0, or 1   × 0.05 = 0.05   ← 1 min

10^1, or 10   × 0.05 = 0.0 5, or 0.5   ← 10 min

10^2, or 100   × 0.05 = 0.05 0, or 5.0   ← 100 min

10^3, or 1,000 × 0.05 = 0.050 0, or 50.0 ← 1,000 min

So, if Tonya maintains her pace, she can walk 0.5 mile in 10 minutes, 5 miles in 100 minutes, and 50 miles in 1,000 minutes.

- What happens to the product as the power of 10 increases?

- What rule can you state for multiplying decimals by powers of 10?

By standing, Mr. McKinney burns 666.6 calories in the 1,000 hours (hr) he teaches each year. How many calories does he burn in 100 hr? in 10 hr? in 1 hr?

Think: 1,000 ÷ 10 = 100; 100 ÷ 10 = 10; 10 ÷ 10 = 1.

Notice the pattern that occurs when you divide decimals by powers of 10.

666.6 ÷ 10^0, or 1   = 666.6   ← 1,000 hr

666.6 ÷ 10^1, or 10   = 66 6.6, or 66.66   ← 100 hr

666.6 ÷ 10^2, or 100   = 6 66.6, or 6.666   ← 10 hr

666.6 ÷ 10^3, or 1,000 = 0 666.6, or 0.6666 ← 1 hr

So, Mr. McKinney burns 66.66 calories in 100 hours, 6.666 in 10 hours, and 0.6666 in 1 hour.

- Does the quotient get larger or smaller as the power of 10 increases?

- What rule can you state for dividing decimals by powers of 10?

Check for Understanding

Complete the pattern.

1. $0.15 \times 10 = 1.5$
   $0.15 \times 100 = $
   $0.15 \times 1{,}000 = $ ■

2. $235 \div 10 = 23.5$
   $235 \div 100 = $ ■
   $235 \div 1{,}000 = $ ■

3. $1.045 \times 1{,}000 = 1{,}045$
   $1.045 \times 100 = $ ■
   $1.045 \times 10 = $ ■

Practice

Copy and complete each table.

×	10^1	10^2	10^3
4. 37.89	■	■	■
5. 0.0643	■	■	■
6. 0.53	■	■	■
7. 0.024	■	■	■

÷	10^1	10^2	10^3
8. 14.5	■	■	■
9. 8.9	■	■	■
10. 0.06	■	■	■
11. 740	■	■	■

Mixed Applications

12. Troy, Alan, and 8 other members of the school's hiking club will share equally the cost of a cabin rental. If the cost is $455.50, how much will each person pay?

13. Fran tried to lift a bag of mail containing 1,000 letters from students concerned about water pollution. If each letter weighed 0.064 pound, how much did all the letters weigh?

LOGICAL REASONING

Use the table for Exercises 14–17.

10 millimeters	= 1 centimeter
100 centimeters	= 1 meter
1,000 meters	= 1 kilometer

14. How many meters are in 4.6 kilometers?

15. How many meters are in 567 centimeters?

16. How many millimeters are in 1 meter?

17. How many millimeters are in 6.4 meters?

How is multiplying a decimal by a power of 10 different from dividing a decimal by a power of 10?

WRAP UP...

EXPLORING

Dividing Decimals by Decimals

Use place-value materials to explore division of decimals by decimals.

WORK TOGETHER

Building Understanding

Talk About It

▶ What decimal total is represented in red? What decimal total is represented in blue?

▶ How many pieces the size of 1.5 can you fit over 7.5?

So, 7.5 ÷ 1.5 = 5, or 7.5 can be divided into 5 pieces the size of 1.5.

Use place-value materials to help you find the quotient.

a. $1.3\overline{)7.8}$

b. $2.4\overline{)7.2}$

c. $3.2\overline{)6.4}$

Talk About It

▶ How many pieces the size of 1.3 can you fit over 7.8?

▶ How many pieces the size of 2.4 can you fit over 7.2?

▶ How many pieces the size of 3.2 can you fit over 6.4?

Making the Connection

You can use a calculator to examine what happens to the quotient when you multiply the divisor and the dividend by the same power of 10.

A. Multiply both 7.5 and 1.5 by 10^1.
B. Divide 75 by 15.
C. Now multiply both 7.5 and 1.5 by 10^2.
D. Divide 750 by 150.

1. How do the quotients of 75 ÷ 15 and 750 ÷ 150 compare with that of 7.5 ÷ 1.5?

2. How does multiplying the divisor and the dividend by the same power of 10 affect the quotient?

Another Example

$4.2 ÷ 0.6 = 7$

Multiply the dividend by 10. ➝ $4.2 × 10 = 42$ Multiply the dividend by 100. ➝ $4.2 × 100 = 420$
Multiply the divisor by 10. ➝ $0.6 × 10 = 6$ Multiply the divisor by 100. ➝ $0.6 × 100 = 60$
The quotient is the same. ➝ $42 ÷ 6 = 7$ The quotient is the same. ➝ $420 ÷ 60 = 7$

Tell whether the quotients will be the same or different. Use a calculator if you wish.

3. $11.5 ÷ 2.3$ 4. $48.6 ÷ 5.4$ 5. $18.4 ÷ 2.3$

   $115 ÷ 23$ $4,860 ÷ 540$ $18.4 ÷ 23$

6. What conclusion can you draw about the quotient when the divisor and the dividend have been multiplied by the same power of 10?

Checking Understanding

Use place-value materials. Find the quotient.

7. $9.9 ÷ 3.3$ 8. $2.2 ÷ 1.1$ 9. $6.8 ÷ 3.4$ 10. $6.9 ÷ 2.3$

Write whether the quotients will be the same or different.

11. $21.7 ÷ 3.1$ 12. $9.9 ÷ 3.03$ 13. $510 ÷ 170$ 14. $135 ÷ 5$

   $217 ÷ 31$ $0.99 ÷ 0.33$ $5.1 ÷ 1.7$ $13.5 ÷ 0.05$

An art teacher gives Bill several containers holding a total of 28.5 liters of paint for a mural and asks him to pour 1.5 liters into each smaller container. How many smaller containers will Bill need?

You have seen that multiplying the divisor and the dividend by the same power of 10 has no effect on the quotient. Think about this relationship when you divide decimals by decimals.

Divide. $1.5\overline{)28.5}$

Step 1	**Step 2**
Make the divisor a whole number. Multiply both the divisor and the dividend by 10.	Place the decimal point in the quotient. Divide as with whole numbers.

Step 1

$1.5 \times 10 = 15 \ (1.5_\curvearrowright)$

$28.5 \times 10 = 285 \ (28.5_\curvearrowright)$

Step 2

$$\begin{array}{r} 19. \\ 15\overline{)285.} \\ -15\downarrow \\ \hline 135 \\ -135 \\ \hline 0 \end{array}$$

Since the remainder is 0, the answer is a whole number, and you do not need to show the decimal point.

So, Bill will need 19 smaller containers.

More Examples

A.
$$\begin{array}{r} 8 \\ 4.3_\curvearrowright\overline{)34.4_\curvearrowright} \\ -34\ 4 \\ \hline 0 \end{array}$$
← whole number

B.
$$\begin{array}{r} 6.6 \\ 0.75_\curvearrowright\overline{)4.95_\curvearrowright 0} \\ -4\ 50\downarrow \\ \hline 45\ 0 \\ -45\ 0 \\ \hline 0 \end{array}$$
Place a zero to continue to divide.

C.
$$\begin{array}{r} 25 \\ 2.38_\curvearrowright\overline{)59.50_\curvearrowright} \\ -47\ 6\downarrow \\ \hline 11\ 90 \\ -11\ 90 \\ \hline 0 \end{array}$$
Place a zero in the dividend to make the divisor a whole number.

Check for Understanding

Write the power of 10 needed to make the divisor a whole number.

1. $1.1\overline{)3.67}$　　2. $52 \div 3.45$　　3. $4.075\overline{)77.88}$　　4. $5.2234 \div 0.06$

5. $17.5 \div 2.5$　　6. $5.55\overline{)49.95}$　　7. $28.16 \div 7.04$　　8. $7.8\overline{)11.7}$

Practice

Place the decimal point in the quotient. Add zeros if necessary.

9. $241.5 \div 4.6 = 525$

10. $1{,}449 \div 1.38 = 1050$

11. $258.5 \div 2.5 = 1034$

12. $0.984 \div 2.4 = 41$

13. $4{,}062.5 \div 0.26 = 15625$

14. $1.25 \div 0.5 = 25$

15. $20.25 \div 1.2 = 16875$

16. $138.75 \div 8.88 = 15625$

17. $56.2152 \div 3.54 = 1588$

Find the quotient.

18. $8.1 \div 0.09$

19. $3.9 \div 0.15$

20. $49.3 \div 0.29$

21. $219.3 \div 5.1$

22. $0.28\overline{)0.42}$

23. $0.063\overline{)15.12}$

24. $11.7\overline{)26.208}$

25. $0.133\overline{)5.32}$

26. $20.7\overline{)107.64}$

27. $0.95\overline{)35.055}$

28. $7.7\overline{)480.48}$

29. $33\overline{)488.4}$

30. $105.6 \div 24$

31. $5.382 \div 9$

32. $0.2835 \div 2.7$

33. $4.563 \div 1.2$

Mixed Applications

34. A school parking lot is 71.3 meters long. If each parking space is 2.3 meters wide, how many cars can be parked side by side?

35. Sori made flags for a school fair out of a strip of material 12.6 meters long. Each flag was 0.7 meter long. How many flags did she make?

36. **Number Sense ● Estimation** Trina's family owns a sailboat that can travel 6.5 kilometers per hour. About how far can the sailboat travel in 4 hours?

37. **Find Data** Use an almanac to find high school graduation rates in your state and in three neighboring states. Organize and display your data in a table.

How do you know by which power of 10 to multiply a divisor and a dividend?

WRAP UP...

A school district is buying 77,250 cases of chalk at a discounted price of $717,867. How much does one case of chalk cost?

Use a calculator to divide large numbers.

717,867 ⎡÷⎤ 77,250 ⎡=⎤ ⎡ 9.2927766 ⎤

Since money is commonly expressed in cents, or hundredths, round the answer to the nearest cent.

So, one case of chalk costs $9.29.

Some division problems will continue to have a remainder no matter the number of places to which you divide. When this happens, round your answer to an appropriate place.

To round a decimal quotient to a given place, divide to the next place-value position. Then round to the given place.

Examples

A. Round to the nearest tenth.

```
        9.44 → 9.4
  4.3)40.6 00
     −38 7↓
        1 9 0
      −1 7 2↓
          1 80      Divide to the
        −1 72       hundredths place.
            8
```

B. Round to the nearest thousandth.

```
      0.8065 → 0.807
  8)6.4520
   −6 4↓↓↓
      052
     −48↓
       40      Divide to the
      −40      ten-thousandths place.
        0
```

Check for Understanding

Find the quotient. Round to the place given.

1. 3.447 ÷ 1.8
   (tenths)

2. 14.5 ÷ 5
   (ones)

3. $14.07 ÷ 8.4
   (cents)

4. 56.77 ÷ 9
   (hundredths)

5. 109.5 ÷ 73
   (ones)

6. 1.4508 ÷ 6.2
   (hundredths)

7. 4.1049 ÷ 9
   (thousandths)

8. 13.2154 ÷ 6
   (thousandths)

Practice

Find the quotient. Round to the nearest whole number or dollar.

9. $8.00 ÷ 3   **10.** 22.1 ÷ 5.6   **11.** 19.5 ÷ 9   **12.** 152 ÷ 5   **13.** 121 ÷ 13

14. 168.7 ÷ 3.5   **15.** 426 ÷ 8   **16.** 87 ÷ 6   **17.** $943 ÷ 7   **18.** $576 ÷ 6.1

Find the quotient. Round to the place given.

19. 113.88 ÷ 73   **20.** 5)14.8   **21.** 52)$87.35   **22.** 31.932 ÷ 6
(tenths)   (ones)   (cents)   (tenths)

23. 1.29 ÷ 5.5   **24.** 1.8)3.446   **25.** 7.263 ÷ 9   **26.** 7)4.104
(hundredths)   (thousandths)   (hundredths)   (ten-thousandths)

Mixed Applications

Choose the place to which you will round for Exercises 27–28. Be prepared to defend your choice. Then solve.

27. The cafeteria staff served 82 liters of salad to 335 students. If the salad was divided equally, about how much did each student receive?

28. The 4 students on a middle school relay team ran the 400-meter dash in 45.19 seconds. What was the average time of each runner?

29. Logical Reasoning   At the school store, pens sell at 3 for $1.53. What is the cost of 1 pen?

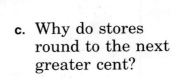

a. To the nearest thousandth, what does 1 pen cost if 3 sell for $1.54?

b. What does a store charge for 1 pen if 3 pens sell for $1.54?

c. Why do stores round to the next greater cent?

MIXED REVIEW

Tell how to move the decimal point to find the answer.

1. 10×1.5 **2.** $3.4 ÷ 100$ **3.** 52.55×10^3 **4.** $5,433 ÷ 10^4$

Estimate the quotient.

5. 448 ÷ 9   **6.** 110 ÷ 58   **7.** 3,496 ÷ 18   **8.** 93,245 ÷ 86

Name an everyday situation in which you round decimals to the hundredths place.

EXPRESSIONS
with Multiplication and Division

You can use what you know about algebraic expressions with addition and subtraction to write algebraic expressions with multiplication and division. Recall that an algebraic expression contains a variable.

Word Expression	Algebraic Expression
Twice a number, y 5.6 times a number, c A number, d, multiplied by 3	$2y$ $5.6c$ $3d$
A number, b, divided by 12 The quotient of a number, x, and 5	$b \div 12$, or $\dfrac{b}{12}$ $x \div 5$, or $\dfrac{x}{5}$

When you write an algebraic expression with multiplication, omit the sign. For example, $4 \times n$ is $4n$.

Rich spent $9.00 for lunches at school this week. He paid the same price each day. What was the daily cost of his lunch?

Since you do not know how many days Rich bought lunch, you can write an algebraic expression for the daily cost of his lunch. Using a variable can help you determine the cost for any number of days. Let n equal the number of days he bought lunch.

The daily cost of Rich's lunch was $\dfrac{9}{n}$.

You can evaluate the expression $\dfrac{9}{n}$ if you know how many days Rich bought his lunch.

Example

Find the daily cost when $n = 5$ days and when $n = 3$ days.

Evaluate $\dfrac{9}{n}$, for $n = 5$.
$\dfrac{9}{5} = 1.8$

Evaluate $\dfrac{9}{n}$, for $n = 3$.
$\dfrac{9}{3} = 3$

So, the daily cost was $1.80 if Rich bought lunch 5 days and $3.00 if he bought lunch 3 days.

- What was the daily cost if Rich bought lunch 2 days? 4 days?

- Suppose Rich spent $24.00 for lunches for 10 days. What was the daily cost of his lunches?

Check for Understanding

Write an algebraic expression for the word expression.

1. 14 times a number, z

2. the quotient of a number, p, and 7

3. a number, h, divided by 12

4. a number, k, multiplied by 54

Evaluate the expression.

5. $x \div 12$, for $x = 60$

6. $8t$, for $t = 7$

7. $4.5m$, for $m = 4$

8. $s \div 10$, for $s = 56.7$

Practice

Evaluate the expression $2.5b$ for each value of b.

9. $b = 21$

10. $b = 33$

11. $b = 153$

12. $b = 722$

13. $b = 17.8$

Evaluate the expression $\frac{b}{6}$ for each value of b.

14. $b = 42$

15. $b = 252$

16. $b = 1{,}503$

17. $b = 48.3$

18. $b = 72.6$

Evaluate the expression.

19. $35a$, for $a = 7$

20. $\frac{a}{4}$, for $a = 144$

21. $72b$, for $b = 3$

22. $\frac{m}{11}$, for $m = 968$

23. $6.5k$, for $k = 2.5$

24. $\frac{c}{3.6}$, for $c = 19.8$

Mixed Applications

For Exercises 25–26, write an algebraic expression.
Then evaluate the expression.

25. Tina traveled m miles to attend 5 track meets at the same place. How far did she travel to attend 1 meet? Evaluate the expression for $m = 378$ miles.

26. Brett has saved b dollars a week from his allowance for 8 weeks. How much has Brett saved? Evaluate the expression for $b = \$4.45$.

27. **Number Sense** Copy the puzzle. Write the missing factors so that the products of the factors both across and down are 144.

4		2	
3	12		2
	3	6	
3			2

If Bill drives m miles to work in 1 day, how far will he drive in 5 days?

WRAP UP...

EXPLORING

Multiplication and Division Equations

Remember that the equals sign in an equation shows that expressions on both sides represent the same value.

An equation is like a balanced scale. You can multiply or divide both sides by the same number to maintain the balance and solve the equation.

$$5 + m = 13$$
$$45 - f = 12$$
$$5n = 30$$
$$\frac{x}{7} = 9$$
$$20 = 2t$$
$$6 = \frac{k}{8}$$

WORK TOGETHER

Building Understanding

Use a balance scale and counters to explore equations.

Each pile on the left side of the scale has the same number of counters.

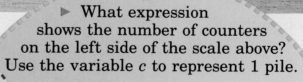

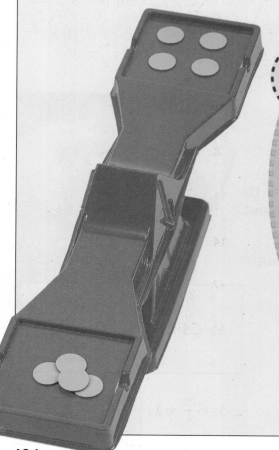

Talk About It

▶ What expression shows the number of counters on the left side of the scale above? Use the variable c to represent 1 pile.

▶ How many counters are on the right side of the scale?

▶ What is an equation that shows the relationship between the left side of the scale and the right side?

▶ Look at the scale on the left. There were 3 piles on the left side. Now there is 1 pile. By what number must you divide $3c$ in order to have only c remaining?

▶ How many counters are now on the right side of the scale?

▶ Since the scale has the same number of counters on each side, how many counters must be on the left side, or what is the value of c?

124

Making the Connection

By using a balance scale, you solved the equation $3c = 12$ and found that $c = 4$.

1. What operation did you use to solve the equation and find the value of c?

2. What is the inverse of multiplication?

Suppose you were asked to solve the equation $\frac{c}{3} = 4$.

3. What is the inverse of division?

4. What operation would you use to solve the equation?

5. How would you find the value of c?

Checking Understanding

Tell how to find the value of the variable.

6. $5x = 25$

7. $\frac{x}{4} = 16$

8. $25w = 15$

9. $\frac{w}{9} = 13$

10. $7d = 133$

11. $\frac{a}{12} = 144$

12. $12a = 144$

13. $\frac{t}{9} = 81$

14. $9t = 81$

15. $\frac{k}{2} = 155$

16. $25y = 625$

17. $\frac{z}{25} = 5$

18. $17s = 153$

19. $\frac{p}{155} = 1$

20. $54n = 432$

Use inverse operations to solve the equation.

21. $2t = 20$

22. $5n = 25$

23. $\frac{c}{3} = 11$

PROBLEM *Solving*

Mrs. Fox, a school cook, has $49.90 left from her paycheck. She paid a 4-week newspaper bill, spent $46.28 for food, and deposited $99.50 in her savings account. If her paycheck is $213.40, what is the weekly cost of the newspaper?

▶ **UNDERSTAND**

What are you asked to find?

What information are you given?

▶ **PLAN**

What strategy will you choose?

Since you know how much Mrs. Fox was paid and how much she spent on other items, *work backward* to find the weekly cost of the newspaper.

▶ **SOLVE**

How can you carry out your plan?

You can make a flowchart to organize the information. Then *work backward* using inverse operations and a calculator to find the weekly cost of the newspaper.

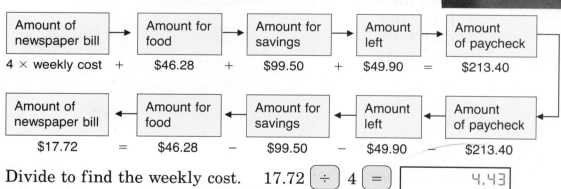

Amount of newspaper bill		Amount for food		Amount for savings		Amount left		Amount of paycheck
4 × weekly cost	+	$46.28	+	$99.50	+	$49.90	=	$213.40

Amount of newspaper bill		Amount for food		Amount for savings		Amount left		Amount of paycheck
$17.72	=	$46.28	−	$99.50	−	$49.90	−	$213.40

Divide to find the weekly cost.   17.72 ÷ 4 = ⟨ 4.43 ⟩

So, the weekly cost of the newspaper is $4.43.

▶ **LOOK BACK**

What other strategy could you use?

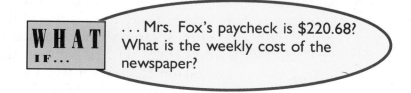

WHAT IF... ... Mrs. Fox's paycheck is $220.68? What is the weekly cost of the newspaper?

Apply

Make a flowchart and *work backward.* Solve.

1 Ben spent $6.00 for school supplies. He spent $3.00 for a notebook and $1.75 for a pen. How much did he spend for other supplies?

2 Carol spent a total of $20.00. She spent $9.45 for tickets, $5.95 for food, and the rest for 2 rings that were on sale at 2 for the price of 1. How much did each ring cost?

Mixed Applications ➤ **STRATEGIES**
- Write a Number Sentence • Guess and Check
- Find a Pattern • Work Backward

Choose a strategy and solve.

3 If the change from a gift purchase was $3.90 and each of 6 students had donated an equal amount, how much change should each student receive?

4 A school has computer lab networks for 4 students and networks for 3 students. If 3 networks hold a total of 10 students, how many 3-student networks are there?

5 Everett has a total of 30 problems for homework. If there are 6 more addition problems than subtraction problems, how many addition problems are there?

6 While working at the school store, Julie sold a jacket for $39.95 and notebooks for $1.39 each. If she collected $109.45, how many notebooks did she sell?

7 A school cafeteria sold 1,280 slices of pizza the first week, 640 the second, and 320 the third. If this pattern continues, in what week will the cafeteria sell 40 slices?

8 At the school store, Yolanda collected $0.85, $1.25, $2.10, and $1.10. She gave $0.25, $0.05, and $0.15 in change. She has $19.85 in the cash box. How much cash was in the box when Yolanda started?

WRITER'S CORNER

9 Students in a science class will expose 35 plants to different environments. Some plants will be kept in natural light, some will be exposed to artificial light, and others will be kept in the dark. Use this situation to write a word problem that can be solved by *working backward.*

CHAPTER REVIEW

Vocabulary Check

Choose a word from the box to complete each sentence.

compatible
divisible
divisor
expression
quotient
remainder

1. The number of times a __?__ divides the dividend is called the __?__ . *(page 96)*

2. Numbers used to estimate that divide without a remainder and are close to the actual numbers are called __?__ numbers. *(page 98)*

3. The __?__ must be less than the divisor. *(page 102)*

4. $\frac{n}{4}$ is an example of an algebraic __?__ . *(page 122)*

5. A number is __?__ by another number if the quotient is a whole number and the remainder is zero. *(page 96)*

I read the words in the box before I read the vocabulary sentences.

Concept Check

6. You can use the inverse operation, __?__ , to check your answer to a division problem. *(page 100)*

7. Since 4.1 and 4.10 are __?__ , you can place zeros to the right of the decimal without changing the value of the number. *(page 112)*

8. When you write an algebraic expression, you can write __?__ for 4 times n. *(page 122)*

9. To solve a multiplication equation, you __?__ each side of the equation by the __?__ number. *(page 124)*

Estimate. Choose the correct number of digits in the quotient. *(page 100)*

10. $12\overline{)1,945}$
    a. 1 digit
    b. 2 digits
    c. 3 digits

11. $3\overline{)12,540}$
    a. 3 digits
    b. 4 digits
    c. 5 digits

12. $25\overline{)53,760}$
    a. 4 digits
    b. 3 digits
    c. 2 digits

13. $173\overline{)945}$
    a. 3 digits
    b. 2 digits
    c. 1 digit

14. $965\overline{)492,906}$
    a. 4 digits
    b. 3 digits
    c. 2 digits

Complete the pattern. *(page 114)*

15. $4.707 \times 1,000 = 4,707$
    $4.707 \times 100 = \blacksquare$
    $4.707 \times 10 = \blacksquare$

16. $543 \div 1,000 = 0.543$
    $543 \div 100 = \blacksquare$
    $543 \div 10 = \blacksquare$

17. $8,505 \div 10 = 850.5$
    $8,505 \div 100 = \blacksquare$
    $8,505 \div 1,000 = \blacksquare$

Skill Check

Determine whether the number is divisible by 2, 3, 5, 9, or 10.
Write all that apply. *(page 96)*

18. 790　　　　　　**19.** 1,845　　　　　　**20.** 2,499　　　　　　**21.** 4,986

Estimate the quotient. *(page 98)*

22. $547 \div 9$　　　**23.** $267 \div 91$　　　**24.** $3,303 \div 16$　　　**25.** $48,139 \div 71$

Find the quotient. *(pages 100, 102, 106, 110, 116, 118)*

26. $12,611 \div 4$　　**27.** $52,836 \div 34$　　**28.** $965.25 \div 5$　　**29.** $649.2 \div 0.03$

Find the quotient. Round to the place given. *(page 120)*

30. $215.09 \div 89$　　**31.** $\$27.15 \div 4.9$　　**32.** $4,561 \div 6.7$　　**33.** $3.819 \div 6.2$
(tenths)　　　　　　(cents)　　　　　　　(hundredths)　　　　　(thousandths)

Evaluate the expression. *(page 122)*

34. $\dfrac{d}{6}$, for $d = 90$　　　　**35.** $9x$, for $x = 12$　　　　**36.** $\dfrac{n}{5.3}$, for $n = 42.4$

Tell how to solve the equation. *(page 124)*

37. $2x = 10$　　**38.** $\dfrac{w}{4} = 36$　　**39.** $6d = 844$　　**40.** $\dfrac{y}{24} = 35$

Problem-Solving Check *(pages 104, 126)*

41. Jim needs to pick up 213 band uniforms and 27 band capes from the dry cleaner. If each item costs $5.20 to clean, what will be Jim's total bill?

42. Tanya has misplaced 62 of a total of 437 booster club notices. How many classrooms of 25 students can receive copies of the notice?

43. Band boosters collected $187.50 by selling T-shirts for $6.00 each and hats for $4.50 each. If 15 students picked up their shirts and 15 students picked up their hats, how many students must still pick up items?

44. Nina spent $25.00 at the school bookstore. She has $3.54 left after buying 5 pencils for $0.20 each, 2 pens for $1.98 each, 2 notebooks for $3.50 each, and a novel. How much did the novel cost?

CHAPTER TEST

Determine whether the number is divisible by 2, 3, 5, 9, or 10.
Write all that apply.

1. 2,815　　　　**2.** 65,808　　　　**3.** 6,780　　　　**4.** 79,209

Estimate the quotient.

5. 334 ÷ 80　　**6.** 370 ÷ 41　　**7.** 35,246 ÷ 13　　**8.** 55,721 ÷ 901

Find the quotient.

9. 633 ÷ 7　　**10.** 14,381 ÷ 45　　**11.** 25,763 ÷ 9　　**12.** 4,515 ÷ 82

13. 76.02 ÷ 42　　**14.** 250.95 ÷ 7.5　　**15.** 118.8 ÷ 54　　**16.** 57.33 ÷ 0.09

17. 35.772 ÷ 22　　**18.** 52.5 ÷ 25　　**19.** 75.5 ÷ 25　　**20.** 68.796 ÷ 4.2

Evaluate the expression.

> I need to replace the variable with the given number.

21. $5x$, for $x = 25$　　**22.** $\frac{45}{a}$, for $a = 9$　　**23.** $8s$, for $s = 2.5$

24. $\frac{b}{10}$, for $b = 90$　　**25.** $4t$, for $t = 13$　　**26.** $82.3c$, for $c = 3$

Tell how to solve the equation.

27. $5t = 25$　　**28.** $\frac{r}{12} = 6$　　**29.** $7y = 11$

Solve. Write a number sentence for Exercises 30–31.

30. Mario collected 210 tennis balls from the locker room to distribute to 35 members of the team. How many tennis balls will each member receive?

31. Four team members took $45 each to a tournament. They spent a total of $75 for food and souvenirs and $75 for tickets. How much did they have left?

32. Jane took $32.79 to the mall. She bought school supplies for a total of $12.34 and lunch for $3.45. Did she have enough money left to buy a skirt that is on sale for $15.99?

33. Mr. Moreno's weekly paycheck is $390. Each week he spends $25 for gasoline, $55 for food, $100 for rent, and $35 for entertainment. If he saves the remaining money, how much does he save weekly?

$\mathcal{T}$eamwork
P-R-O-J-E-C-T

$\mathcal{S}$cience Connection

$\mathcal{T}$here are nine planets in the solar system. Each planet takes a different length of time to go around the sun once. The table shows how many of the Earth's days it takes each planet to go around the sun one time.

Your team's goal is to find how many Earth years it takes each planet to go around the sun once. For this activity, let one Earth year equal exactly 365 days.

Planet	Days to Go Around the Sun once	Earth Years to Go Around the Sun Once
Mercury	87.6 days	■
Venus	222.7 days	■
Earth	365.0 days	■
Mars	693.5 days	■
Jupiter	4,343.5 days	■
Saturn	10,767.5 days	■
Uranus	30,660.0 days	■
Neptune	60,152.0 days	■
Pluto	90,702.5 days	■

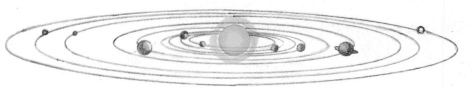

$\mathcal{D}$ecide
Discuss how you should go about solving the problem. Divide the calculations among yourselves. Each team member should do at least one calculation.

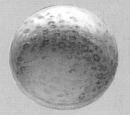

$\mathcal{D}$o
Use your calculations to complete the table. Check your work carefully.

$\mathcal{S}$hare
Compare your team's calculations with those of another team.

Talk About It

What conclusions can you draw about the relationship between the distance of a planet from the sun and the amount of time it takes the planet to go around the sun once?

extend your thinking

Consumer Connection

Many organizations, including some schools, allow people to buy season tickets to sporting events at a discounted rate. For example, a professional basketball organization might sell tickets to individual games for $8.00 but offer season tickets to 81 games for $599.40. If you bought a season ticket, how much would a single game cost?

How much would you save per ticket compared with the single-ticket price?

How much would you save by buying season tickets if you went to every game?

Find an organization in your community or school that offers season tickets. Find out how much the season tickets cost and how much tickets to single events cost. How much does each event cost at season-ticket prices? How much can you save by buying season tickets?

Challenge

Number Puzzle

Find a number that is divisible by all of these numbers:

4, 7, 5, 8, 2, and 10.

Logical Thinking

In a New England harbor, the water level at high tide is 36.8 feet. At low tide, the water level is 24.3 feet. It takes the tide 6 hours to go out. The water level drops steadily, going down the same amount each hour. To the nearest tenth, how far does the water drop in 2 hours?

Write the letter of the correct answer.

1. $112 - 70 \div 5$

   A. 37   B. 98
   C. 99   D. not here

2. What is the value of 10^5?

   A. 1,000   B. 10,000
   C. 100,000   D. 1,000,000

3. Choose the best estimate.
   $9.257 - 2.81$

   A. 5   B. 6
   C. 7.6   D. 8

4. $2,463.88 + 712.49$

   A. 3,175.37   B. 3,176.37
   C. 3,276.37   D. not here

5. Evaluate $b + 21$, for $b = 5.4$.

   A. 15.6   B. 25.4
   C. 26.4   D. 113.4

6. Choose the best estimate.
   $4,263 \times 18.81$

   A. 75,600   B. 76,000
   C. 76,600   D. 80,000

7. 35.4×0.086

   A. 2.9444   B. 3.0444
   C. 3.1444   D. 30.144

8. Choose the best estimate.
   $67.84 \div 8.29$

   A. 7   B. 8
   C. 9.5   D. 80

9. $9.54 \div 11.25$

   A. 0.0085   B. 0.795
   C. 0.848   D. 1.179

10. Evaluate $c \div 32$, for $c = 5.1$.

    A. 0.016   B. 1.59
    C. 159   D. not here

11. Jackie took $6.35 to buy a $1.20
    sandwich, a $0.79 muffin, and an
    $0.80 apple juice. She also bought 2
    pencils. If Jackie had $3.06 left,
    how much did each pencil cost?

    A. $0.25   B. $0.50
    C. $1.00   D. $1.50

12. Jeremy practices band 4 times a
    week for 90 minutes each time and
    for 75 minutes on Friday. If he
    missed 60 minutes on Wednesday,
    how many minutes did he practice
    that week?

    A. 300 minutes   B. 375 minutes
    C. 405 minutes   D. 435 minutes

5

GRAPHING, STATISTICS, AND PROBABILITY

Did you know . . .

. . . that an opinion poll is a popular way to find out how people feel about important issues?

Take an opinion poll in your class. Ask whether students would prefer the 9-month school year or a 12-month school year. What are the results of your poll? Do you think other sixth graders in your school feel the same way? Do you think sixth graders nationwide feel the same way?

COLLECTING AND ORGANIZING DATA

Statistics is a branch of mathematics dealing with the collection, organization, display, and analysis of data.

Mike and Ann are counting election votes. Mike reads the ballots and Ann writes the names, but Ann cannot keep up. What can Ann do to record the data quickly and easily?

The type of facts you want affects how you collect data.

- To collect data to record for an interview, which often requires long answers, use a questionnaire.

- To collect data to record for an opinion poll, which usually requires short answers, use a tally sheet.

Since Ann is recording votes, which are short answers, she can use a tally sheet.

Ann lists the names in alphabetical order on a **tally sheet.** She tallies the votes. Then Mike organizes the information in a frequency table, listing the candidates in order by the number of votes they received.

Tally Sheet

James	Juan	Kris	Teri
||||| |||||	||||| ||||| ||||| |||||	||||| ||||| ||||| ||||| ||||| ||||| ///	||||| ///

Frequency Table

Name	Frequency of Votes
Kris	33
Juan	20
James	10
Teri	8

- In which display are the election results easier to read?

Check for Understanding

1. Why did Ann use alphabetical order on the tally sheet?

2. Why did Mike use numerical order in the frequency table?

3. List three situations in which you would use a tally sheet to collect data for a table.

4. List three situations in which you would use a questionnaire to collect data for an interview.

Practice

Tell how to collect or organize the data.

5. Julio will interview a rock star about her career. Should he use a questionnaire or a tally sheet to gather information about the star? Explain your answer.

6. There are columns labeled *yes* and *no* on a tally sheet. Down the left side are names of several brands of cereal. For what might this tally sheet be used?

Suppose you are making a tally sheet and a frequency table. Use the data in the box for Exercises 7–13.

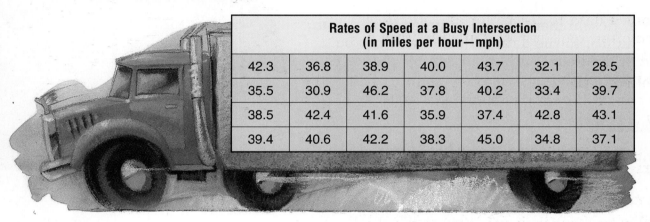

Rates of Speed at a Busy Intersection (in miles per hour—mph)						
42.3	36.8	38.9	40.0	43.7	32.1	28.5
35.5	30.9	46.2	37.8	40.2	33.4	39.7
38.5	42.4	41.6	35.9	37.4	42.8	43.1
39.4	40.6	42.2	38.3	45.0	34.8	37.1

7. Will you write each rate of speed or group the speeds, such as 25 to 30 mph, on your tally sheet? Justify your choice.

8. Will you use decimals or whole numbers to record the rates of speed on your tally sheet? Explain.

9. What will be the lowest rate of speed on your tally sheet?

10. What will be the highest rate of speed on your tally sheet?

11. How will you organize the rates of speed in your frequency table? Explain your answer.

12. Will the number of cars traveling from 40 to 45 mph be easier to find on the tally sheet or in the table?

13. Make a tally sheet for the data in the box. Record the data. Then make a frequency table to organize the data.

Mixed Applications

14. **Find Data** Think of several ways your classmates spend their allowance. Write three questions about spending an allowance. Use a questionnaire to interview at least five classmates.

15. **Organize Data** Use an almanac to find the populations of your state and your surrounding states. Make a table to display the data.

What is a frequency table?

CHOOSING SAMPLES

About 1,000 students attend Blair School. Jon surveyed 100 students by polling 1 out of every 10 as they entered school. He asked whether the student preferred the eagle or the bobcat as the school mascot. Thirty students chose the eagle, and seventy chose the bobcat.

Although the number may vary, people chosen to represent a population or group are called a **sample.** Researchers choose samples at **random,** or by chance, so the data collected will not be biased or slanted. A group chosen by chance is a **random sample.**

WHICH DO YOU PREFER?

Talk About It

▶ What is another method Jon could use to choose a random sample of students?

▶ Do you think the data collected from Jon's sample can be generalized to the whole school? Explain.

▶ If Jon asked the same question of teachers, would his results represent the students? Explain.

▶ If Jon chose to survey only sixth graders, would his results represent the whole school population? Why or why not?

▶ Suppose Jon wanted the eagle to be chosen. If he surveyed only students he knew would vote for the eagle, would his survey represent the whole school population? Explain.

Check for Understanding

Suppose you will survey 1 person out of every 10 for a sample. Tell about how many of each group you will survey.

1. 83 shoppers   2. 521 students   3. 2,987 drivers   4. 326 teachers

Name the people to survey for opinions about each product.

5. diapers   6. dog food   7. chalkboards   8. cereal

Practice

Answer the questions. Give reasons for your answers.

9. Volunteers called 200 voters (1 out of every 10 from a voters' list) to get the data about Mayor Allen's supporters. Is this a random sample? Is the sample large enough for the claim?

10. This billboard advertisement for Oatem cereal is based on a random sample of ten children living in the same block in Dallas, Texas. Is the sample large enough to represent all children?

11. Fay surveys 100 people in a town of 500 and determines that 0.85 of them like to shop at Gee's Grocery. Can Fay claim that 85 out of 100 townspeople like to shop at Gee's?

12. A local radio station polls its audience on issues in the local news. Listeners call in to vote *yes* or *no*. Are the results of these polls representative of all radio listeners?

CONSUMER CONNECTION

The bandwagon technique is a strategy used by advertisers. "Everyone is buying this soap," an ad may claim. Advertisers hope consumers will jump on the bandwagon and buy what "everyone" is buying.

With a team of classmates, discuss the following advertising claims. Are you convinced the product is popular? How specific are the words that tell how many people use the product? Is its popularity a good reason to buy the product? Share your results with other teams.

13. Two out of three people surveyed chose Plastotech toothpaste. Shouldn't you?

14. More and more people are turning to Painfree for headache relief. Shouldn't you get some today?

15. The best athletes and those champions who know quality buy XYZ running shoes.

16. Comfy jeans are the choice of everyone, young and old, who wants to look and feel good.

If you ask twelve boys their opinion, will your results be representative of your class? Explain.

MAKING PICTOGRAPHS AND BAR GRAPHS

Ann and Mike will make graphs of the election results to display on two bulletin boards. What kinds of graphs are appropriate?

The kind of graph you make depends on the type of data you want to show.

To display	You can use
a comparison of data	a bar graph or a pictograph

Advantages and Disadvantages

← can show specific data

← makes an attractive display; difficult to show specific data

Since Ann and Mike will show a comparison of votes, either a bar graph or a pictograph is appropriate.

To make their graphs, both Mike and Ann will follow these guidelines.

- Title the graph.

- Label the vertical axis (from base to top).

- Label the horizontal axis (from left to right).

- In a pictograph, use a key to show the symbol and its value.

- In a bar graph, use bars of equal width.

- In a bar graph, use equal space between bars.

- Use an appropriate numerical scale with equal intervals.

Practice

Use the graph for Exercises 5–7.

5. Does the graph show that more teenagers prefer to watch informational programs or general drama?

6. Does the graph show that more teenagers prefer to watch situation comedies or feature films?

7. What two types of programs appear to be equally liked by teenagers?

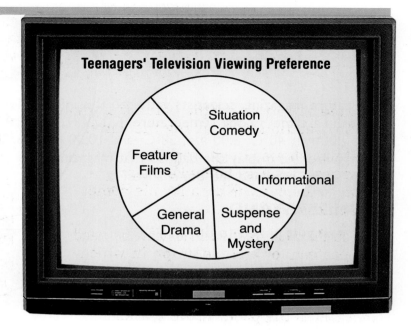

Teenagers' Television Viewing Preference

8. Make a table like the one on page 148 to show how you spend your time during a weekday.

9. Use the table you made in Exercise 8. Trace the pattern for a circle graph on page 148. Make a circle graph to display the data about your activities.

10. Choose the data in *A, B,* or *C.* Trace the pattern for a circle graph on page 148. Make a circle graph to display the data.

A. Favorite Colors

Color	Number of Students
Red	6
Blue	7
Yellow	4
Green	2
Purple	3
Orange	2

B. Favorite Flavors

Flavor	Number of Students
Vanilla	5
Chocolate	6
Strawberry	5
Peach	2
Pecan	4
Banana	2

C. Sue's Budgeted Expenses

Item	Amount Spent
Food	$400
Clothing	$100
Rent	$800
Utilities	$200
Car	$400
Savings	$500

Mixed Applications

11. **Write a Question** Write a question that can be answered by using the *guess and check* or the *work backward* strategy. You may want to use the information in the circle graph you made in Exercise 10.

12. **Making Choices** Look at the graph at the top of the page. Suppose you want to advertise to attract teenage buyers. Which type of program would you want to sponsor? Explain your choice.

How can you decide whether to use a line graph or a circle graph?

WRAP UP...

PROBLEM Solving

Choose an Appropriate Graph

For a nature magazine, scientists gathered this information about changes in a camel's body temperature: 6:00 A.M., 36°C; 10:00 A.M., 39°C; 2:00 P.M., 40°C; 6:00 P.M., 38°C; and 10:00 P.M., 36°C. How can you organize and display the data so that magazine readers will find it easy to read and see the changes?

▶ **UNDERSTAND**

What are you asked to do?

What information is given?

▶ **PLAN**

How can you solve the problem?
You can organize the data by time of day and use a graph to display the data.

▶ **SOLVE**

How can you carry out your plan?
Choose an appropriate type of graph.
Since you will be showing changes in a camel's body temperature over time, you can make a line graph. Organize the data by time of day.

Make a line graph.

1. Label each axis, with time on one axis and temperature on the other.

2. Plot the points.

3. Draw lines connecting the points.

4. Title the graph.

shows that → part of scale is missing

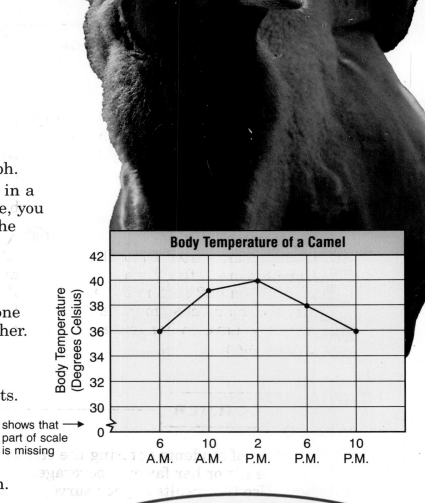

▶ **LOOK BACK**

Is the solution reasonable? Explain.

WHAT IF... ... the magazine asks that the changes in body temperature be displayed in order from highest to lowest? What type of graph would you use?

Apply

Make a table or a graph to organize each set of data so that it is easy to read and compare.

(1) A newspaper reported this data about businesses that have complied with a new law: By the end of June, 45 businesses had complied. By the end of July, 70 had complied. By the end of August, 120 had complied. By the end of September, 150 had complied. By the end of October, 170 had complied.

(2) A group of scientists published a report about bird migration. They caught birds in a net, counted the number of different species, and then released them. They counted birds once a day beginning on March 24. They counted 16, 20, 22, 24, 28, 26, 24, 22, 18, 12, 10, and 10 different species.

Mixed Applications	STRATEGIES	• Make a Table • Write a Number Sentence • Find a Pattern • Work Backward

Choose a strategy and solve.

(3) Nick buys two different nature magazines. The total cost for both is $18.00. The difference in the costs of the magazines is $2.50. How much does each of the magazines cost?

(4) Lisa collects postcards. In May she bought 3. Her aunt gave her 5. Lisa traded 2 of hers for 3 of Betty's. If Lisa has 45 postcards now, how many did she have at the beginning of May?

(5) Julie began her newspaper route with 12 customers. After 2 months she gained 5 more. After 2 more months, Julie had 22 customers. At this rate, how many customers can Julie expect to have on her route after 6 more months?

(6) A newspaper reported the capture of a pet boa constrictor that had been lost in an apartment building. If the pet boa is 0.75 as long as a 24-foot boa (the largest boa ever captured), how long is the pet boa?

WRITER'S CORNER

(7) Take a survey of students entering the cafeteria. Ask each to name his or her favorite beverage, salad, entree, or dessert. Use the results of your survey to write an advertisement for the cafeteria.

1. A newspaper reported that 34 people were running for four local offices. A total of 7 were running for manager, 3 for secretary, and 6 for treasurer. If 2 candidates for commissioner dropped out of the race, how many people were running for commissioner?

2. A town council printed 1,045 ballots for three precincts. In the first precinct, 282 people voted. In the second precinct, 309 people voted. A total of 148 ballots were returned blank. How many votes should a news broadcaster report for the third precinct?

To answer Exercises 1 and 2, I must answer the hidden question.

3. If you were going to record data from an interview, would you use a questionnaire or a tally sheet? Defend your answer.

Tell whether a bar graph or a line graph is more appropriate.

4. most-popular household pets

5. change in car prices over 5 years

Find the quotient. Round your answer to the nearest hundredth.

6. $95.71 \div 5$

7. $52 \div 3.4$

8. $533.24 \div 7.1$

9. $1.9527 \div 40.8$

Evaluate the expression.

10. $\dfrac{k}{11}$, for $k = 55$

11. $5.2x$, for $x = 8.1$

12. $12.5y$, for $y = 7$

13. $\dfrac{c}{2.5}$, for $c = 15.9$

14. $30.3a$, for $a = 2.7$

15. $\dfrac{b}{15}$, for $b = 63$

Use the histogram for Exercises 16–19.

16. How many flights does Midstate have between 6:00 A.M. and noon?

17. How many more flights are there from 8:00–8:59 A.M. than from 6:00–6:59 A.M.?

18. For which flight times are the most tickets available for purchase?

19. For which flight times are the fewest tickets available for purchase?

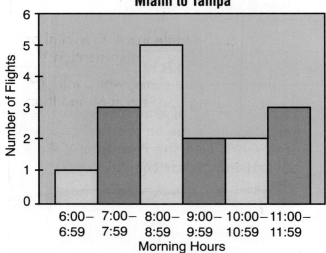

Midstate Flight Schedule
Miami to Tampa

$\mathcal{S}$potlight ON PROBLEM SOLVING

Draw Inferences from Data

Graphs are used to display data. You can often make generalizations from graphs. These generalizations are called inferences.

The double-line graph compares the average monthly temperatures in Miami, Florida, with those in San Antonio, Texas, during a one-year period.

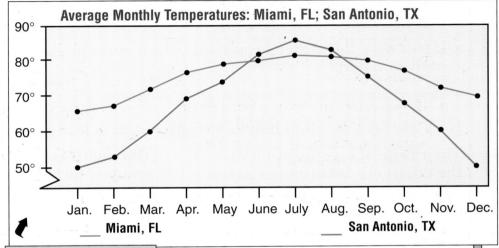

Average Monthly Temperatures: Miami, FL; San Antonio, TX

Miami, FL   San Antonio, TX

↳ indicates that part of the scale is missing

Talk About It

Use the graph and work together to draw inferences for these questions. Defend your answers.

A. Will more people travel to Miami or San Antonio for winter vacations?

B. If rates are the same, when will air-conditioning cost less in Miami than in San Antonio?

C. When might you want to wear a jacket in San Antonio?

D. In which city is freezing rain less likely?

Apply

Some inferences cannot be drawn from the available data. Try to answer the questions by using the graph. Discuss why you can or cannot draw an inference.

1. Is August rainfall higher in San Antonio or Miami?

2. Which of the two cities has a greater number of hurricanes?

3. Which city's economy depends more on light industry?

4. In which city will windchill affect how you dress?

RANGE, MEAN, MEDIAN, AND MODE

Suppose judges gave a figure skater these scores.

    7.9   8.0   8.2   7.9

- If you were the skater's parent, which score might you want to report?

- If you were the skater's opponent, which score might you want to report?

- Describe a fair way of reporting these scores.

Here are four ways to analyze and present data fairly.

The **range** of a group of numbers is the difference between the greatest and least numbers. It measures the distance between extremes.	The **mean** is the average of a group of numbers, or the sum of the group divided by the number of addends in the group.
The range of the scores is $8.2 - 7.9 = 0.3$	The mean of the scores is $(8.2 + 8.0 + 7.9 + 7.9) \div 4 = 8$
The **median** is the middle number in a group of numbers arranged in numerical order. When there are two middle numbers, the median is the mean or average of the two middle numbers.	The **mode** of a group of numbers is the number that occurs most often. There may be more than one mode in a group of numbers, or there may be no mode at all.
7.9 7.9 8.0 8.2 The median of the scores is $(8.0 + 7.9) \div 2 = 7.95$.	The mode of the scores is 7.9.

Check for Understanding

Use the table for Exercises 1–4.

1. Name the gymnast with the median score.

2. Find the mean. Round to the nearest hundredth.

3. What is the range of the scores?

4. What is the mode of the scores?

5. To the nearest hundredth, what is the mean of the three highest scores?

Team "A" Results	
Gymnast	**Score**
Jones	9.1
Dean	8.9
Moss	8.5
Ames	8.1
Keown	7.9
Hilton	6.8
Kent	6.2

 Connection, pages 480–481

Practice

Copy and complete the table.

	Collections of Data	Range	Mean	Median	Mode
6.	27, 27, 30, 85, 46	▦	▦	▦	▦
7.	78, 97, 93, 84, 98	▦	▦	▦	▦
8.	79, 95, 80, 66, 77, 77	▦	▦	▦	▦
9.	86, 95, 59, 74, 58, 83, 70	▦	▦	▦	▦
10.	80, 84, 76, 80, 94, 84, 97	▦	▦	▦	▦
11.	72, 65, 36, 57, 87, 97, 65, 57	▦	▦	▦	▦

Mixed Applications

12. At the *Daily Star,* 2 reporters earn $18,000 a year, 5 earn $22,000, and 3 earn $29,000. What is the mode of the salaries? What is the range?

13. A used-car company advertises 5 cars for sale at $6,212; $5,659; $6,365; $5,719; and $7,140. What is the average price of the used cars? What is the median price?

14. **Logical Reasoning** The LCM of three numbers greater than 1 is 12. What are the numbers?

15. **Number Sense** The range of three numbers is 45. Both the mode and the median are 52. Name each of the three numbers.

MIXED REVIEW

Write whether you would use a tally sheet or a questionnaire to record the information.

1. a day in the life of an airline pilot

2. the number of customers who prefer Brand X to Brand Y

Write whether a bar graph, a line graph, a histogram, or a circle graph is most appropriate to display the data.

3. average monthly value of a corporate stock

4. number sold of the three most popular foreign cars

5. votes counted during 1:00–2:59 P.M., 3:00–4:59 P.M., and 5:00–6:59 P.M.

6. a budget showing how you spend your allowance

How do you find the mean of a set of data?

WRAP
UP...

READING STEM-AND-LEAF PLOTS

The stem-and-leaf plot shows the number of home runs Henry (Hank) L. Aaron hit in each of 23 seasons.

Stem	Leaves
1	0 2 3
2	0 4 6 7 9
3	0 2 4 4 8 9 9
4	0 0 4 4 4 4 5 7

A stem-and-leaf plot is a useful way to organize and display data. In a **stem-and-leaf plot,** the ones digits appear horizontally as leaves. Tens and greater digits appear vertically as stems. In this stem-and-leaf plot, the stems are tens digits, and the leaves are ones digits.

The third stem and its leaves show 30, 32, 34, 34, 38, 39, and 39 home runs.

- How many home runs are shown by the second stem and its leaves?

You can use the stem-and-leaf plot to find the range, median, and mode of the data.

Examples

A. What is the range of the data?

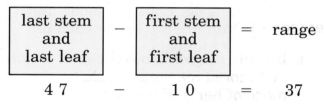

$$\text{4 7} - \text{1 0} = 37$$

So, the range of the data is 37.

B. What is the median of the data?

Since there are 23 leaves, the twelfth leaf shows the median (11 + 1 + 11 = 23).

Count to the twelfth leaf. The twelfth leaf is 4. The stem is 3.

So, the median of the data is 34.

C. What is the mode of the data?

Count the most-repeated leaves for each stem. For the first and second stems, no leaves are repeated. For the third stem, both 4 and 9 appear twice. For the fourth stem, 0 appears twice and 4 appears four times.

So, the mode of the data is 44.

Check for Understanding

Use the stem-and-leaf plot above for Exercises 1–4.

1. Which number occurs more often, 30 or 40?

2. How many leaves does the second stem have?

3. What numbers are shown by the fourth stem and its leaves?

4. Which number occurs less often, 26 or 39?

Idea Bank, page 491, Exercise 13

Practice

This stem-and-leaf plot shows Rella's scores for 20 rounds of golf. Use this plot for Exercises 5–12.

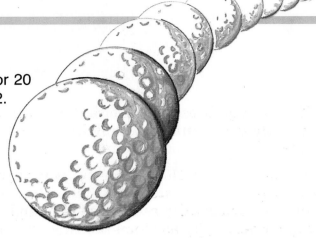

Stem	Leaves
7	6 7 8 9 9 9
8	0 2 3 5 5 6 8 9
9	0 0 1 2 3 8

5. Which score occurs more often, 76 or 85?

6. Which score occurs less often, 79 or 90?

7. What are the scores shown by the first stem and its leaves?

8. What are the scores shown by the second stem and its leaves?

9. What are the scores shown by the third stem and its leaves?

10. What is the range of Rella's golf scores?

11. What is the median of Rella's golf scores?

12. What is the mode of Rella's golf scores?

Mixed Applications

Solve. Use the stem-and-leaf plot above for Exercises 13–15.

13. If Rella played another round of golf and scored 79, what would be the median of her golf scores?

14. If Rella played another round of golf and scored 89, what would be the mode of her golf scores?

15. **Analyze Data**   Use a calculator and the stem-and-leaf plots on page 156 and above. To the nearest hundredth, what is the mean of Aaron's home runs? What is the mean of Rella's golf scores?

16. **Making Decisions**   Rella wants to show the number of times she scored in the seventies, eighties, and nineties. Should she make a line graph or a histogram?

17. Char needs to record the number of different-sized groups entering a mall. Make a tally sheet for recording the number of groups of each size from 1 to 10.

18. Make a stem-and-leaf plot that shows the last ten scores you made on your math tests.

In what everyday situations could you use a stem-and-leaf plot to display data?

WRAP
UP...

At the grand opening of McKool's Frozen Health Food Shoppe, Marcie can buy a large yogurt parfait for $1. She can choose from the selection of flavors and sauces in the table. How many choices does Marcie have?

One way to find the number of choices is to make a tree diagram that shows the total outcomes.

McKool's Yogurt and Sauce	
Yogurt Flavor	Sauce
Vanilla	Apple
Chocolate	Peach
	Blueberry

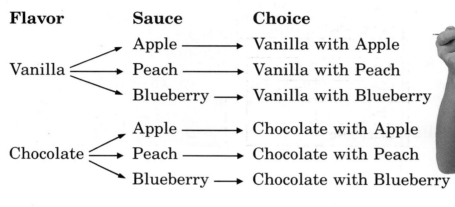

Flavor	Sauce	Choice
Vanilla	Apple →	Vanilla with Apple
	Peach →	Vanilla with Peach
	Blueberry →	Vanilla with Blueberry
Chocolate	Apple →	Chocolate with Apple
	Peach →	Chocolate with Peach
	Blueberry →	Chocolate with Blueberry

So, Marcie has 6 choices.

Another Method

You can also use the counting principle to find the total number of choices. When you use the **counting principle,** you multiply the total outcomes of one set of choices by the total outcomes of the other set of choices.

number of flavors × number of sauces = total choices

$$2 \quad \times \quad 3 \quad = \quad 6$$

Check for Understanding

Find the number of choices by making a tree diagram.

1.
Meat	Gravy
Ham	Redeye
	Mushroom

2.
Crust	Topping
Regular	Pepperoni
Deep-dish	Sausage
	Anchovies

3.
Entree	Beverage
Pizza	Milk
Noodles	Apple juice
Beans	Grape juice

Practice

Make a tree diagram to find the number of choices.

4.

Shoes	Socks
Brown	Argyle
	Black
	White

5.

Entree	Spice
Chicken	Curry
Beef	Mustard
	Garlic

6.

Ink	Paper
Green	Gray
Red	White
Black	

7.

Plate	Napkins
Flowered	Mauve
Checked	Taupe
Polka-dotted	Rust

8.

Shirt	Slacks
Blue	Striped
Red	Checked
Yellow	Plaid

9.

Buttons	Bows
Purple	Striped
Pink	
Chartreuse	

Write the number of choices.

10. 2 vegetables, 3 salads

11. 3 wigs, 5 hats

12. 4 soaps, 7 towels

13. 5 birthdays, 10 cards

14. 5 ink cartridges, 6 pens

15. 150 students, 5 teachers

16. 7 cards, 12 colors

17. 11 pencils, 25 erasers

Mixed Applications

18. Each of 5 airlines offers 3 flights each day from St. Louis to Indianapolis. June wants to take one flight. From how many can June choose?

19. Zed is registering for school. He can choose either English or science at 9:00 A.M. and either art, health, or math at 10:00 A.M. How many pairs of classes can Zed choose from?

20. Logical Reasoning In a recent contest, Gary scored fewer points than Barb, who scored more points than Tina. Tim scored more points than Tina but fewer than Gary. Who won?

21. Make Up a Problem Think of a situation that involves choosing from several alternatives. Make up a problem about the total number of choices.

How can you find the number of choices without drawing a diagram?

PROBABILITY

Probability (P) is a comparison between the number of favorable events or outcomes and the number of possible events or outcomes. The number line shows that the probability of an event ranges from 0, or impossible, to 1, or certain.

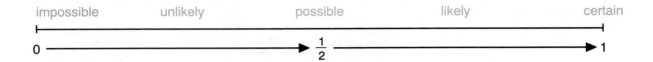

impossible · unlikely · possible · likely · certain

$$0 \longrightarrow \quad \frac{1}{2} \quad \longrightarrow 1$$

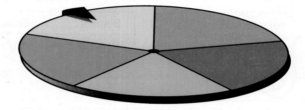

A spinner like this one is used on a television show. What is the probability that the spinner will stop on orange?

$$P(orange) = \frac{\text{number of favorable outcomes}}{\text{number of possible outcomes}} = \frac{1}{5}, \text{ or 1 out of 5}$$

The probability of spinning orange is $\frac{1}{5}$.

Since the outcomes are equally likely, the probability of stopping on any one color is $\frac{1}{5}$, or 1 out of 5.

- Are you more likely to stop on orange if 3 of 5 sections of a spinner are orange or if 1 of 5 sections are orange?

What is the probability of spinning either red or blue?

$$P(red\ or\ blue) = \frac{\text{number of favorable outcomes}}{\text{number of possible outcomes}} = \frac{2}{5}, \text{ or 2 out of 5}$$

So, the probability, P(red or blue), is $\frac{2}{5}$.

Check for Understanding

Use the spinner. Find the probability of each event.

1. stopping on red, blue, or yellow

2. not stopping on green

3. P(red or blue or green or yellow or orange)

4. P(purple, pink, or aqua)

Practice

For Exercises 5–10, think of a number cube labeled 2, 4, 6, 8, 10, and 12.

5. What is the probability of tossing an even number?

6. What is the probability of tossing an odd number?

7. What is the probability of tossing a number less than 8?

8. What is the probability of tossing a number greater than 2?

9. What is the probability of tossing a number greater than 4?

10. What is the probability of tossing 2?

Copy and complete the table.

	Experiment	Possible Outcome	Probabilities
11.	Toss a coin once.	heads or tails	P(heads) = ■ P(tails) = ■
12.	Toss a number cube with faces 1 to 6.	■	P(odd number) = ■ P(even number) = ■ P(3 or 5) = ■
13.	Draw a marble from 3 green, 2 red, and 4 yellow marbles without looking.	■	P(yellow) = ■ P(red or yellow) = ■

Mixed Applications

14. Look at Exercise 13. Which color marble has the greatest probability of being drawn?

15. A coin shows heads five times in a row. What is the probability of heads on the next toss?

16. **Logical Reasoning** The mean of five whole numbers is 16.8. What is the sum of the numbers?

17. **Analyze Data** Toss a coin ten times. Compare your results with the results in Exercise 11.

If you are given a choice of three answers to a problem, what is the probability of choosing the correct answer by chance?

WRAP UP...

INDEPENDENT EVENTS

Rosa cannot decide among program choices of comedy, drama, and mystery to fill prime-time television slots, so she writes the choices on slips of paper and puts them in a bag. Each time she draws a slip of paper, she returns it to the bag. If she has chosen *comedy* in 2 out of 4 draws, what is the probability she will draw *drama* next time?

Events that have no influence on one another are called **independent events.** Because Rosa always returns the slip of paper to the bag, she creates independent events. Since Rosa always has the same number of possible outcomes, drawing *comedy* does not affect the probability of drawing *drama*.

So, the probability of drawing *drama* is still $\frac{1}{3}$.

Rosa will choose from car and cereal commercials to air with the programs. She puts slips of paper in bags marked *programs* and *commercials*. What is the probability she will draw *car* for the commercial and *drama* for the program?

Commercial	Program	Possible Combination
Car	Comedy ⟶	Car commercial, Comedy
	Drama ⟶	Car commercial, Drama
	Mystery ⟶	Car commercial, Mystery
Cereal	Comedy ⟶	Cereal commercial, Comedy
	Drama ⟶	Cereal commercial, Drama
	Mystery ⟶	Cereal commercial, Mystery

So, the probability of choosing *car* and *drama* is $\frac{1}{6}$.

Check for Understanding

Use Rosa's choices of programs and commercials. Find the probability of each event.

1. drawing mystery program after drawing drama 2 times

2. drawing car commercial after drawing cereal 5 times

3. P(car commercial, comedy program)

4. P(car or cereal, comedy)

Practice

Use the situation described for Exercises 5–8.

Arthur will go to a theater to see a movie and have a snack. *Here With the Wind, The Tin Man,* and *Old Blue* are playing at the theater. Arthur's favorite snacks are popcorn, pizza, and burritos.

5. Make a tree diagram to show all of Arthur's possible choices.

6. What is the probability that Arthur will choose *Old Blue* and a burrito?

7. If Claire has the same choices as Arthur, what is the probability she will choose *Here With the Wind* and popcorn?

8. Suppose Claire can choose a fourth movie, *Field Trip*. What is the probability she will choose pizza and *The Tin Man*?

Mixed Applications

9. The weather reporter said the chance of rain is 1 out of 5 this morning. If it rains at 6:00 A.M., what is the probability of rain at 10:30 A.M. and 11:00 A.M.?

10. **Number Sense • Mental Math**
Jeffrey must choose a three-piece outfit from 3 pairs of slacks, 4 shirts, and 2 jackets. How many choices does Jeffrey have?

MIXED REVIEW

Evaluate the algebraic expression.

1. $\frac{m}{12}$, for $m = 108$

2. $6.8b$, for $b = 3.5$

3. $35x$, for $x = 10$

Tell which operation you use to solve the equation.

4. $37y = 333$

5. $\frac{n}{62} = 186$

6. $5.9n = 82.6$

Draw a tree diagram to show the number of choices.

7. 1 problem, 4 answers

8. 3 shirts, 3 slacks

9. 4 cats, 5 dogs

If the probability of red is 1 out of 5, what will be the probability of red at the twelfth event?

PROBLEM *Solving*

Strategy • Find a Pattern

ELECTION UPDATE

A television station will predict the winner in a close election when 17,200 votes are counted. At 7:00 P.M. 8,700 votes had been counted. By 8:00 P.M. 10,200 votes had been counted. By 9:00 P.M. 11,800 votes had been counted, and by 10:00 P.M. 13,500 votes had been counted. If the pattern continues, when will the station predict the winner?

Making a table is often a good strategy for solving a problem when you must find a pattern.

▶ **UNDERSTAND**

What are you asked to find?

What information are you given?

▶ **PLAN**

How will you solve the problem?

You can make a table showing the times and the number of votes counted. Then extend the pattern.

▶ **SOLVE**

How will you find the pattern?

Find the number of votes counted during each interval.

Time	7:00 P.M.	8:00 P.M.	9:00 P.M.	10:00 P.M.
Votes Counted	8,700	10,200	11,800	13,500

+ 1,500   + 1,600   + 1,700

An additional 100 votes are counted each hour.

Extend the pattern.

11:00 P.M.

13,500 ⊞ + ⊟ 1,800 ⊟ = ⊟ | 15300. |

12:00 midnight

15,300 ⊞ + ⊟ 1,900 ⊟ = ⊟ | 17200. |

The television station will predict the winner at 12:00 midnight.

▶ **LOOK BACK**

How can you check your answer?

WHAT IF... ... you were asked how many votes will be counted by 2:00 A.M.? What would be your answer?

164

Apply

Find a pattern and solve.

1 A print shop's presses must be cleaned regularly to keep them working. A service company cleaned them in October 1984, March 1985, August 1985, and January 1986. During which months in 1988 were the print shop's presses cleaned?

2 A city has a total of 7 news offices. There are 6 computer terminals in one office, 8 terminals in the second office, and 11 terminals in the third office. If the pattern continues, what is the total number of computer terminals in all 7 offices?

Mixed Applications | **STRATEGIES** | • Find a Pattern • Guess and Check
• Work Backward • Write a Number Sentence

Choose a strategy and solve.

3 Michael spent a total of $22.70 at a local newsstand. He bought a newspaper for $1.25, a magazine for $3.95, and 2 books that each cost the same. How much did each book cost?

4 Lydia studies twice as long as James. James and Cathy study a total of 7 hours, but Cathy studies 3 hours longer than James. How long does Lydia study?

5 Each NBA team has 5 minutes to choose a player in the draft. If the draft begins at 8:00 P.M. and the Nets get the sixth draft choice, at what time will the Nets choose?

6 Use the information in Exercise 5. Suppose you were the twentieth player chosen in the NBA draft. What is the greatest number of minutes you would have had to wait to be chosen by one of the teams?

7 One world leader will travel 3 hours to get to a summit this year. The second will travel 1 hour more than twice the time traveled by the first, and the third will travel 2 times longer than the second. What is the total travel time for the world leaders?

8 The summit will last 4 days. A 6-hour meeting and a 2-hour luncheon are scheduled each day. There will be a 3-hour reception on the opening day and a 4-hour banquet on the closing day. What is the total amount of time scheduled during the summit?

Vocabulary Check

Choose a word or words from the box to complete each sentence.

circle graph
histogram
line graph
median
mode
probability
range

1. Changes over time can be shown in a __?__ . *(page 146)*

2. The number that occurs most often in a set of data is the __?__ . *(page 154)*

3. A bar graph that shows how often numbers occur within a certain range is a __?__ . *(page 144)*

4. The middle number in a group of numbers arranged in numerical order is the __?__ . *(page 154)*

5. The type of graph used to display parts of a whole and relationships among the parts is a __?__ . *(page 148)*

6. A comparison between the number of favorable events and the number of possible events is called __?__ . *(page 160)*

7. The difference between the greatest and least numbers of a group of numbers is called the __?__ . *(page 154)*

Concept Check

8. If you were graphing changes in amount of light over a 24-hour period, would you use a bar graph, a histogram, or a line graph? *(pages 140, 144, 146)*

Tell whether a bar graph, histogram, line graph, or circle graph is most appropriate to display the data. *(pages 140, 144, 146, 148)*

9. number of babies born during a 24-hour period

10. amount of electricity used from month to month for a year

11. heights of tallest mountains

12. speeds of fastest animals

13. number to finish a race in 5-minute intervals

14. daily relative humidity in Puerto Rico for the month of May

The type of graph I choose will depend on the kind of data to be graphed.

Skill Check

Use the information in the stem-and-leaf plot for Exercises 15–19.

Scholastic Bowl Team "B" Tournament Points Scored

Stem	Leaves
3	3 4 4
4	5 6 7 8
5	2 2 2 8

15. How many points are shown by the second stem and its leaves? *(page 156)*

16. What is the range of the scores? *(pages 154, 156)*

17. What is the median of the scores? *(pages 154, 156)*

18. What is the mode of the scores? *(pages 154, 156)*

19. To the nearest hundredth, what is the mean of the scores in the plot? *(page 154, 156)*

Draw a tree diagram. Tell the number of possible choices. *(page 158)*

20.

Jacket	Hat
blazer	beret
	sock hat
	cap

21.

Ink	Card
blue	postcard
red	birthday
	thank you

22.

Course	Day
science	Monday
English	Tuesday
health	Friday

23. A number cube has faces 1 through 6. What is the probability of tossing a 3 or a 5? *(page 160)*

24. A number cube has faces 1 through 6. What is the probability of tossing a 6 if you have already tossed the cube 4 times? *(page 162)*

Problem-Solving Check *(pages 150, 164)*

25. Wendy will replace a radio newscaster every other Friday night, beginning the second Friday in September. If there are 4 Fridays in each month, will Wendy work the last Friday in October?

26. Ms. Malone is a beekeeper. On Monday she tends 2 hives, on Tuesday 4 hives, on Wednesday 8 hives, and on Thursday 16 hives. If she works five days a week and the pattern continues, how many hives will she tend next Tuesday?

27. Ron asked 24 students to name their favorite type of music. Twelve like rock, 2 like jazz, 4 like country, 5 like rap, and 1 likes classical. Make a bar graph, a histogram, or a circle graph for the data.

28. Dan will survey 1 out of every 10 mail carriers. If there are 450 carriers, how many will he survey?

Tell whether a bar graph, a histogram, a line graph, or a circle graph is most appropriate.

1. four tallest trees

2. changes in air temperature

3. month-to-month attendance at a civic center

4. life cycle of a butterfly

Use the information in the stem-and-leaf plot for Exercises 5–8.

I need to recall the meaning of *mode, range, median,* and *mean.*

5. What is the mode?

6. What is the range?

7. What is the median?

8. What is the mean?

Numbers of Bluejays Feeding in Gardens

Stem	Leaves
1	7 9 9
2	0 2

Make a tree diagram. Tell the number of choices.

9.

Hair Color	Hairstyle
brown	flattop
	mohawk

10.

Dress	Shoes
pink	beige
blue	white

11.

Coat	Tie
tweed	striped
plaid	polka-dot
solid	checked

A number cube has faces 1 through 6. Tell the probability of the event.

12. tossing 5 or 6

13. tossing 2, 5, or 6

14. tossing 2 on the fifth roll

15. tossing 2 or 3 on tenth toss

16. tossing 3

17. tossing 1, 2, 3, 4, or 5

Solve.

18. Gary rides a bus 100 miles on Monday, 150 miles on Tuesday, 250 miles on Wednesday, and 400 miles on Thursday. If the pattern continues, how far will Gary ride on Friday?

19. Paula gave away 96 stickers from her collection in April, 48 in May, 24 in June, and 12 in July. If the pattern continues, how many stickers will Paula give away in August?

20. What group should Ann survey to collect data about student participation in after-school activities? If she wants to survey 1 out of 10 and there are 1,200 in the group, how many should she survey?

Graph the Results

Sometimes you can demonstrate a general rule by testing the rule and making a graph of your results. For example, when you toss a coin, the probability of heads is 1 out of 2.

Work with teammates. Experiment by tossing a coin. Then graph your results.

 Decide

Discuss how to record the data, allowing each member of the team to record his or her own results. Also decide how you will construct your graph.

 Do

Each team member should toss a coin 20 times and record the number of heads and the number of tails. Then the team should make a bar

graph to show the results.
• Use two bars for each group member, shading one bar for heads and one for tails.
• Shade or color the bars differently.

 Share

Compare your results with those of another team.

Talk About It   Are the results easier to understand from each team member's record or from the graph? Explain.

How is your graph similar to the other team's graph?

Is the probability of heads 1 out of 2 in most cases? Why or why not?

Predict Events

If you roll a number cube one time, you will roll 1, 2, 3, 4, 5, or 6.

The probability of rolling a 2 is $\frac{1}{6}$. If you roll the cube 60 times, the best prediction for the number of 2's is 10, because $\frac{1}{6}$ of 60 is 10.

Make a prediction for each situation described below. Then use number cubes to see how close your prediction is to your outcome.

1. How many times will you roll an odd number if you roll one number cube 50 times?

2. How many times will you roll a sum of 7 if you roll two number cubes 180 times?

Challenge

Logical Reasoning

1. A player spins each spinner once. How many possible outcomes are there?

2. A player spins each spinner twice. How many possible outcomes are there?

Problem Solving

1. The mean of Evan's scores on three math tests is 72. His last two scores were 76 and 72. What was his first score?

2. Dale's math teacher counts tests twice as heavily as quizzes. Dale scored 80 and 60 on quizzes, but he has an overall average of 82. What was his score on the test?

CUMULATIVE REVIEW

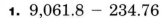

Write the letter of the correct answer.

1. 9,061.8 − 234.76

   A. 8,827.04   **B.** 8,827.42
   C. 8,837.12   **D.** 9,827.42

2. Evaluate 21.4 − b, for $b = 5.9$.

   A. 14.5   **B.** 15.5
   C. 16.5   **D.** not here

3. 215 ÷ 5 − 3

   A. 33   **B.** 40
   C. 107.5   **D.** not here

4. Evaluate $\dfrac{x}{2.4}$, for $x = 7.92$.

   A. 2.3   **B.** 3.0
   C. 3.3   **D.** 3.4

5. What is the mode of the data?
   2   5   7   9   12   12

   A. 7.8   **B.** 9
   C. 10   **D.** 12

6. 0.0153 × 6,729

   A. 102.9537   **B.** 103.9537
   C. 109.5327   **D.** 1,029.537

7. Estimate to place the decimal point.
   453.8337 ÷ 9.01

   A. 5.037   **B.** 50.37
   C. 503.7   **D.** 5,037

8. 2.748 ÷ 45.8

   A. 0.6   **B.** 0.62
   C. 6.02   **D.** not here

9. Which type of graph would you use to show the lengths of the 5 longest rivers?

   A. circle   **B.** histogram
   C. bar   **D.** line

10. What is the probability of choosing a 5 from a bag containing cards with the numbers 1–6?

   A. 6 out of 6   **B.** 2 out of 6
   C. 3 out of 6   **D.** 1 out of 6

11. Sara is twice as old as her brother Sean. Sean is 4 years older than Tracey. If Sara will be 13 years old next year, how old is Tracey?

   A. 2   **B.** 3
   C. 4   **D.** 5

12. Lily scored 4 more points on a quiz than Dora scored. If the sum of their scores is 180, how many points did Lily score on the quiz?

   A. 84   **B.** 88
   C. 90   **D.** 92

CHAPTER

6

NUMBER THEORY

Did you know . . .

. . . that using number theory when you play games can make you a more competitive player?

Talk About It

Suppose the altitude gauge on a flight simulator game shows an increase in altitude of 10 feet for every second you pull back on a joystick. How can you find what your altitude will be if you pull back on the joystick for 15 seconds?

MULTIPLES AND LEAST COMMON MULTIPLE

Nan takes 3 minutes to drive the course of a car-rally video game and return to the starting point. Cladio takes 4 minutes. If they start at the same time, how many minutes will pass until they cross the starting point at the same time?

A list of numbers can help you find multiples of 3 and 4. The multiples show when Nan and Cladio cross the starting point.

Multiples of 3 tell when Nan crosses the starting point. To find multiples of 3, multiply 3 by 1, 2, 3, 4, and so on. Multiples of 3 are shaded.

Multiples of 4 tell when Cladio crosses the starting point. To find multiples of 4, multiply 4 by 1, 2, 3, 4, and so on. An X is put through each multiple of 4.

1	2	3	4	5	6	7	8	9	10
11	12	13	14	15	16	17	18	19	20
21	22	23	24	25	26	27	28	29	30

Numbers that are both shaded and crossed out are **common multiples.** The smallest common multiple of two or more numbers is called the **least common multiple (LCM).**

- Which numbers in the list are common multiples of 3 and 4?

- Which number is the LCM of 3 and 4?

So, 12 minutes will pass before Nan and Cladio cross the starting point at the same time.

Another Method   You can also list multiples of each number to find the LCM of two or more numbers.

What is the LCM of 2 and 5?

Step 1	**Step 2**
List multiples of 2 and 5.	Find the LCM.
2: 2 4 6 8 10 12 14	2: 2 4 6 8 ⑩ 12 14
5: 5 10 15 20 25 30 35	5: 5 ⑩ 15 20 25 30 35

So, the LCM of 2 and 5 is 10.

- Is there an LCM of every pair of numbers? How do you know?

Check for Understanding

Use a list of numbers to find the LCM of the numbers.

1. 3, 5   **2.** 4, 12   **3.** 3, 4   **4.** 2, 3, 7   **5.** 3, 5, 6

List multiples to find the LCM of the numbers.

6. 4, 5   **7.** 3, 7   **8.** 4, 6   **9.** 2, 3, 4   **10.** 2, 8, 12

Practice

Write the first three multiples, excluding the number itself.

11. 3   **12.** 5   **13.** 6   **14.** 7   **15.** 9

16. 10   **17.** 11   **18.** 12   **19.** 15   **20.** 20

Find the LCM of the numbers.

21. 6, 7   **22.** 2, 13   **23.** 8, 12   **24.** 20, 3   **25.** 9, 15

26. 5, 35   **27.** 3, 5   **28.** 4, 20   **29.** 6, 12   **30.** 8, 9

31. 9, 6   **32.** 10, 15   **33.** 15, 45   **34.** 12, 24   **35.** 16, 32

36. 18, 54   **37.** 11, 132   **38.** 16, 64   **39.** 15, 40   **40.** 1, 110

41. 50, 100   **42.** 2, 4, 6   **43.** 3, 6, 9   **44.** 12, 15, 18   **45.** 12, 24, 30

Mixed Applications

46. Bob plays tennis every other day, and Caroline plays every fourth day. Some days they compete with each other. If they both play on Monday, on what day will Bob and Caroline both play again?

47. Justine has 12 card games and 14 board games. Rachel has twice as many board games and half as many card games. How many games does Rachel have?

48. Number Sense If the LCM of a pair of numbers is 4 and the sum of the pair is 6, what are the numbers?

49. Logical Reasoning The LCM of three different numbers is 4. What are the numbers?

How can you find the LCM of three numbers?

EQUIVALENT FRACTIONS

Jody and Lyle follow these steps to make a spinner for a board game.

Fold a circle in half. Shade one part.

Fold the circle in half again.

Fold the circle in half a third time.

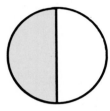

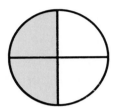

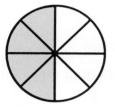

$\frac{1}{2}$ is shaded.

$\frac{2}{4}$ is shaded.

$\frac{4}{8}$ is shaded.

- How can you tell from the circles above that $\frac{1}{2} = \frac{2}{4}$, $\frac{2}{4} = \frac{4}{8}$, and $\frac{1}{2} = \frac{4}{8}$?

- If Jody and Lyle fold the circle in half a fourth time, will the shaded amount remain the same?

- What fraction names the amount shaded if they fold the circle in half a fourth time?

Equivalent fractions are fractions that name the same part. $\frac{1}{2}$, $\frac{2}{4}$, $\frac{4}{8}$, and $\frac{8}{16}$ are equivalent fractions.

Another Method   You can also multiply or divide both the numerator and the denominator by the same number to find equivalent fractions.

A. $\frac{1}{2} = \frac{1 \times 2}{2 \times 2} = \frac{2}{4}$
$\llcorner \frac{2}{2} = 1$

B. $\frac{8}{16} = \frac{8 \div 8}{16 \div 8} = \frac{1}{2}$
$\llcorner \frac{8}{8} = 1$

C. $\frac{4}{8} \overset{\times 2}{\underset{\times 2}{=}} \frac{8}{16}$

Check for Understanding

Fold a sheet of paper with the given amount shaded to find two equivalent fractions.

1. $\frac{1}{4}$

2. $\frac{2}{3}$

3. $\frac{3}{4}$

Multiply or divide to find two equivalent fractions.

4. $\frac{2}{5}$

5. $\frac{5}{10}$

6. $\frac{5}{6}$

Practice

Write a fraction that tells what part is colored. Identify the equivalent fractions by comparing Exercises 7–10.

7.

8.

9.

10.

Complete the number sentence.

11. $\dfrac{2}{3} = \dfrac{\blacksquare}{6}$

12. $\dfrac{1}{2} = \dfrac{4}{\blacksquare}$

13. $\dfrac{5}{8} = \dfrac{\blacksquare}{64}$

14. $\dfrac{30}{35} = \dfrac{\blacksquare}{7}$

15. $\dfrac{4}{5} = \dfrac{\blacksquare}{25}$

16. $\dfrac{1}{2} = \dfrac{38}{\blacksquare}$

17. $\dfrac{13}{8} = \dfrac{\blacksquare}{32}$

18. $\dfrac{2}{3} = \dfrac{16}{\blacksquare}$

19. $\dfrac{30}{36} = \dfrac{5}{\blacksquare}$

20. $\dfrac{3}{24} = \dfrac{\blacksquare}{8}$

21. $\dfrac{17}{34} = \dfrac{1}{\blacksquare}$

22. $\dfrac{39}{52} = \dfrac{\blacksquare}{4}$

Write *yes* or *no* to tell whether the fractions are equivalent. If they are not, write an equivalent fraction for each fraction.

23. $\dfrac{15}{30}, \dfrac{1}{2}$

24. $\dfrac{3}{18}, \dfrac{1}{3}$

25. $\dfrac{2}{3}, \dfrac{12}{18}$

26. $\dfrac{3}{4}, \dfrac{9}{12}$

27. $\dfrac{4}{16}, \dfrac{12}{18}$

28. $\dfrac{10}{12}, \dfrac{13}{24}$

29. $\dfrac{10}{16}, \dfrac{4}{4}$

30. $\dfrac{12}{21}, \dfrac{4}{7}$

Mixed Applications

31. Janis can solve 5 mazes in one day. If she has 45 new mazes to work, how many days will Janis need to solve them?

32. A pizza is cut into fourths. Gwen will cut it into smaller pieces to share equally with 5 friends. Into how many total pieces will Gwen cut the pizza?

33. Logical Reasoning Warren played $\frac{1}{2}$ of 18 holes of golf. Robin assembled $\frac{1}{2}$ of a 500-piece jigsaw puzzle. Are their efforts equal? Explain.

34. Making Decisions You must take the shorter of two routes to a friend's house. One route is $\frac{5}{6}$ mile, and the other is $\frac{1}{3}$ mile. Which route will you take?

How do you know that $\frac{2}{2}$ and $\frac{8}{8}$ are equal to 1?

WRAP UP...

EXPLORING

Least Common Denominator

Name some multiples of 2 and 3. What is the LCM of 2 and 3? In this lesson you will look at multiples of 2 and 3 to explore least common denominator.

WORK TOGETHER

Building Understanding

Use paper, a ruler, and scissors. Draw and cut out two rectangles that are 6 cm by 24 cm each.

Fold one rectangle, or draw a line dividing it into halves. Label each part $\frac{1}{2}$. Then shade $\frac{1}{2}$.

Fold the other rectangle or draw lines dividing it into thirds. Label each part $\frac{1}{3}$. Then shade $\frac{2}{3}$.

$\frac{1}{2}$	$\frac{1}{2}$

Rectangle A

$\frac{1}{3}$	$\frac{1}{3}$	$\frac{1}{3}$

Rectangle B

Talk About It

▶ How can you divide each rectangle so that both rectangles have the same number of sections?

▶ Into how many equal sections has each triangle been folded?

▶ After the fold, what fraction names the shaded part of Rectangle A?

▶ After the fold, what fraction names the shaded part of Rectangle B?

▶ Is $\frac{3}{6}$ the same as $\frac{1}{2}$ of Rectangle A?

▶ Is $\frac{4}{6}$ the same as $\frac{2}{3}$ of Rectangle B?

▶ Look at the denominators of the fractions. How is 6 related to 2 and 3?

178

Making the Connection

A common multiple of the denominators of two or more fractions is called a **common denominator**. You can find a common denominator the same way you find a common multiple.

How can you write $\frac{5}{6}$ and $\frac{1}{9}$ using common denominators?

Find common multiples of 6 and 9.

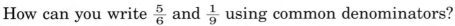

6: 6 12 ⑱ 24 30 ㊱ 42 48
9: 9 ⑱ 27 ㊱ 45 54 63 72

Write equivalent fractions using denominators that are common multiples.

$\frac{5}{6} = \frac{15}{18}$ $\frac{5}{6} = \frac{30}{36}$ $\frac{1}{9} = \frac{2}{18}$ $\frac{1}{9} = \frac{4}{36}$

So, using common denominators, $\frac{5}{6}$ can be written as $\frac{15}{18}$ and $\frac{30}{36}$, and $\frac{1}{9}$ can be written as $\frac{2}{18}$ and $\frac{4}{36}$.

The **least common denominator (LCD)** for two or more fractions is the least common multiple (LCM) of the denominators.

You can find the LCD the same way you find the LCM.

How can you write $\frac{1}{3}$ and $\frac{4}{5}$ using the LCD?

Step 1 Find the LCD.	**Step 2** Write equivalent fractions.
3: 3 6 9 12 ⑮ 18 21 5: 5 10 ⑮ 20 25 30 35	$\frac{1}{3} = \frac{1 \times 5}{3 \times 5} = \frac{5}{15}$ $\frac{4}{5} = \frac{4 \times 3}{5 \times 3} = \frac{12}{15}$

So, with the LCD, $\frac{1}{3}$ is written $\frac{5}{15}$ and $\frac{4}{5}$ is written $\frac{12}{15}$.

1. What is the LCD for $\frac{1}{5}$ and $\frac{9}{15}$?

2. What is the LCD for $\frac{5}{6}$ and $\frac{1}{9}$? Rewrite $\frac{5}{6}$ and $\frac{1}{9}$ using the LCD.

Checking Understanding

Write each pair of fractions by using the LCD.

3. $\frac{1}{2}, \frac{3}{4}$ 4. $\frac{5}{6}, \frac{1}{9}$ 5. $\frac{1}{5}, \frac{3}{10}$ 6. $\frac{1}{3}, \frac{3}{4}$ 7. $\frac{1}{6}, \frac{5}{8}$

8. Name two fractions in which one of the denominators is the LCD for the fractions.

Amber, Ben, and Chad are playing a game with fraction cards. They each draw a card from the stack and turn it faceup. The person with the greatest fraction takes all the cards. Amber draws $\frac{4}{5}$, Ben draws $\frac{1}{5}$, and Chad draws $\frac{3}{5}$. Who takes all the cards?

$\frac{1}{5}$, $\frac{4}{5}$, and $\frac{3}{5}$ are **like fractions.** They have the same denominator. To compare and order like fractions, compare the numerators.

Since $4 > 3 > 1$, then $\frac{4}{5} > \frac{3}{5} > \frac{1}{5}$.

So, Amber takes all the cards.

Suppose Amber draws $\frac{1}{6}$, Ben draws $\frac{1}{4}$, and Chad draws $\frac{1}{3}$. Who takes all the cards?

$\frac{1}{6}$, $\frac{1}{4}$, and $\frac{1}{3}$ are **unlike fractions.** They have different denominators. To compare and order unlike fractions, you can use fraction bars or write equivalent fractions with like denominators.

Fraction Bars

$\frac{1}{3}$	$\frac{1}{3}$	$\frac{1}{3}$

$\frac{1}{4}$	$\frac{1}{4}$	$\frac{1}{4}$	$\frac{1}{4}$

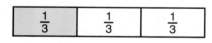

$\frac{1}{3} > \frac{1}{4} > \frac{1}{6}$

So, Chad takes all the cards.

Equivalent Fractions

Use the LCD to write equivalent fractions. The LCD is 12.

$$\frac{1}{6} = \frac{2}{12} \quad (\times 2)$$

$$\frac{1}{4} = \frac{3}{12} \quad (\times 3)$$

$$\frac{1}{3} = \frac{4}{12} \quad (\times 4)$$

$$\frac{1}{3} > \frac{1}{4} > \frac{1}{6}$$

Talk About It

▶ When you compare and order two fractions with a numerator of 1, how can the denominators help you determine which fraction is greater?

▶ How would you order $1\frac{1}{2}$, $2\frac{1}{4}$, and $1\frac{1}{4}$ from least to greatest?

Check for Understanding

Use the LCD to write like fractions. Tell which one is greater.

1. $\frac{3}{5}, \frac{9}{10}$

2. $\frac{4}{9}, \frac{16}{27}$

3. $\frac{6}{7}, \frac{30}{49}$

4. $\frac{2}{3}, \frac{6}{21}$

5. $\frac{5}{6}, \frac{35}{36}$

6. $\frac{4}{7}, \frac{1}{2}$

7. $\frac{3}{5}, \frac{7}{8}$

8. $\frac{4}{15}, \frac{7}{10}$

Practice

Compare. Use < or >.

9. $\frac{2}{3} \bullet \frac{1}{3}$

10. $\frac{5}{8} \bullet \frac{3}{4}$

11. $\frac{4}{7} \bullet \frac{6}{7}$

12. $\frac{39}{40} \bullet \frac{7}{8}$

13. $3\frac{6}{15} \bullet 3\frac{9}{30}$

Use <, >, or = to compare the fractions.

14. $\frac{5}{20} \bullet \frac{6}{20}$

15. $\frac{4}{5} \bullet \frac{2}{3}$

16. $\frac{7}{14} \bullet \frac{4}{6}$

17. $\frac{9}{27} \bullet \frac{11}{33}$

18. $\frac{16}{32} \bullet \frac{9}{12}$

19. $\frac{24}{48} \bullet \frac{27}{36}$

20. $\frac{12}{15} \bullet \frac{10}{12}$

21. $\frac{49}{50} \bullet \frac{56}{100}$

Write in order from least to greatest. Use <.

22. $\frac{4}{5}, \frac{7}{10}, \frac{3}{5}$

23. $\frac{7}{8}, \frac{1}{2}, \frac{2}{3}$

24. $\frac{1}{2}, \frac{1}{3}, \frac{3}{4}$

25. $\frac{4}{6}, \frac{7}{14}, \frac{5}{7}, \frac{1}{3}$

Tell whether the fractions are in order from greatest to least.
Write *yes* or *no*.

26. $\frac{5}{8} > \frac{3}{8} > \frac{5}{6}$

27. $\frac{5}{6} > \frac{3}{4} > \frac{1}{2}$

28. $\frac{2}{3} > \frac{4}{9} > \frac{3}{4}$

29. $\frac{7}{10} > \frac{3}{5} > \frac{4}{15}$

Mixed Applications

30. Of all the markers in Trey's new game, $\frac{1}{6}$ are red, $\frac{1}{2}$ are blue, and $\frac{1}{3}$ are green. Does Trey have more blue markers or green markers?

31. **Making Choices** A board-game card reads, "You must pay the player to your left 0.3 of your earnings or pay the bank 0.42 of your earnings." Which choice will you make?

Why is it easier to order like fractions than unlike fractions?

WRAP UP...

PROBLEM Solving

Teresa, Lea, Bart, and Doug are getting ready for a chess tournament. Before play begins, each player shakes hands with every other player once. How many handshakes are there in all?

When you are solving a problem, it sometimes helps to act out the situation.

▶ **UNDERSTAND**

What are you asked to find?

What information are you given?

▶ **PLAN**

How can you solve the problem?

You can *act it out* by having four students represent the four chess players.

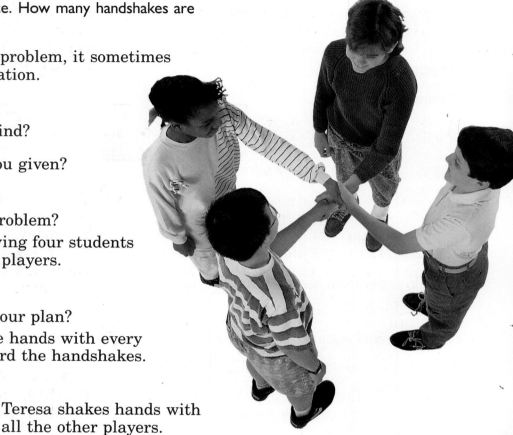

▶ **SOLVE**

How can you carry out your plan?

Have each student shake hands with every other student once. Record the handshakes.

Record of Handshakes

Teresa and ⟨ Lea, Bart, Doug   Teresa shakes hands with all the other players.

Lea and ⟨ Bart, Doug   Lea shakes hands with every player except Teresa.

Bart and — Doug   Bart shakes hands with Doug.

So, there are 6 handshakes in all.

▶ **LOOK BACK**

How can you check your solution?

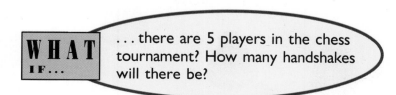

WHAT IF... . . . there are 5 players in the chess tournament? How many handshakes will there be?

Apply

Solve by acting out the situation.

(1) There are five reporters for a television show. Before the first show, each of the reporters had one telephone conversation with every other reporter. How many telephone conversations were there in all?

(2) Six girls sat at a round table. Opal sat at Suzanna's right. Suzanna sat across from Pearl. Barb did not sit next to Pearl, but she did sit next to April. Maria sat between Opal and Pearl. Which of the girls sat at Pearl's right?

Mixed Applications ➔ **STRATEGIES**

- Make a Table   • Work Backward
- Write a Number Sentence
- Act It Out

Choose a strategy and solve.

(3) Tari and Rita have different editions of the same game. Each has 56 markers. Half of Tari's markers are purple, but Rita has 5 fewer purple markers than Tari. How many of Rita's markers are not purple?

(4) Edward and Doris worked crossword puzzles on Monday, Thursday, Sunday, Wednesday, and Saturday. If this pattern continues, when will Edward and Doris work their next crossword puzzle?

(5) Perry had 42 sheets of colored construction paper that he divided among 7 classmates and himself. Could Perry divide the sheets of paper evenly, or did he have some left over? Explain.

(6) When a game was called because of rain, Tom was $\frac{3}{5}$ finished, Mack was $\frac{3}{9}$ finished, Bob was $\frac{1}{3}$ finished, and Dewayne was $\frac{7}{10}$ finished. Which players were tied?

(7) Fanny, Harold, Sandy, and Ted enjoy fishing, hunting, skiing, or tennis. No person's name begins with the first letter of the activity he or she enjoys. Fanny likes tennis. Sandy does not like hunting. Which activity does each person enjoy?

(8) Colette gave 12 marbles to Jim, got 15 from Lenny, got twice that number from Dee, and gave 16 more to Sally than she had given to Jim. Now she has 62 marbles. How many marbles did Colette have before she gave 12 marbles to Jim?

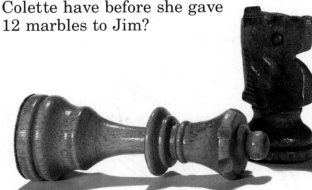

FACTORS, PRIMES, AND COMPOSITES

Sid and Corey are playing "Factor." They draw from a bag containing the numbers 2 to 100 to determine the number of squares with which to play. The object is to use the squares to make as many rectangles as possible. Players get a point for each rectangle they make.

Corey draws the number 5 and uses 5 squares. How many rectangles can Corey make?

Corey can make two rectangles, one that is 5 squares by 1 square and another that is 1 square by 5 squares. The numbers 1 and 5 are factors of 5.

Factors are numbers that are multiplied to find a product.

Since 5 has only two factors, it is a prime number. A **prime number** has exactly two factors, itself and 1.

Another Example

Sid draws the number 12 and uses 12 squares. How many rectangles can Sid make?

Sid can make 6 rectangles: 1 by 12, 12 by 1, 2 by 6, 6 by 2, 3 by 4, and 4 by 3. The numbers 1, 2, 3, 4, 6, and 12 are factors of 12.

A whole number such as 12 is called a **composite number** because it has more than two factors.

NOTE: The numbers 0 and 1 are neither prime nor composite.

Talk About It

Use unit squares to help you model the questions.

▶ When Sid draws a number, will he score more points if he draws a prime number or a composite number?

▶ Will Corey score more points if he draws 6 or 9?

▶ Will Sid score more points if he draws 28 or 30?

  Idea Bank, page 490, Exercises 5–6

Check for Understanding

List the factors. Then tell whether the number is prime or composite.

1. 5   **2.** 14   **3.** 18   **4.** 2   **5.** 16

Practice

Tell whether the number is prime or composite.

6. 12   **7.** 11   **8.** 36   **9.** 37   **10.** 49   **11.** 71   **12.** 83

Write the factors of each number.

13. 9   **14.** 16   **15.** 12   **16.** 21   **17.** 18   **18.** 25   **19.** 121

Mixed Applications

20. Make a list of the prime numbers between 1 and 10.

21. Make a list of the composite numbers between 1 and 10.

22. Alice and Mary have 36 games. Mary has 12 more games than Alice. How many games does Alice have? How many does Mary have?

23. Number Sense Challenge another student to a game of Factor. Draw numbers 2 to 50 from a bag to determine the number of cubes for each player's turn. Keep score.

SOCIAL STUDIES CONNECTION

Eratosthenes was a Greek mathematician who lived about 200 B.C. He devised this system of finding the prime numbers between 1 and 100.

List the numbers 1 to 100 on a sheet of paper. Then follow the instructions in *A–D* and complete Exercise 24.

A. Cross out 1.
B. Cross out all the multiples of 2 that are greater than 2.
C. Cross out all the multiples of 3 that are greater than 3.
D. Do the same for multiples of 5 and 7.

24. The remaining numbers are prime. List all the prime numbers from 1 to 100.

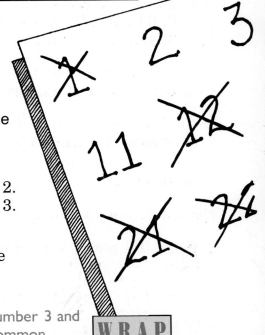

Name two factors that the prime number 3 and the composite number 12 have in common.

WRAP
UP...

More Practice, Lesson 6.6, page H55   185

PRIME FACTORIZATION

A composite number can be expressed as a product of prime numbers. This is the **prime factorization** of the number. You can use a factor tree to find the prime factors of a composite number.

What is the prime factorization of 100?

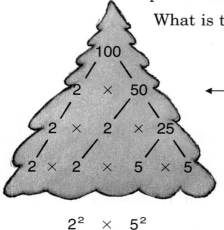

← Choose any two factors of 100. →
Continue until only prime numbers are left.

← prime factorization →

prime factorization written
← with exponents →

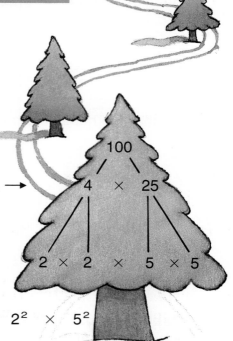

$2^2 \times 5^2$

So, the prime factorization of 100 is $2 \times 2 \times 5 \times 5$, or $2^2 \times 5^2$.

Another Method You can also divide until the quotient is 1 to find the prime factors of a number.

What is the prime factorization of 36?

$36 \div 2 \div 2 \div 3 \div 3 = 1$

prime factors   quotient

The prime factorization of 36 is $2 \times 2 \times 3 \times 3$, or $2^2 \times 3^2$.

Talk About It

▶ How can you use divisibility rules to help you find the prime factorization of a number?

▶ How do you know that you have finished a prime factorization?

Check for Understanding

Complete the prime factorization.

1. $12 = 2 \times \blacksquare \times 3$

2. $2 \times 5 \times \blacksquare = 70$

3. $81 = 3 \times 3 \times 3 \times \blacksquare$

4. $2^\blacksquare = 16$

5. $3 \times \blacksquare \times 7 = 105$

6. $2 \times 7^\blacksquare = 98$

Practice

Write the prime factorization. Use a factor tree.

7. 25   **8.** 16   **9.** 21   **10.** 24   **11.** 49   **12.** 56

13. 36   **14.** 44   **15.** 66   **16.** 42   **17.** 98   **18.** 84

Write the prime factorization in exponent form.

19. 9   **20.** 18   **21.** 12   **22.** 32   **23.** 50   **24.** 49

25. 48   **26.** 98   **27.** 64   **28.** 27   **29.** 56   **30.** 72

Mixed Applications

31. Number Sense If a number x is a prime factor of 12, will x be a prime factor of 36? How do you know?

32. Logical Reasoning A number f is the least common multiple of 3, 5, and 6. What is f?

MATH CONNECTION

You can use prime factorization to find the LCM.

Example Find the LCM of 4, 9, and 50.

Step 1 Write the prime factorizations.	**Step 2** Write an expression using each factor once.	**Step 3** Write the greatest exponent of each factor. Then multiply. $2^2 \cdot 3^2 \cdot 5^2$
$4 = 2^2$ $9 = 3^2$ $50 = 2 \times 5^2$	$2 \cdot 3 \cdot 5$ $\uparrow \quad \uparrow$ Dots mean multiply.	You can use a calculator with an x^2 key.  

So, the LCM of 4, 9, and 50 is 900.

Use prime factorization to find the LCM.

33. 9, 30   **34.** 12, 16   **35.** 10, 15   **36.** 20, 90   **37.** 4, 25, 100

Do the prime factors of a number differ depending on which factors you choose first? Explain.

More Practice, Lesson 6.7, page H56

GREATEST COMMON FACTOR

Rosa will make a game board that is 16 inches by 24 inches for a game she has invented. She wants to use square tiles. What is the largest tile Rosa can use?

You must find the largest number that divides into both 16 and 24 without a remainder.

Factors shared by two or more numbers are called **common factors**. The largest common factor is called the **greatest common factor (GCF)**.

To find the GCF, list the factors of 16 and 24, identify the common factors, and then find the greatest factor.

Factors of 16: 1, 2, 4, 8, 16
Factors of 24: 1, 2, 3, 4, 6, 8, 12, 24

Talk About It

▶ What are the sizes of square tiles that would cover the game board?

▶ What is the largest tile that can cover the game board?

So, the largest tile Rosa can use is an 8-inch square tile.

Another Method You can also use prime factorization to find the GCF. The GCF of two or more numbers is the product of their common factors.

Find the GCF of 18 and 24.

Prime factorization of 18: $2 \times 3 \times 3$ ← Common factors: $2 \times 3 = 6$
Prime factorization of 24: $2 \times 2 \times 2 \times 3$

So, the GCF of 18 and 24 is 6.

Check for Understanding

Find the GCF by listing the factors.

1. 9 and 15 **2.** 24 and 32 **3.** 52 and 78 **4.** 25 and 75

Find the GCF by using prime factorization.

5. 18 and 30 **6.** 12 and 16 **7.** 54 and 72 **8.** 30 and 96

Practice

Write the common factors of each pair of numbers.

9. 9, 12   **10.** 18, 36   **11.** 12, 16   **12.** 32, 60   **13.** 27, 54

14. 9, 64   **15.** 40, 12   **16.** 56, 49   **17.** 25, 50   **18.** 12, 72

Write the GCF of each pair of numbers.

19. 8, 52   **20.** 21, 9   **21.** 18, 99   **22.** 36, 16   **23.** 34, 60

24. 56, 64   **25.** 30, 12   **26.** 33, 99   **27.** 25, 40   **28.** 12, 72

29. 4, 72   **30.** 21, 63   **31.** 24, 72   **32.** 45, 81   **33.** 24, 56

Mixed Applications

34. Rico has 72 red roses and 54 white roses to make bouquets. How many roses can he put in each bouquet if he uses an equal number of each color and makes the largest bouquets possible?

35. Mental Math Sean has six 12-inch pieces of toy train track. Ruth has eight 9-inch pieces of train track. When assembled, will both tracks be the same length? Explain.

MIXED REVIEW

Complete the number sentence.

1. $\frac{1}{3} = \frac{\blacksquare}{6}$ **2.** $\frac{3}{4} = \frac{\blacksquare}{12}$ **3.** $\frac{9}{18} = \frac{1}{\blacksquare}$ **4.** $\frac{4}{5} = \frac{16}{\blacksquare}$ **5.** $\frac{3}{7} = \frac{15}{\blacksquare}$

Write in order from greatest to least. Use >.

6. $\frac{1}{5}, \frac{4}{5}, \frac{3}{5}$ **7.** $\frac{2}{7}, \frac{6}{7}, \frac{5}{7}, \frac{4}{7}$ **8.** $\frac{1}{2}, \frac{3}{5}, \frac{2}{3}$ **9.** $\frac{2}{9}, \frac{3}{4}, \frac{2}{3}$ **10.** $\frac{3}{8}, \frac{1}{4}, \frac{1}{3}, \frac{1}{6}$

Write the factors of each number.

11. 4   **12.** 17   **13.** 27   **14.** 39   **15.** 47

How can you use prime factorization to find the GCF of two numbers?

WRAP UP...

REVIEW AND MAINTENANCE

1. At a closeout sale, you can buy 1 game at the regular price of $7.50, 2 for $13.00, 3 for $18.50, and 4 for $24.00. If the pattern continues, how much can you save over the regular price if you buy 6 games?

2. Quiltz is a game of patterns. Denise drew a card with 32, 31, 29, 26, and 22 written on it. She must find the next three numbers in the pattern to score. What are they?

3. Mary, Emily, and Sue drove to a chess match in their own cars. One car was blue, one gray, and one white. Mary met the white car at a traffic light. The blue car passed Mary. Sue does not drive a white car. Which color car does each person drive?

4. After a contest, five winners lined up in order from the fifth- to the first-prize winner. Will was ahead of Dean but behind Pete. Harold was behind Will but ahead of Dean. Dan was ahead of Pete. Who received each prize?

Use the stem-and-leaf plot for Exercises 5–9.

5. What are the ages shown by the first stem and its leaves?

6. What is the range of the ages?

7. What is the mode of the data?

Ages of Baseball Players

Stem	Leaves
2	0 1 2 3 7 8
3	1 2 4 4 6

I read the direction lines very carefully.

8. What is the median of the data?

9. What is the average age of the baseball players?

Write the number of choices.

10. 2 cars, 4 colors

11. 4 dresses, 6 belts

Write the LCM for each pair of numbers.

12. 20, 40 13. 12, 18 14. 15, 35 15. 9, 10 16. 3, 75

Use the LCD to write like fractions.

17. $\frac{2}{3}, \frac{1}{2}$ 18. $\frac{1}{8}, \frac{3}{10}$ 19. $\frac{4}{21}, \frac{2}{9}$ 20. $\frac{7}{15}, \frac{5}{9}$ 21. $\frac{11}{12}, \frac{7}{8}$

Write the GCF for each pair of numbers.

22. 9, 63 23. 12, 16 24. 25, 60 25. 35, 75 26. 18, 42

Spotlight ON PROBLEM SOLVING

Visualize the Situation

Sometimes visualizing a situation can help you solve a problem. When you visualize a problem, you form a mental picture of the solution.

Heather is buying lunch for 6 of her friends. The pizzeria serves a 12-inch pizza by cutting it into 8 equal slices. Each of Heather's friends ordered 3 slices of pizza.

Talk About It

Work with a classmate to answer the questions. Be prepared to discuss your responses with the class.

A. How many pizzas will Heather need to buy for her 6 friends?

B. How many pizzas would Heather need to buy if she had 3 slices of pizza with her friends?

C. Make a drawing that would serve as the solution to the problem. Include slices of pizza for Heather.

D. Do you think it is easier to visualize a solution or to compute to find the solution?

Apply
Visualize a solution to each problem. Then draw a picture of the solution.

1. Rich bought a dozen eggs. He and two brothers ate $\frac{1}{3}$ of the eggs for breakfast. His mother used $\frac{1}{2}$ dozen eggs in a soufflé. How many eggs are left?

2. In Cozy Shoes' sale, if you buy 2 pairs of shoes, the third pair is free. The Yaws have 6 children. How many pairs must they buy to provide each child with 2 pairs?

3. Susan is preparing for the school's Day of Games. There are 28 students in her class. If she wants to buy enough 6-packs of juice for each student to have 2 drinks, how many 6-packs should Susan buy?

4. The Day of Games will have long tables for board games. These tables seat 8 people on each side and 2 game directors, one at each end. There are 4 of these long tables in the school gym. How many game directors will be needed?

191

FRACTIONS
in Simplest Form

Jim and Alex were playing Simplest-Form Fraction Match. Jim drew these two cards and called them a match. He said $\frac{16}{24}$ is not in simplest form, but $\frac{2}{3}$ is. Alex challenged the play. Who was correct?

A fraction is in **simplest form,** or lowest terms, when the numerator and the denominator have no common factor greater than 1.

- Is $\frac{2}{3}$ in simplest form? How do you know?

- Is $\frac{16}{24}$ in simplest form? How do you know?

To find who was correct, you must write $\frac{16}{24}$ in simplest form. Use repeated division until no common factors other than 1 remain.

$$\frac{16}{24} = \frac{8}{12} = \frac{4}{6} = \frac{2}{3} \leftarrow \text{simplest form}$$

with each step dividing by $\div 2$.

So, Jim was correct.

Another Method

You can also use the GCF to write a fraction in simplest form.

Write $\frac{6}{8}$ in simplest form.

Divide the numerator and the denominator by the GCF.

$$\frac{6 \div 2}{8 \div 2} = \frac{3}{4} \leftarrow \text{simplest form}$$

- Which method of writing a fraction in simplest form is more efficient? Why?

- What is $\frac{12}{8}$ written in simplest form?

- What is $\frac{10}{10}$ written in simplest form? $\frac{a}{a}$?

- Does the value of the fraction remain the same when you divide both the numerator and the denominator by the GCF? How do you know?

Check for Understanding

Find the GCF of each pair of numbers.

1. 12, 24   **2.** 36, 42   **3.** 16, 48   **4.** 18, 72   **5.** 40, 45

Tell which fraction is written in simplest form.

6. $\dfrac{21}{23}, \dfrac{5}{25}$ **7.** $\dfrac{54}{54}, \dfrac{4}{9}$ **8.** $\dfrac{4}{16}, \dfrac{7}{9}$ **9.** $\dfrac{2}{4}, \dfrac{2}{5}, \dfrac{2}{8}$ **10.** $\dfrac{3}{7}, \dfrac{4}{12}, \dfrac{7}{14}$

Practice

Write the GCF of the numerator and denominator.

11. $\dfrac{40}{65}$ **12.** $\dfrac{15}{60}$ **13.** $\dfrac{28}{63}$ **14.** $\dfrac{42}{56}$ **15.** $\dfrac{4}{32}$

16. $\dfrac{9}{54}$ **17.** $\dfrac{16}{80}$ **18.** $\dfrac{20}{70}$ **19.** $\dfrac{8}{32}$ **20.** $\dfrac{48}{54}$

Write the fraction in simplest form.

21. $\dfrac{18}{60}$ **22.** $\dfrac{10}{16}$ **23.** $\dfrac{50}{60}$ **24.** $\dfrac{36}{54}$ **25.** $\dfrac{14}{21}$

26. $\dfrac{64}{72}$ **27.** $\dfrac{16}{32}$ **28.** $\dfrac{40}{32}$ **29.** $\dfrac{15}{24}$ **30.** $\dfrac{25}{30}$

31. $\dfrac{45}{72}$ **32.** $\dfrac{75}{55}$ **33.** $\dfrac{63}{72}$ **34.** $\dfrac{12}{12}$ **35.** $\dfrac{48}{42}$

Write the fraction that is in simplest form.

36. $\dfrac{3}{6}, \dfrac{1}{2}, \dfrac{4}{8}, \dfrac{5}{10}$ **37.** $\dfrac{6}{9}, \dfrac{18}{27}, \dfrac{12}{18}, \dfrac{2}{3}$ **38.** $\dfrac{3}{5}, \dfrac{15}{25}, \dfrac{30}{50}, \dfrac{21}{35}$

39. $\dfrac{4}{24}, \dfrac{2}{12}, \dfrac{1}{6}, \dfrac{3}{18}$ **40.** $\dfrac{15}{20}, \dfrac{3}{4}, \dfrac{9}{12}, \dfrac{6}{8}$ **41.** $\dfrac{12}{27}, \dfrac{8}{18}, \dfrac{16}{36}, \dfrac{4}{9}$

Mixed Applications

42. Beth made 24 blueberry, 12 banana, and 12 chocolate muffins. What part of the muffins are blueberry?

43. **Logical Reasoning** How do you know that $\frac{4}{8}$ written in simplest form is not $\frac{1}{3}$?

44. **Making Decisions** Is $\frac{2}{3}$ greater than $\frac{4}{6}$? Defend your answer.

How do you know that a fraction is in simplest form?

WRAP UP...

MIXED NUMBERS
and Fractions

After a table-tennis tournament, Patty and two friends will share some pizza. How can they share 1 pizza?

Any whole number can be written as a fraction.

$$1 = \frac{3}{3}$$

So, they can share by dividing the pizza into $\frac{3}{3}$.

- If you buy 11 slices of pizza from a restaurant that cuts pizzas into thirds, how many pizzas will have to be cut?

$\frac{11}{3}$ 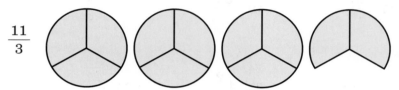 $3\frac{2}{3}$

A fraction is greater than 1 if the numerator is greater than the denominator.

A **mixed number** is a whole number and a fraction.

A fraction greater than 1 can be written as a mixed number.

Write $\frac{15}{4}$ as a mixed number.

Divide the numerator by the denominator.

$$\begin{array}{r} 3 \\ 4\overline{)15} \\ -12 \\ \hline 3 \end{array}$$

Write the remainder as a fraction in simplest form.

$$3\frac{3}{4} \quad 4\overline{)15}$$

A mixed number can be written as a fraction greater than 1.

Write $7\frac{3}{4}$ as a fraction.

Multiply the whole number by the denominator. $7 \times 4 = 28$

Add the numerator to the product. Write the sum as the new numerator. Use the same denominator.

$3 + 28 = 31$

$7\frac{3}{4} = \frac{31}{4}$

Talk About It

▶ How can you tell whether a fraction can be rewritten as a mixed number?

▶ How can you write $\frac{6}{3}$ as a whole number?

Check for Understanding

Write as a mixed number.

1. $\dfrac{13}{4}$ 2. $\dfrac{15}{11}$ 3. $\dfrac{37}{2}$

Write as a fraction.

4. $2\dfrac{2}{3}$ 5. $3\dfrac{5}{8}$ 6. $1\dfrac{4}{5}$

Practice

Find the missing digit.

7. $\dfrac{27}{5} = 5\dfrac{2}{\blacksquare}$ 8. $\dfrac{28}{3} = \blacksquare\dfrac{1}{3}$ 9. $\dfrac{35}{6} = \blacksquare\dfrac{5}{6}$ 10. $7\dfrac{31}{4} = \dfrac{\blacksquare}{4}$

11. $\dfrac{39}{11} = \blacksquare\dfrac{6}{11}$ 12. $\dfrac{29}{10} = 2\dfrac{\blacksquare}{10}$ 13. $13 = \dfrac{\blacksquare}{3}$ 14. $7 = \dfrac{\blacksquare}{1}$

Write the fraction as a mixed number or as a whole number.

15. $\dfrac{31}{9}$ 16. $\dfrac{59}{6}$ 17. $\dfrac{57}{10}$ 18. $\dfrac{56}{7}$ 19. $\dfrac{44}{8}$

Write the mixed number as a fraction.

20. $10\dfrac{4}{5}$ 21. $9\dfrac{1}{3}$ 22. $6\dfrac{5}{6}$ 23. $4\dfrac{2}{7}$ 24. $6\dfrac{8}{9}$

Mixed Applications

25. **Number Sense** Dave has more games than Jill but fewer than Toni. If Toni has $\dfrac{2}{3}$ of the games, can Dave have $\dfrac{3}{4}$ of the games? Defend your answer.

26. **Make Up a Problem** Kim has played checkers after school for 35 days. Make up a problem that can be solved by writing a fraction.

MIXED REVIEW

Write the GCF of each pair of numbers.

1. $3, 9$ 2. $8, 16$ 3. $5, 25$ 4. $45, 54$ 5. $7, 11$

Write the fraction in simplest form.

6. $\dfrac{50}{60}$ 7. $\dfrac{7}{14}$ 8. $\dfrac{15}{45}$ 9. $\dfrac{21}{21}$ 10. $\dfrac{35}{63}$

How can you order $1\dfrac{1}{5}$, $\dfrac{8}{5}$, and $\dfrac{4}{5}$ from least to greatest?

More Practice, Lesson 6.10, page H57

To paint the bleachers in a gym, Joanne stood on a step 2.4 meters (m) from the floor. The steps of the bleachers are 0.25 m apart. She went up 6 more steps to paint the top of the bleachers. How many meters from the floor is the top of the bleachers?

> **Understand**
> **Plan**
> **Solve**
> **Look Back**

Sometimes you can use one of several strategies to solve a problem.

What strategies can you use?
You can write a *number sentence* or *draw a diagram*.

Strategy: Write a Number Sentence

Write a number sentence.

distance between steps	number of steps climbed	distance of first step from floor	height of bleachers from floor
↓	↓	↓	↓
(0.25 ×	6) +	2.4 =	■

0.25 [×] 6 [+] 2.4 [=] [　　　3.9　]

Strategy: Draw a Diagram

Draw a diagram.

Show the distances between the steps of the bleachers.

So, the top of the bleachers is 3.9 meters from the floor.

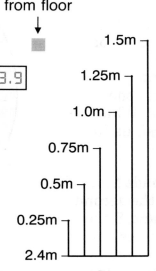

1.5m ¬
1.25m ¬
1.0m ¬
0.75m ¬
0.5m ¬
0.25m ¬
2.4m ¬

WHAT **IF...** ... the steps are 0.3 meters apart? How many meters from the floor is the top of the bleachers?

Choose a strategy and solve.

1. Dylan, Croaker, Legs, and Amos competed in a frog-jumping contest. Dylan finished after Legs but before Croaker. Amos finished just before Croaker. Legs finished first. In what order did the frogs finish?

2. Tammy and Peter are working 45 mazes each. Tammy has completed 7 more than Peter, who has completed 15. How many mazes does Tammy still need to complete?

3. There are 65 games of pachisi and backgammon on a toy-store shelf. If there are 15 more backgammon games than pachisi games, how many boxes of each game are on the shelf?

4. Tim spent $\frac{1}{6}$ of his money on a tic-tac-toe game, $\frac{1}{3}$ on mazes, $\frac{5}{12}$ on puzzles, and $\frac{1}{12}$ on marbles. On which item did Tim spend the most?

5. Guillermo made a spinner with triangles, squares, a circle, and a star. What is the probability he will land on a square if he spins 18 times?

6. Joyce is decorating the border of a game board. She starts with 3 triangles, 4 squares, and 5 circles. Then she repeats the 3 triangles and 4 squares. What will be the next three designs in the pattern?

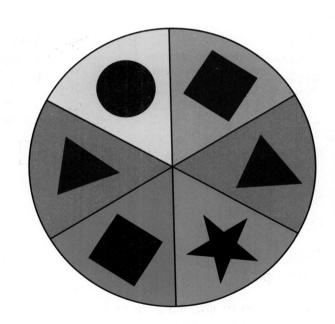

7. Art invents mazes. He made 2 during the first week, 4 the second week, 6 the third week, and 8 the fourth week. If Art continues this pattern of making mazes, how many mazes will he make during the eighth week?

WRITER'S CORNER

8. Think about a game you like to play. Write a problem about the game that can be solved using two different strategies. Be sure to name the strategies.

CHAPTER REVIEW

Vocabulary Check

Choose a word or words from the box to complete each sentence.

| composite |
| greatest common factor (GCF) |
| least common denominator (LCD) |
| least common multiple (LCM) |
| like |
| mixed |
| prime |
| prime factorization |

If you multiply two factors, your answer is a multiple.

1. The smallest number that is a multiple of two or more whole numbers is the __?__. *(page 174)*

2. A number that has only two factors, itself and 1, is a __?__ number. *(page 184)*

3. A whole number that has more than two factors is a __?__ number. *(page 184)*

4. The __?__ is the LCM of the denominators. *(page 179)*

5. The largest common factor of two or more numbers is called the __?__. *(page 188)*

6. Fractions that have the same denominator are called __?__ fractions. *(page 180)*

7. When you express a composite number as the product of prime factors, you are using __?__. *(page 186)*

8. A whole number and a fraction form a(n) __?__ number. *(page 194)*

Concept Check

9. What is the difference between the LCM and the LCD? *(page 180)*

10. What are equivalent fractions? *(page 176)*

11. How can you order fractions with unlike denominators? *(page 180)*

12. What is the difference between prime and composite numbers? *(page 184)*

13. How do you know when a fraction is in simplest form? *(page 192)*

14. When is a fraction greater than 1? *(page 194)*

15. How can you write a fraction as a mixed number? *(page 194)*

Skill Check

Find the LCM for each pair of numbers. *(page 174)*

16. $8, 40$ **17.** $12, 30$ **18.** $10, 16$ **19.** $11, 20$

Complete the number sentence. *(page 176)*

20. $\dfrac{3}{4} = \dfrac{\blacksquare}{12}$ **21.** $\dfrac{2}{3} = \dfrac{\blacksquare}{9}$ **22.** $\dfrac{4}{5} = \dfrac{\blacksquare}{20}$ **23.** $\dfrac{3}{8} = \dfrac{\blacksquare}{24}$

Use $<$, $>$, or $=$ to compare the fractions. *(page 180)*

24. $\dfrac{2}{4} \bullet \dfrac{15}{16}$ **25.** $\dfrac{9}{12} \bullet \dfrac{5}{8}$ **26.** $\dfrac{4}{9} \bullet \dfrac{20}{45}$

27. $\dfrac{3}{5} \bullet \dfrac{2}{15}$ **28.** $\dfrac{1}{9} \bullet \dfrac{7}{12}$ **29.** $\dfrac{3}{8} \bullet \dfrac{5}{12}$

Tell whether the number is prime or composite. Then list the factors. *(page 184)*

30. 18 **31.** 61 **32.** 26 **33.** 97

Write the prime factorization in exponent form. *(page 186)*

34. 63 **35.** 88 **36.** 50 **37.** 120

Write the GCF of each pair of numbers. *(page 188)*

38. $10, 35$ **39.** $15, 90$ **40.** $16, 120$ **41.** $45, 75$

Write the fraction as a mixed number or as a whole number. *(page 194)*

42. $\dfrac{40}{7}$ **43.** $\dfrac{18}{3}$ **44.** $\dfrac{62}{8}$ **45.** $\dfrac{93}{12}$

Problem-Solving Check *(pages 182, 196)*

46. Denny, Greg, and Gene went to a game. One drove, one took a bus, and the other took a train. Greg did not go by bus. Denny did not drive. Gene took a train. Who took a bus?

47. Four girls are running in a marathon. Tora is 10 minutes ahead of Tisha. Tisha is 25 minutes ahead of Lara, and Kim is 15 minutes behind Tora. How far behind Kim is Lara?

48. Maria is working a jigsaw puzzle. If it takes her an average of 7 minutes to assemble 20 pieces, how long will it take her to assemble 160 pieces?

49. Cindy runs 10 miles one day and 4 miles the next. How many days will it take her to run a total of 52 miles if she runs every two days and rests every third day?

CHAPTER TEST

Find the LCM for each pair of numbers.

1. $3, 18$ **2.** $2, 25$ **3.** $12, 15$

Think: What does LCM stand for?

Use $<$, $>$, or $=$ to compare the fractions.

4. $\dfrac{6}{9}$ ⬤ $\dfrac{2}{3}$ **5.** $\dfrac{11}{12}$ ⬤ $\dfrac{6}{7}$ **6.** $\dfrac{3}{8}$ ⬤ $\dfrac{2}{5}$

7. $\dfrac{3}{4}$ ⬤ $\dfrac{2}{3}$ **8.** $\dfrac{5}{9}$ ⬤ $\dfrac{3}{54}$ **9.** $\dfrac{1}{3}$ ⬤ $\dfrac{5}{7}$

Tell whether the number is prime or composite. Then list the factors.

10. 24 **11.** 19 **12.** 42 **13.** 31 **14.** 43

Write the GCF of each pair of numbers.

15. $20, 25$ **16.** $16, 96$ **17.** $24, 60$ **18.** $12, 45$

Write the fraction in simplest form.

19. $\dfrac{5}{45}$ **20.** $\dfrac{18}{24}$ **21.** $\dfrac{25}{80}$

Write the fraction as a mixed number.

22. $\dfrac{42}{8}$ **23.** $\dfrac{37}{5}$ **24.** $\dfrac{62}{15}$ **25.** $\dfrac{87}{7}$

Write the mixed number as a fraction.

26. $7\dfrac{7}{9}$ **27.** $6\dfrac{5}{8}$ **28.** $20\dfrac{1}{6}$ **29.** $14\dfrac{3}{5}$

Solve.

30. Meg, Trish, and Jill take turns driving. Meg drives on Day 2. Trish does not drive on Day 1. Jill does not drive on Day 2 or Day 3. Who drives on Day 3?

31. Ray puts games on the third, or bottom, shelf of a bookcase, 54 inches from the floor. The shelves are 16 inches apart. How far from the floor is the first shelf?

32. Bill, Jim, Ted, and Art are on the same bowling team. In the first game, Jim beat Ted but not Art. Bill beat only Ted. In what order did they finish?

33. Cassandra has a total of 29 games. She has 11 more video games than board games. How many games of each type does Cassandra have?

Teamwork P-R-O-J-E-C-T

Make a Math Game

Creating your own game can be both challenging and fun.

Work with your teammates to create a math game and challenge another team in your classroom.

Decide

As a team, decide on a math concept to structure the game.

Will players compete as individuals or teams? How will a player or a team win?

Decide on the format for the game. Will it contain cards, a board, game pieces?

Decide on a method of scoring.

Discuss and limit the length of the game.

Do

• As a team, design and build the game.

• Make the necessary parts.

• Write a set of rules. State how to score and how to win.

• Play the game. Adjust any features that do not work.

Share

Exchange games with another team. After everyone has had a chance to play, discuss the challenges of both games.

Talk About It

What math skills are required to play each game?

How can you improve your game?

Which game seems to be more popular? Why?

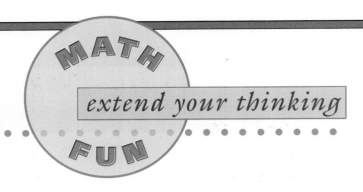

Factor Removal

You can play this game with a partner. Arrange paper squares or other objects in a rectangular array that represents any composite number.

Players take turns removing pieces. Each player can remove a number of pieces equal to a factor of the total number left in the array. However, players cannot remove just one or the total number of pieces. The player who leaves a prime number of pieces in the array is the winner.

Example

In the array shown, the first player may remove 3 pieces of paper (3 × 6 = 18), leaving 15. The other player must remove

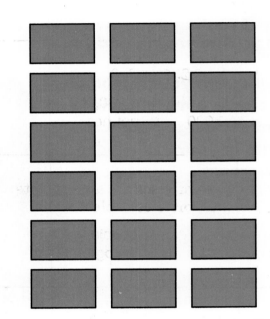

a number of pieces that represents a factor of 15, say 5. Play continues until one player wins.

Challenge

Number Sense

Mirror primes are pairs of prime numbers whose digits are reversed. Find the mirror primes in the table.

Prime Numbers Less Than 150
2 3 5 7 11 13 17 19
23 29 31 37 41 43 47 53
59 61 67 71 73 79 83 89
97 101 103 107 109 113 127 131
137 139 149

Twin primes are pairs of prime numbers with a difference of 2. Name the twin primes that are less than 150.

Logical Reasoning

The numbers below can be written as the sum of two prime numbers. For example, 71 + 11 = 82. Find two prime-number addends for each number.

12	94
24	126
38	176
60	222
82	

Find a second pair of prime numbers whose sum is 222.

Write the letter of the correct answer.

1. $24.2 - (8.1 \times 2) + 8$

    A. 15   **B.** 16
    C. 40.2   **D.** 161

2. Evaluate $b - 6$, for $b = 18.9$.

    A. 12   **B.** 12.9
    C. 18.3   **D.** not here

3. Estimate $6{,}235 \times 240$.

    A. 120,000   **B.** 1,200,000
    C. 1,800,000   **D.** not here

4. 8.8×0.622

    A. 4.4736   **B.** 5.4636
    C. 5.4736   **D.** 54.736

5. What type of graph is appropriate to show favorite car colors?

    A. bar   **B.** double-line
    C. line   **D.** histogram

6. Choose the number of choices. 2 pairs of shoes, 3 pairs of socks

    A. 2 choices   **B.** 3 choices
    C. 5 choices   **D.** 6 choices

7. $9.66 \div 2.1$

    A. 0.46   **B.** 4.5
    C. 46.   **D.** not here

8. Find the LCM of 10 and 12.

    A. 1   **B.** 2
    C. 60   **D.** 120

9. Find the GCF of 8 and 32.

    A. 2   **B.** 4
    C. 8   **D.** 16

10. What is $7\frac{2}{5}$ written as a fraction?

    A. $\frac{14}{5}$ **B.** $\frac{37}{5}$
    C. $\frac{72}{5}$ **D.** $35\frac{2}{5}$

11. Sandy has the greatest number of hits. Jon has fewer than Kirk, who has fewer than Sandy. Mona is ahead of Jon but behind Kirk. Who has the least number of hits?

    A. Jon   **B.** Kirk
    C. Mona   **D.** Sandy

12. A cat was tangled in 36 inches of yarn. With every attempt to get free, he got rid of 15 inches and then re-entangled himself in 8 inches. How many tries did it take the cat to get free?

    A. 3 tries   **B.** 6 tries
    C. 9 tries   **D.** not here

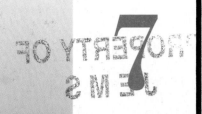

ADDING AND SUBTRACTING FRACTIONS

Did you know ...

... that fractions are commonly used around the home?

Talk About It

Suppose you want to make muffins that contain $1\frac{1}{3}$ cups of raisins and a fruit salad that contains $\frac{3}{4}$ cup of raisins. How can you determine the amount of raisins to buy?

ESTIMATING
Fraction Sums and Differences

You can round to estimate fraction sums or differences. Some fractions that can be rounded to 0, $\frac{1}{2}$, or 1 are given.

$\boxed{\frac{1}{9}}\boxed{\frac{1}{8}}\boxed{\frac{1}{6}}\boxed{\frac{2}{9}}\boxed{\frac{1}{4}}$

The numerator is much less than the denominator. So, round to 0.

$\boxed{\frac{1}{3}}\boxed{\frac{3}{8}}\boxed{\frac{4}{9}}\boxed{\frac{1}{2}}\boxed{\frac{5}{9}}\boxed{\frac{5}{8}}\boxed{\frac{2}{3}}$

The numerator is about one half the denominator. So, round to $\frac{1}{2}$.

$\boxed{\frac{3}{4}}\boxed{\frac{7}{9}}\boxed{\frac{5}{6}}\boxed{\frac{7}{8}}\boxed{\frac{8}{9}}$

The numerator is about the same as the denominator. So, round to 1.

Leon's pieces of wood scrap are $\frac{1}{4}$ yard (yd), $\frac{3}{8}$ yd, and $\frac{5}{6}$ yd long. He determines that he has $1\frac{11}{24}$ yd of wood scrap. Is his answer reasonable?

$$\frac{1}{4} + \frac{3}{8} + \frac{5}{6} = \blacksquare$$

$$\downarrow \qquad \downarrow \qquad \downarrow$$

Estimate. $\quad 0 \;+\; \frac{1}{2} \;+\; 1 \;=\; 1\frac{1}{2}$

So, Leon's answer is reasonable.

You can also round to estimate mixed-number sums and differences.

Example About how much is $9\frac{9}{10} - 5\frac{7}{8}$?

Step 1	Step 2
Round to the nearest whole number.	Subtract.
$9\frac{9}{10}$ is a little less than 10.	$\begin{array}{r} 10 \\ -\ 6 \\ \hline 4 \end{array}$ ← estimate
$-5\frac{7}{8}$ is a little less than 6.	

Check for Understanding

Write *about 0*, *about* $\frac{1}{2}$, or *about 1*.

1. $\frac{14}{27}$

2. $\frac{10}{11}$

3. $\frac{1}{9}$

4. $\frac{11}{24}$

5. $\frac{1}{16}$

6. $\frac{9}{10}$

Practice

Round the fractions to 0, $\frac{1}{2}$, or 1. Then rewrite the problem.

7. $\frac{13}{14} + \frac{10}{17}$

8. $8\frac{1}{3} - 3\frac{1}{15}$

9. $\frac{8}{9} + \frac{1}{2}$

10. $11\frac{4}{5} - 2\frac{7}{9}$

11. $6\frac{1}{4} + 3\frac{2}{9}$

12. $4\frac{1}{20} - 1\frac{4}{5}$

Estimate the sum or difference.

13. $\frac{1}{15} + \frac{9}{20}$

14. $\frac{1}{8} + \frac{5}{6}$

15. $\frac{7}{8} - \frac{4}{9}$

16. $\frac{29}{30} - \frac{9}{10}$

17. $3\frac{3}{7} + 1\frac{1}{14}$

18. $1\frac{5}{26} - \frac{1}{6}$

19. $12\frac{2}{3} - 5\frac{6}{11}$

20. $\frac{4}{5} + \frac{7}{10} + \frac{1}{6}$

21. $4\frac{3}{4} - 1\frac{1}{8}$

22. $\frac{13}{15} + \frac{1}{5}$

23. $3\frac{1}{4} + 4\frac{6}{7}$

24. $5\frac{6}{7} - 2\frac{1}{3}$

25. $\frac{7}{8} - \frac{1}{16}$

26. $4\frac{1}{2} + 2\frac{3}{4}$

27. $9\frac{1}{9} - 7\frac{7}{8}$

28. $\frac{4}{9} - \frac{1}{15}$

Mixed Applications

Estimate to solve.

29. Elsa had $27\frac{7}{8}$ yards of jute. She used $13\frac{1}{4}$ yards to make a plant hanger. Does Elsa have enough jute to make another plant hanger the same size? Defend your answer.

30. Leon has three fabric remnants measuring $2\frac{5}{6}$ yards, $1\frac{1}{4}$ yards, and $1\frac{2}{3}$ yards. He determines that he has a total of about 4 yards. Is his estimate reasonable? Explain.

31. **Number Sense** Prime numbers that differ by two, such as 3 and 5 or 59 and 61, are called **twin primes.** Write 2 other pairs of twin primes between 1 and 50.

32. **Make Up a Problem** Write a problem about everyday life at home that can be solved by estimating fractions. Exchange with a classmate and solve.

Explain how to round fractions.

W R A P
U P . . .

Cher's muffin recipe calls for $\frac{5}{8}$ teaspoon (t) of cinnamon and $\frac{1}{8}$ t of nutmeg. How much spice does she need?

You can use mental math when you add like fractions.

Step 1	Step 2
When the denominators are the same, add the numerators.	Write the answer in simplest form.
$\frac{5}{8} + \frac{1}{8} = \frac{6}{8}$	$\frac{6 \div 2}{8 \div 2} = \frac{3}{4}$

So, the recipe calls for a total of $\frac{3}{4}$ t of spice.

How much more cinnamon than nutmeg is needed for the recipe?

You can also use mental math when you subtract like fractions.

Step 1	Step 2
When the denominators are the same, subtract the numerators.	Write the answer in simplest form.
$\frac{5}{8} - \frac{1}{8} = \frac{4}{8}$	$\frac{4 \div 4}{8 \div 4} = \frac{1}{2}$

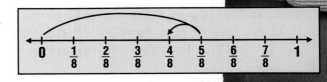

So, $\frac{1}{2}$ t more cinnamon than nutmeg is needed.

More Examples

A. $\frac{5}{7} + \frac{4}{7} = \frac{9}{7}$, or $1\frac{2}{7}$ B. $\frac{10}{12} - \frac{5}{12} = \frac{5}{12}$ C. $\frac{5}{6} + \frac{5}{6} + \frac{4}{6} = \frac{14}{6} = \frac{7}{3}$, or $2\frac{1}{3}$

Check for Understanding

Find the sum or difference. Write your answer in simplest form.

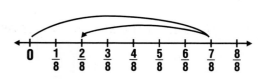

1. $\frac{1}{4} + \frac{1}{4}$ 2. $\frac{2}{6} + \frac{3}{6}$ 3. $\frac{7}{8} - \frac{5}{8}$

Practice

Estimate the sum.

4. $2\frac{1}{12} + 3\frac{1}{12}$ **5.** $3\frac{1}{5} + 4\frac{2}{3}$ **6.** $5\frac{2}{7} + 6\frac{3}{4}$ **7.** $7\frac{2}{3} + 5\frac{1}{9}$

Find the sum.

8. $\begin{array}{r} 3\frac{1}{10} \\ + 2\frac{3}{10} \\ \hline \end{array}$ **9.** $\begin{array}{r} 6\frac{1}{4} \\ + 2\frac{1}{4} \\ \hline \end{array}$ **10.** $\begin{array}{r} 1\frac{3}{8} \\ + 5\frac{1}{8} \\ \hline \end{array}$ **11.** $\begin{array}{r} 2\frac{2}{7} \\ + 3\frac{3}{7} \\ \hline \end{array}$ **12.** $\begin{array}{r} 4\frac{5}{6} \\ + 7\frac{1}{6} \\ \hline \end{array}$

13. $\begin{array}{r} 1\frac{1}{2} \\ + 2\frac{3}{5} \\ \hline \end{array}$ **14.** $\begin{array}{r} 3\frac{3}{8} \\ + 5\frac{3}{4} \\ \hline \end{array}$ **15.** $\begin{array}{r} 2\frac{2}{3} \\ + 1\frac{1}{2} \\ \hline \end{array}$ **16.** $\begin{array}{r} 1\frac{3}{5} \\ + 4\frac{5}{8} \\ \hline \end{array}$ **17.** $\begin{array}{r} 5\frac{1}{4} \\ + 7\frac{3}{16} \\ \hline \end{array}$

18. $\begin{array}{r} 5\frac{1}{8} \\ + 3\frac{3}{4} \\ \hline \end{array}$ **19.** $\begin{array}{r} 11\frac{7}{12} \\ + 5\frac{1}{4} \\ \hline \end{array}$ **20.** $\begin{array}{r} 9\frac{2}{3} \\ + 8\frac{4}{7} \\ \hline \end{array}$ **21.** $\begin{array}{r} 8\frac{3}{7} \\ + 6\frac{2}{3} \\ \hline \end{array}$ **22.** $\begin{array}{r} 4\frac{5}{8} \\ + 7\frac{3}{5} \\ \hline \end{array}$

Mixed Applications

23. Carlos bought $1\frac{2}{3}$ pounds (lb) of potato salad, $2\frac{3}{5}$ lb of coleslaw, and $4\frac{5}{6}$ lb of chicken at a deli. What is the total weight of his purchases?

24. Make Up a Problem Use a newspaper to find the prices of three stocks listed on a stock exchange. Then use the information to write a problem.

CALCULATOR CONNECTION

You can use a calculator designed to operate with fractions.

Example $4\frac{1}{5} + 6\frac{7}{8}$ 

25. What does pressing [Ab/c] do?

26. What keystrokes would you use to add two fractions?

How does adding mixed numbers differ from adding fractions?

WRAP UP...

The steps of a building extend south $20\frac{1}{3}$ yd from the entrance. The south edge of a statue is $15\frac{2}{3}$ yd west of the bottom step. An east-west path begins $24\frac{2}{3}$ yd south of the statue. How far is it from the entrance of the building straight south to the path?

Sometimes drawing a diagram can help you solve a problem. The diagram may help you visualize the solution.

▶ UNDERSTAND

What are you asked to find?

What information are you given?

▶ PLAN

What strategy can you use?

You can *draw a diagram* that shows the building entrance, the statue, and the path.

▶ SOLVE

How will you carry out your plan?

Draw a diagram and label the structures and the distances. Since the direction from the steps to the statue is west, you can ignore it and add the remaining distances.

$$20\frac{1}{3} + 24\frac{2}{3} = 44\frac{3}{3} = 45$$

So, the path is 45 yd from the building entrance.

▶ LOOK BACK

What other strategy can you use to solve the problem?

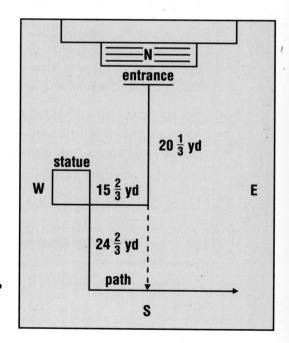

WHAT IF... ... you walk from the entrance straight down the steps, turn right, and walk to the statue? How far will you walk?

Apply

(1) Kirk walked $\frac{9}{10}$ mile north, $1\frac{1}{10}$ miles east, $\frac{3}{10}$ mile south, and $1\frac{6}{10}$ miles west in order to visit friends. How far had he walked when he crossed his own path?

(2) Carrie's room is 12 feet square. A chair that is $2\frac{1}{4}$ feet deep is against one wall. A 2-foot-wide table is $2\frac{3}{4}$ feet from the chair. How far is the table from the opposite wall?

Mixed Applications → **STRATEGIES** • Draw a Diagram • Make a Table • Find a Pattern • Write a Number Sentence

Choose a strategy and solve. Use the table for Exercises 3–4.

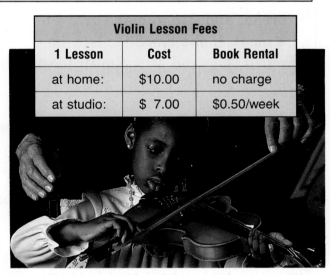

Violin Lesson Fees		
1 Lesson	Cost	Book Rental
at home:	$10.00	no charge
at studio:	$ 7.00	$0.50/week

(3) If Jasmine takes one violin lesson a week, how much will it cost her to take four lessons at the studio?

(4) How much more will it cost Jasmine to take four lessons at her home than at the studio?

(5) Ed wants to put a 1.4-meter chest against a 3.6-meter wall. If he centers the chest, how far will it be from each end of the wall?

(6) Wade's baby brother chewed $\frac{1}{4}$ of Wade's baseball cards. What part of the cards were not chewed?

(7) Dan's record collection includes $\frac{3}{5}$ rock, $\frac{1}{5}$ country, and $\frac{1}{5}$ classical. How much of his collection is not rock music?

(8) Suppose you have 6 blue pens, 5 green pens, and some red pens in your desk. If there is a $\frac{4}{15}$ probability of choosing a red pen from your desk, how many pens are in your desk?

(9) Five pads of paper cost $4.50, 10 pads cost $8.05, 20 pads cost $15.15, and 30 pads cost $22.25. If this pattern continues, how much do 50 pads cost?

WRITER'S CORNER

(10) Write a word problem that can be solved by drawing a diagram. Draw the diagram on a separate sheet of paper and solve. Then ask a classmate to solve the problem. Is his or her diagram similar to yours?

REVIEW AND MAINTENANCE

1. Lamar is standing on a ladder to paint windows. He is 2.9 meters from the ground. The ladder rungs are 0.2 meter apart. If he moves up 3 rungs, how many meters will he be from the ground?

After I read a problem, I choose a strategy to solve it.

2. Mrs. Smith used $1\frac{1}{2}$ cups (c) of flour to make muffins, $4\frac{1}{3}$ c to make bread, and $\frac{3}{4}$ c to make gravy for a meal. If she has $3\frac{1}{4}$ c left, how much flour did Mrs. Smith have before she started the meal?

3. Mr. Evans is painting squares on a wall. The first is 5 inches (in.) square, the second 8 in., the third 13 in., and the fourth 20 in. If the pattern continues, what will be the size of the sixth square?

Write the GCF of the numerator and denominator.

4. $\frac{10}{15}$ 5. $\frac{21}{63}$ 6. $\frac{32}{96}$ 7. $\frac{12}{36}$ 8. $\frac{44}{80}$

Write the fraction as a mixed number.

9. $\frac{62}{10}$ 10. $\frac{81}{6}$ 11. $\frac{79}{9}$ 12. $\frac{24}{5}$ 13. $\frac{54}{7}$

Write the mixed number as a fraction.

14. $4\frac{1}{3}$ 15. $7\frac{1}{4}$ 16. $6\frac{2}{5}$ 17. $11\frac{1}{2}$ 18. $8\frac{4}{9}$

Estimate the sum or difference.

19. $6\frac{2}{3} + 8\frac{9}{11}$ 20. $4\frac{9}{10} - 2\frac{1}{8}$ 21. $8\frac{7}{8} + 2\frac{3}{4}$

Find the sum or difference.

22. $\frac{1}{6} + \frac{2}{6} = \blacksquare$ 23. $4\frac{2}{5} + 3\frac{4}{5} = \blacksquare$ 24. $\frac{9}{10} - \frac{3}{10} = \blacksquare$ 25. $\frac{7}{9} + \frac{2}{5} = \blacksquare$

26. $\frac{6}{15} + \frac{1}{10} = \blacksquare$ 27. $\frac{5}{12} + \frac{1}{4} = \blacksquare$ 28. $\frac{3}{4} - \frac{1}{6} = \blacksquare$ 29. $\frac{2}{3} - \frac{1}{4} = \blacksquare$

30. $\frac{5}{7}$
    $-\frac{1}{14}$

31. $9\frac{2}{3}$
    $+7\frac{1}{4}$

32. $5\frac{1}{9}$
    $+3\frac{2}{3}$

33. $2\frac{3}{4}$
    $+4\frac{3}{5}$

34. $11\frac{3}{8}$
    $+5\frac{2}{16}$

Spotlight ON PROBLEM SOLVING

Identify Relevant and Irrelevant Information

You must understand a problem before you can plan to solve it. The given information should be analyzed to determine what is relevant and what is irrelevant.

Juana is making a snack of raisins and nuts for a slumber party. The nuts are on sale at $2.98 a pound. If Juana buys $\frac{1}{4}$ pound of nuts and $\frac{3}{8}$ pound of raisins, how much of the snack can she make?

Apply

Read each problem. Identify what the problem is asking and what the relevant information is. Then solve.

① Sherry, Frank, and Pete ordered 1 pizza with pepperoni, green peppers, onions, and mushrooms. If Sherry eats $\frac{3}{8}$ of the pizza, Frank $\frac{1}{8}$, and Pete $\frac{1}{4}$, how much will be left?

② Last month a health store sold $\frac{1}{2}$ of a carton of oat bars. This month they sold $\frac{1}{4}$ of a carton. Each carton contains 120 oat bars. How many cartons did the store sell in 2 months?

Talk About It

Work together to analyze the information.

What is the problem asking?

Identify relevant information. Why is this information relevant?

What information is irrelevant? How do you know the information is irrelevant?

How much of the snack can Juana make?

What information would you want to know if you had to make a snack of raisins and nuts for a party?

EXPLORING

Subtraction of Mixed Numbers

Mrs. France has $3\frac{1}{4}$ yards of fabric to make placemats and napkins. If she uses $1\frac{3}{4}$ yards to make placemats, how much fabric will be left to make napkins?

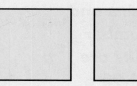

WORK TOGETHER

Building Understanding

Use fraction squares to subtract mixed numbers with like denominators.

Example $3\frac{1}{4} - 1\frac{3}{4}$

Talk About It

▶ What amount in Figure **A** is blue?

▶ What must you do to change Figure **A** so that you can subtract $1\frac{3}{4}$ from it?

▶ How does Figure **B** differ from Figure **A**?

▶ What amount is left in Figure **B** if you remove $1\frac{3}{4}$?

▶ How much fabric will be left to make napkins?

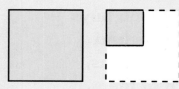

Figure A

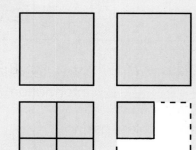

Figure B

Use fraction squares to find the difference.

a. $3 - 1\frac{1}{2}$ b. $3 - \frac{3}{4}$ c. $1\frac{1}{3} - \frac{2}{3}$ d. $3\frac{1}{6} - 2\frac{5}{6}$

218

Making the Connection

Sometimes you must rename mixed numbers before you can subtract. Renaming mixed numbers is similar to regrouping whole numbers.

Examples

Whole number: 234 = 2 hundreds, 3 tens, 4 ones
                   = 1 hundred, 13 tens, 4 ones

Mixed number: $5\frac{3}{5} = 4 + 1 + \frac{3}{5} = 4 + \frac{5}{5} + \frac{3}{5} = 4\frac{8}{5}$

1. Is it necessary to rename if you are subtracting $1\frac{1}{5}$ from $3\frac{4}{5}$? Justify your answer.

2. When must you rename a mixed number before you can subtract?

3. How do you rename a mixed number?

Tell whether or not you must rename the greater number. Then rename if necessary.

4. $2\frac{1}{8} - \frac{7}{8}$

5. $2\frac{3}{4} - 1\frac{1}{4}$

6. $3\frac{1}{3} - 1\frac{2}{3}$

7. $3\frac{2}{5} - 2\frac{1}{5}$

8. $1\frac{11}{12} - \frac{7}{12}$

9. $1\frac{1}{5} - \frac{3}{5}$

Checking Understanding

Rename the greater number.

10. $4 - 2\frac{4}{5}$

11. $2\frac{1}{6} - 1\frac{5}{6}$

12. $5\frac{5}{12} - 3\frac{11}{12}$

13. $5 - 1\frac{2}{3}$

14. $6\frac{3}{10} - 3\frac{7}{10}$

15. $7\frac{2}{9} - 2\frac{7}{9}$

Find the difference.

16. $8 - 6\frac{5}{8}$

17. $11 - 10\frac{2}{3}$

18. $7\frac{1}{3} - 4\frac{2}{3}$

19. $6\frac{1}{5} - 4\frac{3}{5}$

20. $4\frac{1}{4} - 2\frac{3}{4}$

21. $5\frac{5}{8} - 3\frac{7}{8}$

22. $8\frac{1}{8} - 2\frac{7}{8}$

23. $8 - 5\frac{3}{4}$

24. $19 - 15\frac{2}{3}$

25. $12\frac{1}{5} - 1\frac{3}{5}$

26. $15\frac{1}{8} - 12\frac{5}{8}$

27. $7\frac{2}{9} - 5\frac{8}{9}$

SUBTRACTING MIXED NUMBERS
with Like Denominators

Roberto had $6\frac{3}{4}$ quarts of lemonade. He gave $1\frac{1}{4}$ quarts to his sister. How much lemonade was left?

Estimate.

$$6\frac{3}{4} - 1\frac{1}{4} = \blacksquare$$

$$\downarrow \qquad \downarrow$$

$$7 - 1 = 6 \leftarrow \text{estimate}$$

Step 1 Subtract the fractions.	**Step 2** Subtract the whole numbers. Write the fraction in simplest form.
$6\frac{3}{4}$ $-1\frac{1}{4}$ $\overline{\frac{2}{4}}$	$6\frac{3}{4}$ $-1\frac{1}{4}$ $\overline{5\frac{2}{4} = 5\frac{1}{2}}$

So, $5\frac{1}{2}$ quarts of lemonade were left.

Sometimes you must rename the greater mixed number.

Mr. James bought $7\frac{1}{3}$ pounds of ground beef to make sandwiches for a group of scouts. If he used $4\frac{2}{3}$ pounds of the ground beef, how much was left?

Step 1 Decide whether to rename the greater mixed number. Think: $\frac{2}{3} > \frac{1}{3}$. So, rename.	**Step 2** Subtract. If necessary, write the fraction in simplest form.
$7\frac{1}{3} = 6\frac{4}{3}$ $-4\frac{2}{3}$ $\overline{}$	$7\frac{1}{3} = 6\frac{4}{3}$ $-4\frac{2}{3} = 4\frac{2}{3}$ $\overline{2\frac{2}{3}}$

So, $2\frac{2}{3}$ pounds of ground beef were left.

Check for Understanding

Find the difference.

1. $7\frac{4}{5} - 3\frac{1}{5}$

2. $5\frac{1}{3} - 3\frac{2}{3}$

3. $10\frac{5}{8} - 8\frac{3}{8}$

4. $19\frac{1}{5} - 12\frac{4}{5}$

Practice

Find the difference.

5. $16\frac{6}{7}$
   $-\ 3\frac{1}{7}$

6. $5\frac{1}{3}$
   $-1\frac{2}{3}$

7. $7\frac{4}{20}$
   $-5\frac{3}{20}$

8. 9
   $-3\frac{11}{12}$

9. $10\frac{7}{11}$
   $-\ 4\frac{9}{11}$

10. $9\frac{19}{20}$
    $-2\frac{7}{20}$

11. $3\frac{1}{8}$
    $-2\frac{5}{8}$

12. $5\frac{3}{8}$
    $-2\frac{7}{8}$

13. $8\frac{6}{12}$
    $-3\frac{5}{12}$

14. $18\frac{9}{10}$
    $-\ 9\frac{3}{10}$

15. $4\frac{1}{9}$
    $-1\frac{7}{9}$

16. $12\frac{7}{8}$
    $-\ 4\frac{3}{8}$

17. $15\frac{9}{16}$
    $-\ 2\frac{13}{16}$

18. $76\frac{19}{20}$
    $-31\frac{17}{20}$

19. $49\frac{11}{36}$
    $-22\frac{17}{36}$

Mixed Applications

20. Shelby practices the piano $7\frac{3}{4}$ hours a week. He has already practiced $5\frac{1}{3}$ hours. How many more hours will Shelby practice this week?

21. **Number Sense** Look at the fractions. Find the pattern. What are the next three numbers in the pattern?

    $\frac{1}{2}, \frac{2}{3}, \frac{5}{6}$, ▨, ▨, ▨

22. **Logical Reasoning** Two 2-digit numbers have the same digits, only reversed. The sum of the digits is 6. The difference between the 2-digit numbers is 18. What are the two numbers?

NUMBER SENSE

23. Copy the puzzle. Find the missing numbers so that the sum of the first and second numbers across or down equals the third number. Write your answers in simplest form.

24. Use the puzzle as a model. Make a puzzle that can be solved by subtracting across and down.

$1\frac{1}{10}$	+	▨	=	▨
+		+		+
▨	+	$6\frac{7}{10}$	=	10
=		=		=
▨	+	$10\frac{9}{10}$	=	$15\frac{3}{10}$

How do you know that $6\frac{1}{2} - 4\frac{1}{4}$ is more than 2?

WRAP UP...

EXPLORING

More Subtraction of Mixed Numbers

WORK TOGETHER

Building Understanding

Use fraction bars to explore renaming mixed numbers with unlike denominators in order to subtract.

Example $2\frac{1}{3} - 1\frac{1}{2}$

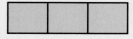

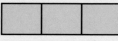
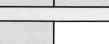

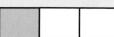

Figure B

Figure A

> **Talk About It**

▶ What amount is shown in Figure **A**?

▶ What amount is shown in Figure **B**?

▶ If you put the blue amount over the pink amount, how can you find the amount of pink still showing?

▶ What size pieces will fit exactly over both $\frac{1}{2}$ and $\frac{1}{3}$?

▶ How many pieces the size of $\frac{1}{6}$ will fit over the amount of pink still showing?

▶ If you remove $1\frac{1}{2}$ from $2\frac{1}{3}$, what amount is left?

Use fraction bars to find the difference.

a. $3 - 1\frac{1}{2}$ **b.** $2\frac{1}{2} - 1\frac{3}{4}$ **c.** $3\frac{1}{3} - 1\frac{3}{4}$

Making the Connection

Sometimes you must write equivalent fractions and rename before you can subtract mixed numbers.

Example $2\frac{1}{6} - 1\frac{5}{12}$

Step 1 Write equivalent fractions using the LCD.	**Step 2** Rename the greater number.	**Step 3** Subtract. Write the fraction in simplest form.
$2\dfrac{1}{6} = 2\dfrac{2}{12}$ $-1\dfrac{5}{12} = 1\dfrac{5}{12}$	$2\dfrac{2}{12} = 1 + \dfrac{12}{12} + \dfrac{2}{12}$ $= 1\dfrac{14}{12}$	$2\dfrac{2}{12} = 1\dfrac{14}{12}$ $-1\dfrac{5}{12} = 1\dfrac{5}{12}$ $\dfrac{9}{12} = \dfrac{3}{4}$

1. Is it necessary to write equivalent fractions using the LCD if you are subtracting $1\frac{1}{2}$ from $2\frac{1}{3}$? Explain.

2. Is it necessary to rename if you are subtracting $1\frac{1}{2}$ from $2\frac{1}{3}$? Justify your answer.

3. Why do you write equivalent fractions before you rename? Can you rename before you write equivalent fractions?

Checking Understanding

Change to the LCD if necessary. Then tell whether you must rename to subtract. Write *yes* or *no*.

4. $2\dfrac{1}{3} - \dfrac{2}{3}$

5. $2\dfrac{3}{5} - 1\dfrac{1}{4}$

6. $3\dfrac{3}{4} - 1\dfrac{1}{10}$

7. $3\dfrac{1}{7} - 2\dfrac{4}{7}$

8. $1\dfrac{4}{5} - \dfrac{1}{12}$

9. $1\dfrac{1}{15} - \dfrac{6}{15}$

Find the difference.

10. $2\dfrac{1}{3} - \dfrac{2}{3}$

11. $6\dfrac{1}{5} - 3\dfrac{7}{10}$

12. $10\dfrac{5}{6} - 6\dfrac{1}{2}$

13. $8\dfrac{5}{6} - 4\dfrac{8}{9}$

14. $16\dfrac{3}{8} - 7\dfrac{1}{2}$

15. $6\dfrac{1}{3} - 1\dfrac{5}{9}$

16. $5\dfrac{3}{4} - 3\dfrac{11}{12}$

17. $18\dfrac{1}{6} - 5\dfrac{3}{4}$

18. $20\dfrac{4}{5} - 17\dfrac{5}{6}$

SUBTRACTING MIXED NUMBERS
with Unlike Denominators

Kele has $1\frac{5}{12}$ yards of colonial molding and $3\frac{2}{3}$ yards of quarter-round molding. How much more quarter-round molding does he have?

Estimate. $3\frac{2}{3} - 1\frac{5}{12} = $ ▨

$$\downarrow \qquad \downarrow$$

$$4 \quad - \quad 1\frac{1}{2} \quad = 2\frac{1}{2} \leftarrow \text{estimate}$$

Step 1 Write equivalent fractions using the LCD.	**Step 2** Subtract. Write the fraction in simplest form.
$3\frac{2}{3} = 3\frac{8}{12}$ The LCD is 12. $-1\frac{5}{12} = 1\frac{5}{12}$	$\begin{array}{l} 3\frac{2}{3} = 3\frac{8}{12} \\ -1\frac{5}{12} = 1\frac{5}{12} \\ \hline \qquad 2\frac{3}{12} = 2\frac{1}{4} \end{array}$

So, Kele has $2\frac{1}{4}$ yards more quarter-round molding.

Another Example $3\frac{2}{3} - 2\frac{8}{9}$

Step 1 Write equivalent fractions using the LCD.	**Step 2** Rename. Subtract. Write the fraction in simplest form.
$3\frac{2}{3} = 3\frac{12}{18}$ The LCD is 18. $-2\frac{8}{9} = 2\frac{16}{18}$	$\begin{array}{l} 3\frac{2}{3} = 3\frac{12}{18} = 2\frac{30}{18} \\ -2\frac{8}{9} = 2\frac{16}{18} = 2\frac{16}{18} \\ \hline \qquad\qquad\qquad\quad \frac{14}{18} = \frac{7}{9} \end{array}$

Check for Understanding

Write equivalent fractions using the LCD.

1. $\begin{array}{r} 1\frac{4}{6} \\ -1\frac{1}{5} \\ \hline \end{array}$

2. $\begin{array}{r} 4\frac{3}{4} \\ -2\frac{1}{2} \\ \hline \end{array}$

3. $\begin{array}{r} 5\frac{1}{8} \\ -3\frac{3}{4} \\ \hline \end{array}$

4. $\begin{array}{r} 7\frac{2}{3} \\ -3\frac{4}{5} \\ \hline \end{array}$

Practice

Estimate the difference.

5. $5\dfrac{1}{6}$
   $-2\dfrac{2}{3}$

6. $7\dfrac{1}{4}$
   $-4\dfrac{2}{5}$

7. $3\dfrac{9}{10}$
   $-1\dfrac{6}{7}$

8. $5\dfrac{7}{10}$
   $-3\dfrac{1}{2}$

9. $8\dfrac{1}{3}$
   $-\dfrac{3}{4}$

Find the difference.

10. $7\dfrac{4}{9}$
    $-3\dfrac{1}{2}$

11. $8\dfrac{2}{5}$
    $-4\dfrac{1}{4}$

12. $5\dfrac{7}{12}$
    $-1\dfrac{1}{6}$

13. $6\dfrac{2}{3}$
    $-2\dfrac{1}{8}$

14. $9\dfrac{5}{9}$
    $-5\dfrac{1}{6}$

15. $18\dfrac{1}{6}$
    $-15\dfrac{3}{4}$

16. $20\dfrac{4}{5}$
    $-16\dfrac{5}{6}$

17. $26\dfrac{1}{2}$
    $-11\dfrac{3}{8}$

18. $32\dfrac{1}{2}$
    $-21\dfrac{7}{8}$

19. $43\dfrac{1}{2}$
    $-32\dfrac{7}{10}$

20. $15\dfrac{1}{6} - 3\dfrac{1}{2}$

21. $19\dfrac{3}{8} - 12\dfrac{3}{4}$

22. $28\dfrac{1}{2} - 21\dfrac{4}{5}$

23. $37\dfrac{2}{3} - 4\dfrac{7}{9}$

24. $36\dfrac{1}{4} - 14\dfrac{3}{4}$

25. $21\dfrac{1}{4} - 13\dfrac{7}{10}$

Mixed Applications

26. Peter lives $1\dfrac{3}{4}$ miles from school. Tony lives $1\dfrac{2}{3}$ miles from school in the same direction. How much farther is Peter's round-trip than Tony's round-trip?

27. **Logical Reasoning** Tim raises chickens and cows. His animals have a total of 25 heads and 70 feet. How many chickens and how many cows does Tim have?

MIXED REVIEW

Estimate the product or quotient.

1. $999 \div 99$

2. 279×19

3. $386 \div 6$

Write the common factors.

4. $6, 12$

5. $9, 15$

6. $9, 18, 27$

7. $12, 16, 24$

8. $36, 54, 72$

How does subtracting mixed numbers with unlike denominators differ from subtracting mixed numbers with like denominators?

WRAP UP...

PROBLEM Solving

A minibus leaves the garage to pick up Louis at the first stop. Then it travels $3\frac{1}{6}$ miles (mi) to pick up Tanya, $4\frac{1}{4}$ mi more to pick up Renee, and $4\frac{5}{12}$ mi more to the school. If the bus travels a total of $21\frac{2}{3}$ mi, what is the distance from the garage to Louis's house?

Sometimes you can use different strategies to solve the same problem.

What strategies can you use?

You can *draw a diagram* or *work backward*. First make the problem easier by writing equivalent fractions using the LCD 12.

$$3\frac{1}{6} = 3\frac{2}{12} \qquad 4\frac{1}{4} = 4\frac{3}{12} \qquad 4\frac{5}{12} = 4\frac{5}{12} \qquad 21\frac{2}{3} = 21\frac{8}{12}$$

Strategy: Draw a Diagram

Garage $\longrightarrow$	Louis $\longrightarrow$	Tanya $\longrightarrow$	Renee $\longrightarrow$	School
0	? mi	$3\frac{2}{12}$ mi	$4\frac{3}{12}$ mi	$4\frac{5}{12}$ mi

$21\frac{8}{12}$ mi

Add the miles to each stop.

$$3\frac{2}{12} + 4\frac{3}{12} + 4\frac{5}{12} = 11\frac{10}{12}$$

Subtract from the total miles.

$$21\frac{8}{12} - 11\frac{10}{12} = 20\frac{20}{12} - 11\frac{10}{12} = 9\frac{10}{12} = 9\frac{5}{6}$$

$\longrightarrow$ rename

Strategy: Work Backward

Miles to Louis	$\rightarrow$	Miles to Tanya	$\rightarrow$	Miles to Renee	$\rightarrow$	Miles to school	$\rightarrow$	Total miles
?	+	$3\frac{2}{12}$	+	$4\frac{3}{12}$	+	$4\frac{5}{12}$	=	$21\frac{8}{12}$

Miles to Louis	$\leftarrow$	Miles to Tanya	$\leftarrow$	Miles to Renee	$\leftarrow$	Miles to school	$\leftarrow$	Total miles
$9\frac{5}{6} = 9\frac{10}{12}$	=	$3\frac{2}{12}$	−	$4\frac{3}{12}$	−	$4\frac{5}{12}$	−	$21\frac{8}{12}$

So, the distance from the garage to Louis's house is $9\frac{5}{6}$ mi.

WHAT
IF...

... you were asked to find the distance from Tanya's house to the school? What strategy would you use?

Choose a strategy and solve.

1 Teresa runs a backyard lemonade stand. She sold $\frac{1}{2}$ of the cups of lemonade before lunch. Then she sold 4 cups after lunch. By evening she had 12 cups left. How many cups of lemonade did Teresa have at the beginning of the day?

2 Melanie swam 1 lap in the pool the first week, 4 laps the second week, 9 laps the third week, and 16 laps the fourth week. If she continues this pattern, how many laps will Melanie swim in weeks five, six, and seven?

3 Esther left her backyard and walked $1\frac{1}{3}$ kilometers (km) north. Then she walked $\frac{3}{4}$ km west, $\frac{1}{3}$ km north, $1\frac{1}{4}$ km east, and $1\frac{2}{3}$ km south. How far from her backyard was she?

4 Mrs. Wilson returned home after $1\frac{1}{2}$ hours. During that time she drove $\frac{1}{4}$ hour to take Jeff to scouts and $\frac{1}{3}$ hour to take Karen to ballet, and she then went shopping. How much time did it take her to shop and return home?

Monty drew a bar graph of the time he spent in a week making one model airplane. Use the bar graph for Exercises 5–7.

5 What is the total amount of time Monty spent making the model from Monday to Friday?

6 What is the median length of time Monty spent making the model during the week?

7 On the average, did Monty spend more time making the model during the five weekdays or during the weekend? How much more or less time did he spend per day?

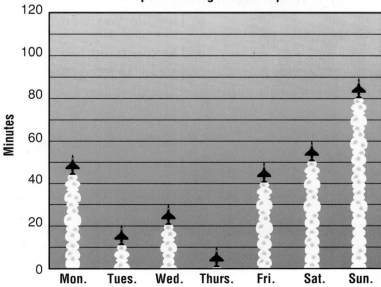

Time Spent Making Model Airplane

Vocabulary Check

Choose a word or words from the box to complete each sentence.

> denominator
> estimate
> renaming
> simplest form
> unlike

1. You can round fractions to 0, $\frac{1}{2}$, or 1 to __?__ sums and differences. *(page 206)*

2. When fractions have the same __?__, you can add or subtract the numerators. *(page 208)*

3. To add mixed numbers with __?__ denominators, find the LCD for the fractions. *(page 212)*

4. You divide the numerator and the denominator by the same number to write a fraction in __?__. *(page 208)*

5. Regrouping whole numbers is similar to __?__ mixed numbers. *(page 219)*

Concept Check

> Think: When do you need to rename the greater number?

6. If the numerator is much less than the denominator, you round to __?__ when estimating fraction sums and differences. *(page 206)*

7. If the numerator is about the same as the denominator, you round to __?__ when estimating fraction sums and differences. *(page 206)*

8. How does adding or subtracting like fractions differ from adding or subtracting unlike fractions? *(pages 208, 210)*

9. How do you write equivalent fractions? *(page 210)*

10. Do you need to find the LCD to answer $2\frac{1}{4} - 1\frac{1}{6}$? What is the LCD for $\frac{1}{4}$ and $\frac{1}{6}$? *(page 223)*

11. What must you do to subtract $2\frac{1}{4}$ from 4? *(page 223)*

Tell whether you must rename to subtract. Write *yes* or *no*.
(page 223)

12. $5\frac{1}{3} - 3\frac{2}{3}$

13. $6\frac{1}{2} - 2\frac{1}{4}$

14. $7 - \frac{3}{5}$

15. $3\frac{4}{9} - 2\frac{1}{9}$

16. $9\frac{7}{10} - 3\frac{11}{15}$

17. $8\frac{2}{3} - 2\frac{1}{2}$

Skill Check

Estimate the sum or difference. *(page 206)*

18. $\dfrac{1}{8} + \dfrac{3}{4}$

19. $\dfrac{9}{10} - \dfrac{1}{9}$

20. $9\dfrac{5}{7} + 1\dfrac{8}{9}$

21. $6\dfrac{1}{6} - 2\dfrac{7}{8}$

22. $5\dfrac{1}{15} + 5\dfrac{4}{5}$

23. $21\dfrac{1}{4} - 9\dfrac{5}{6}$

Find the sum or difference. *(pages 208, 210, 212, 214, 218, 220)*

24. $\dfrac{8}{11} + \dfrac{2}{11}$

25. $\dfrac{8}{15} - \dfrac{2}{15}$

26. $\dfrac{3}{10} + \dfrac{7}{10}$

27. $\dfrac{7}{9} + \dfrac{4}{5}$

28. $\dfrac{4}{5} - \dfrac{1}{2}$

29. $\dfrac{1}{6} + \dfrac{7}{8}$

30. $10\dfrac{1}{8} + 2\dfrac{5}{8}$

31. $3\dfrac{1}{12} + 7\dfrac{5}{12}$

32. $4\dfrac{1}{6} + 8\dfrac{1}{6}$

33. $12\dfrac{2}{3} - 3\dfrac{1}{3}$

34. $12\dfrac{2}{7} - 9\dfrac{5}{7}$

35. $4\dfrac{1}{8} - 2\dfrac{5}{8}$

Tell whether the sum or difference is correct. Write *true* or *false*. If you write *false*, give the correct answer. *(pages 212, 214, 222, 224)*

36. $4\dfrac{3}{4} + 2\dfrac{2}{5} = 7\dfrac{3}{20}$

37. $8\dfrac{1}{6} + 6\dfrac{1}{8} = 14\dfrac{1}{3}$

38. $9\dfrac{3}{5} + 9\dfrac{2}{3} = 19\dfrac{4}{15}$

39. $7\dfrac{2}{3} - 1\dfrac{2}{9} = 6\dfrac{4}{9}$

40. $8\dfrac{1}{6} - 2\dfrac{1}{15} = 6\dfrac{1}{15}$

41. $15\dfrac{1}{2} - 11\dfrac{5}{8} = 4\dfrac{7}{8}$

42. $3\dfrac{1}{8} - 1\dfrac{3}{4} = 1\dfrac{1}{2}$

43. $9\dfrac{1}{7} + 3\dfrac{11}{14} = 12\dfrac{13}{14}$

44. $7\dfrac{1}{3} - 5\dfrac{3}{8} = 1\dfrac{23}{24}$

Problem-Solving Check *(pages 214, 226)*

45. Kim watched as a cat played for $1\dfrac{1}{4}$ hours, ate for $\dfrac{1}{4}$ hour, played again for $\dfrac{1}{4}$ hour, and then slept. If Kim watched the cat for $2\dfrac{1}{2}$ hours, how long did the cat sleep?

46. Sue walked $1\dfrac{2}{3}$ miles (mi) from school to a store. Continuing in the same direction, she walked 1 mi to Rosa's home and then to her own home. Sue walked a total of $3\dfrac{1}{3}$ mi. How far is her home from Rosa's?

47. Bill has 5 shirts and 4 pairs of jeans. All of the shirts go with all of the jeans. How many different shirt-and-jeans outfits can Bill make with this wardrobe?

48. Paul drives from his home $2\dfrac{1}{2}$ mi south. Next, he drives west $\dfrac{1}{3}$ mi. Then, he drives north 3 mi. In which directions must Paul turn to return home?

CHAPTER TEST

Estimate the sum or difference.

An estimate is an approximation, not an exact answer.

1. $2\frac{2}{5} + 4\frac{1}{6}$

2. $6\frac{2}{3} - 3\frac{7}{10}$

3. $\frac{1}{8} + \frac{7}{9}$

4. $7\frac{5}{8} - 5\frac{2}{7}$

5. $10\frac{5}{11} - 1\frac{1}{2}$

Tell whether the sum or difference is correct. Write *true* or *false.*
If you write *false,* give the correct answer.

6. $\frac{1}{8} + \frac{5}{8} = \frac{3}{4}$

7. $\frac{5}{12} - \frac{1}{12} = \frac{1}{4}$

8. $\frac{7}{9} + \frac{5}{9} = \frac{12}{9}$

9. $\frac{1}{6} + \frac{1}{8} = \frac{7}{24}$

10. $\frac{5}{9} - \frac{1}{2} = \frac{1}{9}$

11. $\frac{2}{3} + \frac{2}{5} = 1\frac{1}{15}$

12. $\frac{1}{9} + \frac{2}{3} = \frac{6}{9}$

13. $\frac{3}{4} - \frac{3}{5} = \frac{1}{10}$

14. $\frac{1}{6} - \frac{1}{9} = \frac{1}{18}$

15. $\frac{4}{5} - \frac{2}{3} = \frac{2}{15}$

16. $\frac{3}{8} + \frac{1}{4} = \frac{9}{16}$

17. $1\frac{1}{7} - \frac{6}{7} = \frac{2}{7}$

Find the sum or difference.

18. $2\frac{1}{7}$
   $+ 3\frac{3}{7}$

19. $4\frac{3}{8}$
   $+ 1\frac{2}{3}$

20. $8\frac{3}{4}$
   $+ 6\frac{3}{5}$

21. $18\frac{7}{9}$
   $+ 6\frac{1}{6}$

22. $10\frac{2}{9}$
   $+ 5\frac{1}{3}$

23. $9\frac{1}{2}$
   $+ 2\frac{5}{15}$

24. $10\frac{2}{3}$
   $- 5\frac{1}{3}$

25. $8\frac{5}{16}$
   $- 6\frac{7}{16}$

26. $4\frac{1}{6}$
   $- 3\frac{1}{5}$

27. $16\frac{1}{5}$
   $- 8\frac{1}{4}$

28. $5\frac{3}{4}$
   $- 3\frac{2}{3}$

29. $1\frac{1}{3}$
   $- \frac{6}{7}$

30. Barbara spent 3 hours (hr) studying, including a break. She spent $\frac{3}{4}$ hr on math, $\frac{1}{2}$ hr on science, and 1 hr on music. How long was her break?

31. Yolanda drove 2 mi west, $1\frac{1}{2}$ mi south, $\frac{1}{8}$ mi east, and 3 mi north. How far had she driven when she crossed her own path?

32. The post office is east of Ron's house. A theater is an additional 5 mi east, and a cafe is $2\frac{1}{2}$ mi farther east. A trip from Ron's house to the cafe and back is 33 mi. How far is the post office from Ron's house?

33. Dean, Kathy, and Suzy collect seashells. Dean has 5 more than Suzy, who has twice as many as Kathy. If they have a total of 95 seashells, how many does each person have?

Teamwork P-R-O-J-E-C-T

Create an Invention

Have you ever thought, "If there were only some gadget that would . . . to make my life easier"?

Work with your teammates to create an invention, such as a gadget, a piece of furniture, or an appliance, that could make your lives easier.

Decide	Begin by making a list of common tasks or activities with which you could use some help. What kinds of inventions would help?
	Choose one invention to work on. Describe the purpose of the invention.
Do	As a team, make a model or draw a sketch of your invention.
	Write a description of how the invention would be manufactured and used.
Share	Show your model or sketch to another team. If you made a model, demonstrate it. If you drew a sketch, describe how your invention works. Then let the other team do the same with its model or sketch.

Talk About It

How useful is each invention?

What fraction of the students in your class would find your invention helpful?

Suppose you wanted to manufacture your invention. What do you think would be the cost of manufacturing it?

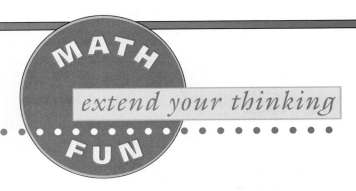

Computer Connection

*T*he decimal system is based on ten numerals. Numbers greater than 9 are written using powers of 10. You can use exponents to show the place values.

$5,469_{10} = 5 \qquad 4 \qquad 6 \qquad 9$

$(5 \times 10^3) + (4 \times 10^2) + (6 \times 10^1) + (9 \times 10^0)$

$5,000 \quad + \quad 400 \quad + \quad 60 \quad + \quad 9$

Some computers calculate in the binary system, or base two, which uses only the digits 0 and 1. Numbers greater than 1 are written using powers of 2.

$1011_2 = 1 \qquad 0 \qquad 1 \qquad 1$

$(1 \times 2^3) + (0 \times 2^2) + (1 \times 2^1) + (1 \times 2^0)$

To convert numbers from binary to base ten, calculate the powers of 2 and then add.

$(1 \times 2^3) + (0 \times 2^2) + (1 \times 2^1) + (1 \times 2^0) = 8 + 0 + 2 + 1 = 11$

Convert these binary numbers to base ten.

1. 10101001   2. 10001010   3. 01101100

What comparisons can you make between the base-ten system and the base-two system?

Challenge

Magic Square

Complete the square so that the sum of the numbers in every row, column, and diagonal is $3\frac{15}{16}$.

■	■	■
$1\frac{1}{16}$	■	■
■	$1\frac{7}{16}$	$1\frac{1}{8}$

Write a Question

Use the picture to write a question. Tell whether to add or subtract to solve.

$\frac{15}{16}$ inch — A

$\frac{11}{16}$ inch — B

Write the letter of the correct answer.

1. Evaluate $3.45 - c$, for $c = 0.5$.

   A. 2.95   **B.** 3.4
   C. 3.95   **D.** not here

2. $3 \times 60.4 - 0.4 + 10$

   A. 150   **B.** 190
   C. 190.8   **D.** 210

3. 2.3×5.04

   A. 1.602   **B.** 11.592
   C. 11.692   **D.** 115.92

4. $39.8 \div 0.4$

   A. 9.95   **B.** 99.5
   C. 995   **D.** not here

5. What is the number of combinations for 3 hats and 4 pairs of shoes?

   A. 3   **B.** 4
   C. 7   **D.** 12

6. Which is the appropriate graph for June temperature readings in Miami?

   A. bar   **B.** line
   C. circle   **D.** histogram

7. What is the LCM of 8 and 12?

   A. 2   **B.** 4
   C. 24   **D.** 96

8. What is the GCF of 15 and 60?

   A. 3   **B.** 5
   C. 15   **D.** not here

9. $12\frac{1}{5} + 3\frac{3}{4}$

   A. $15\frac{4}{9}$ **B.** $15\frac{9}{20}$
   C. 16   **D.** not here

10. $9\frac{1}{3} - 7\frac{7}{8}$

   A. $\frac{11}{24}$ **B.** $1\frac{5}{12}$
   C. $1\frac{11}{24}$ **D.** $2\frac{11}{24}$

11. Jim is in a maze. He goes north 5 ft, west 2 ft, north 2 ft, east 4 ft, and south 3 ft. In what direction should he turn to cross his own path?

   A. east   **B.** west
   C. north   **D.** south

12. Ken drove $25\frac{1}{3}$ mi from his house to the store. He stopped at Lisa's, which is $5\frac{1}{2}$ mi from his house. How far is Lisa's from the store?

   A. $19\frac{1}{6}$ mi   **B.** $19\frac{5}{6}$ mi
   C. $20\frac{5}{6}$ mi   **D.** $30\frac{5}{6}$ mi

MULTIPLYING AND DIVIDING FRACTIONS

 Did you know ...

... that hundreds of marching bands participate in holiday parades in the United States every year?

Suppose $\frac{1}{4}$ of the 144 members of a marching band play percussion instruments. How can you find the number of band members who play percussion instruments?

To find $\frac{1}{2}$ of 6, you multiply. How would you find $\frac{1}{2}$ of $\frac{3}{4}$? In this lesson you will explore multiplying a fraction by a fraction.

Think: What is $\frac{1}{2}$ of $\frac{3}{4}$?

WORK TOGETHER

Building Understanding

You can use a model to help you find the product of $\frac{1}{2} \times \frac{3}{4}$.

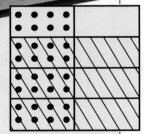

Figure A

Figure B

Talk About It

▶ What part of Figure **A** is represented by diagonal lines?

▶ What part of Figure **B** is represented by dots?

▶ What part of Figure **B** is represented by the area that has both dots and diagonal lines?

▶ What is $\frac{1}{2}$ of $\frac{3}{4}$?

▶ Is your answer less than or greater than each factor?

Talk About It

▶ How does each product compare with the factors?

▶ Will the product of two fractions that are each less than 1 always be less than either factor? How do you know?

Draw a model to represent each problem. Solve.

A. $\frac{1}{2} \times \frac{1}{3}$

B. $\frac{1}{3} \times \frac{2}{3}$

C. $\frac{1}{3} \times \frac{3}{5}$

236

Making the Connection

Multiplying fractions that are less than 1 is similar to multiplying decimals that are less than 1.

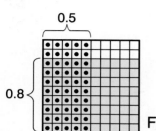

Figure A

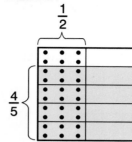

Figure B

a. Think: 0.5 of 0.8,
or 0.5 × 0.8 = 0.40.

b. Think: $\frac{1}{2}$ of $\frac{4}{5}$,

or $\frac{1}{2} \times \frac{4}{5} = \frac{4}{10}$, or $\frac{2}{5}$.

1. How do the numbers in the problem for Figure **A** compare with the numbers for Figure **B**?

2. How does the part that has both shading and dots in Figure **A** compare with the part that has both shading and dots in Figure **B**?

3. Is the product of 0.5 × 0.8 the same as the product of $\frac{1}{2} \times \frac{4}{5}$? How can you tell?

Checking Understanding

Use the model to help you find the product. Write the product in simplest form.

4. $\frac{2}{5} \times \frac{1}{4}$ $\frac{2}{5}$

5. $\frac{1}{6} \times \frac{2}{3}$ $\frac{1}{6}$

6. $\frac{1}{2} \times \frac{4}{7}$ $\frac{1}{2}$

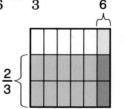

$\frac{1}{4}$ $\frac{2}{3}$ $\frac{4}{7}$

Draw a model for each problem. Tell whether the product in **a** is the same as the product in **b**.

7. a. 0.5 × 0.4 = 0.2

    b. $\frac{1}{2} \times \frac{2}{5} = \frac{1}{5}$

8. a. $\frac{3}{4} \times \frac{1}{3} = \frac{1}{4}$

    b. 0.7 × 0.7 = 0.49

9. a. $\frac{1}{8} \times \frac{4}{5} = \frac{1}{10}$

    b. 0.9 × 0.8 = 0.72

10. a. 0.1 × 0.5 = 0.05

    b. $\frac{1}{10} \times \frac{1}{2} = \frac{1}{20}$

Mrs. Mar buys $\frac{2}{3}$ yard of material to trim costumes for a Fourth of July play. She uses $\frac{5}{6}$ of the material. What part of a yard does she use?

Think: What is $\frac{5}{6}$ of $\frac{2}{3}$?

You can use a model to help you solve the problem.

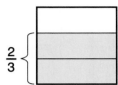
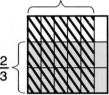

- What part of the model has both shading and diagonal lines?

Another Method   You can also multiply to find $\frac{5}{6}$ of $\frac{2}{3}$.

Step 1 Multiply the numerators.	**Step 2** Multiply the denominators.	**Step 3** Write the answer in simplest form.
$\frac{5}{6} \times \frac{2}{3} = \frac{10}{}$	$\frac{5}{6} \times \frac{2}{3} = \frac{10}{18}$	$\frac{10 \div 2}{18 \div 2} = \frac{5}{9}$

So, Mrs. Mar uses $\frac{5}{9}$ of a yard of material.

- How is $\frac{2}{3}$ represented in the model?

- How is $\frac{5}{6}$ represented in the model?

- How is $\frac{10}{18}$ represented in the model?

- Why do you divide the numerator and denominator by 2 to simplify?

Check for Understanding

Use the model to help you find the product.

1. $\frac{1}{3} \times \frac{1}{2}$

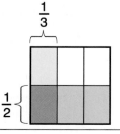

2. $\frac{1}{5} \times \frac{1}{2}$

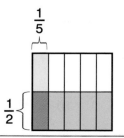

3. $\frac{2}{3} \times \frac{3}{4}$

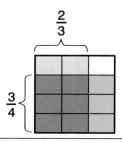

4. $\frac{1}{4} \times \frac{4}{5}$

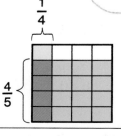

Practice

Complete the multiplication sentence.
Write the product in simplest form.

5. $\dfrac{3}{4} \times \blacksquare = \blacksquare$

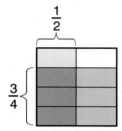

6. $\dfrac{3}{5} \times \blacksquare = \blacksquare$

7. $\blacksquare \times \dfrac{5}{6} = \blacksquare$

Solve. Write the product in simplest form.

8. $\dfrac{1}{3} \times \dfrac{2}{3}$

9. $\dfrac{1}{2} \times \dfrac{1}{2}$

10. $\dfrac{3}{4} \times \dfrac{1}{4}$

11. $\dfrac{1}{5} \times \dfrac{2}{3}$

12. $\dfrac{1}{4} \times \dfrac{2}{7}$

13. $\dfrac{7}{8} \times \dfrac{2}{5}$

14. $\dfrac{3}{8} \times \dfrac{4}{7}$

15. $\dfrac{2}{9} \times \dfrac{3}{4}$

16. $\dfrac{4}{5} \times \dfrac{5}{6}$

17. $\dfrac{6}{7} \times \dfrac{7}{8}$

18. $\dfrac{2}{5} \times \dfrac{5}{7}$

19. $\dfrac{1}{9} \times \dfrac{3}{5}$

20. $\dfrac{5}{9} \times \dfrac{3}{10}$

21. $\dfrac{4}{9} \times \dfrac{3}{5}$

22. $\dfrac{5}{7} \times \dfrac{7}{15}$

Mixed Applications

23. Seth had $\dfrac{1}{2}$ of a display from the festival. He gave $\dfrac{2}{3}$ of what he had to Tim. What part did Seth give to Tim?

24. Beth's dad had $\dfrac{3}{4}$ of a box of sparklers. He used $\dfrac{1}{2}$ of the sparklers last night. What part of the box did he use?

25. Logical Reasoning Write a multiplication problem that has the same answer as $\dfrac{1}{2} + \dfrac{1}{2} + \dfrac{1}{2} + \dfrac{1}{2}$.

26. Number Sense Use the rules for the order of operations to solve $\dfrac{1}{5} + \dfrac{2}{3} \times \dfrac{3}{5} - \dfrac{2}{5}$. Write the answer in simplest form.

VISUAL THINKING

Think of the multiplication of a whole number by a fraction as repeated addition. Use a number line to visualize the answer.

Example $\dfrac{3}{5} \times 6$

$\dfrac{3}{5} \times 6 = \dfrac{18}{5} = 3\dfrac{3}{5}$

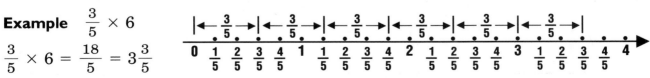

27. Draw a number line to find the product $\dfrac{1}{4} \times 5$.

How do you multiply fractions?

WRAP
U P . . .

The first United States flag was adopted in 1777. Many people remember the occasion on June 14 every year by celebrating Flag Day. Yoshi lives $\frac{4}{5}$ mile from the park where the town celebrates Flag Day. On Flag Day he was $\frac{1}{8}$ of the way to the park on his bike when he had a flat tire. How far did he ride before he had the flat tire?

You can often simplify before you multiply.

Step 1	Step 2	Step 3
Find a common factor of any one numerator and any one denominator.	Divide the numerator and the denominator by the common factor.	Repeat until 1 is the only common factor left. Then multiply.
$\frac{1}{8} \times \frac{4}{5}$ A common factor of 8 and 4 is 2.	$\frac{1}{\underset{4}{8}} \times \frac{\overset{2}{4}}{5}$	$\frac{1}{\underset{2}{\cancel{8}}} \times \frac{\overset{1}{\cancel{4}}}{5} = \frac{1 \times 1}{2 \times 5} = \frac{1}{10}$

So, Yoshi rode $\frac{1}{10}$ mile before he had the flat tire.

Talk About It

▶ What is the product of $\frac{1}{8}$ and $\frac{4}{5}$ if you multiply without simplifying?

▶ What is the greatest common factor (GCF) of 4 and 8?

▶ What fractions would you multiply in Step 2 if you had simplified using the GCF instead of any other common factor?

▶ When you use the GCF, do you need to continue to simplify the fractions? Explain.

More Examples

A. $\frac{5}{8} \times \frac{8}{16} = \frac{5}{\underset{1}{\cancel{8}}} \times \frac{\overset{1}{\cancel{8}}}{16} = \frac{5}{16}$ GCF is 8.

B. $\frac{2}{3} \times \frac{3}{10} = \frac{\overset{1}{\cancel{2}}}{\underset{1}{\cancel{3}}} \times \frac{\overset{1}{\cancel{3}}}{\underset{5}{10}} = \frac{1}{5}$ GCF of 3 and 3 is 3.
GCF of 2 and 10 is 2.

Check for Understanding

Tell what common factors you can use to simplify the fractions.

1. $\frac{1}{2} \times \frac{2}{3}$ **2.** $\frac{1}{5} \times \frac{15}{16}$ **3.** $\frac{14}{27} \times \frac{6}{7}$ **4.** $\frac{4}{9} \times \frac{6}{14}$ **5.** $\frac{6}{4} \times \frac{8}{9}$

Practice

Simplify the factors.

6. $\frac{1}{4} \times \frac{4}{5}$

7. $\frac{1}{2} \times \frac{6}{7}$

8. $\frac{2}{5} \times \frac{3}{4}$

9. $\frac{3}{5} \times \frac{5}{6}$

10. $\frac{2}{3} \times \frac{3}{4}$

11. $\frac{4}{20} \times \frac{5}{8}$

12. $\frac{2}{3} \times \frac{6}{9}$

13. $\frac{4}{9} \times \frac{15}{22}$

14. $\frac{9}{12} \times \frac{6}{18}$

15. $\frac{3}{5} \times \frac{1}{6}$

16. $\frac{4}{5} \times \frac{5}{16}$

17. $\frac{4}{7} \times \frac{21}{28}$

18. $\frac{2}{15} \times \frac{5}{6}$

19. $\frac{5}{12} \times \frac{18}{25}$

20. $\frac{2}{9} \times \frac{27}{28}$

21. $\frac{7}{10} \times \frac{5}{14}$

22. $\frac{3}{4} \times \frac{16}{21}$

23. $\frac{1}{2} \times \frac{12}{13}$

24. $\frac{5}{8} \times \frac{12}{25}$

25. $\frac{6}{8} \times \frac{2}{3}$

Choose a method to find the product.
Write the product in simplest form.

26. $\frac{2}{3} \times \frac{1}{6}$

27. $\frac{5}{6} \times \frac{3}{8}$

28. $\frac{7}{10} \times \frac{5}{7}$

29. $\frac{4}{5} \times \frac{5}{8}$

30. $\frac{8}{9} \times \frac{3}{4}$

31. $\frac{5}{6} \times \frac{3}{10}$

32. $\frac{2}{3} \times \frac{9}{10}$

33. $\frac{6}{7} \times \frac{5}{8}$

34. $\frac{5}{8} \times \frac{4}{15}$

35. $\frac{5}{14} \times \frac{7}{10}$

36. $\frac{8}{9} \times \frac{3}{4}$

37. $\frac{18}{25} \times \frac{5}{9}$

38. $\frac{4}{5} \times \frac{15}{16}$

39. $\frac{21}{22} \times \frac{2}{7}$

40. $\frac{3}{16} \times \frac{8}{15}$

41. $\frac{5}{24} \times \frac{9}{10}$

42. $\frac{7}{26} \times \frac{13}{35}$

43. $\frac{9}{10} \times \frac{5}{27}$

44. $\frac{9}{30} \times \frac{5}{18}$

45. $\frac{11}{28} \times \frac{7}{22}$

Mixed Applications

46. Mark had $\frac{2}{3}$ of his cake left after his birthday party. If he gave $\frac{3}{4}$ of the remaining cake to Rita, what part of the entire cake did Mark give Rita?

47. Mrs. Chen has used all the red candles from a box of candles and still has $\frac{2}{3}$ left. If $\frac{1}{4}$ of the remaining candles are blue, what part of the entire box was blue?

48. **Visual Thinking** Look at the number line. If C and B are less than 1, does A or D correspond to $C \times B$?

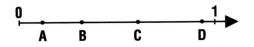

49. **Logical Reasoning** Find the values for a and b if a and b are consecutive even numbers and $\frac{a}{b} = \frac{8}{9}$.

What is the advantage of simplifying before multiplying?

WRAP
UP...

ESTIMATING PRODUCTS OF FRACTIONS

Americans set aside the third Monday of February for Presidents' Day. This is a day to remember all U.S. Presidents throughout history. The park manager has marked off $\frac{7}{8}$ of the park for the Presidents' Day celebration. Of this area, $\frac{3}{5}$ will be used for games and sports. About how much of the park will be used for games and sports?

You can estimate the product of $\frac{7}{8}$ and $\frac{3}{5}$ to answer the question.

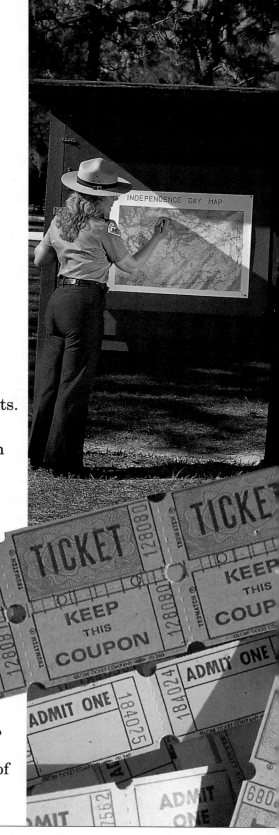

Step 1 Compare the numerator to the denominator.	**Step 2** Round each factor.	**Step 3** Multiply the rounded factors.
$\dfrac{7}{8} \times \dfrac{3}{5}$ about the same as the denominator about one half the denominator	$\dfrac{7}{8} \times \dfrac{3}{5}$ $\downarrow \qquad \downarrow$ $1 \times \dfrac{1}{2}$	$1 \times \dfrac{1}{2} = \dfrac{1}{2}$

So, about $\frac{1}{2}$ of the park will be used for games and sports.

You can also use compatible numbers to estimate. When you estimate using two methods, you can find a range.

Judy had a total of 179 tickets. If she sold about $\frac{4}{9}$ of them, about how many tickets did she sell?

Use rounding.

$\frac{4}{9} \times 179$
$\downarrow \qquad \downarrow$
$\frac{1}{2} \times 200 = 100$

Use compatible numbers.

$\frac{4}{9} \times 179$
$\downarrow \qquad \downarrow$
$\frac{4}{9} \times 180 = 80$

So, Judy sold about 80 to 100 tickets.

Talk About It

▶ What other pairs of compatible numbers can you use?

▶ What method would you use to estimate the product of $\frac{2}{3}$ and 627? Explain your choice.

Check for Understanding

Choose the best range of estimates. Write **a, b,** or **c**.

1. $\frac{5}{6} \times 376$
   a. 350 to 900
   b. 300 to 376
   c. 100 to 300

2. $\frac{2}{3} \times 264$
   a. 150 to 200
   b. 50 to 300
   c. 75 to 100

3. $\frac{3}{8} \times 176$
   a. 30 to 50
   b. 40 to 80
   c. 70 to 100

4. $\frac{3}{5} \times 443$
   a. 100 to 400
   b. 300 to 370
   c. 200 to 270

Practice

Use rounding to estimate the product.

5. $\frac{4}{9} \times \frac{7}{8}$

6. $\frac{2}{3} \times \frac{9}{11}$

7. $\frac{2}{5} \times \frac{7}{16}$

8. $\frac{11}{12} \times \frac{6}{7}$

9. $\frac{5}{12} \times \frac{11}{13}$

Use compatible numbers to estimate the product.

10. $\frac{1}{4} \times 79$

11. $\frac{1}{5} \times 451$

12. $910 \times \frac{3}{4}$

13. $\frac{2}{5} \times 299$

14. $\frac{5}{6} \times 538$

Tell whether the estimate is reasonable. Write *yes* or *no*.

15. $\frac{9}{10} \times 30 \approx 20$

16. $\frac{2}{5} \times 20 \approx 10$

17. $\frac{7}{12} \times 314 \approx 300$

18. $\frac{1}{3} \times 300 \approx 100$

19. $\frac{13}{14} \times \frac{7}{15} \approx 1$

20. $\frac{7}{15} \times 210 \approx 75$

21. $\frac{9}{20} \times 425 \approx 100$

22. $\frac{1}{4} \times 600 \approx 150$

Mixed Applications

23. At a dance contest, $\frac{1}{2}$ of the winners received the third prize, fancy socks. If there were 395 winners, about how many received fancy socks?

24. **Visual Thinking** Write the multiplication sentence that the model represents.

Find the difference.

1. $3\frac{1}{2} - \frac{3}{4}$

2. $5\frac{1}{3} - 1\frac{4}{5}$

3. $6\frac{1}{5} - 4\frac{5}{7}$

4. $1\frac{3}{4} - \frac{7}{8}$

Find the sum. Write your answer in simplest form.

5. $\frac{7}{8} + \frac{1}{2}$

6. $\frac{1}{6} + \frac{5}{18}$

7. $\frac{3}{4} + \frac{2}{3}$

8. $\frac{11}{12} + \frac{3}{4}$

How do you decide which strategy to use when you estimate?

MULTIPLYING
with Mixed Numbers

Gina brought $1\frac{1}{3}$ pans of lasagna to a Kwanzaa festival. If she gave away $\frac{1}{2}$ of the lasagna, how much did Gina give away?

Think: What is $\frac{1}{2}$ of $1\frac{1}{3}$?

You can make a model like this one to determine the answer, or you can multiply $\frac{1}{2}$ and $1\frac{1}{3}$.

• How many parts are in each pan?

• How many parts are shaded red?

• What part of the pans would the entire shaded area be?

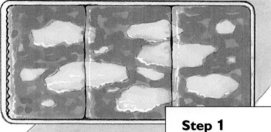

Step 1 Write the mixed number as a fraction.	**Step 2** Simplify.	**Step 3** Multiply.
$\frac{1}{2} \times 1\frac{1}{3}$ $\frac{1}{2} \times \frac{4}{3}$	$\frac{1}{2} \times \frac{4}{3} = \frac{1}{2} \times \frac{\overset{2}{\cancel{4}}}{\underset{1}{3}}$	$\frac{1}{\cancel{2}} \times \frac{\overset{2}{\cancel{4}}}{3} = \frac{1}{1} \times \frac{2}{3} = \frac{2}{3}$

So, Gina gave away $\frac{2}{3}$ of a pan of the lasagna.

• Why is the product, $\frac{2}{3}$, greater than one of the factors?

Another Example $3\frac{1}{3} \times 2\frac{1}{4}$

Estimate. Round to the nearest whole number. $3 \times 2 = 6$ ← estimate

Multiply.

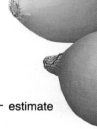

Step 1 Write the mixed numbers as fractions.	**Step 2** Simplify.	**Step 3** Multiply.
$3\frac{1}{3} \times 2\frac{1}{4} = \frac{10}{3} \times \frac{9}{4}$	$\frac{10}{3} \times \frac{9}{4} = \frac{10}{\underset{1}{\cancel{3}}} \times \frac{\overset{3}{\cancel{9}}}{\underset{2}{\cancel{4}}}$	$\frac{\overset{5}{\cancel{10}}}{\underset{1}{\cancel{3}}} \times \frac{\overset{3}{\cancel{9}}}{\underset{2}{\cancel{4}}} = \frac{5}{1} \times \frac{3}{2} = \frac{15}{2}$, or $7\frac{1}{2}$

• Why is the product greater than each factor?

244

Check for Understanding

Rewrite the problem by changing each mixed number to a fraction.

1. $4\frac{3}{4} \times \frac{1}{8}$

2. $\frac{2}{7} \times 6\frac{3}{5}$

3. $1\frac{1}{3} \times 3\frac{3}{4}$

4. $2\frac{1}{3} \times 1\frac{6}{7}$

Practice

Write each mixed number as a fraction. Then simplify the factors.

5. $1\frac{2}{3} \times \frac{3}{4}$

6. $\frac{4}{15} \times 4\frac{3}{8}$

7. $2\frac{2}{3} \times 1\frac{3}{8}$

8. $4\frac{1}{6} \times 2\frac{14}{25}$

Tell whether the product will be less than both factors, between the factors, or greater than both factors.

9. $\frac{1}{8} \times \frac{3}{5}$

10. $\frac{1}{9} \times 2\frac{1}{4}$

11. $\frac{2}{3} \times 1\frac{1}{8}$

12. $2\frac{4}{5} \times 2\frac{1}{2}$

13. $2\frac{1}{3} \times 1\frac{2}{7}$

14. $1\frac{5}{6} \times \frac{1}{11}$

15. $\frac{5}{6} \times 1\frac{1}{3}$

16. $5\frac{1}{4} \times 4\frac{2}{3}$

Solve. Write the product in simplest form.

17. $3\frac{1}{2} \times \frac{4}{5}$

18. $6\frac{1}{4} \times 5\frac{3}{5}$

19. $3\frac{1}{3} \times 2\frac{5}{8}$

20. $\frac{1}{5} \times 3\frac{1}{3}$

21. $4\frac{2}{3} \times 1\frac{3}{4}$

22. $1\frac{7}{8} \times 4\frac{2}{3}$

23. $5\frac{1}{2} \times \frac{1}{6}$

24. $\frac{1}{2} \times 3\frac{1}{7}$

25. $4\frac{1}{6} \times 3\frac{3}{5}$

26. $1\frac{3}{4} \times \frac{1}{3}$

27. $10\frac{1}{5} \times 8\frac{1}{3}$

28. $5\frac{5}{6} \times \frac{1}{5}$

29. $3\frac{1}{3} \times 2\frac{1}{7}$

30. $3\frac{1}{4} \times \frac{2}{5}$

31. $\frac{7}{8} \times 7\frac{3}{7}$

32. $9\frac{3}{8} \times 4\frac{4}{5}$

Mixed Applications

33. Karen and Cami rode bicycles to the picnic. Karen rode $6\frac{1}{2}$ minutes. Cami rode $1\frac{1}{4}$ times as long. How long did it take Cami to ride her bicycle to the picnic?

34. Richard and Hector walked to a picnic. Richard walked $1\frac{3}{5}$ miles. Hector walked $2\frac{1}{2}$ times as far as Richard. How far did Hector walk?

35. **Number Sense • Mental Math** Julie has completed $\frac{2}{3}$ of an 18-week enrichment course. How many weeks has she completed?

36. **Logical Reasoning** Sara has 20 nickels and dimes. The value of the coins is $1.35. How many of each coin does Sara have?

When you multiply two mixed numbers, is the product less than or greater than the factors?

WRAP
UP...

Markie and Bill are on a committee to make favors for a New Year's Eve party. If they use $8\frac{2}{3}$ cups of confetti for every dozen favors, how many cups of confetti will they use for $12\frac{3}{4}$ dozen favors?

▶ **UNDERSTAND**

What are you asked to find?

What information are you given?

▶ **PLAN**

What strategy will you use?

You can write and solve an equation.

▶ **SOLVE**

How will you carry out your plan?

Write an equation. Let c represent the number of cups of confetti that will be used.

$$c = 8\frac{2}{3} \times 12\frac{3}{4} \qquad c = \frac{26}{3} \times \frac{51}{4}$$

Use a standard calculator.
Multiply the denominators.

3 × 4 = 12 M+

26 × 51 = 1326 ←Multiply the numerators.

1326 ÷ MRC = `110.5`

Use a calculator designed to operate with fractions.

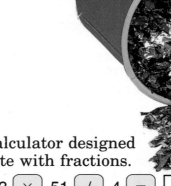

26 / 3 × 51 / 4 = `1326/12`

Ab/c `110 u 6/12`

Simp 6 = `110 u 1/2`

$110.5 = 110\frac{1}{2}$ 0.5 and $\frac{1}{2}$ name the same amount.

So, Markie and Bill will use $110\frac{1}{2}$ cups of confetti.

▶ **LOOK BACK**

How can you check your solution?

WHAT IF... ... Markie and Bill need to make 15 dozen favors? How many cups of confetti will they use?

246

Apply

Write an equation. Then solve.

(1) The employees of a novelty company worked $\frac{1}{2}$ as many hours this week as they worked last week. If they worked 60 hours last week, how many hours did the employees work this week?

(2) Mr. Gonzalez, the manager of a novelty company, will earn $1\frac{1}{2}$ times as much this year as he earned last year. If he earned $15,000 last year, how much will he earn this year?

(3) For Arbor Day, Nora gave one tiny tree each to $\frac{1}{2}$ of her 36 classmates and $\frac{1}{3}$ of the 33 students on her bus. How many trees did Nora give away?

Mixed Applications	STRATEGIES	• Write an Equation • Guess and Check
		• Work Backward • Find a Pattern

Choose a strategy and solve. Use the table for Exercises 6–7.

(4) Nim's Novelty Company employs 16 clerks. Noe's company employs $\frac{3}{4}$ as many clerks as Nim's. How many clerks does Noe's Novelty Company employ?

(5) Amy spent $\frac{1}{3}$ of her allowance for confetti, $\frac{1}{2}$ of what was left for balloons, and the remaining $3.00 for red streamers. How much did Amy spend?

(6) Andy has a package delivery service. If the pattern of delivery charges continues, how much will Andy charge to deliver a package $2\frac{5}{8}$ miles?

(7) Andy delivered a package $2\frac{5}{8}$ miles to one client, returned to the office, and delivered another package 2 miles in the opposite direction. How much money did Andy collect?

Andy's Delivery Service	
Distance	**Fee**
Up to $1\frac{1}{2}$ miles	$1.25
From $1\frac{1}{2}$ to $1\frac{3}{4}$ miles	$1.70
From $1\frac{3}{4}$ to 2 miles	$2.15

(8) Leon placed 2 boxes of party favors on a delivery truck. The boxes weighed a total of 12 pounds. One box was 2 pounds heavier than the other. How much did each of the boxes weigh?

(9) Kevin earns $40 for working an 8-hour day. If he is paid twice his regular rate for overtime, what will Kevin be paid for working a regular 40-hour week and 5 hours of overtime?

REVIEW AND MAINTENANCE

1. A bus leaves a fair to pick up riders at Stop 1. It then goes $2\frac{1}{2}$ miles (mi) to Stop 2, 4 mi to Stop 3, and $3\frac{1}{3}$ mi to Stop 4. If the whole trip is $12\frac{1}{6}$ mi, how far is the fair from Stop 1?

2. Mike sold $\frac{1}{2}$ of his flags on Monday and Tuesday. On Wednesday he sold 3 and had 5 left. How many flags did Mike have before he sold some on Monday?

3. Last year, Tom and Jan ran $1\frac{3}{4}$ mi per hour to come in third in a three-legged race at a Veterans Day picnic. After practicing, they now run $1\frac{3}{5}$ times faster. How fast do they run now?

4. Carla often works 35 hours a week. Since she is taking some of her vacation this week, she will work only 2 hours more than $\frac{1}{5}$ of her usual schedule. How many hours will Carla work this week?

Estimate the difference.

5. $3\frac{1}{3} - 1\frac{2}{3}$

6. $8\frac{1}{6} - 6\frac{1}{8}$

7. $5\frac{3}{5} - 2\frac{1}{4}$

8. $10\frac{1}{5} - 8\frac{7}{8}$

Rename the greater mixed number.

9. $8\frac{1}{4} - 6\frac{3}{4}$

10. $7\frac{1}{3} - 4\frac{2}{3}$

11. $6\frac{1}{6} - 2\frac{5}{6}$

12. $23\frac{1}{8} - 17\frac{5}{8}$

Find the difference. Write your answer in simplest form.

13. $5 - 2\frac{1}{2}$

14. $11\frac{1}{9} - 4\frac{4}{9}$

15. $8\frac{1}{5} - 3\frac{4}{5}$

16. $7\frac{1}{5} - 5\frac{1}{4}$

17. $4\frac{4}{9} - 3\frac{1}{3}$

18. $18\frac{1}{2} - 1\frac{2}{3}$

19. $8\frac{1}{6} - 1\frac{7}{8}$

20. $12\frac{1}{4} - 8\frac{5}{6}$

Tell whether the estimate is reasonable. Write *yes* or *no*.

21. $\frac{3}{4} \times \frac{1}{5} \approx 2$

22. $62 \times \frac{1}{3} \approx 20$

23. $\frac{1}{2} \times 253 \approx 200$

24. $\frac{9}{10} \times \frac{11}{12} \approx 1$

Simplify the factors.

25. $\frac{1}{3} \times \frac{3}{20}$

26. $\frac{2}{5} \times \frac{1}{8}$

27. $\frac{4}{9} \times \frac{3}{10}$

> Remember to multiply both the numerators and the denominators.

Find the product. Write the product in simplest form.

28. $\frac{1}{3} \times \frac{3}{4}$

29. $\frac{3}{5} \times \frac{7}{12}$

30. $\frac{1}{2} \times \frac{7}{8}$

31. $1\frac{2}{3} \times 5$

32. $4\frac{1}{2} \times 3$

33. $6\frac{5}{8} \times \frac{4}{5}$

34. $8\frac{1}{3} \times \frac{1}{5}$

35. $3\frac{5}{6} \times \frac{1}{4}$

36. $2\frac{1}{7} \times 2\frac{2}{5}$

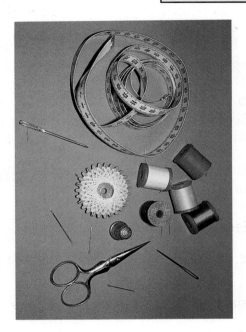

Spotlight ON
PROBLEM SOLVING

Interpret the Remainder

When a division problem does not result in a whole-number answer, you need to interpret the remainder carefully.

Nita has 66 yards of calico to make skirt-and-vest outfits for a Memorial Day production. She needs 4 yards to make each outfit.

Talk About It

Work together to answer the questions. Be prepared to share your responses with the class.

a. How many skirt-and-vest outfits can Nita make?

b. Will Nita have any calico left? If so, how much?

c. How much more calico does Nita need to make another outfit?

d. Do you have to interpret the remainder in order to answer question **a**, **b**, or **c**? Explain.

Apply

Solve. Be prepared to discuss how you interpreted the remainder.

1. Stacey puts 24 party favors in each layer of a box that has 3 layers. If Stacey has 200 favors, how many boxes can she completely fill?

2. Heather has 124 cards to put in boxes. Each box holds 15 cards. How many cards will be left over?

3. A company manufactures giant flags. Employees produce 39 flags in one day. The flags are packed 5 in a box. How many boxes do they fill each day?

4. There are 46 people taking a tour of warehouses where parade floats are being made. The tour company hires vans to transport the people. If a van holds 10 people, how many vans are needed?

EXPLORING

Division of Fractions

An artist is painting a mural in the city park. He has 3 quarts of paint that he wants to put in $\frac{1}{2}$-quart containers. How many $\frac{1}{2}$-quart containers will he need?

- Since you must find how many $\frac{1}{2}$'s are in 3, what operation will you use to solve the problem?

You can use fraction circles to explore dividing whole numbers by fractions.

WORK TOGETHER

Building Understanding

Use fraction circles. Trace complete circles on your paper to represent the whole numbers. Use circle parts to represent fractions.

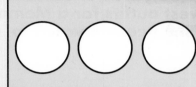

Figure A

Think: $3 \div \frac{1}{2}$.

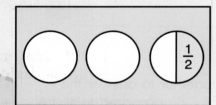

Figure B

> **Talk About It**

> ▶ What amount is represented by the white circles in Figure **A**?

> ▶ What amount is represented by one part of the blue fraction circle in Figure **A**?

> ▶ Look at Figure **B**. Into how many parts the size of $\frac{1}{2}$ can 3 be divided? In other words, how many $\frac{1}{2}$-quart containers will the artist need?

Use fraction circles to model each problem.

a. $2 \div \frac{1}{3}$
How many $\frac{1}{3}$'s are in 2?

b. $4 \div \frac{1}{5}$
How many $\frac{1}{5}$'s are in 4?

c. $3 \div \frac{2}{6}$
How many $\frac{2}{6}$'s are in 3?

d. $5 \div \frac{1}{3}$
How many $\frac{1}{3}$'s are in 5?

You can also use fraction circles to explore
dividing fractions by fractions.

WORK TOGETHER

Building Understanding

Use fraction circles to represent the
divisor and the dividend.

Example $\dfrac{1}{2} \div \dfrac{1}{6}$

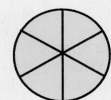

Figure A

Figure B

Talk About It

► What part of a whole is
represented in blue in Figure **A**?

► Into how many parts is the yellow
circle divided in Figure **A**?

► What part of a whole is represented by 1
yellow part? Look at Figure **B**. How many
parts the size of $\frac{1}{6}$ can you fit over $\frac{1}{2}$? In
other words, into how many parts the size
of $\frac{1}{6}$ can $\frac{1}{2}$ be divided?
What is the quotient of
$\frac{1}{2} \div \frac{1}{6}$?

Use fraction circles to model each problem.

a. $\dfrac{3}{4} \div \dfrac{1}{4}$
How many $\frac{1}{4}$'s
are in $\frac{3}{4}$?

b. $\dfrac{1}{3} \div \dfrac{1}{6}$
How many $\frac{1}{6}$'s
are in $\frac{1}{3}$?

c. $\dfrac{1}{2} \div \dfrac{1}{8}$
How many $\frac{1}{8}$'s
are in $\frac{1}{2}$?

d. $\dfrac{3}{4} \div \dfrac{1}{8}$
How many $\frac{1}{8}$'s
are in $\frac{3}{4}$?

Making the Connection

Look for a pattern in the division and multiplication number sentences. Use fraction circles to model the problems.

1. $6 \div 2 = \blacksquare$ $6 \times \dfrac{1}{2} = \blacksquare$

2. $1 \div \dfrac{1}{2} = \blacksquare$ $1 \times \dfrac{2}{1} = \blacksquare$

3. $3 \div \dfrac{3}{4} = \blacksquare$ $3 \times \dfrac{4}{3} = \blacksquare$

4. $\dfrac{1}{4} \div \dfrac{1}{2} = \blacksquare$ $\dfrac{1}{4} \times \dfrac{2}{1} = \blacksquare$

$\dfrac{2}{1} = 2$

Talk About It

▶ What is the relationship between the dividend and the first factor? between the quotient and the product?

▶ Look at the divisor and the second factor. Remember that multiplication and division are inverse operations. What is the product of the divisor and the second factor of each pair of number sentences?

$2 \times \dfrac{1}{2} = \blacksquare$ $\dfrac{1}{2} \times 2 = \blacksquare$ $\dfrac{3}{4} \times \dfrac{4}{3} = \blacksquare$ $\dfrac{1}{2} \times \dfrac{2}{1} = \blacksquare$

Such number relationships are called **reciprocals.** Two numbers are reciprocals if their product is 1.

▶ How can you use multiplication to solve a division problem?

Checking Understanding

Write the reciprocal of the divisor.

5. $7 \div \dfrac{1}{3}$ **6.** $5 \div \dfrac{2}{3}$ **7.** $\dfrac{4}{5} \div 5$ **8.** $\dfrac{5}{6} \div 6$ **9.** $\dfrac{2}{3} \div \dfrac{3}{4}$

10. $\dfrac{1}{2} \div \dfrac{1}{10}$ **11.** $\dfrac{7}{8} \div \dfrac{1}{8}$ **12.** $25 \div \dfrac{1}{5}$ **13.** $36 \div \dfrac{6}{7}$ **14.** $\dfrac{9}{10} \div \dfrac{1}{2}$

Complete the multiplication sentence. Then find the quotient of the division sentence.

15. $\dfrac{3}{4} \div \dfrac{1}{4} = \blacksquare$ $\dfrac{3}{4} \times \blacksquare = \blacksquare$

16. $12 \div \dfrac{3}{4} = \blacksquare$ $12 \times \blacksquare = \blacksquare$

17. $\dfrac{1}{3} \div \dfrac{1}{6} = \blacksquare$ $\dfrac{1}{3} \times \blacksquare = \blacksquare$

18. $15 \div \dfrac{1}{3} = \blacksquare$ $15 \times \blacksquare = \blacksquare$

19. $\dfrac{2}{3} \div \dfrac{1}{9} = \blacksquare$ $\dfrac{2}{3} \times \blacksquare = \blacksquare$

20. $\dfrac{3}{4} \div \dfrac{1}{10} = \blacksquare$ $\dfrac{3}{4} \times \blacksquare = \blacksquare$

More Practice, Lesson 8.7, page H64

In the United States, people celebrate their independence on July 4. In Mexico, people celebrate their independence in September.

Social Studies Connection

Every September 15 and 16, Julio and his family go to Guaymas to celebrate Mexican independence. They participate in festivities that include fireworks, parades, and street dances. Julio enjoys the activities, arts and crafts, and ethnic foods that are found in the crowded marketplaces.

1. Julio sees 8 girls who are waiting for a parade to begin. There are 5 carrying castanets, 3 carrying maracas, and 2 carrying both castanets and maracas. How many of the girls are not carrying either castanets or maracas?

2. Aneta likes to watch the street dancers who wear traditional costumes and dance in groups of 4 or 6. She counted a total of 36 dancers. There were more groups of 6 than of 4. How many groups of 4 and how many groups of 6 did Aneta watch?

3. Julio was among 6 contestants in a men's competition. He finished second, and his friend Luis finished next to last. José finished just before Luis, and Benito finished after Luis. If Carlos did not finish first, in what place did Alejandro finish in the competition?

4. Maria is making tissue-paper flowers. She tears a sheet of tissue paper in half. Then she puts 1 piece on top of the other and tears them in half again. If she continues the same process, how many pieces of tissue paper will Maria have after she makes 5 tears?

5. Octavio and Susana found a cafe that accepts U.S. dollars. They had $20.00 to spend for dinner. They each bought 3 tamales for $1.50, a serving of frijoles for $1.75, 2 tostadas for $1.25 each, and 2 enchiladas for $1.50 each. How much change did they receive?

6. In the final $1\frac{1}{2}$ hours of the celebration, Julio watched a shower of rockets for $\frac{1}{4}$ hour, a brilliant fireworks display for $\frac{1}{2}$ hour, and a pinata party in which his little sister participated. For how long did Julio watch the party?

DIVIDING FRACTIONS

Jesse's family is having an open house. She has 16 cups of grape juice. She wants to make as many batches of Columbus Day punch as possible. Each batch calls for $\frac{2}{3}$ cup of grape juice. How many batches of punch can Jesse make?

Step 1 Use the reciprocal of the divisor to write a multiplication problem. $16 \div \frac{2}{3} = 16 \times \frac{3}{2}$	**Step 2** Simplify. $\frac{\overset{8}{16}}{1} \times \frac{3}{\underset{1}{2}}$	**Step 3** Multiply. $\frac{8}{1} \times \frac{3}{1} = \frac{24}{1}$, or 24

So, Jesse can make 24 batches of punch.

More Examples

A. $\dfrac{3}{8} \div \dfrac{3}{4} = \dfrac{\overset{1}{3}}{\underset{2}{8}} \times \dfrac{\overset{1}{4}}{\underset{1}{3}} = \dfrac{1}{2}$

B. $\dfrac{7}{10} \div \dfrac{2}{5} = \dfrac{7}{\underset{2}{10}} \times \dfrac{\overset{1}{5}}{2} = \dfrac{7}{4}$, or $1\dfrac{3}{4}$

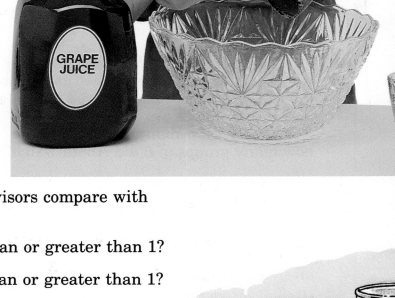

Talk About It

▶ In Examples A and B, how do the divisors compare with the dividends?

▶ In Example A, is the quotient less than or greater than 1?

▶ In Example B, is the quotient less than or greater than 1?

▶ What rule can you write to compare the value of the quotient with the values of the divisor and the dividend?

Check for Understanding

Tell whether the quotient will be less than or greater than 1.

1. $7 \div \dfrac{3}{5}$ 2. $\dfrac{7}{9} \div \dfrac{3}{5}$ 3. $\dfrac{1}{2} \div \dfrac{2}{3}$ 4. $\dfrac{2}{3} \div \dfrac{1}{2}$ 5. $\dfrac{1}{2} \div 5$

Practice

Complete.

6. $\frac{1}{4} \div \frac{1}{2} = \frac{1}{4} \times \frac{2}{1} = \frac{\blacksquare}{\blacksquare}$

7. $6 \div \frac{1}{4} = 6 \times \frac{\blacksquare}{\blacksquare} = \frac{\blacksquare}{\blacksquare}$

8. $3 \div \frac{3}{5} = \blacksquare \times \frac{5}{3} = \frac{\blacksquare}{\blacksquare}$

9. $\frac{1}{2} \div \frac{3}{5} = \frac{1}{2} \times \frac{\blacksquare}{\blacksquare} = \frac{\blacksquare}{\blacksquare}$

Tell whether the quotient will be greater than or less than 1.

10. $15 \div \frac{5}{6}$

11. $10 \div \frac{3}{5}$

12. $\frac{3}{5} \div \frac{1}{8}$

13. $\frac{3}{4} \div \frac{1}{6}$

14. $\frac{5}{6} \div \frac{2}{9}$

15. $\frac{5}{6} \div \frac{7}{3}$

16. $1 \div \frac{4}{3}$

17. $9 \div \frac{3}{8}$

Find the quotient.

18. $10 \div \frac{5}{6}$

19. $4 \div \frac{4}{5}$

20. $\frac{3}{4} \div \frac{1}{3}$

21. $\frac{5}{8} \div \frac{2}{3}$

22. $8 \div \frac{6}{7}$

23. $12 \div \frac{3}{5}$

24. $\frac{3}{4} \div \frac{3}{16}$

25. $\frac{2}{3} \div \frac{4}{5}$

26. $6 \div \frac{3}{4}$

27. $\frac{9}{10} \div \frac{3}{5}$

28. $2 \div \frac{1}{6}$

29. $\frac{1}{10} \div \frac{5}{6}$

Mixed Applications

30. Brian is grilling hamburgers for a block party. How many $\frac{1}{4}$-pound hamburgers can he grill with 12 pounds of ground beef?

31. **Number Sense**   The number 4 is 16 times greater than its reciprocal. If a number is 9 times greater than its reciprocal, what is the number?

NUMBER SENSE

You can use common denominators or the LCD to divide.

A. $\frac{9}{8} \div \frac{3}{8}$ 8 is a common denominator.

B. $\frac{3}{4} \div \frac{1}{8}$ LCD is 8.

$\frac{9}{8} \div \frac{3}{8} = \frac{9 \div 3}{8 \div 8} = \frac{3}{1} = 3$

$\frac{3}{4} \div \frac{1}{8} = \frac{6}{8} \div \frac{1}{8} = \frac{6 \div 1}{8 \div 8} = \frac{6}{1} = 6$

Use the LCD to divide. Show your work.

32. $\frac{3}{4} \div \frac{1}{4}$

33. $\frac{2}{5} \div \frac{1}{5}$

34. $\frac{3}{4} \div \frac{3}{8}$

35. $\frac{14}{15} \div \frac{3}{5}$

Describe how you divide fractions by using reciprocals.

WRAP
UP...

DIVIDING MIXED NUMBERS

Alex is cutting out a picture of American patriot Patrick Henry. The base of the picture is $3\frac{3}{4}$ inches long, and it includes a repeated pattern that is $1\frac{1}{4}$ inches long. How many times does the pattern occur?

You can use a ruler to visualize the answer.

- Into how many parts the size of $1\frac{1}{4}$ inches can $3\frac{3}{4}$ inches be divided?

Or, you can divide $3\frac{3}{4}$ by $1\frac{1}{4}$ to find the answer.

Step 1 Write the mixed numbers as fractions.	**Step 2** Use the reciprocal to write a multiplication problem. Simplify.
$3\frac{3}{4} \div 1\frac{1}{4} = \frac{15}{4} \div \frac{5}{4}$	$\frac{15}{4} \div \frac{5}{4} = \frac{15}{4} \times \frac{4}{5} = \frac{\overset{3}{\cancel{15}}}{\cancel{4}} \times \frac{\cancel{4}}{\cancel{5}}{\underset{1}{}}$

Step 3
Multiply.

$$\frac{\overset{3}{\cancel{15}}}{\underset{1}{\cancel{4}}} \times \frac{\overset{1}{\cancel{4}}}{\underset{1}{\cancel{5}}} = \frac{3}{1} \times \frac{1}{1} = 3$$

So, the pattern occurs 3 times.

More Examples

A. $4\frac{1}{2} \div 3 = \frac{9}{2} \div \frac{3}{1} = \frac{9}{2} \times \frac{1}{3} = \frac{\overset{3}{\cancel{9}}}{2} \times \frac{1}{\underset{1}{\cancel{3}}} = \frac{3}{2},$ or $1\frac{1}{2}$

B. $\frac{4}{5} \div 3\frac{1}{2} = \frac{4}{5} \div \frac{7}{2} = \frac{4}{5} \times \frac{2}{7} = \frac{8}{35}$

- What other method can you use to divide?

- What is the LCD of $\frac{4}{5}$ and $3\frac{1}{2}$?

- How do you use the LCD to divide mixed numbers?

Check for Understanding

Tell whether the multiplication sentence is correct. Write *yes* or *no*.

1. $4\frac{1}{4} \div 2 = \frac{17}{4} \times \frac{1}{2}$
     2. $5\frac{1}{4} \div 1\frac{3}{4} = \frac{4}{21} \times \frac{7}{4}$
     3. $10\frac{1}{3} \div 5\frac{2}{3} = \frac{31}{3} \times \frac{3}{17}$

Practice

Write the multiplication sentence.

4. $1\frac{1}{4} \div \frac{5}{8}$
     5. $\frac{7}{8} \div 1\frac{3}{4}$
     6. $2\frac{2}{3} \div 6$
     7. $1\frac{1}{8} \div 6\frac{3}{4}$

Find the quotient.

8. $1\frac{1}{2} \div \frac{3}{8}$
     9. $3\frac{2}{3} \div \frac{5}{6}$
     10. $3\frac{1}{4} \div 1\frac{3}{8}$
     11. $\frac{7}{8} \div 3\frac{1}{2}$

12. $1\frac{1}{2} \div 6\frac{1}{2}$
     13. $5 \div 1\frac{7}{8}$
     14. $2\frac{1}{2} \div 1\frac{1}{4}$
     15. $\frac{5}{8} \div 1\frac{1}{2}$

16. $8 \div 2\frac{2}{5}$
     17. $4\frac{5}{7} \div 3$
     18. $3\frac{1}{4} \div 2\frac{1}{6}$
     19. $3\frac{3}{7} \div 8$

20. $1\frac{1}{6} \div 5\frac{1}{4}$
     21. $9 \div 3\frac{3}{4}$
     22. $4\frac{2}{7} \div 2\frac{1}{2}$
     23. $1\frac{3}{8} \div 5\frac{1}{2}$

Mixed Applications

24. A board 12 feet long will be cut into sections for bookshelves. Each shelf will be $1\frac{1}{2}$ feet long. How many shelves can be made from the 12-foot board?

25. Bill has $\frac{3}{4}$ of a pizza left. He wants to give $\frac{1}{2}$ of it to Julie. How can you find the amount Bill wants to give Julie?

MIXED REVIEW

Tell whether the product will be greater than or less than 1.

1. $\frac{2}{5} \times \frac{1}{2}$
     2. $\frac{1}{3} \times 97$
     3. $45 \times \frac{1}{8}$
     4. $\frac{9}{10} \times \frac{2}{3}$

Estimate the sum or difference.

5. $\frac{4}{5} + \frac{9}{18}$
     6. $\frac{7}{8} - \frac{9}{10}$
     7. $6\frac{2}{3} + 5\frac{3}{4}$
     8. $10\frac{3}{8} - 2\frac{2}{5}$

Find the sum or difference. Write your answer in simplest form.

9. $\frac{9}{10} - \frac{2}{10}$
     10. $\frac{4}{9} + \frac{2}{9}$
     11. $9\frac{7}{8} - 4\frac{3}{8}$
     12. $5\frac{1}{2} + 1\frac{1}{2}$

When you divide two mixed numbers, will the quotient be less than or greater than the dividend?

WRAP UP...

RELATING
Decimals and Fractions

Jim wants to represent $\frac{3}{4}$ on a standard calculator to determine the cost of each serving of juice.

Use the models to visualize $\frac{3}{4}$ as a decimal.

- What part of Figure **A** is brown?

- What part of Figure **B** is blue?

- How does the amount in Figure **A** compare with the amount in Figure **B**?

So, Jim can use 0.75 to represent $\frac{3}{4}$ on a calculator.

Figure A   Figure B

You can change a fraction to an equivalent decimal by dividing the numerator by the denominator.

You can use paper and pencil, or you can use a calculator.

A. $\frac{1}{4}$

$$\begin{array}{r} 0.25 \\ 4\overline{)1.00} \\ -8 \\ \hline 20 \\ -20 \\ \hline 0 \end{array}$$

$\frac{1}{4} = 0.25$

B. $\frac{1}{3}$

$$\begin{array}{r} 0.33 \\ 3\overline{)1.00} \\ -9 \\ \hline 10 \\ -9 \\ \hline 1 \end{array}$$

← The remainder is always 1. The decimal repeats.

$\frac{1}{3} = 0.\overline{3}$ ← The bar shows that the digit 3 repeats.

C. $\frac{2}{9}$

2 ÷ 9 = $\boxed{0.2222222}$

$\frac{2}{9} = 0.\overline{2}$

Another Method

If the denominator of a fraction is a factor of 10 or 100, write an equivalent fraction using 10 or 100 as the denominator. Then use place value to write the decimal.

A. $\frac{3}{50} = \frac{6}{100} = 0.06$ **B.** $\frac{11}{25} = \frac{44}{100} = 0.44$ **C.** $\frac{1}{5} = \frac{2}{10} = 0.2$

You can change a decimal to an equivalent fraction by using what you know about place value.

A. $0.8 = \frac{8}{10} = \frac{4}{5}$ **B.** $0.25 = \frac{25}{100} = \frac{1}{4}$ **C.** $0.125 = \frac{125}{1,000} = \frac{1}{8}$

Tell how you would change to a decimal or a fraction. Write *division* or *place value.*

1. $\frac{1}{2}$ 2. $\frac{13}{20}$ 3. $\frac{2}{3}$ 4. 0.4   5. 0.64   6. 0.45

Practice

Write as a decimal.

7. $\frac{1}{2}$ 8. $\frac{43}{100}$ 9. $\frac{4}{5}$ 10. $\frac{3}{10}$ 11. $\frac{3}{4}$ 12. $\frac{7}{8}$

13. $\frac{13}{20}$ 14. $\frac{2}{9}$ 15. $\frac{12}{25}$ 16. $\frac{17}{50}$ 17. $\frac{2}{25}$ 18. $\frac{1}{12}$

Use a calculator. Find an equivalent decimal.

19. $\frac{3}{5}$ 20. $\frac{2}{3}$ 21. $\frac{7}{20}$ 22. $\frac{5}{6}$ 23. $\frac{7}{8}$ 24. $\frac{6}{11}$

Write as a fraction in simplest form.

25. 0.5   26. 0.09   27. 0.10   28. 0.15   29. 0.25   30. 0.025

31. 0.8   32. 0.04   33. 0.01   34. 0.75   35. 0.38   36. 1.99

Mixed Applications

37. Marsha needs to know the decimal equivalent of $\frac{1}{4}$ in order to determine the cost of each serving of yogurt. Write the decimal equivalent of $\frac{1}{4}$.

38. **Logical Reasoning** If the repeating decimal that is equivalent to $\frac{1}{3}$ is $0.\overline{3}$, what is the repeating decimal that is equivalent to $\frac{2}{3}$?

39. **Number Sense** A number is between 24 and 25. There is a 6 in the hundredths place, and the sum of the 4 digits is 13. Write the number as a mixed number.

Name some ways you can change a decimal to a fraction or a fraction to a decimal.

WRAP UP...

Charity volunteers are holding a Spring Fair raffle on Flag Day. They sold $\frac{1}{2}$ of the raffle tickets and gave away $\frac{1}{4}$ of the remaining tickets. If the volunteers gave away 2,400 raffle tickets, how many tickets did they have in the beginning?

▶ **UNDERSTAND**

What are you asked to find?

What information are you given?

▶ **PLAN**

What strategy will you use?

You can *solve a simpler problem.* Since 24×100 is 2,400, use 24 for the number of tickets given away.

▶ **SOLVE**

How can you carry out your plan?

Let 24 equal the number of tickets given away.

Think:

$\frac{1}{4}$ of the number of tickets = 24.
If $\frac{1}{4} = 24$, then $\frac{4}{4} = 96$.

Think:

$\frac{1}{2}$ of the number of tickets = 96.
If $\frac{1}{2} = 96$, then $\frac{2}{2} = 192$.

If 24 had been given away, there would have been 192 in the beginning. Since $24 \times 100 = 2,400$ given away, there were $192 \times 100 = 19,200$ tickets in the beginning.

So, the volunteers had 19,200 raffle tickets in the beginning.

▶ **LOOK BACK**

What other strategy could you use?

WHAT IF...

... the volunteers sold $\frac{3}{4}$ and gave away $\frac{1}{3}$ of the remaining tickets? If they gave away 120 raffle tickets, how many did the volunteers have in the beginning?

Apply

Solve by using a simpler problem.

1 Dennis has 500 plastic name tags. He had used $\frac{1}{2}$ of the total for a convention and $\frac{1}{3}$ of the total for a carnival. How many name tags did Dennis have in the beginning?

2 Meg gave away $\frac{1}{2}$ of the pamphlets, and a friend gave away $\frac{1}{3}$ of what was left. If Meg's friend gave away 550 pamphlets, how many did Meg have at first?

Mixed Applications	STRATEGIES	• Solve a Simpler Problem • Guess and Check • Write an Equation • Find a Pattern

Choose a strategy and solve.

3 A group of 10 girls and 10 boys will play tennis. If each girl plays one match with each boy, how many tennis matches will there be?

4 There are $\frac{1}{3}$ as many rides at the carnival as there are games. The total number of games is 51. How many rides are at the carnival?

5 At the carnival 20 students enter a checkers tournament. If each student plays every other student only once, what is the total number of games the students will play?

6 Together two rides hold 64 people. One ride holds 3 times as many as the other. How many people can each ride hold?

7 Keisha is making tea for the carnival. She can make 2 quarts of tea with 1 tea bag, 5 with 2 tea bags, and 9 with 3 tea bags. At this rate, how many quarts of tea can Keisha make with 6 tea bags?

8 A group of adults and students went to a concert. They spent a total of $51 for tickets. Adult tickets cost $12.75 each, and student tickets cost $8.50 each. How many of each kind of ticket did the group buy?

WRITER'S CORNER

9 You and your family have just been to a Thanksgiving celebration. Write a problem that can be solved by multiplying or dividing fractions. Exchange papers with a classmate and solve.

Vocabulary Check

Choose a word or words from the box to complete each sentence.

| decimal |
| divisor |
| fraction |
| less than |
| reciprocals |
| simplify |

Read and think before you write your answer.

1. When the product of two numbers is one, the numbers are __?__. *(page 252)*

2. The product of two fractions that are less than 1 will be __?__ either factor. *(page 236)*

3. To divide by a fraction, you can use the reciprocal of the __?__ and then multiply. *(page 252)*

4. You can change a decimal to an equivalent __?__ by using place value. *(page 258)*

5. You can change a fraction to an equivalent __?__ by dividing the numerator by the denominator. *(page 258)*

6. You can divide the numerator and the denominator by the GCF to __?__ a fraction. *(page 238)*

Concept Check

7. To estimate the product of fractions, you can use __?__ or __?__ numbers. *(page 242)*

8. To avoid having to change the product to simplest form, you can simplify the __?__. *(page 240)*

9. Will the product of two mixed numbers be less than the factors, greater than the factors, or between the factors? Why? *(page 244)*

10. If you must find how many $\frac{1}{3}$'s are in 5, what operation will you use? *(page 250)*

Draw a model to help you find the product. Then solve. *(page 238)*

11. $\frac{1}{2} \times \frac{1}{5} = $ ■

12. $\frac{3}{4} \times \frac{2}{3} = $ ■

13. $\frac{1}{4} \times \frac{3}{4} = $ ■

14. $\frac{1}{2} \times \frac{2}{3} = $ ■

Write the reciprocal of the divisor. *(page 252)*

15. $10\frac{1}{2} \div 2$

16. $6 \div \frac{3}{16}$

17. $\frac{1}{2} \div \frac{1}{12}$

18. $3 \div \frac{1}{4}$

Skill Check

Tell whether the estimate is reasonable. Write *yes* or *no*. (page 242)

19. $\frac{2}{5} \times \frac{7}{11} \approx \frac{1}{4}$

20. $62 \times \frac{7}{8} > 8$

21. $\frac{5}{12} \times \frac{13}{15} < 2$

22. $\frac{1}{6} \times 125 \approx 20$

Simplify the factors. (page 240)

23. $\frac{2}{7} \times \frac{5}{12}$

24. $\frac{8}{20} \times \frac{5}{16}$

25. $\frac{4}{9} \times \frac{3}{10}$

26. $\frac{1}{6} \times \frac{3}{11}$

Find the product. Write your answer in simplest form.
(pages 238, 240, 244)

27. $\frac{3}{10} \times \frac{1}{3}$

28. $\frac{5}{9} \times 6$

29. $\frac{9}{10} \times \frac{1}{18}$

30. $\frac{2}{9} \times \frac{3}{5}$

31. $\frac{1}{3} \times 3\frac{1}{2}$

32. $2\frac{3}{4} \times \frac{2}{3}$

33. $4\frac{2}{5} \times 1\frac{3}{7}$

34. $1\frac{1}{6} \times 6\frac{3}{4}$

Write the reciprocal of the divisor. (page 252)

35. $\frac{7}{8} \div \frac{1}{2}$

36. $\frac{5}{16} \div 3$

37. $1\frac{1}{3} \div \frac{3}{5}$

38. $1\frac{1}{2} \div 4\frac{1}{4}$

Find the quotient. (pages 250, 251, 252, 254, 256)

39. $32 \div \frac{4}{5}$

40. $16 \div \frac{1}{2}$

41. $\frac{1}{8} \div \frac{3}{10}$

42. $45 \div \frac{1}{5}$

43. $2\frac{1}{3} \div \frac{3}{4}$

44. $9\frac{3}{7} \div 4\frac{1}{2}$

45. $5\frac{1}{10} \div \frac{2}{5}$

46. $12\frac{7}{8} \div \frac{1}{3}$

Write as a fraction in simplest form. (page 258)

47. 0.9

48. 0.2

49. 0.45

50. 0.65

51. 0.8

Write as a decimal. (page 258)

52. $\frac{2}{5}$

53. $\frac{1}{8}$

54. $\frac{1}{3}$

55. $\frac{18}{100}$

56. $\frac{1}{9}$

Problem-Solving Check (pages 246, 260)

57. Burt uses $9\frac{1}{2}$ boxes of party streamers to decorate 5 rooms. How many boxes of streamers does he use in each room?

58. Lara received a holiday bonus that was $\frac{1}{6}$ of her monthly pay. If she is paid $420 four times a month, how much was her bonus?

59. Tia gave away 50 cups of juice, which was $\frac{1}{10}$ what she sold at the fair. How many cups of juice did she sell at the fair?

60. There are 15 students planning a party by telephone. Each student talks to every other student once. How many calls are made?

Estimate the product.

1. $\dfrac{4}{5} \times \dfrac{1}{2}$

2. $\dfrac{1}{2} \times 79$

3. $93 \times \dfrac{2}{5}$

Simplify the factors.

4. $\dfrac{2}{3} \times \dfrac{9}{10}$

5. $\dfrac{4}{5} \times \dfrac{5}{13}$

6. $\dfrac{2}{21} \times \dfrac{3}{4}$

Solve. Write the product in simplest form.

7. $\dfrac{1}{4} \times \dfrac{5}{6}$

8. $\dfrac{1}{6} \times \dfrac{2}{3}$

9. $\dfrac{3}{4} \times \dfrac{4}{15}$

10. $25 \times 2\dfrac{3}{4}$

11. $3\dfrac{1}{2} \times 5\dfrac{1}{3}$

12. $4\dfrac{4}{5} \times 4\dfrac{1}{6}$

Find the quotient.

13. $7 \div \dfrac{3}{5}$

14. $\dfrac{1}{6} \div \dfrac{7}{8}$

15. $4\dfrac{1}{3} \div 1\dfrac{1}{6}$

16. $1\dfrac{1}{5} \div 2\dfrac{1}{4}$

17. $12\dfrac{4}{5} \div 5\dfrac{3}{5}$

18. $7\dfrac{7}{9} \div 8\dfrac{1}{6}$

I know I have to use a reciprocal to divide fractions, but how?

Write the decimal as a fraction in simplest form, or write the fraction as a decimal.

19. 0.02

20. $\dfrac{4}{25}$

21. $\dfrac{11}{20}$

Solve.

22. Sue caters parties 6 days a week. Every day, she uses $2\dfrac{1}{2}$ dozen of each of 3 types of paper napkins. How many napkins does Sue use in 2 weeks?

23. Jim barbecued $8\dfrac{1}{2}$ lb of meat for 11 guests. If he serves each guest and himself $\dfrac{5}{8}$ lb of barbecue, how much barbecue will he have left?

24. Dennis works in a card shop. He has 150 birthday cards left over after selling $\dfrac{1}{2}$ of the total on Tuesday and $\dfrac{1}{4}$ of the total on Thursday. How many cards should Dennis order to have the same number he had before he sold any cards on Tuesday?

25. Mary runs a large restaurant. In her stock of dishes, she has $\dfrac{2}{3}$ as many red plates as blue cups, and $\dfrac{1}{4}$ as many blue cups as white cups. She has 120 white cups. How many red plates does she have?

Teamwork PROJECT

Plan Recreational Facilities

Suppose that on Earth Day your community announced plans to build a dome the size of four football fields over your school. Your school building and grounds will be modernized, pollution-free, and environmentally controlled.

You and your teammates have been chosen to plan new recreational activities for your school.

Decide

As a team, discuss the possible choices. Make a list of arts, crafts, and sports you would like to include.

Discuss whether each recreational activity will be in the building or "outdoors," under the dome.

Discuss how to utilize existing facilities and add new ones.

Do

Prepare a plan defining the types of recreation, space, buildings, storage, and equipment needed.

Make a sketch to illustrate your plan.

Share

Compare your team's plan and sketch with those of other teams. Tell why you chose each activity and how each facility will be used.

Talk About It

- Which type of facility will get the most use?
- What fraction of the recreational facilities will be used for arts and crafts? for sports?

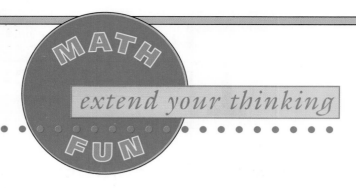

extend your thinking

Patterns of

Repeating Decimals

On Earth Day, a power plant revealed that it sends $\frac{5}{11}$ of its electricity to one city. Use a calculator to write a decimal for $\frac{5}{11}$.

5 ÷ 11 = | 0.4545454 |

The digits 4 and 5 repeat. Put a bar over the digits that repeat, instead of writing them several times, such as $0.\overline{45}$.

Find patterns in repeating decimals.

Use a calculator. Write the fraction as a repeating decimal.

1. $\frac{1}{11}$

2. $\frac{2}{11}$

3. $\frac{3}{11}$

4. $\frac{4}{11}$

5. What pattern do you notice among the numerators and the repeating decimals?

Do not divide. Use the pattern to write the repeating decimal.

6. $\frac{6}{11}$

7. $\frac{7}{11}$

8. $\frac{8}{11}$

9. $\frac{9}{11}$

10. What pattern do you see in in the repeating decimal equivalents of $\frac{1}{9}$, $\frac{2}{9}$, $\frac{3}{9}$, and so on?

As people are influenced by Earth Day, they are becoming more conscious of the need to preserve natural resources.

Challenge

Logical Thinking

In northern California, steam from the earth heats 99 homes, 3 more than last year. Last year 6 times as many homes were heated by the steam than 10 years ago. How many homes were heated by the steam 10 years ago?

Consumer Connection

It takes an average of $2\frac{1}{2}$ T of coal yearly to make enough electricity for a water heater. It takes $\frac{1}{3}$ T for a range, and $\frac{1}{2}$ T each for a dishwasher, a television, and a clothes dryer. Which requires more coal yearly, a water heater alone or a range, dishwasher, television, and clothes dryer combined?

Write the letter of the correct answer.

1. 7.5×9.24

  A. 68.3 B. 69.3

  C. 683 D. 693

2. $20.4 \div 1.6$

  A. 0.1275 B. 1.275

  C. 12.75 D. 127.5

3. $6\frac{1}{8} + 2\frac{1}{3}$

  A. $8\frac{2}{11}$ B. $8\frac{11}{24}$

  C. $8\frac{1}{2}$ D. $8\frac{11}{12}$

4. What is the median of 0, 2, 3, 3, 4?

  A. 0 B. 2

  C. 3 D. 4

5. What are combinations for 3 hats and 5 scarves?

  A. 3 B. 5

  C. 8 D. 15

6. $8\frac{1}{6} - 6\frac{1}{8}$

  A. $1\frac{1}{24}$ B. 2

  C. $2\frac{1}{24}$ D. $2\frac{1}{2}$

7. Which is the estimate for $\frac{7}{15} \times \frac{9}{10}$?

  A. $\frac{1}{2}$ B. 1

  C. $1\frac{1}{2}$ D. not here

8. $2\frac{2}{3} \times 1\frac{1}{8}$

  A. $2\frac{1}{12}$ B. $2\frac{2}{24}$

  C. $\frac{71}{24}$ D. 3

9. $\frac{1}{8} \div 2$

  A. $\frac{1}{4}$ B. 4

  C. 16 D. not here

10. What is the decimal for $\frac{8}{25}$?

  A. 0.032 B. 0.32

  C. 0.33 D. 3.2

11. Loretta drives $3\frac{3}{4}$ mi to work. How far does Loretta drive to pick up a friend if the friend lives at the halfway point?

  A. $1\frac{1}{4}$ mi B. $1\frac{7}{8}$ mi

  C. $1\frac{9}{10}$ mi D. $2\frac{1}{4}$ mi

12. Dan sold $\frac{2}{5}$ of the flowers and Rita sold $\frac{1}{3}$ of what remained. If 600 flowers were left, how many did Dan and Rita have at first?

  A. 80 flowers B. 900 flowers

  C. 1,800 flowers D. 1,500 flowers

9

MEASUREMENT

Did you know ...

... that almost everyone uses measurement every day?

How can you find the difference in water level between the high and low tides?

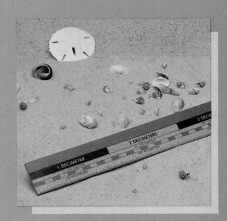

RELATING METRIC UNITS

Metric measurement is based on the decimal system. The relationships among the units are the same as the relationships among place-value positions.

The base unit of length is the **meter.**
The base unit of capacity is the **liter.**
The base unit of mass is the **gram.**

Metric Units of Length	
1 kilometer (km)	= 1,000 meters (m)
	meter (m)
1 decimeter (dm)	= 0.1 meter
1 centimeter (cm)	= 0.01 meter
1 millimeter (mm)	= 0.001 meter

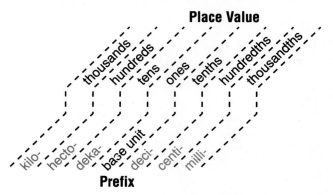

Place Value

thousands, hundreds, tens, ones, tenths, hundredths, thousandths

kilo-, hecto-, deka-, base unit, deci-, centi-, milli-

Prefix

The most commonly used prefixes are *kilo-, deci-, centi-,* and *milli-.* The same prefixes are used for length, capacity, and mass.

Talk About It

► How many times lighter or heavier than a gram is a kilogram?

► How many times greater or less than a liter is a milliliter?

► How many times longer or shorter than a centimeter is a meter?

Use Your Number Sense

a. Name objects in your classroom that are about a meter in length.

b. Name objects in your classroom that are about a centimeter in length.

c. How many of your steps equal about a meter in length?

d. Do you think you could walk a kilometer?

Lea counts her strides as she walks. The distance between her footprints in the sand is 0.75 m. How many centimeters is Lea's stride?

Use place value to change from one unit to another.

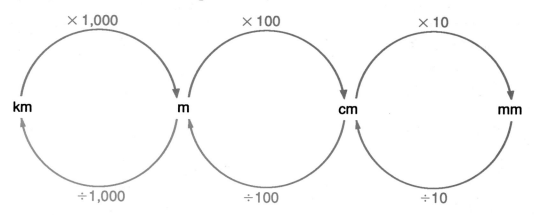

To change from larger units to smaller units, multiply.

To change from smaller units to larger units, divide.

Talk About It

▶ When you change from meters to centimeters, will there be more units or fewer units?

▶ Should you divide or multiply to change from meters to centimeters?

▶ How do you know by what number to multiply or divide?

▶ By what number will you multiply to change from meters to centimeters?

▶ How many centimeters is Lea's stride?

▶ How can you change any metric unit to a smaller unit?

———————————————————

Lea walked 2,800 m. How many kilometers is that?

▶ When you change from meters to kilometers, will there be more units or fewer units?

▶ Should you divide or multiply to change from meters to kilometers?

1,000 m = 1 km
2,800 ÷ 1,000 = 2.8   So, Lea walked 2.8 km.

▶ How can you change any metric unit to a larger unit?

Check for Understanding

Tell which unit is greater.

1. centimeter or decimeter
2. liter or milliliter
3. milligram or kilogram

4. liter or deciliter
5. gram or kilogram
6. meter or millimeter

Tell by what number you must multiply or divide to change the unit.

7. $25 \text{ km} = $  m

8. $2 \text{ L} = $ mL

9. $18 \text{ mg} = $ g

Practice

Complete the pattern.

10. $1 \text{ mL} = 0.001 \text{ L}$
$10 \text{ mL} = $ L
$100 \text{ mL} = $ L
$1,000 \text{ mL} = $ L

11. $0.001 \text{ m} = 0.1 \text{ cm}$
$0.01 \text{ m} = $ cm
$0.1 \text{ m} = $ cm
$1 \text{ m} = $ cm

12. $1,000 \text{ g} = 1 \text{ kg}$
$100 \text{ g} = $ kg
$10 \text{ g} = $ kg
$1 \text{ g} = $ kg

Find the missing number.

13. $0.34 \text{ m} = $ km

14. $480 \text{ cm} = $ m

15. $15 \text{ mL} = $ L

16. $425 \text{ g} = $ mg

17. $37 \text{ cm} = $ mm

18. $16 \text{ L} = $ mL

19. $320 \text{ mm} = $ cm

20. $6 \text{ L} = $ mL

21. $1,000 \text{ g} = $ kg

22. $0.44 \text{ kL} = $ L

23. $1 \text{ km} = $ m

24. $0.086 \text{ kg} = $ g

Mixed Applications

25. If Rosa fills her sand pail with 1.5 L of water, how many milliliters is she using?

26. Jim's beach bag weighs 3,000 g when filled. How many kilograms does it weigh?

27. **Logical Reasoning** To get to a beach resort, Don will travel 4 hours, including a $\frac{1}{4}$-hour stop. If he travels at a rate of 88 km per hour, how far will he travel?

28. **Number Sense • Estimation** Will Donna travel a distance of 250 km if she drives an average of 71 km per hour for $2\frac{1}{4}$ hours?

WRAP UP... Why is the metric system easy to use?

Joan and her family went to the beach for the weekend. While she was sleeping one night, Joan had a math-filled dream about three unusual players in a strange game.

Eight-Arms Octopus wanted to play toss-a-plate on the beach. When he wandered onto the sand, looking for company, he met Two-Hands Mermaid. "How about a game of toss-a-plate?" he asked. "The first to score 20 points gets the Catch of the Day." Two-Hands knew the odds were in Eight-Arms' favor. But she was tempted to try for the Catch of the Day, which she knew was her favorite, Seaweed Surprise. Then Stretch-Neck Seal appeared and wanted to help Two-Hands. He made the odds better, 8 to 3.

1. Two-Hands has two options. Which is the better choice, (a) play alone against Eight-Arms, making the odds 8 to 2 in favor of Eight-Arms, or (b) play with Stretch-Neck, making the odds 8 to 3 in favor of Eight-Arms?

2. Two-Hands has to take a dip in the water every few minutes to keep her scales from drying out. She goes into the water after throws 1, 3, 6, 10, 15, and 21. If this pattern continues, after which throw will she return to the water next?

3. Two-Hands is 150 cm tall. Her reach extends upward 55 cm. If the toss-a-plate is thrown in the air to a height of 268 cm, how far must she jump to catch it?

4. The toss-a-plate playing field is 100 m long. Stretch-Neck ran 20 m less than $\frac{1}{2}$ its length to catch the toss-a-plate. How many meters did Stretch-Neck run?

5. Each team is allowed 30 throws in a half. In the first half, Eight-Arms missed 5 throws. Stretch-Neck missed 15, and Two-Hands missed 5 fewer than Stretch-Neck. In the second half, Eight-Arms missed 1, Stretch-Neck 5, and Two-Hands 2. Make and use a table. Who missed 1 out of 10 throws?

6. Eight-Arms can catch equally well with each of his eight arms, and you can never predict with which arm he will catch the toss-a-plate. What are the chances of his catching one throw of the toss-a-plate with any one of three particular arms?

METRIC UNITS OF LENGTH

Derrick and Harold are planning a vacation at the seashore. They plan to drive along the interstate highway from Knoxville, Tennessee, to Winston-Salem, North Carolina. Derrick determines the distance to be about 350 km. Harold says it is about 250 km. Whose answer is more reasonable?

▶ How can you use the map to find about how many kilometers it is from Knoxville to Winston-Salem?

▶ Whose answer is more reasonable?

▶ Some people visualize the width of a door frame to estimate a meter. What items can you use to visualize a millimeter, a centimeter, a meter, and a kilometer?

Examples

A.

B.

C.

about 1 mm thick   about 1 cm thick   about 1 m wide

• What metric unit would you use to measure the length of your classroom? Why?

• What metric unit would you use to measure the distance from your home to school?

Check for Understanding

Choose the appropriate unit. Write *cm, m,* or *km*.

1. distance from Earth to the moon

2. width of your desk

3. length of a room

Choose the more reasonable estimate. Write **a** or **b**.

4. length of a car
   a. 4 m   **b.** 40 m

5. length of your shoe
   a. 250 cm   **b.** 25 cm

6. length of a pin
   a. 2 mm   **b.** 20 mm

Practice

Choose the most reasonable estimate. Write **a** or **b**.

7. width of a mall hallway
  a. 8 m
  b. 8 km

8. length of a pencil
  a. 14 m
  b. 14 cm

9. a walk around a park
  a. 2.4 km
  b. 240 km

10. thickness of a paper clip
  a. 1 mm
  b. 10 mm

11. distance between two towns
  a. 10 mm
  b. 10 km

12. diameter of a baseball
  a. 10 mm
  b. 10 cm

Choose the appropriate unit. Write *mm, cm, m,* or *km.*

13. length of a house

14. length of a skirt

15. diameter of a penny

16. length of an ant

17. height of a flagpole

18. height of a mountain

Estimate the length.

19.

  _?_ mm

20.

  _?_ cm

21.

  _?_ cm

Mixed Applications

22. Sue needs 3 m of paper to wrap a gift. If she has 195 cm, how much more paper does she need?

23. Analyze Data Measure your classroom. Use a meter stick. Ask a classmate to measure the room. Did you get the same measurement? Why or why not?

CALCULATOR CONNECTION

You can use a calculator to change units.

How many centimeters are in 450 mm?   How many meters are in 0.9 km?

   ← 45 cm   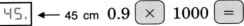 ← 900 m

Use a calculator to change units.

24. 7.9 m = ▦ mm

25. 288 m = ▦ km

26. 402 cm = ▦ m

What are the four most commonly used metric units of length?

Mr. Ray is figuring the cost to build a lattice screen for a client. He made a list of costs for materials, and he noted a labor charge of $12.00 an hour for 6 hours. Mr. Ray will add $15.00 to allow for errors. About how much will his estimate be?

Amount	Materials	Cost	Total Cost
2	lattice panels, $\frac{1}{4}$ in. × $1\frac{1}{2}$ in.	$42.10 each	$84.20
6	boards, 1 in. × 4 in.	2.30 each	13.80
4	boards, 1 in. × 6 in.	3.72 each	14.88
$\frac{1}{2}$	drywall screws, $1\frac{5}{8}$ in., 8 oz	2.08 a lb	1.04
3	concrete mix, 2-lb sack	1.96 a sack	5.88

If weather or changing prices must be considered when determining a total cost, an exact answer is impossible.

▶ **UNDERSTAND**

What are you asked to find?

What information are you given?

▶ **PLAN**

What strategy will you use?

Since you cannot determine an exact answer, you can estimate the cost of the screen.

▶ **SOLVE**

How will you carry out your plan?

Round the total costs to the nearest dollar, write a number sentence, and then use a calculator.

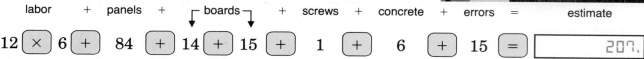

labor + panels + ⌐boards⌐ + screws + concrete + errors = estimate

$12 \times 6 + 84 + 14 + 15 + 1 + 6 + 15 = $ 207.

So, Mr. Ray's estimate will be about $207.

▶ **LOOK BACK**

How will the actual cost relate to the estimate? Why?

WHAT IF... ... Mr. Ray built 2 lattice screens and allowed a total of $10 for errors? How much might his estimate be?

276

Apply

Use estimation to solve.

1 A mechanic tells John that the parts needed to repair his car cost $27.90 and that labor is $37.00 an hour. If it takes the mechanic about $1\frac{1}{2}$ hours, about how much will the repairs cost?

2 Sixth graders will paint sets for the school play, *Sandstorm*. If 1 quart of paint covers 50 square feet and 448 square feet must be painted, is 25 quarts a reasonable estimate of the amount of paint needed? If not, what is?

Mixed Applications → **STRATEGIES** • Use Estimation • Guess and Check • Find a Pattern • Draw a Diagram

Choose a strategy and solve.

3 The distance from Edna's house to Cape Cod is 120 miles. If her car gets 27 miles to a gallon of gasoline, about how many gallons of gasoline will she need to make the round trip?

4 The Jones family always takes 10 towels with them when they go to the beach. If they take 2 more beach towels than bath towels, how many of each do they take?

5 On a scavenger hunt, Lydia found a scarf 3 blocks east of her home. Then, she ran north $1\frac{1}{2}$ blocks for a key ring. Next, she ran east $2\frac{1}{4}$ blocks for a glove, and north $\frac{3}{4}$ block for a left shoe. Finally, she ran $5\frac{1}{4}$ blocks west to the park. How far north of Lydia's home is the park?

6 Together, Ruta's banner and Bill's banner are as long as Gene's banner, which is 60 m long. The length of Bill's banner minus the length of Ruta's banner is equal to the length of Lu's banner. Gene's banner is twice as long as Lu's. How long is Ruta's banner? How long is Bill's banner?

7 A clerk at Cozy Snack Bar sold 92 burritos for $1.90 each and 124 fruit drinks for $1.10 each. The clerk must tell his boss about how much money he collected. What is a reasonable estimate?

8 A civic club is selling tickets to a beach concert. In four days the club has sold 110 tickets, 70 tickets, 40 tickets, and 20 tickets. If the pattern continues, how many tickets will be sold on the fifth day?

More Practice, Lesson 9.3, page H66

METRIC UNITS OF CAPACITY AND MASS

Janet plans to mix a little more than 3 L of orange juice, a little more than 4 L of pineapple juice, and 1,200 mL of papaya juice in an 8-L thermos jug to take to the beach. Will she have enough juice to fill the jug?

Change mL to L. 1,200 mL = 1.2 L

Estimate.

a little more than 3 3^+
a little more than 4 4^+
1.2 is a little more than 1. $+1^+$
                               8^+ ←— more than 8

Janet will have more than enough juice to fill the jug.

- What metric unit would you choose for the capacity of a glass of water?

_____

A sign says, "Win a free fish dinner! Guess the mass of 262 flounder in today's catch." Eric thinks that one flounder has about the same mass as his radio, 0.7 kg. He guesses 175 kg. Is Eric's guess reasonable?

Estimate.

Try an overestimate. $300 \times 1.0 = 300$.

Try an underestimate. Think: $0.7 \approx \frac{1}{2}$.
                        $250 \times \frac{1}{2} = 125$.

The flounder probably weigh between 125 and 300 kg.

So, Eric's guess is reasonable.

Talk About It

▶ Would Eric's best guess be closer to 125 kg or 300 kg? How do you know?

▶ How can you change 125 kg to grams?

▶ What metric unit would you choose for the mass of the sand in an egg timer?

▶ How can you change grams to kilograms?

Capacity

1 L

1 mL

Mass

1 g

1 kg

Check for Understanding

Choose the better estimate. Write **a** or **b**.

1. cup of tea
   a. 240 mL   **b.** 240 L

2. slice of bread
   a. 300 g   **b.** 30 g

3. gold nugget
   a. 25 g   **b.** 25 kg

Practice

Change to the given unit.

4. 2 mL = ▉ L

5. 0.35 L = ▉ mL

6. 1,205 mL = ▉ L

7. 10 kg = ▉ g

8. 0.2 g = ▉ kg

9. 210 g = ▉ kg

10. 24 L = ▉ mL

11. 5.5 L = ▉ mL

12. 10,000 mL = ▉ L

13. 44,000 g = ▉ kg

14. 1.5 kg = ▉ g

15. 620 g = ▉ kg

Mixed Applications

16. Vanna has coins whose total mass of gold is 33 g. If each coin has a mass of gold of about 5.5 g, how many coins does she have?

17. **Logical Reasoning** Amy is without any tools. She must estimate the length and width of a room. How can she determine the dimensions?

SCIENCE CONNECTION

Water has a unique property. The number of units of its capacity is equal to the number of units of its mass. You can verify this. Find the mass of an empty container. Then find the mass of the container filled with water. Determine the mass of the water. To determine the capacity of the water, pour the water into a graduated beaker that measures milliliters. Repeat with containers of different sizes.

1 L = 1 kg

Tell the mass of the water.

18. 1 mL

19. 500 mL

20. 1,000 mL

Tell the capacity of a container filled with each mass of water.

21. 25 g

22. 500 g

23. 2,000 g

Is the capacity of a liter of oil the same as a liter of water? How do you know?

PRECISION

Lisa will use a metric ruler to measure the conch shell. She can measure in centimeters or millimeters. Which would be more precise?

Precision means accuracy.

10 mm = 1 cm

Talk About It

▶ Measure the conch shell. How long is the shell, to the nearest centimeter? to the nearest millimeter?

▶ Which is the smaller unit?

▶ Which measurement is more precise?

So, measuring in millimeters would be more precise.

Suppose you were weighing the conch shell and could use kilograms or grams. Which would be more precise?

▶ Look at the scale. What is the mass of the conch shell, to the nearest kilogram? to the nearest gram?

▶ Which is the smaller unit?

▶ Which measurement is more precise?

So, weighing to the nearest gram would be more precise.

▶ What relationship do you see between the size of the unit and the precision of the measurement?

Examples Name the more precise measurement.

A.

3 cm or 36 mm wide?

36 mm is more precise.

B.

0.5 kg or 575 g?

575 g is more precise.

C.

1.8 L or 2 L?

1.8 L is more precise.

Check for Understanding

Use a centimeter ruler. Write the measurement to the nearest centimeter and to the nearest millimeter.

1. _____   2. _____

3. _____   4. _____

5. _____   6. _____

7. _____   8. _____

Practice

Tell which measurement is more precise.

9. 7 cm or 71 mm

10. 979 m or 1 km

11. 7 km or 7,120 m

12. 53 mm or 5 cm

13. 9 km or 8,903 m

14. 9.1 cm or 90 mm

15. 6.27 cm or 6.2 cm

16. 4 cm or 44 mm

17. 1 km or 1.3 km

18. 2 L or 1.7 L

19. 1 kg or 1.4 kg

20. 3.05 mm or 3.1 mm

Mixed Applications

21. Marty has 60 mL of water in his 1-L thermos. How much water must he add to fill the thermos?

22. Why is 1.8 L more precise than 2 L?

23. Lisa fills a container with 2 L of milk. How many 250-mL glasses can she pour?

24. Jed's 4 books have a mass of 1.5 kg, 2 kg, 2.5 kg, and 1.8 kg. What is their average mass?

25. **Number Sense • Mental Math** Tate wants to stack 4 books that are each 20 mm thick and a lunch box that is 70 mm thick in a beach bag that is 20 cm deep. Will everything fit in the beach bag?

26. **Making Choices** For his pet store, Theo wants to buy a fish tank that is small enough to fit on a stand 2 m long. Should he buy a tank that is 160 cm long or 205 cm long?

Name situations in which you are careful to make precise measurements.

WRAP
UP...

Choosing to estimate or to use a measuring tool is an everyday decision based on the situation. If you decide to use a tool, you must also decide which tool to use.

Talk About It

▶ For each situation, tell whether an estimate is acceptable or if you should use a tool to measure. If you would use a tool, tell which tool.

A. Ian is marking an area 9 m by 18 m so he and some friends can play a game of volleyball.

B. Amy works at a beach boutique that sells gold chains at $35.00 a decimeter.

C. Nicole wonders if the water is too cold for swimming at a Maine beach.

D. Robert checks the time so he will not miss a flight from Los Angeles to New York.

Sometimes you must compute after you have measured.

Hanna has shells that measure 1.5 cm, 3.2 cm, 4.6 cm, and 2.2 cm. If she mounts them edge-to-edge in a row on a large flat shell, how long will the row of small shells be?

$1.5 + 3.2 + 4.6 + 2.2 = 11.5$

So, the row will be 11.5 cm long.

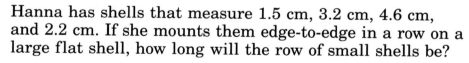

Check for Understanding

Tell whether to estimate or use a tool to measure. If you would use a tool, tell which tool.

1. amount of water to add to a swimming pool

2. time it takes to run a 100-meter dash

3. lengths of boards to make a railing

Practice

Give one example for each type of measurement.

4. mass that must be measured with a tool

5. length that can be estimated

6. capacity that must be measured with a tool

Estimate the sum.

7. $10.3\,g + 8.0\,g + 4.8\,g + 2.3\,g$

8. $7.2\,L + 12.3\,L + 0.32\,L + 0.92\,L$

Find the sum or difference.

9. $60\,m + 201.9\,m + 95.4\,m + 0.31\,m$

10. $0.8\,L + 42\,L + 16.1\,L + 45.9\,L$

11. $10.01\,g - 6.4\,g - 2.03\,g - 0.05\,g$

12. $244.06\,L - 99.2\,L - 2.95\,L - 0.88\,L$

Mixed Applications

13. Jane uses 25 mL of an expensive liquid soap per 1 L of water. Should she estimate or use a tool to measure?

14. Cindy had 305 g of blue sand, 790 g of green sand, and 120 g of white sand. She gave $\frac{1}{3}$ of the sand to Dwight. How much sand did she give Dwight?

15. In second grade, Elliot wore jeans with a 42-cm waist. He has grown taller, and his waist measurement has grown by 5.25 cm each year. If Elliot is in sixth grade, what waist size are his jeans?

MIXED REVIEW

Find the quotient.

1. $2\frac{1}{2} \div 1\frac{2}{3}$

2. $1\frac{2}{7} \div 2\frac{1}{4}$

3. $2\frac{1}{10} \div 1\frac{1}{5}$

4. $1\frac{1}{4} \div 2\frac{1}{2}$

Write as a fraction in simplest form or as a decimal.

5. 0.2

6. 0.8

7. $\frac{3}{5}$

8. $\frac{9}{25}$

9. 0.05

Change to the given unit.

10. $35\,L = \blacksquare\,mL$

11. $2.7\,g = \blacksquare\,kg$

12. $0.4\,cm = \blacksquare\,mm$

What influences your decision to estimate or to choose a tool to measure?

1. Peter rented $\frac{1}{3}$ of his beach chairs. He disposed of $\frac{1}{6}$ of the remaining chairs, which were damaged. If he disposed of 40 chairs, how many did he have before any were rented?

2. Rona mailed $\frac{1}{3}$ of 8,400 letters, and a co-worker mailed $\frac{1}{4}$ of the remainder. There are 4,200 left. How many letters did Rona mail?

The word "about" tells me to find an estimate.

3. A carpenter is estimating the cost of building a ramp. The materials cost $52.29. Labor will be $13.50 an hour for about 7 hr. About how much will she charge?

Write the multiplication problem.

4. $\frac{1}{6} \div \frac{2}{5}$

5. $1\frac{1}{3} \div \frac{4}{9}$

6. $\frac{1}{2} \div 2$

7. $3\frac{1}{6} \div \frac{11}{12}$

Find the quotient.

8. $6 \div \frac{2}{3}$

9. $\frac{1}{4} \div \frac{3}{5}$

10. $\frac{2}{7} \div \frac{1}{10}$

11. $6\frac{1}{8} \div 8\frac{10}{11}$

Write as a fraction in simplest form or as a decimal.

12. $\frac{2}{5}$

13. $\frac{7}{10}$

14. 0.62

15. $\frac{7}{8}$

16. 0.25

17. 0.8

Choose the better estimate. Write **a** or **b**.

18. length of a magazine
    a. 30 cm   **b.** 300 cm

19. capacity of a glass of milk
    a. 200 mL   **b.** 20 L

20. mass of a can of beans
    a. 30 kg   **b.** 0.3 kg

Change to the given unit.

21. 16 cm = ■ m

22. 1.5 g = ■ mg

23. 6 L = ■ kL

24. 90 mm = ■ cm

25. 1.2 kg = ■ dg

26. 81 cL = ■ mL

Tell whether to estimate or to use a tool to measure. If you would use a tool, tell which tool.

27. a picture frame

28. legs for a table

29. milk for cereal

Tell which measurement is more precise.

30. 0.04 g or 50 mg

31. 6 cm or 62 mm

32. 8 kL or 7,920 L

Check for Understanding

Write the time of day, using A.M. or P.M.

1. 8:30 A.M. + 55 min

2. 11:45 P.M. + 1 hr 5 min

3. 12:30 P.M. − 2 hr 25 min

4. 15:20

5. 06:15

6. 20:06

Practice

Change to the given unit. Use a 24-hour clock for Exercises 13–15.

7. 120 min = ▇ sec

8. 1 hr = ▇ sec

9. 144 hr = ▇ days

10. 540 min = ▇ hr

11. 7 days = ▇ hr

12. 24 hr = ▇ min

13. 9:30 A.M. = ▇ : ▇ hr

14. 10:05 P.M. = ▇ : ▇ hr

15. 1:15 P.M. = ▇ : ▇ hr

Find the sum or difference.

16.   4 hr 40 min
       +1 hr 50 min

17.   3 min 50 sec
       +   30 sec

18.   5 min 35 sec
       −4 min 42 sec

Mixed Applications

19. The bell rings for school at 8:30 A.M. Al must be there 15 min before the bell. If the trip to school takes 35 min, when should Al leave for school?

20. Number Sense • Mental Math   What is the difference between the number of hours in 7 days and the number of hours in 5 days?

MIXED REVIEW

Choose the more reasonable estimate. Write **a** or **b.**

1. $3\frac{5}{8} + 5\frac{11}{12}$
   a. 10   **b.** 8

2. $4\frac{3}{4} \times 7\frac{1}{9}$
   a. 24   **b.** 35

3. $5\frac{2}{3} \div 1\frac{7}{8}$
   a. 5   **b.** 3

Tell which measurement is more precise.

4. 5 kL or 4,920 L

5. 750 cm or 8 m

6. 100 g or 99,000 mg

Change to the given unit.

7. 108 in. = ▇ yd

8. 32 oz = ▇ lb

9. 8 c = ▇ pt

How can you find the number of hours you spend traveling to school each year?

WRAP
UP...

PROBLEM Solving

Becky wants to fly from Tampa to Fort Lauderdale. Of the flights listed, which one is the fastest?

Airline Schedule Tampa to Fort Lauderdale		
Flight Number	**Departure Time**	**Arrival Time**
435 (nonstop)	9:50 A.M.	11:20 A.M.
563 (nonstop)	12:30 P.M.	1:40 P.M.
768 (1 stop)	1:00 P.M.	2:55 P.M.

▶ UNDERSTAND

What are you asked to find?

What information are you given?

▶ PLAN

What strategy will you use?

You can use the airline schedule. Subtract each departure time from each arrival time, and compare to determine the fastest flight.

▶ SOLVE

How will you carry out your plan?

Since nonstop flights are faster than the flights that stop, you can eliminate Flight 768 from consideration. Subtract the departure times from the arrival times for the other two flights.

Flight 435:

$$
\begin{array}{r}
11:20 \rightarrow 10:80 \\
-\ 9:50 \rightarrow \underline{\ 9:50} \\
1:30
\end{array}
$$

1 hr 30 min

Flight 563:

$$
\begin{array}{r}
1:40 \rightarrow 13:40 \\
-12:30 \rightarrow \underline{-12:30} \\
1:10
\end{array}
$$

← 1:40 is 1 hr 40 min after 12 noon.
12:00 + 1:40 = 13:40

1 hr 10 min

So, Flight 563 is the fastest flight.

▶ LOOK BACK

How can you check your answer?

WHAT IF...

...you need to know the time difference between the fastest and the slowest flights? What is the difference?

Apply

Use the schedule on page 294 to solve Exercises 1–2.

1 Chad must fly to Fort Lauderdale on business. It takes $\frac{1}{2}$ hr to reach his office from the airport, and his business will take 2 hr. If he will return to Tampa on a 5:30 P.M. flight, should he take Flight 563 or 768?

2 It takes 45 minutes to drive from Fort Lauderdale's airport to Fran's favorite restaurant. If it takes Fran 15 minutes to get her luggage, can she meet a friend for lunch at 12:30 P.M. at the restaurant?

Mixed Applications

STRATEGIES
- Use a Schedule
- Work Backward
- Use Estimation
- Act It Out

Choose a strategy and solve.

3 Randy will pick up his brother at a bus station at 2:00 P.M. The bus spends 1 hr 40 min on the road and makes two stops, one for 15 min and one for 20 min. Bus 1 departs at 11:35 A.M., Bus 2 at 12:00 noon, and Bus 3 at 12:20 P.M. Which bus should Randy's brother take?

4 Jill must take her pets—an alligator, a bird, and a cat—to a pet show. She can carry only one pet at a time on her bike. She cannot leave the alligator with the cat or the cat with the bird. How can Jill get all the pets to the pet show?

5 Kevin sold 12 beach umbrellas on Monday. He put 4 green umbrellas in the storeroom. Then he divided the remaining umbrellas into 2 equal piles of 24 each. How many umbrellas did Kevin have before he opened the store on Monday?

6 If an elevator holds more than 1,000 lb, an alarm goes off. Seven adults whose average weight is 132 lb and five children whose average weight is 93 lb enter the elevator. Does the alarm go off?

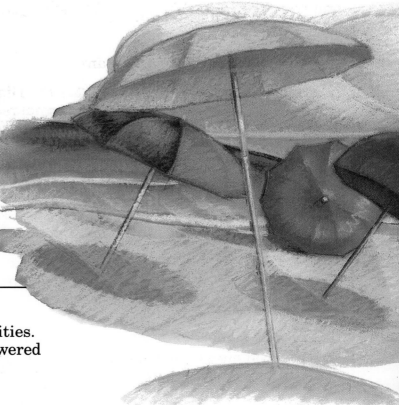

WRITER'S CORNER

7 Make a schedule of your daily activities. Make up a problem that can be answered by using the schedule.

CHAPTER REVIEW

Vocabulary Check

Choose a word or words from the box to complete each sentence.

capacity
customary
gram
inches
liter
meter
metric
ounces
precision
weight

1. The relationships among place-value positions are the same as the relationships among ___?___ units. *(page 270)*

2. The base unit of length in the metric measurement system is the ___?___. *(page 270)*

3. The base unit of capacity in the metric measurement system is the ___?___. *(page 270)*

4. The base unit of mass in the metric measurement system is the ___?___. *(page 270)*

5. The degree of accuracy needed for a particular measurement is called ___?___. *(page 280)*

6. In the ___?___ measurement system, ___?___ and feet are units of length, pints and quarts are units of ___?___, and ___?___ and pounds are units of ___?___. *(pages 286, 288)*

> Remember that metric is different from customary measurement, so read the exercises carefully.

Concept Check

7. On a regular clock, the hours between midnight and noon are ___?___ hours, and the hours between noon and midnight are ___?___ hours. *(page 292)*

8. When you change from centimeters to meters, will there be more or fewer units? *(page 271)*

9. When you change to fewer units, should you multiply or divide? *(page 271)*

10. Within one day's time, would you be able to walk 100 m? 100 km? Explain. *(page 270)*

11. What metric unit would you use to measure the length of a new pencil? What customary unit would you use? *(pages 274, 286)*

Tell by what number to multiply or divide to change the units. *(pages 271, 286, 288)*

12. cm to mm   **13.** mL to L   **14.** in. to ft   **15.** oz to lb   **16.** qt to pt

296 ● **Chapter 9**

Skill Check

Tell which unit is greater. *(page 270)*

17. meters or centimeters   **18.** grams or kilograms   **19.** millimeters or liters

Choose the better estimate. Write a or b. *(pages 274, 288)*

20. baseball bat
    a. 1 m   **b.** 5 m

21. baseball
    a. 5 oz   **b.** 30 oz

22. cup of milk
    a. $\frac{1}{2}$ pt   **b.** 1 gal

Tell whether to estimate or to use a tool to measure. If you would use a tool, tell which tool. *(page 282)*

23. distance from house to mall   **24.** amount of expensive perfume

Tell which measurement is more precise. *(page 280)*

25. 12 cm or 120 mm   **26.** 4 kg or 3,900 g   **27.** 180 mL or 0.18 L

Change to the given unit. *(pages 271, 274, 278, 286, 288, 292)*

28. 2 L = ■ mL   **29.** 620 mm = ■ cm   **30.** 53 g = ■ dg   **31.** 15 m = ■ km

32. 0.26 kL = ■ dL   **33.** 10 mg = ■ g   **34.** 45 in. = ■ ft.   **35.** 120 ft = ■ yd

36. 288 fl oz = ■ qt   **37.** 7 lb = ■ oz   **38.** 10 gal = ■ pt   **39.** 960 min = ■ hr

Find the sum or difference. *(pages 290, 292)*

40.   2 gal 3 qt
    +1 gal 3 qt

41.   5 ft   9 in.
    −2 ft 11 in.

42.   6 lb 8 oz
    +1 lb 8 oz

43.   9 hr 10 min
    −   50 min

Problem-Solving Check *(pages 276, 294)*

44. Kareem delivered 6 T of sand to a construction site. If workers used 3 T 400 lb on Monday and $\frac{1}{2}$ T on Tuesday, about how much sand was left at the site?

45. A regular flight leaves New York at 4:35 P.M., stops in Atlanta for 45 min, and arrives in Miami at 8:15 P.M. How long does it take to travel on this flight?

46. Mia has 52 yd of canvas to cover beach chairs. If it takes $3\frac{1}{4}$ yd of canvas to cover 1 chair, will Mia have enough canvas to cover the 20 chairs on the hotel veranda?

47. Suppose commuter flights arrive in Jackson from Macon every $3\frac{1}{2}$ hr beginning at 7:00 A.M. If the flight takes 45 min, when will the fourth flight leave Macon?

CHAPTER TEST

Choose the better estimate. Write **a** or **b**.

1. length of classroom
   a. 30 m   **b.** 3 km

2. capacity of a bowl of soup
   a. 5 mL   **b.** 300 mL

3. mass of a bicycle
   a. 25 lb   **b.** 2 lb

Tell which unit is greater.

4. dm or m

5. mL or L

6. cm or m

7. g or kg

Tell which measurement is more precise.

8. 2 L or 2.4 L

9. 7 m or 75 cm

10. 5 L or 50 mL

11. 900 g or 0.96 kg

Change to the given unit.

12. 62 g = ■ kg

13. 100 L = ■ mL

14. 33 cm = ■ m

15. 81 cm = ■ mm

16. 810 ft = ■ yd

17. $7\frac{3}{4}$ lb = ■ oz

18. 6 days = ■ hr

19. 300 sec = ■ min

20. 200 fl oz = ■ c

> I must think about whether I am changing to a larger or smaller unit.

Find the sum or difference.

21.   6 ft 2 in.
     −4 ft 5 in.

22.   8 lb   6 oz
     +6 lb 11 oz

23.   4 min 35 sec
     −3 min 59 sec

24.   3 yd 2 ft
     +9 yd 2 ft

25.   2 min 45 sec
     +   33 sec

26.   12 c 3 fl oz
     − 6 c 4 fl oz

Solve.

27. A swimmer must average 35 sec in a 100-m event to make the swim team. In tryouts Travis swam the event in 36.4 sec, 35.2 sec, and 34.9 sec. Did Travis make the swim team?

28. Lorenzo has $500 for cabinets. If the cabinets cost $430 and the installation fee is $12 an hour for 14 hr of labor, does he have enough money to buy and install them?

29. Buses that go downtown leave the mall every hour, from 9:00 A.M. on. Tim wants to walk home from downtown. The bus ride takes 20 min. If Tim must be home by 5:00 P.M. and walking home takes 1 hr 25 min, what is the last bus he should take from the mall?

30. Mary takes a bus that leaves Smithboro at 9:00 A.M. and arrives in Janesville at 10:50 A.M. John takes a bus that leaves Sumner at 10:50 A.M. and arrives in Janesville at 12:35 P.M. Who has the longer ride? How much longer is it?

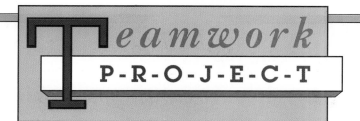

Teamwork PROJECT

Physical Education Connection

Physical fitness is important for a well-rounded and healthful life-style. There are many ways to exercise and keep physically fit. Work with a team to plan a fitness course around a jogging track in your community.

Decide

Discuss the types of exercises that can be done at different stations of a fitness course. Make a list of the exercises.

Decide how many exercise stations will be on your fitness course.

Decide on the exercises and their order.

Do

As a team, draw a map of the fitness course. Divide the exercise stations among yourselves.

Include a description and a diagram of each exercise.

Mark the distances between stations in metric units.

Share

Show your map to another team. Tell why you chose each exercise. Let the other team show you their map.

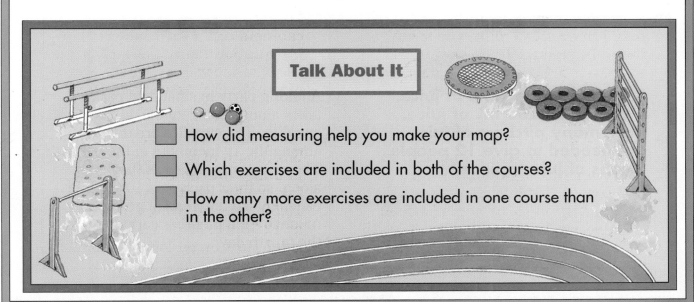

Talk About It

◻ How did measuring help you make your map?

◻ Which exercises are included in both of the courses?

◻ How many more exercises are included in one course than in the other?

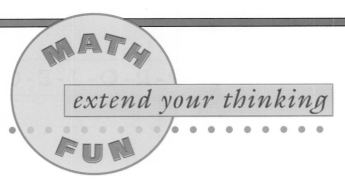

MATH FUN

extend your thinking

Estimate Distance

How many miles do you live from your school? from your favorite shopping mall? from some other location?

Here is a method of estimating the distance of one mile.

1. Measure your normal walking step to the nearest inch. Compare this to the number of inches in a mile to estimate the number of steps you take to walk a mile.

2. Choose a distance you walk frequently. Estimate the distance.

Another Method

Use a pedometer to estimate the same distance.

• Which method do you think gives you the more accurate estimate?

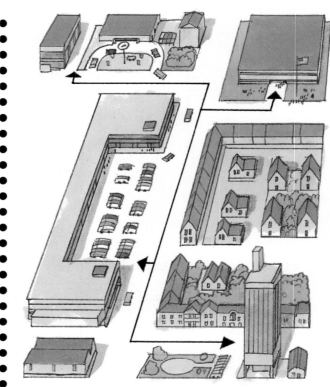

Challenge

Number Sense

A pitcher holds 1.5 L of juice. A cup holds 250 mL of juice. How many pitchers of juice are needed to give 12 people 2 cups of juice apiece?

Logical Reasoning

A hiking party in a national park takes along 299.25 kg of supplies. The supplies are divided among the 19 members of the party. They use the supplies as they go along, so their packs get 10% lighter each day. To the nearest gram, how much is each member carrying on the fourth day?

Write the letter of the correct answer.

1. Evaluate $5.12 - b$, for $b = 2.3$.

   A. 2.3   **B.** 2.82

   C. 2.92   **D.** 3.09

2. $20 \div 4 + 3 \times 5$

   A. 15.2   **B.** 20

   C. 25.5   **D.** 30.5

3. Find the number of combinations.
7 colors, 5 fabrics

   A. 5   **B.** 7

   C. 35   **D.** 53

4. Which fraction is equal to 0.4?

   A. $\frac{1}{5}$ **B.** $\frac{2}{10}$

   C. $\frac{1}{4}$ **D.** $\frac{2}{5}$

5. $3\frac{1}{2} + 2\frac{2}{5}$

   A. $5\frac{3}{10}$ **B.** $5\frac{3}{7}$

   C. $5\frac{9}{10}$ **D.** not here

6. $9\frac{1}{4} - 5\frac{1}{3}$

   A. $3\frac{2}{3}$ **B.** $3\frac{3}{4}$

   C. $3\frac{11}{12}$ **D.** $4\frac{1}{12}$

7. $\frac{1}{5} \times 3\frac{1}{4}$

   A. $\frac{19}{20}$ **B.** $3\frac{1}{20}$

   C. $4\frac{1}{20}$ **D.** not here

8. $\frac{1}{6} \div \frac{11}{12}$

   A. $\frac{2}{11}$ **B.** $\frac{3}{11}$

   C. $\frac{11}{3}$ **D.** $\frac{11}{2}$

9. Change to the given unit.
33 mL = ▇ L

   A. 0.033   **B.** 0.33

   C. 3,300   **D.** 33,000

10. Change to the given unit.
9 pt = ▇ qt

   A. $2\frac{1}{4}$ **B.** $4\frac{1}{2}$

   C. 18   **D.** 36

11. About how much will a custom-made suit cost if fabric is $85, labor is $9 an hour, and 12 hr of labor are needed?

   A. $100   **B.** $185

   C. $285   **D.** $300

12. Maggie's house is 12 min from the station. She is 7 min early for an 11:20 A.M. train. What time did she leave her house?

   A. 10:59 A.M.   **B.** 11:01 A.M.

   C. 11:13 A.M.   **D.** 11:39 A.M.

CHAPTER

10

RATIO, PROPORTION, AND PERCENT

Did you know . . .

. . . that there is a balance in the length and width of the large televisions and the length and width of the small television?

Talk About It

How could you find the number of small televisions it would take to equal the size of one of the large televisions?

RATIOS

In a scene from *Play Basketball,* a camera zooms in on 3 players in white uniforms and 2 players in blue uniforms. What is the ratio of white uniforms to blue uniforms?

A **ratio** is a comparison of two numbers. You can write a ratio to compare one amount to another amount, a part to the whole, or the whole to a part.

There are three ways to write a ratio.

Write: 3 to 2, 3:2, or $\frac{3}{2}$
Read: three to two

So, the ratio of white to blue uniforms is $\frac{3}{2}$.

Another Example

What is the ratio of the number of players wearing blue to the total number of players in the scene?

$$\frac{\text{first term} \longrightarrow 2 \longleftarrow \text{number of players wearing blue}}{\text{second term} \longrightarrow 5 \longleftarrow \text{total number of players}}$$

So, the ratio of the number of players wearing blue to the total number of players is 2:5.

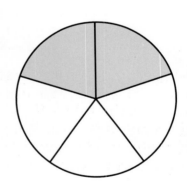

- How would you write the ratio of the number of players jumping to the total number of players?

- What does the ratio $\frac{5}{2}$ compare?

Check for Understanding

Name the items being compared. Then write the ratio by comparing the first amount to the second amount. Use the form ■ : ■.

1. Of the 120 mi Ed drives a week, he drives 80 mi to and from work.

2. A store carries socks that come 3 pairs to a package.

3. The map's scale shows that 2 in. represents 5 mi.

4. Heidi's bicycle travels 42 ft for every 3 pedal revolutions.

5. Of Andrea's 120-card collection of postcards, 45 show pictures of flowers.

6. In Aaron's aquarium, 1 of every 3 fish is a guppy.

Practice

Draw a picture to show the ratio.

7. The ratio of blue boxes to red boxes is 4:6.

8. The ratio of yellow shoes to green shoes is $\frac{7}{2}$.

9. The ratio of stars to crescents is two to five.

10. The ratio of math books to total books is 1:6.

Write the ratio in two other ways.

11. 10:7   **12.** 4:9   **13.** 8:3   **14.** 5:6   **15.** 12:2

16. $\frac{10}{1}$ **17.** $\frac{5}{8}$ **18.** $\frac{9}{5}$ **19.** $\frac{3}{13}$ **20.** $\frac{10}{15}$

21. nine to three   **22.** twelve to fifteen   **23.** twenty-two to fifty

Mixed Applications

24. Lucy buys 4 rolls of color film and 7 rolls of black-and-white film. What is the ratio of color film to the total amount of film?

25. **Making Choices** Suppose apples are your favorite fruit. Would you rather buy a sack where the ratio of apples to oranges is $\frac{1}{2}$ or $\frac{3}{1}$?

MATH CONNECTION

When you solve a probability problem, you are using a ratio. Look at the table. If Mandy is a sixth grader, what is the probability she prefers partially animated movies?

P (partial animation) $= \frac{40}{90}$

So, the probability is $\frac{40}{90}$, or 40:90.

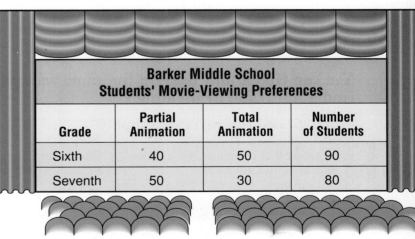

Grade	Partial Animation	Total Animation	Number of Students
Sixth	40	50	90
Seventh	50	30	80

Barker Middle School Students' Movie-Viewing Preferences

Use the table. Find the probability of the event.

26. sixth graders who prefer total animation

27. seventh graders who do not prefer total animation

28. sixth and seventh graders who prefer partial animation

Use your own words to explain the meaning of *ratio*.

WRAP UP...

RATES

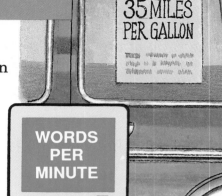

There are 135 students enrolled in 5 photography classes. If the same number of students is enrolled in each class, how many students are in each class?

A **rate** is a ratio that compares one quantity to a different quantity. If the second term of a rate is 1, the rate is called a **unit rate.**

- What are the two different quantities that you must compare to answer this question?

$$\frac{\text{students} \longrightarrow}{\text{classes} \longrightarrow} \quad \frac{135}{5} \longleftarrow \text{rate}$$

- How can you change the rate so that the second term is 1?

$$\frac{135}{5} = \frac{135 \div 5}{5 \div 5} = \frac{27}{1} \longleftarrow \text{unit rate}$$

So, there are 27 students per class.

Best Photo Shop sells 12 rolls of film for $28.68. Ace Photo Shop sells 15 rolls of the same film for $32.85. What is the unit price of film in each shop?

You can find a unit price in the same way you find a unit rate, by dividing.

Step 1	Step 2
Write ratios that compare the number of rolls of film to the price.	Divide the price by the quantity to find the unit price.
Best: $\dfrac{28.68}{12}$	$\dfrac{28.68}{12} = \dfrac{28.68 \div 12}{12 \div 12} = \dfrac{2.39}{1} = 2.39$
Ace: $\dfrac{32.85}{15}$	$\dfrac{32.85}{15} = \dfrac{32.85 \div 15}{15 \div 15} = \dfrac{2.19}{1} = 2.19$

So, the price at Best Photo is $2.39 per roll, and the price at Ace Photo is $2.19 per roll.

- Which is the better buy?

Check for Understanding

Tell how to find the unit rate or unit price.

1. 4 apples for $1.00

2. 310 words per 7 min

3. 16 stickers for $0.80

4. 140 mi per 7 gal of gasoline

Practice

Write a ratio that describes each rate.

5. 5 tickets for $20

6. a dozen eggs for $0.99

7. 3 for a dime

8. 33 mi to a gal

9. 52 words per min

10. 10 for $2

11. 20 pages per 5 min

12. 12 lb per 6 mo

13. 10 for fifty cents

Find the unit rate or unit price. Remember to express the second term.

14. 5 for $1.00

15. $0.95 for 5

16. $1.44 a dozen

17. 200 mi per 8 gal

18. $10 for 2

19. 14 for $31.50

20. $13.05 for 9

21. 900 people per 10 sq mi

22. 350 per 10 sq mi

23. 324 mi per 12 gal

24. 12 lessons for $155.40

25. 1,600 words per 25 min

Mixed Applications

26. Mr. Kerr buys 16 cassette tapes for $79.84. What is the unit price of each tape?

27. Lana has 9 rolls of film developed for $35.91. How much is the cost per roll of film?

28. A drugstore sells photo album pages at 5 for $4.25. If the rate remains the same, how much will 12 pages cost?

29. Chantel has a camera that produces instant photos. If film is $7.45 a roll, how much will 4 rolls cost?

30. At For-Les, the price of video-cassettes is 3 for $28.35. You can buy the same cassettes at Sav-Mor at 5 for $46.75. Which store has the better buy?

31. **Make Up a Problem** On Tuesdays, Fill-It-Up gasoline station sells high-performance gasoline at the special rate of $20.04 for 12 gal.

What is the difference between a ratio and a rate?

EQUIVALENT RATIOS

Ralph works at a video store. On Monday he rented 4 drama videos and 6 comedy videos. On Tuesday he rented 8 dramas and 12 comedies. On Wednesday he rented 16 dramas and 24 comedies. Are the ratios of dramas to comedies rented each day equivalent?

Use counters to visualize whether the ratios are equivalent.

There are 4 red for every 6 blue.

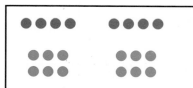

There are 4 red for every 6 blue.

There are 4 red for every 6 blue.

If you can multiply or divide both terms by a common factor, the ratios are equivalent.

$$\frac{\text{dramas} \rightarrow}{\text{comedies} \rightarrow} \quad \frac{4}{6} = \frac{4 \times 2}{6 \times 2} = \frac{8}{12} \qquad \frac{8}{12} = \frac{8 \times 2}{12 \times 2} = \frac{16}{24} \qquad \frac{4}{6} = \frac{8}{12} = \frac{16}{24}$$

So, the ratios of dramas to comedies are equivalent.

Another Example

Ralph rents 3 comedy videos. How many drama videos can he expect to rent if the ratio remains the same?

$$\frac{\text{dramas} \rightarrow}{\text{comedies} \rightarrow} \quad \frac{4}{6} = \frac{\blacksquare}{3} \qquad \frac{4}{6} = \frac{4 \div 2}{6 \div 2} = \frac{2}{3} \quad \leftarrow \text{ratio in simplest form}$$

So, Ralph can expect to rent 2 drama videos.

- How does finding an equivalent ratio compare with finding an equivalent fraction?

- Study the examples. Talk about how you can determine whether two ratios are equivalent.

A. $\dfrac{6}{10} = \dfrac{\blacksquare}{5}$

$\dfrac{6 \div 2}{10 \div 2} = \dfrac{3}{5}$

B. $1:2 = 12:\blacksquare$

$\dfrac{1 \times 12}{2 \times 12} = \dfrac{12}{24}$

C. $\dfrac{4}{32} \stackrel{?}{=} \dfrac{5}{8}$

$\dfrac{5 \times 4}{8 \times 4} = \dfrac{20}{32}$

$\dfrac{4}{32} \neq \dfrac{5}{8} \quad \leftarrow \neq \text{ means "not equal."}$

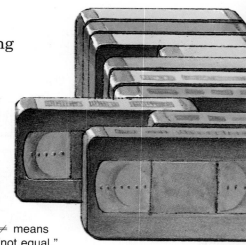

Check for Understanding

Complete. Write = or ≠ to tell whether the ratios are equivalent.

1. $\frac{1}{2}$ ● $\frac{6}{12}$

2. 1:3 ● 5:17

3. 3 to 1 ● 9 to 3

4. 7:2 ● 21:8

Write two ratios that are equivalent to the given ratio.

5. $\frac{1}{2}$

6. 3:4

7. 2 to 3

8. 5:1

9. 3 to 2

10. 2 to 1

11. $\frac{4}{5}$

12. $\frac{7}{2}$

13. 6:12

14. 5 to 9

Tell whether the ratios are equivalent. Write *yes* or *no*.

15. $\frac{2}{1}$; $\frac{8}{4}$

16. 2:5; 6:12

17. 1:3; 7:21

18. $\frac{4}{5}$; $\frac{16}{25}$

19. $\frac{27}{63}$; $\frac{3}{7}$

20. 20:45; 4:9

21. $\frac{16}{32}$; $\frac{2}{4}$

22. 18:48; 3:8

Find the term that makes the ratios equivalent.

23. $\frac{1}{2}$; $\frac{\blacksquare}{10}$

24. $\frac{\blacksquare}{7}$; $\frac{4}{14}$

25. 2 to 5; 6 to ▨

26. 9 to 3; ▨ to 27

27. $\frac{12}{3}$; $\frac{4}{\blacksquare}$

28. $\frac{\blacksquare}{7}$; $\frac{3}{1}$

29. 8 to 4; ▨ to 2

30. 36:15; 12:▨

Mixed Applications

31. Karl took 5 photographs of friends for every 3 photographs of scenery. How many pictures of friends does he have if he has 15 photographs of scenery?

32. Dara's contract calls for her to work in 3 films and then 9 commercials. If her contract is renewed, will her fifteenth job be a film or a commercial?

33. **Analyze Data** The table shows the number of trivia games Sean and Sonia won over five days. The ratio of Sean's winning to Sonia's winning the first day is $\frac{2}{1}$. On which other day is the ratio of Sean's winning to Sonia's winning $\frac{2}{1}$?

Number of Trivia Games					
Day	1	2	3	4	5
Sean won	2	1	6	1	4
Sonia won	1	3	3	2	3

Explain in your own words how to find equivalent ratios.

WRAP UP...

EXPLORING

Proportions

These photographs are in proportion because there is a balance in the relationship of their widths to their lengths. Numbers can help you determine whether items are in proportion.

WORK TOGETHER

Building Understanding

Use counters to help you.
Is $\frac{3}{5}$ equivalent to $\frac{6}{10}$?

Set A

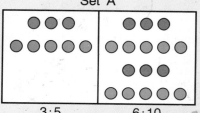

3:5   6:10

Is $\frac{1}{2}$ equivalent to $\frac{2}{3}$?

Set B

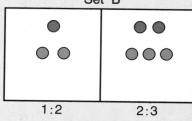

1:2   2:3

Talk About It

▶ In Set A, is the number of red counters in the second box a multiple of the number of red counters in the first box? blue counters?

▶ How does the ratio of red to blue counters on the left compare with the ratio of red to blue counters on the right?

▶ In Set B, is the number of red counters in either box a multiple of the number of red counters in the other box? blue counters?

▶ How does the ratio of red to blue counters on the left compare with the ratio of red to blue counters on the right?

A **proportion** is a number sentence or an equation that states that two ratios are equivalent.

$$\frac{3}{5} = \frac{6}{10} \quad \longleftarrow \text{ a proportion}$$

Use counters. Tell whether the ratios make a proportion. Write = or ≠.

a. $\frac{3}{5}$ ● $\frac{5}{15}$ **b.** $\frac{1}{2}$ ● $\frac{6}{12}$ **c.** $\frac{2}{3}$ ● $\frac{3}{5}$ **d.** $\frac{9}{10}$ ● $\frac{18}{36}$

Making the Connection

You can use cross products to determine whether ratios are proportions. The cross products of a proportion are equivalent.

a. $\dfrac{12}{18} \longleftrightarrow \bullet \longleftrightarrow \dfrac{2}{3}$

$3 \times 12 = \blacksquare$
$18 \times 2 = \blacksquare$
$18 \times 2 \stackrel{?}{=} 3 \times 12$

b. $\dfrac{2}{3} \longleftrightarrow \bullet \longleftrightarrow \dfrac{5}{15}$

$3 \times 5 = \blacksquare$
$2 \times 15 = \blacksquare$
$3 \times 5 \stackrel{?}{=} 2 \times 15$

1. What are the cross products in Example a? in Example b?

2. Do the ratios in each example form a proportion? Explain your answer.

You can use cross products to find the missing term in a proportion.

c. $\dfrac{y}{4} \longleftrightarrow = \longleftrightarrow \dfrac{12}{16}$ Find the cross products.

$16y = 4 \times 12 \longleftarrow 4 \times 12 = 48$
$16y = 48$

d. $\dfrac{18}{6} \longleftrightarrow = \longleftrightarrow \dfrac{n}{2}$ Find the cross products.

3. What equation can you write to show that the cross products of Example d are equal?

4. What would you do to solve the equations?

Checking Understanding

Tell whether the ratios make a proportion. Write *yes* or *no*.

5. $\dfrac{2}{3}; \dfrac{12}{18}$

6. $1:5; 3:15$

7. $\dfrac{4}{5}; \dfrac{32}{8}$

8. $9:2; 15:3$

Write the cross products.

9. $\dfrac{3}{1} = \dfrac{9}{3}$

10. $\dfrac{2}{3} = \dfrac{4}{6}$

11. $\dfrac{1}{8} = \dfrac{t}{40}$

12. $\dfrac{3}{x} = \dfrac{4}{36}$

13. $\dfrac{a}{6} = \dfrac{5}{8}$

14. $\dfrac{4}{b} = \dfrac{7}{9}$

15. $\dfrac{4}{5} = \dfrac{7}{y}$

16. $\dfrac{3}{11} = \dfrac{d}{10}$

Animators made 2,880 drawings for 3 minutes of an animated movie. How many drawings would they make for 15 minutes of animation?

Use what you know about equivalent ratios to find the missing term in a proportion.

Step 1 Write a proportion.	**Step 2** Write the cross products.	**Step 3** Solve the equation.
drawings → $\dfrac{2,880}{3} = \dfrac{n}{15}$ ← minutes	$\dfrac{2,880}{3} \rightleftharpoons \dfrac{n}{15}$ $3n = 2,880 \times 15$	$3n = 2,880 \times 15$ $3n = 43,200$ $n = 14,400$

So, they would make 14,400 drawings.

Another Example For a movie that is set in Chicago, Henk is making scale models of the Sears Tower, which is 550 m tall, and the John Hancock Center, which is 444 m tall. If Henk's model of the Sears Tower is 10 m tall, what will be the height of his model of the John Hancock Center to the nearest hundredth meter?

$\dfrac{\text{model height}}{\text{actual height}} \rightarrow \dfrac{10}{550} \rightleftharpoons \dfrac{t}{444}$ $550t = 444 \times 10$ $t = \dfrac{444 \times 10}{550}$

You can use a calculator to find the answer.

444 10 550 | 8.0727272 |

So, to the nearest hundredth meter, the height of Henk's model of the John Hancock Center will be 8.07 m.

Check for Understanding

Write the cross products.

1. $\dfrac{1}{x} = \dfrac{3}{6}$

2. $\dfrac{3}{8} = \dfrac{t}{24}$

3. $\dfrac{c}{3} = \dfrac{2}{6}$

4. $\dfrac{15}{18} = \dfrac{5}{y}$

5. $\dfrac{a}{16} = \dfrac{1}{4}$

Practice

Tell whether the ratios make a proportion. Write *yes* or *no*.

6. $\dfrac{2}{5}$; $\dfrac{10}{25}$

7. $\dfrac{9}{3}$; $\dfrac{3}{1}$

8. $\dfrac{18}{25}$; $\dfrac{7}{10}$

9. $\dfrac{3}{8}$; $\dfrac{9}{24}$

10. $\dfrac{7}{8}$; $\dfrac{28}{32}$

11. $\dfrac{5}{6}$; $\dfrac{3}{4}$

12. $\dfrac{20}{32}$; $\dfrac{5}{8}$

13. $\dfrac{2}{9}$; $\dfrac{14}{64}$

14. $\dfrac{3}{14}$; $\dfrac{5}{12}$

15. $\dfrac{2}{7}$; $\dfrac{6}{28}$

16. $\dfrac{4}{9}$; $\dfrac{12}{27}$

17. $\dfrac{3}{5}$; $\dfrac{4}{6}$

Write the cross products. Then solve.

18. $\dfrac{6}{8} = \dfrac{n}{12}$

19. $\dfrac{9}{15} = \dfrac{a}{10}$

20. $\dfrac{3}{9} = \dfrac{b}{21}$

21. $\dfrac{12}{9} = \dfrac{t}{12}$

22. $\dfrac{15}{20} = \dfrac{x}{16}$

23. $\dfrac{14}{4} = \dfrac{d}{12}$

24. $\dfrac{p}{6} = \dfrac{2.5}{4}$

25. $\dfrac{4}{m} = \dfrac{1.6}{2.8}$

Mixed Applications

26. The ratio of rolls of film to exposures is 1 to 12. How many exposures are in 7 rolls of film?

27. There are 5 videotapes to a package. If Leon buys 8 packages of videotapes, how many videotapes will he have?

28. **Logical Reasoning** If the ratio of cartoon videos to adventure videos in 2 packages is 6 to 14, how many packages must you buy to have 15 cartoon videos?

MIXED REVIEW

Find the sum or difference.

1. 5 hr 45 min
    −2 hr 30 min

2. 7 min 12 sec
    +6 min 55 sec

3. 12 min 5 sec
    − 8 min 45 sec

4. 2 hr 55 min
    +6 hr 25 min

5. 5 gal − 3 qt

6. 2 T − 1,200 lb

7. 5 km − 3,000 m

Write the ratio in two other ways.

8. four to two

9. five to eight

10. one to nine

11. seven to eleven

How can you tell whether two ratios make a proportion?

More Practice, Lesson 10.5, page H71

EXPLORING

Scale Drawings

Martha is making this scale drawing of an auditorium to use as a prop in a mystery movie.

A **scale drawing** is like a photograph. It can be a reduced or an enlarged version of the actual object.

WORK TOGETHER

Building Understanding

Use centimeter graph paper and a centimeter ruler.

1. Measure the length and the width of the scale drawing.

2. On your graph paper, make a drawing that is twice the size of the scale drawing Martha made.

3. On your graph paper, make a drawing that is half the size of the scale drawing Martha made.

Tell whether you would reduce or enlarge the dimensions to make a scale drawing.

a. a birthstone   **b.** your bedroom

c. an office   **d.** an amoeba

Talk About It

▶ What is the ratio of the length to the width in your first drawing? in Martha's drawing? Are the ratios equivalent?

▶ What is the ratio of the length to the width in your second drawing? in Martha's drawing? Are the ratios equivalent?

▶ Name some examples of scale drawings that you find in everyday life.

▶ If you were making a scale drawing of a classroom, would you reduce or enlarge the dimensions?

▶ If you were making a scale drawing of a thumbtack, would you reduce or enlarge the dimensions?

Making the Connection

The **scale** of a drawing is the ratio of the size of the object in the drawing to the actual size of the object. If you know the scale, you can find a missing dimension.

Use a centimeter ruler and the scale drawing of the office suite.

An interior decorator's drawing of an office suite is 60 mm long. You can write and solve a proportion to find the actual length of the suite.

The scale of the drawing tells you that every distance of 10 mm in the drawing represents an actual distance of 2 m in the office suite.

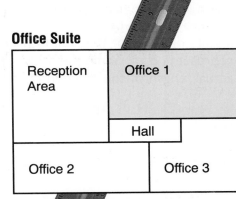

Office Suite

Reception Area	Office 1
Office 2	Hall
	Office 3

Scale: 10 mm = 2 m

$$\frac{\text{mm}}{\text{m}} \rightarrow \frac{10}{2} \overset{\longleftarrow}{\underset{\longleftarrow}{=}} \frac{60}{s} \leftarrow \frac{\text{drawing length}}{\text{actual length}}$$

$$10s = 2 \times 60$$
$$10s = 120$$
$$s = 12$$

So, the actual length of the suite is 12 m.

- What proportion can you write to find the actual length of Office 2?

Checking Understanding

Use the scale drawing of the office suite. Write the proportion you can use to find the actual dimensions.

1. length of the hall

2. width of the suite

3. length of Office 1

4. dimensions of the reception area

Make a scale drawing to enlarge the shape to twice its size.

5.

6.

7.

8.

9.

10.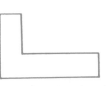

PROBLEM Solving

Denny wants to be an engineer and help companies make decisions about building large structures. Denny made a presentation to his mechanical drawing class about a theater called Bard Production Hall. He used a scale drawing of the hall. In his drawing, 1 cm represents 6 m. Someone asked Denny, "What is the actual length of the makeup room?"

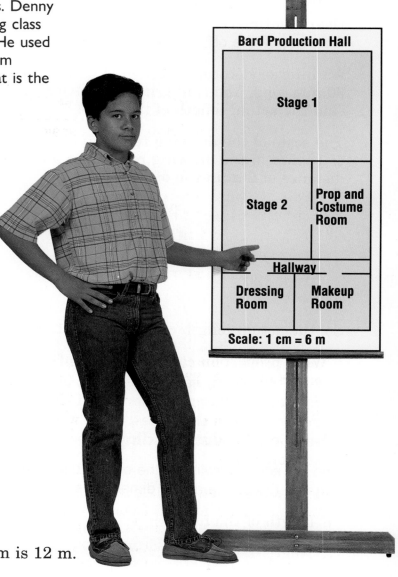

▶ UNDERSTAND

What are you asked to find?

What information are you given?

▶ PLAN

How will you solve the problem?

Use the scale drawing. Measure the length of the makeup room. Then write and solve a proportion.

▶ SOLVE

How will you carry out your plan?

Use a centimeter ruler. The length of the makeup room in the drawing is 2 cm. Write a proportion.

$$\frac{cm}{m} \longrightarrow \frac{1}{6} = \frac{2}{n} \longleftarrow \frac{\text{drawing length}}{\text{actual length}}$$

$$1n = 6 \times 2 \longleftarrow 1 \times n = n$$

$$n = 12$$

So, the actual length of the makeup room is 12 m.

▶ LOOK BACK

How can you check your answer?

WHAT IF... ...the width of the drawing of Stage 2 were 3.5 cm? What would be the actual width of the stage?

Apply

Use a centimeter ruler and the scale drawing on page 316. Solve.

(1) What is the actual width of the prop and costume room?

(2) What is the actual width of the dressing room?

(3) What are the actual length and width of the hallway?

(4) What are the actual length and width of the production hall?

Mixed Applications ▶ **STRATEGIES**
- Write an Equation • Draw a Diagram
- Find a Pattern • Work Backward

Choose a strategy and solve. Use the scale drawing on page 316 for Exercise 6.

(5) A costumer uses $\frac{2}{3}$ yd of fabric to make a blouse and $1\frac{4}{5}$ yd to make a skirt for a turn-of-the-century costume. How much fabric will the costumer use to make the 150 blouses and 75 skirts needed for a crowd scene?

(6) Leanna and Drew are on the set crew for the next production. They are making a blue curtain that will run the entire length of Stage 1. What will be the actual length of the curtain?

(7) To build a long staircase for the filming of *Halt,* the set crew will use 5 blocks for the first step, 10 for the second, 15 for the third, 20 for the fourth, and 25 for the fifth. If the pattern continues, what will be the total number of blocks used for ten steps?

(8) Dan took pictures while on vacation. He used $\frac{3}{4}$ roll of film on day 1, $1\frac{1}{2}$ rolls on day 2, $2\frac{1}{4}$ rolls on day 3, and 3 rolls on day 4. If the pattern continued, how much film did Dan use on day 8?

(9) In a movie scene, an elevator travels from the fifth floor to the first floor. It then travels to the third floor and back down to the first floor. If the floors are 10 ft apart, how far does the elevator travel?

(10) The budget to produce a film is $2,500,000. The producer budgeted $350,000 for costumes; $600,000 for sets; $1,500,000 for actors; and the rest for miscellaneous expenses. How much was budgeted for miscellaneous expenses?

(11) The entire cast of an epic film was invited to the premiere. Of those invited, 4 out of 5 planned to attend. If there were 960 people in the cast, how many planned to attend the premiere?

More Practice, Lesson 10.7, page H71

1. George leaves home for work at 7:30 A.M. He rides a train for 35 min and then walks 10 min to his office. If he is 15 min early, at what time is he supposed to begin work?

2. Train A leaves Nokesville at 9:45 A.M., arriving in the city at 10:57 A.M. Train B leaves at 1:35 P.M. and arrives in the city at 2:53 P.M. Which train takes longer?

3. The blueprints for Jan's house use a scale of 1 cm = 4 m. The kitchen is 6 m long. How long is the kitchen in the drawing?

I would write a proportion to solve Exercise 3.

Change to the given unit.

4. $7.9 \text{ m} = \blacksquare \text{ mm}$

5. $6 \text{ lb} = \blacksquare \text{ oz}$

6. $22{,}000 \text{ g} = \blacksquare \text{ kg}$

Find the sum or difference.

7.
$$\begin{array}{r} 12 \text{ m } 75 \text{ cm} \\ + \ 9 \text{ m } 45 \text{ cm} \\ \hline \end{array}$$

8.
$$\begin{array}{r} 7 \text{ ft } 7 \text{ in.} \\ -4 \text{ ft } 9 \text{ in.} \\ \hline \end{array}$$

9.
$$\begin{array}{r} 6 \text{ min } 45 \text{ sec} \\ +8 \text{ min } 55 \text{ sec} \\ \hline \end{array}$$

10.
$$\begin{array}{r} 5 \text{ lb } 10 \text{ oz} \\ -3 \text{ lb } 11 \text{ oz} \\ \hline \end{array}$$

Write the ratio in two other ways.

11. two to one

12. $5:6$

13. $3:8$

14. three to nine

Find the unit rate.

15. $3.24 a dozen

16. 825 words per 15 min

17. 8 for $12.80

Tell whether the ratios are equivalent. Write *yes* or *no*.

18. $3:2; 9:4$

19. $6:8; 9:12$

20. $4:5; 32:35$

21. $5:15; 20:60$

Find the number that makes the ratios equivalent.

22. $4:3; 32:\blacksquare$

23. $16:8; \blacksquare:2$

24. $5:7; \blacksquare:63$

Tell whether the ratios make a proportion. Write *yes* or *no*.

25. $\dfrac{6}{9}; \dfrac{2}{3}$

26. $\dfrac{1}{9}; \dfrac{2}{5}$

27. $\dfrac{3}{5}; \dfrac{7}{15}$

28. $\dfrac{3}{8}; \dfrac{6}{16}$

Write the cross products.

29. $\dfrac{30}{15} = \dfrac{x}{5}$

30. $\dfrac{n}{4} = \dfrac{9}{1.2}$

31. $\dfrac{21}{9} = \dfrac{a}{3}$

32. $\dfrac{80}{b} = \dfrac{10}{3}$

Make Predictions

$\mathbb{S}$ometimes you can solve problems by using the given information to predict what will happen.

▼ At Northwest Middle School, 350 students will vote for the Movie of the Year. Three weeks ago Lynne surveyed 100 students selected at random to determine their favorite movies. She made this table to show the results of her survey.

Favorite Movies	
Movie	Number of Votes
Planet of the Nerds	30
Fresh Flowers	40
Phantom of West High	24
Undecided	6

Talk About It

Work together to read the table and make the predictions.

A. What movie will be the most popular among the students at Northwest Middle School?

B. What movie will be the least popular among the students at Northwest Middle School?

C. How many students out of 350 do you predict will vote for *Fresh Flowers?*

D. How many students out of 350 do you predict will be undecided in the voting?

Apply

Ask a sample of 10 of your classmates to identify their favorite hobbies, sports teams, or movies. Make a table of your results.

1. Predict the favorite hobby, sports team, or movie among all your classmates.

2. Predict the number of classmates who will select your favorite hobby, sports team, or movie.

EXPLORING
Percent

You can use a 10-by-10 grid to explore percent.

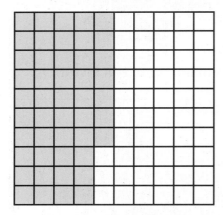

Talk About It

▶ How many squares are in the grid?

▶ How many squares are shaded?

▶ What is the ratio of shaded squares to the total number of squares in the grid?

Percent is the ratio of a number to 100. **Percent** means "per hundred." The symbol for percent is %.

▶ What percent of the grid is shaded?

WORK TOGETHER

Building Understanding

Use graph paper to make a 10-by-10 grid. Color 20 squares red, 50 squares blue, and 5 squares yellow.

Talk About It

▶ How does your grid show 20%? 50%? 5%?

▶ What percent of the grid is not colored?

▶ Does 50% differ from the ratio $\frac{1}{2}$, $\frac{5}{10}$, or $\frac{50}{100}$ when shaded on a grid? Why or why not?

▶ How can you show the ratio $\frac{2}{5}$ on a 10-by-10 grid?

Use graph paper to make three 10-by-10 grids. Color a grid to show the ratio given. Tell what percent is colored.

a. $\frac{75}{100}$ b. $\frac{6}{10}$ c. $\frac{4}{5}$

Making the Connection

The table shows the results of a survey that asked camera users which camera they felt was the most reliable. Use the table for Exercises 1–5.

1. How many people were surveyed?

2. What percent of those surveyed prefer the Minte Maxx?

3. What percent of those surveyed do not prefer the Karron XX?

4. Do more than half of the people surveyed prefer any one type of camera over the others?

Most Reliable Cameras

Type of Camera	Number of Votes*
Codiak AA	30
Insta Pix	10
Karron XX	35
Minte Maxx	20
Reflex	5

*From a total of 100 surveyed

5. Suppose that the table showed that 15 people preferred the Reflex, but nothing else was changed. Would that mean that 15% of those surveyed preferred the Reflex? Why or why not?

Checking Understanding

Tell what percent each is of one dollar.

6. 1 dime and 1 nickel

7. 1 quarter and 1 dime

8. 1 quarter and 2 dimes

9. 2 quarters and 1 nickel

10. 2 dimes and 3 nickels

11. 1 quarter, 2 dimes, and 1 nickel

12. 1 quarter, 1 dime, and 4 pennies

13. 3 quarters, 1 nickel, and 4 pennies

Solve.

14. If sales tax is 6%, how much tax will you pay if you buy an item that costs $1.00?

15. If sales tax is 5%, how much tax will you pay if you buy an item that costs $10.00?

16. If you surveyed 10 people and 8 said yes to a question, what percent of the people said yes? How do you know?

17. If you surveyed 10 people and 6 said yes to a question, what percent of the people said no?

PERCENTS AND DECIMALS

Aliya used a 10-by-10 grid to make a scale drawing of the set of *Tomorrow, Tomorrow, and Tomorrow*. What decimal shows the amount of space taken by the gasoline station?

The gasoline station takes up 12 squares.

12 out of 100 means 12 hundredths or 0.12.

So, 0.12 shows in decimal form the amount of space taken by the gasoline station.

- What percent shows the amount of space taken by the gasoline station?

You can write a decimal as a percent, and you can write a percent as a decimal.

More Examples

A. Write 0.05 as a percent.
0.05 = 5 out of 100

So, 0.05 = 5%.

B. Write 80% as a decimal.
80% = 80 out of 100

So, 80% = $\frac{80}{100}$ = 0.80, or 0.8.

Talk About It

Think of place value when you write a decimal as a percent and a percent as a decimal.

▶ Write 6% and 66% as decimals. By what number do you divide to change a percent to a decimal?

▶ Write 0.07 and 0.7 as percents. How many places did you move each decimal point?

▶ What pattern do you see when you write a percent as a decimal?

▶ What pattern do you see when you write a decimal as a percent?

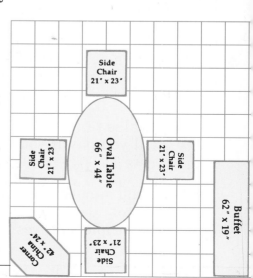

Check for Understanding

Write a decimal and a percent that describe the amount shaded.

1.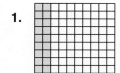
2.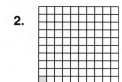
3.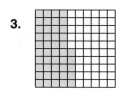
4.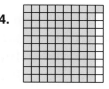

Practice

Use graph paper. Draw a 10-by-10 grid. Then shade the amount.

5. 20%   **6.** 0.6   **7.** 45%   **8.** 75%   **9.** 51%

Write the decimal as a percent.

10. 0.37   **11.** 0.44   **12.** 0.13   **13.** 0.21   **14.** 0.16

15. 0.6   **16.** 0.3   **17.** 0.03   **18.** 0.14   **19.** 1.45

Write the percent as a decimal.

20. 18%   **21.** 37%   **22.** 24%   **23.** 68%   **24.** 94%

25. 3%   **26.** 7%   **27.** 1%   **28.** 25%   **29.** 13%

30. 71%   **31.** 75%   **32.** 8%   **33.** 2%   **34.** 130%

Mixed Applications

35. A local restaurant has 100 autographed photographs of movie stars. Of these, 32 are in color. What percent of the photographs are in color?

36. If you can buy 5 posters for $9, how much does one poster cost?

37. Rich has a poster of a scene from *Dust Busters*. The poster is 150% larger than the original photograph. What decimal expresses the same amount?

38. If you can buy 3 posters for $6, what percent of a dollar does 1 poster cost?

How can you use place value to change a percent to a decimal?

PERCENTS AND FRACTIONS

In one scene from *After the Dance*, $\frac{1}{5}$ of the actors appear in blue makeup and costumes. What percent of the actors appear in blue?

Since percent means per hundred, you can write an equivalent fraction to answer the question.

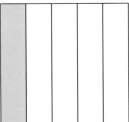 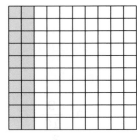

$$\frac{1}{5} = \frac{\blacksquare}{100} \qquad \frac{1 \times 20}{5 \times 20} = \frac{20}{100}$$

So, 20% of the actors appear in blue.

Another Method In another scene $\frac{2}{3}$ of the actors wear hats. What percent of the actors wear hats?

Sometimes you may want to write a fraction as a decimal and then write a percent.

$$0.66\tfrac{2}{3} = 66\tfrac{2}{3}\%$$

Divide to write a
two-digit decimal.
Write the remainder
as a fraction.

$$3\overline{)2.00}$$
$$\underline{1\ 8}$$
$$20$$
$$\underline{18}$$
$$2$$

So, $66\tfrac{2}{3}\%$ of the actors wear hats.

You can change a percent to a fraction by writing the percent as the numerator and 100 as the denominator. Remember to simplify the fraction.

Examples

A. $75\% = \frac{75}{100} = \frac{3}{4}$ **B.** $45\% = \frac{45}{100} = \frac{9}{20}$ **C.** $12\% = \frac{12}{100} = \frac{3}{25}$

- How do you write a decimal as a fraction?

Check for Understanding

Write a fraction in simplest form and a percent that describe the amount shaded.

1. 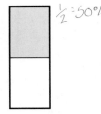 $\frac{1}{2} = 50\%$

2. 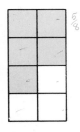 $\frac{5}{8} = 62\frac{1}{2}$

3.

4.

Practice

Write the fraction as a percent.

5. $\frac{1}{10}$ 6. $\frac{1}{5}$ 7. $\frac{1}{4}$ 8. $\frac{9}{10}$ 9. $\frac{4}{5}$

10. $\frac{17}{20}$ 11. $\frac{7}{10}$ 12. $\frac{3}{4}$ 13. $\frac{3}{5}$ 14. $\frac{3}{20}$

Write the percent as a fraction in simplest form.

15. 25% 16. 15% 17. 45% 18. 16% 19. 95%

Mixed Applications

20. A survey of customers at a theater indicates that $\frac{2}{5}$ are preteens. What percent of the customers are preteens?

21. **Number Sense • Mental Math** If $\frac{1}{4}$ of 96 students spend 1 hour a night on homework, what percent of students is this? How many students is this?

NUMBER SENSE

Use a calculator to change a fraction to a percent. Any remainder can be written as a decimal part of the percent.

Write $\frac{1}{3}$ as a percent.

1 ÷ 3 =  `0.3333333`

$0.3333333 = 0.33\overline{3}$

So, $\frac{1}{3}$ can be written as $33.\overline{3}\%$.

The bar shows that the decimal repeats.

Write $\frac{2}{3}$ as a percent.

2 ÷ 3 =  `0.6666666`

$0.6666666 = 0.66\overline{6}$

So, $\frac{2}{3}$ can be written as $66.\overline{6}\%$.

Use a calculator to change the fraction to a percent.

22. $\frac{3}{8}$ 23. $\frac{1}{6}$ 24. $\frac{5}{9}$ 25. $\frac{4}{11}$ 26. $\frac{11}{12}$

How is changing a percent to a fraction similar to changing a decimal to a fraction?

More Practice, Lesson 10.10, page H72

EXPLORING

Percent of a Number

You can find a percent of any number other than 100.

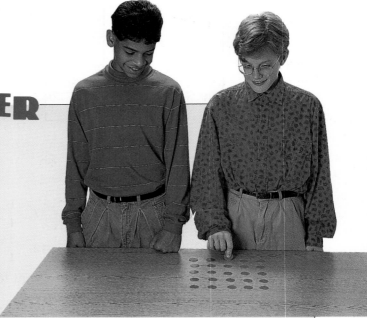

WORK TOGETHER

Building Understanding

What is 20% of 25?

You can use two-color (red and blue) counters to help you model the percent of a number.

How many counters must you turn over so that 20% of the counters are blue?

Talk About It

▶ When you are asked to find part of a number, such as $\frac{1}{2}$ of 30, what operation do you use?

▶ How can you express 20% as a decimal?

▶ How can you express 20% as a fraction?

▶ What is 0.20×25, or $\frac{1}{5} \times 25$?

▶ What is 20% of 25?

▶ Look at the drawing. Which color shows 20%?

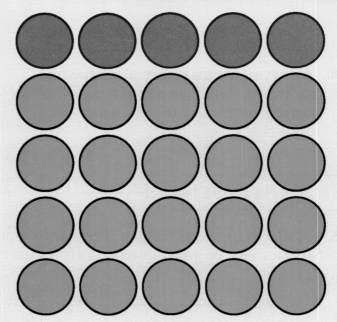

Use two-color counters. Make a model that shows the percent of the number in blue.

a. 10% of 10   **b.** 50% of 20

c. 40% of 65   **d.** 90% of 10

Making the Connection

You can use one of several methods to find a percent of a number.

What is 40% of 85?

Method 1	**Method 2**
Use a ratio in simplest form to name the percent. Then multiply.	Use a decimal to name the percent. Then multiply.
$40\% = \frac{40}{100} = \frac{2}{5}$	$40\% = 0.40$, or 0.4
$\frac{2}{5} \times \frac{85}{1} = \frac{170}{5} = 34$	$\begin{array}{r} 85 \\ \times\ 0.4 \\ \hline 34.0 \end{array}$

Method 3

Use a calculator with a % key.

85 ☒ 40 ☒ | 34. |

So, 40% of 85 is 34.

Checking Understanding

Use a decimal to find the percent of the number.

1. 20% of 55
2. 50% of 200
3. 30% of 40
4. 60% of 400

5. 70% of 120
6. 40% of 40
7. 80% of 200
8. 90% of 150

9. 25% of 140
10. 12% of 165
11. 45% of 90
12. 75% of 144

Use a fraction to find the percent of the number.

13. 10% of 70
14. 50% of 150
15. 25% of 80
16. 75% of 12

17. 25% of 64
18. 90% of 60
19. 80% of 160
20. 45% of 40

Use a calculator to find the percent of the number.

21. 15% of 35
22. 2% of 350
23. 35% of 135
24. 55% of 740

25. 17% of 497
26. 33% of $60
27. 125% of 12
28. 175% of 25

MENTAL MATH
and Percent

You can use benchmarks and mental math to help you find the percent of many numbers.

In Olivia's school 50% of the 440 students polled said their favorite movie was *Dude.* How many students chose *Dude* as their favorite movie?

Benchmarks for Percent

200% means twice as much.

100% is the same as the number.

50% means $\frac{1}{2}$ as much.

25% means $\frac{1}{4}$ as much.

10% means $\frac{1}{10}$ as much.

Talk About It

▶ How can you write 50% as a fraction?

▶ How can you write 50% as a decimal?

▶ Describe two methods you could use to find the answer to the question.

▶ With which method could you find the answer by using mental math?

$50\% = \frac{1}{2}$ ⟶ Multiplying by $\frac{1}{2}$ is the ⟶ $440 \div 2 = 220$
same as dividing by 2.

So, 220 students chose *Dude* as their favorite movie.

More Examples

A. What is 20% of 340?

Think:

10% + 10% = 20%
10% of 340 = 34
34 + 34 = 68

So, 20% of 340 = 68.

B. What is 25% of 400?

Think:

$25\% = \frac{1}{4}$

$400 \div 4 = 100$

So, 25% of 400 = 100.

• How can you find 75% of 400?

• What is 150% of 10?

• What is 200% of 10?

• What is 50% of 10?

Check for Understanding

Tell how you can use benchmarks to find the percent of the number.

1. 25% of 400 **2.** 50% of 100 **3.** 200% of 400 **4.** 30% of 300

Practice

Use mental math to find the percent of the number.

5. 30% of 200 **6.** 5% of 500 **7.** 15% of 500 **8.** 20% of 600

9. 50% of 400 **10.** 10% of 12 **11.** 25% of 800 **12.** 100% of 35

13. 10% of 6 **14.** 25% of 440 **15.** 200% of 100 **16.** 50% of $6.50

17. 75% of $12 **18.** 100% of $9.38 **19.** 10% of $75.45 **20.** 65% of $100

Mixed Applications

21. Carolyn scored 100% on a quiz about movie stars. If 45 questions were on the quiz, how many did she get correct?

22. Of 800 people surveyed, 425 prefer rock theme songs to jazz theme songs in movies. How many prefer jazz theme songs?

23. **Logical Reasoning** Use the information in Exercise 22. What percent of the people do not prefer rock theme songs?

MIXED REVIEW

Find the unit rate.

1. 4 rings for $1.00 **2.** 275 words per 5 min **3.** 285 mi per 15 gal

Tell whether the ratios make a proportion. Write *yes* or *no*.

4. $\frac{1}{5}; \frac{5}{25}$ **5.** $\frac{3}{6}; \frac{2}{5}$ **6.** $\frac{4}{7}; \frac{12}{21}$ **7.** $\frac{35}{45}; \frac{7}{9}$ **8.** $\frac{1}{3}; \frac{3}{16}$

Write as a percent.

9. 0.25 **10.** $\frac{4}{5}$ **11.** $\frac{3}{4}$ **12.** 0.35 **13.** $\frac{3}{10}$

How can you find 110% of a number by using mental math?

WRAP UP...

ESTIMATING PERCENT

Kim reads in the newspaper that the Minte Maxx camera is marked down 9% from the regular price at a local camera shop. If the camera usually sells for $47.99, about how much is the markdown?

Consumers often estimate percents to find a sale price, to compare prices, or to determine how much money to leave as a tip at a restaurant.

$9\% \approx 10\%$ $47.99 is about $50.00. ← Use rounding.

10% of $50.00 = $5.00

Since 9% is rounded to the next ten percent and $47.99 is rounded to the next ten dollars, the estimate is an overestimate.

So, the markdown is about $5.00.

- Suppose the markdown is 12% and the regular price $53.99. If you round to 10% and $50.00, will your estimate be an overestimate or an underestimate?

- Since the markdown is about $5.00, about how much will the camera cost?

Another Example

Karen wants to leave a 15% tip at a restaurant. The bill is $12.34. How much should she leave?

15% is 10% + 5%. $12.34 is about $12.00.

10% of $12.00 = $1.20 ← 0.10 × 12 = 1.2

5% is $\frac{1}{2}$ of 10%, so 5% of $12.00 is $\frac{1}{2} \times$ $1.20 = $0.60.

$1.20 + $0.60 = $1.80

So, Karen should leave about $1.80.

Check for Understanding

Estimate.

1. $12\% \times 111$ **2.** $29\% \times 315$ **3.** $42\% \times 1{,}050$ **4.** $33\frac{1}{3}\% \times 897$ **5.** 50% of 721

Practice

Suppose you know about what 10% of a number is. Tell how you can estimate the given percent.

6. 15%   **7.** 80%   **8.** 20%   **9.** 25%   **10.** 45%

11. 75%   **12.** 40%   **13.** 35%   **14.** 95%   **15.** 12%

Choose the best estimate. Write **a**, **b**, or **c**.

16. 12% of 115
   a. 10% of 100
   b. 20% of 100
   c. 20% of 200

17. 57% of 198
   a. 60% of 150
   b. 60% of 200
   c. 55% of 200

18. 79% of 1,337
   a. 70% of 2,000
   b. 100% of 1,300
   c. 75% of 1,000

19. 28% of 32
   a. 30% of 40
   b. 20% of 35
   c. 30% of 30

20. 19% of 78
   a. 20% of 50
   b. 20% of 80
   c. 20% of 100

21. 82% of $36.85
   a. 80% of $40
   b. 80% of $30
   c. 90% of $40

Tell whether the estimate is an overestimate or an underestimate.

22. 18% of 36 ≈ 8

23. 12% of 124 ≈ 10

24. 98% of 599 ≈ 599

25. 16% of 125 ≈ 25

26. 55% of 700 ≈ 350

27. 25% of 315 ≈ 75

Mixed Applications

28. Reed's advertises 35-mm film for 75% of the regular price of $4.85. About how much is the new price?

29. Fred wants to leave the server at a cafe a 10% tip. If the bill for Fred and his family is $19.85, about how much should he leave?

30. Making Decisions If the price of a poster is 80% of $6 at Store A and 75% of $7 at Store B, where would you get the better buy?

31. Mental Math Sam's Wholesale is having a sale on compact discs. They are marked down 50% below the regular price of $12. What is the sale price of the compact discs?

How can you use the value of 10% of a number to help you estimate other percents of the number?

Jason is making a casserole for an after-the-movie dinner. His recipe calls for 3 tomatoes for every 2 onions, but Jason wants to make more than the recipe yields. How many onions should he use with 15 tomatoes?

Understand
Plan
Solve
Look Back

What strategies can you choose?

You could use one of several strategies. You might *write an equation* in the form of a proportion or *make a table*.

Strategy:

Write an equation.

tomatoes $\longrightarrow \dfrac{3}{2} = \dfrac{15}{n} \longleftarrow$ tomatoes
onions $\longrightarrow$ $\phantom{\dfrac{3}{2}}$ $\phantom{\dfrac{15}{n}}$ $\longleftarrow$ onions

Use cross products to solve.

$3n = 15 \times 2$
$3n = 30$
$n = 10$

Strategy:

Make a table.

You can use multiples of 3 and 2 to extend the table.

Casserole Recipe					
Vegetable	Number Needed				
	× 1	× 2	× 3	× 4	× 5
Tomatoes	3	6	9	12	15
Onions	2	4	6	8	10

So, Jason should use 10 onions with 15 tomatoes.

▶ **LOOK BACK**

What other strategy could you use?

WHAT IF... . . . Jason uses 18 tomatoes? How many onions should he use?

Choose a strategy and solve.

(1) Larry made a scale model of a movie theater, using a scale of 1 in. = 2 ft. The actual length of the theater is 56 ft. What is the length of the model?

(2) Use the information in Exercise 1. Larry's model is three-dimensional. The height of the model is 13 in. What is the actual height of the theater?

(3) Fewer than 300 people attended a movie one Saturday. The next Saturday, about twice as many people attended the movie. If different people attended each Saturday, about how many people attended the movie?

(4) Sue Ann spent the $15 she received on her birthday. Then she bought film for $13 and a flash for $9. She had $3 left. How much money did Sue Ann have before her birthday?

(5) Mr. Sanchez had $\frac{1}{2}$ roll of film left in his camera. He divided it evenly among pictures of his 3 sons. How much of the whole roll of film was used for pictures of each son?

(6) Rita painted the scenery for a play. She used 1 gallon of paint to cover 18 square yards of wall space. How many gallons did she use to cover 54 square yards of wall space?

(7) Mrs. Chen found that a set of camera equipment costs $45.25 at one store and $33.75 at a second store. She needs 12 sets for her class. How much money will she save by buying the equipment at the second store?

(8) Ned wants to buy a $20.00 camera. He plans to save $0.01 the first day. Each day after that he will save double the amount he saved the day before. If he keeps to this plan, how long will it take him to save enough money to buy the $20.00 camera?

WRITER'S CORNER

(9) Write a word problem that can be solved by using two different strategies. Have several classmates solve your word problem. Which strategy was used more often to solve the problem?

Vocabulary Check

Choose a word or words from the box to complete each sentence.

percent
proportion
rate
ratio
scale
unit rate

1. A comparison of two numbers is called a __?__ . *(page 304)*

2. A ratio that compares one quantity to a different quantity is a __?__ . *(page 306)*

3. A number sentence or an equation that states that two ratios are equivalent is a __?__ . *(page 310)*

4. In a __?__ , the second term is 1. *(page 306)*

5. The ratio of the actual size of an object to the size of the object in a drawing is called the __?__ . *(page 315)*

6. The ratio of a number to 100 is called __?__ . *(page 320)*

Concept Check

7. How does finding an equivalent ratio compare with finding an equivalent fraction? *(page 308)*

8. How can you find the percent of a number? *(page 327)*

9. How can you estimate 24% of $79.99? *(page 330)*

Name the items being compared. *(page 304)*

10. Martha drove 5 mi in 3 hr.

11. The gasoline tank of Hal's car holds 17 gal.

12. There are 100 tissues in a box.

Tell how to find the unit rate or unit price. *(page 306)*

13. a dozen oranges for $2.40

14. $21.00 for 15 gal of gasoline

Tell whether the ratios make a proportion. Write *yes* or *no*.
(pages 310, 312)

15. $\frac{2}{5}$; $\frac{5}{15}$

16. $\frac{3}{4}$; $\frac{9}{12}$

17. $\frac{8}{1}$; $\frac{16}{4}$

18. $\frac{2}{26}$; $\frac{4}{50}$

19. $\frac{0.3}{15}$; $\frac{1.2}{60}$

20. $\frac{8}{6}$; $\frac{200}{150}$

Skill Check

Write the ratio in two other ways. *(page 304)*

21. ten to nine

22. $\dfrac{18}{7}$

23. $33:46$

24. five to three

Find the unit rate. *(page 306)*

25. $1.08 a dozen

26. 195 mi per 3 hr

27. 960 words per 12 min

Tell whether the ratios are equivalent. Write *yes* or *no*. *(page 308)*

28. $2:9; 15:45$

29. $\dfrac{7}{27}; \dfrac{21}{81}$

30. $\dfrac{4}{5}; \dfrac{9}{24}$

31. $6:16; 42:112$

Write the cross products. *(page 311)*

32. $\dfrac{10}{c} = \dfrac{5}{10}$

33. $\dfrac{b}{6} = \dfrac{2}{12}$

34. $\dfrac{6}{d} = \dfrac{3}{4}$

35. $\dfrac{1}{7} = \dfrac{x}{5}$

Write the decimal or the fraction as a percent. *(pages 322, 324)*

36. 0.04

37. $\dfrac{11}{20}$

38. $\dfrac{11}{12}$

39. $\dfrac{1}{8}$

40. 1.3

Estimate. *(page 330)*

41. 63% of 196

42. 21% of 27

43. 9% of 81

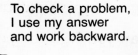

To check a problem, I use my answer and work backward.

Find the percent of the number. *(page 328)*

44. 30% of 30

45. 25% of 44

46. 20% of 15

Problem-Solving Check *(pages 316, 332)*

47. A movie set covers a 20-m by 25-m area of a soundstage. If a scale drawing of the set is 4 cm by 5 cm, what scale was used?

48. Jim used a scale of 1 cm = 0.5 m to make a scale drawing of a stage. If the drawing is 16 cm by 20 cm, what are the actual length and the actual width of the stage?

49. Sue now has 10 theater tickets that cost $18.95 each. If she sold $227.40 worth of tickets yesterday, how many tickets did she have in the beginning?

50. Jill sold 40 more than 6 times as many rolls of film for $2 each as for $4 each. If she sold a total of $144 worth of film, how many rolls of film did Jill sell at each price?

Write the ratio in two other ways.

> Think: A ratio compares two numbers.

1. seven to eleven   **2.** 6:10   **3.** five to four

Find the unit rate.

4. 25 for $10.00   **5.** 24 mi per 2 gal   **6.** 180 words per 3 min

Find the number that makes the ratios equivalent.

7. $1:3 = \blacksquare:9$ **8.** $6:8 = 18:\blacksquare$ **9.** $3:5 = \blacksquare:20$

Write the cross products.

10. $\dfrac{n}{4} = \dfrac{24}{32}$ **11.** $\dfrac{6}{2} = \dfrac{b}{8}$ **12.** $\dfrac{16}{2} = \dfrac{x}{18}$

Write as a percent or as a decimal.

13. 45%   **14.** 0.05   **15.** 350%   **16.** 1.6   **17.** 0.32

Write as a fraction in simplest form or as a percent.

18. 55%   **19.** 35%   **20.** $\dfrac{9}{20}$ **21.** $\dfrac{2}{5}$ **22.** 800%

Estimate.

23. 42% of 109   **24.** 27% of 8,880   **25.** 79% of 175

Find the percent of the number.

26. 50% of 30   **27.** 5% of 20   **28.** 200% of 9   **29.** 75% of 120

Solve.

30. The den in a dollhouse is 1.5 cm long. If the den is a model of a room that is actually 4 m by 5 m, how wide is the den in the dollhouse?

31. Jim made a scale model of his family's garage, using a scale of 1 cm = 10 m. If a window in the garage is actually 1.5 m long, how long is the window in Jim's model?

32. An usher sold 620 programs on Friday, 580 on Saturday, 540 on Sunday, and 500 on Monday. If the pattern continues, how many programs will he sell on Wednesday?

33. Together Shawna and Jane have a collection of 99 rock-and-roll recordings. If Shawna has 20% more recordings than Jane, how many does each girl have?

Teamwork P-R-O-J-E-C-T

Plan a Commercial

Most television commercials are 30 sec to 1 min long.
Work with your teammates to plan a commercial.

Decide

As a team, discuss different products, and decide on a real or make-believe product for your commercial.

Decide on the length of your commercial. Determine the number of frames you will need for filming at 24 frames per second.

Decide on the action in your commercial.

Do

Divide the action into equal parts, and assign each team member a part of the commercial to write.

Describe the action and the roles of the actors. Include in the description the number of frames you will need.

Assemble the parts into one script summary.

Share

Present your summary to other teams. Then watch as other teams present their summaries to you.

Talk About It

What is the difference in the number of frames needed for a 1-min commercial and a 30-sec commercial?

Why do you think commercials are so expensive?

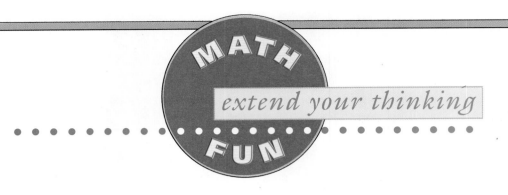

Ratio Concentration

To play this game, you will need an opponent and a deck of 36 cards labeled with equivalent ratios, decimals, and percents. The object of the game is to match more sets of equivalent ratios, decimals, and percents than your opponent. Shuffle the cards and place them facedown in a 6 by 6 rectangular array.

Each player in turn selects three cards in an attempt to find three cards naming an equivalent ratio, decimal, and percent. A player may continue to choose cards as long as the cards match. When a player fails to get a match, the cards are returned facedown to the array and the turn passes to the next player. The player with the most sets of matched cards wins.

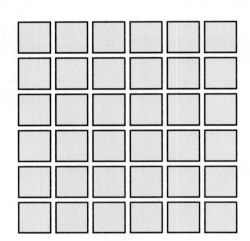

Challenge

Logical Reasoning

In the early days of movies, films were photographed at 16 frames, or pictures, per second. Early movies jumped and jerked on the screen. To improve the picture, movie producers increased the number of frames per second to 24. By what percent did the movie producers speed up the film?

Visual Thinking

Study the geometric figures until you can picture them with your eyes closed. Cover the figures with your hand, and write each of these ratios.

a. circles to triangles

b. triangles to all the figures

c. circles to four-sided figures

d. triangles to four-sided figures

Write the letter of the correct answer.

1. $7\frac{1}{5} + 2\frac{1}{4}$

A. $9\frac{1}{9}$ **B.** $9\frac{2}{9}$

C. $9\frac{9}{20}$ **D.** not here

2. $4\frac{1}{8} - 2\frac{1}{3}$

A. $1\frac{19}{24}$ **B.** 2

C. $2\frac{1}{5}$ **D.** $2\frac{19}{24}$

3. Name the appropriate graph for comparing favorite snacks.

A. bar **B.** line
C. circle **D.** histogram

4. Change to the given unit.
53 cm = ▉ mm

A. 0.53 **B.** 5.3
C. 530 **D.** 5,300

5. $5\frac{1}{7} \times \frac{7}{9}$

A. 4 **B.** $5\frac{1}{9}$

C. $5\frac{7}{63}$ **D.** 6.6

6. $\frac{7}{8} \div \frac{3}{4}$

A. $\frac{1}{8}$ **B.** $1\frac{1}{6}$

C. $1\frac{1}{2}$ **D.** not here

7. Change to the given unit.
240 in. = ▉ ft

A. 12 **B.** 20
C. 80 **D.** 2,880

8. Find one cross product of
$\frac{6}{8} = \frac{96}{x}$.

A. 6×96 **B.** $8x$
C. 6×8 **D.** not here

9. Find the unit rate. $15 for 5

A. $\frac{3}{1}$ **B.** $\frac{5}{1}$

C. $\frac{10}{1}$ **D.** $\frac{15}{1}$

10. What is 20% of 80?

A. 16 **B.** 20

C. 40 **D.** 160

11. A scale model of a house is 40 cm by 60 cm. The scale used was 4 cm = 1 m. What are the actual dimensions of the house?

A. 4 m by 6 m **B.** 10 m by 15 m
C. 16 m by 24 m **D.** 40 m by 60 m

12. The ratio of pens to pencils is 9:3. If 1 pencil is added, how many pens must be added to maintain the same ratio?

A. 1 pen **B.** 3 pens
C. 9 pens **D.** 3:1 pens

CHAPTER

11

GEOMETRY

... Did you know ...

... that without geometric ideas, you would find it difficult to talk about many concepts in nature that you take for granted?

Talk About It

How can you describe the relationship of the shape of one daisy petal to the other daisy petals?

BASIC IDEAS OF GEOMETRY

The North Star is at the end of the Little Dipper's handle. The stars in the Little Dipper suggest points in planes.

These words and symbols will help you describe geometric figures.

The Little Dipper

North Star

Geometric Ideas			
Description	**Example**	**Symbol**	**Read**
A **point** is an exact location.	•P	no symbol	point P
A **line** is a straight path that goes on forever in both directions. It has no endpoints.	A B	$\overleftrightarrow{AB}$ or $\overleftrightarrow{BA}$	line AB or line BA
A **line segment** is part of a line. It has two endpoints.	X Y	$\overline{XY}$ or $\overline{YX}$	line segment XY or line segment YX
A **ray** is part of a line that begins at one endpoint and goes on forever in only one direction.	M N	$\overrightarrow{MN}$	ray MN
An **angle** is formed by two rays that have a common endpoint. The endpoint is the **vertex.**	P M Q	∠PMQ, ∠QMP, or ∠M	angle PMQ, angle QMP, or angle M
A **plane** is a flat surface that goes on forever in all directions.	•G •F •M	no symbol	plane FGM

Talk About It

▶ Look at the picture of the Little Dipper. What geometric figure is suggested by a line from star A, through star B, continuing forever?

▶ Name objects in nature that suggest a line segment and an angle.

▶ How does knowing these geometric terms help you describe what you see?

Check for Understanding

Name the figure suggested by each in the drawing of the Little Dipper on page 342.

1. North Star   **2.** ABC **3.** B of ABC **4.** A to D

Practice

Tell what geometric figure is suggested.

5. sunbeam   **6.** straight road   **7.** tabletop   **8.** fork in the road

Use Figure **A** for Exercises 9–10.

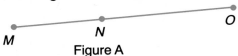

Figure A

9. Name three points.

10. Name three line segments.

Use Figure **B** for Exercises 11–12.

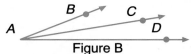

Figure B

11. Name three rays.

12. Name three angles.

Mixed Applications

Use the map for Exercises 13–18. Name the geometric figure suggested by each example.

13. Brian's house

14. a straight path from Brian's house north

15. path from Brian's house to Betty's house

16. Courtney Street intersected by Elm Drive

17. the baseball field

18. Main Street

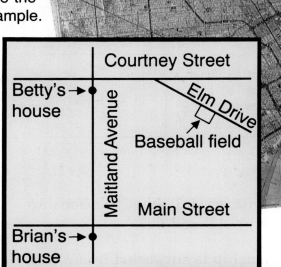

19. **Write a Question** Describe Figure C. Ask a classmate to draw the figure from your description.

20. To get to school, Tisha must climb steps to walk across an overpass. Is her path in one plane? Explain.

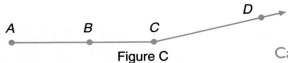

Figure C

Can a line segment be part of a ray?

WRAP UP...

Sometimes we do not think about the fact that points and lines make up much of what we see around us. Lines are everywhere in nature and everyday life, even in these crystals.

These words and symbols will help you describe the relationships among lines.

Description	Example	Symbol	Read
Parallel lines are lines in a plane that are always the same distance apart. They never intersect and have no common points.		$\overleftrightarrow{AB} \parallel \overleftrightarrow{CD}$	Line *AB* is parallel to line *CD*.
Intersecting lines are lines that cross at exactly one point.		no symbol	Line *RS* intersects line *PQ* at point *X*.
Perpendicular lines are lines that intersect to form 90° angles, or right angles.		$\overleftrightarrow{EF} \perp \overleftrightarrow{GH}$	Line *EF* is perpendicular to line *GH*.
Skew lines are not parallel and do not intersect. Skew lines are in different planes.		no symbol	Line *AB* and line *CE* are skew lines.

Talk About It

▶ In the cerussite crystal, what relationship is suggested by $\overline{AB}$ and $\overline{CD}$?

▶ What relationship is suggested by $\overline{EF}$ and $\overline{GH}$?

▶ What relationship is suggested by $\overline{AB}$ and $\overline{EF}$?

▶ What relationship is suggested by $\overline{JK}$ and $\overline{LM}$?

▶ If two lines are in the same plane, must they be either intersecting or parallel? Explain.

Constructing Congruent Line Segments

All line segments of the same length are **congruent.**

Place the compass point on point A. Open the compass to the length of $\overline{AB}$. Without changing the compass opening, move the compass to an endpoint of $\overline{EF}$. Use the compass to measure the length of $\overline{EF}$.

Talk About It

▶ What is the relationship between the length of $\overline{AB}$ and the length of $\overline{EF}$?

_____

You can use a compass and a straightedge to construct congruent line segments. Trace $\overline{AB}$.

Construct a line segment congruent to $\overline{AB}$.

Step 1	**Step 2**	**Step 3**
Draw a ray that is longer than $\overline{AB}$. Label the endpoint C.	Place the compass point on point A. Open the compass to the length of $\overline{AB}$.	Using the same opening, put the compass point on point C. Make a mark where the compass meets the ray. Label it X.
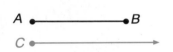	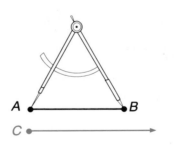	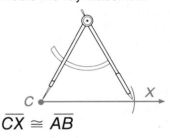 $\overline{CX} \cong \overline{AB}$ $\cong$ means "is congruent to."

Talk About It

▶ In Step 1, why should you draw the ray longer than $\overline{AB}$ instead of shorter than $\overline{AB}$?

▶ Why might you need to know how to construct a pair of congruent line segments?

▶ What are some examples of congruent line segments that you can see in your classroom?

▶ What are some careers in which people must know how to construct geometric figures?

345

Bisecting a Line

You can also use a compass and a straightedge to bisect a line segment. When you bisect a line segment, you divide it into two equal segments. Trace $\overline{RS}$.

Bisect $\overline{RS}$.   R •————————————• S

Step 1	**Step 2**	**Step 3**
Place the compass point on point R. Open the compass to a little more than half the distance from R to S on $\overline{RS}$. Draw an arc through $\overline{RS}$ as shown.	Keep the same compass opening. Place the compass point on point S. Draw an arc as shown. Label the points T and U where the arcs intersect.	Use a straightedge to draw a line from T to U. Label the point P where $\overline{TU}$ intersects $\overline{RS}$.
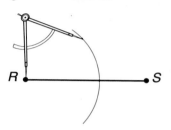	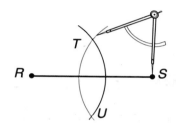	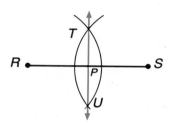 $\overline{TU}$ bisects $\overline{RS}$.

Talk About It

▶ Would you describe $\overline{RS}$ and $\overline{TU}$ as parallel or intersecting?

▶ $\angle TPS$, $\angle SPU$, $\angle UPR$, and $\angle RPT$ are right angles. How many degrees are in each angle?

▶ In addition to intersecting, what other line relationship exists between $\overline{RS}$ and $\overline{TU}$?

Check for Understanding

Look at objects in your classroom. Find examples of these relationships among lines.

1. intersecting   **2.** parallel   **3.** perpendicular   **4.** skew

Tell whether $\overline{XY}$ bisects the line segment. Write *yes* or *no*.

5. 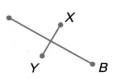   **6.** 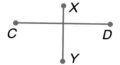   **7.** 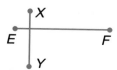   **8.**

346

Practice

Tell what the blue symbol means.

9. $\overrightarrow{CD}$

10. $\angle ABC$

11. $\overline{AB}$

12. $\overrightarrow{AB}$

13. $\overleftrightarrow{EF}$

14. $\overleftrightarrow{KL} \perp \overrightarrow{MN}$

15. $\overline{RS} \parallel \overline{TU}$

16. $\angle D$

17. $\overline{DE} \perp \overline{FG}$

18. $\overrightarrow{PQ} \parallel \overleftrightarrow{RS}$

Use the drawing for Exercises 19–22.
Tell whether the lines are parallel or skew.

19. $\overleftrightarrow{CD}$ and $\overleftrightarrow{GH}$

20. $\overleftrightarrow{BC}$ and $\overleftrightarrow{EH}$

21. $\overleftrightarrow{EF}$ and $\overleftrightarrow{CG}$

22. $\overleftrightarrow{AE}$ and $\overleftrightarrow{GH}$

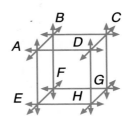

Use a compass and a straightedge.

23. Construct $\overline{AB}$ congruent to $\overline{MN}$.   M •————————————• N

24. Use $\overline{AB}$, which you constructed in Exercise 23. Now, bisect $\overline{AB}$. Label point P where the lines intersect.

25. What is the relationship between $\overline{AP}$ and $\overline{PB}$?

Mixed Applications

Use the drawing for Exercises 26–31. Find two examples of each.

26. angle

27. plane

28. parallel lines

29. perpendicular lines

30. intersecting lines

31. skew lines

32. Dan has striped wallpaper in his dining room. There are 125 stripes along one wall. If 60% of the stripes are blue, how many stripes along the wall are blue?

33. $\overline{AB} \perp \overline{CD}$, $\overline{AB} \perp \overline{EF}$, and $\overline{GH} \perp \overline{CD}$. What is the relationship between $\overline{AB}$ and $\overline{GH}$?

What relationship exists between the two line segments of a bisected line segment?

EXPLORING
Angles

Look at this clock. What geometric shape is suggested by the hands?

An acute angle is less than 90°.

A right angle is 90°.

⌐ means 90° angle.

You can use a clock to help you visualize angles.

An obtuse angle is more than 90° and less than 180°.

Angles are measured in degrees.

A straight angle is 180°.

WORK TOGETHER

Building Understanding

You can use a protractor to measure angles.

1. Trace the angle formed by the hands on the clock and extend the hands.

2. Place the base of the protractor along the hour hand, with the center of the base at the vertex.

3. Read the protractor scale from right to left, starting at 0, to find the measure of the angle.

Talk About It

▶ What is the measure of the angle formed by the clock hands? What type of angle is it?

▶ How could you use a protractor to measure the angle formed by the unshaded area on the clock? What is the measure of this angle?

▶ How could you find the total number of degrees around the clock?

▶ How many degrees are around the clock? Will any circle have the same number of degrees?

Try This

Use a protractor and a straightedge to draw an acute angle, a right angle, and an obtuse angle. Label the rays and write the number of degrees.

Making the Connection

Angles in the same plane sometimes show special relationships with one another, just as lines in the same plane show special relationships.

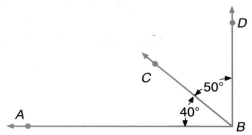

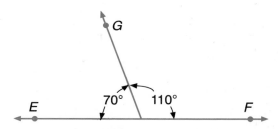

Complementary angles are two angles whose sum is 90°.

Supplementary angles are two angles whose sum is 180°.

Not all supplementary or complementary angles share the same ray. The sum of the measures of ∠JKL and ∠MNO is 90°. So, ∠JKL and ∠MNO are complementary. The sum of the measures of ∠PQR and ∠STU is 180°. So, ∠PQR and ∠STU are supplementary.

Trace the angles and extend the rays.
Find the measure of each angle.

1.

2.

3.

4. Which two angles form complementary angles?

5. Which two angles form supplementary angles?

Checking Understanding

Measure the angles. Write *acute, right,* or *obtuse.*

6.

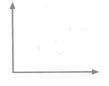

7.

8.

9.

10.

11.

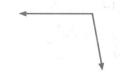

12. Use a protractor to draw two complementary angles.

13. Use a protractor to draw two supplementary angles.

CONSTRUCTING
Congruent Angles

The shapes of the two large peaks suggest congruent angles.

- You know what congruent line segments are. What are congruent angles?

- What other objects in nature suggest congruent angles?

You have used a compass and a straightedge to construct congruent line segments and to bisect a line segment. Now you will learn how to construct congruent angles.

Trace ∠XYZ. Construct an angle congruent to ∠XYZ.

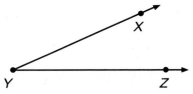

Step 1 Draw $\overrightarrow{MN}$. 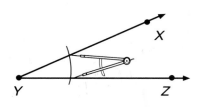	**Step 2** Draw an arc through ∠XYZ. 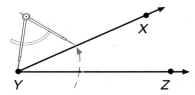	**Step 3** Use the same opening to draw an arc through $\overrightarrow{MN}$. 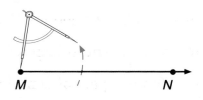
Step 4 Use a compass to measure the arc. 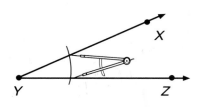	**Step 5** Use the same opening to locate point O. 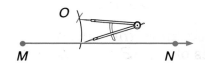	**Step 6** Draw $\overrightarrow{MO}$. 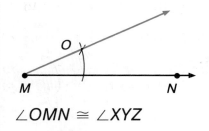 ∠OMN ≅ ∠XYZ

Check for Understanding

Use a protractor to measure each pair of angles. Tell whether the two angles are congruent. Write *yes* or *no.*

1.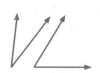

2.

3.

Practice

Use a protractor to measure each pair of angles. Tell whether the angles are congruent. Write *yes* or *no*.

4.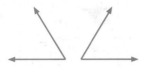

5.

6.

Use a compass and a straightedge.

7. Construct $\angle ABC \cong \angle XYZ$.

8. Construct $\angle DEF \cong \angle UVW$.

9. Construct $\angle GHI \cong \angle RST$.

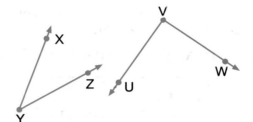

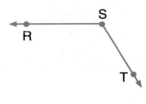

Mixed Applications

Use a protractor and the drawing of the kite for Exercises 10–16.

10. What is the relationship of $\overline{AB}$ to $\overline{CD}$?

11. Name a pair of complementary angles.

12. Name a pair of supplementary angles.

13. Name two acute angles whose vertex is B.

14. Name two obtuse angles.

15. Name one right angle whose vertex is not E.

16. Number Sense How do you know the measure of $\angle CAD$ is the sum of the measures of $\angle CAB$ and $\angle BAD$?

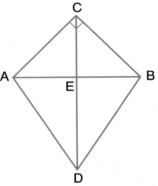

MIXED REVIEW

Tell whether the ratios make a proportion. Write *yes* or *no*.

1. $\dfrac{1}{3}$; $\dfrac{4}{12}$
2. $\dfrac{1}{2}$; $\dfrac{14}{24}$
3. $\dfrac{5}{3}$; $\dfrac{25}{12}$
4. $\dfrac{32}{28}$; $\dfrac{8}{7}$
5. $\dfrac{2}{4}$; $\dfrac{25}{50}$

Tell what the blue symbols mean.

6. $\overline{CD}$
7. $\angle ABC$
8. $\overleftrightarrow{EF} \parallel \overleftrightarrow{GH}$
9. $\overline{JK} \perp \overline{LM}$
10. $\overrightarrow{DE}$

Explain how to construct congruent angles.

WRAP UP...

PROBLEM Solving

Mr. Morris's hobby is mineralogy. He hunts for minerals in his spare time. His collection includes 55% nuggets, 35% crystals, and 10% fibers. How can he present this information in a graph?

▶ **UNDERSTAND**

What are you asked to do?

What facts are you given?

▶ **PLAN**

How will you solve the problem?
You can make a circle graph.

▶ **SOLVE**

How can you carry out your plan?

First you must find the number of degrees represented by each percent. Since there are 360° in a circle, multiply each percent by 360° to find the number of degrees for each type of mineral.

Write each percent as a decimal. Then multiply.

$10\% = 0.10 \rightarrow 0.10 \boxed{\times} 360 \boxed{=}$ | 36. | ← fibers, 36°

$35\% = 0.35 \rightarrow 0.35 \boxed{\times} 360 \boxed{=}$ | 126. | ← crystals, 126°

$55\% = 0.55 \rightarrow 0.55 \boxed{\times} 360 \boxed{=}$ | 198. | ← nuggets, 198°

Make the graph. Use a compass to draw a circle. Draw one radius. Place the center of the base of a protractor on the center of the circle and an edge along the radius.

1. Draw a 36° angle.

2. Place the protractor on the new radius. Draw a 126° angle.

3. Title and label the graph.

• Why did you not have to draw the last angle?

Forms of Minerals

crystals 35%

fibers 10%

nuggets 55%

▶ **LOOK BACK**

What other type of display could you use?

WHAT
IF...

... 25% of the minerals are nuggets, 50% are crystals, and 25% are fibers? How many degrees would be needed to represent each in a circle graph?

352

Apply

1 Dennis determines that when he goes fishing, he catches large fish 5% of the time, medium fish 60%, small fish 25%, and no fish 10% of the time. Make a circle graph showing what happens when Dennis goes fishing.

2 Suppose that the U.S. gross national product (GNP) for this year indicates that industry accounts for 40%, services for 45%, and agriculture for 15%. Make a circle graph showing this GNP.

Mixed Applications

STRATEGIES
- Make a Circle Graph
- Write an Equation
- Work Backward
- Guess and Check

Choose a strategy and solve.
Use the graph for Exercises 3–5.

3 If there are 300 flowers in the garden, how many are zinnias?

4 If there are 100 flowers in the garden, how many are either marigolds or zinnias?

5 If there are 60 tulips in the garden, how many daisies are there?

Julie's Flower Garden

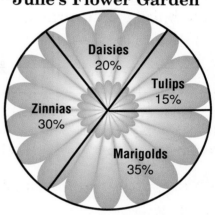

Daisies 20%
Tulips 15%
Zinnias 30%
Marigolds 35%

6 In all, 70 girls and boys belong to Shell-Finders' Club. The ratio of boys to girls is 3:11. How many boys and how many girls are in the club?

7 Maria spent $260 on clam-digging equipment. She sold her first catch for $350. If she spends 10% of her profit on more equipment, how many dollars will she spend?

8 The Simons had $3,000 in savings. They added $460 in June and then spent 25% of the total to buy camping equipment for a family vacation. How much is left in the Simons' savings account?

9 Pete and Dan went fishing with their father. Pete caught 5 more fish than his father. His father caught 2 fewer fish than Dan, who caught 5 fish. How many fish did Pete and his father each catch?

10 Lita divides her rock collection according to shape. She has 12 cone-shaped, 44 spherical, 8 triangular, 32 fan-shaped, and 4 oddly shaped rocks. Make a circle graph for the shapes.

11 Rich is a forester. He planted 25 trees one day and 36 the next day. He gave Tina 62 trees. He gave Sam $\frac{1}{2}$ as many as he planted the second day. If Rich will plant the remaining 46 trees tomorrow, how many trees did he have before he began to plant?

TRIANGLES

The shape of these pines suggests a certain triangle. A **triangle** is a three-sided closed plane figure whose sides are line segments. A triangle can be named by its vertices. The table shows how to classify triangles by sides and by angles.

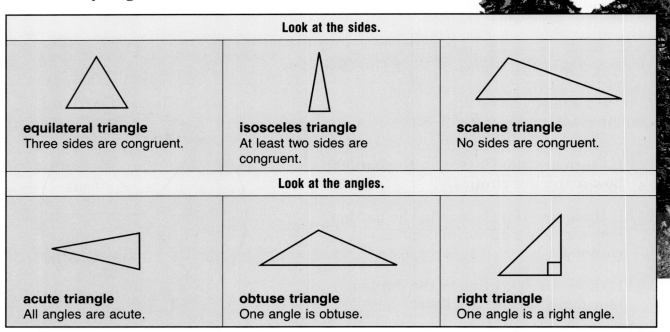

Look at the sides.		
equilateral triangle Three sides are congruent.	**isosceles triangle** At least two sides are congruent.	**scalene triangle** No sides are congruent.

Look at the angles.		
acute triangle All angles are acute.	**obtuse triangle** One angle is obtuse.	**right triangle** One angle is a right angle.

Work Together

Trace three of the triangles in the chart. Extend the sides so that you can use a protractor to measure each angle. Record the measure of each angle. Then label the angles.

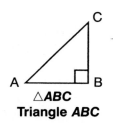

△*ABC*
Triangle *ABC*

Talk About It

▶ What is the sum of the measures of the angles of each of the three triangles you traced and measured?

▶ What conclusion can you draw about the sum of the measures of the angles of a triangle?

▶ The measure of one angle of triangle *ABC* is 90°, and the measure of another angle is 45°. What is the measure of the third angle of △*ABC*?

▶ How can a triangle be both right and isosceles?

▶ Can a triangle be both right and equilateral?

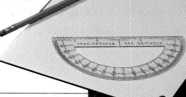

Check for Understanding

Classify the triangle by the sides and then the angles.

1. $9\frac{1}{2}$ 8 2

2. 5 3 5

3. 5 5 5

4. 7 5 5

Practice

Use the drawing for Exercises 5–10. Find and name each type of triangle.

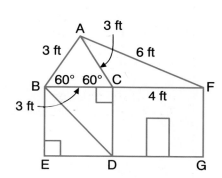

5. equilateral

6. scalene

7. acute

8. right

9. obtuse

10. isosceles

Write the measure of the third angle of the triangle.

11. $100°, 35°, \blacksquare°$

12. $90°, 60°, \blacksquare°$

13. $45°, 45°, \blacksquare°$

14. $25°, 15°, \blacksquare°$

Mixed Applications

15. Don is building a birdhouse of equilateral triangles. The angles of an equilateral triangle are congruent. What is the measure of each angle?

16. Visual Thinking Name several examples where triangles are used in the structure and design of homes and other buildings with which you are familiar.

CHALLENGE

In the triangle, ∠1, ∠2, and ∠3 are **exterior** angles. ∠4 is an **interior** angle. ∠1 is supplementary to ∠4.

17. What is the sum of the measures of the angles of a triangle?

18. What is the measure of ∠4?

19. What is the sum of the measures of supplementary angles?

20. What is the measure of ∠1?

21. What is the sum of the measures of the exterior angles?

Can one of the interior angles of a right triangle be obtuse?

OTHER POLYGONS

A **polygon** is a closed plane figure whose sides are line segments. Polygons are classified by the number of their sides and angles.

Use geoboards and rubber bands to model examples of each type of polygon. Copy your polygons on dot paper.

Just as there are many types of triangles, there are many types of quadrilaterals.

Common Polygons	
Name	**Sides and Angles**
Triangle	3
Quadrilateral	4
Pentagon	5
Hexagon	6
Octagon	8

Quadrilaterals				
parallelogram	**rectangle**	**rhombus**	**square**	**trapezoid**
Opposite sides parallel and congruent	Parallelogram that has four right angles	Parallelogram that has four congruent sides	Rectangle that has four congruent sides	Only two sides parallel

Use geoboards and rubber bands to model examples of each type of quadrilateral. Copy them on dot paper.

A **diagonal** is a line segment that joins two vertices (plural) of a polygon but is not a side.

A **regular polygon** has all sides congruent and all angles congruent.

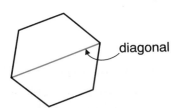

Regular Hexagon

diagonal

Talk About It

▶ Look at the examples of quadrilaterals on your dot paper. If you draw one diagonal in each, what new shapes will you make?

▶ Show how you can use a diagonal to divide a pentagon into a square and a triangle.

▶ Use a geoboard and a rubber band to model a quadrilateral with no sides equal. Is the quadrilateral a regular polygon? What new shapes will a diagonal create?

▶ What kind of triangle can be made by drawing one diagonal of a trapezoid?

Check for Understanding

Name the new figures formed by the diagonal $\overline{AD}$.

1.

2.

3.

4.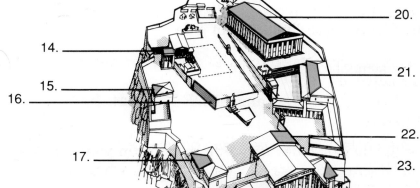

Practice

Name the quadrilateral.

5. 4 right angles and 4 congruent sides

6. 2 sides parallel, 2 sides not parallel

7. opposite sides congruent and parallel

8. 4 right angles and 2 congruent sides

9. 4 congruent sides

10. right angles, opposite sides congruent

Tell whether the figure is a regular or an irregular polygon.

11.

12.

13.

Look at the drawing of the ancient Greek Acropolis. Each number points to a different triangle or quadrilateral. Name the figure.

14. ____
15. ____
16. ____
17. ____
18. ____
19. ____
20.
21.
22.
23.

Mixed Applications

24. Logical Reasoning Is a square also a quadrilateral? a rectangle? a polygon? a parallelogram?

25. Look at the quilt pattern. What is the ratio of triangles to squares?

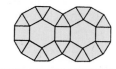

Name 3 quadrilaterals that are types of parallelograms.

More Practice, Lesson 11.7, page H76

357

REVIEW AND MAINTENANCE

1. When Tom goes for walks in the desert, he applies 10 mL of sunscreen every 30 min. If he used 35 mL of sunscreen today, how many hours did he walk?

2. Sue mixed 4 oz of strawberries with 8 oz of yogurt. She added 2 oz of banana slices. How much yogurt must she add to keep the ratio of fruit to yogurt 1 to 2?

3. A circle graph shows stamps in a collection. It shows 144° for animal stamps, 108° for flowers, and 54° each for ships and for airplanes. What percent of each type of stamp is in the collection?

To solve Exercise 3, I need to know the number of degrees in a circle.

Write as a percent or as a decimal.

4. 0.81   5. 0.2   6. 1.52   7. 18%   8. 108%

Write as a percent or as a fraction in simplest form.

9. $\frac{1}{4}$ 10. $\frac{7}{10}$ 11. 12%   12. $\frac{3}{8}$ 13. 35%

Estimate.

14. 53% of 110   15. 29% of 280   16. 81% of 27   17. 62% of 112

Find the percent of the number.

18. 30% of 30   19. 10% of 80   20. 6% of 20   21. 200% of 50

Write the symbol for each figure.

22. ray *AB*   23. angle *CDE*   24. line *FG*   25. triangle *HIJ*

Name the angle. Write *acute*, *right*, *obtuse*, or *straight*.

26. 110°   27. 90°   28. 25°   29. 180°   30. 91°

Name the figure.

31. 3 congruent sides, 3 congruent angles

32. one of 3 angles obtuse

33. none of 3 sides congruent

34. only 2 of 4 sides parallel

35. parallelogram with 4 right angles

36. rectangle with 4 congruent sides

Spotlight ON PROBLEM SOLVING

Prioritize the Information

When you plan a solution to a problem, it is important to follow the directions provided. When you do this, you often **prioritize,** or order, the information according to importance.

Use paper and a ruler. Follow the directions for making a birdhouse in the order given.

1. Draw five 8-in. squares. Label the squares *front, back, side 1, side 2,* and *floor.*

2. Draw an entrance hole centered $2\frac{1}{2}$ in. from the top of the square labeled *front.* Mark a point for a perch $1\frac{1}{2}$ in. below the entrance.

3. Draw a 9-in. square. Label it *roof.*

Talk About It

Work with a classmate to answer the questions. Be prepared to discuss your responses with the class.

a. Are the directions clear? If not, explain why.

b. Are the directions given in order of importance? How would you change the order of the directions?

c. Which direction is the most difficult to follow?

d. What shapes are used to construct the birdhouse?

Apply   Write a prioritized list of directions.

1. Find 150% of $50.

2. Solve. $\frac{2}{3} \div \frac{4}{5}$

3. Describe how to draw Figure A.

4. Describe how to draw Figure B.

Figure A

Figure B

SIMILAR AND CONGRUENT FIGURES

These photos show different sizes of the same image, Pike's Peak. Are the images similar or congruent?

Congruent figures have the same size and shape. **Similar** figures have the same shape. Two shapes that are congruent are also similar. However, two similar shapes may not be congruent.

Since the images are the same shape but not the same size, they are similar but not congruent.

● Think of the relationship of any one circle to any other circle. Are the circles similar or congruent?

Work Together

Discover the relationship among the sides and among the angles of similar polygons.

1. Draw any polygon. Label it *A*.

2. Make a transparency of *A*. Show it on a wall by using an overhead projector. Trace the image on a sheet of paper. Label the tracing *B*.

3. Use a ruler to measure the length of the sides and a protractor to measure the angles of polygons *A* and *B*.

Talk About It

▶ Do you think polygons *A* and *B* are similar? Why?

▶ Are the sides of polygon *A* congruent to the sides of polygon *B*? Are the angles of polygon *A* congruent to the angles of polygon *B*?

▶ What conclusion can you draw about similar polygons?

▶ Is a square a regular polygon? How do you know?

▶ Are all squares congruent? similar? How do you know?

▶ Are all regular polygons that have the same number of sides congruent? How do you know?

▶ What conclusions can you draw about regular polygons that have the same number of sides?

Check for Understanding

Name the figure.

1.

2.

3.

4.

Practice

Complete the table by naming the type of solid figure.

	Type of Solid Figure	Number of Bases and Faces	Number of Edges	Number of Vertices
5.	■	2 square bases 4 square faces	12	8
6.	■	1 base 3 other faces	6	4
7.	■	2 bases	none	none
8.	■	2 bases 5 other faces	15	10
9.	■	2 bases 6 other faces	18	12
10.	■	2 rectangular bases 4 other faces	12	8

Mixed Applications

11. Della has 30 pieces of igneous rock in her collection. If 60% of her collection is igneous rock, how many rocks does she have in her collection?

12. **Logical Reasoning** Why do you think contractors choose materials in the shape of prisms rather than pyramids to build walls?

MIXED REVIEW

Write the ratio. Then find the unit rate or unit price.

1. $12 for 3

2. 90 per 2 min

3. $24 a dozen

4. 420 mi per 12 gal

Why is food stored in cans instead of cone-shaped containers?

WRAP UP...

EXPLORING

Stretching, Shrinking, and Twisting

What would happen if you drew a square on a piece of elastic and then stretched the elastic? What would the square look like?

In this lesson, you will explore what happens when you change the shape of a figure.

WORK TOGETHER

Building Understanding

Use a geoboard, a ruler, and rubber bands.

1. Place a rubber band on the center peg of the top row of the geoboard. Loop the rubber band around the second and fourth pegs of the fourth row of the geoboard.

2. Measure the length of each side of the triangle.

3. Now stretch the triangle by moving the rubber band from the fourth row to the first and last pegs of the fifth row.

4. Measure the length of each side of the stretched triangle.

5. Now shrink the triangle by moving the rubber band from the last row to the second and fourth pegs of the third row.

6. Measure the length of each side of this reduced triangle.

Talk About It

▶ How is the stretched triangle the same as the original triangle? How is it different?

▶ How is the reduced triangle the same as the original triangle? How is it different?

▶ Suppose you drew a square on a balloon and then blew up the balloon. What would happen to the square?

▶ Suppose you drew a circle on an inflated balloon and then let out the air. What would happen to the circle?

Making the Connection

Twisting is a more complex way to change the shape of a figure than stretching or shrinking. Cut newspaper into three strips that are each 3 in. wide by 18 in. long.

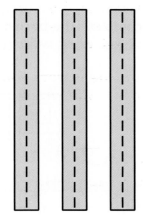

Tape the ends of one strip together, making a loop. Draw a line down the center of the outside surface.

Twist the ends of another strip one time and then tape them together, making a second loop. Draw a line down the center of the outside surface.

1. How does the line on the second loop differ from the line on the first loop?

Cut along the center line of each loop.

2. What happens to the first loop? the second loop?

Twist the ends of the last strip two times and then tape them together, making a third loop. Draw a line down the center of the outside surface.

3. Is the line on the third loop like the line on the first loop or the line on the second loop?

Cut along the center line of the third loop.

4. What happens to the third loop?

5. A conveyor belt is one example of twisting rectangles. Where are conveyor belts used? You may want to use an encyclopedia.

Checking Understanding

Use a geoboard and rubber bands. Begin with a 3-by-3 square. Make changes as directed. Then name the new shape.

6. Stretch both bases the same amount.

7. Stretch both ends of one base the same amount.

8. Shrink one base to a point.

9. Move one base to the left or right without stretching or shrinking it.

Patricia made a painting of a house. She wanted to add a
border with a repeated geometric design. She drew a simple
design and then used translations, reflections, and rotations to
complete the border. She has finished eight images in the
series. What will be the ninth image?

▶ **UNDERSTAND**

What are you asked to find?

What information are you given?

▶ **PLAN**

How will you solve the problem?
You must *find the pattern* in the series of images.

▶ **SOLVE**

How will you carry out your plan?

You can copy and number the images and then
compare each image to the one before.

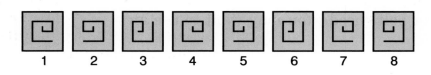

| 1. original design | 3. reflection/rotation | 5. reflection | 7. rotation |
| 2. reflection | 4. rotation | 6. reflection/rotation | 8. reflection |

The pattern is reflection, rotation, rotation.
The eighth image is a reflection.

So, the ninth image in the series will be a rotation.

▶ **LOOK BACK**

What other strategy
could you use?

 **WHAT** *IF...*   . . . you are asked to find the twelfth
image? What will be your answer?

370

Apply

1 Monty watches birds daily. Monday he saw 2 wrens, Tuesday he saw 5 wrens, Wednesday he saw 3 wrens, Thursday he saw 6 wrens, and Friday he saw 4 wrens. If the pattern continues, how many wrens will he see Sunday?

2 Kay is using black tiles and gray tiles to cover her floor. If the pattern she uses is B, G, B, B, G, B, B, G, B, B, what will be the color of the twentieth tile?

Mixed Applications	STRATEGIES	• Write an Equation • Find a Pattern • Work Backward • Draw a Diagram

Choose a strategy and solve.

3 A triangular prism has 6 vertices. A rectangular prism has 8. How many vertices are there in a 12-sided prism?

4 A certain pyramid has 9 faces, including its base. What is the shape of the pyramid's base?

5 Jane buys 5 gal of gasoline to travel 135 mi. Sally's car uses gasoline at the same rate. How much gasoline must Sally buy to take a 675-mi trip to the mountains?

6 Rangers found that $\frac{3}{4}$ of the giraffes in an African animal preserve stay in one area. What percent of the giraffes do not stay in that area?

7 Paul made a flower bed in the shape of an equilateral triangle. Then he divided the triangle, using all possible lines of symmetry. If he plants 1 rose in each of the newly formed triangles, how many roses will he need?

8 Mrs. Smith went to a nursery, where she spent $5.30 for pansies, $3.98 for daisies, $6.75 for begonias, and $11.50 for geraniums. If she had $22.47 when she returned home, how much money did she take with her when she went to the nursery?

9 Don sends messages to Greg, using a secret code: A=2, B=3, C=6, D=8, E=9, F=12, G=14, H=15, I=18, and J=20. If the pattern continues, how would Don use the code to write the word *school*?

10 Carrie's aunt sent her some samples of moon rocks. Carrie gave half to her brother and divided the rest equally among herself and 2 friends. She has 6 rocks left. How many rocks did her aunt send?

WRITER'S CORNER

11 Write a problem that can be solved by finding and extending the pattern shown.

More Practice, Lesson 11.13, page H77

Vocabulary Check

Choose a word or words from the box to complete each sentence.

congruent
diagonal
isosceles
obtuse
perpendicular
plane
polygon
ray
rotational
similar
skew

1. A part of a line that begins at one endpoint and goes on forever in one direction is called a(n) __?__. *(page 342)*
   Ray

2. A flat surface that goes on forever in all directions is a(n) __?__. *(page 342)*
   Plane

3. An angle that is more than 90° but less than 180° is __?__. *(page 348)*
   obtuse

4. Two lines that intersect to form right angles are __?__ lines. *(page 344)*
   Perpendicular

5. A closed plane figure whose sides are line segments is a(n) __?__. *(page 356)*
   Polygon

6. Figures with the same size and shape are __?__. Figures with the same shape are __?__. *(page 360)* *congruent*
   similar

7. A triangle that has two congruent sides is a(n) __?__ triangle. *(page 354)*
   isosceles

8. Lines that are in different planes, are not parallel, and do not intersect are __?__ lines. *(page 344)*
   skew

9. A line segment that joins two vertices of a polygon but is not a side is called a(n) __?__. *(page 356)*
   diagonal

10. If a figure can be turned less than 360° around a point and still match the original, it has __?__ symmetry. *(page 362)*
    rotational

Think: What is the sum of the measures of two supplementary angles?

Concept Check

11. Can each of two supplementary angles be acute? Why or why not? *(page 349)*

12. Why is a trapezoid not a parallelogram? *(page 356)*

13. If two triangles are similar, are their angles congruent? How do you know? *(page 360)*

14. The sum of the measures of all the angles of a triangle is __?__°. *(page 354)*

Skill Check

Identify the geometric shape. Use Figure A for Exercises 15–20.
(pages 342, 344)

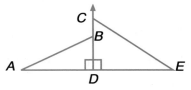

Figure A

15. $\overline{BD}$ **16.** $\overrightarrow{DC}$ **17.** $\overline{AB}$ and $\overline{CD}$

18. $\angle\,ABD$ **19.** $\triangle\,ABD$ **20.** $\angle\,ADB$

Use a compass and a straightedge. Use Figure B for
Exercises 21–22. *(pages 345, 350)*

Figure B

21. Construct $\overline{AB} \cong \overline{YZ}$.   **22.** Construct $\angle\,CAB \approx \angle\,XYZ$.

Classify the triangle by the sides and by the angles. *(page 354)*

23.

24.

25.

Name the polygon. *(page 356)*

26. 6 sides, 6 angles   **27.** 4 sides, 4 angles   **28.** parallelogram with 4 congruent sides

Tell whether the second figure is a translation, rotation, or
reflection. *(page 364)*

29.   **30.**   **31.**

32. Name the solid figure with one hexagonal base. *(page 366)*

Problem-Solving Check *(pages 352, 370)*

33. A circle graph shows the membership of the Save-the-Whales Club. A 288° section shows members who have paid their dues. What percent have paid their dues?

34. Make a circle graph to show that the membership of a recycling club is 45% men, 30% women, 10% boys, and 15% girls.

35. Four hikers reached camp on Day 1, 6 on Day 2, 10 on Day 3, 12 on Day 4, 16 on Day 5, and 18 on Day 6. If the pattern continues, how many hikers will reach camp on Day 7?

36. Dan drove 2 mi Monday, 4 mi Tuesday, 8 mi Wednesday, 16 mi Thursday, and 32 mi Friday. If the pattern continues, how far will he drive next Tuesday?

CHAPTER TEST

Tell whether the angle is acute, right, or obtuse.

1. 60°   **2.** 35°   **3.** 120°   **4.** 90°   **5.** 55°

Identify the type of triangle by the sides and angles.

6.   **7.**   **8.**   **9.**   **10.**

Name the polygon.

11. 5 sides, 5 angles   **12.** 4 sides, opposite sides parallel   **13.** 3 sides congruent, 3 angles congruent

Tell whether the figures are similar or congruent.

14.   **15.**   **16.**

Tell whether the second figure is a translation, rotation, or reflection.

A reflection is what I see in a mirror.

17.   **18.**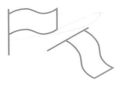

Name the type of solid figure.

19. 1 base, 3 faces   **20.** 2 bases, 5 faces   **21.** 2 round bases

Solve.

22. Of the pets in a neighborhood, 50% are dogs, 30% cats, 15% birds, and 5% other. Make a circle graph to show the data.

23. In a circle graph of night-time weather for a month, 216° shows the number of clear nights. What percent of the nights were clear?

24. The order of four shapes in a pattern is square, triangle, hexagon, and octagon. If this pattern continues, what will be the fifteenth shape?

25. The word *pop* can be reflected to spell *bob*. If you reflect the word *pop* five times, will it spell *pop* or *bob*?

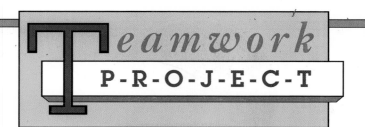
Three-Dimensional Figures

The patterns make a prism, a cylinder, a cone, and a pyramid.

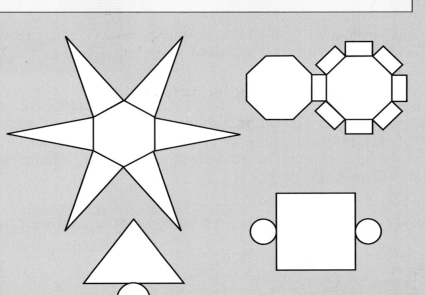

Decide

As a team, discuss which pattern makes each figure.

Each team member should choose one figure to make.

Brainstorm ways to build each figure from objects such as toothpicks or straws and connectors such as gumdrops or clay.

Do

Build the figure. Do not use an object that is already the shape you need.

Make sure the figures that you build have the same properties as the solid shapes you have learned about.

Share

Show the figure and explain its properties to your teammates.

Talk About It

▇ **Are some figures easier to build than others? Which ones?**

▇ **How did building the figure make you more aware of the shapes of everyday objects?**

The Golden Ratio

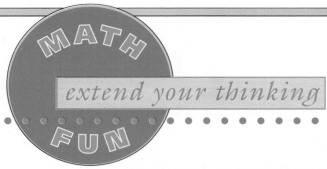

Architects and artists in ancient Greece discovered that some rectangles are more pleasing to the eye than others. The ratio of the sides of the pleasing rectangles is called the Golden Ratio. This Ratio is about $1:1\frac{1}{2}$ or, more precisely, 1:1.6.

1 The ancient Parthenon still stands in Athens, Greece. The width is about 101 feet, and the height is about 60 feet. Is the Parthenon an example of the Golden Ratio?

2 Examine these common rectangular objects. Measure the length and the width of each object. Which items are examples of the Golden Ratio?

a. television   **b.** license plate
c. American flag   **d.** window
e. framed artwork   **f.** sign on building

Challenge

—Logical Thinking—

Drawing one straight line across a circle creates two regions, or parts. Drawing two straight lines across a circle creates three or four regions.

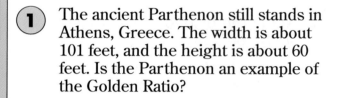

Draw three straight lines across a circle to create the following.

   a. four regions   b. five regions
   c. six regions   d. seven regions

—Number Puzzles—

What is this creature? Solve the code to find the answer.

For each geometric symbol or shape, substitute the first letter in its name (*t* for triangle, for example). Each number stands for a letter's place in the alphabet ($a = 1$, $b = 2$, $c = 3$, and so on).

Write the letter of the correct answer.

1. $2\frac{1}{2} \times 1\frac{3}{10}$

   A. $2\frac{3}{20}$ **B.** $3\frac{1}{4}$

   C. 3.3   **D.** not here

2. $2\frac{1}{12} \div 1\frac{1}{4}$

   A. $\frac{3}{5}$ **B.** 0.6

   C. $1\frac{2}{3}$ **D.** $2\frac{1}{3}$

3. Change to the given unit.
2.09 g = ▪ mg

   A. 0.00209   **B.** 20.9
   C. 209   **D.** 2,090

4. Change to the given unit.
3,520 yd = ▪ mi

   A. 1   **B.** 2
   C. 3   **D.** not here

5. Find the missing number.
$$\frac{3}{5} = \frac{18}{\blacksquare}$$

   A. 6   **B.** 11
   C. 30   **D.** 90

6. Name the triangle with angles of 45°, 60°, and 75°.

   A. equilateral   **B.** isosceles
   C. obtuse   **D.** not here

7. What is 12% of 80?

   A. 0.96   **B.** 9.6
   C. 96   **D.** 960

8. Name the figure that connects two endpoints.

   A. angle   **B.** line segment
   C. ray   **D.** plane

9. Describe lines that never meet.

   A. bisect   **B.** parallel
   C. intersect   **D.** perpendicular

10. Which figure has two circular bases?

   A. cone   **B.** cube
   C. pyramid   **D.** cylinder

11. A circle graph shows that a cereal contains 5% fiber, 25% whey, and 70% oat bran. What is the measure of the largest angle in the graph?

   A. 75°   **B.** 126°
   C. 252°   **D.** 324°

12. A design has two trapezoids followed by one circle, three pentagons, and one rhombus. The design is then repeated. What is the twelfth shape in the design?

   A. circle   **B.** pentagon
   C. rhombus   **D.** trapezoid

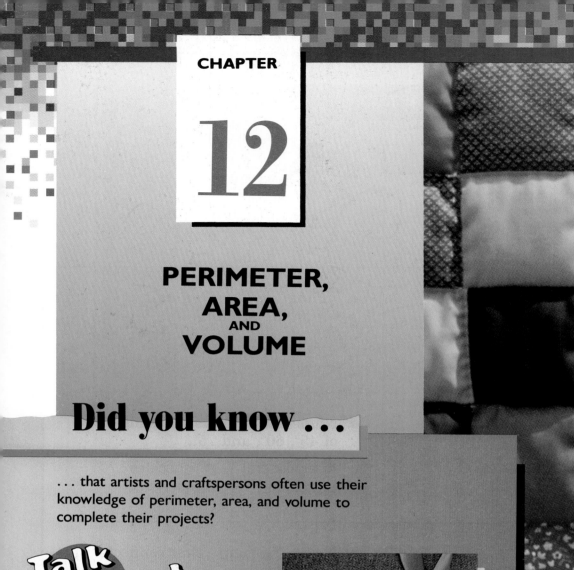

CHAPTER

12

PERIMETER, AREA, AND VOLUME

Did you know . . .

. . . that artists and craftspersons often use their knowledge of perimeter, area, and volume to complete their projects?

Talk About It

How can you find the number of inches of ribbon you would need to wrap one time around the outside of the quilt?

Zack paced off two display booths at a craft fair. For a jewelry booth, he walked 9, 12, and 15 paces. For a leather-crafts booth, he walked 16 paces for each of four sides. How many paces did Zack walk for each booth?

Perimeter (P) is the distance around a polygon. To determine the perimeter, find the sum of the lengths of the sides.

You can write a formula to find $$P = a + b + c$$ the perimeter of the jewelry booth.

- If you use the variable s for the length of each of the four sides, what formula can you write to find the perimeter of the leather-crafts booth?

Jewelry booth | Leather-crafts booth
$P = 9 + 12 + 15$ | $P = 16 + 16 + 16 + 16$
$P = 36$ paces | $P = 64$ paces

So, Zack walked 36 paces for the jewelry booth and 64 paces for the leather-crafts booth.

Talk About It

▶ Would the perimeter of the booths be different if someone other than Zack paced the distances? Why?

▶ How can you determine the actual perimeter of the jewelry and the leather-crafts booths?

▶ If you use the variable s for the length of each of the five sides, what formula can you write to find the perimeter of a regular pentagon?

▶ When might you need to find the perimeter of an object?

Check for Understanding

Write a formula for finding the perimeter of the figure.

1.

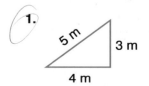

5 m 3 m 4 m

2.

4 in. 4 in. 4 in. 4 in. 4 in.

3.

7 ft 7 ft 7 ft 7 ft 7 ft 7 ft

4.

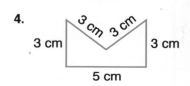

3 cm 3 cm 3 cm 3 cm 5 cm

Practice

Estimate the perimeter of the polygon. Round to the nearest whole number.

5.

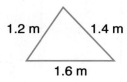

1.2 m 1.4 m 1.6 m

6.

0.75 in. 1.26 in.

7.

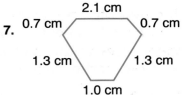

2.1 cm 0.7 cm 0.7 cm 1.3 cm 1.3 cm 1.0 cm

Find the perimeter of the polygon.

8.

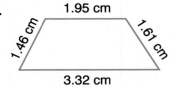

1.95 cm 1.46 cm 1.61 cm 3.32 cm

9.

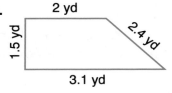

2 yd 1.5 yd 2.4 yd 3.1 yd

10.

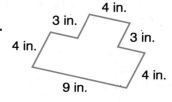

4 in. 3 in. 3 in. 4 in. 4 in. 9 in.

11.

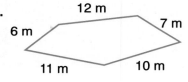

12 m 6 m 7 m 11 m 10 m

12.

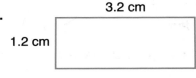

3.2 cm 1.2 cm

13.

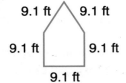

9.1 ft 9.1 ft 9.1 ft 9.1 ft 9.1 ft

Mixed Applications

14. When Sue leaves home, she drives 6 km, turns right, and drives 8 km more to a crafts fair. Her route home is a straight road that is 4 km shorter than her route to the crafts fair. How long is her round trip?

15. Logical Reasoning If a square picture frame measures 1 ft on each side, would the perimeter of the frame be more than a yard?

CHALLENGE

---

16. The perimeter of the regular hexagon in the figure is 42 cm. The star is made from two equilateral triangles whose sides are 21 cm each. What is the perimeter of the star?

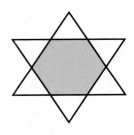

Can you use the formula $P = 5s$ to find the perimeter of an irregular pentagon? Explain.

WRAP UP...

AREA OF RECTANGLES

Phil is making a mosaic tile design with square centimeter tiles. Part of his design is in the shape of a rectangle that is 4 cm wide and 6 cm long. What is the area of the rectangle?

Area is the number of square units needed to cover a surface. Square units are shown as m², ft², and so on.

Look at the rectangle outlined on the graph paper.

• How many square units are needed to cover the rectangle?

So, the area of the rectangle is 24 cm².

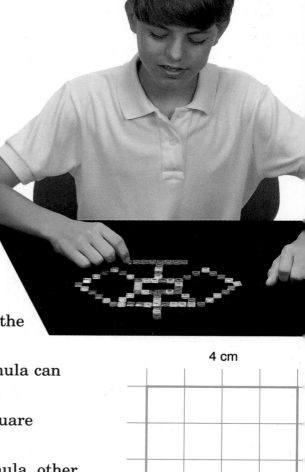

4 cm

6 cm

Talk About It

▶ What is the length of the rectangle? the width?

▶ What is the relationship between the length and the width of the rectangle and its area?

▶ If you use l for length and w for width, what formula can you write to find the area, A, of a rectangle?

▶ A square is a special rectangle. What makes a square special?

▶ If you use s for the length of each side, what formula, other than $A = lw$, can you write to find the area of a square?

▶ When might you or your family need to find the area of an object?

Use your formulas to find the area of rectangles. You can check your answers by using graph paper to count the square units.

Examples

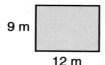

9 m

12 m

A. $A = lw$ ← length × width
$= 12 \text{ m} \times 9 \text{ m}$
$= 108 \text{ m}^2$

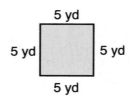

5 yd

5 yd   5 yd

5 yd

B. $A = s^2$ ← side squared
$= 5 \text{ yd} \times 5 \text{ yd}$
$= 25 \text{ yd}^2$

Checking for Understanding

Write a formula for finding the area of the figure.

1.
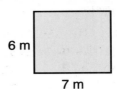
5 in.

5 in.

2.
10 ft

17 ft

3.
6 m

7 m

4.
12 cm

12 cm

Practice

Find the area.

5.
7 ft

15 ft

6.
12 yd

12 yd

7.
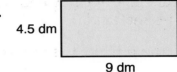
4.5 dm

9 dm

8.
3.1 cm

3.1 cm

9.
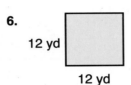
1.4 in.

5.9 in.

10.
8 m

6.2 m

11. $l = 9$ ft, $w = 3$ ft

12. $l = 18$ cm, $w = 8$ cm

13. $l = 25$ yd, $w = 40$ yd

14. $l = 162$ m, $w = 95$ m

15. $l = 20$ cm, $w = 20$ cm

16. $l = 8$ m, $w = 0.12$ m

Mixed Applications

17. A square box lid has a length and width of 4 cm. What is the area of the box lid?

18. The area of a square table is 25 ft^2. What is the perimeter?

19. Sally and Todd have 26 art prints. If Sally has 4 more than Todd, how many prints does Todd have?

20. A rectangle has a width of 3 cm. The length is 3 less than 4 times the width. What is the area?

21. The width of a rectangle is x. The length is $x + 5$. If the perimeter is 18 yd, what are the length and the width of the rectangle?

22. **Number Sense** The area of a rectangle is 20 cm^2. If the lengths of the sides are whole numbers, what lengths and widths could they be?

If you know the area of a square, how can you find the length of the sides?

Kirsten wants to cover this parallelogram with decorative foil. How much decorative foil does she need?

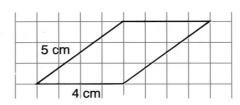

Copy the parallelogram on graph paper and draw a dotted line as shown. Cut along the line.

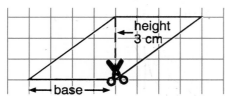

Slide the cutting across the original figure as shown. Label the new figure ABCD.

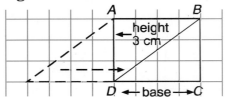

- What new shapes does the dotted line create?

- What new shape does the translation create?

Talk About It

▶ What is the line relationship between $\overline{AD}$ or $\overline{BC}$ and the base of the parallelogram?

▶ How can you find the area of rectangle ABCD?

▶ Is the area of the parallelogram the same as the area of rectangle ABCD? How do you know?

▶ If you use b for the base and h for the height, what formula can you write to find the area of the parallelogram?

$A = bh$ ← base times height

$A = 4 \times 3 = 12$ So, Kirsten needs 12 cm² of foil.

> You cut the parallelogram into two congruent triangles.

What is the area of △ BCD?

- How does the area of triangle BCD compare with the area of parallelogram ABCD? What formula can you write for the area of the triangle?

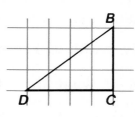

$A = \frac{1}{2}bh$ $\frac{1}{2} \times 4 \times 3 = 6$ The area of △ BCD is 6 cm².

The height is measured on a segment perpendicular to the base.

- What is the height of △ EFG?

Checking for Understanding

Write a formula for finding the area of the figure.

1.
9 cm
12 cm

2.
3 in.   5 in.
4 in.

3.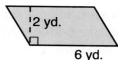
6 m
7 m

4.
2 yd.
6 yd.

Practice

Find the area of the parallelogram.

5. $b = 2\,\text{cm}, h = 3\,\text{cm}$

6. $b = 12\,\text{ft}, h = 8\,\text{ft}$

7. $b = 1.5\,\text{m}, h = 2.6\,\text{m}$

8.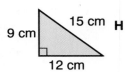
2 cm
4 cm

9.
$4\frac{1}{2}$ ft   6 ft

10.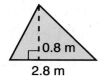
3.3 m
4.2 m

Find the area of the triangle.

11. $b = 10\,\text{yd}, h = 7\,\text{yd}$

12. $b = 82\,\text{m}, h = 4.8\,\text{m}$

13. $b = 6\,\text{in.}, h = 20\,\text{in.}$

14.
9 cm   15 cm   **H**
12 cm

15.
6 in.   2.4 in.

16.
0.8 m
2.8 m

Mixed Applications

17. A baseball field is divided into two congruent triangles. If the area of one triangle is 50 m², what is the area of the baseball field?

18. **Logical Reasoning** You wrote a formula for finding the area of a parallelogram by making a rectangle. Into what 2 familiar figures could you divide a trapezoid to find its area?

MIXED REVIEW

Find the sum or difference.

1. $34.23 - 9.07$

2. $12\frac{5}{9} + 6\frac{2}{3}$

3. $2.073 + 0.909$

4. $8\frac{1}{2} - 6\frac{5}{6}$

5. $45.07 + 12.909$

6. $121 - 12.35$

7. $3.5 + 1.059$

8. $30 - 27.989$

How can you find the area of a rhombus?

WRAP UP...

Nancy is tiling a rectangular tabletop and a square bench with imported tile. The tabletop has a width of 18 in. and a length of 22 in. The sides of the bench are each 20 in. long. How many square inches of tile will she need?

Using a formula is a common problem-solving strategy. You can use the formulas you wrote in previous lessons to help you solve problems.

▶ UNDERSTAND

What are you asked to find?

What information are you given?

▶ PLAN

What strategy can you use?

Since you need to find the area of two figures, you can use the formulas for finding the area of a rectangle and the area of a square. Then add the two areas.

▶ SOLVE

How can you carry out your plan?

Use the formulas for finding the area of a rectangle and the area of a square.

rectangle: $A = lw$ square: $A = s^2$
$\qquad A = 22 \times 18$ $\qquad\qquad A = 20^2$
$\qquad A = 396$ $\qquad\qquad\quad A = 400$

$$396 + 400 = 796$$

So, Nancy needs 796 in.^{2} of tile.

▶ LOOK BACK

What other strategy can you use?

WHAT IF... ... the lengths of the sides of the tabletop were increased? What would happen to the area?

Apply

(1) Liza has a rectangular toolbox with a base 21 in. long and 9 in. wide. She wants to cover the bottom of the tool box with felt material. How many square inches of felt does she need to cover the bottom of the toolbox?

(2) The beads Jose bought to make jewelry came in a container with a lid shaped like a right triangle. If the base of the triangle is 4 cm and its area is 16 cm², what is the height of the lid?

Mixed Applications	**STRATEGIES**	• Use a Formula • Write an Equation
		• Work Backward • Draw a Diagram

Choose a strategy and solve.

(3) Fencing is on sale at a local lumber yard. Maria wants to fence a square section of her yard that is 42 ft on each side. How many feet of fencing should Maria buy?

(4) Dean roped a 215-ft by 170-ft rectangular section of a parking lot to make an unloading zone. What is the area of the unloading zone?

(5) Burt found a store where he can purchase a package of 5 carriage bolts for $2.78. If he needs 13 carriage bolts to complete his project, how much will he spend on the carriage bolts?

(6) During three days, Lani sold 35 picture frames and gave away 9 as samples. If she sold 12 frames on the third day, how many frames did she sell the first two days?

(7) Lindsay's goal was to sell $250 worth of aprons and pot holders. Aprons sell for $5 and pot holders for $3. If she has sold 35 aprons, how many pot holders must she sell to reach her goal?

(8) An express bus travels at a speed of 50 mi an hour. If James takes the 9:00 A.M. express bus to travel 45 mi, at what time will he reach his destination?

WRITER'S CORNER

(9) Use the figure shown. Write a problem that can be solved by using formulas. Exchange with a classmate. Solve. What formulas did your classmate use?

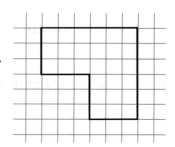

EXPLORING
Area of Irregular Figures

One way to find the area of an irregular figure is to use graph paper and count the number of square units.

WORK TOGETHER

Building Understanding

Look at the shaded figures that are drawn on graph paper. Each figure covers a certain number of square units.

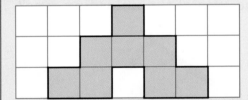

Figure A

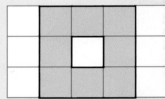

Figure B

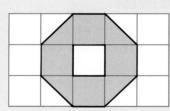

Figure C

Talk About It

▶ How can you find the area of Figure **A**?

▶ What is the area of Figure **A**?

▶ How can you find the area of Figure **B** without counting?

▶ What is the area of Figure **B**?

▶ How can you find the area of Figure **C**?

▶ What is the area of Figure **C**?

▶ Can two figures with different shapes have the same area? Explain.

Tell how to find the area of the figure.

A. 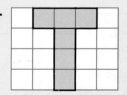   **B.** 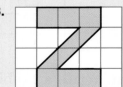   **C.**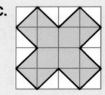

Making the Connection

You can also find the area of an irregular figure that is not drawn on graph paper. Divide the figure into familiar shapes. Measure and then find the area of the familiar shapes. Then add the areas together or subtract the areas from each other.

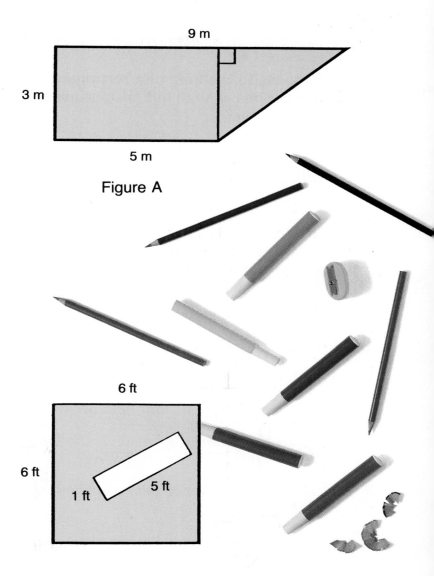

Figure A

1. Into what familiar shapes does the blue line divide Figure **A**?

2. What is the area of each shape?

3. How do you find the area of Figure **A**?

4. What is the area of Figure **A**?

Look at Figure **B**.

How can you find the area of the shaded part of Figure **B**?

5. What familiar shapes do you see in Figure **B**?

6. What is the area of each shape?

7. How do you find the area of the shaded part of Figure **B**?

8. What is the area of the shaded part of Figure **B**?

Figure B

Checking Understanding

Find the area of the shaded part of the figure.

9.

6 mi
8 mi
6 mi
11 mi

10.

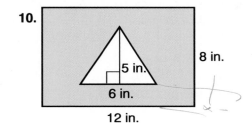

8 in.
5 in.
6 in.
12 in.

11.

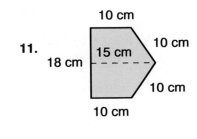

10 cm
10 cm
15 cm
18 cm
10 cm
10 cm

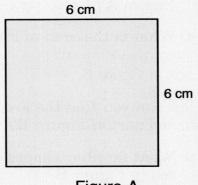

EXPLORING

Relating Perimeter and Area

What happens to the area of a rectangle if the dimensions change but the perimeter remains the same?

WORK TOGETHER

Building Understanding

Look at the rectangles.

- What is the perimeter of each of the rectangles?

- What type rectangle is Figure **A**?

- What is the area of Figure **A**? Figure **B**? Figure **C**?

- Which figure has the greatest area?

- Which figure has the smallest area?

- What is the difference between the length and the width of Figure **A**? Why?

- What is the difference between the length and the width of Figure **B**?

- What is the difference between the length and the width of Figure **C**?

Talk About It

▶ As the difference between the length and the width of each rectangle becomes greater, what happens to the area of the rectangle?

▶ How do you think the area of a square compares with the area of other rectangles with the same perimeter?

6 cm

6 cm

Figure A

8 cm

4 cm

Figure B

10 cm

2 cm

Figure C

Making the Connection

What happens to the area of a rectangle
if you double its length and width?

Draw rectangle *ABCD* 3 cm wide and 5 cm long. Double the
dimensions to draw rectangle *EFGH* 6 cm wide and 10 cm long.

1. What is the perimeter of rectangle *ABCD*? of rectangle
   EFGH?

2. How much greater is the perimeter of rectangle *EFGH*
   than the perimeter of rectangle *ABCD*?

3. What is the area of rectangle *ABCD*? rectangle *EFGH*?

4. How much greater is the area of rectangle *EFGH* than
   the area of rectangle *ABCD*?

Try doubling the dimensions of other rectangles to see what
happens to the area.

Talk About It

▶ What conclusions can you draw about what happens to the
perimeter of a rectangle when the dimensions are
doubled?

▶ What conclusions can you draw about what happens to the
area of a rectangle when the dimensions are doubled?

Checking Understanding

Draw the rectangle with the greatest area using the perimeter
given. Label the lengths of the sides. You may want to use
graph paper.

5. $P = 20$ 6. $P = 32$ 7. $P = 60$ 8. $P = 8$ 9. $P = 100$

Draw a rectangle that has double the dimensions of the given
rectangle. Find the perimeter of each.

10. $l = 3 \text{ cm}; w = 1 \text{ cm}$ 11. $l = 15 \text{ mm}; w = 9 \text{ mm}$ 12. $s = 4 \text{ cm}$

Double the dimensions of the given rectangle. Find the area of
each. Tell what happens to the area.

13. $l = 5 \text{ mm}; w = 1 \text{ mm}$ 14. $s = 2 \text{ yd}$ 15. $l = 6 \text{ in.}; w = 3 \text{ in.}$

1. George swims 7 days a week. He swam 6 laps on Sunday. By Saturday he was swimming 24 laps. If George increased the laps by the same number each day, what was that number?

2. Mary uses a design in four ways for a quilt. First she uses the design itself, second a rotation, third a reflection, and fourth another rotation. What is the tenth pattern?

3. A hexagon is divided into 6 equilateral triangles. One triangle has a 5-cm base and a 4-cm height. What is the area of the hexagon?

4. A rectangle has a length 7 in. less than twice the width. The perimeter is 34 in. What is the length?

In Exercise 1, I must find the intervals in the pattern.

Tell which figures are similar and which are congruent.

5.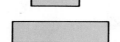

6.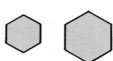

7.

Name the solid figure.

8. 1 base, 5 faces

9. 1 base, 3 faces

10. 2 bases, 6 faces

Find the perimeter of the polygon.

11.
5 m
5 m

12.
3 ft
2 ft · 2 ft
3 ft · 4 ft

13.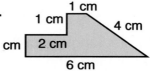
1 cm
1 cm · 4 cm
1 cm · 2 cm
6 cm

Find the area of the square or the rectangle.

14. $l = 10\,\text{cm}, w = 2\,\text{cm}$

15. $l = 11\,\text{m}, w = 5\,\text{m}$

16. $s = 12\,\text{ft}$

Find the area of the parallelogram.

17. $b = 4\,\text{cm}, h = 7\,\text{cm}$

18. $b = 8\,\text{in.}, h = 6\,\text{in.}$

19. $b = 16\,\text{ft}, h = 10\,\text{ft}$

Find the area of the triangle.

20. $b = 8\,\text{cm}, h = 2\,\text{cm}$

21. $b = 15\,\text{m}, h = 4\,\text{m}$

22. $b = 9\,\text{in.}, h = 6\,\text{in.}$

Spotlight ON PROBLEM SOLVING

Identify Relationships

Sometimes identifying relationships among geometric shapes can help you solve problems.

▶ Richard made this tangram puzzle from leftover scraps of construction paper. He noticed that all the shapes were polygons. He placed the shapes in different combinations to see how they were related to each other and what new shapes he could make.

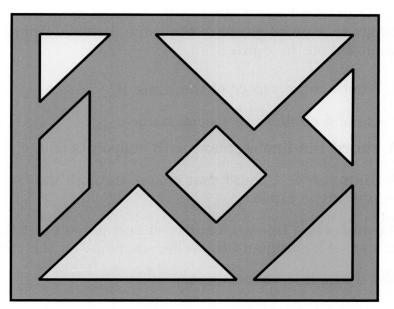

Trace the shapes, color them, and cut them out. Use the shapes to help you answer the questions.

Talk About It

Work with a classmate to answer the questions.

a. Can the orange square fit inside one of the blue triangles?

b. How can you rearrange the yellow triangles to form a parallelogram congruent to the red parallelogram?

Apply

Trace the shapes to illustrate your answers. Be prepared to share your results.

1. How can you rearrange the yellow triangles to cover the orange square?

2. How can the yellow triangles be placed to form a triangle that is similar to the blue triangles?

3. How can the yellow triangles be placed to form an isosceles triangle that is congruent to the green triangle?

4. How can you rearrange all the shapes to form a square? HINT: You may flip any of the figures.

CIRCLES

Needlecrafters use embroidery hoops, which are often in the shape of circles, to hold fabric in place as they embroider.

A **circle** is a special closed figure made up of all the points in a plane that are the same distance from a point called the **center**.

• Where is the center of the circle B?

Parts of a circle have special names.

A **chord** is a line segment with endpoints on a circle.

A **diameter** is a chord that passes through the center of the circle.

A **radius** is a line segment with one endpoint at the center of a circle and the other endpoint on the circle.

Use a compass to construct a circle.

A. Open the compass to the width you desire for the radius.
B. Using the point of the compass as the center of the circle, rotate the pencil.

Talk About It

▶ How is the diameter related to the radius?

▶ Name two chords in Circle *B*. Which is longer?

▶ Name a radius and a diameter in Circle *B*. How is a radius related to a diameter?

▶ Can a radius be a chord? How do you know?

▶ Are all diameters chords? Are all chords diameters? Why?

NOTE: A circle is named by its center.

Check for Understanding

Label the circle you constructed *M*. Using a straightedge, draw and label each part.

1. a diameter, $\overline{JK}$ **2.** two chords, $\overline{RS}$ and $\overline{TU}$ **3.** two radii, $\overline{MN}$ and $\overline{MP}$

Practice

Use Figure A for Exercises 4–10. Identify each.

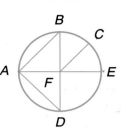

Figure A

4. the center

5. two diameters

6. two radii

7. two chords

8. the circle

9. intersecting line segments

10. If $FE = 6$ cm, what is AE? CF?

Copy and use Figure **B** for Exercises 11–16.

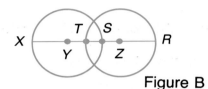

Figure B

11. What is $\overline{XS}$?

12. What is $\overline{RT}$?

13. What is $\overline{XY}$?

14. What is $\overline{TZ}$?

15. Draw one chord that is in each of the two circles.

16. Name a radius in Circle Y that intersects Circle Z.

Mixed Applications

17. A museum is square shaped. The entry doors cover $\frac{1}{2}$ the length of one side. If the perimeter of the building is 440 ft, what is the length of the entry doors?

18. **Number Sense** Think about a circle. How many diameters would you have to draw through the circle to divide it into 8 parts?

MIXED REVIEW

Write each percent as a decimal.

1. 33%   2. 48%   3. 6%   4. 80%   5. 30%   6. 12%

Write each percent as a fraction in simplest form.

7. 25%   8. 50%   9. 20%   10. 30%   11. 28%   12. 55%

Write = or ≠.

13. $\frac{1}{8}$ ● $\frac{3}{24}$ 14. $\frac{4}{7}$ ● $\frac{2}{3}$ 15. $\frac{5}{9}$ ● $\frac{4}{7}$ 16. $\frac{6}{20}$ ● $\frac{3}{10}$ 17. $\frac{5}{10}$ ● $\frac{3}{6}$

Name some everyday items that would not work if they were not in the shape of a circle.

EXPLORING

Circumference of a Circle

Perimeter is found by adding the lengths of the sides of a polygon. Circles do not have sides, so you must find the distance around a circle by using a different method. The distance around a circle is called **circumference**.

WORK TOGETHER

Building Understanding

Use a compass, string, paper, and a ruler to explore the circumference of a circle.

Construct a circle with a $3\frac{1}{2}$-in. radius. Wrap string around the circle. Use a ruler to measure the length of string.

Construct a circle with a different diameter. Use string to measure the circumference and a ruler to measure the string.

- How many times longer than the diameter is the circumference?

Talk About It

▶ What is the length of the diameter of the circle?

▶ What is the circumference of the circle?

▶ Use a calculator. How many times longer than the diameter is the circumference?

Choose four circular objects in your classroom. You might use a roll of tape, a clockface, a coin, or the rim of a trash can. Copy the table. List and measure the objects. Then use a calculator and complete the table.

	Object	Diameter (*d*)	Circumference (*C*)	*C* ÷ *d*
a.	?	■	■	■
b.	?	■	■	■
c.	?	■	■	■
d.	?	■	■	■

396

Making the Connection

You know that the circumference of a circle is always a little more than three times the diameter. This means that the ratio of the circumference to the diameter is a little more than 3. This ratio, $\frac{C}{d}$, is called pi, π. To find the circumference of a circle, you can use the formula $\frac{C}{d} = \pi$, $C = \pi d$, or $C = 2\pi r$.

Use a calculator with a π key, $\frac{22}{7}$, or 3.14 as an approximation for π, whichever makes a calculation easier. Since π is an approximation, write $\approx$ instead of $=$ in your answer.

Examples

A. Find the circumference of a circle with a diameter of 7 in. Use $\frac{22}{7}$ for π.

$C = \pi d$
$C \approx \frac{22}{7} \times 7$
$C \approx 22$ in.

B. To the nearest whole number, what is the circumference of a circle with a diameter of 5 cm? Use a calculator.

Standard calculator

$C \approx 15.7$ cm

Calculator with a π key

$\llcorner$ The display shows $\boxed{3.1415927}$

$C \approx 15.707963$ cm

So, to the nearest whole number, the circumference is 16 cm.

Checking Understanding

Find the circumference. Round your answer to the nearest tenth. You may want to use a calculator.

1.

7 m

2.
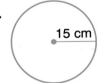
15 cm

3.

5 in.

4. diameter = 8 in.

5. diameter = 25 cm

6. radius = 12 ft

7. diameter is 14 m

8. radius is 10 yd

9. radius is 19 in.

More Practice, Lesson 12.8, page H80

AREA OF CIRCLES

Denise had a circular piece of leather 4 inches in diameter. She cut it into 8 equal pieces and sewed the pieces together to make a bracelet.

A circle can be rearranged as an approximate parallelogram. You can use the formula for the area of a parallelogram to develop the formula for the area of a circle.

Talk About It

▶ In relation to the circle, what is the length of the base of the approximate parallelogram?

▶ How can you find the circumference of a circle when you know the radius?

▶ In relation to the circle, what is the height of the approximate parallelogram?

Now you can develop the formula for the area of a circle. Recall that the area of a parallelogram is $A = bh$.

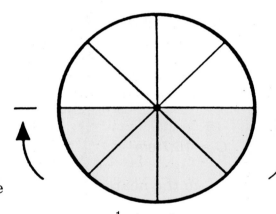

$\frac{1}{2}$ circumference

Think how the base and the height of the approximate parallelogram relate to the parts of the circle.

base $(b) = \frac{1}{2}$ the circumference of a circle $(\frac{1}{2} \times C)$
height (h) = radius (r) of a circle

$$A = bh \quad \longleftarrow \text{ Replace with terms relating to the circle.}$$
$$= (\frac{1}{2} \times C) \times r \quad \longleftarrow C = 2\pi r$$
$$= \frac{1}{2} \times 2\pi r \times r \quad \longleftarrow \frac{1}{2} \times 2\pi r = \pi r$$
$$= \pi r \times r, \text{ or } \pi r^2 \quad \text{Area of a circle} \longrightarrow A = \pi r^2$$

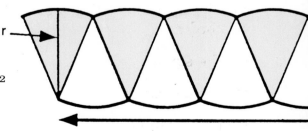

$\frac{1}{2}$ circumference

What was the area of Denise's circle?

$$A = \pi r^2 \quad \longleftarrow r = 2 \text{ and } \pi \approx 3.14$$
$$\approx 3.14 \times 2^2$$
$$\approx 3.14 \times 4$$
$$\approx 12.56$$

So, the area of Denise's circle was about 12.56 in.^{2}

Check for Understanding

Find the area of the circle. Round to the nearest tenth.

1.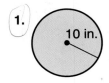
10 in.

2.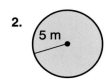
5 m

3.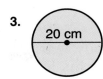
20 cm

Practice

Find the area of the circle. Round to the nearest tenth.

4. $r = 2$ in.

5. $d = 14$ in.

6. $r = 7$ m

7. $d = 8$ ft

8. $r = 3.1$ cm

9. $r = 0.5$ m

10. $r = 12$ cm

11. $r = 12.4$ in.

Mixed Applications

12. Logical Reasoning Consuela has two flat, round griddle pans. One has a radius of 8 in., and the other has a diameter of 12 in. Which pan has the greater area?

14. Visual Thinking Look at Figure *A*. If a square represents one square mile, about how many square miles is the area of Lake Walton?

13. Jon has a square coin whose sides measure 2.3 cm. What is the area of the coin? What is the perimeter?

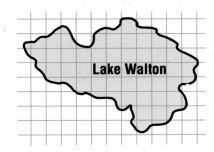
Lake Walton

Figure A

LOGICAL REASONING

You can use what you know about finding the area of polygons and circles to find the number of square meters in the shaded area of this figure. Find the area of each part in this order.

15. the square

16. the circle

17. the triangle

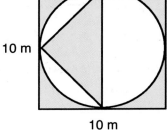
10 m

10 m

Now add and subtract to find the shaded area.

18. How many square meters are in the shaded area?

If you know the area of a circle, what other parts of the circle can you compute?

WRAP
UP...

EXPLORING
Surface Area

You have already learned how to find the area of polygons. In this lesson you will learn how to find the surface area of a rectangular prism.

Surface area is the sum of the areas of the faces of a solid figure.

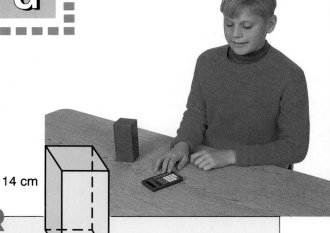

14 cm

6 cm

6 cm
Figure A

WORK TOGETHER

Building Understanding

Use the drawings and a calculator to help you find the surface area.

Figure B

		Top Base	6 cm
6 cm	6 cm	6 cm	6 cm
Back Face	Left Face	Front Face	Right Face
		Bottom Base	6 cm

14 cm

Talk About It

▶ Counting the bases, how many faces does the rectangular prism in Figure A have?

▶ In Figure A, what is the area of the front face of the prism?

Look at Figure B. What faces are congruent to the front face?

▶ What is the combined area of the four faces?

▶ What is the area of the bottom base of the prism?

Look at Figure B. What base is congruent to the bottom base?

▶ What is the combined area of the two bases?

▶ How can you find the surface area of the rectangular prism?

▶ What is the surface area of the rectangular prism?

Find the surface area of the rectangular prism.

a.
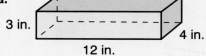
3 in.
4 in.
12 in.

b.
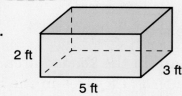
2 ft
3 ft
5 ft

c.
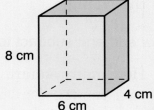
8 cm
6 cm
4 cm

400

Skill Check

Find the perimeter or the circumference. Use $\frac{22}{7}$ for π. *(pages 380, 396)*

16.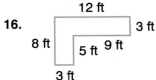

17.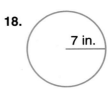

18.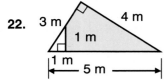

Find the area of the parallelogram. *(page 384)*

19. $b = 3\,\text{ft}, h = 4\,\text{ft}$

20. $b = 12\,\text{m}, h = 8.1\,\text{m}$

21. $b = 2.2\,\text{m}, h = 2.1\,\text{m}$

Find the area of the shaded part of the figure. *(page 388)*

22.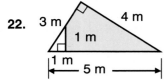

23.

24.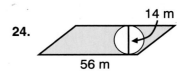

Find the area of the circle. Use 3.14 for π, and round your answer to the nearest tenth. *(page 398)*

25. $r = 2\,\text{yd}$ **26.** $d = 12\,\text{cm}$ **27.** $r = 3.2\,\text{ft}$ **28.** $r = 4.4\,\text{cm}$ **29.** $r = 1.5\,\text{m}$

Find the surface area. *(page 400)*

30.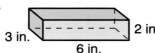

31.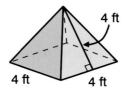

32.

33. Find the volume of the rectangular prism in Exercise 31. *(page 402)*

Problem-Solving Check *(pages 386, 404)*

34. Ray sells bowls with a circumference of 11 in. What size lid is needed to fit the bowls if the lids are sized by the radius? Use $\frac{22}{7}$ for π.

35. Carla added a square room to her house. The room is 100 ft². What is the perimeter of Carla's new room?

36. Lena wants to fill a sandbox that is 4 ft long, 3 ft wide, and $\frac{1}{2}$ ft deep. If sand is sold by the cubic foot, how much sand does she need?

37. Larry left a chair to walk 27 ft west to a bird feeder. He turned south and walked 36 ft to a bush. Then he walked 45 ft back to the chair. How far did he walk?

Find the perimeter or the circumference.

1. 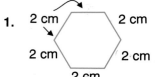 2 cm 2 cm 2 cm 2 cm 2 cm

2. 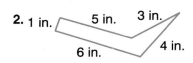 1 in. 5 in. 3 in. 6 in. 4 in.

3. 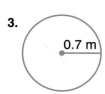 0.7 m

Find the area of the square or the rectangle.

4. $s = 9$ m

5. $l = 4$ ft, $w = 3$ ft

6. $l = 8$ cm, $w = 1.2$ cm

Find the area of the triangle.

7. $b = 6$ cm, $h = 10$ cm

8. $b = 2.7$ m, $h = 7$ m

9. $b = 8$ cm, $h = 1.6$ cm

Find the area of the shaded part of the figure.

10. 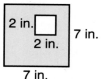 2 in. 2 in. 7 in. 7 in.

11. 4 cm 6 cm 4 cm 6 cm

12. 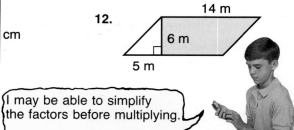 14 m 6 m 5 m

Find the area of the circle. Use $\frac{22}{7}$ for π.

I may be able to simplify the factors before multiplying.

13. $r = 7$ ft

14. $r = 14$ in.

Find the volume of the rectangular prism.

15. $l = 12$ m, $w = 8$ m, $h = 2$ m

16. $l = 2$ m, $w = 1.8$ m, $h = 1.6$ m

Solve.

17. Dale wants to cover the rim of a can lid with decorative paper. If the radius of the can is 7 in., how long a sheet of paper does she need? Use $\frac{22}{7}$ for π.

18. John made a seat for a tool bench. The bench seat is 7 ft long and 5 ft wide. What is the area of the seat?

19. Germaine can take two routes to work. He can go north 5 mi, west 4 mi, south 2 mi, and west 4 mi. Or, he can go west 6 mi, north 3 mi, and west 2 mi. How far from work is he where the routes meet?

20. A game map is 6 squares long and 6 squares wide. From left to right, the squares in each row are red, blue, yellow, brown, blue, red. How many squares are red?

Teamwork P-R-O-J-E-C-T

Make Posters

Work as a team to design a poster. Complete this title for your poster: "How to Determine the Area of _?_."

Decide

Discuss the figures that were presented in this chapter.

Choose one of the figures as the subject of your poster.

Decide what information is necessary to find the area of your chosen figure.

Design your poster. Different parts should be assigned to different team members.

Draw your poster, making it colorful, appealing, and easy to understand.

Do

Use poster board, or tape smaller sheets of paper together to make your poster.

Share

Compare your poster with those of other teams. Tell why you chose the figure you did.

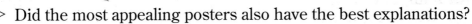
Talk About It

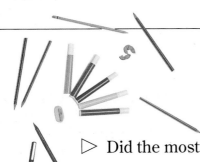

▷ Did the most appealing posters also have the best explanations?

▷ Did any team present a new idea for finding the area of a figure?

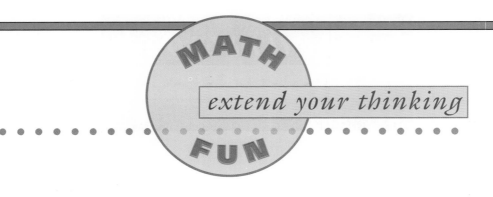

Use Polygons and Circles

You can use polygons to draw almost any figure. Doing this can help you find the area of a complex figure.

If you know the areas of the individual polygons, you can add them together to find the area of the whole figure. What is the area of the tree?

Draw the figure by using polygons. Then find the area of the figure.

1. a dog
2. a shoe
3. a telephone
4. a rabbit

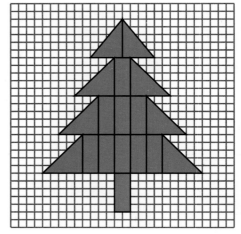

Use circles and polygons to draw these figures.

5. a calculator
6. a school bus
7. an airplane
8. a lamp

Find the area of each figure in Exercises 5–8. Exchange drawings and area calculations with a classmate. Did each of you use the same polygons for the same purposes?

Challenge

Problem Solving

If the mass of an object is less than the mass of an equal volume of water, the object will float; otherwise, the object will sink. For 1 mL of water, mass = 1 g and volume = 1 cm³.

A cube has edges measuring 2 cm. If it has a mass of 5 g, will it sink or float?

Logical Reasoning

Sometimes you can place congruent shapes next to each other to make a larger shape that is similar. How can you do this by using the triangle below four times?

Write the letter of the correct answer.

1. $1\frac{1}{2} \div 2\frac{1}{4}$

  A. $\frac{2}{3}$ **B.** $1\frac{1}{2}$

  C. $2\frac{1}{8}$ **D.** $2\frac{1}{4}$

2. 15 lb = ▨ oz

  A. $\frac{15}{16}$ **B.** 1.8

  C. 120   **D.** 240

3. What is 15% of 100?

  A. 1.5   **B.** 15
  C. 150   **D.** not here

4. Which parallelogram has 4 congruent sides?

  A. triangle   **B.** pentagon
  C. rhombus   **D.** trapezoid

5. $5\frac{1}{3} \times 4\frac{1}{4}$

  A. $20\frac{2}{3}$ **B.** $22\frac{2}{3}$

  C. $22\frac{11}{12}$ **D.** $23\frac{1}{6}$

6. 16:12 = ▨:3

  A. 4   **B.** 6

  C. 9   **D.** 12

7. What is the volume of the rectangular prism?
$l = 5$ m, $w = 4$ m, $h = 7$ m

  A. 16 m^3 **B.** 32 m^3
  C. 60 m^3 **D.** not here

8. What is the perimeter of the square?
$s = 6$ cm

  A. 6 cm   **B.** 12 cm
  C. 24 cm   **D.** 36 cm

9. What is the circumference of the circle? $r = 3$ cm

  A. 9.42 cm   **B.** 18 cm
  C. 18.84 cm   **D.** 28.26 cm

10. What is the area of the triangle?
$b = 6$ ft, $h = 18$ ft

  A. 6 ft^2 **B.** 12 ft^2
  C. 27 ft^2 **D.** 54 ft^2

11. John has an oriental carpet that is 6 ft long and 10 ft wide. What is the area of the carpet?

  A. 16 ft   **B.** 32 ft^2
  C. 60 ft^2 **D.** 120 ft^2

12. Sue put a small box 12 in. long, 8 in. wide, and 4 in. high inside a box 20 in. long, 15 in. wide, and 9 in. high. How many cubic inches of space are left in the larger box?

  A. 1,200 in.^{3} **B.** 2,316 in.^{3}
  C. 2,341 in.^{2} **D.** 1,500 in.^{2}

13

INTEGERS

Did you know ...

... that temperatures vary with altitude?

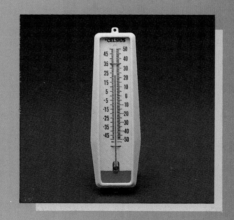

How could you find the difference in temperature between the place where the family is fishing and the place where the snow is on the mountain?

INTEGERS

The highest point in the United States is Mount McKinley in Alaska. It is 20,320 ft above sea level. The lowest point in the United States is in Death Valley, California, where the elevation is 282 feet below sea level. If you consider sea level to be zero, what numbers can you use to represent these two elevations?

You can use integers to represent the elevations. **Integers** include all whole numbers, their opposites, and zero. For example, the opposite of $^+10$ is $^-10$.

So, the elevation of Mount McKinley can be represented as $^+20{,}320$ and that of Death Valley as $^-282$.

An integer that is greater than 0 is called a **positive integer**. An integer that is less than 0 is called a **negative integer**. Zero is neither positive nor negative.

Many situations arise in daily life where both positive and negative integers can be used.

Examples Name an integer to represent each situation.

A. a loss of 5 yd in a football game

$^-5$

B. a temperature of 3 degrees below zero

$^-3$

C. a bank deposit of $100

$^+100$

Talk About It

▶ Describe the opposite of the situation in Examples A, B, and C.

▶ Name an integer to represent the opposite situation.

▶ Name some situations in everyday life where positive and negative integers are useful.

Check for Understanding

Name an integer to represent the situation.

1. a gain of 7 yd

2. a loss of 10 yd

3. a profit of $100

4. a loss of $50

5. a bank deposit of $75

6. a withdrawal of $25

Practice

Describe the opposite of the situation.

7. 3 steps forward

8. 6 degrees above 0

9. 81 ft above sea level

Name an integer to represent the situation. Then describe the opposite situation and give an integer to represent it.

10. up 2 flights of stairs

11. 19 ft above sea level

12. 68 ft below ground

13. 252 ft above ground

14. an increase of $250

15. a loss of $28

16. a weight loss of 6 lb

17. a 6-yd gain in football

Mixed Applications

18. If you deposit $25 and later withdraw $25, what is the new account balance?

19. If the temperature is 0° and drops 5 degrees, what will be the new temperature?

20. New York's Holland tunnel is 8,557 ft long. Virginia's Midtown Tunnel is 4,194 ft long. How much longer is the Holland Tunnel than the Midtown Tunnel?

21. Find Data Use an almanac to find the elevations for the highest and lowest points in the world. Then use integers to name each elevation.

MIXED REVIEW

Find the product or the quotient.

1. $\frac{3}{4} \times \frac{8}{15}$

2. $\frac{9}{15} \div \frac{1}{5}$

3. $1\frac{3}{8} \times 4\frac{4}{11}$

4. $10\frac{2}{3} \div 1\frac{5}{6}$

Tell whether whole numbers, decimals, and fractions are integers.

More Practice, Lesson 13.1, page H82

415

PROBLEM Solving

The Tigers took possession of the football on the Cougars' 45-yd line. On the first play they gained 34 yd. On the second play they lost 12 yd. They gained 9 yd on the third play but lost 5 yd on the fourth play. On what yard line were the Tigers after four plays?

▶ **UNDERSTAND**

What are you asked to find?

What information are you given?

▶ **PLAN**

What strategy will you use?

You can act out the situation to help you visualize how the events are related to each other.

▶ **SOLVE**

How can you carry out your plan?

Draw a diagram of half a football field. Cut a small piece of paper in the shape of a football. Model the play action. Move your football toward the goal line for all the yards the Tigers gained. Move it away from the goal line for all the yards the Tigers lost.

So, after four plays the Tigers were on the Cougars' 19-yd line.

▶ **LOOK BACK**

What other strategy could you use?

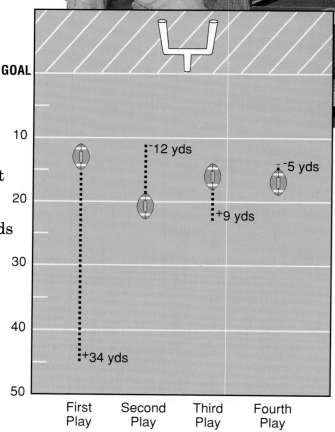

| First Play | Second Play | Third Play | Fourth Play |

WHAT IF... ... the Tigers started on the Cougars' 32-yd line, gained 10 yd, 15 yd, and 5 yd, and then lost 2 yd? On what yard line would they be after the four plays?

416

Apply

Act out the situation to solve each problem.

1 Jan is exploring a mountain cave. One room is a 30-ft wide and 50-ft long rectangle. The long sides face north and south. Jan enters the exact center of the south side and walks 20 ft north. Then she walks 15 ft east. How far is she from the east side of the cave's room?

2 Matt leaves a guest ranch and rides horseback 5 mi west, where he finds a cow's skull, and then 8 mi south, where he finds a cave. Then he rides 1 mi east and 11 mi north and 4 mi east to a large stone mesa. How far north is the mesa from the guest ranch?

Mixed Applications	**STRATEGIES**	• Draw a Diagram • Guess and Check • Act It Out • Work Backward

Choose a strategy and solve.

3 The water flow at an electric plant is increased by 2,000 gal per sec at 7 A.M. At 8 A.M. the water flow is doubled to 8,000 gal per sec. What was the water flow per second before 7 A.M.?

4 Ann, Joe, Luis, and Juana won the first four prizes in a design contest. Joe won second prize. Luis did not win third prize. Juana won fourth prize. What prize did Ann win?

5 A cave has 8 columns along one wall. The columns are each 3 ft wide, and they are spaced 7 ft apart. The columns at each end are 12 ft from the cave walls. How wide is the cave?

6 The road from Sun City extends south 20 mi, where it becomes a divided highway, and continues 15 mi to King City. The road extends 4 mi through King City and then another 24 mi south to Jewett. How far is Jewett from Sun City?

WRITER'S CORNER

7 Draw a diagram of a football field. Describe the result of 4 plays. Write a word problem about the plays. Exchange with a classmate. Solve. Then check your classmate's solution.

8 Write a problem similar to Exercise 4. Exchange with a classmate and solve.

COMPARING AND ORDERING INTEGERS

The lowest recorded temperature in Florida is ⁻2 degrees Fahrenheit. The lowest recorded temperature in Georgia is ⁻17 degrees Fahrenheit. Which temperature is the warmer of the two?

You can use a number line to help you visualize integers. As you move to the right on the number line, the value of the integers becomes greater.

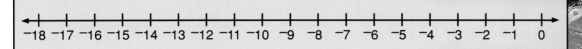

Talk About It

▶ Do the numbers become less or greater as you move to the right on the number line?

▶ Is ⁻2 to the left or to the right of ⁻17?

▶ Is ⁻2 greater than or less than ⁻17?

▶ Which temperature is warmer, ⁻2 degrees Fahrenheit or ⁻17 degrees Fahrenheit?

So, ⁻2 degrees Fahrenheit is warmer.

You can use the symbols $<$, $>$, and $=$ to compare and order integers.

Examples

A. Compare. Write $<$, $>$, or $=$.

$$⁻10 \bullet ⁻2$$
$$⁻10 < ⁻2$$

⁻2 is to the right of ⁻10.

B. Order from least to greatest. Use $<$.

$$⁻3, {}^+7, {}^+15, ⁻20$$
$$⁻20 < ⁻3 < {}^+7 < {}^+15$$

Pairs of integers that are the same distance from 0 on the number line are called **opposites**. For example, ⁻5 and ⁺5 are opposites.

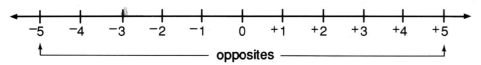

opposites

Check for Understanding

Tell which number is greater.

1. ⁻5 or ⁻3   **2.** ⁻5 or 0   **3.** ⁻10 or ⁺10   **4.** ⁻5 or ⁻8

Name the opposite of the given integer.

5. ⁻10   **6.** ⁺8   **7.** ⁺4   **8.** ⁻7   **9.** ⁺16   **10.** ⁻12

Practice

Use the number line. Write an integer for the given point.

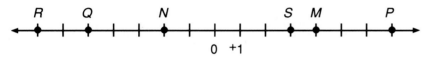

11. M **12.** N **13.** P **14.** Q **15.** R **16.** S

Compare. Use <, >, or =.

17. ⁻7 ● ⁻9   **18.** ⁻8 ● ⁺8   **19.** ⁺2 ● ⁻9   **20.** ⁺3 ● ⁻4   **21.** ⁻12 ● ⁺2

22. ⁻10 ● ⁻9   **23.** 0 ● ⁻6   **24.** ⁻7 ● ⁺1   **25.** ⁻5 ● ⁻5   **26.** ⁻15 ● ⁻10

Order the integers from least to greatest. Use <.

27. 0, ⁻5, ⁺7, ⁻1   **28.** ⁺9, ⁻7, ⁺5, ⁻3

29. ⁺10, ⁻10, 0, ⁺7, ⁻2   **30.** ⁻8, ⁻4, ⁻7, ⁻9, 0

31. ⁻3, ⁺4, ⁻1, ⁺7, ⁻12   **32.** ⁺8, ⁻6, ⁻9, ⁻5, ⁺10, ⁺15

Mixed Applications

Write *sometimes*, *always*, or *never* for Exercises 33–34.

33. A negative integer is less than a positive integer.

34. A negative integer is less than another negative integer.

35. A submarine is 120 ft below the surface of the water. A helicopter is 100 ft above the surface of the water. Which is farther from the surface of the water?

36. **Number Sense** Numbers in a pattern are 1, 2, 3, 5, 8, 13, and 21. What are the next two numbers?

Tell why ⁺2 is greater than ⁻3.

WRAP UP...

EXPLORING

Addition of Integers

Adding **positive integers** is similar to adding whole numbers.

WORK TOGETHER

Building Understanding

Use blue counters. Let each blue counter represent ⁺1. What is ⁺5 and ⁺3?

You can show addition of positive integers on a number line.

Talk About It

▶ How many counters do you need to model ⁺5? ⁺3?

▶ How can you use counters to model ⁺5 + ⁺3?

▶ What is ⁺5 + ⁺3?

▶ How does ⁺5 + ⁺3 compare to ⁺3 + ⁺5?

▶ Is addition of positive integers commutative?

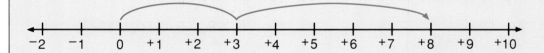

```
 ←—+——+——+——+——+——+——+——+——+——+——+——+——→
   -2  -1   0  +1  +2  +3  +4  +5  +6  +7  +8  +9  +10
```

▶ Use the number line. At what point do you begin?

▶ In what direction do you move to model positive integers?

▶ How would you show ⁺3 + ⁺5 on the number line?

▶ Think about the number line. Why is the sum of two positive integers always positive?

Use counters or a number line to model adding positive integers. Find the sum.

a. ⁺2 + ⁺7

b. ⁺1 + ⁺5

c. ⁺6 + ⁺2

d. ⁺8 + ⁺2

Making the Connection

Addition and subtraction of integers are related.

Examples

Study these examples. Think about the relationship between an integer and its opposite.

A. $^-7 - {}^-3 = {}^-4$ and $^-7 + {}^+3 = {}^-4$
So, $^-7 - {}^-3 = {}^-7 + {}^+3$.

B. $^-6 - {}^+2 = {}^-8$ and $^-6 + {}^-2 = {}^-8$
So, $^-6 - {}^+2 = {}^-6 + {}^-2$.

1. Write a rule telling how to subtract integers.

Checking Understanding

2. Tell which model to use to find $^-5 - {}^+3$.

a.  **b.** 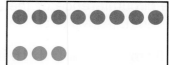 **c.**

3. The model below shows $^-4$. How can you use counters to find $^-4 - {}^+2$?

Use counters to find the difference.

4. $^-7 - {}^-5$ **5.** $^-8 - {}^-7$ **6.** $^-5 - {}^+3$ **7.** $^-2 - {}^-5$

Complete each of the following.

8. $^+7 - {}^-4 = {}^+7 + \blacksquare$ **9.** $^-8 - {}^-6 = {}^-8 + \blacksquare$ **10.** $^-4 - {}^+2 = {}^-4 + \blacksquare$

11. $^-6 - {}^+3 = {}^-6 + \blacksquare$ **12.** $^+6 - {}^+3 = {}^+6 + \blacksquare$ **13.** $^-2 - {}^-5 = {}^-2 + \blacksquare$

Rewrite each subtraction expression as an addition expression. Then solve.

14. $^-7 - {}^-10$ **15.** $^-9 - {}^+4$ **16.** $^+14 - {}^+8$ **17.** $^-14 - {}^-12$

18. $^+17 - {}^+9$ **19.** $^-7 - {}^+9$ **20.** $^+8 - {}^-7$ **21.** $^+9 - {}^+25$

1. Devan has a box 9 in. long, 4 in. wide, and 2 in. high. He has another box 7 in. long, 5 in. wide, and 1 in. high. Will the small box fit inside the large box?

2. Estella has cut a piece of yellow ribbon 25 in. long to wrap around a tree that has an $8\frac{1}{2}$-in. diameter. Will the ends of the ribbon touch when wrapped around the tree?

3. Carole travels 200 mi west of the city. Then she visits an uncle who lives 24 mi off her route. She backtracks and then continues traveling west for another 153 mi to the mountains. What is the direct distance from the city to the mountains?

4. Wade threw a ball 15 ft south to Cal, who caught it and threw it 9 ft east to Jason. Jason threw it 20 ft north to Gene. Gene threw it to Cal. The boys remain in the same positions. How far must Cal throw to reach Wade?

Find the circumference or the area. Round your answer to the nearest tenth.

5. $r = 5$ cm
   $A \approx$ ▪

6. $r = 16$ in.
   $C \approx$ ▪

7. $r = 0.2$ m
   $C \approx$ ▪

8. $r = 1.8$ cm
   $A \approx$ ▪

9. $r = 22$ in.
   $C \approx$ ▪

Find the volume of the rectangular prism.

10. $l = 4$ m, $w = 3$ m, $h = 5$ m

11. $l = 9$ cm, $w = 6$ cm, $h = 1$ cm

Volume is expressed in cubic units.

Name an integer to represent the situation.

12. temperature of 8 degrees above 0

13. a weight loss of 2 lb

Compare. Use $<$, $>$, or $=$.

14. $^-6$ ● $^-10$

15. $^+9$ ● $^-1$

16. $^-12$ ● $^-12$

17. $^+5$ ● $^-5$

18. $^+9$ ● $^+9$

Rewrite each subtraction expression as an addition expression.

19. $^-20 - {}^+4$

20. $^-10 - {}^+6$

21. $^-12 - {}^-2$

22. $^-7 - {}^-15$

23. $^+2 - {}^-9$

Find the sum or difference.

24. $^+12 + {}^+8$

25. $^-10 + {}^-6$

26. $^+15 - {}^+5$

27. $^-22 - {}^+9$

28. $^-15 + {}^+27$

29. $^-13 + {}^+7$

30. $^+32 - {}^-17$

31. $^-5 + {}^+2$

32. $^-7 - {}^-29$

33. $^+6 - {}^-54$

Account for Other Possibilities

ome problems have more than one answer. You may need to account for several possibilities in order to solve a problem.

Look at the numbers in the circles on the triangle. The sum of the numbers on each side of the triangle is 17. Is more than one arrangement possible?

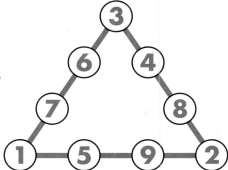

Talk About It

Look at each side of the triangle.

❑ What numbers can be traded without affecting the sum of each side?

❑ How can you use what you know about rotational symmetry to find two other possible arrangements?

❑ Name two other possible arrangements.

So, more than one arrangement is possible.

Apply

Account for other possibilities to solve Exercises 1–4. Share your results with a classmate.

1. The magic puzzle has the same sum horizontally, vertically, and diagonally. Solve, using integers. Are other arrangements possible? How do you know?

■	⁻12	■
■	0	+6
⁻3	■	■

2. Fill in the circles in the pattern so that the sum of each line equals the sum of every other line. Use each number from 1 to 12 only once.

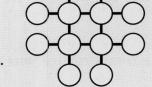

3. A magic number has three digits, and its digits sum to 20. The first digit is 9. What are two possible numbers?

4. Ralph has $1.30 in dimes and nickels. How many combinations of dimes and nickels could he possibly have?

The highest recorded temperature occurred in Libya, where the temperature reached 136°F. The lowest recorded temperature occurred in Antarctica, where the temperature reached ⁻129°F. What is the difference between the highest and lowest temperatures?

Since you need to find the difference in temperatures, you must subtract.

136 − ⁻129   When the sign is not written, the integer is always positive.

Subtract the integer by adding its opposite.

$$136 - {}^-129 = 136 + 129$$
$$= 265$$

So, the difference in the temperatures is 265°F.

136° F

Another Method

You can use a calculator to add and subtract integers. To enter a negative number into a calculator, press the +/− key after entering the number.

136 − ⁻129

136 − 129 +/− = ⬚ 265.

A temperature of ⁻4°F was recorded one morning. By noon the temperature had risen 7°F. What was the temperature at noon?

Since the temperature rose, you must add the integers.

$$^-4 + 7 = 3$$

So, the temperature was 3°F at noon.

Talk About It

▶ When would you press +/− when entering ⁻4 + 7 on a calculator?

⁻129° F

428

Check for Understanding

Find the sum.

1. ⁻8 + ⁻2

2. 17 + ⁻3

3. 20 + 10

4. ⁻13 + ⁻12

Find the difference.

5. 7 + ⁺3

6. ⁻16 + 3

7. ⁻21 − ⁺3

8. ⁻11 − 5

Practice

Find the sum or difference.

9. ⁻20 + 12

10. 12 − 19

11. 3 + ⁻12

12. ⁻17 + ⁻12

13. 21 + ⁻13

14. 16 − ⁺12

15. 14 + ⁻28

16. 19 − ⁻3

17. ⁻26 + ⁺16

18. ⁻12 + 6

19. 20 + ⁻7

20. ⁻14 − ⁻7

21. ⁻15 + ⁻3

22. 25 + ⁺6

23. ⁻31 − 6

24. 21 + ⁻5

25. 16 + ⁻14

26. 12 + 9

27. 12 + ⁻9

28. ⁻12 − ⁻9

29. 7 + ⁻6 + ⁻2

30. ⁻8 + ⁻5 + 1

31. ⁻2 + ⁻9 + ⁻10

Mixed Applications

Write a number sentence to solve Exercise 32.

32. A mountain climber climbs up 15 yd to a ledge. Then she climbs down 7 yd, 8 yd, and 9 yd to get to another ledge. Which ledge is higher, the first or the second?

33. Write a Question The highest recorded temperature in California is 134°F. The lowest recorded temperature is ⁻45°F.

CONSUMER CONNECTION

A bank account is said to be in the black if the balance is positive and in the red if the balance is negative.

34. Heather's account had a balance of $120. Then she made withdrawals of $25, $45, and $30. Use a calculator to find her new balance. Is Heather's final balance in the red or in the black?

How is subtraction of integers related to addition?

WRAP UP...

EXPLORING

Ordered Pairs

This map shows a city divided into blocks.

WORK TOGETHER

Building Understanding

Use the map to follow and give directions to different locations in the city.

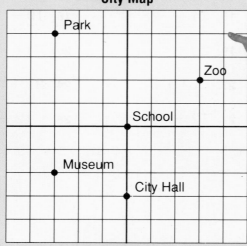

City Map

Park
Zoo
School
Museum
City Hall

Talk About It

▶ Start at the school. Go 3 blocks east and then 2 blocks north. Where will you be?

▶ Start at the school. Go 3 blocks west and then 2 blocks south. Where will you be?

▶ How are the directions for locating the zoo similar to the directions for locating the museum?

▶ How are the directions for locating the zoo different from those for locating the museum?

▶ If you tell someone to walk 3 blocks from the school, does he or she have enough information to find City Hall? Explain.

▶ What directions would guide someone from the school to the park?

430

Making the Connection

Points on a map can be located by an **ordered pair** of numbers. The first number tells the number of blocks east or west of the starting point. The second number tells the number of blocks north or south of the starting point.

Use the map. How would you tell someone how to get from the starting point to the baseball field?

From start, go 6 blocks east. Then go 2 blocks south.

So, to get from the starting point to the baseball field, you would go 6 blocks east and 2 blocks south.

The ordered pair that names the location of the baseball field is $(6, {}^-2)$.

Checking Understanding

Use the map. Tell the directions needed to get from the starting point to the given location.

1. pool   **2.** mall   **3.** fire station   **4.** post office

Trace the map. Locate each point on the map by following the given directions. Name the ordered pairs.

5. Go 4 blocks west and then 3 blocks south.

6. Go 1 block east and then 4 blocks north.

7. Go 3 blocks east and then 3 blocks south.

8. Go 5 blocks east and then 3 blocks south.

9. Go 3 blocks west and then 0 blocks north.

10. Go 3 blocks east and then 2 blocks north.

THE COORDINATE PLANE

The city of Chicago, Illinois, is laid out in a grid. Locations are given east or west of State Street and north or south of Madison Street. For example, a location of 800 west and 1600 south is 8 blocks west of State Street and 16 blocks south of Madison Street.

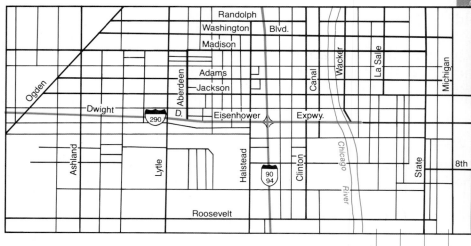

Just as points on a map can be located by an ordered pair of numbers, points on a **coordinate plane**, or grid, can be located by an ordered pair of numbers.

A coordinate plane is formed with two perpendicular lines, called **axes**. The point where both axes intersect is called the **origin**. The ordered pair describing the origin is (0,0).

The horizontal axis is called the **x-axis.** The vertical axis is called the **y-axis.** Ordered pairs tell you how far and in what direction to move from the origin.

Order is important! The first number in the ordered pair always tells you how far to move horizontally. The second number tells you how far to move vertically.

The ordered pair (⁻4,2) gives the location of point *A* in the coordinate plane shown. The first number, the *x*-coordinate, means you start at the origin and move 4 units to the left, since ⁻4 is negative. The second number, the *y*-coordinate, tells you to move 2 units up, since 2 is positive.

Connection, pages 476–477

Examples

A. How would you locate the point (3, ⁻4) in the coordinate plane?

Since the first number in the ordered pair is positive, move 3 units to the right (horizontally). Since the second number is negative, move 4 units down (vertically).

B. How would you locate the point (⁻5,7) in the coordinate plane?

Since the first number in the ordered pair is negative, move 5 units to the left. Since the second number is positive, move 7 units up.

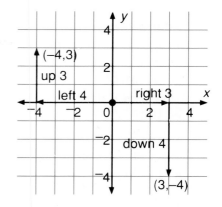

More Examples

C. What ordered pair names each point on the coordinate plane at the right?

1. The ordered pair for point *D* is (1,1).

2. The ordered pair for point *E* is (4,4).

3. The ordered pair for point *F* is (2,⁻4).

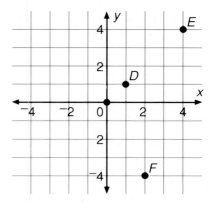

D. What ordered pair names each point on the coordinate plane at the right?

1. The ordered pair for point *R* is (⁻2,⁻4).

2. The ordered pair for point *S* is (⁻4,⁻2).

3. The ordered pair for point *T* is (⁻2,4).

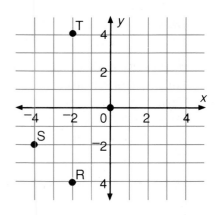

Talk About It

▶ Why is the location of the point (3,⁻4) different from the location of the point (⁻4,3)?

▶ Look at the ordered pairs for points *R* and *S*. How are the ordered pairs similar?

▶ How are the ordered pairs for points *R* and *S* different?

▶ How are the ordered pairs for points *S* and *T* similar? different?

Check for Understanding

Tell the ordered pair that names each point on the coordinate plane.

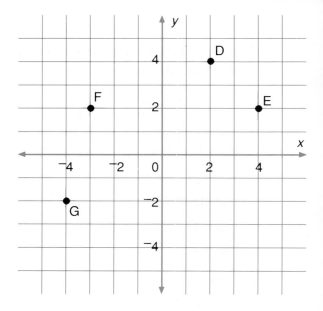

1. point D
2. point E
3. point F
4. point G
5. What is the ordered pair for the origin?
6. On what axis is the point (6,0)?
7. On what axis is the point (0,6)?
8. How would you locate the point (⁻2,⁻5)?

Practice

Write the ordered pair for each point.

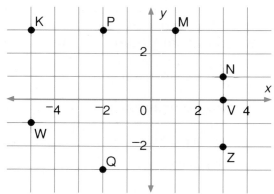

9. point M
10. point N
11. point P
12. point Q
13. point W
14. point Z
15. point K
16. point V

Use graph paper to make a coordinate plane. Locate the point for each ordered pair.

17. $A\,(5,7)$
18. $B\,(4,⁻6)$
19. $C\,(3,⁻5)$
20. $D\,(⁻1,⁻1)$
21. $E\,(⁻6,6)$
22. $F\,(3,7)$
23. $G\,(5,0)$
24. $H\,(0,5)$
25. $J\,(⁻2,⁻2)$

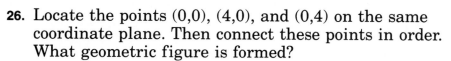

Remember to move to the left or right first.

26. Locate the points (0,0), (4,0), and (0,4) on the same coordinate plane. Then connect these points in order. What geometric figure is formed?

27. Use the figure you made in Exercise 26. Add a point to make the figure a square. What are the coordinates of the new point?

28. Locate the points (1,1), (5,1), (5,5), and (1,5) on the same coordinate plane. Then connect these points in order. What geometric figure is formed?

Mixed Applications

Copy the figure on a coordinate plane that is at least 8 units square.

29. Name the coordinates for points *A*, *B*, and *C*.

30. Add 5 to the *x*-coordinate of points *A*, *B*, and *C*. Graph the new figure. How does adding 5 to the *x*-coordinates affect the figure?

31. Subtract 5 from the original *x*-coordinates of each point. Graph the figure. How does subtracting 5 from the *x*-coordinates affect the figure?

32. Add 5 to the *y*-coordinates of each point. Graph the figure. How does adding 5 to the *y*-coordinates affect the figure?

33. What do you think would happen to the figure if you subtracted 5 from the original *y*-coordinates?

34. Visual Thinking If you reflect the word WOW over a line of symmetry, the word becomes MOM. How else can you move WOW so that it becomes MOM?

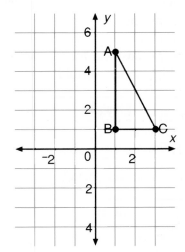

GEOMETRY CONNECTION

Remember that triangles can be classified as equilateral, isosceles, or scalene.

Use graph paper. Plot each set of ordered pairs on a separate coordinate plane. Then connect each set of points.

a. $(4,0)$, $(^-4,0)$, $(0,7)$
b. $(^-3,^-1)$, $(3,2)$, $(2,^-1)$
c. $(^-6,^-2)$, $(0,3)$, $(6,^-2)$
d. $(^-2,0)$, $(0,3\frac{1}{2})$, $(2,0)$

35. Which triangle is scalene?

36. Which triangles are isosceles?

37. Which triangle is equilateral?

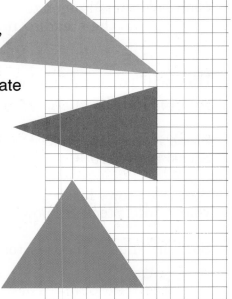

Explain how to locate the point $(3, ^-5)$ on a coordinate plane.

Lori wants to invest $20 in stock that shows a steady increase in price per share. Her broker listed the original price of two stocks and their gains and losses over a four-year period. Which stock should Lori choose?

Stock A—Price per Share				
Original Price	Yr 1	Yr 2	Yr 3	Yr 4
$15	$^+5$	$^-6$	$^+10$	$^-4$

Stock B—Price per Share				
Original Price	Yr 1	Yr 2	Yr 3	Yr 4
$10	$^+1$	$^+1$	$^+1$	$^+2$

▶ **UNDERSTAND**

What are you asked to find?

What information are you given?

▶ **PLAN**

How can you solve the problem?

Add to find the present price of each stock. Compare the changes to determine which stock shows the steadier increase per share.

▶ **SOLVE**

How will you carry out your plan?
Add to find the current price of each stock.

Stock A → $15 + $^+5$ + $^-6$ + $^+10$ + $^-4$ $\doteq$ $20
Stock B → $10 + $^+1$ + $^+1$ + $^+1$ + $^+2$ = $15

Stock A shows large gains and losses from year to year while Stock B shows slight gains each year.

So, Lori should choose Stock B.

▶ **LOOK BACK**

What other factors might Lori consider?

WHAT IF...

... Lori wants to buy stock that will give her the highest return on her money in one year? How will this affect her choice?

Apply

Ramon plans to play golf for 8 weeks this summer. He can buy a pass, pay regular fees, or buy a permit. He made a table to analyze the fees.

Choice 1

A season pass costs $290.

Choice 2

The regular fee is $18 per round.

Choice 3

A permit costs $90 in advance. Then the cost is $11 per round.

Copy and complete the table.

Times Played per Week	Cost		
	Choice 1	Choice 2	Choice 3
(1) 1	▦	▦	▦
(2) 2	▦	▦	▦
(3) 3	▦	▦	▦
(4) 4	▦	▦	▦

(5) What does the table show about the cost of the three choices for the golfer who wants to play more than twice a week?

(6) Ramon decided he would play twice a week. He selected Choice 1. Give one advantage of this choice.

Mixed Applications ➤ **STRATEGIES**
- Guess and Check
- Draw a Diagram
- Make a Table
- Write an Equation

Choose a strategy and solve.

(7) Use the table. Eve plans to play golf about twice a week for 8 weeks. She selected Choice 3. Give one of the advantages of her choice.

(8) Mountain climbers lead tours for 6 people and for 4 people. If there are 4 tours with a total of 22 people, how many 4-person tours are there?

(9) Bill enters a fun house and walks 4.5 m along a ground-level passage. The passage rises vertically 3 m and then is horizontal for 5.5 m. Suddenly, the passage drops 1 m and opens into a room. How far above ground is the room?

(10) One year a forest ranger planted 10 trees. Every year he plants 3 more trees. How many trees will he plant in 6 years?

Vocabulary Check

Choose a word or words from the box to complete each sentence.

axes
coordinate
plane
negative
opposites
origin
positive

1. An integer that has a value greater than zero is called a(n) __?__ integer. *(page 414)*

2. You can locate points on a(n) __?__ by using an ordered pair of numbers. *(page 432)*

3. The point where both axes of a coordinate plane intersect is called the __?__ . *(page 432)*

4. An integer that has a value less than 0 is __?__ . *(page 414)*

5. A coordinate plane is formed with two perpendicular lines called __?__ . *(page 432)*

6. Two integers that are the same distance from 0 on a number line are __?__ . *(page 418)*

Concept Check

I think about a number line when answering questions about integers.

7. Is zero a positive integer or a negative integer? *(page 414)*

8. The sum of opposite integers is always __?__ . *(page 422)*

9. Is 8 a positive or a negative integer? *(page 428)*

10. Explain how to change subtraction of integers to addition of integers without changing the results. *(page 428)*

11. If you tell someone to turn to the title page of this book, have you given him or her enough information to find the copyright date? *(page 430)*

12. On a coordinate plane, how does the *x*-axis differ from the *y*-axis? *(page 432)*

13. How do you make a coordinate plane from a sheet of plain graph paper? *(page 432)*

14. Why is it important to use an ordered pair to name a point on a coordinate plane? *(page 432)*

15. Explain how to locate the point ($^-$2,6) on a coordinate plane. *(page 432)*

Skill Check

Name an integer to represent the situation. *(page 414)*

16. a loss of 3 yards   **17.** a bank deposit of $6   **18.** 4 degrees below 0

Order the integers from least to greatest. Use <. *(page 418)*

19. $^-1, ^-3, 7, 0, 11$ **20.** $12, ^-6, 8, ^-7, ^-9$ **21.** $7, 3, ^-4, ^-9, ^-12$

765 43 21 0 1 2 3 456 7 8 9 10 11

Use the number line. Write an integer for the given point. *(page 418)*

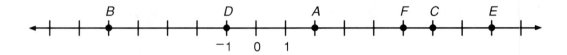

22. A **23.** B **24.** C **25.** D **26.** E **27.** F

Find the sum or difference. *(pages 420, 422, 424, 428)*

28. $^-4 + 9$ **29.** $^-5 + ^-1$ **30.** $^-5 + 7$ **31.** $^-7 + 3$ **32.** $15 + ^-9$

33. $^-10 + ^+2$ **34.** $8 + ^+10$ **35.** $^-1 + ^+3$ **36.** $20 + ^-12$ **37.** $^-2 + ^-46$

Use graph paper to make a coordinate plane. Locate the point for each ordered pair. *(page 432)*

38. $A\,(2,6)$ **39.** $B\,(4,^-2)$ **40.** $C\,(^-6,2)$ **41.** $D\,(^-1,^-5)$

Problem-Solving Check *(pages 416, 436)*

42. On Saturday Jayne hiked 4 mi north, 3 mi west, and 2 mi farther north. On Sunday she hiked 2 mi east and 6 mi south. Over the two-day period, how many miles had Jayne hiked when she crossed her own path?

43. Paul's team began on their own 25-yd line. Then they gained 10 yd, lost 26 yd, lost 4 yd, and gained 5 yd. On what yard line are they?

44. Jo must rent a car. Car 1 rents for $139.00 a week, including mileage. Car 2 rents for $109.00 a week plus $0.05 a mile after the first 50 mi. If Jo plans to drive 500 mi, which car option is less expensive?

45. Mr. Kim plans to attend 5 plays. A season ticket costs $175.00 for 7 plays. Individual tickets cost $35.50 each. Which option is less expensive, buying a season ticket or buying an individual ticket to each of 5 plays?

Name an integer to represent the situation.

1. a profit of $200
2. a withdrawal of $35
3. 2 degrees above 0

Order the integers from least to greatest. Use $<$.

4. $2, 0, {}^-7, {}^-4$
5. ${}^-9, 3, {}^-5, 1$
6. $8, {}^-8, 5, {}^-3, 6$

Find the sum or difference.

7. $8 + {}^-10$
8. $24 - {}^-9$
9. $12 + {}^-6$
10. ${}^-4 - 20$
11. ${}^-22 - {}^-25$

Write the ordered pair for each point on the coordinate plane.

12. point A
13. point B
14. point C
15. point D
16. point E

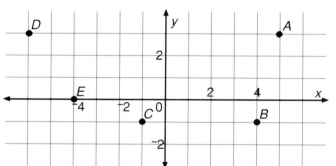

When a problem can be solved by using more than one strategy, choose the one that is easier for you.

Solve.

17. Lynette will meet a friend at a museum. She tells her friend to start at Main Street and go east $\frac{1}{8}$ mi, then north $\frac{1}{4}$ mi, and east another $\frac{3}{4}$ mi. How far east of Main Street is the museum?

18. Mike is at the center of an old Spanish mission courtyard. He walks 21 ft south, 10 ft west, and 11 ft north, where he looks at pottery. Then he walks 15 ft east and 10 ft north. How far is he from the center of the courtyard?

19. Quincy wants to hire 5 guitar players. He tells the musicians they can split between $1,000 and $1,200 a week, or he will pay them each $200 a week plus 5% of $1,500. With which offer can the guitar players make more money?

20. Mary asked her father to give her an allowance for school lunches. One option he has is to give Mary $0.01 on the first day of each month and double the amount for 15 days. The other option is to give her $10.00 a week. Which option is more reasonable?

Teamwork PROJECT

Use a Coordinate Plane

Use a coordinate plane to make a scale drawing of your classroom.

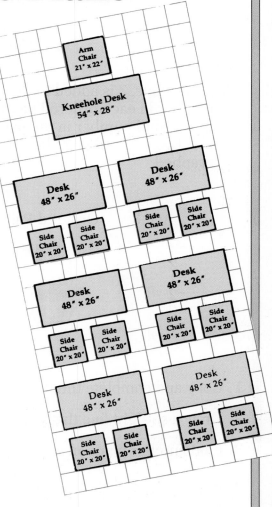

Decide

Decide how to show the exact center of your classroom. This will be (0,0) on your scale drawing.

Decide how your team will work together to complete the scale drawing.

Let one unit on the coordinate plane equal 3 feet in your classroom.

Do

You will need to show chalkboards, tables, bookcases, sinks, and the other large objects in your classroom.

Use ordered pairs to locate the objects on the scale drawing.

Write the ordered pairs for the classroom door, the teacher's desk, and each teammate's desk.

Share

Compare your scale drawing with those of other teams.

TALK ABOUT IT

In what ways is your team's scale drawing similar to those of other teams?

Did you expect most of the drawings to be similar? Why or why not?

Are most of the drawings actually similar?

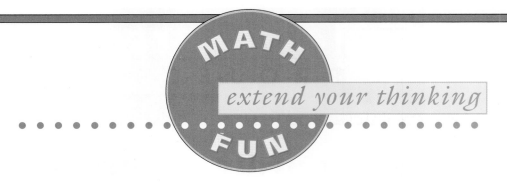
Points on a Straight Line

*I*n this table, 3 is added to the first number in each ordered pair to make the second number in the pair. The first two ordered pairs have been graphed.

Add 3		Ordered Pair
⁻4	⁻1	(⁻4,⁻1)
2	5	(2, 5)
⁻1	■	(■, ■)
⁻2	■	(■, ■)
0	■	(■, ■)
⁻3	■	(■, ■)

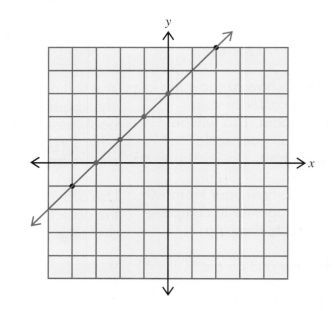

1. Copy and complete the table and the graph of ordered pairs.

2. Draw a straight line that goes through all the points on your graph.

3. Find another point on the line. Write the ordered pair for that point.

4. Make a table of six ordered pairs of integers that have a sum of 0. Locate the ordered pairs on a graph. Can you draw a straight line through all the points?

Challenge

Number Puzzle

Arrange integers to complete the magic square so that the sums for the rows, columns, and diagonals are the same.

4	■	■
■	⁻5	8
■	0	⁻14

Problem Solving

A positive integer is twice as many units from 0 on a number line as a negative integer. The two integers are 48 units apart. Find the two integers.

Write the letter of the correct answer.

1. $3\frac{1}{4} \times 2\frac{1}{2}$

   A. $5\frac{1}{8}$ **B.** $5\frac{5}{8}$

   C. $8\frac{1}{8}$ **D.** $8\frac{3}{4}$

2. 93 yd = ■ ft

   A. 7.75   **B.** 31

   C. 279   **D.** 1,116

3. $\dfrac{■}{9} = \dfrac{2}{3}$

   A. 3   **B.** 4

   C. 5   **D.** 6

4. What is 20% of 16?

   A. 0.32   **B.** 3.2

   C. 8   **D.** not here

5. Which shows the symbol for parallel lines?

   A. $\overleftrightarrow{AB} \parallel \overleftrightarrow{CD}$ **B.** $\overleftrightarrow{AB} \perp \overleftrightarrow{CD}$

   C. $\overleftrightarrow{AB} \cong \overleftrightarrow{CD}$ **D.** not here

6. What is the third angle in the triangle? 60°, 45°, ■

   A. 15°   **B.** 105°

   C. 155°   **D.** not here

7. What is the area of the circle? $r = 5$ cm

   A. 15 cm   **B.** 15.7 cm^2

   C. 78.5 cm   **D.** 78.5 cm^2

8. What is the area of the rectangle? $l = 12$ ft, $w = 10$ ft

   A. 22 ft   **B.** 44 ft

   C. 60 ft^2 **D.** 120 ft^2

9. On what axis is (7,0)?

   A. x-axis   **B.** y-axis

   C. z-axis   **D.** not here

10. $6 - {}^-2$

   A. $^-2$ **B.** 4

   C. 6   **D.** 8

11. A football team began on their own 20-yd line. First, they gained 10 yd. Next, they lost 5 yd. Then, they gained 15 yd. On what yard line are they?

   A. 20-yd line   **B.** 35-yd line

   C. 40-yd line   **D.** 50-yd line

12. At Ace, Greta can buy 3 brushes for $1.99. At Deuce, she can buy the same kind of brushes at 4 for $2.29. At which store will Greta get the better buy?

   A. Ace   **B.** Deuce

   C. same   **D.** need more facts

14

GETTING READY
FOR ALGEBRA

Did you know ...

. . . that in the future your homes may be powered completely by solar energy cells that are controlled by a personal computer?

Suppose a 1 m² solar panel can collect 1,000 watts of power per day. How can you find the number of panels needed to provide power for your home for a day?

Cable television did not gain popularity until the late 1960's when the high costs began to decrease. By the year 2020, the cost of cable television may decrease by $12 a month. What expression can you write to show the decrease in cost?

To solve the problem, first choose a variable to represent the present cost of cable television. Then write the expression.

Let the variable c represent the present cost of cable television.

Word expression: c decreased by twelve

Algebraic expression: $c - 12$

So, the algebraic expression $c - 12$ shows the decrease in cost.

More Examples

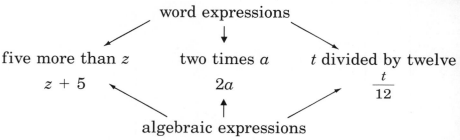

word expressions

five more than z two times a t divided by twelve

$z + 5$ $2a$ $\dfrac{t}{12}$

algebraic expressions

When you use variables to represent unknown quantities, you are using **algebra**. Solving equations and evaluating expressions are ways to find unknown quantities.

Remember that an equation is a number sentence. It has an equals sign.

$$y + 8 = 20 \qquad 3 + 5 = 8 \qquad 22 - w = 11 \qquad d \div 2 = 12$$

Talk About It

▶ Does the variable in an expression always represent the same number? Explain.

▶ How is an equation different from an expression?

Check for Understanding

Write a word from the box to complete each sentence.

| algebra | equation | expression | variable |

1. The number sentence $x + 8 = 12$ is a(n) __?__.

2. In the equation $x + 8 = 12$, x is called a(n) __?__.

3. In the equation $x + 8 = 42$, $x + 8$ is a(n) __?__.

4. When you use variables to represent unknown quantities, you are using __?__.

Practice

Write a word expression for the algebraic expression.

5. $x - 4$

6. $t + 8$

7. $7 + s$

8. $y - 10$

9. $3 - w$

10. $5b$

11. $10a$

12. $\dfrac{x}{5}$

13. $z + 6$

14. $8m$

15. $\dfrac{r}{6}$

16. $10 - y$

Copy and complete the table. Write an algebraic expression, an equation, or a word phrase.

	Word Expression or Sentence	Algebraic Expression or Equation
17.	y plus twelve	■
18.	n and seven equals nine	■
19.	__?__	$^-4 + \dfrac{1}{2}n$
20.	five less than p is 12	■
21.	d divided by four	■
22.	16 is four times h	■

Mixed Applications

23. Jane Tallchief was 7 years old in 1990. How old will she be in 2020?

24. **Mental Math**   Use c for cost. Write an expression to show an increase of $5.

How can you change the expression $a + 6$ to an equation?

WRAP UP...

RATIONAL NUMBERS

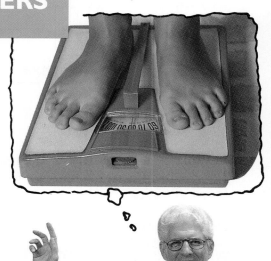

Raphael Perez is an economist who studies future trends. Recently, he predicted that by the year 2000, 90% of all Americans will be overweight. Is 90% a rational number?

A **rational number** can be written as the ratio $\frac{a}{b}$ where a and b are integers and $b \neq 0$. Rational numbers include whole numbers, decimals, fractions, mixed numbers, percents, and integers.

You can write 90% as the ratio $\frac{9}{10}$.

Since you can write 90% as $\frac{90}{100}$, or $\frac{9}{10}$, 90% is a rational number.

Examples

Write the number in the form $\frac{a}{b}$.

$$12 = \frac{12}{1} \qquad 1\frac{3}{5} = \frac{8}{5} \qquad 2.5 = \frac{25}{10}, \text{ or } \frac{5}{2} \qquad 75\% = \frac{3}{4} \qquad {}^-3 = \frac{{}^-3}{1}$$

The type of rational number you use depends on the situation.

Examples

A. Money is usually expressed in decimal form, such as $12.35.

Sometimes, you use fractions to express money amounts, such as $\frac{1}{2}$ dollar.

B. When you use a standard calculator, a fraction is expressed as a decimal. For example, $\frac{3}{5}$ is expressed as 0.6.

$$3 \boxed{\div} 5 = \boxed{0.6}$$

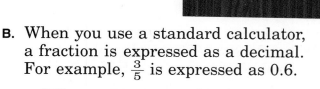

Talk About It

▶ Which rational numbers do you use to count?

▶ Which rational numbers do you use to measure when you cook?

Check for Understanding

Write in the form $\frac{a}{b}$.

1. 0.2   **2.** $1\frac{3}{4}$ **3.** 25%   **4.** 1.5   **5.** $3\frac{1}{3}$

Practice

Write the rational number in the form $\frac{a}{b}$.

6. 0.99   **7.** 1.2   **8.** 0.6   **9.** 0.75   **10.** 0.95

11. $\frac{4}{5}$ **12.** $5\frac{11}{12}$ **13.** 90%   **14.** $1\frac{9}{11}$ **15.** 0.11

16. 7%   **17.** $4\frac{1}{2}$ **18.** 16%   **19.** 10.3   **20.** 100%

Tell which rational numbers you would use in the given situation.

21. to express the amount in your bank account

22. to express the amount of spice needed to make muffins

23. to express your shoe size

24. to express a temperature below 0°

25. Is every rational number a whole number? Explain.

26. Is every integer a rational number? Explain.

Mixed Applications

27. Logical Reasoning Can you write all the possible fractions equivalent to $\frac{1}{2}$? Explain. Write five fractions equivalent to $\frac{1}{2}$.

28. Logical Reasoning The normal body temperature for a human is 98.6°F. Show that 98.6 is a rational number.

29. Only 2% of the apples in a market are bruised. How many apples are bruised if the market has 100 apples?

30. Number Sense How many degrees must the maker of a circle graph use to show 25%?

MIXED REVIEW

Find the least common multiple (LCM) for each pair of numbers.

1. 3, 5   **2.** 15, 45   **3.** 24, 48   **4.** 10, 15   **5.** 2, 18

Find the missing number.

6. 240 mg = ■ g   **7.** 50 cm = ■ mm   **8.** 0.2 kL = ■ L   **9.** 50 cm = ■ m

Explain why you usually use fractions instead of decimals to express part of a foot.

VARIABLES AND EXPRESSIONS

In the future, jets will travel much faster than today's jets. The Concorde travels at 1,500 mph. How fast will jets travel if they travel 100 mph faster than the Concorde? 500 mph faster? 1,000 mph faster?

You know the speed of the Concorde is 1,500 mph. Since you must find three possible speeds for jets of the future, you can use an expression.

Write an expression. Let c represent the number of miles per hour faster a jet of the future will travel than the Concorde.

speed of the Concorde + number of miles per hour faster

$$1,500 + c$$

To evaluate an algebraic expression, replace the variable with the given value for the variable. Then perform the operation. Use a calculator with memory keys.

Enter 1,500 M+.

	Replace.	Perform the operation.

1,500 + c

MRC	+	100	=	1600.
MRC	+	500	=	2000.
MRC	+	1,000	=	2500.

So, the jets of the future will travel at 1,600 mph, 2,000 mph, or 2,500 mph.

Examples

Evaluate the expressions for $d = 10$, $z = \frac{1}{2}$, and $t = {}^{-}12$.

A. $\dfrac{d}{2.5}$

$10 \div 2.5 = 4$

B. $13z$

$13 \times \dfrac{1}{2} = \dfrac{13}{2}$, or $6\dfrac{1}{2}$

C. $t + 10$

$^{-}12 + 10 = {}^{-}2$

- Why is $y + 12$ the same as $12 + y$?

Check for Understanding

Evaluate the expression.

1. $8 + x$, for $x = 5$

2. $y + 10$, for $y = 12$

3. $z - 3$, for $z = 15$

4. $5w$, for $w = 6$

5. $\dfrac{81}{t}$, for $t = 3$

6. $\dfrac{b}{5}$, for $b = 55$

Practice

Evaluate the expression $y - 12$ for each value of y.

7. $y = 24$

8. $y = 36$

9. $y = 15\dfrac{2}{5}$

10. $y = 33.05$

11. $y = {}^{-}2$

Evaluate the expression $d \div 3$ for each value of d.

12. $d = 24$

13. $d = \dfrac{1}{3}$

14. $d = 6\dfrac{2}{3}$

15. $d = 27.9$

16. $d = 111$

Evaluate the expression $7s$ for each value of s.

17. $s = 9$

18. $s = 3\dfrac{1}{5}$

19. $s = 5.5$

20. $s = 45\%$

21. $s = 4.02$

Mixed Applications

22. **Logical Reasoning** The dimensions of Bette's rectangular yard are twice the dimensions of Ian's rectangular yard. How does the area of Bette's yard compare with the area of Ian's yard?

23. John has 9 more apples than Rose. Let x equal the number of apples John has. Write an equation, using 9 for the number of apples Rose has.

CHALLENGE • GEOMETRY CONNECTION

Look at the figure. Try to visualize it as a combination of familiar geometric figures.

Let A = area, P = perimeter, r = radius, s = side, and d = diameter.

24. Write a formula for finding the perimeter of Figure **A**.

25. Write a formula for finding the area of Figure **A**.

26. Use your formulas to find the perimeter and the area of Figure **A**.

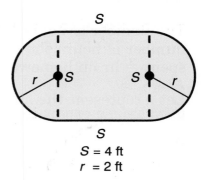

$S = 4\text{ ft}$
$r = 2\text{ ft}$

If the value of x changes, will the value of $x - 5$ remain the same? Explain.

WRAP UP...

EQUATIONS
with Whole Numbers and Fractions

Marshall thinks a twenty-first century baseball player will reach a lifetime record of 807 home runs, beating Henry Aaron's record of 755. The new record would be a meaningful increase over Aaron's record. What would be the increase in the number of home runs?

You can write and solve an equation to answer this question. Let n represent the increase.

Talk About It

▶ What expression, using n and 755, shows the increase in the number of home runs?

▶ How can you use the expression and 807 to form an equation?

▶ What is the inverse of the operation in the equation?

Use the inverse operation to solve the equation.

$$n + 755 = 807$$
$$n + 755 - 755 = 807 - 755 \quad \leftarrow \text{Subtract 755 from each side of the equation.}$$
$$n = 52$$

So, the increase would be 52 home runs.

___

You can solve equations with fractions in the same way you solve equations with whole numbers.

The number of hours Lily spent reading decreased by the number of hours she spent doing homework is $1\frac{3}{4}$. If she spent $\frac{3}{4}$ hr on homework, how long did she read?

Let r represent the amount of time for reading.

$$r - \frac{3}{4} = 1\frac{3}{4}$$
$$r - \frac{3}{4} + \frac{3}{4} = 1\frac{3}{4} + 1\frac{3}{4}$$
$$r = 2\frac{2}{4} = 2\frac{1}{2}$$

So, Lily read for $2\frac{1}{2}$ hr.

Check for Understanding

Tell how to solve the equation.

1. $x - 50 = 127$

2. $122 + y = 200$

3. $x - 1\frac{1}{2} = 4$

4. $m + \frac{3}{4} = 3$

5. $w - 10\frac{3}{8} = 10\frac{7}{8}$

6. $a + 1\frac{1}{5} = 3\frac{4}{5}$

Practice

Tell the inverse of the operation in the equation.

7. $x - 4 = 1$

8. $t + 8 = 17$

9. $\frac{3}{7} + s = 9$

10. $a - 12 = 62$

11. $y - \frac{1}{10} = 25$

12. $w - 3 = 17\frac{1}{3}$

13. $18 = x + 6$

14. $11 + c = 45$

Solve the equation. Use inverse operations.

15. $x + 321 = 500$

16. $y - 212 = 347$

17. $a + 347 = 459$

18. $b + 13 = 500$

19. $x + \frac{3}{8} = \frac{7}{8}$

20. $y - \frac{5}{6} = 1$

21. $m + 2\frac{1}{2} = 6$

22. $y - \frac{1}{2} = \frac{3}{4}$

23. $a + \frac{1}{5} = \frac{7}{20}$

24. $x - \frac{2}{3} = \frac{3}{4}$

25. $w + 3\frac{5}{12} = 7\frac{1}{3}$

26. $z - 2\frac{1}{5} = 11\frac{6}{10}$

27. $m + 17{,}345 = 28{,}000$

28. $a - 76{,}298 = 100{,}000$

29. $n + 7\frac{5}{12} = 23$

Mixed Applications

30. By the year 2000, U.S. exports of wheat, rice, and corn may increase by 15,000,000 tons. If exports now total 45,763,000 tons, how much may be exported by 2000?

31. **Write a Problem** Write a problem that can be solved by writing an equation involving fractions.

MIXED REVIEW

Write the greatest common factor (GCF) for each pair of numbers.

1. $9, 33$

2. $7, 35$

3. $24, 60$

4. $18, 99$

5. $5, 45$

Write the prime factorization in exponent form.

6. 15

7. 45

8. 60

9. 54

10. 75

Explain how to use inverse operations to solve equations.

WRAP UP...

More Practice, Lesson 14.4, page H87

453

The fastest trains in the world today can travel at an average speed of 135 mph. In the future, underground vacuum tubes may travel at an average speed of 14,000 mph. How much faster than today's trains could the vacuum tubes travel?

Sometimes you can solve a problem by writing an equation that relates the quantities you know to the quantity you are trying to find.

▶ UNDERSTAND

What are you asked to find?

What facts are given?

▶ PLAN

What strategy will you use?

You can *write an equation* that shows how the average speed of trains relates to the average speed of vacuum tubes. To do this, choose a variable to represent the amount of increase.

▶ SOLVE

How will you solve the problem?

Let n represent the increase in speed. Then *write an equation* relating the given facts to n.

$$n + 135 = 14,000$$

Use the inverse of addition. Subtract 135 from each side.

$$n + 135 - 135 = 14,000 - 135$$
$$n = 13,865$$

So, the vacuum tubes could travel 13,865 mph faster than today's trains.

▶ LOOK BACK

How can you check your answer?

WHAT IF... ...you write the equation $135 + n = 14,000$ instead of $n + 135 = 14,000$? How will this affect your answer?

Apply

Write an equation. Then solve.

1 Suppose that a football player breaks Fran Tarkenton's lifetime record of 47,003 yd gained. If the new record is 50,000 yd gained, what is the increase over Tarkenton's record?

2 Alice is saving money to buy a computer printer that costs $399. She has already saved $150. How much more does she need to save?

Mixed Applications ➤ | **STRATEGIES** | • Write an Equation • Make a Table • Guess and Check • Draw a Diagram

Choose a strategy and solve.

3 Mike will save $10 this month, $20 next month, $30 the third month, and so on. If the pattern continues, how much will Mike save the sixth month?

4 The temperature was 28°F at 6 A.M. By noon it was 40°F. How much did the temperature increase during the six hours?

5 Thea walks 5 blocks east, 2 blocks north, 4 blocks west, and 5 blocks north. Is she north or south of the point where she began?

6 Aldo has 10 coins in his pocket. He has only dimes and quarters. The total value of the coins is $1.30. How many quarters does he have?

7 The sum of Angelo's age and Mai's age is 29. Angelo is 3 years younger than Mai. How old are Angelo and Mai?

8 A square patio has an area of 121 ft². What is the length of each side of the patio?

WRITER'S CORNER

9 Today's jet planes travel between New York and Los Angeles in 378 min. In the future, underground vacuum tubes may travel the same distance in 54 min. Use this information to write a problem that can be solved by writing an equation.

REVIEW AND MAINTENANCE

Use the table for Exercises 1–2.

> I need to determine the total cost of each option.

1. Saoni wants to buy a robot. She has $50 and earns $60 a month at a part-time job. Which option could Saoni choose? Why?

2. Which of the options is the most expensive? the least expensive?

Robot Purchase Options

1. Pay $145 cash.
2. Pay $18 a month for 12 months.
3. Pay $45 down and $12 a month for 12 months.

3. Paul starts a salad while he microwaves his dinner for 15 min. The salad is ready in 21 min. How much longer does it take Paul to make the salad than to microwave the dinner?

4. A monorail car at an amusement park holds 45 passengers. The park manager wants to be sure he has enough cars to accommodate 1,255 passengers. How many monorail cars does he need?

Find the sum or difference.

5. $2 + {}^-3$

6. ${}^-10 + 8$

7. $11 + {}^+9$

8. ${}^-12 + {}^-6$

Write the ordered pair for each point on the coordinate plane.

9. point A

10. point B

11. point C

12. point D

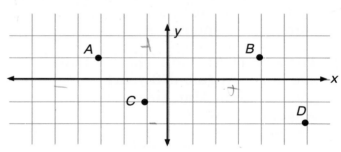

Write an algebraic expression for the word expression.

13. 12 times a

14. 9 more than r

15. 8 less than d

16. c divided by 16

Write the rational number in the form $\frac{a}{b}$.

17. 0.33

18. 5%

19. 2,1

20. 0.35

21. $1\frac{1}{2}$

22. 0.10

Evaluate the expression.

23. $10 - x$, for $x = 9$

24. $y + 4$, for $y = {}^-2$

25. $2z$, for $z = 52$

Solve the equation. Use inverse operations.

26. $a - \frac{3}{4} = \frac{1}{8}$

27. $x + 99 = 220$

28. $y - 9 = {}^-18$

29. $\frac{3}{5} + w = 3\frac{1}{3}$

Spotlight ON PROBLEM SOLVING

Understand
Plan
Solve
Look Back

Recognize Relationships

Some people say that studying math is really recognizing relationships. When people study math in the future, they will continue to look for relationships such as this one.

For every number greater than 1, there is at least one prime number between the number (*n*) and twice the number (2*n*).

Talk About It

Work with a classmate to discover the relationships. Be prepared to discuss your results with the class.

a. How do prime numbers differ from composite numbers?

b. Pick a prime number (*n*). Double it (2*n*).

c. What prime number comes between your number and its double?

d. Find a number that has only one prime number between it and its double.

Apply

Discover the relationship and solve the problem. Discuss your results with the class.

1. Each time a customer rents a film at See-All Video, he or she can choose a card with one of these numbers: 1, 3, 9, 18, 24, 51, 63, 72. The store gives a free video to each customer whose cards total 100. What is the least number of cards you could choose to win? What are the cards?

2. Choose one of these relationships. Give at least three examples.
   a. Every even number greater than 4 can be expressed as the sum of two odd prime numbers.
   b. The sum of any four consecutive whole numbers must have a factor of 2.

EQUATIONS
with Integers

Homes of the future may be built beneath the ocean's surface. Suppose the entrance to an ocean home is 15 m below the surface. The base of the home is 25 m lower than the entrance. How far below the ocean's surface is the base of the home?

You can use integers to write and solve an equation. Let n represent how far the base is from the surface.

Talk About It

▶ What is an expression that shows how far the base is beneath the ocean's surface?

▶ How can you use the expression and n to write an equation?

$$^-15 + \,^-25 = n \quad \longleftarrow \text{ Add the integers.}$$
$$^-40 = n$$

So, the base of the home of the future is 40 m beneath the ocean's surface.

More Examples

A. $x + \,^-8 = \,^-2$

Use the inverse operation.
Subtract $^-8$ from each side.

$x + \,^-8 - \,^-8 = \,^-2 - \,^-8$

Rewrite as addition.
Then add.

$x + \,^-8 + 8 = \,^-2 + 8$
$\qquad x = 6$

B. $y - \,^-45 = 52$

Rewrite as addition.

$y + 45 = 52$

Use the inverse operation.
Subtract 45 from each side.

$y + 45 - 45 = 52 - 45$
$\qquad y = 7$

Talk About It

▶ In Example **A**, how can you solve the equation by adding the same integer to each side?

▶ In Example **B**, how can you solve the equation by adding the same integer to each side?

Check for Understanding

Tell how to solve the equation.

1. $n = {}^-6 + 8$

2. ${}^-8 + {}^-6 = y$

3. $n - 2 = {}^-8$

4. $x - {}^-6 = 10$

5. $y + {}^-2 = {}^-9$

6. $m + 4 = 1$

Practice

Tell what integers to add or subtract to solve the equation.

7. $a = 10 + {}^-3$

8. $m = {}^-14 + {}^-5$

9. $x = {}^-12 + 2$

10. $x - 5 = 2$

11. $m - {}^-7 = 8$

12. $c - 3 = {}^-4$

13. $r + {}^-20 = 13$

14. $x + {}^-5 = {}^-9$

15. $n + 29 = 20$

Solve the equation.

16. $a = 17 + {}^-3$

17. $x = 17 - {}^-2$

18. $r = {}^-8 - {}^-1$

19. $b = {}^-11 - {}^+12$

20. $x + {}^-8 = {}^-11$

21. $x - 8 = {}^-6$

22. $m + {}^-70 = 100$

23. $x - {}^-9 = 33$

24. $x - 13 = 2$

25. $a + {}^-7 = {}^-17$

26. $a + 7 = 1$

27. $x + 9 = {}^-33$

28. $x + 14 = 3$

29. $m - 12 = 2$

30. $r - {}^-6 = 10$

31. $s + {}^-12 = 35$

32. If x is 7, what is $x + 12$?

33. If y is 22, what is $56 - y$?

34. If b is ${}^-5$, what is $b + 9$?

35. If c is ${}^-6$, what is $15 - c$?

Mixed Applications

36. **Number Sense** Look at these numbers: 2, 3, 5, 8, and 12. What are the next two numbers in the pattern?

37. A diver was 78 ft below the surface of the water. She rose to 50 ft below the surface. How many feet did the diver ascend?

38. **Write a Question** Daytime temperatures on the moon reach 250°F. At night, temperatures on the moon drop to ${}^-260$°F.

Tell how to solve the equation
$x - {}^-7 = 4$.

WRAP UP...

INEQUALITIES

A scientist predicts that the United States will begin to explore Mars in less than 12 years. What inequality can you write to represent the statement?

Remember that an equation has an equals sign. An inequality has either $<$ or $>$.

Since you do not know the exact number of years, you can use the variable n to represent the number of years. Then write the inequality.

$$n < 12$$

An inequality may have more than one solution. For $n < 12$, there are 11 whole-number solutions.

$1 < 12$	$2 < 12$	$3 < 12$	$4 < 12$	$5 < 12$	$6 < 12$
$7 < 12$	$8 < 12$	$9 < 12$	$10 < 12$	$11 < 12$	

The choices of fraction, mixed-number, and decimal solutions continue forever.

Another Method

You can use a number line to visualize solutions.

$$n < 12$$

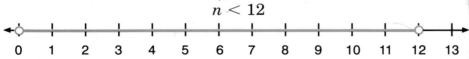

The circles above 0 and 12 show that those numbers are not included. The line segment between 0 and 12 shows that all numbers less than 12 and greater than 0 are included.

- Why are negative numbers not included?

- Are $4\frac{1}{2}$, 2.7, and $\frac{14}{5}$ also solutions of $n < 12$?

Example

$$y < 8$$

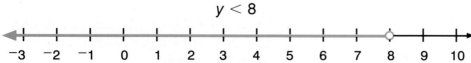

- How will the number line that shows $y > 8$ differ from the number line that shows $y < 8$? Draw the number line.

Check for Understanding

Tell whether the given number is a solution of the inequality in the box. Write *yes* or *no*.

$$x < 5$$

1. 0   **2.** $2\frac{1}{2}$ **3.** 7   **4.** $^-5$ **5.** 5   **6.** 10   **7.** 2

$$x + 4 > {}^-2$$

8. 0   **9.** $^-4$ **10.** $^-2$ **11.** $^-5$ **12.** 20   **13.** $^-15$ **14.** $^-3$

Practice

Tell whether $^-1$ is a solution of the inequality. Write *yes* or *no*.

15. $y > 0$ **16.** $x < {}^-2$ **17.** $x + 3 > 1$ **18.** $y < 12$

Tell whether 3 is a solution of the inequality. Write *yes* or *no*.

19. $x - 2 < 0$ **20.** $y + 5 > {}^-4$ **21.** $m - 3 > 0$ **22.** $n - 4 > {}^-2$

23. Tell which number line shows solutions of $x < 2$.

a.

b.

c.

24. Tell which number line shows solutions of $y > {}^-3$.

a.

b.

c.

Draw a number line that shows the solutions of the inequality.

25. $m > {}^-4$ **26.** $x < {}^-2$ **27.** $m > 5$ **28.** $b + 2 > 0$

29. $a < 3\frac{1}{2}$ **30.** $t > 1\frac{2}{3}$ **31.** $x < 10$ **32.** $d - 5 < 10$

Mixed Applications

33. Use the variable x to write an inequality. The amount in Sally's savings account is less than $50.

34. **Write a Problem** Write a problem that can only be solved by using negative integers.

Explain why 3.4 and $2\frac{1}{2}$ are solutions of $a < 4$.

WRAP UP...

EXPLORING

Relations

When you use algebra, you are exploring how numbers relate to one another and often create patterns.

WORK TOGETHER

Building Understanding

Use the rectangular prism to explore relations.

> **Talk About It**

▶ How many cubes are in each layer? How many layers are in the prism?

▶ If the prism had 6 layers, how many cubes would there be?

Copy and complete the table to find the pattern.

Number of layers	1	2	3	4	5
Total number of cubes	■	■	■	■	■

▶ How is the total number of cubes related to the number of layers?

▶ Let n represent the number of layers. What expression can you write to describe the number of cubes?

Another Activity

Brett is 11 years old, and his sister Heather is 9.

Copy and complete the table to show the pattern.

> **Talk About It**

▶ How is Brett's age related to Heather's age?

▶ Let h represent Heather's age. What expression can you write to describe Brett's age?

Brett's age	11	12	13	14	15
Heather's age	9	■	■	■	■

Making the Connection

When two quantities create a pattern, they are said to form a **relation**. One way to show a relation is to write an expression.

In the rectangular prism, the total number of cubes can be represented by the expression $20n$.

Likewise, Brett's age can be represented by the expression $h + 2$.

Another Example

Suppose the car of the future uses 15 watts of solar power for each mile it travels. What expression can you write to show the number of watts used?

Let x represent the number of miles.

Let y represent the number of watts.

x	1	2	3	4	5
y	15	30	45	60	75

$\longrightarrow 15x$

So, the expression $15x$ shows the number of watts used.

Checking Understanding

Copy and complete the table. Then write an expression using x to show the value of y.

1.

x	3	4	5	6	7	8	9
y	7	8	9	■	■	■	■

2.

x	0	1	2	3	4	5	6
y	0	3	6	9	■	■	■

3.

x	2	3	4	5	6	7	8	9
y	0	1	2	3	■	■	■	■

4.

x	5	10	15	20	25	30
y	1	2	3	■	■	■

5.

x	0	1	2	3	4	5	6	7	8
y	0	$\frac{1}{2}$	1	$\frac{3}{2}$	2	■	■	■	■

6. In Exercise 3, what expression can you write, using y, to show the value of x?

GRAPHING RELATIONS

Engineers can add cars to a monorail to accommodate any number of passengers. A total of 5 passengers can occupy 1 car on a monorail. This relation is shown in the table.

Number of passengers	5	10	15	20	25
Number of cars	1	2	3	4	5

Let p represent the number of passengers. Then the expression $\frac{p}{5}$ shows the number of cars needed.

This relation can also be shown by a set of ordered pairs.

(5,1)   (10,2)   (15,3)   (20,4)   (25,5)

You can use the set of ordered pairs to graph a relation.

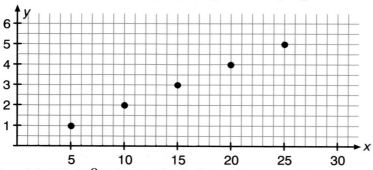

- Should $(13,2\frac{3}{10})$ be included in the set of ordered pairs? Why or why not?

Example

Name the ordered pairs in the table.

x	⁻3	⁻2	⁻1	0	1	2
y	3	2	1	0	⁻1	⁻2

The ordered pairs are (⁻3,3), (⁻2,2), (⁻1,1), (0,0), (1,⁻1), and (2,⁻2).

Talk About It

▶ What expression, using x, can you write to show the value of y in the example?

Idea Bank, page 490, Exercises I-4

Check for Understanding

Name the ordered pairs in the table.

1.

x	8	7	6	5	4
y	5	4	3	2	1

2.

x	4	8	12	16	20
y	1	2	3	4	5

3. What expression, using y, can you write to show the value of x in Exercise 1?

4. What expression, using y, can you write to show the value of x in Exercise 2?

5–6. Use graph paper to make two coordinate planes. Then graph the relation in Exercise 1 and in Exercise 2.

Practice

Use the expression to help you complete the table.

7. $x + 2$

x	0	1	2	3	4
y	2	3	▨	▨	▨

8. $2x$

x	1	2	3	4	5
y	2	4	▨	▨	▨

9. $x - 5$

x	15	14	13	12	11
y	10	9	▨	▨	▨

10. $2x + 1$

x	2	3	4	5	6
y	5	7	▨	▨	▨

11. $2x - 1$

x	1	2	3	4	5
y	1	3	▨	▨	▨

12. $3x - 3$

x	1	2	3	4	5
y	0	3	▨	▨	▨

13–18. Use graph paper. Draw a coordinate plane for each exercise. Graph the ordered pairs for Exercises 7–12.

Mixed Applications

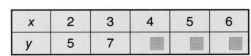

Scientists (s)	1	2	3	4	5
Moons explored (m)	5	8	11	14	17

Use the table for Exercises 19–20.

19. What expression, using s, describes the number of moons explored?

20. Use Data If the pattern continues, how many moons can 10 scientists explore?

What expression can you write to describe the number of students per table in your school cafeteria?

WRAP
UP...

PROBLEM Solving

The sixth-grade class has 28 students. There are 14 who play in the band, 9 who are on the swim team, and 4 who participate in both activities. Kay drew this diagram to show student participation. How many students do not participate in either activity?

Some problems involving relationships among groups (or sets) of people can be solved by using logical reasoning.

Band Participants   Swim Team Participants

10   4   5

▶ UNDERSTAND

What are you asked to find?

What information are you given?

▶ PLAN

How can you solve the problem?

Use logical reasoning to determine the number of students not participating in either activity.

▶ SOLVE

How can you carry out your plan?

The overlap of the circles shows that 4 students participate in both activities.

There are 10 students in the band who are not on the swim team. There are 5 students on the swim team who are not in the band.

Therefore, there are 4 + 10 + 5, or 19, students in the band or on the swim team or both. This leaves 28 − 19, or 9, students who do not participate in either activity.

So, 9 students in the sixth-grade class do not participate in either activity.

▶ LOOK BACK

What other strategy could you use?

WHAT IF... . . . you were asked the number of students who participate in only one activity? What would be your answer?

Apply

Solve. Use logical reasoning.

1 A language club has 35 members. Of these members, 15 speak Spanish, 11 speak French, and 5 speak both Spanish and French. How many members do not speak Spanish or French?

2 The results of a survey of 50 people show 11 who ski but do not play tennis, 8 who play tennis but do not ski, and 3 who do both. How many people do not ski or play tennis?

Mixed Applications	STRATEGIES	• Draw a Picture • Guess and Check
		• Make a Table • Find a Pattern

Choose a strategy and solve.

3 The difference between two numbers is 10. Their sum is 90. What are the numbers?

4 The first number in a pattern is 7. Each number thereafter increases by 4. What is the seventh number in the pattern?

5 If the area of a square picture is 81 in.^{2}, what is the length of each side of the picture?

6 Anna is 4 years older than Julio. If the sum of their ages is 22, how old is Julio?

7 Adult tickets to a concert cost $5. Student tickets cost $2. A group of 10 people will attend the concert. The total cost is $29. How many students will attend?

8 Wallace plans to practice his trumpet 3 hr in Week 1 and 4 hr in Week 2. He will add 1 hr to his practice time each week for 10 weeks. For how many hours will he practice in Week 7?

9 In a group of 60 students, 16 are in the choir, 25 are in the computer club, and 12 are in both. How many students do not participate in either the choir or the computer club?

10 Jalim walks 3 blocks north, 5 blocks east, 2 blocks south, and 6 blocks west. How many blocks will he have walked when he crosses his own path?

11 Look at the table. How many passengers will fit in 5 personal jets?

Personal jets	1	2	3	4
Passengers	1	4	9	16

Vocabulary Check

Choose a word from the box to complete each sentence.

algebra
equation
inequality
rational
relation
variable

1. When you use variables to represent unknown quantities, you are using __?__ . *(page 446)*

2. A number that can be written in the form $\frac{a}{b}$ where a and b are integers and $b \neq 0$ is a(n) __?__ number. *(page 448)*

3. When two quantities create a pattern, they form a(n) __?__ . *(pages 462, 463)*

4. A letter that represents an unknown number is a(n) __?__ . *(pages 446, 450)*

5. A mathematical number sentence that uses < or > is a(n) __?__ . *(page 460)*

6. A mathematical number sentence that uses an equals sign is a(n) __?__ . *(page 446)*

7. What is the difference between an expression and an equation? *(page 446)*

8. How do you know whether a number is a rational number? *(page 448)*

9. How do you evaluate algebraic expressions? *(page 450)*

10. How do you solve the equation $t - 5 = 12$? *(page 452)*

Inequalities have more than one correct answer.

Tell whether the given number is a solution to the inequality in the box. Write *yes* or *no*. *(page 460)*

$$x + 2 > 4$$

11. 10   12. 2   13. 18   14. ⁻5   15. 0   16. 3

Write an expression using x that shows the value of y. *(page 462)*

17.

x	2	4	6	8	10	12	14
y	1	2	3	4	5	6	7

18.

x	2	5	10	15	20	25	30
y	4	10	20	30	40	50	60

Skill Check

Write a word expression for the algebraic expression. *(page 446)*

19. $8 - y$
20. $9 + x$
21. $\dfrac{z}{7}$
22. $(a + 6) - 10$

Write an algebraic expression for the word expression. *(page 446)*

23. six less than b
24. x plus eleven
25. twelve divided by a

Write the number in the form $\dfrac{a}{b}$. *(page 448)*

26. $9\dfrac{1}{5}$
27. 9%
28. $7\dfrac{1}{2}$
29. $10\dfrac{1}{2}$
30. 0.55
31. 25

Evaluate the expression. *(page 450)*

32. $x + 16$, for $x = 5$
33. $\dfrac{y}{0.5}$, for $y = 28$
34. $z - {}^-3$, for $z = 50$

Solve the equation. Use inverse operations. *(pages 452, 458)*

35. $x + 75 = 205$
36. $y - {}^-54 = 55$
37. $z - \dfrac{1}{9} = \dfrac{1}{3}$

Tell whether $^-7$ is a solution of the inequality.
Write *yes* or *no*. *(page 460)*

38. $x > {}^-1$
39. $y < 10$
40. $z + 11 > {}^-7$
41. $r > 1$

42. $b > {}^-7$
43. $c < {}^-8$
44. $h - 20 < 45$
45. $d < {}^-7$

46. Copy and complete the table. Then write the expression that shows the value of y. *(page 462)*

x	1	2	3	4	5	6	7	8
y	2	4	6	8	■	■	■	■

Problem-Solving Check *(pages 454, 466)*

47. The winning football team was ahead 35 to 10. Then the losing team scored 10 points. How many more points must the losing team score to tie the game?

48. Mona had 10 yd of material. She used 4.8 yd to make a suit. How much material does she have left?

49. A survey of 130 people showed that 55 carried only umbrellas, 50 carried only briefcases, and 15 carried both. How many people did not carry umbrellas or briefcases?

50. Of the 51 people who ate in a cafeteria, 32 had salads, 10 had hot meals, 3 had both, and the rest had sandwiches. How many people had sandwiches?

CHAPTER TEST

Write an algebraic expression for the word expression.

1. x plus two   **2.** 18 times d **3.** 9 less than c **4.** b divided by 16

Write the number in the form $\frac{a}{b}$.

5. $1\frac{2}{3}$ **6.** 27%   **7.** 0.35   **8.** 8

Evaluate the expression.

9. $7n$, for $n = 5$ **10.** $8 + d$, for $d = 4$ **11.** $x - 20$, for $x = {}^-20$

Solve the equation.

12. $x + 60 = 44$ **13.** $b - 25 = 45$ **14.** $y - {}^-26 = 71$

Tell whether 2 is a solution of the inequality. Write *yes* or *no*.

15. $x > 3$ **16.** $y < 11$ **17.** $c - 5 > {}^-5$

Write an expression using x that shows the value of y.

18.

x	1	2	3	4
y	2	3	4	5

19.

x	1	2	3	4
y	$^-1$	$^-2$	$^-3$	$^-4$

To write an expression, I must find how y relates to x.

20.

x	4	5	6	7	8
y	2	2.5	3	3.5	4

21. Copy and complete the table.

x	100	90	80	70	60	50	40	30	20	10
y	95	85	75	65	■	■	■	■	■	■

22. A Pullman car holds 54 passengers. Each car behind it holds 5 more than the first car. How many passengers will the first 5 cars hold?

23. John saved $15 a week. He now has $210. For how many weeks has John been saving?

24. Of the 75 students studying French, 42 only speak French, 18 only write French, and 10 can do both. How many can do neither?

25. A survey of 88 pet owners shows that 53 own dogs, 20 own cats, and 9 own both. How many do not own dogs or cats?

Twenty-First Century Products

n 1975 who could have believed there would be a pocket-size color television set? Let your mind wander into the twenty-first century. What kinds of products will you be using? Work with your teammates to design a future-products catalog.

Decide

Brainstorm products that you might expect to see in the future.

Think about the products' durability, price, and usefulness.

Discuss what products should be in the catalog. Choose ten products.

Decide the products' prices, sizes, and descriptions.

Do

Design and make a catalog that shows or explains these ten products.

Share

Compare your team's catalog with those of other teams. Tell why you chose each product. Did other teams include similar products?

Talk About It

How did you determine the price of the products?

What new technology will be required to produce the products?

How did you use rational numbers in your catalog?

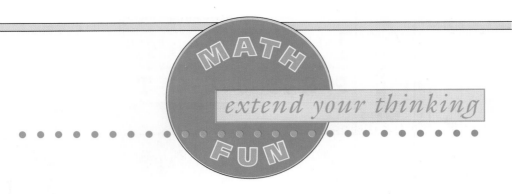

7	14	12	3	16
19	6	1	20	9
2	13	5	11	15
17	10	18	4	8

Four Square

You can play this game with one or two classmates. Make a large gameboard like the one shown and a set of cards with the numbers 1 through 20. Provide each player with a set of small markers and a worksheet. The object of the game is to place four markers in four squares that form a larger square.

Players take turns. After mixing the cards, the first player draws five number cards and arranges them to form an expression equal to a number on the gameboard. Then the player places a marker on the gameboard number. The five cards are mixed with the others for the next player's draw, and play continues. More than one player can place a marker in the same square. The first to mark four squares in a larger square wins. You can use an egg timer to limit the time of each play.

Challenge

Starring Equations

Copy the equations. Use three of the four numbers in the box to replace the stars in each equation, making it correct. You can make the numbers positive or negative. You may want to use a calculator.

2	5	8	11

$$* + * + * = {}^+15$$
$$* + * + * = {}^+2$$
$$* + * + * = {}^-8$$
$$* + * + * = {}^-11$$

Algebraic Patterns

Use the expressions to continue each pattern.

$2n$ 2, 4, 6, 8, ■, ■, ■
$2n + 1$ 3, 5, 7, 9, ■, ■, ■
$2n - 1$ 1, 3, 5, 7, ■, ■, ■

Continue this pattern.
  1, 4, 9, 16, ■, ■, ■

Write an algebraic expression to show the pattern.

Continue this pattern.
  0, 3, 8, 15, ■, ■, ■

Write an algebraic expression to show the pattern.

Write the letter of the correct answer.

1. $1\frac{2}{3} + 2\frac{1}{5}$

   A. $3\frac{3}{8}$ B. $3\frac{13}{15}$

   C. $4\frac{13}{15}$ D. not here

2. $3\frac{3}{4} \times \frac{4}{9}$

   A. $1\frac{2}{3}$ B. $2\frac{1}{3}$

   C. 3   D. not here

3. What is the decimal for $\frac{7}{5}$?

   A. 0.14   B. 0.71
   C. 1.4   D. 7.1

4. What is the GCF of 9 and 21?

   A. 3   B. 9
   C. 21   D. 189

5. Solve. $a + 8 = {}^-12$

   A. $a = {}^-20$ B. $a = {}^-12$
   C. $a = 12$ D. $a = 20$

6. What is 12% of 27?

   A. 0.324   B. 3.24
   C. 32.4   D. not here

7. What is the area of a circle with a radius of 11?

   A. 6.908   B. 37.994
   C. 69.08   D. 379.94

8. What is the area of a triangle with $b = 2$ and $h = 6$?

   A. 6   B. 12
   C. 18   D. 36

9. Evaluate $2x$, for $x = 1.6$.

   A. 0.8   B. 0.32
   C. 32   D. not here

10. Which is a solution of $x > {}^-7\frac{1}{2}$?

    A. $^-12$ B. $^-9$

    C. $^-7\frac{1}{2}$ D. $^-7$

11. Apples cost $3.00 a dozen. Oranges cost $0.10 less than $\frac{1}{2}$ the price of apples. How much does a dozen oranges cost?

    A. $1.30   B. $1.40
    C. $1.50   D. $1.75

12. Of the 48 people surveyed, 33 like corn, 11 like tomatoes, and 3 like corn and tomatoes. How many people do not like either?

    A. 4 people   B. 7 people
    C. 10 people   D. 12 people

COMPUTER
Connection

Computers are powerful tools for doing many kinds of tasks quickly and accurately. They are used by programmers, graphic artists, word processors, accountants, doctors, and even by students in mathematics.

In this section you will explore LOGO, use a word processing program, make a spreadsheet, and build a data base. You will be using the same types of software that many people use at home and at work.

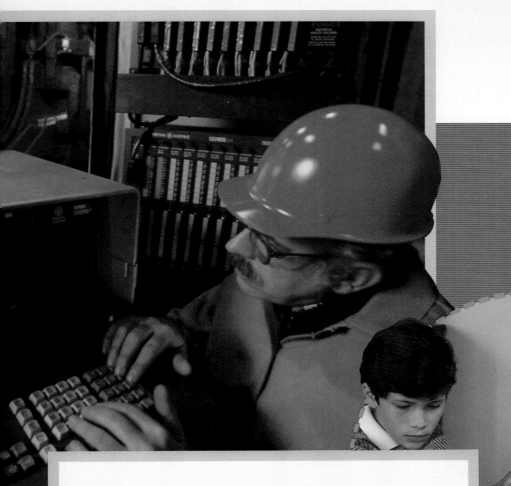

Table of Contents

LOGO Graphics
Subprocedures

A **subprocedure** is a group of commands or a procedure that the computer can do over and over. The subprocedure is written once somewhere outside of the procedure that calls the commands. For example, the procedure STAR calls two subprocedures that are procedures themselves. The subprocedures are called TRIANGLE and MOVE.

At the Computer

Type the procedures TRIANGLE, MOVE, and STAR in that order to draw the picture below.

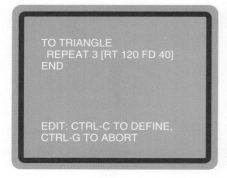

```
TO TRIANGLE
  REPEAT 3 [RT 120 FD 40]
END




EDIT: CTRL-C TO DEFINE,
CTRL-G TO ABORT
```

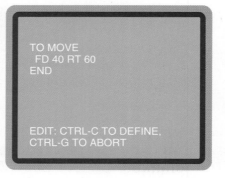

```
TO MOVE
 FD 40 RT 60
END






EDIT: CTRL-C TO DEFINE,
CTRL-G TO ABORT
```

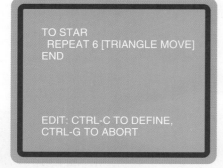

```
TO STAR
  REPEAT 6 [TRIANGLE MOVE]
END




EDIT: CTRL-C TO DEFINE,
CTRL-G TO ABORT
```

```
PLEASE WAIT...
STAR DEFINED
?STAR
?
```

Talk About It

▶ Does it matter which procedure you type first?

▶ What do you think the computer does when it reads the name of the subprocedure in the procedure?

▶ Why are subprocedures useful?

Applying Math

The following computer screens illustrate how to draw a coordinate grid by using LOGO. The procedure GRAPH contains a subprocedure called LINE, which draws the segments on each axis. The lines are 10 turtle steps apart.

The LOGO program has a command called SETXY that directs the turtle to a point on the graph.

At the Computer

1. Type the procedures to make the graph.

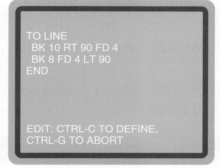

```
TO ARROW
  LT 135 FD 8 BK 8 RT 270
  FD 8 BK 8 LT 135
END



EDIT: CTRL-C TO DEFINE,
CTRL-G TO ABORT
```

```
TO LINE
  BK 10 RT 90 FD 4
  BK 8 FD 4 LT 90
END



EDIT: CTRL-C TO DEFINE,
CTRL-G TO ABORT
```

```
TO GRAPH
  HOME FD 100 ARROW
  BK 180 RT 180 ARROW
  HOME RT 90 FD 100
  ARROW BK 200 RT 180
  ARROW REPEAT 19 [LINE] HOME
  FD 100 REPEAT 17 [LINE] HOME
END

EDIT: CTRL-C TO DEFINE,
CTRL-G TO ABORT
```

2. After you have a grid on your computer screen, you can use the SETXY command to direct the turtle to a point on the graph. The command SETXY 20 (–30) tells the turtle to move 20 steps to the right and 30 steps down. (Some LOGO programs require that the second negative number be enclosed by parentheses.) The ordered pair (20,⁻30) describes the point where the turtle stops.

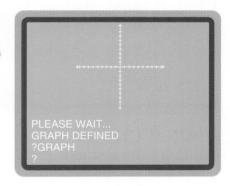

```
PLEASE WAIT...
GRAPH DEFINED
?GRAPH
?
```

3. Using the SETXY command, write four commands, each sending the turtle to a different section of the graph. Bring the turtle home after each command. For example, SETXY –30 (–10) HOME will draw a line from the center, (0,0), to the stopping point, (⁻30,⁻10), in the left lower section of the grid. HOME brings the turtle back to (0,0) ready for the next command.

Notice that the negative signs in computer commands are not raised as in ordered pairs.

4. Write commands for these ordered pairs.

      a. (⁻50,70)   b. (40,60)

      c. (⁻30,⁻50)   d. (10,⁻20)

Recursion is a way of repeating a group of commands over and over. To understand what that means, apply computer recursion to a number sequence discovered by Leonardo Fibonacci in the thirteenth century. The Fibonacci sequence (1, 1, 2, 3, 5, 8, 13, 21, 34, 55, . . .) is recursive because the relationship between the numbers can be expressed in a formula that can be repeated over and over.

At the Computer

1. Type the procedure FIBONACCI1, which prints the sequence.

2. Type the procedure FIBONACCI2, which uses a counter to limit the numbers in the sequence.

```
TO FIBONACCI1 :NUM1 :NUM2
  PRINT :NUM1 + :NUM2
  FIBONACCI1 :NUM2 :NUM1 + :NUM2
END




EDIT: CTRL-C TO DEFINE,
CTRL-G TO ABORT
```

```
TO FIBONACCI2 :NUM1 :NUM2 :COUNTER
  IF :COUNTER = 0 THEN STOP
  PRINT :NUM1 + :NUM2
  FIBONACCI2 :NUM2 :NUM1 + :NUM2 :COUNTER - 1
END




EDIT: CTRL-C TO DEFINE,
CTRL-G TO ABORT
```

FIBONACCI1 1 1
will start the sequence.

FIBONACCI2 1 1 10
will start the sequence.

Talk About It

▶ How are the Fibonacci numbers related?

▶ How can you stop printing the sequence in FIBONACCI1?

▶ Explain what the procedure FIBONACCI1 does.

▶ Why is the procedure FIBONACCI1 recursive?

▶ What are the names of the variables used in FIBONACCI1?

▶ How can you pick out a variable name in a LOGO procedure?

Talk About It

▶ Is the procedure FIBONACCI2 recursive? Why or why not?

▶ Why did the program stop at 144?

▶ What steps in the procedure tell the computer to stop printing the numbers in the sequence?

▶ What can you do to print 20 numbers in the sequence?

▶ What would happen if you start the sequence with two numbers other than 1 and 1?

Many number patterns or sequences are found in architecture, music, or nature. In the nineteenth century, scientists began to discover the Fibonacci sequence in spirals of sunflower heads and snail shells, in pine cones, and even in animal horns. The Fibonacci sequence is found in the chambered nautilus shell. The following procedure uses the sequence to draw the pattern found in the shell.

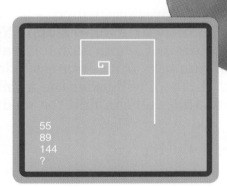

At the Computer

3. Type the procedure FIBONACCI3, which will draw a design of the number sequence found in nature.

```
TO FIBONACCI3 :NUM1 :NUM2 :COUNTER :ANGLE
  IF :COUNTER = 0 THEN STOP
  PRINT :NUM1 + :NUM2
  FD :NUM1 + :NUM2
  RT :ANGLE
  FIBONACCI3 :NUM2 :NUM1 + :NUM2 :COUNTER - 1 :ANGLE
END


EDIT: CTRL-C TO DEFINE,
CTRL-G TO ABORT
```

```
55
89
144
?
```

FIBONACCI3 0 1 11 90
will draw a spiral.

4. Use the procedure FIBONACCI3 to experiment with different number values to make your own designs.

5. Write a procedure to print your own number sequence.

6. Use the number sequence from the procedure written for Exercise 5 to draw a design. Use FIBONACCI3 as a guide.

Spreadsheet

Sorting

Jay organized baseball batting information for some of the players of the Chicago White Sox in the spreadsheet below. He will use the data to find the mean, median, mode, and range for these baseball statistics: Average (AVG), At Bat (AB), Runs (R), Hits (H), Home Runs (HR), Runs Batted In (RBI).

```
File: BASEBALL            REVIEW/ADD/CHANGE           Escape: Main Menu
====== A ====== B ========= C ======== D ======== E ========= F ====== G =====
 1| CHICAGO WHITE SOX
 2|
 3| BATTING      AVG        AB        R        H        HR       RBI
 4| BOSTON       .252       218       34       55        5        23
 5| CALDERON     .286       622       83      178       14        87
 6| FISK         .293       375       47      110       13        68
 7| FLETCHER     .253       546       77      138        1        43
 8| GALLAGHER    .266       601       74      160        1        46
 9| GUILLEN      .253       597       63      151        1        54
10| JOHNSON      .300       180       28       54        0        16
-----------------------------------------------------------------------------
A4:   (Label) BOSTON
Type entry or use ☼ commands                              ☼-? for Help
```

The spreadsheet program has a tool that will sort the information in a particular column. You can tell the computer to sort a column of words alphabetically. It will also sort a column of numbers from greatest to least or from least to greatest. This tool will order the numbers in each of the columns so that you can find the median, mode, and range.

At the Computer

1. Use an almanac or a newspaper to collect information about a baseball team, and make a spreadsheet like the one shown.

2. Type the example spreadsheet (or your own) so that the names of the people are not in alphabetical order. Then use the arrange or sorting tool on *your* computer to alphabetize the list.

3. Using the layout tools, align the numbers and titles on your spreadsheet. Numbers with decimals should have the same number of decimal places, and whole numbers should not have decimals.

4. Use the sorting command on *your* computer to arrange the numbers in column B from greatest to least.

At the Computer

5. Sort the numbers in each of the columns to help you find the mode and range for each baseball statistic. Keep track of your discoveries on a separate sheet of paper or on another section of the same spreadsheet.

6. Finally, copy a formula that will calculate the mean for each column of numbers. For example, the following formula in cell B13 calculates the mean for the numbers in column B.

$$((B4+B5+B6+B7+B8+B9+B10)/7)$$

You can make a relative, or similar, copy of this formula in other columns.

The following baseball spreadsheet shows where the mean, median, mode, and range for the first column of numbers are organized.

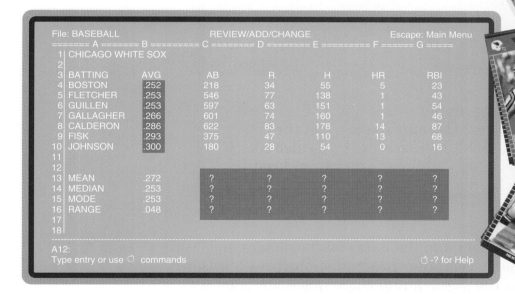

```
File: BASEBALL                  REVIEW/ADD/CHANGE              Escape: Main Menu
======= A ======= B ========== C ======== D ======== E ========= F ====== G =====
 1| CHICAGO WHITE SOX
 2|
 3| BATTING        AVG          AB            R           H          HR         RBI
 4| BOSTON        .252         218           34          55          5          23
 5| FLETCHER      .253         546           77         138          1          43
 6| GUILLEN       .253         597           63         151          1          54
 7| GALLAGHER     .266         601           74         160          1          46
 8| CALDERON      .286         622           83         178         14          87
 9| FISK          .293         375           47         110         13          68
10| JOHNSON       .300         180           28          54          0          16
11|
12|
13| MEAN          .272          ?            ?           ?           ?           ?
14| MEDIAN        .253          ?            ?           ?           ?           ?
15| MODE          .253          ?            ?           ?           ?           ?
16| RANGE         .048          ?            ?           ?           ?           ?
17|
18|
A12:
Type entry or use ⌂ commands                               ⌂ -? for Help
```

Talk About It

▶ How can you be sure a formula is working correctly in a spreadsheet?

▶ When you arrange a column, what happens to the information in the other columns?

▶ How does ordering the numbers help you to find the median, the mode, and the range?

▶ What happens to the formulas when you sort a column?

Spreadsheet
A Checkbook Register

Tammy set up the following spreadsheet to use as a checkbook register. She started with a balance of $514.00 in the bank account. Withdrawals and bank fees are subtracted from the balance. Deposits are added to the balance.

At the Computer

Use the following guidelines to finish Tammy's spreadsheet.

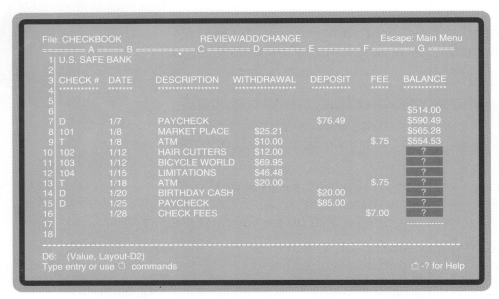

```
File: CHECKBOOK                 REVIEW/ADD/CHANGE                 Escape: Main Menu
======A=====B============C========D========E========F========G=====
 1| U.S. SAFE BANK
 2|
 3| CHECK #   DATE     DESCRIPTION    WITHDRAWAL    DEPOSIT    FEE    BALANCE
 4| ********* *******  ************** *************  *******  *****  ***********
 5|
 6|                                                                  $514.00
 7| D          1/7     PAYCHECK                      $76.49          $590.49
 8| 101        1/8     MARKET PLACE   $25.21                         $565.28
 9| T          1/8     ATM            $10.00                  $.75   $554.53
10| 102        1/12    HAIR CUTTERS   $12.00                         ?
11| 103        1/12    BICYCLE WORLD  $69.95                         ?
12| 104        1/15    LIMITATIONS    $46.48                         ?
13| T          1/18    ATM            $20.00                  $.75   ?
14| D          1/20    BIRTHDAY CASH                 $20.00          ?
15| D          1/25    PAYCHECK                      $85.00          ?
16|            1/28    CHECK FEES                             $7.00  ?
17|                                                                  ------------
18|
------------------------------------------------------------------------------
D6:   (Value, Layout-D2)
Type entry or use ⌂ commands                                 ⌂ -? for Help
```

ATM stands for Automated Teller Machine.

1. Type the check numbers and the dates as characters, not number values. Some computer programs interpret 1/7 as 0.14286 instead of the date January 7. In most spreadsheet programs if you type a " symbol before the number, the computer will read the number as a character.

2. Most spreadsheet programs align the number values at the right of a column. Align the number values and titles into a neat format.

3. Add *** or ---- patterns to highlight titles.

4. Use $ and . symbols for dollar values.

5. Type a formula in cell G7 that will subtract or add withdrawals, deposits, and fees, and adjust the balance. HINT: (G6-__+__-__)

6. Copy the formula to cells G7 through G16.

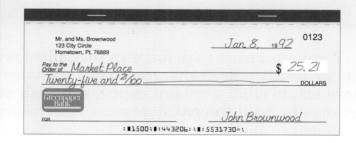

ITEM NO. OR TRANS CODE	DATE	TRANSACTION DESCRIPTION	SUBTRACTIONS AMOUNT OF PAYMENT OR WITHDRAWAL (–)	FEE IF ANY	ADDITIONS AMOUNT OF DEPOSIT OR INTEREST (+)	BALANCE
D	1/7	Paycheck				514.00
					76.49	590.49
101	1/8	Market Place	25.21			565.28
T	1/8	ATM	10.00	75		554.53
102	1/12	Hair cutters	12.00			
103	1/12	Bicycle World	69.95			
104	1/16	Limitations	46.48			
T	1/18	ATM	20.00	75		
D	1/20	Birthday cash			20.00	
D	1/20	Paycheck			85.00	
	1/28	Check fees		7.00		

Mr. and Ms. Brownwood
123 City Circle
Hometown, Pt. 76889

Jan. 8, 1992   0123

Pay to the Order of Market Place $ 25.21

Twenty-five and 21/100   DOLLARS

Greenpaper Bank

FOR _____   John Brownwood

⑆1500⑆ ⑈443206⑆ ⑈5531730⑉

At the Computer

Work in a group of three or four people. Make a checkbook spreadsheet that will record transactions for one month. Follow these steps.

7. Imagine that as a group you will get $200 a month from extra chores, recycling paper and aluminum cans, and allowances.

8. Make a list of six or eight activities to do as a group. Write down how much each activity will cost the group. For example, a trip to a movie might cost $20.00 for four people.

9. Put the transactions to pay for the activities in a spreadsheet. Make up dates and check numbers for your checks. Decide when you can get cash from an Automated Teller Machine (ATM) to pay for an activity.

10. Type a formula that will subtract the costs of the activities from the balance.

11. Include these unexpected transactions.
   a. bank fee $ 0.75   b. work bonus $10.00
   c. check fee $ 8.00   d. bank fee $ 0.75

Talk About It

▶ What happens if the total cost of the activities is greater than the current balance?

▶ What can you do if you forget to type in a transaction?

▶ What happens to the balance if you change the amount of one of the transactions?

Word processors have features that allow you to add or replace text (words or characters) in a document. You can also move text to other word processing, spreadsheet, or data base documents. A **clipboard** stores text to be moved from one document to another.

Before you can move information from one document to another, you must create the files. A **desktop index** will let you choose which files you want to work with. To avoid retyping, the workers at U.S. Safe Bank copied the highlighted list of checks from the CHECKBOOK file to the word processing file CHECK SUMMARY.

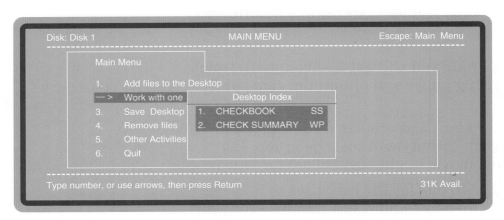

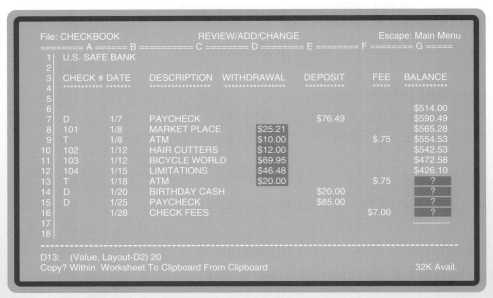

At the Computer

Here is the word processing file that contains information taken directly from the spreadsheet file.

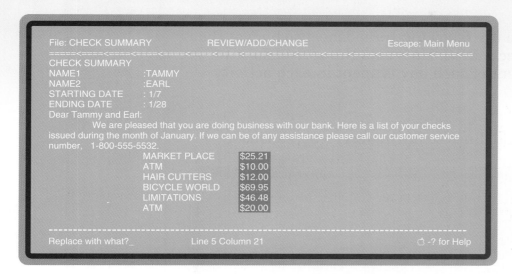

```
File: CHECK SUMMARY          REVIEW/ADD/CHANGE              Escape: Main Menu
=====<====<====<====<====<====<====<====<====<====<====<====<====<====<==
CHECK SUMMARY
NAME1              :TAMMY
NAME2              :EARL
STARTING DATE      : 1/7
ENDING DATE        : 1/28
Dear Tammy and Earl:
          We are pleased that you are doing business with our bank. Here is a list of your checks
issued during the month of January. If we can be of any assistance please call our customer service
number,   1-800-555-5532.
                        MARKET PLACE      $25.21
                        ATM               $10.00
                        HAIR CUTTERS      $12.00
                        BICYCLE WORLD     $69.95
                        LIMITATIONS       $46.48
                        ATM               $20.00

----------------------------------------------------------------------------
Replace with what?_          Line 5 Column 21                    ⌘ -? for Help
```

Suppose that U.S. Safe Bank wants to send Tammy and Earl a summary of their checks every month by changing only certain information. Most word processors have a function that will find and replace characters or numbers.

1. Type the CHECK SUMMARY file on your word processor.

2. Use the **find** and **replace** functions to change January information to February information.

   a. 1/7   2/8
   b. 1/28   2/22
   c. 1-800-555-5532   1-800-555-5528
   d. $25.21 $35.81
   e. $20.00 $30.00

Talk About It

▶ What is the difference between moving information and copying it?

▶ What happens if the word or number you need to find and replace occurs more than once in the file?

▶ If you use a long word like *mathematics* in a document many times, how can the code *mmm* and the find and replace tool help?

Spreadsheet
Budgeting Time

Jerry Kent set up the following spreadsheet to budget the time he spends on recreation. He wants the spreadsheet to calculate what percent of each day is spent in each activity.

At the Computer

Use the following guidelines to finish Jerry's spreadsheet.

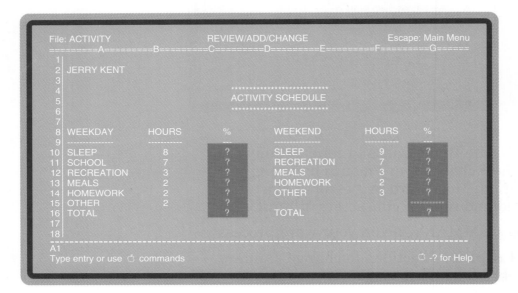

```
File: ACTIVITY                 REVIEW/ADD/CHANGE              Escape: Main Menu
=========A=========B=========C=========D=========E=========F=========G======
 1
 2  JERRY KENT
 3
 4                           ****************************
 5                           ACTIVITY SCHEDULE
 6                           ****************************
 7
 8  WEEKDAY        HOURS       %        WEEKEND        HOURS       %
 9  --------       -----      ---       --------       -----      ---
10  SLEEP            8          ?        SLEEP            9          ?
11  SCHOOL           7          ?        RECREATION       7          ?
12  RECREATION       3          ?        MEALS            3          ?
13  MEALS            2          ?        HOMEWORK         2          ?
14  HOMEWORK         2          ?        OTHER            3          ?
15  OTHER            2          ?                      --------
16  TOTAL            ?          ?        TOTAL                       ?
17
18
---------------------------------------------------------------------------
A1
Type entry or use ⌘ commands                              ⌘ -? for Help
```

1. Align the number values and titles in a neat format. Most spreadsheet programs will align the number values at the right of a column. Therefore, you can tell the computer to also align the titles of these columns at the right.

2. Add *** or --- patterns to highlight titles.

3. Type a formula in cell B16 that will check that the sum of the hours in each day is 24. Copy a variation of the formula to cell F16.

4. Type a formula in cells C10 through C15 that will calculate the percent of time spent on each activity each weekday. HINT: Try (B10/B16). Tell the computer to translate decimals into percents.

5. Repeat Exercise 4 to calculate the percent of time spent on each activity for weekend days.

Applying Math

Some software programs will translate data from the spreadsheet to a circle graph, or pie chart. Make a circle graph showing Jerry's activities. Use a sheet of paper or a graphing computer program.

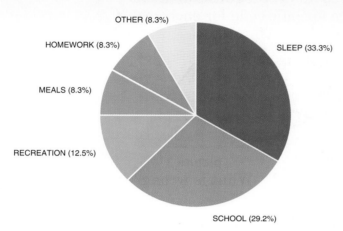

WEEKDAY ACTIVITY SCHEDULE
PERCENT OF TIME

OTHER (8.3%)

HOMEWORK (8.3%)

SLEEP (33.3%)

MEALS (8.3%)

RECREATION (12.5%)

SCHOOL (29.2%)

Use the circle graphs or the spreadsheet on page 486 to answer the following questions about Jerry's schedule.

6. About what percent of time does Jerry spend on recreation and eating during a weekday? a weekend day?

7. What cells contain information about the time Jerry spends on homework?

8. What cells contain 8.3%? Which activities take up this percent of time?

9. About how much more time does Jerry spend sleeping than doing homework and other things during the week?

Talk About It

▶ What happens to the value of the percent on the spreadsheet if you change the number of hours of sleep time from 8 to 7?

▶ How would you add one hour of soccer practice to the weekday schedule?

▶ Why is a spreadsheet an effective way to analyze your daily activities?

Jenny and Dave conducted a survey to investigate how different groups of people view optical illusions. They asked a group of middle school students to answer a question about these three pictures. They used a specific code for each result to establish consistency in the answers.

 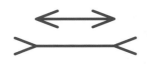 

| picture 1 | picture 2 | picture 3 |
| What do you see? | Which line is longer? | What is wrong? |

ANSWER CODES

FA - faces	SA - same	TH - the
VA - vase	TO - top	NO - nothing

They also used codes to collect information about the people they interviewed.

INTERVIEWEE CODES

Age Group		Gender	Eye Color
10	12	MA - male	BL - blue
11	13	FE - female	BR - brown
			GR - green

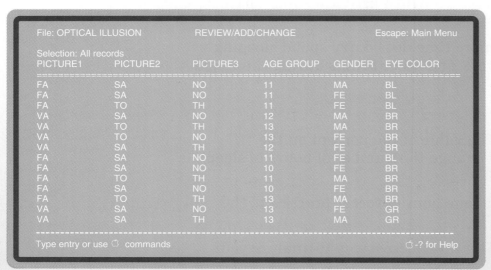

This data base shows how Jenny and Dave organized the results of the optical illusions survey.

File: OPTICAL ILLUSION   REVIEW/ADD/CHANGE   Escape: Main Menu

Selection: All records

PICTURE1	PICTURE2	PICTURE3	AGE GROUP	GENDER	EYE COLOR
FA	SA	NO	11	MA	BL
FA	SA	NO	11	FE	BL
FA	TO	TH	11	FE	BL
VA	SA	NO	12	MA	BR
VA	TO	TH	13	MA	BR
VA	TO	NO	13	FE	BR
VA	SA	TH	12	FE	BR
FA	SA	NO	11	FE	BL
FA	SA	NO	10	FE	BR
FA	TO	TH	11	MA	BR
FA	SA	NO	10	FE	BR
FA	TO	TH	13	MA	BR
VA	SA	NO	13	FE	GR
VA	SA	TH	13	MA	GR

Type entry or use ⌂ commands   ⌂-? for Help

Investigate

1. Look at the code descriptions and the data base on page 488 to answer these questions.

   a. How many females with blue eyes thought picture 1 was two faces?

   b. How many 13-year-olds thought picture 1 was a vase, or that the lines in picture 2 were the same?

   c. How many people with green eyes thought the lines in picture 2 were the same and that there was nothing wrong with picture 3?

   d. Why is a data base program better for answering the questions?

2. What does the following computer screen show?

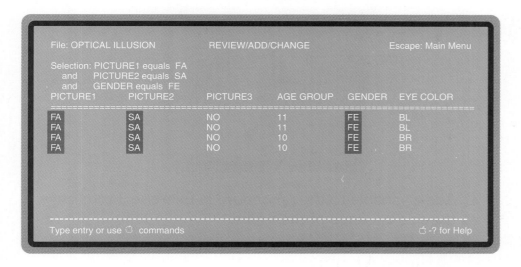

At the Computer

3. Trace the optical illusions on page 488. Conduct a survey like the example, and put your results in a data base.

4. Create your own format and layout. Decide which categories give you valuable information. Determine the widths of the fields.

5. Sort each of the picture fields to see whether there are any interesting results.

6. Print lists of the selections that show patterns or trends.

IDEA BANK

LOGO IDEAS

1. Use a TRIANGLE or SQUARE procedure in a subprocedure for drawing a triangle or a square.

2. Add a variable to the procedure in Exercise 1 to change the size or shape of the figure.

3. Using recursion, write a procedure to draw a figure like this one.

PLEASE WAIT...
CORNERS DEFINED
?CORNERS
?

4. Add a variable to the procedure in Exercise 3 to change the size or shape of the figure.

WORD PROCESSING IDEAS

5. Write directions explaining how to find factors of a large number like 2,464 with a calculator. Type example problems.

6. Use the find and replace functions to change the example problems in Exercise 5.

7. Write a plan for a survey about sports. Make a list of the questions you will ask and the people you will interview. Think about how you can organize the information in a data base program.

8. Write directions on how to copy text from one document to another with your word processor.

SPREADSHEET AND DATA BASE IDEAS

9. Collect statistics from an almanac or a newspaper about your favorite athlete. Put the information in a spreadsheet.

10. Conduct the survey from Exercise 7. Organize the information in a data base.

11. Make a schedule of your day at school. Organize it in a spreadsheet.

12. To the spreadsheet in Exercise 11, add the percent of time each class takes up in the school day.

13. Project. Keep track of your television viewing for one week. Use a spreadsheet to find the total hours you watched television during the week. Calculate the mean, median, range, and mode for the week.

14. Make a data base of the television shows you watch every week. Answer these questions.

    a. How long does each show last?

    b. Who is your favorite performer in the show?

    c. How many years or months have you been watching the show?

    d. How many of your classmates watch the show?

15. Make a data base containing this information about your family and friends.

    a. name

    b. address

    c. phone number

    d. birth date

    e. age

Student **H**andbook

CHAPTER 1

Place Value: Whole Numbers and Decimals

Rounding

A newspaper office reports a circulation of 36,475 newspapers. To the nearest ten thousand, how many newspapers are circulated?

You can use a number line to help you.

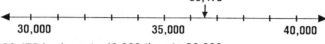

36,475 is closer to 40,000 than to 30,000.

You can also use rounding rules.
Look at the digit to the right of the place to which you are rounding.

36,475

6 > 5

If that digit is less than 5, the digit being rounded remains the same.

If that digit is 5 or greater, the digit being rounded increases by 1.

So, to the nearest ten thousand, 40,000 newspapers are circulated.

Newspaper ads vary in length. Sally wants to place three ads at the lengths given in the table. Estimate each length to the nearest centimeter.

You can use the rules for rounding whole numbers to round decimals.

Newspaper Ads	
Display Ad	**Length (in cm)**
Car	12.3
Grocery	12.5
Tire	12.7

Examples

Car ad

digit to be rounded —— 3 < 5

12.3
↓
12

Since 3 is less than 5, round 12.3 to 12 centimeters.

Grocery ad

digit to be rounded —— 5 = 5

12.5
↓
13

Since 5 is equal to 5, round 12.5 to 13 centimeters.

Tire ad

digit to be rounded —— 7 > 5

12.7
↓
13

Since 7 is greater than 5, round 12.7 to 13 centimeters.

- The price of gasoline at a gasoline pump may appear as $1.239. Why is the total amount purchased rounded to the nearest cent?

Practice

Round to the nearest ten thousand.

1. 37,205   **2.** 58,936   **3.** 324,520   **4.** 845,625

Round to the nearest hundred thousand.

5. 483,267   **6.** 678,090   **7.** 449,300   **8.** 12,786,500

Round to the nearest million.

9. 35,458,936   **10.** 20,843,267   **11.** 135,984,600   **12.** 1,452,935,278

Round to the nearest tenth.

13. 84.07   **14.** 89.93   **15.** 0.98   **16.** 0.32

17. 103.506   **18.** 165.094   **19.** 2,045.055   **20.** 1,390.039

Round to the nearest hundredth.

21. 0.934   **22.** 7.783   **23.** 37.839   **24.** 45.005

25. 0.014   **26.** 0.996   **27.** 93.097   **28.** 198.894

Round to the nearest dollar.

29. $2.93   **30.** $11.67   **31.** $0.98

32. $4.02   **33.** $32.39   **34.** $199.49

Round to the nearest whole number.

35. 3.75   **36.** 87.42   **37.** 18.9   **38.** 42.09   **39.** 100.54

Use the table for Exercises 40–41.

40. Which kinds of magazines have a circulation of about 5,000,000?

41. Round to the nearest million, and write about how many more news magazines are sold than travel magazines.

42. The number 149 is the greatest three-digit number that can be rounded to 100. What is the greatest four-digit number that can be rounded to 1,000?

Circulation of Magazines	
Kinds of Magazines	**Number Circulated**
News magazines	5,748,324
Sports magazines	4,928,165
Food magazines	1,875,692
Travel magazines	1,379,685

Multiplying Whole Numbers and Decimals

Multiplying Multiples of Ten

Bucky found that the average person uses about 40 gallons of hot water for a shower. If each of 5 family members takes a shower daily, about how much hot water would the family use for showers in one day?

You know about how much hot water 1 person uses. Multiply to find about how much a family of 5 uses.

Find $5 \times 40 = n$.

$$
\begin{array}{r}
4 \text{ tens} \\
\times\ 5 \\
\hline
20
\end{array}
\longrightarrow
\begin{array}{r}
40 \\
\times\ 5 \\
\hline
200
\end{array}
$$

Think:
Since $5 \times 4 = 20$,
$5 \times 40 = 200$.

So, the family of 5 would use about 200 gallons of hot water for showers in one day.

You can use a calculator to find patterns with multiples of 10.

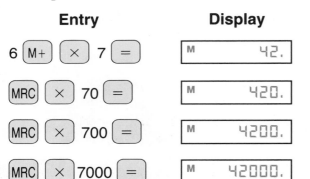

Entry	Display	
6 M+ × 7 =	M 42.	The M+ key stores one factor in memory.
MRC × 70 =	M 420.	The MRC key recalls that factor from memory.
MRC × 700 =	M 4200.	
MRC × 7000 =	M 42000.	

Examples

A.
$8 \times 1 = 8$
$8 \times 10 = 80$
$8 \times 100 = 800$
$8 \times 1,000 = 8,000$

B.
$9 \times (3 \times 1) = 9 \times 3 = 27$
$9 \times (3 \times 10) = 9 \times 30 = 270$
$9 \times (3 \times 100) = 9 \times 300 = 2,700$
$9 \times (3 \times 1,000) = 9 \times 3,000 = 27,000$

Talk About It

▶ How is the pattern in Example B different from the pattern in Example A?

▶ How can you use mental math to find 5×7, 5×70, 5×700, and $5 \times 7,000$?

Practice

Use mental math to find the product.

1.	50	2.	30	3.	800	4.	900	5.	500
	$\times\ 5$		$\times\ 7$		$\times\ 2$		$\times\ 4$		$\times\ 6$

6.	400	7.	900	8.	4,000	9.	2,000	10.	7,000
	$\times\ 8$		$\times\ 3$		$\times\ 6$		$\times\ 7$		$\times\ 9$

Complete the number sentence.

11. $700 \times 9 = $ ▨

12. $400 \times 5 = $ ▨

13. ▨ $\times 30 = 240$

14. $3 \times 200 = $ ▨

15. $500 \times 5 = $ ▨

16. $800 \times$ ▨ $= 4,800$

17. $2 \times$ ▨ $= 600$

18. ▨ $\times 40 = 320$

19. $6 \times$ ▨ $= 3,000$

Multiply each number by 10, 100, and 1,000.

20. 2　　**21.** 4　　**22.** 5　　**23.** 7　　**24.** 9

25. 10　　**26.** 15　　**27.** 23　　**28.** 45　　**29.** 123

Use a calculator to complete the pattern.

30. $7 \times 1 = 7$
$7 \times 10 = $ ▨
$7 \times 100 = $ ▨
$7 \times 1,000 = $ ▨

31. $8 \times (6 \times 1) = 48$
$8 \times (6 \times 10) = $ ▨
$8 \times (6 \times 100) = $ ▨
$8 \times (6 \times 1,000) = $ ▨

32. $11 \times (11 \times 1) = 121$
$11 \times (11 \times 10) = $ ▨
$11 \times (11 \times 100) = $ ▨
$11 \times (11 \times 1,000) = $ ▨

Use the table to solve Exercises 33–34.

Cost of Gas and Electricity at Bucky's House	
Month	Amount
January	$150
April	$ 95
July	$200
October	$ 90

33. There are 10 houses on Bucky's block. If each household paid the same amount for gas and electricity in October, how much would all the households on the block have paid?

34. Suppose 1,000 households have the same average gas and electricity bill as Bucky. How much would all the households have paid in January? in July?

CHAPTER 3

Multiplying Whole Numbers and Decimals

Multiplying by One-Digit Numbers

Solar collectors attached to the roof of a house capture
energy from sunlight. If the system for one house uses
6 collectors, how many solar collectors are needed to supply
213 houses with the same kind of solar energy system?

Estimate. $6 = 6$ $213 \approx 200$
$$6 \times 200 = 1,200 \longleftarrow \text{estimate}$$

You can use four different colors of counters to make
a model to solve the problem.

Let $\bullet = 1,000$, $\bullet = 100$, $\bullet = 10$, and $\circ = 1$.

Step 1
Model the problem.
6 groups of 213

$$\begin{array}{r} 213 \\ \times\ \ 6 \end{array}$$

Step 2
Group all counters by color.

Hundreds	Tens	Ones

6 groups of 200, | 6 groups of 10, | 6 groups of 3,
or 12 hundreds | or 6 tens | or 18 ones

Step 3 Thousands   Hundreds   Tens   Ones
Regroup.

1   2   7   8

$$\begin{array}{r} 213 \\ \times\ \ 6 \\ \hline 18 \longleftarrow 6 \times 3 \\ 60 \longleftarrow 6 \times 10 \\ +1{,}200 \longleftarrow 6 \times 200 \\ \hline 1{,}278 \end{array}$$

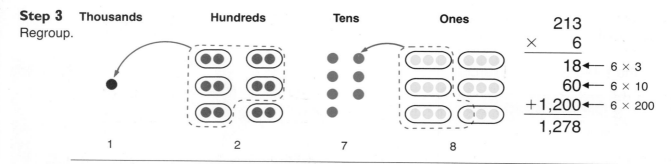

You can also use the standard method of multiplication to
find the number of solar collectors needed.

$$\begin{array}{r} 1 \\ 213 \\ \times\ \ 6 \\ \hline 1{,}278 \end{array}$$ So, 1,278 solar collectors are needed.

• How is regrouping done in the standard method?

Practice

Solve. Use counters to model each regrouping.

1. $2 \times 346 = \blacksquare$ **2.** $3 \times 604 = \blacksquare$ **3.** $6 \times 365 = \blacksquare$

Estimate each product by rounding.

4. $\begin{array}{r} 37 \\ \times\ 4 \\ \hline \end{array}$ **5.** $\begin{array}{r} 63 \\ \times\ 5 \\ \hline \end{array}$ **6.** $\begin{array}{r} 367 \\ \times\ \ 7 \\ \hline \end{array}$

7. $\begin{array}{r} 276 \\ \times\ \ 3 \\ \hline \end{array}$ **8.** $\begin{array}{r} 129 \\ \times\ \ 3 \\ \hline \end{array}$ **9.** $\begin{array}{r} 649 \\ \times\ \ 8 \\ \hline \end{array}$

10. $\begin{array}{r} 592 \\ \times\ \ 7 \\ \hline \end{array}$ **11.** $\begin{array}{r} 2,105 \\ \times\ \ \ \ 5 \\ \hline \end{array}$ **12.** $\begin{array}{r} 7,952 \\ \times\ \ \ \ 6 \\ \hline \end{array}$

Multiply.

13. $\begin{array}{r} 42 \\ \times\ 3 \\ \hline \end{array}$ **14.** $\begin{array}{r} 28 \\ \times\ 7 \\ \hline \end{array}$ **15.** $\begin{array}{r} 64 \\ \times\ 6 \\ \hline \end{array}$ **16.** $\begin{array}{r} 102 \\ \times\ \ 5 \\ \hline \end{array}$

17. $\begin{array}{r} 63 \\ \times\ 5 \\ \hline \end{array}$ **18.** $\begin{array}{r} 77 \\ \times\ 4 \\ \hline \end{array}$ **19.** $\begin{array}{r} 702 \\ \times\ \ 4 \\ \hline \end{array}$ **20.** $\begin{array}{r} 200 \\ \times\ \ 5 \\ \hline \end{array}$

21. $\begin{array}{r} 401 \\ \times\ \ 8 \\ \hline \end{array}$ **22.** $\begin{array}{r} 4,623 \\ \times\ \ \ \ 9 \\ \hline \end{array}$ **23.** $\begin{array}{r} 1,982 \\ \times\ \ \ \ 6 \\ \hline \end{array}$ **24.** $\begin{array}{r} 3,746 \\ \times\ \ \ \ 7 \\ \hline \end{array}$

25. $\begin{array}{r} 582 \\ \times\ \ 2 \\ \hline \end{array}$ **26.** $\begin{array}{r} 1,045 \\ \times\ \ \ \ 5 \\ \hline \end{array}$ **27.** $\begin{array}{r} 3,456 \\ \times\ \ \ \ 8 \\ \hline \end{array}$ **28.** $\begin{array}{r} 8,143 \\ \times\ \ \ \ 4 \\ \hline \end{array}$

29. $2 \times 453 = \blacksquare$ **30.** $7 \times 2,450 = \blacksquare$ **31.** $3,129 \times 7 = \blacksquare$ **32.** $9,767 \times 8 = \blacksquare$

33. Sally has a recipe that makes 54 whole-wheat rolls. She will make 6 recipes for a bake sale. How many rolls will she make?

34. Suppose that a row of seats on a jetliner will seat 9 passengers. How many passengers can be seated in 43 rows?

35. Americans recycle 78 million aluminum cans daily. At this rate, how many aluminum cans do Americans recycle in one week?

36. Is 37,000 a reasonable product for the factors 740 and 5? Explain.

## CHAPTER 4

Dividing Whole Numbers and Decimals

Exploring Decimal Division

WORK TOGETHER

You can use base-ten blocks to explore dividing with decimals.

Divide. $5.36 \div 4 = n$

Work with a classmate. Model 5.36 using base-ten blocks.

If you let the flat represent 1, you can make the following chart.

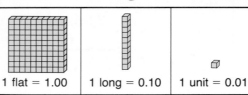

| 1 flat = 1.00 | 1 long = 0.10 | 1 unit = 0.01 |

- What blocks can you use to model 5.36?

- How many flats can be sorted evenly into 4 groups?

- Are there any flats left over?

- What regrouping can be made?

Regroup.
- How many longs are there now?

- How many longs can be sorted evenly into each of the 4 groups?

- Are there any longs left over?

- What regrouping can be made to use the other long?

Regroup.
- How many units are there now?

- How many units can be sorted evenly into each of the 4 groups?

- Did you use all of the blocks?

- What blocks are in each of the 4 groups?

Talk About It

▶ What decimal number represents the amount in each of the 4 equal groups?

▶ How can you compare division to this sorting process?

Practice

Use base-ten blocks to model the problem. Let one flat represent 1, one long represent 0.10, and one unit represent 0.01. Find the quotient.

1. $1.5 \div 5$

2. $3.2 \div 8$

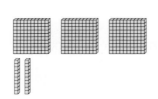

3. $4.4 \div 2$

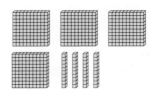

4. $3.74 \div 2$

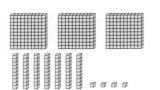

5. $5.28 \div 3$

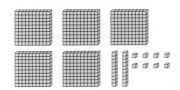

6. $2.10 \div 6$

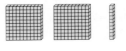

7. $3\overline{)7.5}$

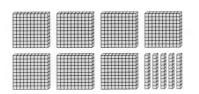

8. $4\overline{)4.8}$

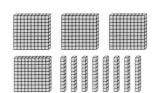

9. $3\overline{)6.3}$

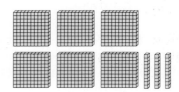

10. $3\overline{)2.79}$

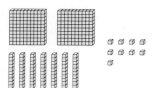

11. $4\overline{)5.36}$

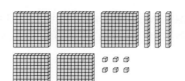

12. $5\overline{)2.95}$

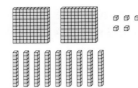

13. Painters at a new school took 9 hours to paint a section of a wall that is 26.1 meters long. How long a section of wall did they paint in 1 hour?

14. A school district administration building is 37.2 meters tall. It was built by attaching 12 identical concrete sections together. How tall is each section?

15. A small van will deliver 2,541.6 kilograms of supplies to the school today. If the van makes 6 trips, what is the average amount of supplies it will carry on each trip?

16. Amy has $1.44. She bought 3 notebooks, a package of pencils for $1.98, and a pen for $3.25. Amy had $16.00 to begin, and each notebook cost the same amount. What did each notebook cost?

CHAPTER 5

Graphing, Statistics, and Probability

Range, Mode, Median, and Mean

Carla surveyed sixth-grade students to find out how many hours a week they watch television. The frequency table shows the results of Carla's survey.

Analyze the data so that you can prepare a report.

Use connecting cubes to model the number of hours each student watches television.

Find the difference between the number of cubes in the tallest and the shortest stacks. This is called the **range.**

$10 - 2 = 8$ The range is 8.

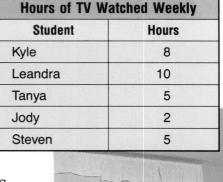

Hours of TV Watched Weekly	
Student	Hours
Kyle	8
Leandra	10
Tanya	5
Jody	2
Steven	5

Look for any stacks that have the same number of cubes. The number that appears most often is called the **mode.** The number 5 appears most often.
So, 5 is the mode.

Place the stacks of cubes in order from greatest to least. The number in the middle stack is called the **median.** The middle stack contains 5 cubes.
So, 5 is the median.

Put the cubes in one stack. Separate the stack into five equal stacks. Count the cubes in each new stack. This number, called the **mean,** is the average number of cubes in the original stacks. To compute the mean, follow these steps.

Step 1	**Step 2**
Find the total number of cubes.	Divide the sum of the data by the number of addends.
$8 + 10 + 5 + 2 + 5 = 30$	$30 \div 5 = 6$ ⌐ mean

So, the mean is 6.

Talk About It

▶ If you wanted a station to carry more programs of interest to sixth graders, which number would you report? Why?

Practice

Use the data from each table to find the range, mean, median, and mode.

1.

Pet Owners	
Student	Number Of Pets
Peggy	7
Ella	3
Rafael	2
Dennis	3
Kelko	5

Range ▪
Mean ▪
Median ▪
Mode ▪

2.

School Clubs	
Name	Membership
Computer	19
Math	9
Reading	7
Stamp	5
Yearbook	5

Range ▪
Mean ▪
Median ▪
Mode ▪

3.

Fifth-Grade Classes	
Teacher	Number of Students
Mrs. Larson	27
Ms. Stone	31
Mr. Freeman	34
Mrs. Lo	31
Mrs. Ortiz	32

Range ▪   Mean ▪

Median ▪   Mode ▪

4.

Girls' Heights	
Name	Inches
Adela	55
Sandy	59
Melba	60
Luanne	59
Gloria	57

Range ▪   Mean ▪

Median ▪   Mode ▪

Find the range, mean, median, and mode.

5. 24, 37, 42, 37, 15

6. $28, $42, $59, $42, $64

7. $270, $299, $271, $270, $275

8. 575, 630, 720, 575, 525

9. A football team has scored 14 points, 7 points, 10 points, and 17 points in its last four games. Find the mean of the points scored in the four games.

10. Sheila scored 95, 82, 90, and 83 on four tests. After the fifth test, the mode of her scores was 83. What did she score on the fifth test?

11. Use the information in Exercise 9. What is the range of the points that the football team scored?

12. Use the information in Exercise 10. What is the mean of Sheila's five test scores?

13. Use the information in Exercise 10. What is the range of Sheila's five test scores?

14. Use the information in Exercise 10. What is the median of Sheila's five test scores?

CHAPTER 6

Number Theory

Comparing Fractions

Simon and Takenya played a round of Plan-a-Garden. Simon planted watermelon seeds in $\frac{4}{5}$ of the garden. Takenya planted $\frac{2}{5}$ of the garden with cantaloupe seeds. Is more of the garden planted with watermelon or cantaloupe?

To compare fractions with like denominators, compare numerators or use fraction bars.

$\frac{1}{5}$	$\frac{1}{5}$	$\frac{1}{5}$	$\frac{1}{5}$	$\frac{1}{5}$

$\frac{1}{5}$	$\frac{1}{5}$	$\frac{1}{5}$	$\frac{1}{5}$	$\frac{1}{5}$

The fraction bars show that $\frac{4}{5}$ is greater than $\frac{2}{5}$. Also, look at the numerators. $4 > 2$

So, more of the garden is planted with watermelons.

You can also use fraction bars to compare fractions with unlike denominators.

Which is greater, $\frac{2}{3}$ or $\frac{3}{9}$?

$\frac{1}{3}$	$\frac{1}{3}$	$\frac{1}{3}$

$\frac{1}{9}$	$\frac{1}{9}$	$\frac{1}{9}$	$\frac{1}{9}$	$\frac{1}{9}$	$\frac{1}{9}$	$\frac{1}{9}$	$\frac{1}{9}$	$\frac{1}{9}$

The fraction bars show that $\frac{2}{3}$ is greater than $\frac{3}{9}$.

So, $\frac{2}{3} > \frac{3}{9}$.

Another Method

You can also compare $\frac{2}{3}$ and $\frac{3}{9}$ by writing equivalent fractions with like denominators.

Step 1	Step 2	Step 3
Find the least common multiple (LCM) of 3 and 9.	Write an equivalent fraction. Use the LCM as the denominator.	Compare the numerators.
3: 3, 6, 9 9: 9	$\frac{2}{3} = \frac{\blacksquare}{9}$ $\frac{2}{3} = \frac{6}{9}$	$\frac{6}{9} > \frac{3}{9}$ So, $\frac{2}{3} > \frac{3}{9}$

Practice

Use fraction bars to model the problem. Tell which fraction is greater.

1. $\dfrac{3}{4}, \dfrac{1}{4}$

2. $\dfrac{1}{2}, \dfrac{2}{3}$

3. $\dfrac{3}{4}, \dfrac{1}{3}$

4. $\dfrac{5}{6}, \dfrac{3}{8}$

Use the least common denominator (LCD) to write equivalent fractions.

5. $\dfrac{1}{8}, \dfrac{5}{6}$
LCD = 24

6. $\dfrac{2}{9}, \dfrac{5}{6}$
LCD = 18

7. $\dfrac{1}{3}, \dfrac{3}{7}$
LCD = 21

8. $\dfrac{5}{8}, \dfrac{3}{16}$
LCD = 16

9. $\dfrac{3}{8}, \dfrac{5}{6}$
LCD = ▨

10. $\dfrac{1}{9}, \dfrac{1}{5}$
LCD = ▨

11. $\dfrac{2}{3}, \dfrac{3}{7}$
LCD = ▨

12. $\dfrac{5}{8}, \dfrac{9}{16}$
LCD = ▨

Compare. Write <, >, or = for ●.

13. $\dfrac{2}{4}$ ● $\dfrac{3}{4}$

14. $\dfrac{1}{4}$ ● $\dfrac{1}{8}$

15. $\dfrac{2}{3}$ ● $\dfrac{5}{6}$

16. $\dfrac{7}{8}$ ● $\dfrac{5}{6}$

17. $\dfrac{5}{6}$ ● $\dfrac{3}{4}$

18. $\dfrac{1}{2}$ ● $\dfrac{3}{6}$

19. $\dfrac{5}{8}$ ● $\dfrac{2}{3}$

20. $\dfrac{6}{8}$ ● $\dfrac{3}{4}$

21. $\dfrac{3}{4}$ ● $\dfrac{5}{8}$

22. $\dfrac{1}{8}$ ● $\dfrac{1}{6}$

23. $\dfrac{1}{2}$ ● $\dfrac{3}{8}$

24. $\dfrac{2}{3}$ ● $\dfrac{4}{6}$

25. Anna used $\frac{2}{3}$ bag of fertilizer for her apple trees and $\frac{4}{6}$ bag for her pear trees. Did she use more for her apple or her pear trees?

26. Derek made some fruit sauce for his pancakes. He used $\frac{3}{4}$ cup of lemons and $\frac{7}{8}$ cup of limes. Did he use more lemons or more limes?

27. The members of the buyers' club are purchasing vegetables. One catalog advertises $\frac{5}{6}$ pound of chard for $1, and another catalog offers $\frac{7}{8}$ pound of chard for $1. Which is the better buy?

28. Brent planted $\frac{1}{3}$ of his garden with tomato plants, and Jill planted $\frac{2}{5}$ of her garden with tomato plants. Who has more tomato plants if they both have the same number of plants in their gardens?

Number Theory

Mixed Numbers

You can use fraction circles and fraction bars to help you understand mixed numbers.

Some fractions greater than 1 can be written as whole numbers.

Method 1

Here is one way to rename $\frac{16}{8}$.

$$\frac{8}{8} = 1 \qquad \frac{8}{8} = 1$$

$$\frac{8}{8} \;+\; \frac{8}{8} \;=\; \frac{16}{8}$$
$$1 \;+\; 1 \;=\; 2$$

Method 2

You can also divide to rename a fraction greater than 1 as a whole number.

$$\frac{16}{8} \;\longrightarrow\; 8\overline{)16} \atop \begin{array}{r} 2 \\ -16 \\ \hline 0 \end{array}$$

So, another name for $\frac{16}{8}$ is 2.

Some fractions greater than 1 can be written as mixed numbers.

Method 1

A **mixed number** is a whole number with a fraction. Here is one way to rename $\frac{9}{8}$.

$$\frac{8}{8} = 1 \qquad \frac{1}{8}$$

$$1 \;+\; \frac{1}{8} \;=\; 1\frac{1}{8}$$

Method 2

You can also divide to rename a fraction greater than 1 as a mixed number.

$$\frac{9}{8} \;\longrightarrow\; 8\overline{)9} \atop \begin{array}{r} 1 \\ -8 \\ \hline 1 \end{array} \qquad \frac{1}{8}$$

So, another name for $\frac{9}{8}$ is $1\frac{1}{8}$.

All mixed numbers can be written as fractions greater than 1.

Method 1

$$2\frac{1}{3} \qquad 1 = \frac{3}{3} \qquad 1 = \frac{3}{3} \qquad \frac{1}{3}$$

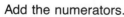

Add the numerators.

$$\frac{3}{3} + \frac{3}{3} + \frac{1}{3} = \frac{3 + 3 + 1}{3} = \frac{7}{3}$$

The denominator remains 3.

Method 2

You can also use multiplication and addition to change a mixed number to a fraction greater than 1.

$$2\frac{1}{3} = \frac{(3 \times 2) + 1}{3} = \frac{6 + 1}{3} = \frac{7}{3}$$

So, another name for $2\frac{1}{3}$ is $\frac{7}{3}$.

Practice

Use the model. Rewrite as a whole number.

1. $\dfrac{5}{5}$

2. $\dfrac{12}{4}$

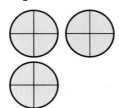

3. $\dfrac{8}{2}$

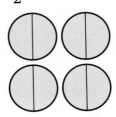

Use the model. Rewrite as a mixed number in simplest form.

4. $\dfrac{3}{2}$

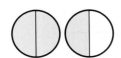

5. $\dfrac{15}{6}$

6. $\dfrac{11}{3}$

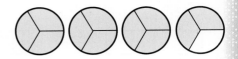

Use the model. Rewrite as a fraction.

7. $3\dfrac{1}{2}$

8. $2\dfrac{1}{3}$

9. $1\dfrac{4}{5}$

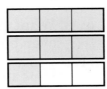

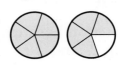

Rewrite as a whole number or a mixed number in simplest form.

10. $\dfrac{6}{6}$ **11.** $\dfrac{12}{3}$ **12.** $\dfrac{24}{4}$ **13.** $\dfrac{36}{6}$ **14.** $\dfrac{81}{9}$

15. $\dfrac{9}{7}$ **16.** $\dfrac{14}{4}$ **17.** $\dfrac{21}{2}$ **18.** $\dfrac{39}{5}$ **19.** $\dfrac{52}{7}$

Rewrite as a fraction.

20. 2 **21.** $1\dfrac{3}{5}$ **22.** $2\dfrac{1}{4}$ **23.** $1\dfrac{2}{3}$ **24.** $3\dfrac{5}{6}$

25. A cook uses $5\dfrac{1}{4}$ loaves of bread to make sandwiches. How many fourths of loaves is this?

26. There are $6\dfrac{2}{3}$ baskets of apples to be divided. How many thirds of baskets will there be?

27. Some students share a pizza. There are $3\dfrac{1}{3}$ pizzas. Each student receives $\dfrac{1}{3}$ of a pizza. How many students can share?

28. There are $2\dfrac{3}{8}$ pounds of spaghetti. One serving takes $\dfrac{1}{8}$ of a pound. How many servings are there?

Adding and Subtracting Fractions

Adding and Subtracting Unlike Fractions

WORK TOGETHER

You can use fraction bars to model addition and subtraction
of unlike fractions.

Addition	**Subtraction**
$\frac{1}{2} + \frac{2}{5}$	$\frac{1}{2} - \frac{1}{3}$

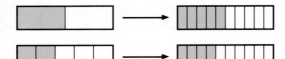

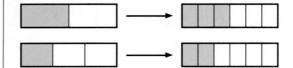

Talk About It

▶ What fraction bars will fit exactly over both $\frac{1}{2}$ and $\frac{2}{5}$?

▶ How many tenths does it take to make $\frac{1}{2}$? $\frac{2}{5}$?

▶ What is $\frac{5}{10} + \frac{4}{10}$?

So, $\frac{1}{2} + \frac{2}{5} = \frac{9}{10}$.

Talk About It

▶ What fraction bars will fit exactly over both $\frac{1}{2}$ and $\frac{1}{3}$?

▶ How many sixths does it take to make $\frac{1}{2}$? $\frac{1}{3}$?

▶ What is $\frac{3}{6} - \frac{2}{6}$?

So, $\frac{1}{2} - \frac{1}{3} = \frac{1}{6}$.

Another Method Write equivalent fractions, using the least
common multiple (LCM). Then add or subtract.

A. $\frac{1}{5} + \frac{2}{3}$

$\frac{1}{5}$ Multiples of 5: 5, 10, 15

$\frac{2}{3}$ Multiples of 3: 3, 6, 9, 12, 15

$$\frac{1}{5} = \frac{3}{15}$$
$$+\frac{2}{3} = \frac{10}{15}$$
$$\overline{\phantom{+\frac{2}{3}=}\ \frac{13}{15}}$$

B. $\frac{3}{4} - \frac{1}{6}$

$\frac{3}{4}$ Multiples of 4: 4, 8, 12

$\frac{1}{6}$ Multiples of 6: 6, 12

$$\frac{3}{4} = \frac{9}{12}$$
$$-\frac{1}{6} = \frac{2}{12}$$
$$\overline{\phantom{-\frac{1}{6}=}\ \frac{7}{12}}$$

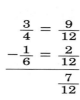
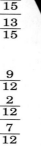

Bridge Lesson

Practice

Use fraction bars to find the sum or difference.

1. $\dfrac{1}{4} + \dfrac{1}{2}$

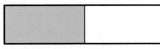

2. $\dfrac{1}{2} - \dfrac{3}{10}$

3. $\dfrac{1}{4} + \dfrac{1}{3}$

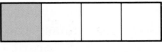

4. $\dfrac{3}{4} - \dfrac{1}{3}$

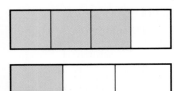

5. $\dfrac{5}{6} - \dfrac{1}{3}$

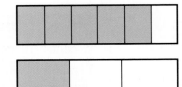

6. $\dfrac{3}{4} + \dfrac{5}{6}$

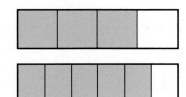

Find the least common denominator (LCD).

7. $\dfrac{1}{5}, \dfrac{2}{3}$

8. $\dfrac{3}{4}, \dfrac{4}{10}$

9. $\dfrac{2}{9}, \dfrac{5}{6}$

10. $\dfrac{1}{2}, \dfrac{4}{5}$

11. $\dfrac{2}{5}, \dfrac{3}{10}$

12. $\dfrac{1}{5}, \dfrac{2}{7}$

13. $\dfrac{1}{6}, \dfrac{2}{5}$

14. $\dfrac{1}{2}, \dfrac{3}{7}$

15. $\dfrac{1}{3}, \dfrac{7}{9}$

Rewrite the problem, using equivalent fractions.
Then find the sum or difference.

16. $\dfrac{1}{5} + \dfrac{2}{3}$

17. $\dfrac{3}{4} - \dfrac{1}{10}$

18. $\dfrac{2}{9} + \dfrac{5}{6}$

19. $\dfrac{4}{5} - \dfrac{1}{2}$

20. $\dfrac{2}{5} + \dfrac{3}{10}$

21. $\dfrac{2}{3} - \dfrac{1}{5}$

22. An explorer in the Arctic needed electricity to power some scientific equipment. He used a windmill to produce the electricity. Suppose the wind blew $10\frac{2}{5}$ hours one day and $8\frac{1}{3}$ hours the next day. How many more hours did the wind blow the first day?

23. A reporter is traveling by nonstop train from Rome to Paris to cover an international summit meeting. The trip to Paris takes $5\frac{1}{4}$ hours, and the return takes $4\frac{3}{8}$ hours. What is the total time for the round trip?

## CHAPTER 9

Measurement

The Metric System

Math Club members worked on a project, using only units from the **metric system.** They used metric units of length, capacity, and mass. They discovered that the same prefixes are used with different base units to name all the other units in the system. The prefixes relate to place value.

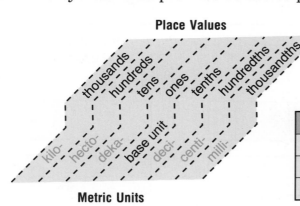

Place Values

Metric Units

Prefix	Base Unit	Measurement
centi-	meter	0.01 meter
milli-	liter	0.001 liter
kilo-	gram	1,000 grams

Metric measurements are given using a prefix and a base unit.

centi*meter*   milli*liter*   kilo*gram*

Decimals show how the prefix relates to the base unit.

centimeter	milliliter	kilogram
0.01 meter	0.001 liter	1,000 grams
(one hundredth of a meter)	(one thousandth of a liter)	

Examples

1 centimeter = 0.01 meter   1 milliliter = 0.001 liter   1 kilogram = 1,000 grams
4 centimeters = ■ meter   3 milliliters = ■ liter   7 kilograms = ■ grams
4 × 0.01 = 0.04 meter   3 × 0.001 = 0.003 liter   7 × 1,000 = 7,000 grams

Talk About It

▶ Which prefixes are used to show units that are smaller than the base units?

▶ Which prefix shows a unit 1,000 times greater than the base units?

▶ Which prefix shows a unit 100 times smaller than the base units?

Practice

Choose the smaller unit of measure. Write **a** or **b**.

1. **a.** milliliter
   b. liter

2. **a.** gram
   b. milligram

3. **a.** kilometer
   b. meter

4. **a.** kilogram
   b. milligram

5. **a.** kilometer
   b. centimeter

6. **a.** liter
   b. kiloliter

Choose the larger unit of measure. Write **a** or **b**.

7. **a.** gram
   b. kilogram

8. **a.** milliliter
   b. liter

9. **a.** decimeter
   b. centimeter

10. **a.** gram
    b. milligram

11. **a.** kilometer
    b. centimeter

12. **a.** liter
    b. kiloliter

Complete the table.

		km	m	dm	cm	mm
13.	3 m	0.003	3	30	300	
14.	9 m	0.009	9	90		9,000
15.	15 m	0.015	15		1,500	15,000
16.	25 m		25	250	2,500	25,000
17.	30 m	0.03	30		3,000	
18.	45 m		45			

Use the place-value poster on page H18. Write each as a decimal, using the base unit.

19. 5 dm

20. 3 mL

21. 8 g

22. 2 mm

23. 9 mg

24. 2 mL

25. 13 mL

26. 6 cm

27. 12 mg

28. 25 mg

29. Kristen and Sara need string for their projects. Kristen needs 2.5 m of string, and Sara needs 3.4 m of string. How much string do both girls need?

30. For her science project, Lois needs a board that is 1 m long. Alex needs a board that is 1 dm long. Who needs a longer board?

31. Ricardo is painting his display board. He already has 0.25 L of paint. If the board requires 1.5 L of paint, how much more paint does he need?

32. Cornelius is using an object that weighs 1 kg. Mark is using an object that weighs 1 mg. Who is using the lighter object?

Measurement

Using a Customary Ruler

Lisa did an experiment on plant growth. She measured and recorded the height of a plant in five different ways over four weeks.

Customary Units of Length	
12 inches (in.)	= 1 foot (ft)
3 ft	= 1 yard (yd)
5,280 ft or 1,760 yd	= 1 mile (mi)

Plant Height		
Measurement	**Week 1**	**Week 4**
To the nearest inch.	4 in.	4 in.
To the nearest $\frac{1}{2}$ in.	4 in.	4 in.
To the nearest $\frac{1}{4}$ in.	$3\frac{3}{4}$ in.	$4\frac{1}{4}$ in.
To the nearest $\frac{1}{8}$ in.	$3\frac{7}{8}$ in.	$4\frac{1}{8}$ in.
To the nearest $\frac{1}{16}$ in.	$3\frac{13}{16}$ in.	$4\frac{3}{16}$ in.

1 inch
$\frac{1}{2}$ inch
$\frac{1}{4}$ inch
$\frac{1}{8}$ inch
$\frac{1}{16}$ inch

- If Lisa measures to the nearest inch or to the nearest $\frac{1}{2}$ in., what would she record?

- Why are some measurements from Week 1 the same as Week 4?

- Using precise measurements, what was the height of the plant in Week 1? Week 4?

- To the nearest $\frac{1}{16}$ in., how much did Lisa's plant grow in four weeks?

Measure the width of your math book to the nearest inch, $\frac{1}{2}$ in., $\frac{1}{4}$ in., $\frac{1}{8}$ in., and $\frac{1}{16}$ in.
Record the measurements.

Talk About It

▶ Which measurement is the most precise?

▶ Why is measuring to the nearest $\frac{1}{16}$ in. more precise than measuring to the nearest $\frac{1}{2}$ in., $\frac{1}{4}$ in., or $\frac{1}{8}$ in.?

▶ When is a precise measurement necessary? When are precise measurements less important?

Practice

Measure each line segment to the part of the inch that gives the most precise measurement.

1. _____

2. _____

3. _____

4. _____

Draw a line to the given length.

5. $5\frac{1}{4}$ in. **6.** $2\frac{3}{8}$ in. **7.** $6\frac{1}{2}$ in. **8.** $7\frac{5}{16}$ in. **9.** $\frac{3}{4}$ in.

10. $4\frac{3}{4}$ in. **11.** $1\frac{3}{8}$ in. **12.** $\frac{5}{16}$ in. **13.** $7\frac{1}{2}$ in. **14.** $4\frac{5}{8}$ in.

Measure the given part of the figure to the nearest $\frac{1}{16}$ in.

15. the length of the straight yellow bar

16. the long sides of the blue triangle

17. the short side of the blue triangle

18. the red line

19. the green line

20. the purple line

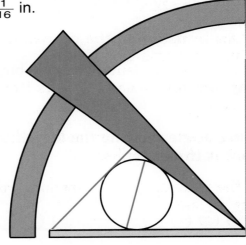

Solve. For Exercises 21–23, complete the riddle.

21. I measure long distances. There are 5,280 ft in me. My name is __?__, and my abbreviation is __?__.

22. I measure small things. There are 12 of me in 1 ft. My name is __?__, and my abbreviation is __?__.

23. I measure large things. There are 3 ft in me. My name is __?__, and my abbreviation is __?__.

24. Caroline measured a butterfly's wing span at $2\frac{3}{8}$ in. What is the measurement to the nearest $\frac{1}{2}$ in.?

25. Mills measured his plant twice a week. If the plant grew $2\frac{1}{3}$ in. each time he measured it, how much did the plant grow in 4 weeks?

26. Dillan measured the height of 5 flowers in his mother's garden. They measured 7 in., 5 in., $8\frac{3}{4}$ in., $7\frac{1}{4}$ in., and 7 in. What is the average height of the flowers?

## CHAPTER 10

Ratio, Proportion, and Percent

Ratios

In Mrs. Appleton's class, 3 of the 5 students who ride bicycles to school ride red bicycles.

You can compare the number of students who ride red bicycles to the total number of students who ride bicycles. A **ratio** is a comparison of two numbers.

WORK TOGETHER

Draw pictures to show comparisons and to explore ratio.

- Draw a rectangle and divide it into five equal parts. Let each part represent one student.
- Shade the number of parts equal to the number of students with red bicycles.

Talk About It

▶ How many students who ride bicycles do *not* ride red bicycles?

_____

The rectangle showing the bicycle riders in Mrs. Appleton's class has three sections.

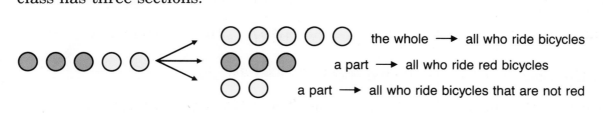

the whole → all who ride bicycles

a part → all who ride red bicycles

a part → all who ride bicycles that are not red

Here are other ratios for Mrs. Appleton's class.	part:whole not red:all 2:5	whole:part all:red 5:3	part:part red:not red 3:2

Talk About It

▶ For Mrs. Appleton's class, what does the ratio $\frac{5}{2}$ describe?

▶ Does the ratio $\frac{5}{2}$ describe the same comparison as the ratio $\frac{2}{5}$? Explain.

Practice

Use the shapes in the box. Write the ratio in three ways.

1. stars to circles

2. circles to all shapes

3. all shapes to stars

4. squares to stars

5. squares to all shapes

6. all shapes to squares

7. circles to stars

8. stars to all shapes

9. circles to squares

10. all shapes to circles

11. stars to squares

12. squares to circles

Describe the comparison by using the shapes in the box. Write *part to whole, whole to part,* or *part to part.*

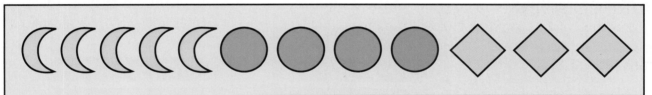

13. crescents to circles

14. circles to crescents

15. circles to diamonds

16. circles to all shapes

17. all shapes to crescents

18. diamonds to all shapes

19. diamonds to circles

20. diamonds to crescents

21. crescents to diamonds

22. all shapes to diamonds

23. crescents to all shapes

24. all shapes to circles

Choose shapes of your own. Draw a picture to show the ratio.

25. The ratio of red to green is $1:2$.

26. The ratio of red to all is $\frac{3}{10}$.

27. The ratio of short to long is $5:2$.

28. The ratio of fat to thin is $\frac{2}{9}$.

29. The ratio of small to all is $\frac{4}{11}$.

30. The ratio of all to thin is $30:25$.

31. Jane and Angela have 2 pairs of yellow shoelaces, 3 pairs of orange shoelaces, and 2 pairs of skates. What is the ratio of pairs of orange shoelaces to pairs of skates? What information is not needed to answer the question?

32. There are 2 wooden bowls, 3 wooden statues, and 4 metal bowls in the garage. What is the ratio of wooden objects to metal objects?

## CHAPTER 11

Geometry

Quadrilaterals

Quadrilaterals are closed plane figures that have four sides and four angles. There are several different kinds of quadrilaterals. Some of them you already know.

WORK TOGETHER

Building Understanding

Make larger drawings of these figures. Make cardboard strips from your drawings. Punch holes in the cardboard strips and connect them with fasteners. Record the figures on a sheet of paper.

Make a rectangle.

Make a square.

Make a trapezoid.

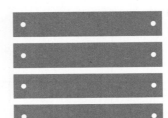

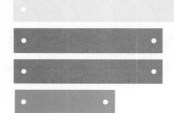

Talk About It

► How many different shapes did you make?

► Which figures have four right angles?

► Which figure has acute and obtuse angles?

► Which figures have two pairs of parallel sides?

► Which figure has only one pair of parallel sides?

Adjust the cardboard strips of the square and the rectangle to form a different kind of quadrilateral for each. Trace these new figures on a sheet of paper.

► Describe the new figures you made.

► Do your new figures have any right angles?

► Do any of your figures have parallel sides? If so, how many?

Practice

Describe the relationship among the sides of the quadrilaterals.

Quadrilaterals Classified by Sides		
Name	**Example**	**Description**
1. Rectangle		?
2. Square		?
3. Trapezoid		?
4. Parallelogram		?
5. Rhombus		?

Describe the relationship among the angles of the quadrilaterals.

Quadrilaterals Classified by Angles		
Name	**Example**	**Description**
6. Rectangle	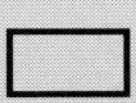	?
7. Square	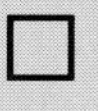	?
8. Trapezoid		?
9. Parallelogram		?
10. Rhombus		?

11.  parallelogram   trapezoid

Compare the sides of a parallelogram with the sides of a trapezoid. How is the trapezoid different?

12.  parallelogram   rectangle

Compare the sides of a parallelogram with the sides of a rectangle. How are they the same?

13. 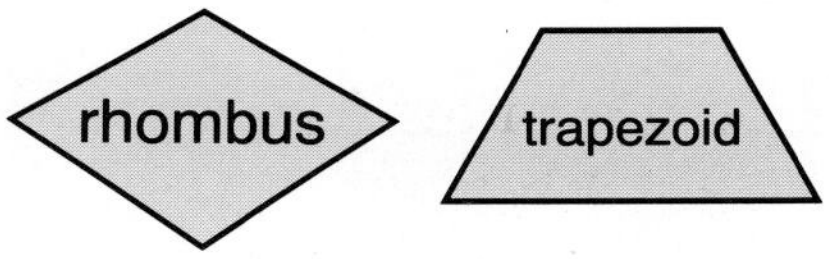 rhombus   trapezoid

Compare the sides of a rhombus with the sides of a trapezoid. How is the rhombus different?

14.  rectangle   square

Compare the angles of a rectangle with the angles of a square. What are their measures?

CHAPTER 1

Place Value: Whole Numbers and Decimals

Application: Comparing Yearly Salaries

The figures in the table are for 1989. These figures, from the Bureau of Labor, show the average yearly salary of workers in five different states.

Write the names of the states in order from the state with the highest average salary to the state with the lowest.

State	Average Yearly Salary
Connecticut	$27,000
Florida	$20,072
Mississippi	$17,047
New York	$27,303
South Dakota	$15,810

Now Try This

What factors do you think affect the salaries of people in a particular state?

Look at employment advertisements in your newspaper. What salaries are listed for jobs you might like to have when you finish school?

CHAPTER 2

Adding and Subtracting Whole Numbers and Decimals

Application: Using a Budget

Budgeting helps you manage your money. A budget shows whether you have enough money to pay for expenses and to save for extras.

If your income is $25 a week and you need money for school lunches, clothes, school supplies, and extras, your budget might be like this.

Budget	
Lunches	$10
Clothes	7
School supplies	3
Extras	+ 5
TOTAL	$25

Now Try This

Suppose your allowance is $7 a week. Make a budget to show how you would spend your allowance during four weeks.

CHAPTER 3

Multiplying Whole Numbers and Decimals

Application: Making Change

Knowing how to make change is an everyday life skill. When making change, use as few bills and as few coins as possible. Suppose you must give your parent $6.46 in change. You might use any of these combinations.

a. six $1 bills, 1 quarter, 2 dimes, 1 penny
b. six $1 bills, 4 dimes, 1 nickel, 1 penny
c. one $5 bill, one $1 bill, 1 quarter, 2 dimes, 1 penny

Which combination is the best way to make the change?

Now Try This

Make a table like the one below. Show the best way to make change of $3.22, $2.36, $6.73, and $5.98.

Change Due	Change: Number of					
	$5 bills	$1 bills	Quarters	Dimes	Nickels	Pennies
$3.22	▪	▪	▪	▪	▪	▪

CHAPTER 4

Dividing Whole Numbers and Decimals

Application: Planning for Transportation

If you are planning a trip for a group of people, you must arrange for transportation. Suppose 35 people in your neighborhood are planning a trip. They will travel in vans that each hold 6 people. How many vans will they need?

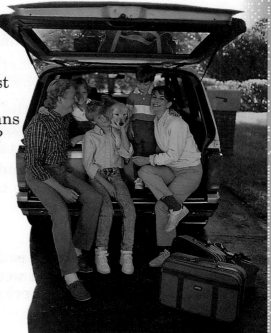

$$\begin{array}{r} 5.8 \\ 6{\overline{\smash{\big)}\,35.0}} \end{array} \leftarrow \text{They will need 6 vans.}$$

Now Try This

Plan a trip for a group of people in your neighborhood. The people will ride in vans. How many vans will you need to rent? Will all the vans be full? What else will you need to consider if the people ride in vans?

CHAPTER 5

Graphing, Statistics, and Probability

Application: Reading Stock Reports

A stock consists of shares of a company that are bought and sold on a stock market. The prices are listed in the newspaper each day. A line in the stock listings may look like this.

Stock	Div.	PE	Sales hds.	High	Low	Close	Chg.
ABC	1.68	13	63	14	13	14	$+\frac{3}{4}$

The column labeled *Div.* indicates the value of the annual dividend for one share. It is based on the most recent quarterly or semiannual dividend. ABC paid $1.68 per share.

Now Try This

Look in the financial pages of a newspaper for the stock listings. Find the section that tells you how to read the listings. What does each column heading mean?

CHAPTER 6

Number Theory

Application: Adjusting Shutter Speed

On some cameras there is an adjustment for shutter speed. The shutter speed determines how long the shutter remains open to receive light. The larger the number on the dial, the less time the shutter is open.

A setting of 250 means the shutter will be open for $\frac{1}{250}$ of a second. A setting of 15 means the shutter will be open for $\frac{1}{15}$ of a second. Which setting will let more light into the camera? If you take a picture in a dark room, which setting will you use?

Now Try This

Look at a camera your family or a friend owns. Does it have an adjustment for the shutter speed, or is the shutter speed automatic? What do you think are some advantages of an automatic shutter? some disadvantages?

School-Home Connection

CHAPTER 7
Adding and Subtracting Fractions

Application: Egyptian Fractions

Scientists discovered an ancient document in Egypt that they call the Rhind Papyrus. This document shows how Egyptians wrote fractions. It was written in 1700 B.C., so you know that people have been using fractions for a long time.

Egyptians used ⬯ to represent a numerator of 1. They used their whole-number symbols to represent the value of the denominator.

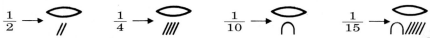

How did the ancient Egyptians write $\frac{1}{14}$?

Now Try This

Make up your own system and symbols for writing fractions. Make a poster that explains your system. What are some advantages of your system?

CHAPTER 8
Multiplying and Dividing Fractions

Application: Adjusting Recipes

Most recipes are written to provide 4 to 6 servings. If you cook for a larger number of people, you must adjust the recipe so you will have enough food to serve everyone.

Suppose a casserole recipe calls for $\frac{3}{4}$ cup of broccoli for each serving. How much broccoli would you need for a casserole large enough to serve 15 people?

$\frac{3}{4} \times 15 = 11\frac{1}{4}$ ← You will need $11\frac{1}{4}$ cups of broccoli.

Now Try This

Find a casserole recipe. Divide the amount of each ingredient by the number of servings the recipe makes. This will give you the amount needed for 1 serving. Then adjust the amounts so that the casserole will serve 15 people.

CHAPTER 9

Measurement

Project: Ordering Carpet

Carpet is sold in 9-ft and 12-ft widths. You can buy almost any length. To buy carpet, first measure the length and the width of a room. Next, determine which measurement is less than or equal to 9 ft or 12 ft. Then, use the other measurement to determine the length of carpet needed.

Suppose you want to carpet the floor of a room that is 8 ft wide and 18 ft long. Would you order carpet that has a 9-ft or a 12-ft width? What length would you order if you wanted to have 1 more foot than is actually needed?

Now Try This

Measure one room in your home to determine how much carpet you would need to cover the floor. Suppose that you can order the carpet in 9-ft widths and in 12-ft widths. How much carpet of each width would you need?

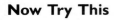

CHAPTER 10

Ratio, Proportion, and Percent

Application: Tipping

When you purchase a meal in a restaurant, you usually tip the server for good service. The amount of the tip is usually between 10% and 20% of the bill.

Suppose a meal costs $18.00 and the service was good. You may decide to leave a 15% tip.

Think: $18 \times 0.10 = 1.80$ (10%)
$\frac{1}{2} \times 1.80 = \underline{0.90}$ (5%)   You would leave
$\phantom{\frac{1}{2} \times 1.80 =} 2.70$ $2.70 for a tip.

Now Try This

The next time your family goes to a restaurant, ask if you can figure the tip. Ask a family member what percent to leave for the tip, and then determine the amount by multiplying the bill by the percent.

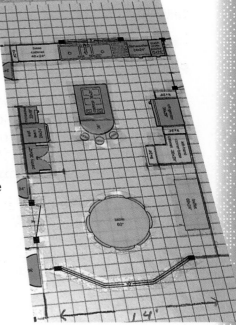

CHAPTER 11

Geometry

Application: Making a Scale Drawing

A scale drawing is usually smaller than the actual object. The scale of the drawing relates the size of the drawing to the size of the object.

Suppose the scale of a drawing is 1 in. = 20 ft. This means that a length of 1 in. in the drawing represents 20 ft in the actual object.

Now Try This

Make a scale drawing of two or three rooms in your home. Use the scale $\frac{1}{2}$ in. = 1 ft. Leave spaces in your drawing where there are doorways.

CHAPTER 12

Perimeter, Area, and Volume

Application: Measuring Volume of Containers

Suppose you want to know if several small items will fit in a container. You can find out by comparing the volume of the container to the volume of the items.

Denny has 85 1-in. cubes and a box that is 2 in. wide, 5 in. long, and 10 in. deep. Will all the cubes fit in the box?

Volume of the cubes
$85 \times 1 \times 1 = 85$
85 in.^{3}

Volume of the box
$2 \times 5 \times 10 = 100$
100 in.^{3}

Since 100 in.^{3} is greater than 85 in.^{3}, the cubes will fit in the box.

Now Try This

Find several differently shaped boxes that look as if they have the same volume. Then measure to determine the volume of each box. Do the boxes actually have about the same volume?

CHAPTER 13

Integers

Application: Watching Stock Changes

A stock consists of shares of a company that are bought and sold on a stock market. The prices are listed in the newspaper each day. Lines in the stock listings may look like this.

Stock	Div.	PE	Sales hds.	High	Low	Close	Chg.
ABC	1.68	13	63	14	13	14	$+\frac{3}{4}$
XYZ	1.00	58	5557	$49\frac{7}{8}$	$48\frac{7}{8}$	$49\frac{1}{8}$	$-\frac{7}{8}$

Chg. means "change." It is the difference between the closing price shown (Close) and the closing price of the day before.

Now Try This

Choose a stock and follow it for two weeks. Record the change each day. Are the changes, or differences, mostly gains (positive) or mostly losses (negative)?

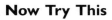

CHAPTER 14

Getting Ready for Algebra

Application: Computing Commission

In many sales jobs, employees are paid a salary plus a commission. A commission is an amount of money equal to a percent of the employee's sales.

Suppose Josh receives a weekly salary of $250 plus a commission of 5% of his sales. How much would he be paid if he sold $2,500 of merchandise in one week?

salary + (5% × sales) = salary + commission
250 + (0.05 × 2,500) = 250 + 125 = 375

So, Josh would be paid $375 for one week.

Now Try This

In your town, what are some sales jobs in which employees are paid a salary and a commission? Why do you suppose employers want to pay their employees this way? Why do you think people in sales like to be paid this way?

CHAPTER I

Lesson 1.1 *(pages 2–5)*

Write the Roman numeral.

1. 32   2. 568   3. 9   4. 97

5. 411   6. 1979   7. 39   8. 2010

9. 1546   10. 250   11. 1887   12. 780

13. 19   14. 2915   15. 44   16. 907

Lesson 1.2 *(pages 6–7)*

Write the value of the underlined digit.

1. 245,<u>9</u>86   2. 5,7<u>86</u>,341   3. 6,4<u>3</u>5

4. 4,<u>3</u>75,129   5. 10,916,<u>4</u>89   6. 29,633,824

7. 11,924,01<u>5</u>   8. 6,<u>8</u>12   9. 8<u>9</u>,542

Write the number in short word form.

10. 1,908,665   11. 761,249   12. 396

13. 300,000,268   14. 45,836,000   15. 1,032

16. 12,801   17. 90,100,010   18. 6,008

Write the number in standard form.

19. seven thousand, ninety-five

20. six million, four hundred fifty-two thousand, three hundred sixty-nine

21. forty-thousand, six hundred eight

22. two hundred fifteen billion, one million, three thousand two

23. $22,000,000,000 + 55,000,000 + 600 + 20 + 5$

24. $4,000,000 + 600,000 + 70,000 + 200 + 40 + 3$

Lesson 1.3 *(pages 8–9)*

Write the number in short word form.

1. 0.4　　　　　　　　**2.** 0.8925　　　　　　**3.** 0.468

4. 2.63　　　　　　　**5.** 0.482　　　　　　　**6.** 0.69

7. 11.03　　　　　　　**8.** 0.6253　　　　　　**9.** 6.812

Write the value of the underlined digit.

10. 0.3<u>9</u>　　　　**11.** 0.56<u>8</u>　　　**12.** <u>2</u>.03　　　　**13.** 0.234<u>5</u>

14. 4.<u>1</u>5　　　　**15.** 0.0<u>2</u>4　　　**16.** 10.999<u>9</u>　　**17.** 9.75<u>2</u>

Write the number in standard form.

18. 96 thousandths　　　　**19.** 21 hundredths　　　**20.** 6 tenths

21. 402 ten-thousandths　　　　　　**22.** seventy-two and three tenths

23. 1 and 15 hundredths　　**24.** 612 thousandths　　**25.** 5 hundredths

26. 10 and 8 ten-thousandths　　　　**27.** six and twelve hundredths

Lesson 1.4 *(pages 10–11)*

Compare the numbers. Write $<$, $>$, or $=$.

1. 10.009 ● 10.090　　　**2.** 3,232 ● 3,323　　　**3.** 40.345 ● 40.354

4. 39.0045 ● 39.0450　　**5.** 6.120 ● 6.1200　　**6.** 0.550 ● 0.549

7. 9.350 ● 9.35　　　　**8.** 4.854 ● 4.844　　**9.** 600,910 ● 609,100

List the numbers in order from least to greatest. Use $<$.

10. 33,546; 33,645; 33,564　　**11.** 0.020; 0.200; 0.002　　**12.** 4,698; 4,869; 4,689

13. 0.301; 0.0301; 0.101　　**14.** 2,421; 2,412; 2,422　　**15.** 6.009; 6.090; 6.008

16. 4,532; 5,234; 3,254　　　　　　**17.** 160,329; 180,528; 610,329

18. 2.911; 2.191; 1.921　　　　　　**19.** 395.005; 295.005; 352.009

20. 0.195; 0.095; 0.189　　　　　　**21.** 6.918; 6.098; 9.006

22. 0.071; 0.171; 0.0018　　　　　　**23.** 600,201; 601,002; 600,120

24. 2.3077; 2.0377; 2.3773　　　　　**25.** 2,738; 2,728; 2,078

Lesson 1.5 *(pages 12–13)*

1. Sue wants to make a report on the heights and weights of some of her classmates. Later she will gather facts about their parents' and grandparents' heights and weights. Make a table from the information below.

> Report: Linda is 5 feet 4 inches and weighs 120 pounds; Alex is 6 feet 2 inches and weighs 190 pounds; Jason is 5 feet 7 inches and weighs 180 pounds; Herb is 5 feet 8 inches and weighs 200 pounds; Michelle is 5 feet 5 inches and weighs 120 pounds.

Use your table for Exercises 2–5.

2. Which classmates' weights are between 150 pounds and 210 pounds?

3. Compare Michelle's height with that of Alex. Use < or >.

4. List all the heights from tallest to shortest. Use >.

5. Which classmates weigh the same?

Lesson 1.6 *(pages 14–15)*

Estimate by rounding to the place indicated.

1. $4.68
   10 cents

2. 451
   hundreds

3. 84
   tens

4. $3.63
   dollar

5. 890,000,000,000
   hundred billions

The number has been rounded to the place indicated. Write the range of numbers that round to the given number.

6. 600
   hundred

7. 55,000
   thousand

8. 700,000
   hundred thousand

9. 4,000,000
   million

10. 100
    hundred

11. $8.50
    ten cents

12. $2.00
    dollar

13. 8,000,000
    million

Lesson 1.7 *(pages 18–19)*

Solve.

1. $6 \times 5 + 3$

2. $3 \times 4 + 5$

3. $36 \div 3 - 10$

4. $(7 + 4) \times 2$

5. $(5 - 2) \div 3$

6. $12 + 5 \times 3$

7. $66 \div (14 - 3)$

8. $4 \times (3 + 2)$

9. $(6 - 4) \times (4 + 6)$

10. $18 - 2 \times 6$

11. $7 + 10 \div 2$

12. $(8 + 2) \times 10$

Lesson 1.8 (pages 20–21)

Tell how many zeros will be in the number when written in standard form.

1. 10^5 **2.** 10^6 **3.** ten squared   **4.** ten to the sixth power

5. $10 \times 10 \times 10$ **6.** $10 \times 10 \times 10 \times 10$ **7.** 10^8

8. ten to the twelfth power   **9.** $10 \times 10 \times 10 \times 10 \times 10$ **10.** 10^{10}

Write the number in standard form.

11. $10 \times 10 \times 10 \times 10 \times 10$ **12.** ten to the eighth power   **13.** 10^{12}

14. ten to the third power   **15.** $7 \times 10 \times 10 \times 10$ **16.** 6×10^2

Lesson 1.9 (pages 22–23)

Use a calculator. Write the square or the square root of the number in standard form.

1. 21^2 **2.** 1.01^2 **3.** 40^2 **4.** 3.2^2

5. $\sqrt{36}$ **6.** $\sqrt{0.25}$ **7.** $\sqrt{169}$ **8.** $\sqrt{0.0025}$

9. $\sqrt{324}$ **10.** $\sqrt{1.21}$ **11.** $\sqrt{256}$ **12.** $\sqrt{4.41}$

13. 60^2 **14.** 0.7^2 **15.** 2.8^2 **16.** 12^2

Lesson 1.10 (pages 24–25)

Find the pattern. Then solve.

1. Pat spent 10 minutes on her rowing machine the first time she used it. If she increases her workout by 4 minutes each time, for how many minutes will she exercise on the sixth time?

2. You plant 2 flowers on the first day and then plant 3 more each day than the day before. If you follow this pattern, how many flowers will you plant on day 8?

3. A stamp collector buys 25 stamps the first month. After that, he buys 15 more stamps every month than the month before. How many stamps does he buy in the sixth month?

4. Tom builds 3 miniature car models the first day and 4 more cars each day than the day before. If he follows this pattern how many cars does he build on the fifth day?

CHAPTER 2

Lesson 2.1 *(pages 34–35)*

Find the sum or difference. Use mental math when possible.

1. $(3 + 10) - 12$ **2.** $6 + (5 + 9)$ **3.** $12 + 13 + 5$ **4.** $42 + (8 + 4)$

5. $(7 + 5) + 10$ **6.** $22 + 35 + 8$ **7.** $15 + 35 + 9$ **8.** $18 - 6 - 2$

9. $(6 + 24) + 7$ **10.** $43 - 13 - 7$ **11.** $68 - 9$ **12.** $46 - 27$

13. $35 + 20 + 65$ **14.** $54 - 27$ **15.** $23 + 35 + 17$ **16.** $50 - 10 - 15$

Lesson 2.2 *(pages 36–37)*

Use front-end estimation to estimate the sum or difference.

1. 8,545	**2.** 2,989	**3.** 3,849	**4.** 3,758	**5.** 9,243
−5,328	+4,156	−1,314	+2,455	−6,411

6. 3,971	**7.** 12,810	**8.** 2,178	**9.** 20,244	**10.** 6,954
+6,428	− 4,202	+8,695	− 8,127	+9,821

Round to estimate the sum or difference.

11. 32,564	**12.** 42,345	**13.** 18,941	**14.** 29,310	**15.** 14,258
+26,383	−13,859	+17,865	−12,980	+17,637

16. 78,432	**17.** 3,932	**18.** 62,403	**19.** 8,526	**20.** 9,645
−10,927	−2,121	+ 7,380	+1,254	−4,462

Lesson 2.3 *(pages 38–39)*

Find the sum or difference. Use the inverse operation to check.

1. 631	**2.** 291	**3.** 547	**4.** 4,546	**5.** 9,341
+348	−156	−396	+5,219	−8,934

6. 43,642	**7.** 3,101	**8.** 32,675	**9.** 245,147	**10.** 683,473
−29,835	−1,898	+48,325	− 96,639	−197,789

11. 541	**12.** 2,539	**13.** 3,568	**14.** 45,109	**15.** 999,999
63	1,983	2,479	31,802	876,543
+371	+ 818	+10,238	+23,005	+ 5

Lesson 2.4 *(pages 40–41)*

Solve. Use estimation, paper and pencil, mental math, or a calculator. Justify your choice.

1. Yolanda's three deposits last month were $239.00, $154.00, and $175.00. How much money did Yolanda deposit last month?

2. Steven gives a clerk $20.00 to pay for a $1.49 pack of pencils. How much change will he receive?

3. Adam gave a clerk $10.00 for frozen yogurt and received $7.01 in change. How much was the frozen yogurt?

4. Marcy bought 3 tapes for $36.97. The first tape cost $12.99 and the second cost $10.99. How much did the third tape cost?

Lesson 2.5 *(pages 42–43)*

Use front-end estimation to estimate the sum or difference.

1. 0.893
$+0.145$

2. 3.92
-1.25

3. 0.83
-0.192

4. 4.1
$+2.85$

5. 0.435
$+1.569$

6. 62.62
$+31.90$

7. 7.15
-6.05

8. 12.44
$+3.78$

9. 3.75
-2.16

10. 0.0862
$+0.228$

Round to estimate the sum or difference.

11. 2.54
-1.23

12. 4.72
$+3.01$

13. 41.6
-29.8

14. 1.59
$+0.33$

15. 4.15
-3.91

16. 75.9
$+20.6$

17. 54.07
-28.05

18. 32.16
$+61.4$

19. 90.01
-82.15

20. 99.81
$+6.95$

Lesson 2.6 *(pages 46–47)*

Find the sum.

1. $2.05 + 6.453$

2. $6.8 + 5.234$

3. $0.45 + 9.761$

4. $\$12.99 + \$65.36$

5. $3.2 + 1.684$

6. $0.003 + 6.58$

7. 1.024
3.913
$+0.276$

8. 4.5
0.013
$+2.46$

9. 39.126
0.486
$+23.725$

10. 435.1
1.7
$+0.452$

11. 39.62
1.01
$+456.789$

12. $0.015 + 2.5 + 32.16$

13. $\$3.19 + \$4.28 + \$5.07$

Lesson 2.7 (pages 48–49)

Find the difference.

1. $6.12 - 0.054$ **2.** $61.39 - 3.4$ **3.** $215.62 - 9.8$

4. $21 - 0.025$ **5.** $0.78 - 0.678$ **6.** $45.4 - 29.489$

7. $0.5 - 0.4982$ **8.** $7.25 - 5.025$ **9.** $8.1 - 0.467$

10. $6.315 - 3.125$ **11.** $4.2 - 3.199$ **12.** $234.1 - 0.927$

13. $\begin{array}{r} 0.09 \\ -0.008 \\ \hline \end{array}$ **14.** $\begin{array}{r} 32.12 \\ -29.98 \\ \hline \end{array}$ **15.** $\begin{array}{r} 89.6 \\ -\ 1.998 \\ \hline \end{array}$

Lesson 2.8 (pages 50–51)

Find the balance. Use a calculator with memory keys.

1.

Checks	Deposits
375.00	510.91
80.00	
69.79	490.91
12.03	
Balance: ▨	

2.

Checks	Deposits
35.49	425.00
68.87	
119.13	
387.34	400.00
Balance: ▨	

3.

Checks	Deposits
679.85	2,930.14
498.39	
215.67	
3.04	
Balance: ▨	

Lesson 2.9 (pages 52–53)

Write an algebraic expression for the word expression.

1. 8 less than a number, t **2.** the sum of 39 and a number, x

3. m fewer than 42   **4.** b more than 85

5. the sum of 0.5 and a number, g **6.** 25 fewer than a number, k

7. d less than 145   **8.** a more than 300

Write a word expression for the algebraic expression.

9. $41 + t$ **10.** $95 - m$

11. $1.2 + x$ **12.** $e - 35.2$

13. $n + 4.56$ **14.** $d - 33$

15. $x - 1$ **16.** $b + 409$

Lesson 2.10 *(pages 54–55)*

Evaluate the expression.

1. $b + 3.5$, for $b = 0.7$

2. $a + 99$, for $a = 3$

3. $d - 65$, for $d = 65$

4. $g - 19$, for $g = 50$

5. $46 - x$, for $x = 24$

6. $403 - y$, for $y = 108$

7. $29.3 - w$, for $w = 29$

8. $m + 0$, for $m = 16$

9. $n + 5$, for $n = 5$

10. $(10 + x) + 5$, for $x = 3$

11. $(6 - m) + 11$, for $m = 2.5$

12. $43 - (n + 2.1)$, for $n = 0.9$

13. $51 + (t + 25)$, for $t = 7.6$

14. $(a - 6) + 8$, for $a = 12$

15. $b - (21 - 9)$, for $b = 31.6$

16. $b + (8 - 3)$, for $b = 15$

17. $37 - (z - 12)$, for $z = 24$

Lesson 2.11 *(pages 56–57)*

Tell how to solve the equations.

1. $x - 12 = 4$

2. $y + 3 = 5$

3. $m + 9 = 33$

4. $4.3 + b = 9.2$

5. $a + 5.6 = 23.7$

6. $d - 4 = 5$

7. $8.2 + k = 10$

8. $z - 2.5 = 1$

9. $g + 3.2 = 5.3$

Use inverse operations. Solve the equations.

10. $y - 9 = 20$

11. $6 + c = 13$

12. $d + 4 = 25$

13. $a + 35 = 42$

14. $b - 10 = 2$

15. $x + 16 = 26$

Lesson 2.12 *(pages 58–59)*

Solve. Use the strategy *guess and check.* Record your guesses and checks.

1. Pam and Lew collect buttons. Pam has 17 more buttons than Lew. Together they have a total of 267 buttons. How many buttons does Lew have?

2. Of the 90 members of the marching band, there are 20 more female members than males. How many males are there?

3. John bought two banners at the baseball game. The total cost for both was $10. One banner cost $2 more than the other banner. What was the cost of each banner?

4. A hiking club hikes 15 miles in two days. On the second day they hike twice as far as they did on the first day. How far do they hike each day?

CHAPTER 3

Lesson 3.1 *(pages 68–69)*

Find the missing factor. Name the property used.

1. $15 \times 11 = \blacksquare \times 15$ 2. $39 \times 1 = \blacksquare$ 3. $\blacksquare \times 8 = (4 \times 2) + (4 \times 6)$

4. $9 \times \blacksquare = 0$ 5. $16 \times (2 \times 8) = (16 \times \blacksquare) \times 8$ 6. $5 \times (6 \times 8) = (8 \times \blacksquare) \times 6$

7. $16 \times \blacksquare = 16$ 8. $\blacksquare \times 5 = (8 \times 5) + (7 \times 5)$ 9. $36 \times 5 = 5 \times \blacksquare$

Use mental math and the properties of multiplication to find the product.

10. $18 \times 12 \times 0$ 11. 15×1 12. 40×3 13. 50×4

14. 10×80 15. 5×12 16. $6 \times 8 \times 1$ 17. $11 \times 5 \times 2$

18. $6 \times 3 \times 3$ 19. 3×15 20. $40 \times 6 \times 0$ 21. 36×3

22. 12×20 23. $2 \times 2 \times 7$ 24. $10 \times 9 \times 2$ 25. $5 \times 5 \times 2$

Lesson 3.2 *(pages 70–71)*

Estimate the product.

1. $\begin{array}{r}42 \\ \times\ 3 \\ \hline\end{array}$	2. $\begin{array}{r}31 \\ \times\ 5 \\ \hline\end{array}$	3. $\begin{array}{r}49 \\ \times\ 4 \\ \hline\end{array}$	4. $\begin{array}{r}99 \\ \times\ 8 \\ \hline\end{array}$	5. $\begin{array}{r}324 \\ \times\ \ 3 \\ \hline\end{array}$
6. $\begin{array}{r}685 \\ \times\ \ 7 \\ \hline\end{array}$	7. $\begin{array}{r}6,215 \\ \times\ \ \ \ 4 \\ \hline\end{array}$	8. $\begin{array}{r}22 \\ \times 56 \\ \hline\end{array}$	9. $\begin{array}{r}291 \\ \times\ 52 \\ \hline\end{array}$	10. $\begin{array}{r}615 \\ \times 481 \\ \hline\end{array}$
11. $\begin{array}{r}45 \\ \times\ 5 \\ \hline\end{array}$	12. $\begin{array}{r}62 \\ \times\ 8 \\ \hline\end{array}$	13. $\begin{array}{r}82 \\ \times 15 \\ \hline\end{array}$	14. $\begin{array}{r}54 \\ \times 59 \\ \hline\end{array}$	15. $\begin{array}{r}312 \\ \times\ 45 \\ \hline\end{array}$
16. $\begin{array}{r}42,108 \\ \times\ \ \ \ \ 97 \\ \hline\end{array}$	17. $\begin{array}{r}3,920 \\ \times\ \ \ \ 35 \\ \hline\end{array}$	18. $\begin{array}{r}4,086 \\ \times\ \ \ \ 24 \\ \hline\end{array}$	19. $\begin{array}{r}450 \\ \times\ 82 \\ \hline\end{array}$	20. $\begin{array}{r}18,420 \\ \times\ \ \ \ \ 62 \\ \hline\end{array}$

Estimate to compare. Use $<$ or $>$.

21. $8 \times 28 \, \bullet \, 240$ 22. $50 \times 19 \, \bullet \, 800$ 23. $63 \times 31 \, \bullet \, 1,800$

24. $215 \times 52 \, \bullet \, 10,000$ 25. $85 \times 9 \, \bullet \, 810$ 26. $38 \times 68 \, \bullet \, 2,800$

27. $45 \times 5 \, \bullet \, 250$ 28. $9 \times 27 \, \bullet \, 300$ 29. $11 \times 82 \, \bullet \, 800$

30. $190 \times 5 \, \bullet \, 1,000$ 31. $41 \times 32 \, \bullet \, 1,200$ 32. $680 \times 97 \, \bullet \, 70,000$

Lesson 3.3 *(pages 72–73)*

Find the product.

1. 85 ×41	**2.** 39 ×97	**3.** 247 ×368	**4.** 1,236 × 39	**5.** 3,039 × 165
6. 46,164 × 58	**7.** 6,352 × 24	**8.** 3,815 × 242	**9.** 4,998 × 906	**10.** 136,761 × 525
11. 81 ×32	**12.** 618 × 79	**13.** 9,845 × 68	**14.** 259 × 28	**15.** 8,954 × 71
16. 486 ×351	**17.** 5,876 × 34	**18.** 8,644 × 142	**19.** 9,514 × 529	**20.** 1,012 × 426

Lesson 3.4 *(pages 74–75)*

Frederick wants to buy a television that costs $469. He has $250 in a savings account. He saves $60 from his paycheck each week. He is considering these options.

Option 1: Continue to save until he can pay for the television in full.
Option 2: Pay $30 per month for 18 months.
Option 3: Pay $100 down and $23 per month for 18 months.

1. How much will the television cost using Option 2?

2. With which option will he pay the least amount of money each month?

3. How much will he save by choosing Option 3 instead of Option 2?

4. Which option is the least expensive of all the options?

Lesson 3.5 *(pages 76–77)*

Estimate. Choose the correct product. Write **a**, **b**, or **c**.

1. 43.6×38
   a. 16.568
   b. 165.68
   c. 1,656.8

2. 8.234×8.25
   a. 67.9305
   b. 6.79305
   c. 679.305

3. 3.24×6.76
   a. 219.024
   b. 21.9024
   c. 2.19024

4. 841×5.13
   a. 43.1433
   b. 431.433
   c. 4,314.33

Estimate the product.

5. 34.2×9.6

6. 2.1×5.9

7. 4.3×12.4

8. 1.6×48.6

9. 6.75×4.93

10. 37.2×9.5

11. 49.6×1.23

12. 3.6×8.7

Lesson 3.6 *(pages 80–81)*

Use mental math and multiplication to estimate the sum.

1.
```
  390
  412
  420
+375
```

2.
```
  885
  902
  873
+900
```

3.
```
 1,954
 2,431
 2,145
+1,837
```

4.
```
 12,342
 11,785
 12,040
+11,827
```

5.
```
 8.91
 8.82
 8.75
+8.69
```

6.
```
$3.75
 4.19
 3.68
+ 4.19
```

7.
```
 0.8
 1.4
 0.06
+0.9
```

8.
```
 44.001
 43.631
 43.72
+44.26
```

9.
```
 34,800
 35,020
 34,641
+35,293
```

10.
```
 810,462
 777,888
 763,141
+782,205
```

11.
```
$ 9.97
 10.21
  9.80
+ 10.12
```

12.
```
 721,108
 681,926
 662,044
+710,802
```

13.
```
 5.9
 5.7
 6.3
+6.1
```

14.
```
 3.03
 3.09
 2.8
+2.7
```

15.
```
 9,105
 9,080
 8,970
+8,790
```

16.
```
 160.8
 158.9
 162.1
+159.4
```

Lesson 3.7 *(pages 82–83)*

Find the product. Round money amounts to the nearest cent.

1.
```
 4.3
×7.6
```

2.
```
 6.578
× 2.8
```

3.
```
 437.2
× 9.8
```

4.
```
$22.69
× 9.5
```

5.
```
 67.89
× 45
```

6.
```
$49.95
× 0.4
```

7.
```
$492.45
× 5.12
```

8.
```
 0.38
× 0.6
```

9.
```
 22.61
× 0.52
```

10.
```
 0.047
× 0.63
```

11.
```
 4.28
×0.75
```

12.
```
 22.2
×2.78
```

13.
```
 29.5
× 38
```

14.
```
 42.91
× 0.03
```

15.
```
 286.5
× 2.91
```

16.
```
 4.76
× 59
```

17. 38.76×4.6

18. 0.125×0.65

19. 5.1×0.06

20. 33.33×0.003

21. 1.01×99

22. 6.008×0.2

23. 200.8×3.45

24. 106×3.03

25. 4.9×0.01

26. 4.02×1.6

27. $\$11.20 \times 6.2$

28. 1.5×0.002

Lesson 3.8 (pages 84–85)

Place the decimal point in the product. Write zeros where necessary.

1. 0.02 × 6.7 ——— 134	2. 0.004 × 25.2 ——— 1008	3. 0.054 × 2.3 ——— 1242	4. 0.0013 × 1.43 ——— 1859
5. 0.0006 × 35 ——— 21	6. 0.006 × 16 ——— 96	7. 0.302 × 0.03 ——— 906	8. 0.012 × 0.82 ——— 984
9. 120.1 × 3.3 ——— 39633	10. 0.8 ×1.6 ——— 128	11. .011 ×0.55 ——— 605	12. 8.18 ×2.07 ——— 169326

Find the product.

13. 0.015 × 10	14. 63.75 × 1.93	15. 0.06 × 8	16. 13.68 × 0.03
17. 0.062 × 0.2	18. 0.0049 × 331	19. 6.8 ×0.5	20. 0.64 ×3.48
21. 0.031 × 60.4	22. 0.89 × 316	23. 0.55 ×0.93	24. 200.75 × 0.26

25. 1.2×10 26. 0.005×100 27. $1.425 \times 1,000$

28. 0.23×100 29. 0.006×10 30. $3.002 \times 10,000$

31. 33.06×10 32. 0.79×100 33. 0.5132×100

Lesson 3.9 (pages 86–87)

1. A hospital held a bake sale to raise money for a new nursery. It sold 240 breadsticks at $0.75 each, 125 muffins at $0.89 each, and 500 rolls at $0.25 each. How much money did the hospital raise?

2. Mirriam bought 12 cucumbers at 4 for $1.00 and 3 pounds of tomatoes at $0.89 a pound. How much more money did Mirriam spend for cucumbers than she spent for tomatoes?

3. Jim drove 132 miles to the city. His father drove twice as many miles to the next big city. How far did they drive in all?

4. Rose bought 10 rolls of film. There are 24 pictures on each roll. If she used all except 2 rolls of film, how many pictures did she take?

CHAPTER 4

Lesson 4.1 (pages 96–97)

Determine whether the number is divisible by 2, 3, 5, 9, or 10.
Write all that apply.

1. 779　　　**2.** 302　　　**3.** 2,515　　　**4.** 891　　　**5.** 640

Lesson 4.2 (pages 98–99)

Estimate the quotient.

1. $259 \div 9$　　**2.** $625 \div 3$　　**3.** $4,749 \div 7$　　**4.** $321 \div 6$　　**5.** $428 \div 5$

6. $1,125 \div 21$　　**7.** $353 \div 8$　　**8.** $614 \div 7$　　**9.** $412 \div 9$　　**10.** $514 \div 6$

11. $1,254 \div 22$　　**12.** $740 \div 19$　　**13.** $430 \div 18$　　**14.** $3,119 \div 60$　　**15.** $461 \div 15$

16. $19,350 \div 90$　　**17.** $16,500 \div 220$　　**18.** $185 \div 8$　　**19.** $961 \div 9$　　**20.** $2,624 \div 24$

21. $13,629 \div 14$　　**22.** $822 \div 5$　　**23.** $2,618 \div 12$　　**24.** $839 \div 7$　　**25.** $64,877 \div 29$

Lesson 4.3 (pages 100–101)

Find the quotient.

1. $639 \div 2$　　**2.** $408 \div 8$　　**3.** $414 \div 6$　　**4.** $807 \div 3$　　**5.** $2,564 \div 4$

6. $777 \div 5$　　**7.** $1,920 \div 8$　　**8.** $2,532 \div 2$　　**9.** $3,402 \div 6$　　**10.** $3,000 \div 7$

11. $2,067 \div 3$　　**12.** $272 \div 4$　　**13.** $5,589 \div 9$　　**14.** $2,835 \div 8$　　**15.** $2,996 \div 7$

16. $6,242 \div 6$　　**17.** $5,326 \div 4$　　**18.** $5,476 \div 3$　　**19.** $26,547 \div 5$　　**20.** $43,852 \div 7$

Lesson 4.4 (pages 102–103)

Find the quotient.

1. $162 \div 54$　　**2.** $584 \div 40$　　**3.** $475 \div 19$　　**4.** $154 \div 11$

5. $984 \div 82$　　**6.** $3,787 \div 71$　　**7.** $182 \div 13$　　**8.** $1,854 \div 36$

9. $2,755 \div 19$　　**10.** $522 \div 23$　　**11.** $9,027 \div 51$　　**12.** $918 \div 27$

13. $273 \div 39$　　**14.** $1,701 \div 27$　　**15.** $18,397 \div 28$　　**16.** $13,425 \div 15$

17. $502 \div 31$　　**18.** $2,244 \div 18$　　**19.** $7,295 \div 51$　　**20.** $6,271 \div 11$

21. $2,791 \div 62$　　**22.** $20,780 \div 18$　　**23.** $8,188 \div 33$　　**24.** $42,927 \div 26$

Lesson 4.5 *(pages 104–105)*

Write a number sentence. Then solve.

1. Christian's car averages 312 miles on 12 gallons of gasoline. How many miles does his car average on 1 gallon?

2. Renee makes $5.35 an hour working as a cashier. How much will Renee make if she works 32 hours?

3. Sallie earned $281.25 working 45 hours as a pharmacy technician. How much does Sallie earn per hour?

4. Zach picked 15 three-leaf clovers and 8 four-leaf clovers. How many clover leaves does he have in all?

Lesson 4.6 *(pages 106–107)*

Find the quotient.

1. $8\overline{)5{,}120}$
2. $9\overline{)1{,}082}$
3. $3\overline{)603}$
4. $7\overline{)763}$

5. $14\overline{)2{,}870}$
6. $21\overline{)4{,}368}$
7. $26\overline{)13{,}239}$
8. $33\overline{)2{,}314}$

9. $5\overline{)7{,}500}$
10. $12\overline{)1{,}680}$
11. $4\overline{)3{,}080}$
12. $8\overline{)6{,}448}$

13. $18\overline{)36{,}414}$
14. $37\overline{)15{,}133}$
15. $50\overline{)2{,}502}$
16. $29\overline{)8{,}912}$

Lesson 4.7 *(pages 110–111)*

Find the quotient.

1. $3.2 \div 4$
2. $0.96 \div 8$
3. $43.7 \div 46$
4. $450.8 \div 98$

5. $93.24 \div 18$
6. $3.528 \div 84$
7. $75.02 \div 62$
8. $155.4 \div 42$

9. $0.416 \div 16$
10. $243.46 \div 47$
11. $35.28 \div 84$
12. $146.4 \div 8$

13. $131.2 \div 82$
14. $89.54 \div 74$
15. $0.7 \div 10$
16. $9.45 \div 63$

Lesson 4.8 *(pages 112–113)*

Divide until the remainder is zero.

1. $1.075 \div 5$
2. $0.336 \div 12$
3. $25.555 \div 19$
4. $5.35 \div 2$
5. $90.662 \div 22$

6. $0.3 \div 4$
7. $2.064 \div 16$
8. $6.015 \div 3$
9. $56.25 \div 18$
10. $35.595 \div 35$

11. $0.448 \div 8$
12. $1.225 \div 7$
13. $0.2208 \div 32$
14. $19.067 \div 46$
15. $150.75 \div 18$

16. $15.025 \div 5$
17. $147.24 \div 6$
18. $0.546 \div 12$
19. $1.7567 \div 11$
20. $6.8835 \div 15$

Lesson 4.9 (pages 114–115)

Copy and complete each table.

	×	10^1	10^2	10^3
1.	15.27	■	■	■
2.	0.038	■	■	■
3.	0.004	■	■	■
4.	1.2	■	■	■

	÷	10^1	10^2	10^3
5.	2.3	■	■	■
6.	0.6	■	■	■
7.	67.4	■	■	■
8.	480	■	■	■

Lesson 4.10 (pages 116–117)

Use place-value materials. Find the quotient.

1. $8.8 \div 2.2$ 2. $2.8 \div 1.4$ 3. $3.9 \div 1.3$

Write whether the quotients will be the same or different.

4. $640 \div 320$
$6.4 \div 3.2$

5. $34.5 \div 1.15$
$3.45 \div 11.5$

6. $6.6 \div 2.2$
$0.66 \div 0.022$

Lesson 4.11 (pages 118–119)

Place the decimal point in the quotient. Add zeros if necessary.

1. $134.3 \div 3.4 = 395$ 2. $1.475 \div 2.5 = 59$ 3. $3.933 \div 1.9 = 207$

4. $9.057 \div 0.3 = 3019$ 5. $60.84 \div 0.15 = 4056$ 6. $40.12 \div 5.9 = 68$

Find the quotient.

7. $4.8 \div 0.08$ 8. $5.922 \div 0.94$ 9. $62.712 \div 13.4$

Lesson 4.12 (pages 120–121)

Find the quotient. Round to the nearest whole number or dollar.

1. $135 \div 8$ 2. $\$16.00 \div 5$ 3. $22.1 \div 6.7$ 4. $\$13.00 \div 6$

Find the quotient. Round to the place given.

5. $68.3 \div 9$
(ones)

6. $4.591 \div 1.41$
(hundredths)

7. $25.63 \div 15$
(tenths)

8. $\$93.45 \div 12$
(cents)

9. $9.965 \div 8$
(ten-thousandths)

10. $245.82 \div 39$
(thousandths)

Lesson 4.13 *(pages 122–123)*

Write an algebraic expression for the word expression.

1. a number, m, divided by 9

2. a number, t, multiplied by 3

3. the quotient of a number, y, and 8

4. 35 times a number, w

Evaluate the expression.

5. $23a$, for $a = 14$

6. $2.9d$, for $d = 6.8$

7. $86a$, for $a = 2$

8. $\dfrac{n}{14}$, for $n = 126$

9. $\dfrac{b}{5}$, for $b = 235$

10. $\dfrac{a}{7.2}$, for $a = 48.96$

11. $15.3x$, for $x = 12$

12. $\dfrac{15}{t}$, for $t = 3$

13. $0.5y$, for $y = 35$

Lesson 4.14 *(pages 124–125)*

Tell how to solve the equation.

1. $3x = 99$

2. $\dfrac{x}{5} = 45$

3. $11c = 121$

4. $\dfrac{t}{6} = 144$

5. $9d = 369$

6. $\dfrac{m}{12} = 48$

7. $\dfrac{d}{15} = 225$

8. $29a = 435$

9. $\dfrac{n}{4} = 240$

Use inverse operations. Solve the equation.

10. $4m = 100$

11. $3x = 18$

12. $\dfrac{t}{6} = 9$

13. $91x = 910$

14. $\dfrac{b}{5} = 7$

15. $\dfrac{y}{10} = 55$

Lesson 4.15 *(pages 126–127)*

Make a flowchart and *work backward.* Solve.

1. Bea spent a total of $30.00. She spent $12.95 for a blouse, $9.95 for a T-shirt, $5.95 for a book, and the rest for a birthday card. How much was the birthday card?

2. Jane collected $119.10 for selling 3 jackets at $29.95 each and $29.25 for 15 souvenir pins. How much does one souvenir pin cost?

3. A sandwich shop sells a 6-inch sandwich for $2.95 and a 12-inch for $4.95. On Monday they sold 48 6-inch sandwiches. How many 12-inch sandwiches did they sell if they sold $314.85 worth of sandwiches that day?

4. Emilio bought $15.00 worth of school supplies. He bought 4 book binders at $2.75 each and spent the rest on scratch pads that sell for 3 pads for $1.00. How many pads did Emilio buy?

CHAPTER 5

Lesson 5.1 *(pages 136–137)*

Suppose you are making a tally sheet and a frequency table.
Use the data in the box for Exercises 1–4.

1. Will you write the number of pages in groups of 10 pages, such as 200-210, on your tally sheet? Justify your choice.

2. What will be the highest group of 10 pages on your tally sheet?

3. How will you organize the number of pages in your frequency table?

Number of Pages in Paperback Books				
245	127	200	395	218
392	195	229	456	376
369	248	345	512	189
412	341	420	259	526

4. Will the number of books with 512 pages be easier to find on the tally or the table?

Lesson 5.2 *(pages 138–139)*

Answer the questions. Give reasons for your answers.

1. A local TV station polls its audience on issues in national politics. Viewers call a 900 number to vote *yes* or *no*. Are the results of these polls representative of the whole country?

2. Farrah polled voters in a predominantly Republican neighborhood about the governor who is a Democrat. Will their opinions be biased?

3. Byron surveys 500 people in a town of 20,000 and determines that 0.75 of the group like coffee. Can Byron claim that 75 out of 100 townspeople like coffee?

4. Sarah determines that 10 out of 10 students in the drama club like to read. Can she claim that 100% of the school population likes to read? Why or why not?

Lesson 5.3 *(pages 140–143)*

Choose the data in A and B. Make one bar graph and one pictograph.

A.

Throwing Contest	
Name	Distance (feet)
Kim	98
John	110
Frank	105
Mac	120
Carol	115

B.

Bowling Scores	
Name	Score
Lee	145
Jamie	210
Joe	199
Mary	125
Barb	188

Lesson 5.4 (pages 144–145)

Use the data in A to make a bar graph. Use the data in B to make a histogram.

A.

Amount of Sales	
Store	Sales
Store A	$25,000
Store B	$10,000
Store C	$45,000
Store D	$22,000
Store E	$60,000

B.

Number of Shoppers	
Time	Number
8:00–9:59 A.M.	35
10:00–11:59 A.M.	49
12:00–1:59 P.M.	92
2:00–3:59 P.M.	54

Lesson 5.5 (pages 146–147)

Choose the data in A or B. Make a line graph.

A.

Jay's Bank Balance	
Month	Balance
March	$ 659.95
April	$1,635.00
May	$1,392.49
June	$ 848.11
July	$ 900.56

B.

Jane's Weight Loss	
Month	Weight Loss (pounds)
December	7
January	5
February	6
March	4
April	8

Lesson 5.6 (pages 148–149)

Choose the data in A or B. Make a circle graph.

A.

Favorite Sports	
Sport	Number of Students
Football	40
Tennis	20
Bowling	10
Baseball	20
Skiing	6

B.

Favorite Vacation	
Vacation	Number of Travelers
Beach	36
Ranch	6
City	15
Cruise	15
Europe	24

Lesson 5.7 (pages 150–151)

Make a table or a graph to organize each set of data so that it is easy to read and compare.

1. An ice-cream store sold 1,500 cones in July, 1,800 in August, 1,200 in September, 900 in October, and 600 in November.

2. The Sooner family rode their exercycle 50 miles on Monday, 60 on Tuesday, 80 on Wednesday, 100 on Thursday, and 150 on Friday.

Lesson 5.8 (pages 154–155)

Copy and complete the table.

	Collection of Data	Range	Mean	Median	Mode
1.	75, 86, 73, 80, 86, 80	▦	▦	▦	▦
2.	86, 90, 76, 42, 98, 88	▦	▦	▦	▦
3.	48, 52, 75, 47, 83, 49	▦	▦	▦	▦
4.	16, 20, 19, 16, 15, 19, 15, 16	▦	▦	▦	▦

Lesson 5.9 (pages 156–157)

This stem-and-leaf plot shows 20 students' heights in inches. Use this plot for Exercises 1–6.

Stem	Leaves
5	8 8 9 9
6	0 0 0 1 2 3 4 5 6 6
7	0 0 1 2 2 3

1. How many leaves does the second stem have?

2. What numbers are shown by the third stem and its leaves?

3. Which height occurs more often, 60 in. or 59 in.?

4. What is the range of the students' heights?

5. What is the median of the students' heights?

6. What is the mode of the students' heights?

Lesson 5.10 (pages 158–159)

Make a tree diagram to find the number of choices.

1.

Purses	Shoes
Black	Navy
Beige	White
Blue	Brown

2.

Curtains	Paint
Orange	Green
White	Mauve
	Taupe

3.

Paper	Pen
Blue	Red
Pink	Black

Write the number of choices.

4. 5 brands, 6 sizes

5. 20 scarves, 12 pairs of earrings

6. 9 slacks, 21 shirts

7. 8 pens, 4 colors

Lesson 5.11 *(pages 160–161)*

Use the spinner. Find the probability of each event.

1. stopping on 1

2. stopping on an even number

3. stopping on a number less than 5

4. stopping on a number greater than 8

5. stopping on a number less than or equal to 8

6. stopping on a number greater than 1

7. stopping on 1, 2, or 4

8. stopping on 1, 2, 3, 4, 5, 6, 7, or 8

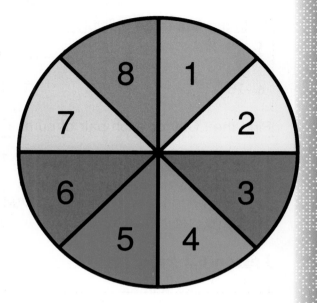

Lesson 5.12 *(pages 162–163)*

Use the situation in the box for Exercises 1–4.

1. Make a tree diagram to show all of Judy's possible choices.

2. How many choices does Judy have for interior and exterior colors?

3. What is the probability that Judy will choose white exterior and red interior?

> Judy bought a new car. The color choices for the interior of the car were blue, red, gray, and white. Her choices for the exterior were light blue, black, and white.

4. What is the probability that Judy will choose white interior and white exterior?

Lesson 5.13 *(pages 164–165)*

Find a pattern and solve.

1. Jean worked 12 hours the first week, 15 hours the second week and 18 hours the third week. How many hours will she work in the sixth week if the pattern continues?

2. Alan saved $100 in March, $125 in April, $160 in May and $205 in June. If the pattern continues, how much money will he save in September?

3. A worker lays 4 design bricks in the first row of a patio, 6 in the third row, and 8 in the fifth row. If the pattern continues, in which row will he lay 12 design bricks?

4. A video store rents one movie for $1.50, 2 movies for $2.00, and 3 for $2.50. If the pattern continues, how much will 6 movies cost?

CHAPTER 6

Lesson 6.1 (pages 174–175)

Write the first three multiples, excluding the number itself.

1. 2   **2.** 4   **3.** 8   **4.** 13   **5.** 14

6. 16   **7.** 17   **8.** 18   **9.** 19   **10.** 21

Find the LCM for each pair of numbers.

11. 4, 5   **12.** 3, 17   **13.** 6, 13   **14.** 7, 15   **15.** 8, 10

16. 4, 16   **17.** 3, 9   **18.** 7, 9   **19.** 7, 21   **20.** 6, 18

21. 12, 16, 24   **22.** 25, 50   **23.** 2, 3, 12   **24.** 1, 4, 32   **25.** 7, 13, 91

Lesson 6.2 (pages 176–177)

Complete the number sentence.

1. $\dfrac{2}{5} = \dfrac{\blacksquare}{10}$ **2.** $\dfrac{1}{3} = \dfrac{\blacksquare}{9}$ **3.** $\dfrac{3}{4} = \dfrac{\blacksquare}{32}$ **4.** $\dfrac{\blacksquare}{24} = \dfrac{5}{6}$

5. $\dfrac{8}{9} = \dfrac{\blacksquare}{72}$ **6.** $\dfrac{\blacksquare}{33} = \dfrac{5}{11}$ **7.** $\dfrac{4}{13} = \dfrac{\blacksquare}{39}$ **8.** $\dfrac{\blacksquare}{45} = \dfrac{8}{15}$

9. $\dfrac{21}{23} = \dfrac{\blacksquare}{92}$ **10.** $\dfrac{5}{12} = \dfrac{\blacksquare}{144}$ **11.** $\dfrac{19}{38} = \dfrac{\blacksquare}{2}$ **12.** $\dfrac{28}{48} = \dfrac{\blacksquare}{12}$

Write *yes* or *no* to tell whether the fractions are equivalent. If they are not, write an equivalent fraction for each fraction.

13. $\dfrac{6}{8}, \dfrac{18}{32}$ **14.** $\dfrac{1}{5}, \dfrac{5}{25}$ **15.** $\dfrac{4}{6}, \dfrac{24}{36}$ **16.** $\dfrac{33}{120}, \dfrac{11}{10}$

17. $\dfrac{7}{49}, \dfrac{2}{7}$ **18.** $\dfrac{10}{30}, \dfrac{1}{3}$ **19.** $\dfrac{25}{115}, \dfrac{5}{23}$ **20.** $\dfrac{4}{16}, \dfrac{2}{32}$

21. $\dfrac{3}{5}, \dfrac{2}{10}$ **22.** $\dfrac{8}{12}, \dfrac{2}{3}$ **23.** $\dfrac{24}{32}, \dfrac{8}{16}$ **24.** $\dfrac{18}{27}, \dfrac{6}{9}$

25. $\dfrac{75}{100}, \dfrac{2}{4}$ **26.** $\dfrac{1}{3}, \dfrac{3}{24}$ **27.** $\dfrac{20}{21}, \dfrac{40}{42}$ **28.** $\dfrac{7}{8}, \dfrac{15}{16}$

Lesson 6.3 (pages 178–179)

Write each pair of fractions by using the LCD.

1. $\dfrac{3}{7}, \dfrac{1}{14}$ **2.** $\dfrac{5}{8}, \dfrac{2}{4}$ **3.** $\dfrac{6}{9}, \dfrac{1}{3}$ **4.** $\dfrac{6}{10}, \dfrac{3}{5}$

5. $\dfrac{7}{11}, \dfrac{10}{22}$ **6.** $\dfrac{3}{5}, \dfrac{5}{6}$ **7.** $\dfrac{4}{7}, \dfrac{1}{4}$ **8.** $\dfrac{6}{9}, \dfrac{5}{6}$

9. $\dfrac{3}{8}, \dfrac{5}{6}$ **10.** $\dfrac{12}{18}, \dfrac{1}{6}$ **11.** $\dfrac{2}{3}, \dfrac{3}{7}$ **12.** $\dfrac{6}{8}, \dfrac{2}{4}$

Lesson 6.4 *(pages 180–181)*

Use the LCD to write like fractions.

1. $\dfrac{1}{3}, \dfrac{5}{18}$ 2. $\dfrac{4}{6}, \dfrac{1}{24}$ 3. $\dfrac{5}{12}, \dfrac{11}{24}$ 4. $\dfrac{1}{2}, \dfrac{5}{16}$

5. $\dfrac{3}{8}, \dfrac{1}{24}$ 6. $\dfrac{7}{15}, \dfrac{8}{45}$ 7. $\dfrac{3}{4}, \dfrac{2}{5}$ 8. $\dfrac{11}{13}, \dfrac{1}{2}$

9. $\dfrac{2}{3}, \dfrac{4}{5}$ 10. $\dfrac{6}{10}, \dfrac{1}{15}$ 11. $\dfrac{3}{4}, \dfrac{5}{7}$ 12. $\dfrac{7}{8}, \dfrac{1}{12}$

13. $\dfrac{1}{6}, \dfrac{3}{10}$ 14. $\dfrac{5}{6}, \dfrac{5}{9}$ 15. $\dfrac{3}{4}, \dfrac{5}{6}$ 16. $\dfrac{2}{12}, \dfrac{1}{8}$

Use <, >, or = to compare the fractions.

17. $\dfrac{1}{3} \bigcirc \dfrac{2}{9}$ 18. $\dfrac{4}{7} \bigcirc \dfrac{10}{21}$ 19. $\dfrac{5}{6} \bigcirc \dfrac{3}{4}$ 20. $\dfrac{8}{24} \bigcirc \dfrac{2}{6}$

21. $\dfrac{15}{24} \bigcirc \dfrac{18}{32}$ 22. $\dfrac{5}{30} \bigcirc \dfrac{13}{78}$ 23. $\dfrac{8}{25} \bigcirc \dfrac{16}{45}$ 24. $\dfrac{12}{25} \bigcirc \dfrac{7}{9}$

25. $\dfrac{5}{6} \bigcirc \dfrac{4}{5}$ 26. $\dfrac{4}{12} \bigcirc \dfrac{7}{12}$ 27. $\dfrac{5}{8} \bigcirc \dfrac{11}{12}$ 28. $\dfrac{3}{4} \bigcirc \dfrac{7}{9}$

29. $\dfrac{1}{9} \bigcirc \dfrac{2}{15}$ 30. $\dfrac{2}{3} \bigcirc \dfrac{3}{4}$ 31. $\dfrac{6}{10} \bigcirc \dfrac{8}{40}$ 32. $\dfrac{11}{12} \bigcirc \dfrac{7}{8}$

33. $\dfrac{4}{8} \bigcirc \dfrac{5}{10}$ 34. $\dfrac{5}{8} \bigcirc \dfrac{7}{10}$ 35. $\dfrac{7}{8} \bigcirc \dfrac{6}{7}$ 36. $\dfrac{7}{9} \bigcirc \dfrac{21}{27}$

Lesson 6.5 *(pages 182–183)*

Solve by acting out the situation.

1. Five students, A through E, just put their papers on the teacher's desk. B was not first but was before A. C put his paper on the desk between A and E. D was before A. Whose paper is at the bottom of the stack?

2. There are 6 students taking part in a school debate. Each student shook hands with every other student. How many handshakes were there in all?

Lesson 6.6 *(pages 184–185)*

Tell whether the number is prime or composite.

1. 19   2. 17   3. 45   4. 9   5. 121   6. 13   7. 27

Write the factors of each number.

8. 22   9. 36   10. 8   11. 28   12. 42   13. 65   14. 100

Lesson 6.7 *(pages 186–187)*

Write the prime factorization. Use a factor tree.

1. 34
2. 26
3. 14
4. 45
5. 52
6. 81
7. 80
8. 75
9. 69
10. 105
11. 38
12. 54
13. 40
14. 49
15. 32
16. 42
17. 60
18. 22
19. 28
20. 34

Write the prime factorization in exponent form.

21. 4
22. 20
23. 63
24. 68
25. 76
26. 88
27. 108
28. 243
29. 128
30. 40
31. 30
32. 18
33. 42
34. 110
35. 400
36. 44
37. 96
38. 56
39. 90
40. 24

Lesson 6.8 *(pages 188–189)*

Write the common factors of each pair of numbers.

1. 4, 16
2. 12, 60
3. 3, 27
4. 9, 27
5. 25, 100
6. 8, 48
7. 7, 56
8. 45, 65
9. 23, 69
10. 18, 90
11. 21, 15
12. 18, 20
13. 15, 95
14. 2, 30
15. 9, 21
16. 20, 32
17. 16, 24
18. 24, 30
19. 16, 30
20. 15, 45

Write the GCF of each pair of numbers.

21. 18, 20
22. 30, 27
23. 15, 24
24. 24, 32
25. 14, 35
26. 33, 55
27. 60, 72
28. 44, 60
29. 36, 63
30. 60, 42
31. 60, 75
32. 48, 68
33. 62, 124
34. 42, 56
35. 36, 120
36. 48, 54
37. 4, 12
38. 24, 28
39. 9, 15
40. 32, 48
41. 15, 24
42. 12, 18
43. 15, 21
44. 16, 20
45. 4, 48
46. 21, 15
47. 15, 45
48. 18, 90

Lesson 6.9 (pages 192–193)

Write the GCF of the numerator and denominator.

1. $\dfrac{24}{30}$
2. $\dfrac{14}{42}$
3. $\dfrac{9}{63}$
4. $\dfrac{6}{18}$
5. $\dfrac{8}{48}$

6. $\dfrac{25}{50}$
7. $\dfrac{18}{20}$
8. $\dfrac{12}{72}$
9. $\dfrac{110}{130}$
10. $\dfrac{15}{25}$

Write the fraction in simplest form.

11. $\dfrac{20}{50}$
12. $\dfrac{6}{18}$
13. $\dfrac{42}{49}$
14. $\dfrac{16}{18}$
15. $\dfrac{21}{72}$

16. $\dfrac{25}{100}$
17. $\dfrac{33}{36}$
18. $\dfrac{21}{24}$
19. $\dfrac{5}{5}$
20. $\dfrac{40}{44}$

21. $\dfrac{48}{52}$
22. $\dfrac{20}{25}$
23. $\dfrac{42}{90}$
24. $\dfrac{10}{24}$
25. $\dfrac{18}{21}$

Lesson 6.10 (pages 194–195)

Write the fraction as a mixed number or a whole number.

1. $\dfrac{44}{9}$
2. $\dfrac{65}{4}$
3. $\dfrac{39}{13}$
4. $\dfrac{68}{11}$
5. $\dfrac{31}{4}$

6. $\dfrac{57}{11}$
7. $\dfrac{28}{12}$
8. $\dfrac{49}{7}$
9. $\dfrac{145}{15}$
10. $\dfrac{192}{8}$

Write the mixed number as a fraction.

11. $6\dfrac{1}{3}$
12. $3\dfrac{11}{12}$
13. $4\dfrac{7}{8}$
14. $8\dfrac{1}{3}$
15. $2\dfrac{13}{25}$

16. $5\dfrac{3}{8}$
17. $6\dfrac{2}{3}$
18. $7\dfrac{5}{9}$
19. $12\dfrac{1}{2}$
20. $17\dfrac{2}{3}$

Lesson 6.11 (pages 196–197)

Choose a strategy. Then solve.

1. Guy spent $\frac{2}{5}$ of his time reading, $\frac{1}{3}$ writing, $\frac{1}{4}$ talking and $\frac{3}{8}$ dreaming. On which activity did Guy spend the most time?

2. There are 48 rolls on the shelf. If there are 24 more sourdough rolls than French rolls, how many French rolls are on the shelf?

3. Camille and Pierre will work 30 hours each this month at the beach picking up trash. Camille has already worked 5 more hours than Pierre, who has worked 18 hours. How many more hours does Camille need to work?

4. Tammy had 60 marbles. She gave $\frac{1}{5}$ of her marbles to John. She gave $\frac{1}{3}$ of what she had left to Yakov and the rest to Paula. How many marbles did Paula receive?

CHAPTER 7

Lesson 7.1 (pages 206–207)

Tell whether the estimate is a little less than or a little more than the answer given. Write < or >.

1. $\frac{15}{16} + \frac{1}{4}$ ● 1

2. $6\frac{1}{2} - 3\frac{3}{4}$ ● 3

3. $1\frac{1}{3} + 2\frac{1}{6}$ ● 3

4. $8\frac{3}{8} - 2\frac{1}{3}$ ● 6

5. $5\frac{1}{9} + 6\frac{3}{7}$ ● 11

6. $4\frac{1}{6} - 3\frac{2}{3}$ ● 1

Estimate the sum or difference.

7. $\frac{1}{9} + \frac{5}{8}$

8. $\frac{5}{6} + \frac{7}{8}$

9. $\frac{8}{9} - \frac{1}{6}$

10. $\frac{5}{6} - \frac{5}{8}$

11. $2\frac{11}{12} - \frac{1}{9}$

12. $3\frac{1}{3} + 4\frac{1}{8}$

13. $5\frac{7}{9} - 4\frac{12}{13}$

14. $4\frac{3}{13} + 5\frac{2}{15}$

Lesson 7.2 (pages 208–209)

Find the sum or difference. Write your answer in simplest form.

1. $\frac{1}{7} + \frac{3}{7}$

2. $\frac{8}{13} - \frac{5}{13}$

3. $\frac{4}{10} + \frac{5}{10}$

4. $\frac{3}{7} - \frac{2}{7}$

5. $\frac{5}{9} + \frac{8}{9}$

6. $\frac{9}{11} - \frac{3}{11}$

7. $\frac{5}{6} + \frac{1}{6}$

8. $\frac{2}{3} - \frac{1}{3}$

9. $\frac{3}{4} + \frac{2}{4}$

10. $\frac{7}{8} - \frac{3}{8}$

11. $\frac{4}{5} + \frac{3}{5}$

12. $\frac{2}{15} + \frac{3}{15}$

Lesson 7.3 (pages 210–211)

Find the sum or difference. Write your answer in simplest form.

1. $\begin{array}{r} \frac{3}{8} \\ -\frac{1}{12} \\ \hline \end{array}$

2. $\begin{array}{r} \frac{2}{3} \\ +\frac{5}{12} \\ \hline \end{array}$

3. $\begin{array}{r} \frac{5}{6} \\ +\frac{8}{9} \\ \hline \end{array}$

4. $\begin{array}{r} \frac{11}{12} \\ -\frac{5}{6} \\ \hline \end{array}$

5. $\begin{array}{r} \frac{4}{5} \\ -\frac{1}{4} \\ \hline \end{array}$

6. $\begin{array}{r} \frac{2}{3} \\ +\frac{5}{7} \\ \hline \end{array}$

7. $\begin{array}{r} \frac{3}{4} \\ -\frac{2}{5} \\ \hline \end{array}$

8. $\begin{array}{r} \frac{1}{3} \\ +\frac{2}{5} \\ \hline \end{array}$

9. $\begin{array}{r} \frac{7}{10} \\ -\frac{1}{4} \\ \hline \end{array}$

10. $\begin{array}{r} \frac{7}{8} \\ +\frac{5}{6} \\ \hline \end{array}$

11. $\begin{array}{r} \frac{1}{6} \\ +\frac{1}{2} \\ \hline \end{array}$

12. $\begin{array}{r} \frac{3}{4} \\ +\frac{1}{6} \\ \hline \end{array}$

13. $\begin{array}{r} \frac{5}{6} \\ +\frac{2}{3} \\ \hline \end{array}$

14. $\begin{array}{r} \frac{3}{15} \\ +\frac{2}{5} \\ \hline \end{array}$

15. $\begin{array}{r} \frac{5}{6} \\ +\frac{3}{4} \\ \hline \end{array}$

16. $\begin{array}{r} \frac{1}{3} \\ +\frac{1}{9} \\ \hline \end{array}$

Lesson 7.4 *(pages 212–213)*

Find the sum. Write your answer in simplest form.

1. $4\frac{1}{2}$
   $+ 5\frac{1}{4}$

2. $3\frac{2}{5}$
   $+2\frac{7}{10}$

3. $2\frac{6}{7}$
   $+1\frac{3}{14}$

4. $8\frac{1}{3}$
   $+ 1\frac{1}{3}$

5. $1\frac{1}{8}$
   $+ 2\frac{3}{8}$

6. $3\frac{5}{6}$
   $+1\frac{5}{6}$

7. $4\frac{1}{5}$
   $+2\frac{3}{10}$

8. $9\frac{2}{3}$
   $+ 8\frac{1}{5}$

9. $5\frac{1}{6}$
   $+ 2\frac{2}{3}$

10. $2\frac{6}{7}$
    $+ 3\frac{1}{3}$

11. $6\frac{4}{9}$
    $+ 2\frac{2}{9}$

12. $8\frac{1}{6}$
    $+ 2\frac{1}{2}$

13. $7\frac{3}{10}$
    $+ 4\frac{1}{2}$

14. $4\frac{1}{3}$
    $+ 5\frac{3}{5}$

15. $1\frac{1}{2}$
    $+ 1\frac{2}{9}$

16. $10\frac{9}{10}$
    $+ \quad \frac{3}{5}$

17. $22\frac{4}{5}$
    $+ 17\frac{5}{9}$

18. $32\frac{11}{12}$
    $+25\frac{5}{6}$

19. $47\frac{7}{8}$
    $+ \ 39\frac{3}{5}$

20. $23\frac{10}{11}$
    $+ \ 9\frac{1}{2}$

21. $1\frac{3}{8} + 1\frac{2}{3}$

22. $5\frac{2}{5} + 6\frac{7}{10}$

23. $6\frac{2}{3} + 2\frac{3}{4}$

Lesson 7.5 *(pages 214–215)*

Draw a diagram for Exercises 1–4. Then solve.

1. Merle wants to hang a 1.5-foot poster on a 6.5-foot wall. If she centers the poster, how far will it be from each end of the wall?

2. Laurie walked $1\frac{1}{9}$ miles south, and $2\frac{4}{9}$ miles east. How many more miles does she need to walk to complete her 5-mile walk?

3. Ely has a total of 320 books. He says that $\frac{3}{16}$ of his book collection consists of novels, and $\frac{3}{8}$ of the collection are biographies. The rest are reference books. How many are reference books?

4. Eric wants to mount a 3-inch decal on a square window with 51-inch sides. If he centers the decal, how far will it be from each end of the window?

Lesson 7.6 *(pages 218–219)*

Rename the larger number.

1. $6 - 1\frac{1}{3}$

2. $4\frac{1}{8} - 2\frac{3}{8}$

3. $3\frac{2}{15} - 2\frac{4}{15}$

4. $5\frac{1}{6} - 3\frac{5}{6}$

5. $2\frac{1}{3} - 1\frac{2}{3}$

6. $6 - 1\frac{3}{16}$

Find the difference.

7. $6 - 4\frac{1}{8}$

8. $10 - 3\frac{1}{6}$

9. $8\frac{1}{5} - 4\frac{4}{5}$

10. $3\frac{1}{8} - 1\frac{2}{8}$

11. $3\frac{1}{3} - 1\frac{2}{3}$

12. $5\frac{2}{7} - 2\frac{5}{7}$

Lesson 7.7 *(pages 220–221)*

Find the difference. Write the answer in simplest form.

1. $8\frac{7}{8}$
$-2\frac{5}{8}$

2. $8\frac{11}{12}$
$-5\frac{7}{12}$

3. $6\frac{6}{15}$
$-5\frac{11}{15}$

4. $2\frac{1}{8}$
$-\frac{3}{8}$

5. 6
$-2\frac{3}{10}$

6. $6\frac{2}{13}$
$-3\frac{7}{13}$

7. $4\frac{1}{6}$
$-1\frac{5}{6}$

8. $7\frac{12}{13}$
$-5\frac{6}{13}$

9. $3\frac{1}{7}$
$-1\frac{5}{7}$

10. 12
$-8\frac{3}{8}$

Lesson 7.8 *(pages 222–223)*

Change to the LCD if necessary. Then tell whether you must rename to subtract. Write *yes* or *no.*

1. $6\frac{4}{5} - 2\frac{1}{2}$

2. $3\frac{1}{6} - 1\frac{5}{6}$

3. $2\frac{5}{6} - 1\frac{1}{3}$

4. $2\frac{1}{8} - 1\frac{5}{8}$

5. $3\frac{1}{7} - 1\frac{4}{7}$

6. $4\frac{3}{4} - 2\frac{5}{6}$

Find the difference. Write the answer in simplest form.

7. $3\frac{1}{5} - \frac{4}{5}$

8. $4\frac{1}{8} - 2\frac{7}{24}$

9. $5\frac{7}{8} - 2\frac{1}{4}$

10. $6\frac{1}{3} - 1\frac{5}{6}$

11. $6\frac{4}{15} - 3\frac{2}{5}$

12. $7\frac{1}{8} - 3\frac{15}{24}$

13. $2\frac{1}{2} - 1\frac{8}{9}$

14. $5\frac{2}{3} - 4\frac{2}{5}$

15. $9\frac{1}{10} - 3\frac{9}{20}$

16. $8\frac{1}{6} - 7\frac{7}{12}$

17. $1\frac{1}{4} - \frac{1}{3}$

18. $20\frac{1}{12} - 6\frac{1}{8}$

Lesson 7.9 *(pages 224–225)*

Find the difference.

1. $8\frac{11}{12}$
    $-7\frac{3}{4}$

2. $10\frac{1}{4}$
    $-3\frac{1}{12}$

3. $5\frac{5}{8}$
    $-1\frac{1}{3}$

4. $9\frac{3}{4}$
    $-4\frac{1}{6}$

5. $8\frac{1}{6}$
    $-5\frac{1}{3}$

6. $3\frac{4}{5}$
    $-2\frac{9}{10}$

7. $10\frac{1}{3}$
    $-6\frac{5}{6}$

8. $6\frac{3}{8}$
    $-3\frac{1}{2}$

9. $5\frac{1}{4}$
    $-4\frac{5}{6}$

10. $8\frac{2}{3}$
    $-6\frac{7}{8}$

11. $9\frac{1}{8}$
    $-7\frac{1}{3}$

12. $6\frac{7}{8}$
    $-1\frac{7}{12}$

13. $5\frac{5}{6}$
    $-1\frac{1}{4}$

14. $5\frac{3}{4}$
    $-2\frac{1}{2}$

15. $6\frac{1}{2}$
    $-2\frac{1}{16}$

16. $8\frac{6}{15}$
    $-2\frac{7}{9}$

17. $22\frac{4}{5}$
    $-17\frac{1}{9}$

18. $32\frac{1}{12}$
    $-25\frac{5}{6}$

19. $47\frac{1}{8}$
    $-39\frac{3}{5}$

20. $23\frac{2}{11}$
    $-9\frac{1}{2}$

21. $4\frac{1}{5} - 2\frac{4}{5}$

22. $8\frac{1}{3} - 2\frac{1}{6}$

23. $3\frac{2}{3} - 1\frac{1}{3}$

Lesson 7.10 *(pages 226–227)*

Choose a strategy. Then solve.

1. Josie painted $\frac{1}{3}$ of her fence in the morning and $\frac{1}{2}$ of what was left in the afternoon. What fraction of the fence does she still need to paint to finish the job?

2. Maria spent $15.00 at the pet store. She bought dog food with $\frac{2}{5}$ of her money, a dog collar for $\frac{1}{5}$, and flea shampoo with the rest of her money. How much was the shampoo?

3. Mr. Jones spent $3\frac{1}{2}$ hours running errands. He spent $1\frac{1}{4}$ hours at the grocery store and $\frac{5}{8}$ hour at the hardware store. The rest of the time was spent driving. How long did Mr. Jones spend driving?

4. Corey left her front door and walked $1\frac{1}{3}$ miles east. Then she walked $\frac{1}{2}$ mile south, $\frac{2}{3}$ mile east, $\frac{1}{6}$ mile south and 2 miles west. How far from her front door is she?

CHAPTER 8

Lesson 8.1 (pages 236–237)

Draw a model for each problem. Tell whether the product in **a** is the same as the product in **b**.

1. **a.** $0.6 \times 0.4 = 0.24$
   b. $\dfrac{3}{5} \times \dfrac{2}{5} = \dfrac{6}{25}$

2. **a.** $\dfrac{5}{8} \times \dfrac{1}{2} = \dfrac{5}{16}$
   b. $0.6 \times 0.5 = 0.3$

3. **a.** $0.2 \times 0.4 = 0.08$
   b. $\dfrac{1}{5} \times \dfrac{2}{5} = \dfrac{2}{25}$

4. **a.** $\dfrac{2}{3} \times \dfrac{1}{5} = \dfrac{2}{15}$
   b. $0.65 \times 0.5 = 0.325$

Lesson 8.2 (pages 238–239)

Solve. Write the product in simplest form.

1. $\dfrac{7}{12} \times \dfrac{6}{7}$

2. $\dfrac{1}{4} \times \dfrac{1}{4}$

3. $\dfrac{2}{5} \times \dfrac{5}{8}$

4. $\dfrac{1}{6} \times \dfrac{2}{5}$

5. $\dfrac{8}{9} \times \dfrac{9}{10}$

6. $\dfrac{5}{7} \times \dfrac{14}{25}$

7. $\dfrac{3}{10} \times \dfrac{20}{30}$

8. $\dfrac{4}{9} \times \dfrac{3}{8}$

9. $\dfrac{1}{6} \times \dfrac{3}{4}$

10. $\dfrac{2}{9} \times \dfrac{6}{10}$

11. $\dfrac{1}{8} \times \dfrac{4}{5}$

12. $\dfrac{3}{7} \times \dfrac{14}{21}$

13. $\dfrac{1}{9} \times \dfrac{2}{3}$

14. $\dfrac{3}{5} \times \dfrac{1}{2}$

15. $\dfrac{4}{11} \times \dfrac{1}{4}$

16. $\dfrac{1}{6} \times \dfrac{7}{8}$

Lesson 8.3 (pages 240–241)

Simplify the factors.

1. $\dfrac{1}{5} \times \dfrac{5}{6}$

2. $\dfrac{1}{3} \times \dfrac{3}{5}$

3. $\dfrac{1}{2} \times \dfrac{8}{15}$

4. $\dfrac{6}{11} \times \dfrac{2}{3}$

5. $\dfrac{3}{7} \times \dfrac{7}{15}$

6. $\dfrac{7}{12} \times \dfrac{3}{14}$

7. $\dfrac{7}{8} \times \dfrac{24}{49}$

8. $\dfrac{2}{6} \times \dfrac{9}{18}$

9. $\dfrac{1}{2} \times \dfrac{2}{3}$

10. $\dfrac{11}{12} \times \dfrac{6}{8}$

11. $\dfrac{1}{8} \times \dfrac{4}{9}$

12. $\dfrac{3}{4} \times \dfrac{8}{9}$

13. $\dfrac{5}{7} \times \dfrac{14}{10}$

14. $\dfrac{2}{5} \times \dfrac{15}{4}$

15. $\dfrac{7}{12} \times \dfrac{6}{21}$

16. $\dfrac{7}{8} \times \dfrac{16}{6}$

Choose a method. Then find the product. Write the product in simplest form.

17. $\dfrac{3}{4} \times \dfrac{1}{2}$

18. $\dfrac{7}{8} \times \dfrac{4}{5}$

19. $\dfrac{2}{3} \times \dfrac{3}{8}$

20. $\dfrac{3}{8} \times \dfrac{4}{13}$

21. $\dfrac{4}{9} \times \dfrac{3}{5}$

22. $\dfrac{5}{6} \times \dfrac{19}{20}$

23. $\dfrac{3}{7} \times \dfrac{14}{21}$

24. $\dfrac{3}{7} \times \dfrac{5}{9}$

25. $\dfrac{14}{25} \times \dfrac{5}{7}$

26. $\dfrac{8}{9} \times \dfrac{3}{16}$

27. $\dfrac{11}{24} \times \dfrac{12}{22}$

28. $\dfrac{5}{9} \times \dfrac{3}{15}$

Lesson 8.4 *(pages 242–243)*

Use rounding to estimate the product.

1. $\dfrac{5}{6} \times \dfrac{2}{5}$ **2.** $\dfrac{1}{3} \times \dfrac{10}{11}$ **3.** $\dfrac{1}{4} \times \dfrac{5}{12}$ **4.** $\dfrac{15}{16} \times \dfrac{9}{10}$ **5.** $\dfrac{6}{11} \times \dfrac{8}{17}$

Use compatible numbers to estimate the product.

6. $\dfrac{1}{3} \times 89$ **7.** $\dfrac{1}{2} \times 101$ **8.** $\dfrac{2}{5} \times 69$ **9.** $\dfrac{5}{6} \times 131$ **10.** $\dfrac{3}{4} \times 158$

Tell whether the estimate is reasonable. Write *yes* or *no*.

11. $\dfrac{2}{5} \times 40 \approx 20$ **12.** $\dfrac{4}{9} \times 200 \approx 180$ **13.** $\dfrac{1}{4} \times 800 \approx 200$ **14.** $\dfrac{1}{8} \times 30 \approx 4$

15. $\dfrac{7}{8} \times \dfrac{2}{5} \approx 1$ **16.** $\dfrac{6}{11} \times 120 \approx 70$ **17.** $\dfrac{3}{8} \times 50 \approx 20$ **18.** $\dfrac{3}{4} \times 100 \approx 30$

Lesson 8.5 *(pages 244–245)*

Tell whether the product will be less than both factors, between both factors, or greater than both factors.

1. $\dfrac{1}{6} \times \dfrac{2}{3}$ **2.** $\dfrac{1}{8} \times 4\dfrac{1}{2}$ **3.** $\dfrac{5}{6} \times 2\dfrac{3}{4}$ **4.** $2\dfrac{1}{3} \times 2\dfrac{1}{2}$

5. $5\dfrac{5}{6} \times \dfrac{3}{5}$ **6.** $3\dfrac{7}{8} \times \dfrac{5}{6}$ **7.** $4\dfrac{1}{12} \times 1\dfrac{3}{7}$ **8.** $6\dfrac{1}{3} \times 4\dfrac{4}{7}$

Find the product.

9. $2\dfrac{1}{6} \times 3\dfrac{1}{3}$ **10.** $5\dfrac{1}{5} \times 6\dfrac{7}{8}$ **11.** $3\dfrac{3}{4} \times 2\dfrac{1}{8}$ **12.** $1\dfrac{9}{11} \times 1\dfrac{1}{10}$

13. $1\dfrac{2}{11} \times 1\dfrac{9}{13}$ **14.** $\dfrac{3}{7} \times 4\dfrac{5}{11}$ **15.** $5\dfrac{1}{2} \times 7\dfrac{1}{3}$ **16.** $\dfrac{1}{9} \times 3\dfrac{3}{5}$

17. $2\dfrac{1}{3} \times 3\dfrac{1}{5}$ **18.** $8\dfrac{1}{6} \times 6\dfrac{1}{2}$ **19.** $1\dfrac{3}{4} \times 2\dfrac{3}{5}$ **20.** $9\dfrac{1}{10} \times 6\dfrac{1}{3}$

Lesson 8.6 *(pages 246–247)*

Write an equation. Then solve.

1. This week, Karim worked $2\dfrac{1}{3}$ times more than the 15 hours he worked last week. How many hours did he work this week?

2. Natalie earned $1\dfrac{1}{8}$ times more this year than she did last year. If she earned \$16,000 last year, how much did she earn this year?

3. Rob walks $11\dfrac{2}{5}$ miles every day. How many miles does he walk in 5 days?

4. Maria sold twice as many toys as her age. She is $24\dfrac{1}{2}$ years old. How many toys did she sell?

Lesson 8.7 (pages 250–252)

Write the reciprocal of the divisor.

1. $4 \div \frac{1}{5}$
2. $6 \div \frac{2}{7}$
3. $8 \div \frac{2}{3}$
4. $1 \div \frac{1}{10}$
5. $\frac{2}{5} \div \frac{5}{6}$

Complete the multiplication sentence. Then find the quotient of the division sentence.

6. $\frac{1}{8} \div \frac{1}{16} = \blacksquare$ $\frac{1}{8} \times \frac{\blacksquare}{\blacksquare} = \blacksquare$

7. $\frac{1}{2} \div \frac{1}{4} = \blacksquare$ $\frac{1}{2} \times \frac{\blacksquare}{\blacksquare} = \blacksquare$

Lesson 8.8 (pages 254–255)

Tell whether the quotient will be greater than or less than 1.

1. $12 \div \frac{1}{8}$
2. $3 \div \frac{1}{10}$
3. $\frac{8}{9} \div \frac{1}{3}$
4. $\frac{5}{8} \div \frac{3}{4}$
5. $\frac{2}{3} \div \frac{5}{12}$
6. $\frac{1}{8} \div \frac{2}{3}$
7. $\frac{2}{7} \div \frac{1}{3}$
8. $6 \div \frac{11}{12}$

Find the quotient.

9. $6 \div \frac{1}{4}$
10. $8 \div \frac{2}{5}$
11. $\frac{3}{10} \div \frac{6}{7}$
12. $\frac{7}{8} \div \frac{3}{4}$
13. $\frac{11}{12} \div \frac{1}{6}$
14. $\frac{3}{4} \div \frac{7}{8}$
15. $\frac{5}{6} \div \frac{11}{12}$
16. $\frac{5}{9} \div \frac{2}{3}$
17. $9 \div \frac{1}{3}$
18. $6 \div \frac{1}{8}$
19. $\frac{5}{11} \div \frac{15}{20}$
20. $12 \div \frac{3}{4}$
21. $\frac{1}{2} \div 10$
22. $\frac{1}{8} \div \frac{7}{16}$
23. $\frac{9}{10} \div \frac{4}{5}$
24. $\frac{8}{9} \div \frac{1}{3}$

Lesson 8.9 (pages 256–257)

Write the multiplication sentence.

1. $3\frac{1}{6} \div \frac{1}{2}$
2. $4\frac{4}{5} \div 2\frac{1}{3}$
3. $5\frac{1}{3} \div \frac{4}{9}$
4. $\frac{1}{3} \div 3\frac{3}{5}$

Find the quotient.

5. $3\frac{1}{8} \div 2\frac{1}{4}$
6. $3\frac{1}{2} \div \frac{1}{2}$
7. $4\frac{4}{5} \div \frac{9}{10}$
8. $\frac{5}{8} \div 6\frac{1}{4}$
9. $2\frac{2}{9} \div 1\frac{2}{3}$
10. $9\frac{1}{4} \div \frac{1}{8}$
11. $\frac{2}{5} \div 6\frac{1}{4}$
12. $4\frac{1}{8} \div \frac{3}{7}$
13. $1\frac{7}{8} \div 5\frac{1}{2}$
14. $2\frac{2}{3} \div 5\frac{1}{6}$
15. $9\frac{1}{6} \div 4\frac{1}{3}$
16. $\frac{5}{3} \div 8\frac{1}{3}$
17. $3\frac{1}{4} \div 5\frac{1}{2}$
18. $8\frac{1}{6} \div \frac{11}{12}$
19. $\frac{1}{4} \div 1\frac{3}{5}$
20. $1\frac{7}{8} \div 6\frac{1}{3}$
21. $11\frac{1}{7} \div \frac{2}{21}$
22. $12\frac{1}{8} \div \frac{1}{16}$
23. $1\frac{2}{3} \div 1\frac{7}{15}$
24. $6\frac{1}{8} \div \frac{7}{10}$

Lesson 8.10 (pages 258–259)

Write as a decimal.

1. $\dfrac{19}{100}$ 2. $\dfrac{1}{25}$ 3. $\dfrac{2}{5}$ 4. $\dfrac{14}{20}$ 5. $\dfrac{11}{50}$ 6. $\dfrac{41}{100}$

7. $\dfrac{4}{9}$ 8. $\dfrac{1}{100}$ 9. $\dfrac{1}{20}$ 10. $\dfrac{27}{40}$ 11. $\dfrac{13}{250}$ 12. $\dfrac{7}{9}$

13. $\dfrac{4}{5}$ 14. $\dfrac{2}{3}$ 15. $\dfrac{3}{5}$ 16. $\dfrac{7}{8}$ 17. $\dfrac{2}{9}$ 18. $\dfrac{11}{12}$

Use a calculator. Find an equivalent decimal.

19. $\dfrac{15}{30}$ 20. $\dfrac{1}{9}$ 21. $\dfrac{4}{5}$ 22. $\dfrac{3}{11}$ 23. $\dfrac{27}{100}$ 24. $\dfrac{23}{50}$

25. $\dfrac{2}{3}$ 26. $\dfrac{7}{11}$ 27. $\dfrac{1}{12}$ 28. $\dfrac{1}{6}$ 29. $\dfrac{9}{40}$ 30. $\dfrac{9}{100}$

31. $\dfrac{1}{250}$ 32. $\dfrac{6}{50}$ 33. $\dfrac{8}{75}$ 34. $\dfrac{1}{50}$ 35. $\dfrac{5}{12}$ 36. $\dfrac{4}{11}$

37. $\dfrac{1}{15}$ 38. $\dfrac{5}{9}$ 39. $\dfrac{9}{11}$ 40. $\dfrac{7}{100}$ 41. $\dfrac{4}{9}$ 42. $\dfrac{9}{15}$

Write as a fraction in simplest form.

43. 0.66   44. 0.9   45. 0.08   46. 0.05   47. 0.125   48. 0.038

49. 0.15   50. 0.2   51. 0.75   52. 0.35   53. $0.3\overline{3}$ 54. 0.54

55. 0.45   56. 0.55   57. $0.08\overline{3}$ 58. 0.4   59. $0.\overline{36}$ 60. 0.875

61. $0.91\overline{6}$ 62. 0.11   63. 0.625   64. 0.16   65. 0.01   66. 0.18

Lesson 8.11 (pages 260–261)

Solve by using a simpler problem.

1. Anna gave away $\frac{1}{5}$ of the yellow ribbons the club had, and Tina gave away $\frac{7}{10}$ of what was left. If Tina gave away 840 ribbons, how many ribbons did the club have when it started?

2. Patrick read $\frac{1}{3}$ of his book on Saturday and $\frac{1}{5}$ on Sunday. He still has 280 pages to read. What is the total number of pages in the book?

3. Ms. Hollingsworth, the manager of a retail store, pledged to give $\frac{1}{10}$ of the store's sales for the day to the school fund-raiser for band uniforms and $\frac{1}{20}$ of the store's sales that day to a local youth organization. If Ms. Hollingsworth's store gave away $750, what were the store's sales for that day?

4. Randy is a stock clerk at a discount store. His boss gave him 140 packages of price stickers. There are 240 stickers in each package, and Randy had 30 packages left over. How many stickers did Randy use?

CHAPTER 9

Lesson 9.1 (pages 270–272)

Find the missing number.

1. $15\,\text{m} = \blacksquare\,\text{dm}$
2. $40\,\text{cm} = \blacksquare\,\text{dm}$
3. $40\,\text{L} = \blacksquare\,\text{mL}$

4. $35\,\text{g} = \blacksquare\,\text{kg}$
5. $4{,}583\,\text{mm} = \blacksquare\,\text{m}$
6. $35.28\,\text{kg} = \blacksquare\,\text{g}$

7. $12\,\text{cm} = \blacksquare\,\text{mm}$
8. $500\,\text{mL} = \blacksquare\,\text{L}$
9. $3\,\text{m} = \blacksquare\,\text{km}$

10. $0.385\,\text{kg} = \blacksquare\,\text{g}$
11. $675\,\text{g} = \blacksquare\,\text{mg}$
12. $1{,}000\,\text{m} = \blacksquare\,\text{km}$

Lesson 9.2 (pages 274–275)

Choose the most reasonable estimate. Write **a, b,** or **c.**

1. length of a closet   **a.** 2 mm   **b.** 2 m   **c.** 2 km

2. height of a newborn   **a.** 40 m   **b.** 40 mm   **c.** 40 cm

3. thickness of a dime   **a.** 1 dm   **b.** 1 cm   **c.** 1 mm

4. walk around the block   **a.** 300 mm   **b.** 30 dm   **c.** 0.25 km

Choose the appropriate unit. Write *cm, m,* or *km.*

5. height of a table
6. diameter of a dime
7. height of a skyscraper

8. length of a bookcase
9. length of a road
10. width of a book

11. height of a tree
12. distance between cities
13. length of a skirt

Lesson 9.3 (pages 276–277)

Solve by using estimation.

1. A computer technician tells Lisa that the part needed to repair her computer is $145.90 and labor is $95.00 an hour. If it takes the technician 2 hours, about how much will the repair cost?

2. The distance between Carol's house and Key West is 300 miles. If her car gets 34 miles to a gallon of gasoline, about how many gallons of gasoline will she need to make the round trip?

3. Joey's car holds 12 gallons of gasoline and gets 28 miles per gallon. About how many full tanks will he need for a 1,500 mile trip?

4. Betty makes $4.75 per hour. About how many hours does she need to work to make $250?

Lesson 9.4 *(pages 278–279)*

Change to the given unit.

1. $35 \text{ kg} = \blacksquare \text{ g}$

2. $95 \text{ L} = \blacksquare \text{ mL}$

3. $12{,}000 \text{ g} = \blacksquare \text{ kg}$

4. $4 \text{ mL} = \blacksquare \text{ L}$

5. $675 \text{ g} = \blacksquare \text{ kg}$

6. $3{,}645 \text{ mL} = \blacksquare \text{ L}$

7. $0.69 \text{ L} = \blacksquare \text{ mL}$

8. $4.8 \text{ kg} = \blacksquare \text{ g}$

9. $6.2 \text{ L} = \blacksquare \text{ mL}$

10. $1{,}000 \text{ g} = \blacksquare \text{ kg}$

11. $0.9 \text{ g} = \blacksquare \text{ kg}$

12. $500 \text{ g} = \blacksquare \text{ kg}$

13. $0.1 \text{ L} = \blacksquare \text{ mL}$

14. $0.05 \text{ kg} = \blacksquare \text{ g}$

15. $21 \text{ mL} = \blacksquare \text{ L}$

Lesson 9.5 *(pages 280–281)*

Tell which measurement is more precise.

1. 6 km or 5,980 m

2. 0.2 L or 200 mL

3. 45 mm or 4 cm

4. 1,508 m or 1.5 km

5. 8.2 cm or 82.5 mm

6. 400 m or 0.4 km

7. 4 km or 4.1 km

8. 6.98 mm or 6.9 mm

9. 30 cm or 300 mm

10. 30 mg or 325 mg

11. 6 cm or 65 mm

12. 1 kg or 500 g

13. 5 km or 4,902 m

14. 30 L or 30.5 L

15. 160 mL or 0.2 L

Lesson 9.6 *(pages 282–283)*

Tell whether to estimate or use a tool to measure. If you would use a tool, tell which tool.

1. amount of fabric to make a dress

2. time it takes to get to the theater

3. length of dresser for bedroom

Describe an everyday situation to fit the requirements.

4. capacity that requires a precise measurement

5. length that can be estimated

6. measuring mass with a tool

Estimate the sum.

7. $40 \text{ m} + 9.5 \text{ m} + 1.25 \text{ m} + 3.9 \text{ m}$

8. $2.3 \text{ g} + 0.1 \text{ g} + 1.04 \text{ g} + 3.9 \text{ g}$

Find the sum or difference.

9. $40 \text{ mg} + 200.1 \text{ mg} + 3.59 \text{ mg} + 1 \text{ mg}$

10. $5 \text{ g} - 0.256 \text{ g} - 3.25 \text{ g} - 1.22 \text{ g}$

11. $200 \text{ L} - 12.23 \text{ L} - 100.6 \text{ L} - 50.156 \text{ L}$

12. $59.5 \text{ m} + 0.12 \text{ m} + 12.69 \text{ m} + 5.3 \text{ m}$

Lesson 9.7 *(pages 286–287)*

Estimate the product or the quotient.

1. $50 \, \text{ft} \times 12$

2. $6{,}008 \, \text{in.} \div 36$

3. $92 \, \text{yd} \times 3$

4. $551 \, \text{ft} \div 3$

5. $48 \, \text{mi} \times 5{,}280$

6. $8 \, \text{yd} \times 1{,}760$

Tell by what number to multiply or divide. Then change the units.

7. 15 feet to inches

8. 108 inches to yards

9. 27 yards to feet

10. 20 miles to feet

11. 10,560 feet to miles

12. 8 yards to inches

Change to the given units.

13. $459 \, \text{in.} = \blacksquare \, \text{ft} \, \blacksquare \, \text{in.}$

14. $10{,}569 \, \text{ft} = \blacksquare \, \text{mi} \, \blacksquare \, \text{yd}$

15. $5 \, \text{mi} = \blacksquare \, \text{yd}$

16. $395 \, \text{in.} = \blacksquare \, \text{ft} \, \blacksquare \, \text{in.}$

17. $430 \, \text{ft} = \blacksquare \, \text{yd} \, \blacksquare \, \text{ft}$

18. $672 \, \text{in.} = \blacksquare \, \text{yd} \, \blacksquare \, \text{ft}$

19. $320 \, \text{ft} = \blacksquare \, \text{yd} \, \blacksquare \, \text{ft}$

20. $216 \, \text{in.} = \blacksquare \, \text{yd} \, \blacksquare \, \text{ft}$

21. $7 \, \text{mi} = \blacksquare \, \text{yd}$

Change to the given unit. Write any remainder in fraction form.

22. $1{,}760 \, \text{ft} = \blacksquare \, \text{mi}$

23. $33 \, \text{in.} = \blacksquare \, \text{ft}$

24. $27 \, \text{in.} = \blacksquare \, \text{yd}$

25. $122 \, \text{in.} = \blacksquare \, \text{ft}$

26. $156 \, \text{in.} = \blacksquare \, \text{yd}$

27. $31 \, \text{ft} = \blacksquare \, \text{yd}$

28. $288 \, \text{in.} = \blacksquare \, \text{yd}$

29. $205 \, \text{ft} = \blacksquare \, \text{yd}$

30. $21{,}120 \, \text{ft} = \blacksquare \, \text{mi}$

Lesson 9.8 *(pages 288–289)*

Change to the given unit.

1. $4 \, \text{oz} = \blacksquare \, \text{lb}$

2. $30 \, \text{qt} = \blacksquare \, \text{c}$

3. $6 \, \text{lb} \, 8 \, \text{oz} = \blacksquare \, \text{oz}$

4. $5\frac{1}{8} \, \text{lb} = \blacksquare \, \text{oz}$

5. $3\frac{1}{4} \, \text{gal} = \blacksquare \, \text{pt}$

6. $42 \, \text{oz} = \blacksquare \, \text{c}$

7. $10\frac{1}{2} \, \text{pt} = \blacksquare \, \text{c}$

8. $33 \, \text{qt} = \blacksquare \, \text{gal}$

9. $108 \, \text{oz} = \blacksquare \, \text{pt}$

10. $9{,}500 \, \text{lb} = \blacksquare \, \text{T}$

11. $49 \, \text{pt} = \blacksquare \, \text{qt}$

12. $2\frac{1}{2} \, \text{T} = \blacksquare \, \text{lb}$

13. $5 \, \text{lb} \, 3 \, \text{oz} = \blacksquare \, \text{oz}$

14. $36 \, \text{c} = \blacksquare \, \text{qt}$

15. $96 \, \text{oz} = \blacksquare \, \text{lb}$

16. $6\frac{1}{2} \, \text{qt} = \blacksquare \, \text{pt}$

17. $5 \, \text{c} = \blacksquare \, \text{fl oz}$

18. $16\frac{1}{2} \, \text{pt} = \blacksquare \, \text{c}$

19. $1\frac{1}{2} \, \text{lb} = \blacksquare \, \text{oz}$

20. $10 \, \text{lb} \, 6 \, \text{oz} = \blacksquare \, \text{oz}$

21. $7 \, \text{pt} = \blacksquare \, \text{fl oz}$

22. $8 \, \text{oz} = \blacksquare \, \text{lb}$

23. $1{,}000 \, \text{lb} = \blacksquare \, \text{T}$

24. $1 \, \text{qt} = \blacksquare \, \text{gal}$

Lesson 9.9 (pages 290–291)

Find the sum or difference.

1. 4 ft 3 in.
   +2 ft 5 in.

2. 2 ft 8 in.
   +3 ft 1 in.

3. 6 ft 6 in.
   +5 ft 6 in.

4. 2 yd 1 ft
   +3 yd 1 ft

5. 4 yd 2 ft
   +5 yd 1 ft

6. 6 yd 2 ft
   +1 yd 2 ft

7. 7 ft 2 in.
   −4 ft 10 in.

8. 4 yd 1 ft
   −1 yd 2 ft

9. 9 ft 6 in.
   −3 ft 9 in.

Lesson 9.10 (pages 292–293)

Change to the given unit.

1. 50 min = ■ sec

2. 360 min = ■ hr

3. 15 hr = ■ min

4. 6:30 A.M. = ■:■ hours

5. 4 days = ■ hr

6. 7:15 P.M. = ■:■ hours

7. 264 hr = ■ days

8. 3:25 P.M. = ■:■ hours

9. 3 hr = ■ sec

Find the sum or difference.

10. 2 hr 15 min
    +3 hr 55 min

11. 7 min 20 sec
    −6 min 25 sec

12. 3 hr 5 min
    −1 hr 40 min

13. 1 min 30 sec
    +   90 sec

14. 2 min 59 sec
    +9 min 5 sec

15. 6 hr 18 min
    −1 hr 26 min

Lesson 9.11 (pages 294–295)

Use the following schedule to solve Exercises 1–4.

1. Of the flights listed, which one is the fastest?

2. Karen has a meeting this morning at 10 A.M. that will last 3 hours. It takes her 45 minutes to get to the airport from the meeting. What is the earliest flight she can take?

3. What is the difference in time between the departure of Flight 139 and Flight 494?

Airline Schedule Atlanta to Miami		
Flight #	Departs	Arrives
265 (1 stop)	11:55 A.M.	2:10 P.M.
139 (nonstop)	1:40 P.M.	3:30 P.M.
494 (nonstop)	2:05 P.M.	4:10 P.M.

4. If the meeting lasted only $2\frac{1}{2}$ hours, which flights could Karen take?

CHAPTER 10

Lesson 10.1 *(pages 304–305)*

Draw a picture to show the ratio.

1. The ratio of red roses to yellow roses is 8:2.

2. The ratio of 9-year-olds to 10-year-olds is 5:6.

3. The ratio of tinted glass to clear glass is 10:15.

4. The ratio of salads to soups is 11:5.

Write the ratio in two other ways.

5. 30:7

6. three to six

7. $\frac{8}{9}$

8. ten to twelve

9. 10:3

10. eleven to two

Lesson 10.2 *(pages 306–307)*

Write a ratio that describes each rate.

1. 4 for a quarter

2. 60 mi per 120 min

3. 15 for $2.00

4. 10 muffins for $2.99

5. 45 words per min

6. 10 for $1.00

Find the unit rate or unit price. Remember to express the second term.

7. $1.25 for 10

8. 12 for $60.60

9. 900 mi per 15 hr

10. 3 for $9.00

11. 405 mi for 15 gal

12. $3.95 for 5

13. $4.20 a dozen

14. 1,750 words per 35 min

15. 600 people per sq mi

Lesson 10.3 *(pages 308–309)*

Tell whether the ratios are equivalent. Write *yes* or *no.*

1. $\frac{3}{5}$; $\frac{9}{25}$

2. $\frac{4}{3}$; $\frac{100}{75}$

3. 1:4; 16:64

4. 4:9; 24:54

5. 8:5; 12:15

6. $\frac{3}{2}$; $\frac{6}{3}$

7. 7:12; 21:36

8. $\frac{4}{5}$; $\frac{81}{100}$

Find the term that makes the ratio equivalent.

9. $\frac{5}{4}$; $\frac{\blacksquare}{8}$

10. $\frac{1}{9}$; $\frac{\blacksquare}{63}$

11. 9:4; 36:■

12. 3 to 8; 60 to ■

13. 2 to 9; ■ to 72

14. 40:5; 200:■

15. $\frac{12}{15}$; $\frac{24}{\blacksquare}$

16. $\frac{60}{45}$; $\frac{\blacksquare}{15}$

Lesson 10.4 *(pages 310–311)*

Write the cross products.

1. $\dfrac{4}{6} = \dfrac{2}{3}$

2. $\dfrac{8}{12} = \dfrac{2}{3}$

3. $\dfrac{1}{2} = \dfrac{m}{16}$

4. $\dfrac{12}{x} = \dfrac{32}{40}$

Tell whether the ratios make a proportion. Write *yes* or *no*.

5. $\dfrac{2}{45}; \dfrac{6}{130}$

6. $\dfrac{6}{9}; \dfrac{9}{12}$

7. $\dfrac{2}{3}; \dfrac{12}{18}$

8. $\dfrac{8}{5}; \dfrac{40}{25}$

Lesson 10.5 *(pages 312–313)*

Tell whether the ratios make a proportion. Write *yes* or *no*.

1. $\dfrac{5}{7}; \dfrac{15}{21}^{105}$

2. $\dfrac{10}{11}; \dfrac{100}{101}^{1100}$

3. $\dfrac{43}{100}; \dfrac{22}{50}^{2200}$

4. $\dfrac{24}{29}; \dfrac{72}{87}^{2088}$

5. $\dfrac{9}{3}; \dfrac{45}{15}^{135}$

6. $\dfrac{17}{12}; \dfrac{51}{36}^{612}$

7. $\dfrac{8}{19}; \dfrac{16}{38}^{304}$

8. $\dfrac{7}{16}; \dfrac{15}{30}^{240}$

Write the cross products. Then solve.

9. $\dfrac{2}{3} = \dfrac{n}{120}$

10. $\dfrac{4}{11} = \dfrac{28}{n}$

11. $\dfrac{6}{n} = \dfrac{42}{35}$

12. $\dfrac{4}{20} = \dfrac{16}{n}$

13. $\dfrac{7}{12} = \dfrac{x}{108}$

14. $\dfrac{x}{35} = \dfrac{3}{7}$

15. $\dfrac{x}{15} = \dfrac{10}{150}$

16. $\dfrac{8}{x} = \dfrac{96}{36}$

Lesson 10.6 *(pages 314–315)*

Use the scale drawing of the lot, the house, and the garage. Write the proportion you can use to find the actual dimensions.

1. width of the lot

2. length of the lot

3. width of the house

4. length of the garage

1 cm = 6 m

Lesson 10.7 *(pages 316–317)*

Use a centimeter ruler and the scale drawing for Lesson 10.6. Solve.

1. What is the actual width of the garage?

2. What is the actual length of the lot?

3. What is the actual width of the house?

4. What is the actual width of the lot?

Lesson 10.8 (pages 320–321)

Tell what percent is shaded.

1. 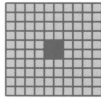 2. 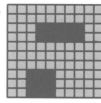 3.  4.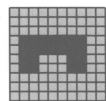

Lesson 10.9 (pages 322–323)

Write the decimal as a percent.

1. 0.28   **2.** 0.5   **3.** 0.19   **4.** 0.04   **5.** 1.28

6. 0.4   **7.** 0.45   **8.** 0.75   **9.** 0.8   **10.** 2.05

Write the percent as a decimal.

11. 10%   **12.** 43%   **13.** 12%   **14.** 6%   **15.** 35%

16. 9%   **17.** 85%   **18.** 90%   **19.** 79%   **20.** 155%

Lesson 10.10 (pages 324–325)

Write the fraction as a percent.

1. $\frac{13}{50}$ **2.** $\frac{4}{25}$ **3.** $\frac{2}{5}$ **4.** $\frac{13}{20}$ **5.** $\frac{9}{10}$

6. $\frac{7}{10}$ **7.** $\frac{9}{20}$ **8.** $\frac{8}{25}$ **9.** $\frac{47}{50}$ **10.** $\frac{1}{25}$

Write the percent as a fraction in simplest form.

11. 50%   **12.** 32%   **13.** 44%   **14.** 75%   **15.** 12%

Lesson 10.11 (pages 326–327)

Use a decimal to find the percent of the number.

1. 10% of 20   **2.** 30% of 60   **3.** 60% of 35   **4.** 50% of 96

5. 70% of 200   **6.** 20% of 100   **7.** 80% of 40   **8.** 40% of 70

Use a fraction to find the percent of the number.

9. 35% of 120   **10.** 65% of 80   **11.** 45% of 120   **12.** 55% of 900

13. 25% of 32   **14.** 70% of 140   **15.** 15% of 40   **16.** 75% of 60

Lesson 10.12 *(pages 328–329)*

Use mental math to find the percent of the number.

1. 25% of 400
2. 20% of 40
3. 2% of 200
4. 50% of $3.50

5. 10% of 65
6. 30% of 300
7. 200% of 12
8. 75% of 24

9. 100% of 10
10. 40% of 60
11. 150% of 20
12. 20% of $5.50

13. 200% of 40
14. 50% of $9.00
15. 30% of 120
16. 1% of 1,000

Lesson 10.13 *(pages 330–331)*

Suppose you know about what 10% of a number is. Tell how you can estimate the given percent.

1. 35%
2. 16%
3. 24%
4. 55%
5. 28%

Choose the most compatible numbers. Write **a**, **b**, or **c**.

6. 18% of 95
   a. 10% of 100
   b. 20% of 200
   c. 20% of 100

7. 46% of 130
   a. 40% of 150
   b. 50% of 150
   c. 50% of 100

8. 27% of 41
   a. 30% of 40
   b. 20% of 45
   c. 20% of 40

9. 39% of $45.95
   a. 40% of $50
   b. 30% of $40
   c. 30% of $50

10. 52% of 95
    a. 50% of 200
    b. 50% of 50
    c. 50% of 100

11. 78% of 2,842
    a. 70% of 2,000
    b. 80% of 2,500
    c. 80% of 3,000

Tell whether the estimate is an overestimate or underestimate.

12. 6% of 790 ≈ 48
13. 97% of 50 ≈ 50
14. 15% of 190 ≈ 40

Lesson 10.14 *(pages 332–333)*

Choose a strategy and solve.

1. Maureen made a scale model of her patio, using a scale of 1 in. = 4 ft. The length of the model is 11 inches. What is the actual length of Maureen's patio?

2. Leonore spent $40 on a gift for her mother. Then she bought computer paper for $27 and ribbons for $38. She had $15 left. How much money did she have to start?

3. James travels 60 mi a day to and from work. He works 5 days a week. His car gets 25 mi per gallon of gasoline. How many gallons does James use every week?

4. Rob bought a stereo on credit. His payments are $25.75 per month for 24 months. If Rob had paid cash for the stereo, he would have saved $68. What is the cash price of the stereo?

CHAPTER 11

Lesson 11.1 *(pages 342–343)*

Tell what geometric figure is suggested.

1. star in the sky   **2.** stove top   **3.** open scissors   **4.** piece of pipe

Use Figure A for Exercises 5–6.

Figure A

5. Name three points.

6. Name three line segments.

Use Figure B for Exercises 7–8.

Figure B

7. Name three rays.

8. Name three angles.

Lesson 11.2 *(pages 344–347)*

Tell what the blue symbol means.

1. $\overleftrightarrow{AB}$ **2.** $\angle E$ **3.** $\overrightarrow{AB}$ **4.** $\overleftrightarrow{AB} \perp \overleftrightarrow{CD}$ **5.** $\overleftrightarrow{EF} \parallel \overleftrightarrow{GH}$

6. $\overline{KL} \perp \overline{MN}$ **7.** $\overline{OP}$ **8.** $\overleftrightarrow{AB} \parallel \overleftrightarrow{CD}$ **9.** $\angle ABC$ **10.** $\overleftrightarrow{AB} \perp \overleftrightarrow{CD}$

Use Figure C for Exercises 11–14. Tell whether the lines are
parallel, perpendicular, intersecting, or skew.

11. $\overleftrightarrow{AB}$ and $\overleftrightarrow{CD}$ **12.** $\overleftrightarrow{AB}$ and $\overleftrightarrow{GH}$

13. $\overleftrightarrow{AB}$ and $\overleftrightarrow{EF}$ **14.** $\overleftrightarrow{EF}$ and $\overleftrightarrow{RS}$

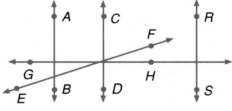

Use a compass and a straightedge.

15. Trace $\overline{CD}$. Construct $\overline{AB}$ congruent to $\overline{CD}$.

C _____ D

16. Trace $\overline{RS}$. Then bisect it.

R _____ S

Lesson 11.3 *(pages 348–349)*

Name the angles. Write *acute*, *right*, or *obtuse*.

1.    **2.**    **3.**

4.   **5.** 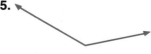   **6.**

Lesson 11.4 *(pages 350–351)*

Use a protractor to measure each pair of angles. Write <, >, or ≅.

1.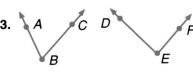

   ∠ABC ● ∠DEF

2. ∠ABC ● ∠DEF

3. ∠ABC ● ∠DEF

Use a compass and a straightedge.

4. Trace ∠DEF. Construct ∠ABC ≅ ∠DEF.

5. Trace ∠RST. Construct ∠KLM ≅ ∠RST.

6. Trace ∠XYZ. Construct ∠MNO ≅ ∠XYZ.

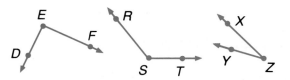

Lesson 11.5 *(pages 352–353)*

Make a circle graph.

1. Zach spends 60% of his monthly budget on rent, 25% on a car payment, 10% on food, and 5% on miscellaneous expenses. Make a circle graph showing his monthly expenses.

2. Adam spent 30% of his vacation in London, 25% in Paris, and 45% in Geneva. Make a circle graph showing how much time was spent in each city.

3. In a living room, 20% of the floor space is covered by a couch, 30% by a bookcase, and 10% by a coffee table. The remaining 40% is empty. Make a circle graph showing this.

4. Jackie's wardrobe consists of 20% dresses, 10% skirts, 45% slacks, and 25% shirts. Make a circle graph showing her wardrobe contents.

Lesson 11.6 *(pages 354–355)*

Use the drawing for Exercises 1–6. Find and name each type of triangle.

1. right

2. obtuse

3. acute

4. scalene

5. equilateral

6. isosceles

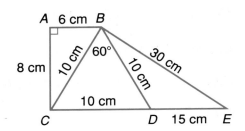

Write the measure of the third angle of the triangle.

7. 10°, 70° ■°

8. 30°, 40° ■°

9. 60°, 60° ■°

10. 90°, 20° ■°

Lesson 11.7 (pages 356–357)

Name the polygon.

1.
2.
3.
4.
5.

Lesson 11.8 (pages 360–361)

Using graph paper draw a polygon similar to the one shown and a polygon congruent to the one shown.

1.   2.   3.   4.

 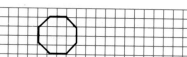

Lesson 11.9 (pages 362–363)

Trace the figure. Then draw the lines of symmetry.

1.
2.
3.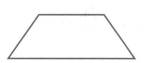
4.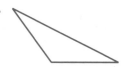

Tell whether the figure has rotational symmetry. Write *yes* or *no.*

5.
6.
7.
8.

Lesson 11.10 (pages 364–365)

Tell whether the second figure is a translation, a rotation, or a reflection.

1.
2.
3.

Trace and label a translation, a rotation, and a reflection of the given figure.

4.
5.
6.
7.

Lesson 11.11 *(pages 366–367)*

Complete the table.

	Figure	Number of Faces	Number of Edges	Number of Vertices
1.	Rectangular prism	■	■	■
2.	Triangular pyramid	■	■	■
3.	Rectangular pyramid	■	■	■
4.	Cone	■	■	■
5.	Triangular prism	■	■	■

Lesson 11.12 *(pages 368–369)*

Use a geoboard and rubber bands. Begin with a 3-by-2 rectangle.
Make changes as directed. Then name the new shape.

1. Stretch both bases the same amount.

2. Shrink one base to a point.

3. Move one base to the right without stretching or shrinking.

4. Stretch both ends of one base the same amount.

5. Move the center of one side one unit away from the rectangle.

6. Move the center of each side one unit away from the rectangle.

Lesson 11.13 *(pages 370–371)*

Find a pattern and solve.

1. Mike is using red and white tiles to cover his kitchen floor. If the pattern Mike uses is R, R, W, R, R, W, what will be the color of the eighteenth tile?

2. Jane runs every day. Monday she ran 2 mi, Tuesday 3 mi, Wednesday 5 mi, and Thursday 8 mi. If the pattern continues, how many miles will she run on Saturday?

3. Mark is building a model of a tower out of blocks. He used 65 blocks in the first layer, 60 blocks in the second layer, 54 blocks in the third layer, and 47 blocks in the fourth layer. If the pattern continues, how many blocks will he use in the seventh layer?

4. Silvia saved $1 her first week at work, $2 the second week, and $4 the third week. If the pattern continues, how much will she save the sixth week?

CHAPTER 12

Lesson 12.1 *(pages 380–381)*

Find the perimeter of the polygon.

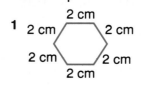

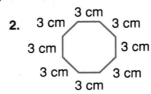

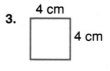

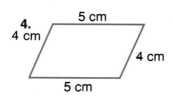

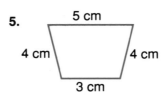

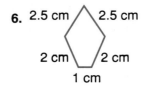

7. regular pentagon
   11 cm each side

8. equilateral triangle
   $12\frac{1}{2}$ in. each side

9. rectangle
   $l = 8$ m, $w = 7$ m

Lesson 12.2 *(pages 382–383)*

Find the area of the rectangle.

1. 6 in. / 2 in.

2. 16 yd. / 10 yd.

3. 9 m / 1.5 m

4. $l = 3$ in., $w = 15$ in.

5. $l = 6$ m, $w = 5$ m

6. $l = 13$ m, $w = 12$ m

7. $l = 5$ yd, $w = 12$ yd

8. $l = 7$ cm, $w = 8$ cm

9. $l = 35$ m, $w = 14.5$ m

Lesson 12.3 *(pages 384–385)*

Find the area of the parallelogram.

1. $b = 4$ m, $h = 8$ m

2. $b = 5$ m, $h = 3$ m

3. $b = 0.5$ m, $h = 3$ m

4. $b = 3$ in., $h = 1.8$ in.

5. $b = 6$ in., $h = 8.5$ in.

6. $b = 3.8$ m, $h = 2.3$ m

7. $b = 15$ cm, $h = 3.3$ cm

8. $b = 1.2$ in., $h = 6$ in.

9. $b = 2.1$ m, $h = 32$ m

Find the area of the triangle.

10. $b = 5$ yd, $h = 6$ yd

11. $b = 3$ yd, $h = 9$ yd

12. $b = 4$ m, $h = 12$ m

13. $b = 9$ in., $h = 20$ in.

14. $b = 6.5$ m, $h = 12$ m

15. $b = 2.4$ m, $h = 6.6$ m

16. $b = 6.2$ m, $h = 2.6$ m

17. $b = 1.1$ cm, $h = 2.4$ cm

18. $b = 9.9$ m, $h = 1.2$ m

Lesson 12.4 *(pages 386–387)*

Use a formula and solve.

1. Bill is carpeting a rectangular room that has a width of 11 ft and a length of 16 ft. How many square feet of carpeting will he need?

2. Jane wants to cover her front window with solar film. Her window is 6.5 ft by 3.2 ft. How much solar film does she need?

3. Claude needs a new triangular mainsail for his sailboat. His mainsail is 20 ft high and 10 ft wide. What is the area of his mainsail?

4. Louise wants to screen her 8 patio windows. Each is 6 ft by 5 ft. How much screen does she need?

Lesson 12.5 *(pages 388–389)*

Find the area of the shaded part of the figure.

1.
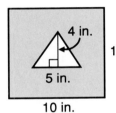
4 in.
12 in.
5 in.
10 in.

2.
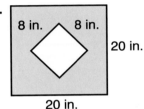
8 in.   8 in.
20 in.
20 in.

3.
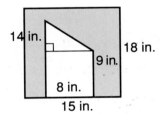
14 in.
18 in.
9 in.
8 in.
15 in.

Lesson 12.6 *(pages 390–391)*

Draw the rectangle with the greatest area. Label the length of the sides.

1. $P = 40$ units   2. $P = 68$ units   3. $P = 88$ units   4. $P = 12$ units   5. $P = 96$ units

Draw a rectangle that has double the dimensions of the given rectangle. Find the perimeter of both.

6. $l = 4$ cm, $w = 8$ cm   7. $l = 2$ cm, $w = 8$ cm   8. $l = 5$ cm, $w = 9$ cm

9. $l = 13$ cm, $w = 11$ cm   10. $s = 6$ cm   11. $l = 7$ cm, $w = 9$ cm

Double the dimensions of the given rectangle. Find the area of both.

12. $l = 8$ in., $w = 6$ in.   13. $s = 5$ cm   14. $l = 9$ cm, $w = 2$ cm

15. $l = 2\frac{1}{2}$ ft, $w = 1\frac{3}{4}$ ft   16. $s = 35$ mm   17. $l = 5.2$ m, $w = 3.7$ m

Lesson 12.7 (pages 394–395)

Use Figure A for Exercises 1–6. Find and name the circle and its parts.

1. two diameters
2. two radii
3. two chords
4. center
5. circle
6. intersecting line segments

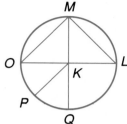

Figure A

Lesson 12.8 (pages 396–397)

Find the circumference. Round your answer to the nearest tenth. You may want to use a calculator.

1.

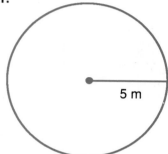

5 m

2.

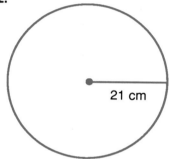

21 cm

3.

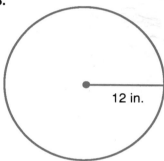

12 in.

4. diameter = 9 in.
5. diameter = 4 m
6. radius = 16 in.

7. diameter = 20 in.
8. diameter = 13 in.
9. radius = 10 in.

Lesson 12.9 (pages 398–399)

Find the area of the circle. Round to the nearest tenth.

1.

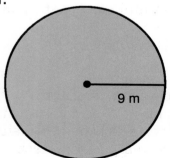

9 m

2.

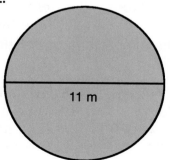

11 m

3.

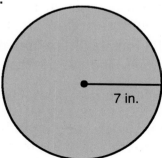

7 in.

4. $r = 4$ in.
5. $d = 6$ m
6. $r = 9$ yd
7. $r = 2.8$ in.

8. $d = 25$ in.
9. $r = 7.4$ yd
10. $d = 3.2$ m
11. $r = 0.8$ m

Lesson 12.10 *(pages 400–401)*

Find the surface area.

1.
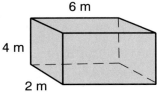
6 m
4 m
2 m

2.
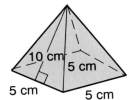
10 cm
5 cm
5 cm
5 cm

3.
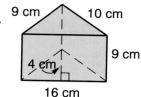
9 cm
10 cm
9 cm
4 cm
16 cm

Lesson 12.11 *(pages 402–403)*

Find the volume.

1.
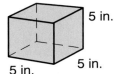
5 in.
5 in.
5 in.

2.
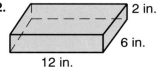
2 in.
6 in.
12 in.

3.

4 m
2 m
1 m

4. $l = 3$ cm, $w = 2$ cm, $h = 5$ cm

5. $l = 9$ m, $w = 7$ m, $h = 1$ m

6. $l = 8$ in., $w = 6$ in., $h = 10$ in.

7. $l = 12$ in., $w = 2$ in., $h = 1$ in.

Lesson 12.12 *(pages 404–405)*

Make a model and solve.

1. The dining room is a rectangle 10 ft long and 8 ft wide. A table 2 ft long and 3 ft wide will be put inside the room. How many square feet of space will be left after the table is placed in the dining room?

2. Corey wants to store a glass bowl in a cube-shaped box. The widest point of the bowl has a diameter of 12 in. The height is 9 in. What is the smallest box Corey can use?

3. Stuart made a basket in the shape of a rectangular prism 8 in. long, 6 in. wide, and 7 in. high. He wants to cover the bottom with plastic cubes that are 3 in. long on each side. Stuart has 15 cubes. Does he have enough cubes to cover the bottom of the basket?

4. The sitting room is a rectangle 8 ft wide and 9 ft long. A bookcase 6 ft long and 2 ft wide will be put inside the room. How many square feet will be left after the bookcase is placed in the sitting room?

CHAPTER 13

Lesson 13.1 *(pages 414–415)*

Describe the opposite of the situation.

1. gaining 5 pounds
2. 10 steps up
3. 3 miles north

Give an integer to represent the situation. Then describe the opposite situation and give an integer to represent it.

4. 45 ft underground
5. stock market up 100 points
6. loss of $50
7. 4 ft up the flagpole
8. 1,500 ft above sea level
9. increase of 10 members
10. weight loss of 10 pounds
11. up 3 flights

Lesson 13.2 *(pages 416–417)*

Act out the situation to solve each problem.

1. The Igloos took possession of the football on their own 10-yd line. They gained 20 yd, lost 5 yd, gained 28 yd, and lost 6 yd. On what yard line were the Igloos after those 4 plays?

2. Joyce leaves her front door and walks 3 blocks east, 1 block south, 2 blocks west, 3 blocks south, and one block west. How far is she from her front door?

3. Anna leaves her front door and walks $\frac{1}{2}$ block east, 3 blocks north, 10 blocks west, 2 blocks south, 4 blocks east, and 1 block south. How far is she from her front door?

4. Ryan left his garage and drove 6 miles south, 2 miles east, 10 miles south, and 2 miles west. How far was he from his garage?

Lesson 13.3 *(pages 418–419)*

Compare. Use < or >.

1. 0 ● ⁻4
2. ⁻3 ● ⁺2
3. ⁻1 ● 0
4. ⁺5 ● ⁻3
5. ⁻6 ● ⁺6
6. ⁻4 ● ⁻5
7. ⁻8 ● ⁻9
8. ⁺1 ● ⁻2

Order the integers from least to greatest. Use <.

9. 3, ⁻1, ⁻2, ⁻4
10. ⁺6, ⁻5, ⁺4, ⁻1
11. ⁻7, ⁺5, ⁻3, ⁻4, 0
12. ⁺20, ⁺10, ⁺15, ⁻10, ⁻15

Lesson 13.4 (pages 420–423)

Use counters or a number line. Find the sum.

1. $^+4 + {}^+5$
2. $^+3 + {}^-5$
3. $^-6 + {}^-7$
4. $^-5 + {}^+10$
5. $^-1 + {}^+2$
6. $^+11 + {}^-8$
7. $^+13 + {}^-9$
8. $^-8 + {}^-11$
9. $^-15 + {}^-10$
10. $^+23 + {}^-14$
11. $^-41 + {}^+26$
12. $^-8 + {}^+11$
13. $^+9 + {}^-2$
14. $^+25 + {}^+1$
15. $^-16 + {}^-4$
16. $^+7 + {}^-14$
17. $^+11 + {}^+5$
18. $^-18 + {}^+20$
19. $^-8 + {}^-8$
20. $^-13 + {}^-15$
21. $^+7 + {}^+11$
22. $^+8 + {}^+16$
23. $^-3 + {}^+5$
24. $^-2 + {}^-7$
25. $^+12 + {}^-12$
26. $^-19 + {}^+5$
27. $^+23 + {}^+15$

Lesson 13.5 (pages 424–425)

Use counters to find the difference.

1. $^-3 - {}^+2$
2. $^-9 - {}^-8$
3. $^-4 - {}^-1$

Complete each of the following.

4. $^-3 - {}^+6 = {}^-3 + \blacksquare$
5. $^+10 - {}^-4 = {}^+10 + \blacksquare$
6. $^+5 - {}^-10 = {}^+5 + \blacksquare$
7. $^-2 - {}^+3 = {}^-2 + \blacksquare$
8. $^-7 - {}^-5 = {}^-7 + \blacksquare$
9. $^+9 - {}^+4 = {}^+9 + \blacksquare$
10. $^+6 - {}^-10 = {}^+6 + \blacksquare$
11. $^-3 - {}^-18 = {}^-3 + \blacksquare$
12. $^+8 - {}^+7 = {}^+8 + \blacksquare$
13. $^-5 - {}^+11 = {}^-5 + \blacksquare$
14. $^+2 - {}^-1 = {}^+2 + \blacksquare$
15. $^+16 - {}^-9 = {}^+16 + \blacksquare$

Rewrite each subtraction expression as an addition expression. Solve.

16. $^+12 - {}^-8$
17. $^+7 - {}^+5$
18. $^+16 - {}^-24$
19. $^-5 - {}^-1$
20. $^+6 - {}^-20$
21. $^+11 - {}^+1$
22. $^+100 - {}^+1$
23. $^-3 - {}^+2$
24. $^+8 - {}^-7$
25. $^-4 - {}^-9$
26. $^+18 - {}^+2$
27. $^+10 - {}^-2$

Lesson 13.6 *(pages 428–429)*

Find the sum or difference.

1. $6 + 3$

2. $^-8 + ^-5$

3. $9 - ^-4$

4. $4 + ^-5$

5. $8 + 9$

6. $^-7 + ^-7$

7. $^-10 + ^-8$

8. $11 - ^-3$

9. $0 + ^-9$

10. $3 - 8$

11. $^-2 - ^-7$

12. $12 - 5$

13. $^-7 + 3$

14. $^-7 + ^-8$

15. $6 + ^-5$

16. $^-14 + 8$

17. $6 + ^-6$

18. $^-9 - 6$

19. $9 - 4$

20. $9 - ^-2$

21. $^-6 + 4$

22. $^-10 - ^-8$

23. $5 - ^-2$

24. $^-14 + ^-3$

25. $^-15 + ^-6$

26. $^-35 + ^-20$

27. $15 + ^-45$

Lesson 13.7 *(pages 430–431)*

Use the map. Tell the directions needed to get from the starting point to the given location.

1. theater

2. park

3. zoo

4. stadium

5. pool

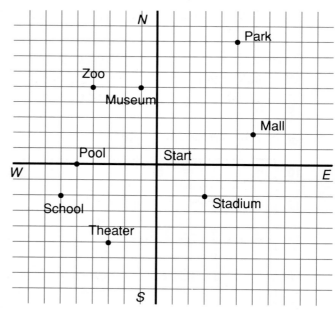

Trace the map. Locate each point on the map by following the given directions.

6. Go 6 blocks east, 2 blocks north

7. Go 3 blocks east, 2 blocks south

8. Go 5 blocks west

9. Go 1 block west, 5 blocks north

10. Go 6 blocks west, 2 blocks south

11. Go 5 blocks east, 8 blocks north

Lesson 13.8 (pages 432–435)

Write the ordered pair for each point.

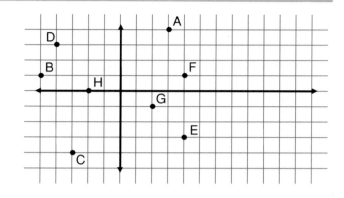

1. point A
2. point E
3. point B
4. point F
5. point C
6. point G
7. point D
8. point H

Use graph paper to make a coordinate plane. Locate the point for each ordered pair.

9. $A\,(4,3)$
10. $B\,(5,^-4)$
11. $C\,(4,0)$
12. $D\,(^-2,5)$

13. $E\,(^-3,^-5)$
14. $F\,(^-4,2)$
15. $G\,(^-2,^-8)$
16. $H\,(4,^-6)$

17. $I\,(0,^-5)$
18. $J\,(3,0)$
19. $K\,(0,4)$
20. $L\,(0,2)$

21. $M\,(^-4,^-2)$
22. $N\,(^-3,6)$
23. $P\,(7,7)$
24. $Q\,(^-6,0)$

Lesson 13.9 (pages 436–437)

Sean plans to use the health spa during his 6-week vacation to play racquetball. He can buy a pass, pay regular fees, or use a permit.

Choice 1
A 6-week pass costs $100.

Choice 2
The regular fee is $8 per game.

Choice 3
A permit costs $50 in advance. Then the cost is $4 per game.

Copy and complete the table.

	Times played per week	Cost for Six Weeks		
		Choice 1	Choice 2	Choice 3
1.	1	■	■	■
2.	2	■	■	■
3.	3	■	■	■
4.	4	■	■	■

5. What does the table show about the cost of the three choices for a player who plays racquetball two times a week or less?

6. Sean decides he would play 3 times a week. He selected Choice 2. Give one advantage of this choice over Choice 3.

CHAPTER 14

Lesson 14.1 (pages 446–447)

Write a word expression for the algebraic expression.

1. $4h$

2. $\dfrac{x}{5}$

3. $n + 3$

4. $y + 10$

5. $d - 8$

6. $m - 5$

7. $6b$

8. $\dfrac{12}{y}$

9. $25 - x$

10. $a + 6$

11. $7c$

12. $8 + a$

Copy and complete the table. Write an algebraic expression or an equation.

	Word Expression	Algebraic Expression or Equation
13.	b less than 2 is 15	■
14.	y divided by 5	■
15.	eighteen is three times g	■
16.	a and eight equals twelve	■
17.	c plus nine	■
18.	six more than x is ten	■
19.	b divided by 6 = 5	■

Lesson 14.2 (pages 448–449)

Write the number in the form $\dfrac{a}{b}$.

1. 3.5

2. 0.68

3. 0.39

4. $5\dfrac{6}{11}$

5. 25.2

6. $4\dfrac{5}{8}$

7. 0.93

8. $2\dfrac{12}{13}$

9. 58%

10. 4.7%

Tell what rational numbers you would use in the given situation.

11. to express flight numbers

12. to express sale prices

13. to express hat sizes

14. to express a business loss

15. to express a comparison between games won and games played

16. to express mass on a gram scale

Lesson 14.3 *(pages 450–451)*

Evaluate the expression $x - 17$ for each value of x.

1. $x = 9$ **2.** $x = {}^-5$ **3.** $x = 1\frac{1}{3}$ **4.** $x = 25.06$ **5.** $x = {}^-90$

Evaluate the expression $m \div 4$ for each value of m.

6. $m = 25$ **7.** $m = 12.5$ **8.** $m = \frac{1}{16}$ **9.** $m = 3\frac{1}{8}$

10. $m = 16$ **11.** $m = \frac{2}{3}$ **12.** $m = 15$ **13.** $m = 24.9$

Evaluate the expression $9b$ for each value of b.

14. $b = 27$ **15.** $b = 6\frac{1}{8}$ **16.** $b = 25.4$ **17.** $b = 90\%$

18. $b = 4.5$ **19.** $b = \frac{2}{3}$ **20.** $b = 4.02$ **21.** $b = \frac{5}{18}$

Lesson 14.4 *(pages 452–453)*

Tell the inverse of the operation in the equation.

1. $x + 2 = 90$ **2.** $y - 4 = 10$ **3.** $\frac{1}{2} + z = 7$

Use inverse operations. Solve the equation.

4. $x - 253 = 792$ **5.** $y + 29 = 148$ **6.** $x + 6\frac{1}{3} = 25\frac{1}{2}$

7. $x - \frac{7}{8} = 3$ **8.** $y + \frac{5}{12} = \frac{7}{12}$ **9.** $y - \frac{9}{10} = \frac{1}{10}$

10. $y + 3{,}400 = 6{,}876$ **11.** $x - \frac{3}{8} = 16\frac{1}{2}$ **12.** $x - 356 = 0$

13. $y + \frac{1}{9} = 4\frac{1}{3}$ **14.** $x - 46 = 46$ **15.** $y + 39\frac{1}{2} = 48\frac{1}{16}$

Lesson 14.5 *(pages 454–455)*

Write an equation. Then solve.

1. Monica wants to read a 500-page novel in 3 days. She reads 145 pages the first day and 198 pages the second day. How many pages must she read the third day to meet her goal?

2. Al is saving money to buy a bicycle that costs $295. He has already saved $179. How much more does he need to save?

3. Yves wrote 90 words fewer than Chuck in his book report. Chuck wrote 625 words. How many words did Yves write?

4. Rita has $230 more than her brother who has $190. How much money does Rita have?

Lesson 14.6 *(pages 458–459)*

Tell what integers to add or subtract to solve the equation.

1. $x = 2 + 3$

2. $y - 5 = 9$

3. $z - 1 = 15$

4. $c + 4 = 5$

5. $g - 13 = 1$

6. $a + 8 = 20$

Solve the equation.

7. $x = 14 + {}^-9$

8. $y + {}^-6 = {}^-20$

9. $x = {}^-2 + {}^-3$

10. $x = 21 + {}^-12$

11. $y - 16 = 49$

12. $x + {}^-35 = 215$

13. $y + {}^-3 = {}^-41$

14. $x - 16 = {}^-9$

15. $y + 3 = 15$

16. $y - {}^-7 = 26$

17. $x - 13 = 15$

18. $y + 6 = 2$

Lesson 14.7 *(pages 460–461)*

Tell whether $^-3$ is a solution of the inequality. Write *yes* or *no.*

1. $x < 0$

2. $x < {}^-5$

3. $x + 5 > 1$

Tell whether 5 is a solution of the inequality. Write *yes* or *no.*

4. $y + 3 > 10$

5. $y - 10 < 0$

6. $y - 1 < 0$

Draw a number line that shows the solutions of the inequality.

7. $x > 4$

8. $a < 0$

9. $b < 2\frac{1}{3}$

10. $y > 7$

11. $x < {}^-3$

12. $d > {}^-5$

13. $c > 2.5$

14. $x < 1.2$

15. $b > {}^-1.5$

Lesson 14.8 *(pages 462–463)*

Copy and complete the table. Then write an expression using *y* to show the value of *x.*

1.

x	2	3	4	5	6	7	8
y	4	6	8	10	■	■	■

2.

x	0	1	2	3	4	5	6	7
y	$^-2$	$^-1$	0	1	2	■	■	■

3.

x	0	1	2	3	4	5	6	7	8
y	3	4	5	6	7	■	■	■	■

Lesson 14.9 *(pages 464–465)*

Name the ordered pairs in each table.

1.

x	12	9	6	3
y	4	3	2	1

2.

x	5	6	7	8
y	1	2	3	4

3. What expression using y can you write to show the value of x in Exercise 1?

4. What expression using y can you write to show the value of x in Exercise 2?

Use the expression to help you complete the table. Then graph the ordered pairs on a coordinate plane.

5. $x - 3$

x	3	4	5	6	7
y	0	▨	▨	▨	▨

6. $\dfrac{x}{2}$

x	10	12	14	16	18
y	5	6	▨	▨	▨

7. $2x + 6$

x	2	3	4	5	6
y	10	12	▨	▨	▨

8. $3x + 1$

x	2	3	4	5	6
y	7	10	▨	▨	▨

Lesson 14.10 *(pages 466–467)*

Solve. Use logical reasoning.

1. A chess club has 25 members. Of these members, 5 have played in a state tournament, 8 have played in a city tournament, and 4 have played in both kinds of tournaments. How many members have never played in a tournament?

2. The results of a survey of 75 people show 31 collect only stamps, 26 collect only postcards, and 8 do both. How many people do not collect stamps or postcards?

3. The results of a survey of 90 people show 30 attend only football games, 20 attend only soccer games, and 8 do both. How many people do not attend football or soccer games?

4. A survey of 120 computer programmers shows that 50 write Cobol, 30 write Pascal, and 15 do both. How many programmers do not write Cobol or Pascal?

The Learning Resources can be traced, colored, and cut out. These resources can be used as tools to help you understand math concepts and solve problems.

Plane Geometric Shapes

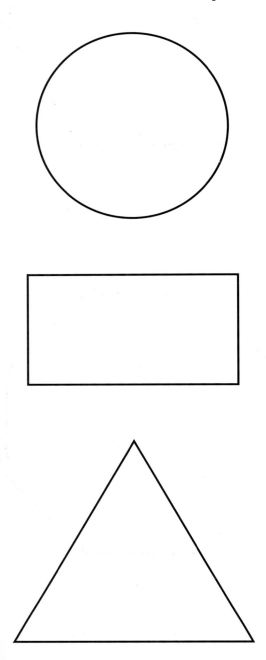

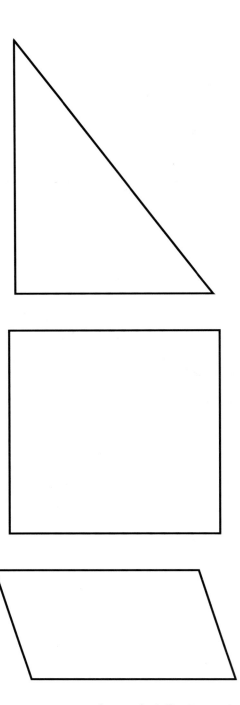

Regular Polygons

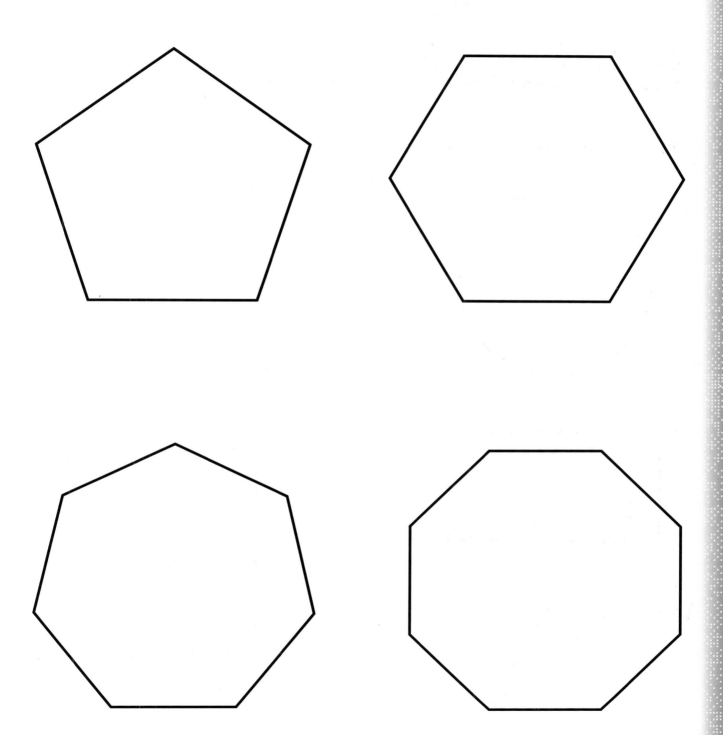

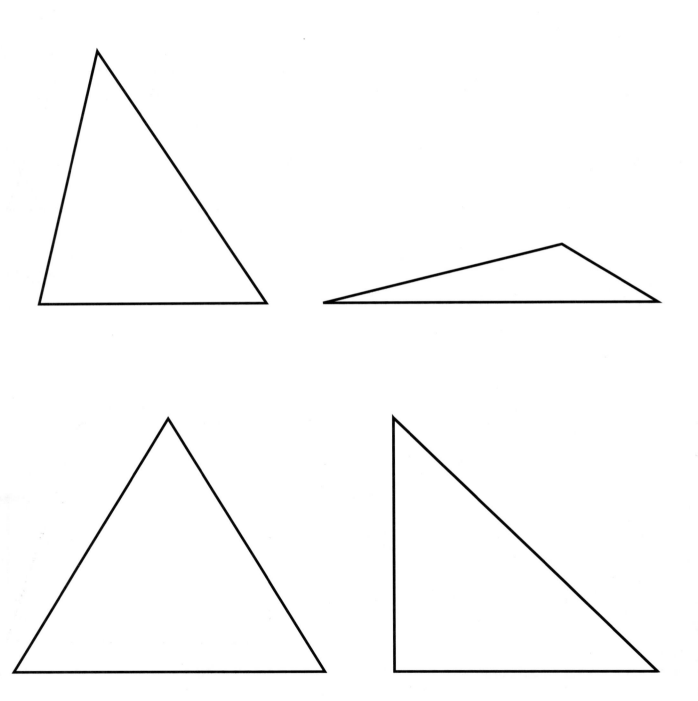

More Polygons

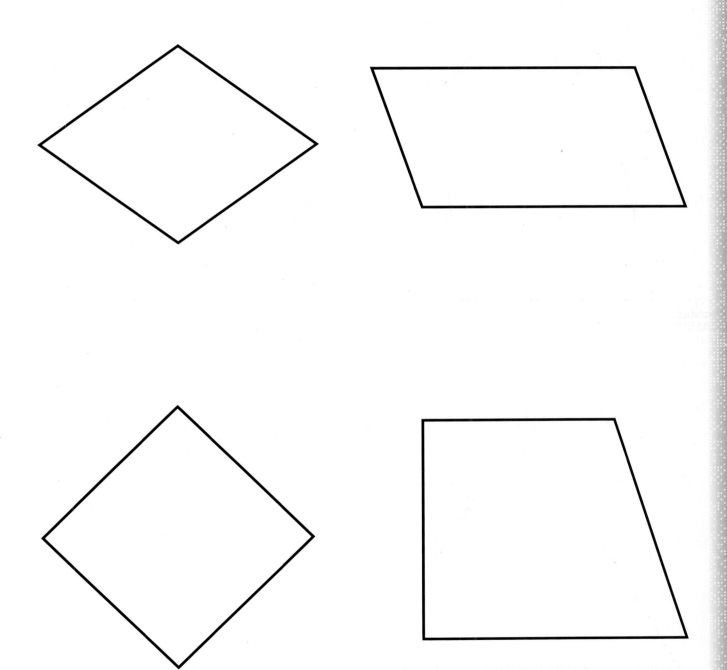

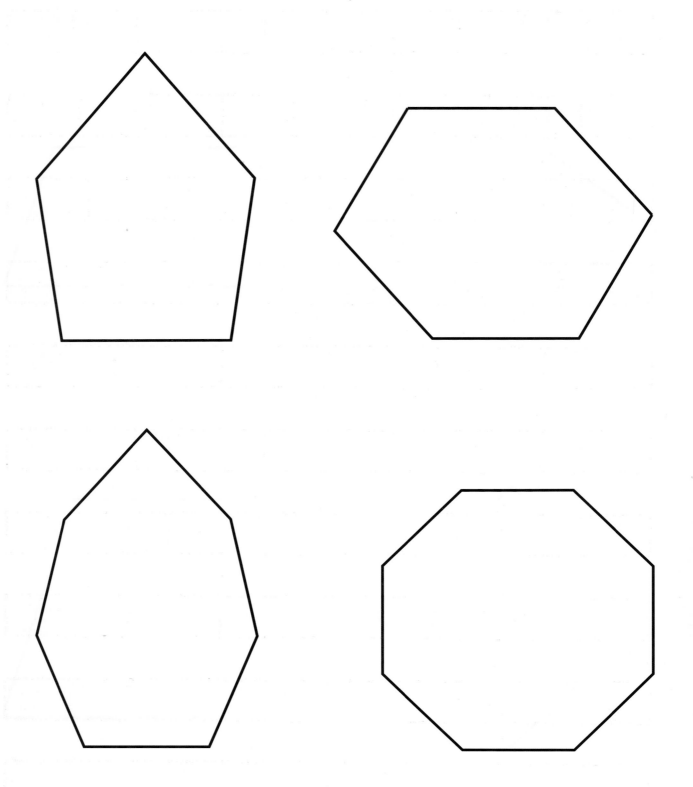

Fraction Bars

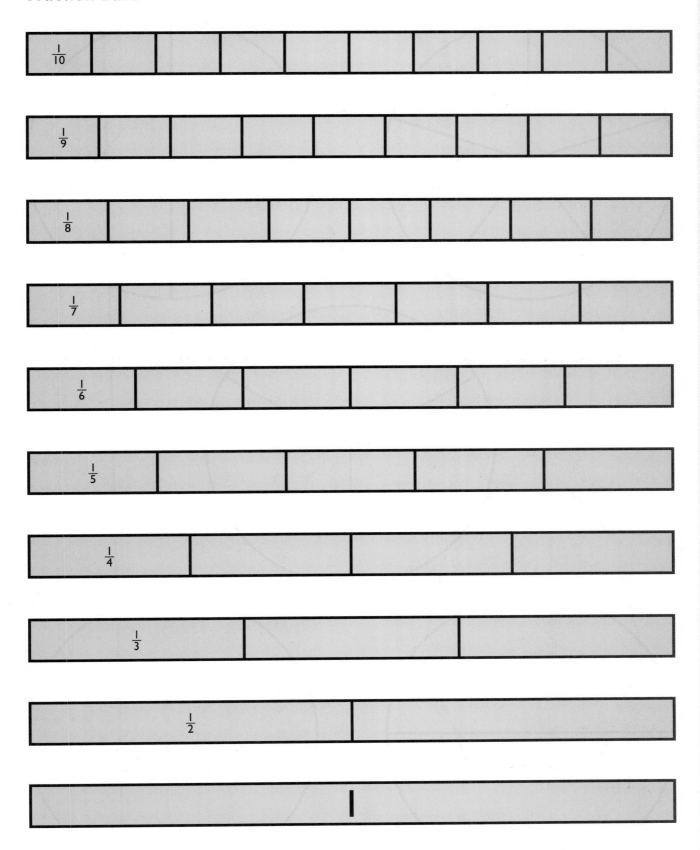

Fraction Circles

More Fraction Circles

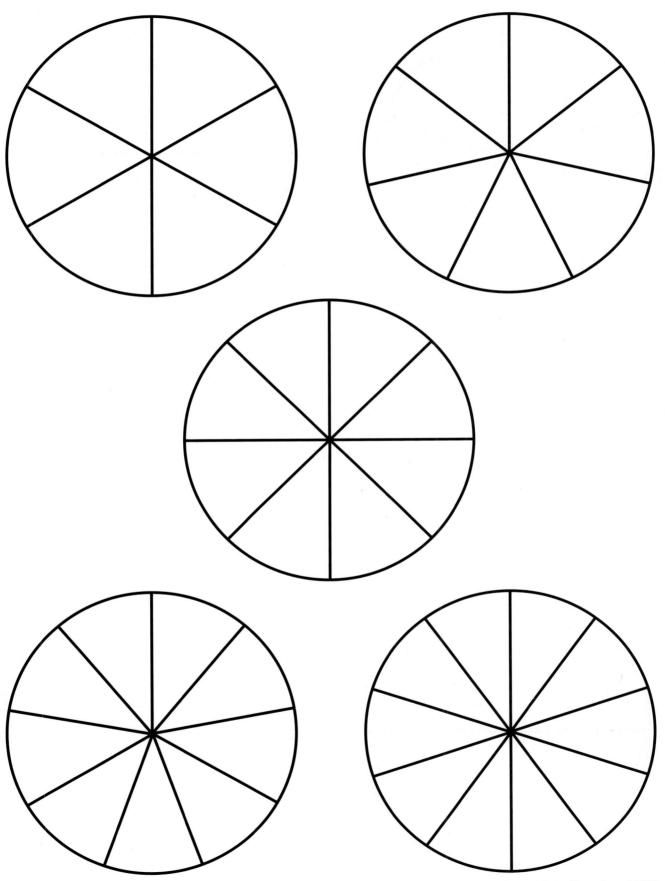

Circles

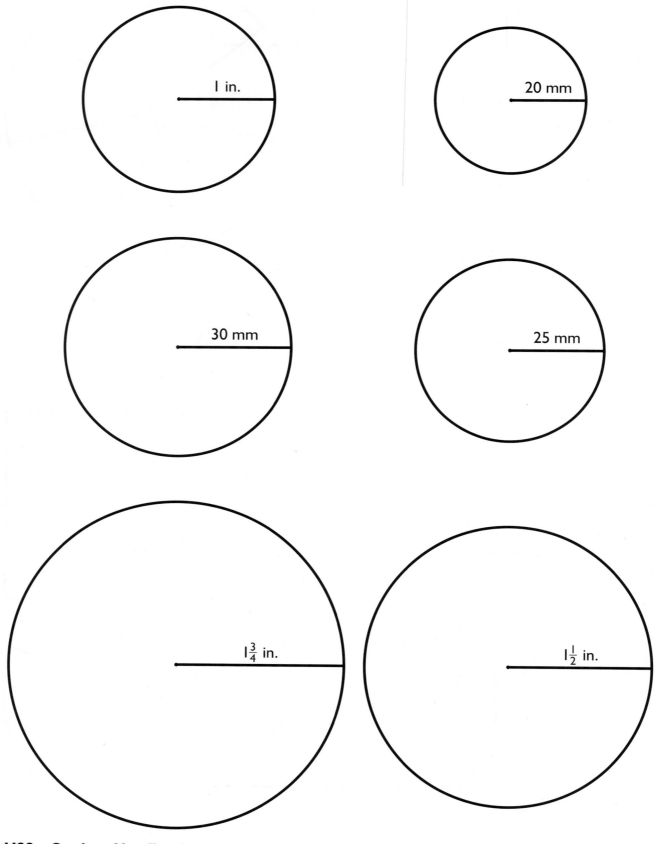

Solid Geometric Shape

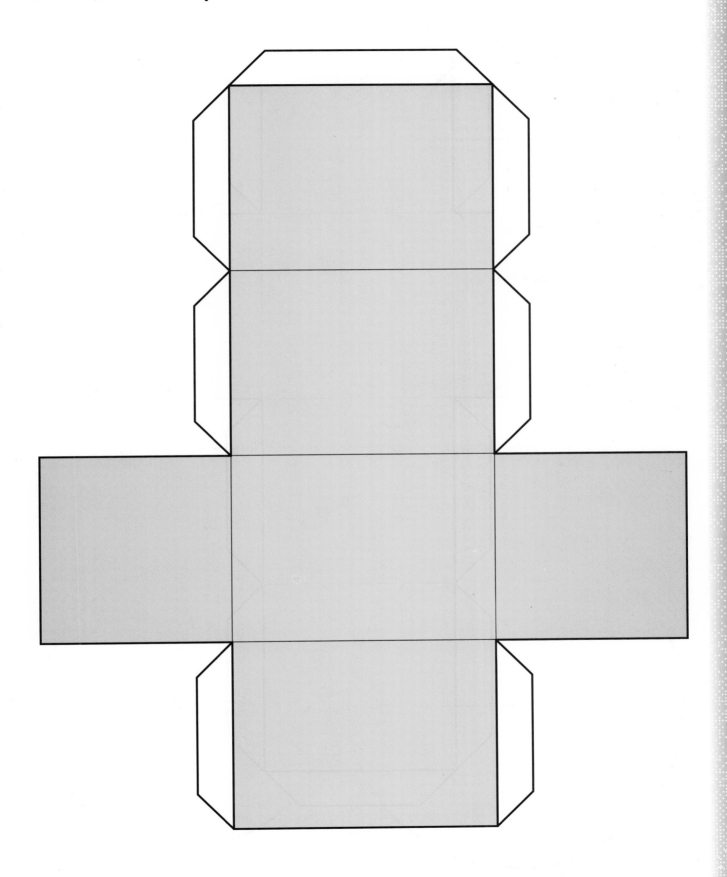

Solid Geometric Shape

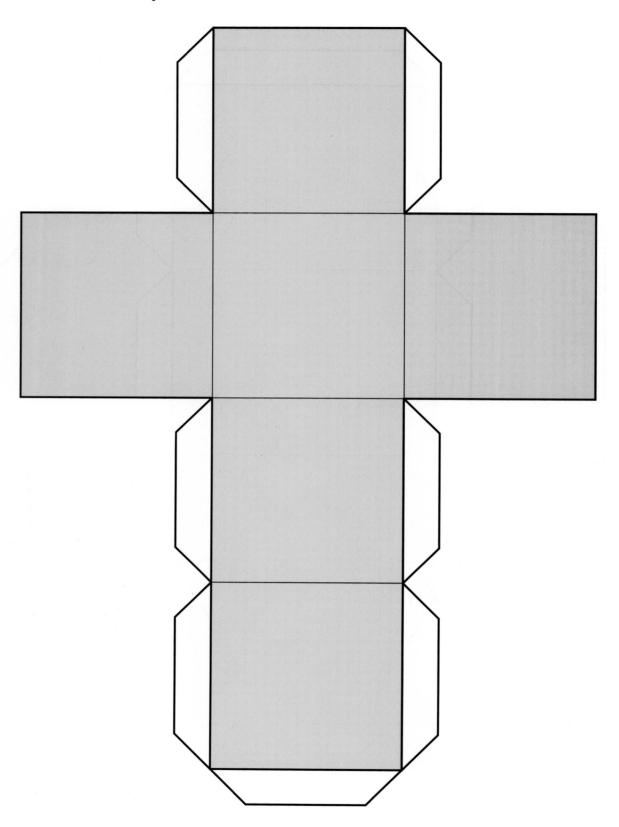

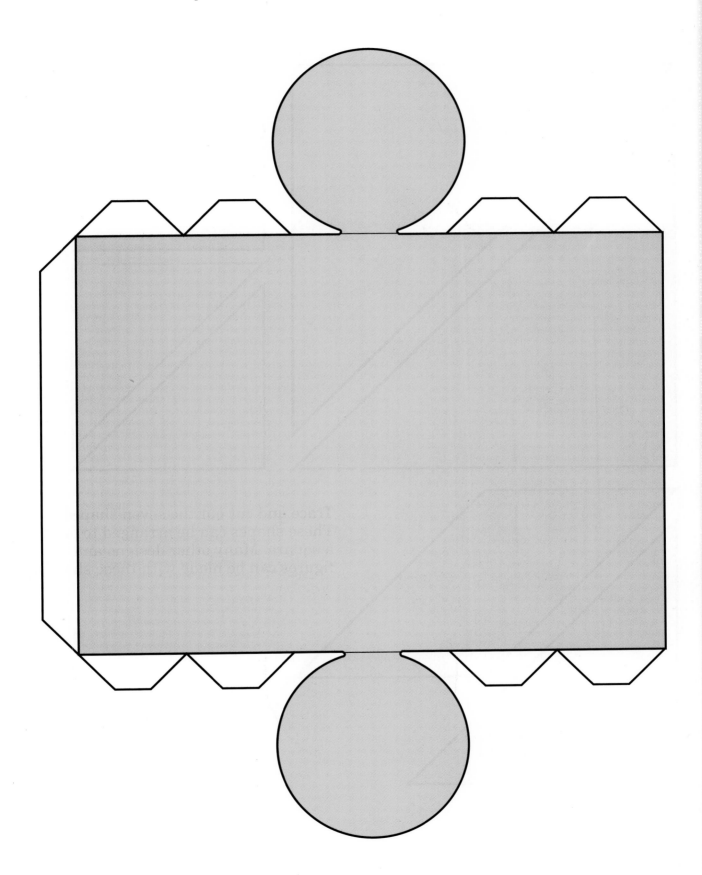

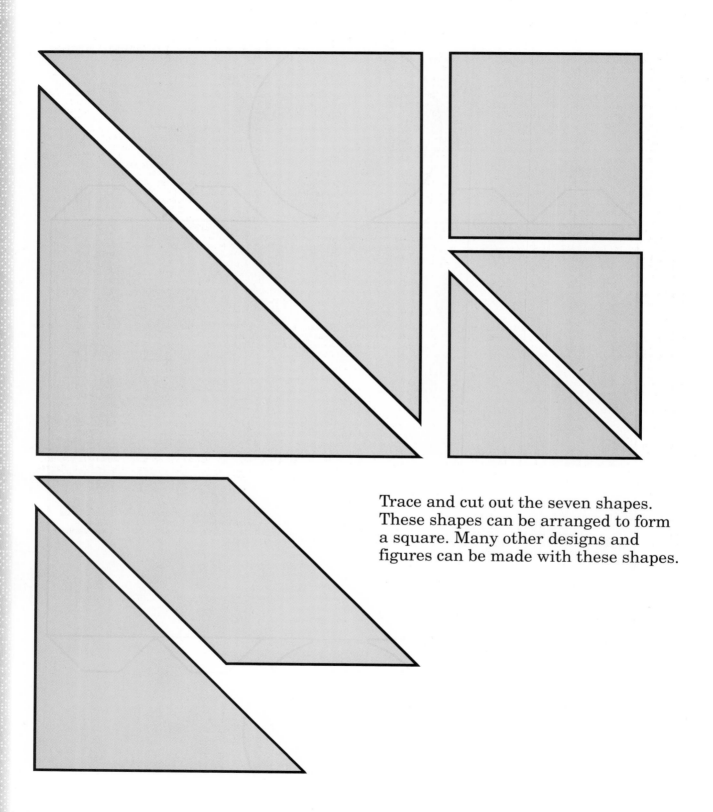

Trace and cut out the seven shapes.
These shapes can be arranged to form
a square. Many other designs and
figures can be made with these shapes.

Table of Measures

METRIC

CUSTOMARY

Length

1 kilometer (km) = 1,000 meters (m)
1 decimeter (dm) = 0.1 meter
1 centimeter (cm) = 0.01 meter
1 millimeter (mm) = 0.001 meter

1 foot (ft) = 12 inches (in.)
1 yard (yd) = 3 feet, or 36 inches
1 mile (mi) = 1,760 yards, or 5,280 feet

Capacity

1 kiloliter (kL) = 1,000 liter (L)
1 milliliter (mL) = 0.001 liter

1 cup (c) = 8 fluid ounces (fl oz)
1 pint (pt) = 2 cups
1 quart (qt) = 2 pints
1 gallon (gal) = 4 quarts

Mass/Weight

1 kilogram (kg) = 1,000 grams (g)
1 milligram (mg) = 0.001 gram

1 pound (lb) = 16 ounces (oz)
1 ton (T) = 2,000 pounds

Time

1 hour (hr) = 60 minutes (min)
1 minute = 60 seconds (sec)

Formulas

$P = a + b + c$
$A = lw$
$A = \frac{1}{2} bh$
$\pi = \pi r^2$

$P = 2l + 2w$
$A = bh$
$C = \pi d$, or $2\pi r$
$V = lwh$

Symbols

=	is equal to	$\overset{\leftrightarrow}{AB}$	line AB
≠	is not equal to	$\overline{AB}$	line segment AB
>	is greater than	∠ABC	angle ABC
<	is less than	‖	is parallel to
10^2	ten squared	△ABC	triangle ABC
10^3	ten cubed	⊥	is perpendicular to
10^4	ten to the fourth power	≅	is congruent to
$2.\overline{6}$	repeating decimal	π	pi (about 3.14)
P(Y)	probability of event Y	°	degrees
≈	is approximately equal to	$^+2$	positive 2
1:3	ratio of 1 to 3	$^-2$	negative 2
$\overset{\rightarrow}{AB}$	ray AB	(⁻5,3)	ordered pair ⁻5,3

Glossary

······**A**······

absolute copy   A copy of a cell or a group of cells in a spreadsheet; the computer makes an exact copy of the information *(page 481)*

acute angle   An angle whose measure is greater than 0° and less than 90° *(page 348)*

acute triangle   A triangle in which all angles are acute *(page 354)*

algebraic expression   An expression that is written using one or more variables *(pages 52, 446)*

angle   A figure formed by two rays that meet at a common endpoint called a vertex *(page 342)*
   Example:

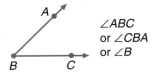

area   The number of square units needed to cover a surface *(page 382)*

Associative Property of Addition   The property which states that three or more addends can be grouped in any order without changing their sum *(page 34)*
   Example: $(2 + 3) + 5 = 2 + (3 + 5)$

Associative Property of Multiplication   The property which states that three or more factors can be grouped in any order without changing their product *(page 68)*
   Example: $(5 \times 2) \times 6 = 5 \times (2 \times 6)$

average   The number obtained by dividing the sum of a set of numbers by the number of addends *(page 11)*

······**B**······

bar graph   A graph that uses separate bars (rectangles) of different heights (lengths) to show and compare data *(page 140)*

base   A number used as a repeated factor *(page 20)*
   Example: $8^3 = 8 \times 8 \times 8$
   The base is 8. It is used as a factor three times.

base   The standard grouping of a numeration system *(page 5)*

base   A side of a polygon or a face of a solid figure by which the figure is measured or named *(pages 366, 384)*
   Examples:

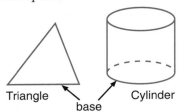

bisect   To divide into two equal parts *(page 346)*

······**C**······

capacity   The amount a container will hold when filled *(page 278)*

category (or field)   A type of information in a data base, such as names or phone numbers *(page 489)*

cell   In a spreadsheet, a block area in which data or formulas can be entered; the cell is located by an address consisting of a letter and a number *(page 481)*

center of a circle   The point inside a circle that is the same distance from each point on the circle *(page 394)*
   Example:

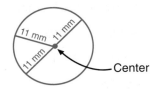

chord A line segment whose endpoints lie on a circle *(page 394)*
   Example:

circle The set of points in a plane that are the same distance from a given point called the center of the circle *(page 394)*

circle graph A graph using a circle that is divided into pie-shaped sections showing percents or parts of the whole *(pages 148, 352)*

circumference The distance around a circle *(page 396)*

clipboard An area in a computer's memory in which the program stores information to be moved or copied from one location or document to another location or document *(page 484)*

common denominator A number that is a multiple of the denominators of two or more fractions *(page 179)*

common factor A number that is a factor of two or more numbers *(page 188)*

common multiple A number that is a multiple of two or more given numbers *(page 174)*

Commutative Property of Addition The property of addition which states that when the order of two addends is changed, the sum is the same *(page 34)*
   Example:
      $9 + 4 = 4 + 9$

Commutative Property of Multiplication The property of multiplication which states that when the order of two factors is changed, the product is the same *(page 68)*
   Example:
      $3 \times 5 = 5 \times 3$

compatible number A number that is close to the actual number and is easy to compute mentally *(page 98)*

compensation Changing one addend and adjusting the other addend to keep the balance *(page 34)*
   Example: $16 + 9$
      $(16 - 1) + (9 + 1)$
      $15 + 10 = 25$

complementary angles Two angles whose measures have a sum of 90° *(page 349)*

composite number A whole number greater than 1 with more than two whole-number factors *(page 184)*

cone A solid figure with a circular base and one vertex *(page 366)*
   Example:

congruent figures Figures that have the same size and shape *(page 360)*

coordinate plane A plane formed by a horizontal line (*x*-axis) that intersects a vertical line (*y*-axis) at a point called the origin *(page 432)*
   Example:

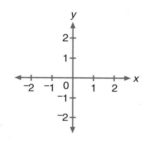

counting principle The process of multiplying the number of choices in one set by the number of choices in another set to find the total number of outcomes *(page 158)*

cross products Two equal products obtained by multiplying the second term of each ratio by the first term of the other ratio in a proportion *(page 311)*
   Example: $\dfrac{2}{3} = \dfrac{6}{9}$
      $2 \times 9 = 3 \times 6$
      $18 = 18$

cube A rectangular solid figure with six congruent square faces *(page 366)*
   Example:

customary measurement system A measurement system that measures length in inches, feet, yards, and miles; capacity in cups, pints, quarts, and gallons; weight in ounces, pounds, and tons; and temperature in degrees Fahrenheit *(pages 286, 418)*

cylinder A solid figure with two parallel bases that are congruent circles *(page 366)*

data A set of information *(page 136)*

data base A computer program used to organize, sort, and find the kind of information that is normally kept in a list or on file cards *(page 488)*

decimal system A numeration system based on grouping by tens *(page 4)*

degree A unit for measuring angles *(page 348)*

degree Celsius (°C) A metric unit for measuring temperature *(pages 13, 418)*

degree Fahrenheit (°F) A customary unit for measuring temperature *(pages 13, 418)*

denominator The number below the fraction bar in a fraction; tells the total number of equal parts or groups into which the whole or group has been divided *(page 176)*

desktop An area in a computer's memory in which documents or files are stored *(page 484)*

diagonal A line segment that joins the vertices of a polygon but is not a side *(page 356)*
    Example:

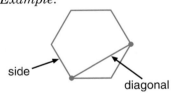

side
    diagonal

diameter A chord that passes through the center of a circle *(page 394)*

difference The answer in a subtraction problem *(page 35)*

Distributive Property of Multiplication over Addition The property which states that multiplying a sum by a number is the same as multiplying each addend by the number and then adding the products *(page 68)*
    Example: $4 \times (3 + 5) = 32$
        $(4 \times 3) + (4 \times 5) = 32$

dividend The number to be divided in a division problem *(page 96)*

divisible A number is divisible by another number if the quotient is a whole number and the remainder is zero *(page 96)*

divisor The number by which a dividend is divided in a division problem *(page 96)*

edge The line segment where two faces of a solid figure meet *(page 366)*

equation A mathematical sentence that uses an equals sign to show that two quantities are equal *(page 56)*

equilateral triangle A triangle in which all three sides are congruent *(page 354)*

equivalent fractions Two or more fractions that name the same number *(page 176)*

equivalent ratios Ratios that name the same comparisons *(page 308)*

estimate An answer that is close to the exact answer and is found by rounding, by using front-end digits, or by using compatible numbers *(page 14)*

expanded form A number written as the sum of the products of its digits and powers of 10 *(page 6)*
    Example:
    3,251
    3,000 + 200 + 50 + 1

exponent A number that tells how many times a base is to be used as a factor *(page 20)*
    Example: $2^3 = 2 \times 2 \times 2 = 8$
    The exponent is 3 because 2 is multiplied by itself 3 times.

expression A name for a number that contains at least one of the operations of addition, subtraction, multiplication, and division *(page 122)*
    Examples: $n + 5, a - b, 8 \times 4$

face One of the polygons of a solid figure *(page 366)*

factor A number that is multiplied by another number to find a product *(page 184)*

factor tree   A diagram that shows the prime factors of a number *(page 186)*
Example:

file   The electronic form of information stored together as a group on a disk or on a computer's hard drive *(page 484)*

formula   In a spreadsheet, a set of instructions that tells the computer to do a calculation or to perform a task *(page 486)*

fraction   A number that names part of a group or part of a whole *(page 192)*

gram   A metric unit for measuring mass *(pages 270, 278)*

greater than (>)   More than in size, quantity, or amount; the symbol > stands for *is greater than (page 10)*
Example: Read $7 > 5$ as *seven is greater than five.*

greatest common factor (GCF)   The largest number that is a factor of two or more numbers *(page 188)*
Example:
18 is the GCF of 54 and 72.

height   The length of a perpendicular segment from the base to the opposite side or vertex of a polygon or solid figure *(pages 384, 403)*
Examples:

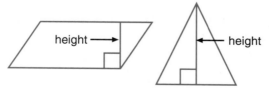

hexagon   A six-sided polygon *(page 356)*

histogram   A bar graph that shows the number of times data occurs within certain ranges or intervals *(page 144)*

independent events   Events that have no influence on each other *(page 162)*

inequality   A mathematical sentence containing < (less than) or > (greater than) to show that two expressions do not represent the same quantity *(page 460)*
Examples:
$2 \times 3 < 8; 6 + 5 > 9$

integers   The set of whole numbers and their opposites *(page 414)*
Examples:
$\ldots, {}^-3, {}^-2, {}^-1, 0, 1, 2, 3, \ldots$

intersecting lines   Lines that cross at exactly one point *(page 344)*
Example:

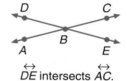

$\overleftrightarrow{DE}$ intersects $\overleftrightarrow{AC}$.

inverse operations   Operations that undo each other; addition and subtraction are inverse operations; multiplication and division are inverse operations *(page 38)*
Examples:
$29 - 13 = 16, 16 + 13 = 29$
$15 \div 3 = 5, 5 \times 3 = 15$

isosceles triangle   A triangle in which at least two sides and two angles are congruent *(page 354)*

label   In a spreadsheet, text read as characters, not as a number value *(page 480)*

least common denominator (LCD)   The smallest number, other than zero, that is a multiple of two or more denominators *(page 179)*

least common multiple (LCM)   The smallest number, other than zero, that is a multiple of two or more given numbers *(page 174)*

less than (<)   Smaller in size, quantity, or amount; the symbol < stands for *is less than (page 10)*
Example: Read $6 < 8$ as *six is less than eight.*

line A straight path that goes on forever in opposite directions *(page 342)*
    Example:

    Read: line *MN*

line graph A graph in which line segments are used to show changes over time *(page 146)*

line of symmetry A line that divides a figure into two congruent parts *(page 362)*

liter A metric unit for measuring capacity *(pages 270, 278)*

LOGO A computer language used primarily to draw graphic designs; it can also perform calculations *(page 476)*

mass The amount of matter in an object *(page 278)*

mean The average of a group of numbers *(page 154)*

median The middle number or the mean of the two middle numbers of a group of numbers arranged in numerical order *(page 154)*

meter A metric unit for measuring length *(page 270)*

metric system A measurement system that measures length in millimeters, centimeters, meters, and kilometers; capacity in liters and milliliters; mass in grams and kilograms; and temperature in degrees Celsius *(page 270)*

mixed number A number that is made up of a whole-number part and a fraction or a decimal part *(page 194)*

mode The number or numbers that occur most often in a collection of data; there can be more than one mode or none at all *(page 154)*

multiple The product of a given number and a whole number *(page 174)*

negative integer The opposite of a positive whole number; zero is neither positive nor negative *(page 414)*

numeration system A system of reading and writing numbers *(page 2)*

numerator The number above the fraction bar in a fraction; tells how many of the equal parts of a whole are being considered *(page 176)*

obtuse angle An angle whose measure is greater than 90° and less than 180° *(page 348)*

obtuse triangle A triangle in which exactly one angle is obtuse *(page 354)*

octagon An eight-sided polygon *(page 356)*
    Example:

opposites Two numbers whose points on the number line are the same distance from 0, but are on opposite sides of 0 *(page 418)*

ordered pair A pair of numbers used to locate a point on a coordinate plane *(page 431)*

order of operations The order in which operations are done; first, do the operations within parentheses; then, multiply and divide from left to right; and last, add and subtract from left to right *(page 18)*

origin The point on the coordinate plane where the *x*-axis and the *y*-axis intersect, (0,0) *(page 432)*

outcome A possible result in a probability experiment *(page 160)*

overestimate An estimate that is greater than the actual answer *(page 36)*

parallel lines Lines in a plane that do not intersect *(page 344)*
    Example:

    Read: *AB* is parallel to *CD*.

parallelogram A quadrilateral in which opposite sides are parallel and congruent (*page 356*)

pentagon A five-sided polygon (*page 356*)
  Example:

percent The ratio of a number to 100; percent means per hundred (*page 320*)

perimeter The distance around a polygon (*page 380*)

perpendicular lines Lines that intersect to form 90°, or right, angles (*page 344*)
  Example:

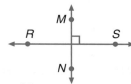

$$\overleftrightarrow{RS} \perp \overleftrightarrow{MN}$$
  Read: *RS* is perpendicular to *MN*.

pi (π) The ratio of the circumference of a circle to its diameter; π≈3.14 or $\frac{22}{7}$ (*page 397*)

pictograph A graph that uses pictures or symbols to represent numbers (*page 140*)

place value The value of a digit as determined by its position in a number (*page 6*)

plane A flat surface that goes on forever in all directions (*page 342*)
  Example:

  Read: plane *P*

point An exact location in space; usually represented by a dot (*page 342*)
  Example:

  • *P*

  Read: point *P*

polygon A closed plane figure whose sides are line segments (*page 356*)

positive integer A whole number that is greater than 0 (*page 414*)

precision A property of measurement that is related to the unit of measure used; the smaller the unit of measure used, the more exact the measurement is (*page 280*)

prime factorization A number written as the product of all its prime factors (*page 186*)
  Example: $24 = 2 \times 2 \times 2 \times 3$,
    or $2^3 \times 3$

prime number A whole number greater than 1 whose only factors are itself and 1 (*page 184*)

prism A solid figure whose bases are congruent, parallel polygons and whose other faces are parallelograms (*page 366*)
  Examples:

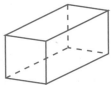

Rectangular Prism   Triangular Prism

probability (P) The chance that an event will occur expressed as the ratio of the number of favorable outcomes to the number of possible outcomes (*page 160*)

procedure A set of commands that directs the computer (*page 476*)

product The answer in a multiplication problem (*page 68*)

Property of One for Multiplication The property which states that the product of 1 and any factor is the factor (*page 68*)
  Examples:
    $3 \times 1 = 3; 1 \times a = a$

proportion An equation which states that two ratios are equivalent (*page 310*)

  Example: $\frac{2}{3} = \frac{4}{6}$

pyramid A solid figure whose base is a polygon and whose other faces are triangles with a common vertex (*pages 366, 401*)
  Examples:

Triangular Pyramid   Rectangular Pyramid

quadrilateral A four-sided polygon *(page 356)*

quotient The answer in the division operation *(page 96)*

radius A line segment with one endpoint at the center of a circle and the other endpoint on the circle *(page 394)*
Example:

random sample A group chosen by chance so that each item has an equal chance of being chosen *(page 138)*

range The difference between the greatest and least numbers in a set of numbers *(page 154)*

rate A ratio that compares different kinds of units, such as miles per hour, beats per minute, or students per class *(page 306)*

ratio A comparison of two numbers *(page 304)*
Examples: 3 to 5, 3:5, $\frac{3}{5}$

rational number Any number that can be expressed as a ratio in the form of $\frac{a}{b}$ where a and b are integers and $b \neq 0$ *(page 448)*

ray A part of a line that has one endpoint and goes on forever in only one direction *(page 342)*
Example:

A •————— B $\overrightarrow{AB}$
Read: ray *AB*

reciprocal One of two numbers whose product is 1 *(page 252)*

rectangle A parallelogram with four right angles *(page 356)*

recursion The ability of a procedure to repeat a set of commands by calling itself *(page 478)*

reflection A flip of a geometric figure across a line of symmetry to obtain a mirror image *(page 364)*
Example:

line of symmetry

regular polygon A polygon in which all sides and all angles are congruent *(page 356)*

relation A set of ordered pairs *(page 463)*

repeating decimal A decimal in which one digit or a series of digits repeats endlessly *(page 258)*
Example: 0.333 . . ., or $0.\overline{3}$

rhombus A parallelogram with four congruent sides *(page 356)*

right angle An angle whose measure is 90° *(page 348)*

right triangle A triangle in which exactly one angle is a right angle *(page 354)*

rotation (turn) A turn of a figure about a fixed point without reflection *(page 364)*
Example:

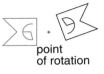

point of rotation

rotational symmetry A figure has rotational symmetry if it matches exactly when turned less than 360° about a point *(page 362)*

sample A group of people or objects chosen from a larger group to provide data to make predictions about the larger group *(page 138)*

scale The ratio of the size of the object or the distance in a drawing to the actual size of the object or the actual distance *(page 315)*

scale drawing A reduced or enlarged drawing whose shape is the same as an actual object and whose size is determined by the scale *(page 314)*

scalene triangle A triangle in which no sides are congruent *(page 354)*

similar figures Figures having the same shape but not necessarily the same size *(page 360)*

simplest form A fraction is in simplest form when the numerator and denominator have no common factor greater than 1 *(page 192)*

skew lines Lines that are in different planes, are not parallel, and do not intersect *(page 344)*

Examples:

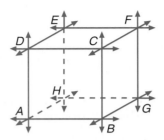

$\overleftrightarrow{AB}$ and $\overleftrightarrow{FG}$,
$\overleftrightarrow{DA}$ and $\overleftrightarrow{BG}$,
$\overleftrightarrow{EH}$ and $\overleftrightarrow{BG}$, and
$\overleftrightarrow{CB}$ and $\overleftrightarrow{AH}$
are skew lines.

solid figure   A geometric figure that exists in three or more planes *(page 366)*

spreadsheet   A computer program that organizes information in rows and columns and does calculations with numbers and formulas *(page 480)*

square   A rectangle with four congruent sides *(page 356)*

square   To square a number means to multiply it by itself *(page 22)*
   Example:
      25 is the square of 5 because $5^2 = 25$.

square root   One of the two equal factors of a number *(page 22)*
   Example: 5 is the square root of 25 because $5^2 = 25$ and $\sqrt{25} = 5$.

standard form   The form in which numerals are usually written, with digits 0 through 9, separated into periods by commas *(page 6)*
   Example: 634,578,910

stem-and-leaf plot   A method of organizing data in order to make comparisons; the ones digits appear horizontally as leaves, and tens and greater digits appear vertically as stems *(page 156)*
   Example:

Stem	Leaves
1	3 4 4 6 7
2	1 2 2 3 3
3	0 0 2 3 4

straight angle   An angle whose measure is 180° *(page 348)*

supplementary angles   Two angles whose measures have a sum of 180° *(page 349)*

surface area   The sum of the areas of all the faces or surfaces of a solid figure *(page 400)*

·······T·······

translation (slide)   A movement of a geometric figure to a new position without turning or flipping it *(page 364)*

Example:

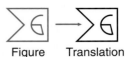

Figure   Translation

trapezoid   A quadrilateral with only two parallel sides *(page 356)*

tree diagram   A diagram that shows all the possible outcomes of an event *(page 158)*
   Example:

coin toss — heads / tails

triangle   A three-sided polygon *(page 354)*

·······U·······

underestimate   An estimate that is less than the actual answer *(page 36)*

unit rate   A rate in which the second term is 1 *(page 306)*

unlike fractions   Fractions whose denominators are not the same *(page 180)*

·······V·······

variable   A letter used to represent one or more numbers *(page 52)*

vertex   The point where two rays meet; the point of intersection of two sides of a polygon; the point of intersection of three edges of a solid figure *(page 342)*

volume   The number of cubic units that can fill a container *(page 402)*

··W··X··Y··Z··

weight   The measure of the force of gravity on an object *(page 289)*

x-axis   The horizontal axis on the coordinate plane *(page 432)*

y-axis   The vertical axis on the coordinate plane *(page 432)*

Zero Property of Addition   The property which states that the sum of any number and zero is that number *(page 34)*
   Example: $3 + 0 = 3$

Zero Property of Multiplication   The property which states that the product of 0 and any number is 0 *(page 68)*
   Example: $3 \times 0 = 0$

Index

MATH FUN MAGAZINE

These brainteasers don't stump me!

Have fun solving these brain teasers!

▶ As you learn
new things this year,
you will be able
to solve problems
that might have
stumped you at first.
So, keep trying!

Double SCOOP DILEMMA

Be a detective and use the given clues to solve this puzzle. You may find it helpful to make a table of choices.

George, Hiram, and Leeanna walk into an ice cream shop to buy double dip ice cream cones. They have a choice of five different flavors and two kinds of cones. Each friend chooses a different combination of two flavors and a cone.

Use the clues given below to determine what kind of double dip ice cream cone each friend chooses.

FEATURED FLAVORS

- **MINT CHOCOLATE CHIP**
- **BANANA NUT**
- **ROOT BEER MARBLE**
- **FUDGE MARSHMALLOW**
- **CHERRY SWIRL**

CLUES

- George does not like fruit in his ice cream.
- Hiram is allergic to nuts.
- Leeanna does not like chocolate or root beer.
- Hiram likes root beer and chooses it.
- George loves chocolate, so he chooses both chocolate flavors.
- Hiram's other choice is cherry swirl.
- The two friends who choose the same flavor choose sugar cones.
- One person chooses a plain cone.

NUMBER

I'VE GOT YOUR

Here are some puzzles for those with a calculating mind. Use a calculator to help you solve each puzzle.

1 Continue these calculations to reveal an interesting pattern. Show the final computation and its result.

$9 \times 9 + 7 = 88$
$98 \times 9 + 6 = 888$
$987 \times 9 + 5 = 8,888$

2 Copy the numbers and circles onto your own paper. Insert operation signs $(+, -, \times)$ to make the number sentences correct.

a. 12 ◯ 3 ◯ 4 ◯ 5 ◯ 67 ◯ 8 ◯ 9 = 100

b. 12 ◯ 3 ◯ 4 ◯ 5 ◯ 6 ◯ 7 ◯ 89 = 100

c. 123 ◯ 4 ◯ 5 ◯ 67 ◯ 89 = 100

d. 1 ◯ 2 ◯ 34 ◯ 56 ◯ 7 ◯ 8 ◯ 9 = 100

3 Follow these steps.

Step 1 Choose any four-digit number. Write it.
Step 2 Rearrange the digits to form another four-digit number. Write it.
Step 3 Subtract the lesser number from the greater number. Write the difference.
Step 4 Add the digits of the difference.
Step 5 If the sum of the digits of the difference is a two-digit number, rearrange the digits of the difference and repeat Steps 3 and 4 until the sum of the digits of the difference is a one-digit number.

What do you notice about the sum of the digits?

THE RIGHT STUFF

See if you have the right stuff to solve these number arrangement puzzles.

1 Copy this figure onto your own paper. Arrange the numbers 1–9 in the nine empty spaces to get a sum of 17 along each side.

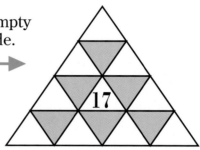

2 Copy this figure onto your own paper. Arrange the numbers 1–9 in the nine empty spaces to get a sum of 23 along each side.

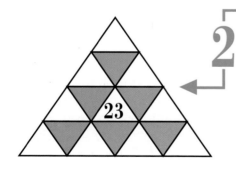

3 Copy the 3 x 3 grid onto your own paper. Fill in the three spaces with the given numbers as shown. Nine consecutive counting numbers form a path through the grid. The three given numbers are part of that path. All the numbers follow only a vertical or a horizontal path.
Complete the grid to make a path of consecutive counting numbers.

	29	30
	33	

PUZZLES That Make CENTS

Here are four brainteasers about money. See if you can solve each one without passing the buck!

1. Mike has six American coins for a total amount of $1.15. With his coins, Mike cannot give Jill exact change for a dollar bill. He cannot give Tim exact change for a 50-cent piece. He cannot give Shawn change for a quarter, or Maria change for a dime, or Cindy change for a nickel. What are Mike's six coins?
HINT: Some of the coins may be the same kind.

2. Mary Lou has two cans of equal size. One can is full of nickels. The other can is half full of dimes. Which can has more money in it? How do you know?

3. Mr. Parks was about to begin a job that would last 30 days. His boss said, "I will give you a choice of salary plans. You can be paid $1,000 a day for the entire job, or you can start with a wage of 1 cent for the first day and have your pay double for each day afterward." Which salary plan offers Mr. Parks the most money? Explain.

4. An archaeologist found two gold coins while digging in Rome, Italy. Each coin was dated 32 B.C. The archaeologist realized the coins were fake. How did she know?

What's Next?

Sometimes you can predict what comes next
if you detect a pattern.
Try to solve each of these puzzles involving a pattern.
Look for clues to help you.

1 What letter comes next?
Once you find the pattern,
the answer is as simple
as one, two, three!

O T T F F S S __

2 What design comes next?
Look carefully at the figures.
Take time to reflect on each one.

3 Below are all the letters of the alphabet, except *Z*.
Each letter has been placed above or below the line for a
reason. Does *Z* belong above or below the line?
Don't let this pattern throw you a curve!

A   E F   H I   K L M N   T   V W X Y
_____
  B C D   G   J   O P Q R S U

4 Copy the figures
onto your own paper.
Draw the next figure
in the pattern.
Don't stumble
end- over-end looking
for the answer!

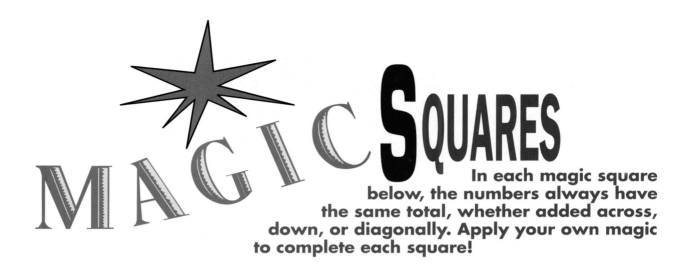

MAGIC SQUARES

In each magic square below, the numbers always have the same total, whether added across, down, or diagonally. Apply your own magic to complete each square!

1.	In Square A, the sum of each row is 34. Copy Square B onto your own paper. Then fill in numbers that are	35% of each number in Square A. Do the new numbers still make a magic square? If so, what is the sum of each row?

7	6	11	10
14	9	8	3
12	15	2	5
1	4	13	16

Square A

Square B

2. Copy the square onto your paper. Write a fraction in each box so that each row, column, and diagonal adds up to 1. One fraction is given.

	$\frac{5}{15}$	

3. Magic squares work with both positive and negative numbers. Copy this square onto your paper. Fill the square with numbers so that each row, column, and diagonal adds up to ‾24. Two numbers are given.

	‾8	
		32

4. Magic squares also work with decimals. Copy this square onto your paper. Fill in numbers so that each row, column, and diagonal adds up to 3.3. Three numbers are given.

	1.1	
	1.3	0.8

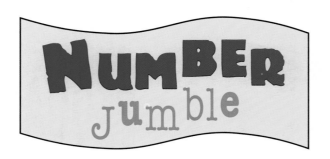

The problems below have all the right numbers, but the numbers are out of order. Can you help?

Jake cut out dozens of numbers and arranged the numbers for a class display on division. Unfortunately, the wind blew Jake's divisors and dividends off the board.

Rearrange the numbers in each box below so that they equal the quotient shown.

Example: | 8 8 3 | = 4.75 $\longrightarrow$ $8\overline{)38}$ with 4.75 above

1. | 4 6 9 | = 24   7. | 1 8 5 | = 16.2

2. | 0 9 9 | = 10   8. | 7 1 0 | = 0.7

3. | 1 5 8 | = 3.6   9. | 7 6 2 | = 33.5

4. | 2 4 8 | = 20.5   10. | 3 0 4 | = 7.5

5. | 6 1 2 | = 0.5   11. | 0 2 5 | = 0.25

6. | 2 9 8 | = 3.625   12. | 1 1 1 | = 11

Jake also cut out numbers to arrange for a class display on addition. Each problem used the digits 1 through 9. This time, the wind blew away all but one digit in each problem. Supply the missing numbers for Jake. The sum of the numbers is given. The sum of the digits in each number is given to the right.

13.
```
    ■■■■ (13)
     6 ■■ (23)
  +   ■■ (9)
   8,055
```

14.
```
    5 ■■■ (14)
     ■■■ (15)
  +   ■■ (16)
   5,724
```

Now just suppose...

**These problems contain true facts about animals.
Now just suppose something weird happened.
Could you find the solution?**

1 A swarm of 50,000 bees weighs 10 pounds.
Now just suppose an overweight bee decided to go on a diet.
If the bee weighed twice as much as an average bee,
what would be the weight of the overweight bee?

2 A grasshopper can jump a distance of 2 feet.
Now just suppose a grasshopper got the hiccups
and jumped 1,000 times without stopping. How many yards
would the grasshopper have jumped?

3 A camel can drink 25 gallons of water in half an hour.
If your job is to give a camel water from a quart pitcher,
how many times will you need to fill the pitcher with water
for the camel to drink for an hour?

4 All ants have 6 legs. Now just suppose you were buying
ant shoes. Naturally, each ant needs 3 pairs. The Acme Ant
Shoe Store is having a sale. You can buy 2 pairs of shoes
for $4 each and get a third pair for half price. How much
would you spend to buy shoes for one dozen ants?

5 A dog is as old at 12 years as a person is at 84.
Now just suppose your dog is having his actual
100th birthday. How old is your dog in "dog years"?

GOING AROUND IN SQUARES

**All of the puzzles below are about squares.
See if you can "square off" with each puzzle and solve it!**

1 Which two of these shapes, when connected to each other, will make exactly four squares?

2 Copy this dot grid onto your own paper. How many squares can you draw within the dots? Each corner of the square must touch a dot. One square has been drawn for you.

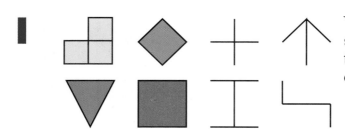

3 How many other squares contain exactly the same design as the square bordered by bold lines?
HINT: the squares can be in any position.

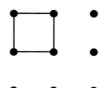

4 Carefully copy or trace the five shapes shown. Cut out the shapes. Then fit them together to make a square. It can be done!

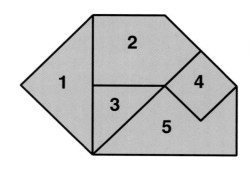

GETTING INTO SHAPE

Here are some picture puzzlers of all shapes and sizes. Study them closely before answering, and you will be in fine shape yourself!

1 How many squares and how many triangles can you find in each of these figures?

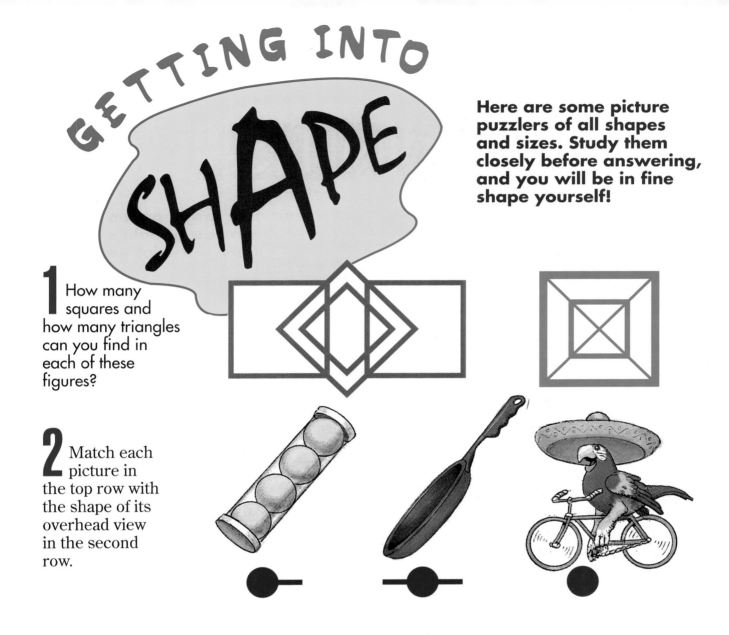

2 Match each picture in the top row with the shape of its overhead view in the second row.

3 Copy this figure onto your own paper. Divide the figure into five sections so that all five numbers (1, 2, 3, 4, and 5) are included in each section.

2	1	3	4	3
5	2	5	2	4
4	3	1	4	1
3	5	2	1	3
1	4	5	2	5

4 Copy this figure onto your own paper. How many circles of the same size as these can you add that will be touching, but not crossing, both of these circles?

Coordination COUNTS!

Copy the coordinate plane below onto your own graph paper.
Plot each pair of coordinates. Then connect each pair of points
with a straight line. The first pair of points has been done for you.
The message you spell answers this riddle:

If you buy only 10¢ worth of nails, what do you want for them?

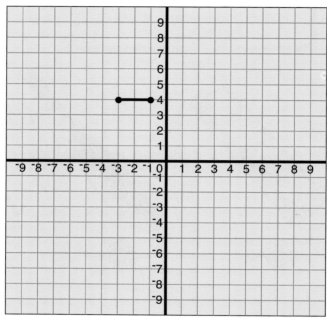

1.	(⁻3,4) (⁻1,4)	14.	(⁻3,⁻1) (⁻3,⁻4)
2.	(⁻2,1) (⁻2,4)	15.	(⁻3,⁻4) (⁻1,⁻4)
3.	(1,1) (1,4)	16.	(⁻3,⁻2) (⁻1,⁻2)
4.	(1,4) (3,4)	17.	(1,⁻1) (⁻1,⁻4)
5.	(1,3) (3,3)	18.	(1,⁻1) (2,⁻4)
6.	(1,1) (3,1)	19.	(2,⁻1) (2,⁻4)
7.	(4,1) (4,4)	20.	(3,⁻1) (5,⁻1)
8.	(4,4) (5,1)	21.	(4,⁻1) (4,⁻4)
9.	(5,1) (5,4)	22.	(8,⁻1) (6,⁻1)
10	(⁻4,⁻1) (⁻6,⁻1)	23.	(6,⁻1) (6,⁻3)
11.	(⁻6,⁻1) (⁻6,⁻4)	24.	(6,⁻3) (8,⁻3)
12.	(⁻6,⁻4) (⁻4,⁻4)	25.	(8,⁻3) (8,⁻4)
13.	(⁻1,⁻1) (⁻3,⁻1)	26.	(8,⁻4) (6,⁻4)

TOOTH PiCK REMOVAL

Arrange 24 toothpicks to form the figure below.

1   **Remove 10 toothpicks so that 2 squares remain.**

2   **Remove 12 toothpicks so that 2 squares remain.**

3   **Remove 8 toothpicks so that 2 squares remain.**

4   **Remove 7 toothpicks so that 3 squares remain.**

Catchy PUZZLERS

Here are some "catchy" problems that may seem impossible to solve. Yet each one has a logical answer. All you must do is find the "catch"!

1 During a half-inning in a softball game, 7 players came to bat, but no man crossed home plate. How was this possible?

2 A bus driver picked up 23 passengers along his bus route. Only 1 passenger got off the bus before the end of the line. At the end of the route, there were still 23 people on the bus. How was this possible?

3 Eight adults were huddled under an umbrella measuring only 2 feet in diameter. No one got wet. How was this possible?

4 Rita had 2 coins in her purse. They totaled 35¢. One of the coins was not a dime. How was this possible?

5 Jennifer was born in 1960, but by 1990 she had had only 7 birthdays. How was this possible?

Letter Perfect

The puzzles on this page have mysterious letters
that will surely challenge you.
See if you can find some "letter-perfect" solutions!

 For each statement below, figure out what the letters stand for. The subject might be weights, measures, science, sports, music, or anything else!

Example:

52 = W in a Y | **Weeks in a Year**

a. 12 = I in a F
b. 16 = O in a P
c. 9 = P in the S S
d. 4 = Q in a D
e. 11 = P on a F T
f. 100 = C in a M

g. 2,000 = P in a T
h. 180 = D in a S A
i. 50 = S in the U S
j. 29 = D in F in a L Y
k. 8 = P in a G

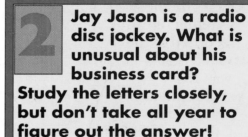

Jay Jason is a radio disc jockey. What is unusual about his business card? Study the letters closely, but don't take all year to figure out the answer!

J. JASON

DJ FM / AM

 Spell an animal's name from each telephone number below. Choose letters that correspond to the numbers on a telephone.

Example:

243-3824   CHEETAH

a. 447-2333
b. 365-7446
c. 678-7424

d. 536-7273
e. 467-4552
f. 885-8873

Strange But True

These word problems contain facts that may seem strange, but the facts are all true. Can you solve each problem?

1 The highest temperature recorded in the United States was 134° Fahrenheit. How many degrees Celsius was this?

2 A piece of pie eaten just once a week will add 3 pounds of body weight in a year. How many ounces of body weight are gained after each piece of pie is eaten?

3 The longest recorded flight by a pigeon was 5,400 miles in 55 days. What was the pigeon's average speed in miles per hour, assuming the bird slept 8 hours a day?

5 Suppose you spent one dollar per minute. About how many years would it take you to spend one billion dollars?

I solved every problem! Did you?

4 The average American makes 382 telephone calls in a year. How many telephone calls does a person average in a month?